ENCYCLOPEDIA OF
THE INTERWAR YEARS
FROM 1919 TO 1939

ENCYCLOPEDIA OF
THE INTERWAR YEARS
FROM 1919 TO 1939

Mark Grossman

☑®

Facts On File, Inc.

Encyclopedia of the Interwar Years

Copyright © 2000 by Mark Grossman

Facts On File, Inc.
11 Penn Plaza
New York NY 10001

Library of Congress Cataloging-in-Publication Data

Grossman, Mark.
Encyclopedia of the interwar years / by Mark Grossman.
p. cm.
ISBN 0-8160-3576-8
1. History, Modern—20th century—Encyclopedias. I. Title.
D727.G745 2000
909.82'2'03—dc21
99-085998

Facts On File books are available at special discounts when purchased in bulk
quantities for businesses, associations, institutions or sales promotions.
Please call our Special Sales Department in New York at 212/967-8800 or
800/322-8755.

You can find Facts On File on the World Wide Web at
http://www.factsonfile.com

Text design by Joan Toro
Cover design by Cathy Rincon

Printed in the United States of America.

VB Hermitage 10 9 8 7 6 5 4 3 2 1

This book is printed on acid-free paper.

CONTENTS

LIST OF ENTRIES

INTRODUCTION

"Civilization exists by geological consent, subject to change without notice."

—Will Durant, American historian.

The Paris edition of the *New York Herald* for March 6, 1933, announced two lead stories: newly inaugurated American president Franklin Delano Roosevelt had ordered all U.S. banks to close to stem the growing bank crisis and a rush of withdrawals of deposits; in Germany, Adolf Hitler and his Nazi Party had come to power. These two stories were distinctly unrelated, but they can be seen as the start of an era that would lead to the rise of two of the most important leaders of the 20th century, and to World War II. But the events of that March day were merely a continuation of events that had begun long before the world knew of Adolf Hitler. When, on November 11, 1918, Germany surrendered and World War I ended, the world entered a period of 20 years of "peace"—but it was a peace that was tinged by friction and small conflicts and that was in essence a buildup for a war far worse. The year 1919 has been of great interest to me. In my many years as a student of American and world history, I can see that much of the world's 20th-century chronicle divides around the year 1919. It was the first year after the end of World War I; it was the start of the war against bolshevism in the United States; it was the beginning of the Weimar Republic in Germany; it was the year of the Versailles Peace Conference and the Senate fight over ratification of the treaty exacted there. And it began a 20-year period of peace (or semi-peace) around the world that ended with the onset of World War II in the dark days of September 1939. While historians have studied with fascination the years just after World War I and the years just prior to World War II, never before, in one volume, has the entire era of the years between the world wars been scrutinized with such depth. This volume is the first work dealing with an era that has undergone little investigation and analysis.

The years just after World War I were a "return to normalcy," as President Warren G. Harding called them. For the United States, it was a time of incredible economic growth and the rise of organized crime during the Prohibition years; all over the world, however, nations were recovering from the war and fostering the rise of numerous dictatorships, in Germany, in Italy, in Japan, and in the Soviet Union. All these factors would collide in the 1930s.

But in 1920s America, bathtub gin and flappers ruled the day. It was "The Jazz Age"—an era in which everything seemed possible, all fueled by a stock market that seemed to have no limit in its increasing value. But that was the 1920s. The following decade was so much different: an era dominated by the stock market crash, an end to Prohibition, the Depression, the "New Deal," court-packing, social welfare in the United States, appeasement abroad. It was as if the global self-flagellation that characterized World War 1 was not enough, and the world proceeded headlong into the military buildup that led to World War II.

Yet during these years other events were occurring: sports; politics; motion pictures (in which we came out of the silent era and entered the age of the "talkie") and the development of radio; labor unrest and the growth of unions, both in the United States and England. From the Treaty of Versailles to Adolf Hitler's final ultimatum to Poland to acquiesce to German demands before the blitzkrieg of September 1, 1939, the events and people that made up this little-explored age are covered here.

This work is meant to fully document the years between the wars. Accordingly, in addition to the more than 400 entries on people, places, court cases, and other matters, it contains verbatim tracts of the era's most important speeches, writings, and treaties. As a historian, researcher, and author, I have noticed that the people and places and events of the interwar era, the pieces that form the smaller parts of that amazing puzzle we call "history," are frequently forgotten; only the "big picture" is presented. In this work, through the use of entries, graphs, and appendices, I have attempted to color in this panorama, to give shape to that history, to include those who normally get left off the list of persons involved in the era. When this work began in March 1996, I set out with a varied list of entries that were to be completed; as work progressed, new entries were added, and some from the original list were deleted as their importance (or lack thereof) became clear. This has been my way of drafting a book since I began writing more than a decade ago.

In the beginning, I did not conceive the immense amount of work that would be needed to realize the completion of this book. It included two trips to London—one in 1996, and a second in 1999—and several excursions to Washington, D.C., and New York, all to visit some of the world's best institutions for research. The result, from three years of researching, compiling, and writing, is this work. And in starting any work, I as the author and researcher must set certain goals and boundaries. I look at a blank page on a computer screen as a canvas, waiting to be filled in with the paint of words. How the subjects for this book, from the people to the events to the places to other topics, came to be chosen, deserves explanation and discussion. Generally my method is, first, to delve into the history of an era, consulting contemporary sources (books printed at that time, newspapers, and magazines) and making numerous lists which are then pared down to those entries that are *most* important to the main topic of the book. For this work in particular, an international scope was demanded, so the world, as the old phrase goes, was my oyster. Famous international statesmen, Nobel Prize winners, speeches, economic plans, artists, musicians, singers, cultural people, labor unrest, revolutions, assassinations—all had merit, and perhaps another author would have included others which I did not. Some statesmen were culled because while they served during the period between the world wars and may have been important in their respective nations, as a whole they did not fit into a comprehensive history of the era. Important art movements, the history of the silent and talking screens during the period, and sports all receive coverage. The elections in three important countries—the United States, Great Britain, and Germany—are covered with text and graphs devoted to votes received and seats won. Any typographical error or incorrect information is my fault alone.

It should be noted that this book uses the Wade-Giles transliteration system for Chinese names because it was the system most widely used during the period in question. Thus, *Mao Tse-tung* appears here rather than the currently acceptable pinyin *Mao Zedong*. Further, for Japanese names, I have utilized the Western form of the name, rather than the Japanese. For instance, the entry "Korekiyo Takahashi" is filed as "Takahashi, Korekiyo."

I would like to thank the following persons and institutions, without whose kind assistance and dedication this work would not have been possible: the wonderful staff of the British Library, London, and the British Newspaper Library, Colindale (just outside of London), for their appreciated assistance while I was in Great Britain (a note: during my 1996 visit, the British Library was located in the British Museum; in 1999, it had moved to its new home at St. Pancras); the Library of Congress, particularly the Main Reading Room, where the thousands of copies which make up the main part of the research in this book were made, as well as the Manuscript Reading Room, where research was conducted into various manuscript collections; the National Archives, where the files of government agencies of the New Deal period and Senate and House committees were extensively searched; the staff of the New York Public Library, where books and papers were examined; the staff of the Nicholas Butler Library of Columbia University, where thousands of books were pulled and copied; Professor Barry Cushman, of the Saint Louis University School of Law in St. Louis, Missouri, who shared with me a copy of his discourse on "The Hughes Court and Constitutional Consultation"; Barbara, Bill, Steve, and all the great folks at the Maricopa County Library in Phoenix, Arizona, who endured my haggling, pestering, and usually illegible interlibrary loan requests, not to mention my years of searching through reels of films and piles of books, all in the library's wonderful collections; the staff of the Hayden Library at Arizona State University in Tempe, Arizona, where much of the newspaper research on this book was conducted; the staff of the Nebraska State Historical Society in Lincoln, Nebraska, for sharing with me some of the papers of Governor Charles Wayland Bryan, who ran for vice president in 1924; the staff of the Franklin D. Roosevelt Library in Hyde Park, New York, who furnished me copies of several letters from Roosevelt during his unsuccessful campaign for the vice presidency in 1920; Michael Keepper, library director of the Herrin City Library in Herrin, Illinois, for his help in assembling information on the Herrin coal strike of 1922; the Westminster Reference Library near Trafalgar Square in London, which saved the day by allowing me to use its collections while the British Library's workers were on strike in 1999; and the Public Record Office in the village of Kew outside of London, which allowed me free access to many of their books and papers during my two visits in 1996 and 1999.

Mark Grossman

Abbott, Edith (1876–1957)

American social worker, known for her work during the interwar years in helping to establish the Social Security system. A noted author and educator, she was born in Grand Island, Nebraska, on September 26, 1876, one of four children of Othman Ali Abbott, a Civil War veteran, attorney, and later the first lieutenant governor of Nebraska, and Elizabeth (Griffin) Abbott. Her family's prosperity made it possible for her to attend the prestigious Brownell Hall, a girls' boarding school in Omaha. Although Abbott wished to enter college after graduating in 1893, a severe economic depression prevented this. Instead, she began to teach in her hometown of Grand Island. At the same time, she took correspondence courses and summer classes, and in 1901 she received a bachelor's degree from the University of Nebraska. She also studied at the University of Chicago, where she received a doctorate in 1905, as well as the University of London and the London School of Economics. While in London, she studied the development of a modern welfare system for the poor, which, upon her return to the United States in 1907, she desired to implement while teaching economic theory at Wellesley College.

After a short stint at Wellesley, however, Abbott became acquainted with the reformist attorney and social worker Sophonisba Preston Breckinridge and the pioneering social worker Julia Lathrop, both of whom asked Abbott to join them in Chicago to work at the Chicago School of Civics and Philanthropy. There, Abbott joined her sister Grace ABBOTT, who was earning a degree at the University of Chicago, and who had come to feel a similar desire to help the poor. From 1907 until 1920 both sisters worked at Hull House, a model community for the poor established by Jane ADDAMS. In 1920, Edith Abbott and Breckinridge helped incorporate their school into the University of Chicago as the School of Social Service Administration. Four years later Abbott became the school's first dean, serving until 1942. In 1927, as an extension of

the school, the women established the *Social Service Review,* the official journal of American social work. She served two terms as president of the National Association of Social Workers and edited the journal from its inception until 1954.

During the GREAT DEPRESSION, Abbott spoke out on the need for a government social program to prevent the poor from becoming homeless. Her constant writings printed in such influential magazines as *The Nation* and *The New Republic,* as well as her views distributed in other forums, led to her support for the Social Security system established by Congress in 1935. That year, she published economist Simon Leland's lecture addressing funding concerns for the new legislation.

The death of her sister Grace in 1939 was a devastating blow to Abbott. She continued to work as a teacher, activist, and editor until 1954. After retiring, she returned to Grand Island, where she died on July 28, 1957.

References: Lela B. Costin, *Two Sisters for Social Justice: A Biography of Grace and Edith Abbott* (Urbana: University of Illinois Press, 1983); Grace Weatherford, *American Women's History* (New York: Prentice Hall, 1994); James Stuart Olson, *Historical Dictionary of the 1920s: From World War I to the New Deal, 1919–1933* (Westport, Conn.: Greenwood, 1988); 1; Lela B. Costin, "Abbott, Edith," in Walter I. Trattner, ed., *Biographical Dictionary of Social Welfare in America* (Westport, Conn.: Greenwood, 1986), 3–6; Steven Diner, "Scholarship in the Quest for Social Welfare: A Fifty-Year History of the Social Service Review," *Social Service Review* 51, no. 1 (1977): 1–66; Walter I. Trattner, *From Poor Law to Welfare State: A History of Social Welfare in America* (New York: Free Press, 1994).

Abbott, George Francis (1887–1995)

American theater writer, producer, and director, known for his numerous Broadway shows that he presented over a nearly 70-year career, including such interwar productions as *Broadway* (1926) and *Three Men and a Horse* (1935). Born in Forestville, New York, on June 25, 1887, Abbott graduated from the University of Rochester in 1911 and began working in the theater two years later as both a playwright and an actor. For a time he studied under George Pierce Baker, a noted drama teacher, at Harvard. After a year in the Boston theater, and with a prize under his hat for a one-act play he had written, Abbott went to New York City to work on Broadway.

While working for producer John Golden, Abbott wrote and acted. In 1925 he collaborated with fellow writer James Gleason to compose the play *The Fall Guy*. In 1926 he wrote the play *Love 'Em and Leave 'Em,* rewrote Philip Dunning's *Broadway,* and directed the productions of *Chicago* and *Cowboy Crazy*. Abbott admitted in later years that he "was not a successful playwright until I took parasitical advantage of other people's ideas." In 1930 he went to Hollywood and worked with others on the script for Erich Maria Remarque's novel *All Quiet on the Western Front* (for which Abbott received an Academy Award nomination for Best Achievement in Writing). A year later he returned to the stage. From 1935 until 1963, writes Jack Kroll, Abbott "always had at least one play running on Broadway as a director or writer."

During his lifetime, Abbott was awarded four Tony Awards and a Pulitzer Prize. He was involved in more than 120 Broadway plays and worked well into his nineties. Abbott died from a stroke in Miami Beach, Florida, on January 31, 1995. His autobiography, *Mister Abbott*, was published in 1963.

References: "Abbott, George," in Charles Moritz, ed., *Current Biography 1965* (New York: H. W. Wilson Company, 1965), 1–2; George Abbott, *Mister Abbott* (New York: Random House, 1963); Ephraim Katz, *The Film Encyclopedia* (New York: HarperPerennial, 1994), 1–2; Jack Kroll, "Mister Broadway," *Newsweek*, February 13, 1995, p. 61.

Abbott, Grace (1878–1939)

American social worker and advocate for the poor, the highest-ranking female to serve in the Harding administration, as director of the U.S. Children's Bureau. The sister of Edith ABBOTT, Grace Abbott was born on November 17, 1878, in Grand Island, Nebraska, the daughter of Othman Ali Abbott, a lawyer and Nebraska politician, and Elizabeth (Griffin) Abbott. She attended local schools before graduating from Grand Island College in 1898. She taught locally (a period interrupted by a bout of typhoid), and in 1907 moved to Chicago, where she earned a master's degree in political science at the University of Chicago.

That same year Abbott joined her sister Edith at Hull House, a community for the poor established by reformer Jane ADDAMS. The following year, working closely with other Chicago reformers, Abbott was appointed head of the Immigrants' Protective League, where she remained until 1917, when then head of the U.S. Children's Bureau Julia Lathrop asked Abbott to come to join her in the nation's capital, where Abbott eventually worked with such luminaries as Martha Eliot and Katharine Lenroot. Much of her work over the next fifteen years focused on child labor and immigration issues; in particular, she advocated a constitutional amendment banning children from paid work and helped draft the CHILD LABOR ACT of 1919. In 1921 she assumed the directorship of the bureau, serving until 1934.

In 1930 Abbott was considered a popular candidate to become the U.S. secretary of labor, which would have made her the first woman to serve in the cabinet, but she was passed over. She often lectured at the University of Chicago. When Abbott retired from the Children's Bureau, she joined the faculty of the University of Chicago's School of Social Service Administration, where her sister Edith was dean. During her final years President Franklin D. ROOSEVELT sent her to several conferences, including the seventh Pan-American Child Congress in Mexico in 1935, and the 1936 and 1937 meetings of the International Labour Organization. This heavy schedule, combined with two bouts of tuberculosis, may have contributed to Abbott's early death. She died of a multiple myeloma in Chicago on June 19, 1939.

References: Martha M. Eliot, "Abbott, Grace," in Allen Johnson et al., eds., *Dictionary of American Biography* (New York: Charles Scribner's Sons, 1930–95), 2: 1–2; Susan Wladaver-Morgan, "Grace Abbott" in Frank Magill, ed., *Great Lives from History: American Women Series* (Pasadena, Calif.: Salem Press, 1985), 1: 6–10; Eugene P. Trani and David L. Wilson, *The Presidency of Warren G. Harding* (Lawrence: University Press of Kansas, 1977), 51; Susan Ware, *Beyond Suffrage: Women in the New Deal* (Cambridge: Harvard University Press, 1987); Grace Weatherford, *American Women's History* (New York: Prentice Hall, 1994), 1–2; James Stuart Olson, *Historical Dictionary of the 1920s: From World War I to the New Deal, 1919–1933* (Westport, Conn.: Greenwood, 1988), 1–2; Julia Lathrop, *The United States Children's Bureau, 1912–1972* (New York: Arno, 1972).

Abbott, Robert Sengstacke (1868–1940)

American newspaper publisher and editor, founder of the weekly *Chicago Defender,* one of the most influential newspapers devoted to the interests of the black community during the interwar period. Abbott, the second child of former slaves, was born on November 28, 1868, on St. Simon's Island, Georgia. His father, Thomas Abbott, died when Abbott was but a few months old. He was reared by his stepfather, John Hermann Henry Sengstacke, and took the name as his own middle name. His mother, Flora Butler Abbott, worked in a printing shop. Her work, as well as his stepfather's stint on a short-lived newspaper in Georgia, may have influenced Abbott to enter publishing.

Abbott studied at the Beach Institute in Savannah, Georgia, and at Claflin University in Orangeburg, South Carolina, and learned the printing trade at the Hampton Institute (now Hampton University) in Virginia. In 1898 he received a degree from the Kent College of Law in Chicago; however, probably because of his race, Abbott was deterred from becoming a lawyer. On May 6, 1905, with a total of 25 cents in capital, he founded the *Chicago Defender,* working as the paper's reporter, editor, and publisher. His editorial mission was to use the newspaper to fight against "segregation, discrimination, disenfranchisement."

The mass migration of southern blacks to northern cities, particularly Chicago, set off a panic for jobs that led to the Chicago Race Riot of 1919, in which dozens of whites and blacks were murdered. In the pages of the *Defender,* Abbott kept his readers informed of events, and it was such evenhanded reporting that led him to be named to the Chicago Commission on Race Relations by the governor of Illinois to investigate racial matters in the city. The 1922 commission report, *The Negro in Chicago,* is considered a landmark work in investigating the sources of racial tension.

According to biographer Harry Amana, "During the years between World War I and World War II, the heyday of the black press, the *Defender* was the single most influential national black newspaper in America. At its peak during that period it had a paid circulation in excess of 230,000, and researchers agree that its readership was anywhere from two to five times that number." Abbott's role in the black press has been compared with that of William Randolph Hearst's in the mainstream press. He successfully parlayed the *Defender* into a moneymaker that adequately survived the Great Depression, allowing Abbott in 1930 to introduce *Abbott's Monthly,* which lasted until 1933, and in the following year, *Abbott's Weekly and Illustrated News,* which folded after only five months.

In 1932 he contracted tuberculosis and a few years later developed Bright's disease, a kidney ailment. Abbott died on February 29, 1940.

References: Doris E. Saunders, "Abbott, Robert Sengstacke" in Rayford W. Logan and Michael R. Winston, eds., *Dictionary of American Negro Biography* (New York: W. W. Norton, 1982), 1–2; Harry Amana, "Robert S. Abbott" in Sam G. Riley, ed., *American Magazine Journalists, 1900–1960* (Detroit, Mich.: Bruccoli Clark Layman, 1995), 3–10; Roland Edgar Wolseley, *Black Achievers in American Journalism* (Nashville, Tenn.: James C. Winston Publishing, 1995); James Stuart Olson, *Historical Dictionary of the 1920s: From World War I to the New Deal, 1919–1933* (Westport, Conn.: Greenwood, 1988), 2; Kenneth L. Kusmer, ed., "The Great Migration and After" in Kenneth L. Kusmer, gen. ed., *Black Communities and Urban Development in America, 1720–1990* (New York: Garland, 1990), 4: 220; "Robert S. Abbott Dies; Publisher of Negro Paper," *New York Herald-Tribune,* March 1, 1940, 16.

Abd el-krim (1882:–1963)

Moroccan Berber independence leader, born Muhammad Ibn Abd al-Karim al-Khattabi, organized resistance against the Spanish and French for control of Morocco. Except that he was the eldest son of a member of the Ait Warayaghar, a Tamazight-speaking Berber tribe of the Rif mountains in northeastern Morocco, little is known about Abd el-Krim's upbringing.

In 1860, Frederick Hardman wrote of the Spanish war in Morocco and of "an enemy whose qualities are but imperfectly known, and whom it would be rashness, to despise." By 1893 this enemy, composed of Muslim Berbers called the Riff, or Rif, people, initiated a war against the Spanish occupiers of Morocco's El Rif region. By November of that year, Spain was forced to send twenty-five thousand men to drive back the Rif. The Treaty of Fez (1894) ended the short war and left the Rif homeless. By 1919, Abd el-Krim, who was known by the nickname "the Wolf of the Rif Mountains," had joined the Moroccan leader Ahmed ibn-Muhammad Raisuli in attacking the Spanish on two fronts. Although the Spanish troops under Damaso Berenguer were able to contain Raisuli, those under General Fernandez Silvestre, some twelve thousand out of a force of twenty thousand, were slaughtered by Abd el-Krim's forces at Annoval on July 21, 1921. This collapse forced a Spanish withdrawal, and Abd el-Krim's formation of the Republic of the Rif, of which Abd el-Krim served as president from 1921 until 1926. This pushed the Spanish government toward the civil war. Abd el-Krim took his force of twenty thousand and moved toward Fez to drive French troops out of Morocco, which forced the Spanish and French—long rivals for control of the area—to coordinate their activities against Abd el-Krim. From one side a contingent led by the Spanish dictator Miguel Primo de Rivera landed a combined Spanish-French force at Alhucemas Bay on Morocco's Mediterranean coast in September 1925. From the other side was French commander Marshal Philippe Pétain's larger force of 160,000. Boxing in Abd el-Krim's now smaller army, the contingent seemed ready to destroy the Rif and its leader. On May 26, 1926, Abd el-Krim surrendered; he was exiled to Réunion Island until 1947, after which the French government granted him amnesty, allowing him to live in Egypt. There he helped to form the North African Liberation Committee.

Abd el-Krim was a skilled tactician whose moves for independence were thwarted only by his opposition's military and technological superiority. He died in Cairo on February 6, 1963. "[His] legacy . . . is an ambiguous one.

His brave and resourceful struggle served as an inspiration to Moroccan contemporaries, notably the young nationalists," writes historian Edmund Burke, "but the idea of a Rifian republic has also been seen as a potentially divisive one in independent Morocco."

References: Edmund Burke, III, "Abd El-Krim" in John L. Esposito, ed., *The Oxford Encyclopedia of the Modern Islamic World,* 5 vols. (New York: Oxford University Press, 1995), 1: 8–10; Frederick Hardman, *The Spanish Campaign in Morocco* (Edinburgh and London: William Blackwood and Sons, 1860), 1; C. R. Pennell, *A Country with a Government and a Flag: The Rif War in Morocco, 1921–1926* (Wisbech, England: Middle East and North African Studies, 1986); "French Crush Krim Attacks in Torrid Sun," New York *Herald* (European edition), July 22, 1925, 1; George C. Kohn, *Dictionary of Wars* (New York: Facts On File, 1986), 372–73.

Abrams v. United States (1919)

Landmark United States Supreme Court decision that held that revolutionary literature could not be circulated in the United States if it met the so-called "clear and present danger" test. In 1917 the U.S. Congress enacted the Espionage Act and, along with an amendment in 1918, outlawed the publication of any material "intended to incite, provoke and encourage resistance to the United States" during World War I. Jacob Abrams, and four others sympathetic to the Bolshevist regime in Russia, printed and distributed a pamphlet that called for an end to the war in Europe. Under the Espionage Act, they were arrested, tried on charges of printing material of incitement, and convicted of two of four charges. The men appealed to the Supreme Court, which heard arguments on October 21 and 22, 1919. In one of the most important free-speech cases to come before the Court in the 20th century, and perhaps in U.S. history, the Court held on November 10, 1919 (ironically almost one year to the day of the war's end, which the plaintiffs had fought for), that the Espionage Act was constitutional and that the government had had sufficient proof to convict Abrams and his allies for breaking the law. In a dissent famed for its eloquence, Justice Oliver Wendell HOLMES (joined by Justice Louis D. Brandeis) "urged toleration . . . convinced that the First Amendment [to the U.S. Constitution] established a national policy favoring a search for the truth, while balancing social interests and individual interests." *Abrams* was the fourth in a series of six free-speech cases heard by the Court from 1919 to 1920.

See also CLARKE JR., JOHN HESSIN; PALMER RAIDS; RED SCARE; SCHENCK V. UNITED STATES.

References: Elder Witt, ed., *Congressional Quarterly's Guide to the U.S. Supreme Court* (Washington, D.C.: Congressional Quarterly, 1979), 398; Martin Shapiro, "*Abrams v. United States*" in Leonard W. Levy, ed., *Encyclopedia of the American Constitution* (New York: Macmillan, 1986–92), 1: 7–8; Thomas F. Carroll, "Freedom of Speech and of the Press in War Time: The Espionage Act," *Michigan Law Review* 17 (June 1919): 621–65; Paul L. Murphy, *World War I and the Origin of Civil Liberties in the United States* (New York: W. W. Norton, 1979), 267; *Abrams v. United States,* 250 US 616 (1919).

Academy Awards

Since 1929 the Academy of Motion Picture Arts and Sciences has held an annual awards presentation. The awards, called Oscars, recognize excellence in filmmaking achievement in more than 20 categories that honor outstanding individual or collective efforts. In their first year the awards were presented at a private dinner at the Hollywood Roosevelt Hotel, with fewer than 250 people in attendance. Public interest proved so great, however, that the following year the Academy permitted a radio broadcast of the event. The presentation was first televised in 1953, and since 1969 has been telecast throughout the world.

Achuapa, Battle of   *See* NICARAGUA, AMERICAN OCCUPATION OF.

Ådalen Strike

Period of labor unrest. Ådalen, an area of Ångermanland in northern Sweden, was the center of the nation's paper pulp industry. When the strike started in 1931, and the employers brought in "strike breakers"—nonunion workers—to fill union positions, communist agitators started boisterous demonstrations. The Swedish army was called in and opened fire on the demonstrators, killing five civilians. The news was taken badly in the capital, Stockholm, leading to the collapse of Prime Minister Carl Gustav Ekman's minority Liberal government in the 1932 elections and the Social Democratic Party's forty-year reign of power.

Reference: Irene Scobbie, *Historical Dictionary of Sweden* (Metuchen, N.J.: Scarecrow, 1995), 25.

Adams, Franklin Pierce (1881–1960)

American journalist and humorist, known by his initials "F. P. A." Born in Chicago on November 15, 1881, the son of Moses and Clara Adams, he attended local schools and the University of Michigan before dropping out to enter the business world. For several years he bounced around performing odd jobs. His writing career began in 1903, when he went to work for the Chicago *Journal* writing a column called "A Little About Everyting," earning $25 a week. The following year he moved to New York and

	BEST ACTOR	BEST ACTRESS	BEST DIRECTOR	BEST PICTURE
		OSCAR WINNERS, 1927–1940		
1927–28	Emil Jannings (*The Way of All Flesh*)	Janet Gaynor (*Seventh Heaven*)	Frank Borzage (*Seventh Heaven*) Lewis Milestone (*Two Arabian Knights*)	*Wings*
1928–29	Warner Baxter (*In Old Arizona*)	Mary Pickford (*Coquette*)	Frank Lloyd (*The Divine Lady*)	*Broadway Melody*
1929–30	George Arliss (*Disraeli*)	Norma Shearer (*The Divorcee*)	Lewis Milestone (*All Quiet on the Western Front*)	*All Quiet on the Western Front*
1930–31	Lionel Barrymore (*A Free Soul*)	Marie Dressler (*Min and Bill*)	Norma Taurog (*Skippy*)	*Cimarron*
1931–32	Frederic March (*Dr. Jekyll and Mr. Hyde*) Wallace Berry (*The Champ*)	Helen Hayes (*The Sin of Madelon Claudet*)	Frank Borzage (*Bad Girl*)	*Grand Hotel*
1932–33	Charles Laughton (*The Private Life of Henry VIII*)	Katharine Hepburn (*Morning Glory*)	Frank Lloyd (*Cavalcade*)	*Cavalcade*
1934	Clark Gable (*It Happened One Night*)	Claudette Colbert (*It Happened One Night*)	Frank Capra (*It Happened One Night*)	*It Happened One Night*
1935	Victor McLaglen (*The Informer*)	Bette Davis (*Dangerous*)	John Ford (*The Informer*)	*Mutiny on the Bounty*
1936	Paul Muni (*The Story of Louis Pasteur*)	Luise Rainer (*The Great Ziegfeld*)	Frank Capra (*Mr. Deeds Goes to Town*)	*The Great Ziegfeld*
1937	Spencer Tracy (*Captains Courageous*)	Luise Rainer (*The Good Earth*)	Leo McCarey (*The Awful Truth*)	*The Life of Emile Zola*
1938	Spencer Tracy (*Boys Town*)	Bette Davis (*Jezebel*)	Frank Capra (*You Can't Take It with You*)	*You Can't Take It with You*
1939	Robert Donat (*Goodbye Mr. Chips*)	Vivien Leigh (*Gone with the Wind*)	Victor Fleming (*Gone with the Wind*)	*Gone with the Wind*
1940	James Stewart (*The Philadelphia Story*)	Ginger Rogers (*Kitty Foyle*)	John Ford (*The Grapes of Wrath*)	*Rebecca*

began working for several of the city's dailies. Adams started at *The Evening Mail*, with his "Always in Good Humor" column, but in 1913 he moved to the *New York Tribune* (which became the *New York Herald, New York Tribune* in 1924 and the *New York Herald Tribune* from 1926 to 1966), where he worked until 1937. His column, containing bits on local events, was called "The Conning Tower" and was essentially the forerunner of the modern newspaper column with a byline.

He also wrote a column for the military newspaper *Stars and Stripes* from 1923 to 1931. After a dispute with the *Herald Tribune* in 1937, he moved his column to the *New York Post*, where it appeared until 1941. Historians Stanley Kunitz and Howard Hatcraft wrote in 1942: "It is as 'F.P.A.,' the conductor, versifier, wit, and sometimes scholar of 'The Coming Tower,' that he remains best known. In this, long our senior and most respected newspaper 'column,' appeared the early contributions to many of the celebrated Americans of today."

Adams's published works include *Tobogganing on Parnassus* (1911), *Women I'm Not Married To* (1922), *The Conning Tower Book* (1926), *The Second Conning Tower* (1927), and the two-volume *The Diary of Our Own Samuel Pepys* (1935). He died on March 23, 1960.

References: "Adams, Franklin Pierce" in Charles Moritz, ed., *Current Biography 1941* (New York: H. W. Wilson, 1941), 7–9; William F. Steirer, "Adams, Franklin Pierce" in Allen Johnson and Dumas Malone et al., eds., *Dictionary of American Biography* (New York: Charles Scribner's Sons, 1930–95), 6: 4–6; Stanley J. Kunitz and Howard Haycraft, eds., *Twentieth Century Authors: A Biographical Dictionary of Modern Literature* (New York: H. W. Wilson, 1942), 5–6; "Franklin P. Adams, Columnist, 78, Dies," *New York Times,* March 24, 1960, pp. 1, 33.

Addams, Jane (1860–1935)

American social worker, peace activist, and advocate for the poor. The daughter of John Huy Addams, a mill owner, and his wife Sarah (Weber) Addams, both Quakers, she was born on September 6, 1860, in Cedarville, Illinois. Addams suffered from a spinal deformity that left her disabled for life. Brought up and educated at home until she was 17, she entered the Rockford Female Seminary in Rockville, Illinois, in 1881, and graduated on the day that it was renamed Rockville College.

From an early age, Addams thought that she could improve the world through doctoring, and she studied medicine until a spinal operation left her bedridden for six months. She then visited Toynbee Hall in London, where historian and professor Arnold Toynbee had opened "the first of the world's great social settlements," and came to understand that she had to follow this course of reform. Returning to the United States, Addams and a friend and schoolmate, Ellen Gates Starr, planned a similar settlement community in Chicago for immigrants and the poor. They purchased a house on Halstead and Polk Streets, where on September 14, 1889, they opened Hull House. Addams remained its resident head until her death. Biographer Harriet Hyman Alonso writes: "The settlement boasted an array of clubs and functions, a day nursery, a gymnasium, and a cooperative boarding house for single working women." Addams described her labors at Hull House in numerous works, including the interwar classic, *Peace and Bread in Time of War* (1922).

A founding member of the Woman's Peace Party in 1915, Addams became the head of the Woman's International League for Peace and Freedom in 1919. A lifelong pacifist who fervently believed in civil liberties, she was also a founding member of the American Civil Liberties Union in 1920. During the 1920s and early 1930s Addams remained a powerful voice in these circles, and for this she shared the 1931 Nobel Peace Prize with Nicholas Murray Butler. In honoring her life's work, Nobel committee spokesperson Professor Halvdan Koht said, "We also render homage to the work which women can do for peace and human brotherhood." Addams lived only four years beyond the bestowal of the Nobel. She died on May 21, 1935.

Jane Addams holds a child at Hull House, 1930. *(CORBIS/Bettmann)*

References: Tyler Wasson, ed., *Nobel Prize Winners: An H. W. Wilson Biographical Dictionary* (New York: H. W. Wilson, 1987), 1–3; Mona Kerby, "Addams, Laura Jane" in Bernard S. and June H. Schlessinger, eds., *The Who's Who of Nobel Prize Winners* (Phoenix, Ariz.: Oryx, 1986), 135; Thomas Watson MacCallum, and Stephen Taylor, eds., *The Nobel Prize-Winners and the Nobel Foundation, 1901–1937* (Zurich, Switzerland: Central European Times Publishing, 1938), 377–78; James Weber Linn, *Jane Addams: A Biography* (New York and London: Appleton-Century Company, 1935); John C. Farrell, *Beloved Lady: A History of Jane Addams' Ideas on Reform and Peace* (Baltimore, Md.: Johns Hopkins University Press, 1967); Nancy Ann Slote, "Addams, Jane" in Harold Josephson, ed., *Biographical Dictionary of Modern Peace Leaders* (Westport, Conn.: Greenwood, 1985), 5–8; "Jane Adams" in Nancy L. Roberts, *American Peace Writers, Editors and Periodicals* (Westport, Conn.: Greenwood, 1991), 4–5; Harriet Hyman Alonso, "Addams, Jane" in Bruce W. Jentleson and Thomas G. Paterson, eds., *Encyclopedia of U.S. Foreign Relations* (New York: Oxford University Press, 1997), 1: 19–20; "Jane Addams, Peace Crusader and Foe of Slums, Dead at 74; Famous Founder of Hull House Loses Valiant Fight for Life After Operation at Chicago; Co-Winner of Nobel Prize," *Washington Post,* May 22, 1935, p. 1.

Adjusted Compensation Act of 1924

U.S. congressional legislation, also known as the World War Adjusted Compensation Act, enacted May 19, 1924, in a second attempt to provide a "bonus" to American veterans of World War I. The first attempt, in 1921, was called the Soldier's Compensation Bill, and although it passed through Congress (with opposition from conservative Republicans, who first demanded a balanced budget), the bill was vetoed by President Warren HARDING, who claimed that cutting the nation's taxes was a higher priority: "We may rely on the sacrifices of patriotism in war, but to-day we face new markets, and the effects of supply and demand, and the inexorable law of credits in time of peace. . . . A modest offering to the millions of service men is a poor palliative to more millions who may be out of employment."

In 1924, Congress enacted such a law, which was then passed over President Calvin COOLIDGE's veto, establishing a system of bonuses based on the length of service, with a higher share of the bonuses going to men who served overseas. If the bonus was $50 or less, it was to be paid in cash; above that amount was to be paid in certificates that would mature in 1945. To pay for these certificates, Congress enacted that 20 annual installments of $112 million would have to be appropriated. This was done and by 1932 Congress had put $896 million into the bonus account. Added to interest of $95 million, the account held $991 million.

See also BONUS MARCH.

Reference: Andrew Sinclair, *The Available Man: The Life behind the Masks of Warren Gamaliel Harding* (New York: Macmillan, 1965), 212.

Adjusted Compensation Act of 1936

U.S. congressional legislation enacted January 27, 1936, over President Franklin D. ROOSEVELT's veto that provided a bonus to American veterans of World War I. Also known as the Vinson-Patman-McCormack Act, the enactment was passed after veterans expressed that a bonus would help them through the GREAT DEPRESSION. During the 1932 election President Herbert HOOVER used troops to put down the BONUS MARCH riot by veterans of World War I who wanted their bonuses, promised by Congress, at that time instead of in 1945 when they were due. The military response ended any hope Hoover had of winning the presidential election. With Roosevelt in office, many veterans who had voted for him seemed to believe that a more sympathetic voice would be there to help. But one source on Roosevelt's attitude toward the veterans writes, "Roosevelt believed that the veterans' demands constituted an unwarranted raid on the federal treasury by a special interest group which jeopardized his efforts to bring an end to the depression."

In 1933, Roosevelt told the AMERICAN LEGION that "no person, because he wore a uniform, must thereafter be placed in a special class of beneficiaries over and above all other citizens." In 1935, however, Congress passed, over Roosevelt's veto, a restoration of veterans' pensions cut in 1933. "The following year [1936], Congress yielded to election-year pressures and passed legislation providing bonus payments to veterans," reports the source on the president. "Again Roosevelt vetoed the bill but this time quietly and in full recognition that Congress would override." Almost 20 years after the war, the American veterans who had fought for their country received their bonus.

References: James MacGregor Burns, *Roosevelt: The Lion and the Fox* (New York: Harcourt, Brace, 1956); Otis L. Graham, Jr., and Meghan Robinson Wander, eds., *Franklin D. Roosevelt: His Life and Times: An Encyclopedic View* (Boston: G. K. Hall, 1985), 436.

Adkins v. Children's Hospital

Landmark U.S. Supreme Court decision that struck down the right of Congress to enact minimum-wage legislation for women as violative of the Fifth Amendment to the Constitution. By the end of World War I, women earned far less than men in the United States; Congress sought to remedy the situation by enacting the Minimum Wage Act of September 19, 1918, which "authorize[d] the fixing of minimum wage standards for adult women, in any occupation in the District of Columbia." Two parties in Washington, D.C., came forward to challenge the law: Children's Hospital, which sought to enjoin the local Minimum Wage Board from enforcing the act on its nurses, and a maid at the Congress Hall Hotel who was earning $35 a week but was laid off because the board demanded she be paid more for her work. (She felt that the pay was adequate for the "short hours" she was working at the hotel.) Children's Hospital asked the District Court to hear the facts of the case; that court then struck down the law in both cases, and Adkins, head of the Minimum Wage Board, appealed to the U.S. Supreme Court. Arguments were heard before the Court on March 14, 1923.

Less than a month later, on April 9, the Court held that the minimum-wage law violated the Fifth Amendment, in which the Court found "that the right to contract about one's affairs is part of the liberty protected" by that section of the Constitution. Justice George Sutherland delivered the 6–2 opinion (Chief Justice William Howard Taft was joined in dissent by Justice Oliver Wendell HOLMES, while Justice Louis D. Brandeis did not participate). Sutherland wrote: "It has been said that legislation of the kind now under review is required in the interest of social justice, for whose ends freedom of contract may lawfully be subject to restraint. The liberty of the individual to do as he pleases, even in innocent matters, is not absolute. It must frequently yield to the common good, and the line beyond which the power of interference may not be pressed is neither definite nor unalterable, but may be made to move, within limits not well defined, with changing need and circumstance. Any attempt to fix a rigid boundary would be unwise, as well as futile. But, nevertheless, there are limits to the power, and when these have been passed, it becomes the plain duty of the courts in the proper exercise of their authority to so declare. To sustain the individual freedom of action contemplated by the Constitution is not to strike down the common good, but to exalt it, for surely the good of society as a whole cannot be better served than by the preservation against arbitrary restraint of the liberties of its constituent members." In 1937, at the height of the so-called COURT-PACKING CONTROVERSY, the Court essentially overruled the standard established in *Adkins* in *West Coast Hotel Co. v. Parrish*.

References: Grace Weatherford, *American Women's History* (New York: Prentice Hall, 1994), 6–7; Harold W. Chase, and Craig R. Ducat, *Constitutional Interpretation: Cases-Essays-Materials* (St. Paul, Minn.: West Publishing Company, 1979), 674–75; Alpheus Thomas Mason, *The Supreme Court from Taft to Warren* (Baton Rouge: Louisiana State University Press, 1958); Joel Francis Paschal, *Mr. Justice Sutherland: A Man against the State* (Princeton: Princeton University Press, 1951); *Adkins v. Children's Hospital* 261 US 525 (1923).

Adrian, Edgar Douglas (1889–1977)

English physiologist, corecipient (with Sir Charles Scott SHERRINGTON) of the 1932 Nobel Prize for physiology or medicine for his "discoveries regarding the function of the neurons" and how they operated inside the human body. The son of Alfred Douglas Adrian and Flora Lavinia (Barton) Adrian, Edgar Adrian was born in London, England, on November 30, 1889. He attended the prestigious Westminster School and Trinity College at Cambridge University, from which he received a bachelor's degree in 1911.

For two years Adrian studied the action of nerves inside the human body, after which he was elected to a fellowship at Trinity College, where he studied medicine. He then continued his medical training at St. Bartholomew's Hospital in London before earning his medical degree in 1915. After World War I, Adrian used wounded soldiers to test his work on nerves and nerve injuries. In 1920 he began what became a 55-year career as a professor at Cambridge University, where he continued his studies of nerves and neuron impulses. At this same time Professor Sherrington was performing the same research at Oxford University. In 1932 both men were honored for their breakthroughs. In presenting the award, Professor G. Lilestrand of the Royal Caroline Institute remarked, "Edgar Douglas

Adrian has attempted to illuminate the question of the nature of the processes connected with the lines to and from the stations and also within the receiving apparatuses, i.e., the sense organs. He has availed himself of the fact which has been well known since the middle of last century, that activity in an organ is usually accompanied by electric changes, in that a region in action becomes negatively charged in relation to one that is at rest."

Adrian, who was made a baron in 1955, worked until two years before his death on August 4, 1977.

References: Tyler Wasson, ed., *Nobel Prize Winners: An H. W. Wilson Biographical Dictionary* (New York: H. W. Wilson, 1987), 3–5; Rashell Karp, "Adrian, Edgar Douglas, Baron" in Bernard S. and June H. Schlessinger, eds., *The Who's Who of Nobel Prize Winners* (Phoenix, Ariz.: Oryx, 1986), 87–88; Thomas Watson MacCallum and Stephen Taylor, eds., *The Nobel Prize-Winners and the Nobel Foundation, 1901–1937* (Zurich, Switzerland: Central European Times Publishing, 1938), 226.

Agricultural Adjustment Act of 1933

U.S. congressional legislation, enacted May 12, 1933, which established the Agricultural Adjustment Administration (AAA) as part of Franklin Delano ROOSEVELT's NEW DEAL plan to end the GREAT DEPRESSION. Passed in the first two months of Roosevelt's administration in an attempt to subsidize farmers, the act was an omnibus farm-relief bill that embodied the plans of many national farm organizations to save the food production resource in the United States. Because more food was being produced, prices dropped, pushing many farmers out of business. The act created the AAA, which, under the control of the U.S. Agriculture Department, subsidized farmers by requiring that they cut their output. At the same time, the COMMODITY CREDIT CORPORATION gave loans and established storage programs.

By 1936 the program had lent farmers some $1.5 billion. However, in the case of *United States v. Butler et al.*, the U.S. Supreme Court held the act to be unconstitutional. Congress then enacted the AGRICULTURAL ADJUSTMENT ACT OF 1938, which was intended to pass constitutional muster.

References: Van L. Perkins, *Crisis in Agriculture: The Agriculture Adjustment Administration and the New Deal, 1933* (Berkeley: University of California Press, 1969); Theodore Saloutos and John D. Hicks, *Agricultural Discontent in the Midwest, 1900–1939* (Madison: University of Wisconsin Press, 1951).

Agricultural Adjustment Act of 1938

U.S. congressional legislation, enacted in response to the U.S. Supreme Court's striking down of the AGRICULTURAL

ADJUSTMENT ACT OF 1933 as unconstitutional in the case of *United States v. Butler et al.* This was followed by the passing of the Soil Conservation and Allotment Act, which sought to pay farmers to improve the soil quality, limit their yield, and increase prices—a key component of the 1933 act. When the Soil Act did not work well enough, President ROOSEVELT asked Congress to pass a second AAA, which he signed into law on February 16, 1938. Historian James Olson writes: "Titles I and II established the 'ever-normal granary' principle. The secretary of agriculture could set marketing quotas whenever the price of a particular crop was threatened by surplus production. Acreage allotments for individual farmers went into effect once two-thirds of the affected farmers had approved them in referendum elections." The act also established the COMMODITY CREDIT CORPORATION, which loaned farmers stipends to tide them over until prices stabilized.

References: William E. Leuchtenberg, *Franklin D. Roosevelt and the New Deal, 1932–1940* (New York: Harper & Row, 1963); Edward L. Schapsmeier and Frederick H. Schapsmeier, *Henry A. Wallace of Iowa: the Agrarian Years, 1910–1940* (Ames: Iowa State University Press, 1968); James Stuart Olson, *Historical Dictionary of the New Deal: From Inauguration to Preparation for War* (Westport, Conn.: Greenwood, 1985), 8–9.

Aiken, Conrad Potter (1889–1973)

American poet, critic, and writer, awarded the Pulitzer Prize in 1929 for *Selected Poems*. Born in Savannah, Georgia, on August 5, 1889, Aiken was haunted in his childhood when he discovered his parents' bodies—his father had killed his mother, then taken his own life. He went to private schools, then attended Harvard University, where he was a friend of T. S. ELIOT. After leaving Harvard, Aiken lived either in New York or in England until 1947, after which he returned to Savannah.

Starting in 1915, Aiken wrote a series of "symphonies" in which his poetry seemed to resemble music. In 1920 he turned to fiction, writing a series of short stories that were highly popular. His collected works—ranging from *Punch: The Immortal Liar, Documents in His History* (1921) and *Priapus and the Pool* (1922) to *The Pilgrimage of Festus* (1923) and *Bring! Bring! And Other Stories* (1925)—earned him wide praise. His 1929 *Selected Poems* won the Pulitzer Prize for poetry. In the 1930s perhaps his greatest work was *Among the Lost People* (1934), which included the short story "Mr. Arculis."

Aiken remained an active literary force through the late 1960s. He died in Savannah on August 17, 1973.

References: Conrad Aiken (Louis Untermeyer, ed.), *Conrad Aiken* (New York: Simon & Schuster, 1927); Jay Martin, *Conrad Aiken: A Life of His Art* (Princeton, N.J.: Princeton University Press, 1962); Florence W. Bonnell, *Conrad Aiken: A Bibliography (1902–1978)* (San Marino, Calif.: Huntington Library, 1982); "Conrad Aiken, Poet and Novelist, Dies," *New York Times,* August 18, 1973, pp. 1, 24.

Al-Banna, Hasan (1906–1949)

Egyptian nationalist leader, founding member of the Muslim Brotherhood, a leading nationalist organization in the Middle East in the 1920s and 1930s. Born in 1906 in the village of Mahmudiyah near Alexandria, Egypt, he was a nationalist from an early age. Al-Banna attended the Damanhur Teachers' Training College and the Dar al-Ulum University in Cairo. In 1927 he began teaching, at the same time working as a correspondent for the Cairo Muslim Youth magazine *Al-fath* ("The Beginning"). He also helped establish the Young Men's Muslim Association (YMMA).

In March 1928, al-Banna founded the Muslim Brothers, which historian David Commins said was done "with the purpose of promoting true Islam and launching a struggle against foreign domination" of Egypt. The following year, it was being renamed the Muslim Brotherhood (Jamiyat al-Ikhwan al-Muslimun) in underground newspapers. By 1945 the Brotherhood had an estimated five hundred thousand members. As the movement's head, Al-Banna himself was called the *murshid* (guide). However, he had to compete with the Wafd Party, which ruled Egypt, and the British, who controlled the nation for most of al-Banna's life. In the late 1930s he called on King Farouk and the rest of the nation's leadership to disband the government and formulate an Islamic state, free from secular and Western influences. In 1939, al-Banna took over the editorial duties of the journal *Al-manar* ("The Lighthouse") for two years.

As political tensions worsened over the next decade, the government saw al-Banna as a continuing threat. On February 12, 1949, the Egyptian secret police executed him on a Cairo street. He was just 43 years old. For years al-Banna was regarded as a martyr by his supporters and the Muslim Brotherhood, which was dissolved by the British government in 1955 but still exists in closed circles, considered by many a terrorist organization.

References: Nazih N. Ayubi, "Muslim Brotherhood," and Oliver Carré, "Banna, Hasan al-" in John L. Esposito, ed., *The Oxford Encyclopedia of the Modern Islamic World* (New York: Oxford University Press, 1995), 1: 195–99; Edmund Jan Osmañczyk, *The Encyclopedia of the United Nations and International Agreements* (Philadelphia: Taylor and Francis, 1985), 531; Joan Wucher King, *Historical Dictionary of Egypt* (Metuchen, N.J.: Scarecrow, 1984), 348–53; David Commins, "Hasan al-Banna" in Ali Rahnema, ed., *Pioneers of Islamic Revival* (London: Zed Books Ltd., 1994), 125–53.

Alexander of Yugoslavia (1888–1934)

Yugoslavian king, who helped to unite the disparate ethnic minorities of the Balkans into the state that later became Yugoslavia. Born in Cetinje, Serbia (now part of the reformulated Yugoslavia), on December 16, 1888, Alexander was the son of Peter I of the Karageorgević royal family, the king of Serbia (1903–21), and the grandson of Alexander Karageorgević. In exile with his father, Alexander spent much of his youth in St. Petersburg, Russia. In 1909, when his family was reinstated to the throne and his older brother renounced the royal title, Alexander returned to Serbia as the heir apparent. In charge of Serbia's forces during World War I, he was at the head of the army that entered Belgrade in triumph on October 31, 1918. On December 1, he proclaimed the establishment of the Kingdom of Serbs, Croats, and Slovenes.

On August 16, 1921, following an unsuccessful attempt on his life, Alexander was crowned as king of this kingdom, which on October 3, 1929, he renamed *Yugoslavia* ("Land of the Slavs"). That same year, he married Princess Marie, daughter of Ferdinand I of Romania. During the 1920s he was forced to deal with the different ethnic divisions inside his artificial nation, as well as the assassinations of Croat officials by a Montenegrin deputy in the parliament. This forced Alexander to disband the parliament, abolish the constitution that he had promulgated in 1921, and establish a royal dictatorship. By the end of the decade, he had banned all political parties based on ethnic or religious differences, standardized schools across the entire nation, and calmed relations with Bulgaria (1933), with Czechoslovakia and Romania in the so-called Little Entente (1920–21), and with Greece, Romania, and Turkey in the Balkan Entente (1934).

At home, Alexander established a police state and became a despised oppressor of many of the minorities that he had sought to bring under one authority. In the 1931 constitution, he established this dictatorship in the rule of law. The worldwide financial depression that began in the early 1930s swept over Yugoslavia and made matters worse. By 1934, Alexander was considering restoring the parliamentary form of government that he had once overseen. He worked closely with French Foreign Minister Jean-Louis BARTHOU to establish peace in the Balkans. While motoring through the streets of Marseille on October 9, 1934, to meet with Barthou, Alexander fell to a Macedonian terrorist, Vlada Gheorghieff, who shot both men while cameras were rolling. Alexander died in the car; Barthou died later that evening. Gheorghieff was wrestled to the ground by the police and beaten fatally, dying later of his wounds.

References: Stephen Graham, *Alexander of Yugoslavia: The Story of the King Who was Murdered at Marseilles* (New Haven: Yale University Press, 1939); Allen Roberts, *The Turning Point: The Assassination of Louis Barthou and King Alexander I of Yugoslavia* (New York: St. Martin's Press, 1970); Harry M. Lentz, III, *Assassinations and Executions: An Encyclopedia of Political Violence, 1865–1986* (Jefferson, N.C.: McFarland & Company, 1988), 62–63; "King of Yugoslavia Murdered. M. Barthou Fatally Wounded. Croat Assassin's Attack at Marseilles. Criminal Cut Down," *The Times* (London), October 10, 1934, p. 14; "Obituary: King Alexander of Yugoslavia. Statesmanship and Diplomacy," *The Times* (London), October 10, 1934, p. 19; "After The Murders. Moving Ceremonies at Marseilles. King Alexander's Voyage Home Begun. The Queen and Her Son," *The Times* (London), October 11, 1934, p. 14.

Alexandretta   *See* ISKENDERUN.

Alfonso XIII (1886–1941)

Spanish king, ruled 1902–31. He was born on May 17, 1886, seven months after the death of his father, Alfonso XII, and immediately proclaimed as the Spanish monarch, under the regency of his mother, María Cristina, until 1902. Much of his reign was drowned in strife. During the early 1920s uprisings by the Rif tribesmen in Spanish Morocco led to a military campaign to crush the insurrection and to a military disaster for the Spanish army, capped off by ABD EL-KRIM's victory at Annoval in 1921. Two years later the military situation led to a coup d'état by General Miguel Primo de Rivera and the establishment, with Alfonso's consent, of a military government. In 1925 this was replaced by a more civil dictatorship, led by José Calvo Sotelo and Rafael Benjumea conde de Guadalhorce, among others. De Rivera led an expedition to Morocco, landing at Alhucemas Bay and defeating the Rif warriors. In 1930 de Rivera was forced to step down and was succeeded by General Dámaso Berenguer y Fusté and Admiral Juan Bautista Aznar, who called for municipal elections. The peace in Spain did not last. When the elections, held on April 12, 1931, returned an overwhelming Republican majority, Alfonso lost the army's support and went into voluntary exile to avoid a civil war. After he left, however, war did break out, scarring the nation and making way for General Francisco FRANCO's Fascist government.

Alfonso never returned to his native land. Although Franco reinstated him as a Spanish citizen and returned his lands and property to him, Alfonso abdicated the Spanish throne to his third son, Don Juan. Alfonso died in Rome on February 28, 1941.

See also SPANISH CIVIL WAR.

References: Vicente R. Pilapil, *Alfonso XIII* (New York: Twayne Publishers, 1969); Vicente Blasco Ibáñez (Leo Ongley, trans.), *Alfonso XIII Unmasked: The Military Terror in Spain* (New York: E. P. Dutton, 1924); "Alfonso Abandons Throne and Leaves Spain; Republic Established Under Provisional Premier; King Renounces Claims of Self and Son and Leave to Board Ship for England; Zamora Forms Cabinet and Takes Control," New York *Herald* (European Edition), April 15, 1931, p. 1.

Algonquin Round Table

Informal group of American literary figures who met from 1919 to 1943 for lunch and discussions of literature and other topics in the Algonquin Hotel in New York City. The group began lunching in 1919 at a huge table in the hotel, and within a few years had grown into a large and comprehensive crowd, embracing many of the leading literary figures in New York City. Among the people who met at the round table were Franklin Pierce ADAMS, humorist Robert Benchley, Heywood BROUN, Marc CONNELLY, *New York Evening Post* columnist Russel Crouse, novelist Edna Ferber, George S. Kaufman, comedian Harpo MARX, Dorothy PARKER, *New Yorker* editor Harold Wallace Ross, playwright and *Life* magazine editor Robert Emmet Sherwood, and journalist and drama critic Alexander Woollcott. The celebrated offshoot of the round table, where those members played cards, was called the Thanatopsis Inside Straight Literary and Chowder Club. The group last met at the Algonquin in 1943, after which the living members went their separate ways.

References: Margaret Case Harriman, *The Vicious Circle: The Story of the Algonquin Round Table* (New York: Rinehart, 1951); James R. Gaines, *Wit's End: Days and Nights of the Algonquin Round Table* (New York: Harcourt Brace Jovanovich, 1977).

Allen, Frederick Lewis (1890–1954)

American editor, author, and historian. Born in Boston on July 1, 1890, Allen attended the prestigious Groton School, then received his bachelor's and master's degrees from Harvard University, where he befriended fellow writer Robert Benchley and cartoonist Gluyas Williams. He then worked for a time for the editor of *Atlantic* magazine. Although opposed to U.S. intervention in World War I, Allen left the magazine in 1917 to become director of publicity for the Council of National Defense in Washington, D.C.

After the war he moved back to Cambridge, where he served for a time as director of publicity for Harvard University. In 1923 Harper and Brothers, the major New York publishing house at the time, offered him a position with the company as the assistant editor of *Harper's Magazine.* He worked under Thomas B. Wells and Lee Hartman before becoming editor in 1941. The STOCK MARKET CRASH of 1929 inspired Allen to write a history of the 1920s. *Only Yesterday* (1931), now considered a landmark chronicle of that era, sold more than a million copies. In 1933 he published, *The American Procession,* a photographic history of

the United States from the Civil War to the U.S. intervention in World War I. His *The Lords of Creation* (1935) told the story of the rise of American economic power from the 1890s until the GREAT DEPRESSION. His later works include *Since Yesterday* (1940), a continuation of his first major book, and *The Big Change* (1952), which explained American science and technology in the first half of the twentieth century. Allen died on February 13, 1954.

References: Leonard Weeks, "Allen, Frederick Lewis," in Allen Johnson and Dumas Malone et al., eds., *Dictionary of American Biography* (New York: Charles Scribner's Sons, 1930–95), 5: 16–17; Darwin Payne, *The Man of Only Yesterday: Frederick Lewis Allen, Former Editor of Harper's Magazine, Author, and Interpreter of His Times* (New York: Harper & Row, 1975).

All Quiet on the Western Front

Landmark interwar novel, published in Germany in 1929 as *Im Western Nichts Neues* (and released in the United States six months later with the English translation by A. W. Wheen), by German writer Erich Maria Remarque. The work is considered the leading antiwar book—and, later, film—of the period. It deals with the emotions and attitudes of several young Germans who fight at the front during World War I. In the introduction, Remarque penned: "This story is neither an accusation nor a confession, and least of all an adventure, for death is not an adventure to those who stand face to face with it. It will try simply to tell of a generation of men who even though they may have escaped its shells, were destroyed by the war." Lewis Milestone directed the 1930 Oscar-winning motion picture based on the work, which starred Lew Ayres as the lead character Paul Bäumer.

References: Richard Arthur Firda, *All Quiet on the Western Front: Literary Analysis and Cultural Context* (New York: Twayne, 1993); Leonard Maltin, ed., "Movie and Video Guide 1996 Edition" (New York: Plume, 1995), 25.

alphabet agencies

Through U.S. president Franklin D. ROOSEVELT's national economic policy known as the NEW DEAL, a series of programs was enacted to combat the crippling effects of the GREAT DEPRESSION on agriculture, banking, and employment. These programs were carried out through the creation of dozens of agencies and commissions, such as the Agricultural Adjustment Administration (AAA), the CIVILIAN CONSERVATION CORPS (CCC), the FARM SECURITY ADMINISTRATION (FSA), the NATIONAL RECOVERY ADMINISTRATION (NRA), the Tennessee Valley Authority (TVA), and the WORKS PROGRESS ADMINISTRATION (WPA). These agencies were referred to as "alphabet agencies" because of their numerous acronyms.

Scene from the influential film *All Quiet on the Western Front* (*CORBIS/Bettmann*)

The table below lists the New Deal's "alphabet soup" acronyms and their proper names.

American Association for Old Age Security   *See* SOCIAL SECURITY ACT.

American Civil Liberties Union (ACLU)
Preeminent American civil liberties and civil rights organization, formed by American activists Jane ADDAMS, Helen Keller, Norman Mattoon Thomas, Felix Frankfurter, and Roger Nash BALDWIN, among others, in 1920.

ACRONYMS OF THE NEW DEAL AGENCIES

AAA	Agricultural Adjustment Administration		FCA	Farm Credit Administration
BCLB	Bituminous Coal Labor Board		FCC	Federal Communications Commission
BOB	Bureau of the Budget		FCIC	Federal Crop Insurance Program
CAA	Civil Aeronautics Authority		FDIC	Federal Deposit Insurance Corporation
CCC	Civilian Conservation Corps		FERA	Federal Emergency Relief Agency
CCC	Commodity Credit Corporation		FFMC	Federal Farm Mortgage Administration
CWA	Civil Works Administration		FHA	Federal Housing Administration

FLA	Federal Loan Agency
FSA	Farm Security Administration
FSA	Federal Security Agency
FTC	Federal Trade Commission
FWA	Federal Works Agency
HOLC	Home Owners Loan Corporation
MLB	Maritime Labor Board
NBCC	National Bituminous Coal Commission
NLB	National Labor Board
NLRB	National Labor Relations Board
NRAB	National Railroad Adjustment Board
NRA	National Recovery Administration
NRB	National Resources Board
NRC	National Resources Committee
NRPB	National Resources Planning Board
NYA	National Youth Administration
PWA	Public Works Administration
RA	Resettlement Administration
REA	Rural Electrification Administration
RFC	Reconstruction Finance Corporation
RRB	Railroad Retirement Board
SCS	Soil Conservation Service
SEC	Securities and Exchange Commission
SSB	Social Security Board
TNEC	Temporary National Economic Committee
TVA	Tennessee Valley Authority
USEP	United States Employment Service
USHA	United States Housing Authority
USMC	United States Maritime Commission
WPA	Works Progress Administration

Source: Otis L. Graham, Jr. and Meghan Robinson Wander, eds., *Franklin D. Roosevelt: His Life and Times: An Encyclopedic View* (Boston: G. K. Hall, 1985), 287.

The ACLU was founded amid an atmosphere of governmental crackdowns on fundamental civil liberties. Originally constituted as the American Union Against Militarism (AAUM) during World War I, the group later became the National Civil Liberties Bureau, dedicated to fighting government oppression. Joined by such liberal luminaries as Crystal Eastman (whose brother, Max Forrester Eastman, was then a leading American communist), an original member of the AAUM, the ACLU was formed in 1920 to fight the RED SCARE and the U.S. government's attempts to deport suspected communists. Perhaps its most famous case during the interwar period was the SCOPES TRIAL—the "monkey trial"—in which a Tennessee teacher was prosecuted for teaching evolution in school. The group also opposed the censorship in the United States of the James JOYCE novel *Ulysses.* The ACLU aided in the defense of Italian anarchists Nicola SACCO and Bartolomeo VANZETTI in 1921 and the SCOTTSBORO BOYS in Alabama in 1931. In the late 1930s, the ACLU defended the right of the children of Jehovah's Witnesses not to salute the U.S. flag in public schools.

References: Donald Johnson, "American Civil Liberties Union: Origins, 1914–1924" (Ph.D. diss., Columbia University, 1960); Samuel Walker, *In Defense of American Liberties: A History of the ACLU* (New York: Oxford University Press, 1990); Robert K. Murray, *Red Scare: A Study in National Hysteria, 1919–1920* (Minneapolis: University of Minnesota Press, 1955).

American Farm Bureau Federation (AFBF)

U.S. farm advocacy association, established 1920 by agricultural leaders in the United States, among them Henry Cantwell Wallace, editor of *Farm and Dairy Journal,* an influential farming and agricultural publication and future secretary of agriculture (1921–24) in the Harding administration. Growing out of the country farm bureau movement, which sought in the early years of the twentieth century to advocate farmers' rights, the AFBF was organized at a convention of state farm bureaus in Chicago in 1919. During the 1920s the federation supported reform of farming laws and lent their endorsement of the McNary-Haugen Act, a leading piece of profarm legislation that was vetoed by President Calvin COOLIDGE. In the 1930s the AFBF supported the passage of the AGRICULTURAL ADJUSTMENT ACT OF 1933 and the AGRICULTURAL ADJUSTMENT ACT OF 1938. Today, the group calls itself "the world's largest voluntary organization of farmers and ranchers." In 1998 more than 4.5 million family farms belonged to more than 2,700 farm bureaus across the United States that belong to separate state bureau organizations in all 50 states and Puerto Rico.

References: Christiana McFadyen Campbell, *The Farm Bureau and the New Deal: A Study of the Making of National Farm Policy, 1933–1940* (Urbana: University of Illinois Press, 1962); Samuel R. Berger, *Dollar Harvest: The Story of the Farm Bureau* (Lexington, Mass.: Heath Lexington Books, 1971).

American Federation of Labor

Premier U.S. labor union during the 1920s and 1930s, organized by Samuel Gompers in 1886. Begun as the Knights of Labor, the group soon became one of the leading American unions, unifying U.S. labor as never before. In the 1920s the nation enjoyed prosperity, but the AFL did not. For example, the United Mine Workers saw much of their financial security lost in bitter wage reductions forced by mine owners. After the STOCK MARKET

CRASH in 1929 and the massive unemployment that followed, the labor union saw the potential end of any power they might have held. Then came the administration of Franklin D. ROOSEVELT. Under Roosevelt the national government saw labor not as a threat but as a partner in the effort to restimulate the sagging economy. With such enactments as the NATIONAL RECOVERY ADMINISTRATION, the Tennessee Valley Association, and other "back-to-work" laws, the government sought to aid in the nation's industrial recovery. Under section 7 of the National Industrial Recovery Act, the unions saw the rights to organize and to strike. Roosevelt established a NATIONAL LABOR RELATIONS BOARD with the signing of Executive Order 6763 on June 29, 1934.

One of the most important union leaders at this time was John Llewellyn Lewis, head of the United Mine Workers. In 1935 he formed inside the AFL the Congress of Industrial Organizations (CIO), which represented those workers in the steel, automobile, and other "mass production industries." A tough battle went on between the two groups until 1955, when the AFL and the CIO merged to form the AFL-CIO.

References: Philip Taft, *The A.F. of L. from the Death of Gompers to the Merger* (New York: Octagon Books, 1970); Lewis L. Lorwin, *The American Federation of Labor: History, Policies, and Prospects* (Washington, D.C.: The Brookings Institution, 1933); Irving Bernstein, *The Lean Years: A History of the American Worker, 1920–1933* (Boston: Houghton Mifflin, 1960).

Americanization

Campaign sponsored by U.S. Federal, local, and private organizations, launched after the end of World War I, mainly to teach immigrants to the United States the English language and other basic skills. Between 1890 and 1920 a wave of immigrants, particularly from eastern and southern European nations, brought to the United States people who were different from many of the immigrants who had come earlier in the century. A national committee as well as countless local civic organizations, settlement houses, domestic science classes, English language classes, and immigrant protective services embraced the movement. Some viewed these new immigrants as a potential threat if they did not quickly "Americanize," or learn the language and customs of their new land.

Sinclair LEWIS, in his 1920 work *Main Street,* called Americanization the method by which "the sound American customs absorbed without one trace of pollution another alien invasion." At first, the Americanization program sought to interpret America to the new settlers to elicit voluntary consent to citizenship, and to cultivate a patriotic loyalty. For example, settlement house workers such as Lillian Wald and Jane ADDAMS taught language,

civics, and housekeeping classes in efforts to Americanize the female immigrant. In many ways the movement hinged on immigrant women, who would raise the next generation of citizens. The program often focused on replacing the immigrants' "antimodern" or "Old World" customs with more efficient, "American" traditions. But as time went on, the laws behind the movement became more restrictive against those immigrants who resisted, and began to include the requirement of speaking English to hold a job or to vote. Although the movement never found its way into the mainstream, the immigrants endeavored to find their own definitions of "being American" within their or their children's generation.

References: Edward George Hartmann, *The Movement to Americanize the Immigrant* (New York: Columbia University Press, 1948); William Spencer Bernard, ed., *Americanization Studies: The Acculturation of Immigrant Groups into American Society* (Montclair, N.J.: Patterson Smith, 1971); John F. McClymer, "Gender and the 'American Way of Life': Women in the Americanization Movement," *Journal of American Ethnic History* 10, no. 3 (1991): 3–20.

American Legion

American veterans' organization, founded in Paris in 1919. On March 15, 1919, just four months after the end of World War I, members of the former American Expeditionary Force—the units of U.S. soldiers who first served on the front lines of the war in 1917—gathered for a three-day conference that culminated in the founding of the American Legion. On September 16 of that year the U.S. Congress granted the organization a charter, which was changed in later years to admit veterans of World War II, Korea, and Vietnam. Its only membership prerequisite is that one has to have been an honorably discharged service member. The largest such association of its kind, representing some three million veterans by the 1990s, the American Legion has a national headquarters in Indianapolis, Indiana, as well as seven regional offices, 51 state bureaus, and more than 16,000 local posts. It lobbies for good health care and benefits on behalf of these veterans.

In 1921, British war veterans founded the British Legion (modeled after the American counterpart), headquartered in London.

References: Thomas A. Rumer, *The American Legion: An Official History, 1919–1989* (New York: M. Evans, 1990); Raymond Moley, *The American Legion Story* (New York: Duell, Sloan and Pearce, 1966); Roscoe Baker, *The American Legion and American Foreign Policy* (New York: Bookman Associates, 1954); Richard S. Jones, *A History of the American Legion* (Indianapolis: Bobbs-Merrill, 1947); "American Legion, The" in Louis Filler, *A Dictionary of American Conservatism* (Secaucus, N.J.: Citadel Press, 1988), 33; Jerel A. Rosati, "American

Legion" in Bruce W. Jentleson and Thomas G. Paterson, senior eds., *Encyclopedia of U.S. Foreign Relations* (New York: Oxford University Press, 1997), 1: 65–66.

American Mercury   *See* MENCKEN, H. L.

Amritsar Massacre   *See* JALLIANWALA BAGH MASSACRE.

Amundsen, Roald (1872–1928)

Norwegian explorer who navigated the Northwest Passage, noted for Flying over the North Pole (1926) along with the American Lincoln Ellsworth and the Italian Umberto Nobile. Born in the village of Vedsten, in Ostfold, Norway, on July 16, 1872, Amundsen studied medicine for two years at the University of Christiana (now the University of Oslo), then joined the Norwegian naval service in 1893. Four years after entering the service, he was named first officer on the *Belgica*, a ship involved in the Belgian South Polar Expedition. Starting in 1901, Amundsen began to make oceanographic researches off the coast of Greenland in the *Gjoa*, a small research vessel, and in 1903 he set out to find the position of the magnetic North Pole. He became the first to successfully navigate a ship from the Atlantic Ocean to the Pacific Ocean through the Northwest Passage. With the triumphant expedition to the North Pole of Robert E. Peary in 1909, Amundsen announced in 1910 that he would attempt to discover the South Pole, which he did on December 14, 1911.

In 1918, he attempted to sail from Norway to the North Pole but did not succeed. Amundsen sought to cross over the North Pole in an airplane in 1925 and was unsuccessful. In the following year, starting on May 11, he flew from Spitsbergen in the Italian dirigible *Norge* ("Norway"), and two days later crossed over the Pole with fifteen other men, including Ellsworth, Nobile, and the Norwegian Hjalmar Riiser-Larsen, landing in Teller, Alaska. The ship's captain, Oscar Wisting, had also been with Amundsen during his trip to the South Pole. They became the first men to see both poles. Amundsen claimed that he was the first across in the name of Norway, while Nobile claimed it in the name of Italy. The two men quarreled and never spoke again. In 1928, when Amundsen heard that Nobile and the *Norge* had crashed, he set out to rescue his old friend. Instead, his plane disappeared. Nobile was rescued but Amundsen was never heard from again.

References: Bellamy Partridge, *Amundsen* (London: R. Hale, 1953); Charles Turley, *Roald Amundsen, Explorer* (London: Methuen & Co., 1935); Helmer Julius Hanssen, *Voyages of a Modern Viking* (London: G. Routledge & Sons, 1936).

Anderson, Carl David, Jr. (1905–1991)

American physicist, corecipient (with Victor Franz HESS) of the 1936 Nobel Prize in physics for his discovery of the positron. Born in New York City on September 3, 1905, Anderson was educated at the California Institute of Technology, which awarded him a bachelor's degree (1927) and doctorate (1930). There he served as a physics professor as well as an administrator from 1930 until his retirement in 1977.

According to his biographer, Sarah Spurgin: "In August 1932 Anderson photographed a charged particle moving upward, and because cosmic rays only move downward, he concluded that this must be a positively charged particle released inside the cloud chamber. The particle appeared to have the mass of an electron, and its ionizing power was too weak to be a proton or alpha particle. Carl Anderson had discovered the positive electron which would become a significant contribution to the understanding of atomic structure." Prof. H. Pleijel, chairman of the Nobel Committee for Physics of the Royal Swedish Academy of Sciences, in presenting the Nobel to Anderson, said, "In the course of your comprehensive studies on the nature and qualities of cosmic radiation you have made important and material contributions to the elucidation of the questions involved, and by utilizing ingenious devices you have succeeded in finding one of the buildingstones of the universe, the positive electron. We congratulate you on this great success attained in your young years and we wish to express the hope that your further investigations will bring to science many new and equally important results."

Anderson died in San Marino, California, on January 11, 1991.

References: Tyler Wasson, ed., *Nobel Prize Winners: An H. W. Wilson Biographical Dictionary* (New York: H. W. Wilson, 1987), 19–20; Sarah H. Spurgin, "Anderson, Carl David" in Bernard S. and June H. Schlessinger, eds., "The Who's Who of Nobel Prize Winners" (Phoenix, Ariz.: Oryx, 1986), 162; Thomas Watson MacCallum, and Stephen Taylor, eds., *The Nobel Prize-Winners and the Nobel Foundation, 1901–1937* (Zurich, Switzerland: Central European Times Publishing, 1938), 103; "[Obituary:] Carl D. Anderson, 85, Physicist, 1936 Nobel Laureate," *Boston Globe,* January 13, 1991, p. 43.

Anderson, Marian (1897–1993)

American contralto, early civil rights advocate for African Americans. Born in Philadelphia, Pennsylvania, on February 17, 1897, Anderson began to sing when she was only three and joined her church choir three years later. Her father died when she was 12, after which she sang to financially support her family. Anderson's talent was discovered in 1925, when she won first prize at a competition sponsored by the New York Philharmonic Orchestra. Her debut that year was hailed as a success, and in the early 1930s she toured Europe. From 1935 she toured the United States, eventually reaching New York's Carnegie Hall. During this period she became the best-known contralto in the world.

In 1939, Howard University sought to have her sing at Constitution Hall in Washington, D.C., an auditorium run by the Daughters of the American Revolution (DAR). When the DAR turned down the request because of Anderson's skin color, First Lady Eleanor ROOSEVELT resigned her DAR membership in protest. She then asked Secretary of the Interior Harold Ickes to arrange an outdoor concert for Anderson. On Easter Sunday in 1939 some seventy-five thousand people appeared before the Lincoln Memorial to hear Anderson sing. She began the concert with the patriotic *My Country 'Tis of Thee;* countless others heard the broadcast on radio. Later that year the First Lady presented Anderson with the Spingarn Medal of the National Association for the Advancement of Colored People. Four years later, the DAR, contrite over the incident, invited Anderson to sing at Constitution Hall, an offer which was accepted.

Anderson's professional career continued through the early 1960s, and she received numerous awards in recognition of both her talent and her work on behalf of human rights. She died in Portland, Oregon, on April 8, 1993.

References: Catherine Udall Turley, "Marian Anderson" in Frank Magill, ed., *Great Lives from History—American Women Series* (Pasadena, Calif.: Salem Press, 1985), 1: 55–59; Grace Weatherford, *American Women's History* (New York: Prentice Hall, 1994), 12–13; David Bianco, "Marian Anderson" in Barbara Carlisle Bigelow, ed., *Contemporary Black Biography* (Detroit: Gale Research, 1992), 2: 5–9: Mildred Denby Green, "Anderson, Marian" in Darlene Clark Hine, ed., *Black Women in America: An Historical Encyclopedia* (Brooklyn, N.Y.: Carlson Publishing, 1993), 1: 29–33; Allan Kozinn, "Marian Anderson Is Dead at 96; Singer Shattered Racial Barriers," *New York Times*, April 9, 1993, p. A1.

Andrews, Roy Chapman (1884–1960)
American naturalist, explorer, and author, noted for his 1920s excavations in China and Central Asia. Born in Beloit, Wisconsin, on January 26, 1884, the son of Charles Ezra Andrews and Cora May (Chapman) Andrews, Roy Andrews received his bachelor's degree from Beloit College in 1906 and immediately went to work for the American Museum of Natural History in New York.

With his first assignment, that of unearthing a whale skeleton at Amagansett, on New York's Long Island, Andrews began a life of archaeological research. He served as a naturalist on an expedition to the Dutch East Indies from 1909 to 1910 on the U.S.S. *Albatross,* investigated unexplored areas in northern Korea in 1911, and exca-

vated for dinosaur bones during six trips into the Gobi Desert in central China from 1921 to 1930. On these latter explorations, Andrews discovered the first dinosaur eggs seen by humans, as well as the skeleton of the baluchitherium, then the largest known mammal. In a letter written during one of his dinosaur hunts, Andrews explained, "These beasts we are digging up out here—only their bones, of course—were certainly as big as dragons, and twice as ugly. They lived at least 10,000,000 years ago; and they must have been very fat and well-fed to judge from their enormous size. For instance, one we just dug up had a jaw seven feet long and teeth more than a foot wide!" He wrote several books of his research, including *Across Mongolian Plains* (1921), *On the Trail of Ancient Man* (1926), *The Ends of the Earth* (1929), and *This Business of Exploring* (1935). Of these, one critic wrote, "Roy Chapman Andrews has never written a dull book or an unscientific one."

Andrews served as director of the American Museum of Natural History until his retirement in 1941. He spent his final years in California's Carmel Valley, where he died of a heart attack on March 11, 1960.

See also BEEBE, Charles William.

References: John Whiteclay Chambers III, "Andrews, Roy Chapman" in Allen Johnson and Dumas Malone et al., eds., *Dictionary of American Biography* (New York: Charles Scribner's Sons, 1930–95), 6: 17–19; Roy Chapman Andrews, *Ends of the Earth* (New York: G. P. Putnam's Sons, 1929); Fitzhugh Green, *Roy Chapman Andrews: Dragon Hunter* (New York: G. P. Putnam's Sons, 1930), iii; "Dr. Roy Chapman Andrews, Explorer, Naturalist, Dies," *New York Herald-Tribune,* March 12, 1960, p. 1.

Angell, Sir Norman (1872–1967)
British economist, writer, and lecturer, awarded the Nobel Peace Prize in 1933 for his numerous writings. Born Ralph Norman Angell Lane on December 26, 1872, in Holbeach, Lincolnshire, England, he attended local schools and then the Geneva University. In 1889 he borrowed 50 pounds from his father and traveled to the United States, where he held a series of odd jobs in the Southwest. Angell returned to Europe in 1898, setting up a printing press in Paris and pumping out an English-language newspaper called *The Daily Messenger.* He eventually rose to become editor in 1904 of *The Continental Daily Mail.*

In 1903 he wrote his first book, *Patriotism under Three Flags,* which was published under the name Norman Lane. Six years later he released *Europe's Optical Illusion,* rereleased in 1910 under the title *The Great Illusion.* Angell sought to explain in this work the reasoning behind the threat of war in Europe. Writes biographer Irwin Abrams, "The book made Angell famous. It was translated into twenty-five foreign languages, sold more than two million copies, and produced a peace movement called 'Norman Angellism.'"

World War I seemed to vindicate Angell's idea that a comprehensive world body was needed to make sure such a war was never fought again. As biographer Frank Hardie explains, "Angell was one of the pioneers of the idea of the League of Nations. . . . From the creation of the League of Nations onwards Angell's main doctrinal emphasis was on the putting of force in international affairs behind the law rather than the litigants. By this emphasis he hoped, but failed, to merge the ranks of 'internationalists' and pacifists." After the war, Angell published *The Fruits of Victory* (1921) and *The Unseen Assassins* (1932).

In 1931 he was knighted, and two years later he was awarded the Nobel Prize. The award was not given until 1934, however, when it was presented with the 1934 winner. Ironically, it was at this time that Angell was arguing, unlike other pacifists, that war against fascist dictators was acceptable if freedom was defended. In the last two decades of his life, he became more of a supporter of Anglo-American internationalism, claiming that the strength of the two nations could help deter another world war. He died at his home in Croydon, England, on October 7, 1967.

References: Frank L. Turner, "Angell, Norman, Sir" in Bernard S. and June H. Schlessinger, eds., "The Who's Who of Nobel Prize Winners" (Phoenix, Ariz.: Oryx, 1986), 135–36; Frank Hardie, "Angell, Sir (Ralph) Norman" in Sir Leslie Stephen and Sir Sidney Lee et al., eds., *The Dictionary of National Biography* (Oxford, England: Oxford University Press, 1917–1993), 7: 31–32; Thomas Watson MacCallum and Stephen Taylor, eds., *The Nobel Prize-Winners and the Nobel Foundation, 1901–1937* (Zurich, Switzerland: Central European Times Publishing Co. 1938), 381–82; "The Reminiscences of Norman Angell," Oral History Memoir, Oral History Research Office, Columbia University; Ralph Norman Angell, *The Great Illusion, 1933: A Study of the Relation of Military Power in Nations to their Economic and Social Advantage* (London: Heinemann, 1934), ix–xiii; Irwin Abrams, *The Nobel Peace Prize and the Laureates: An Illustrated Biographical History, 1901–1987* (Boston: G. K. Hall & Co., 1988), 121.

Anglo-Egyptian Treaty

Pact that restored British troops to Egypt twelve years after they were removed. In 1899, Great Britain established a *condominium* (defined as "a joint dominion . . . joint sovereignty by two or more nations") with Egyptian authorities under which London would provide governors-general to oversee the combined Egyptian-Sudanese government, while Egypt would provide four-fifths of the operating budget. This arrangement remained intact for nearly half a century.

Under the treaty—agreed to in Cairo on August 26, 1936, and signed in Montreux, Switzerland, in May 1937—Britain was allowed to station some 10,000 troops in Egypt, with the condition that Egyptian independence would be established at the end of the fifty-year period ending in 1949. Accordingly, the treaty increased anti-British sentiment in Egypt. Britain was also allowed to impose martial law and censorship in the event of a military emergency and was permitted to retain control over its naval base at Alexandria until 1944. Britain agreed to name an ambassador to Cairo to replace the high commissioner and, after the period of transition to independence passed, foreigners would become subject to Egyptian law. The condominium was ended with the proclamation of the Republic of the Sudan on January 1, 1956.

References: Afaf Lutfi Sayyid-Marsot, *Egypt and Cromer: A Study in Anglo-Egyptian Relations* (London: Murray, 1968); John Marlowe, *A History of Modern Egypt and Anglo-Egyptian Relations, 1800–1956* (Hamden, Conn.: Archon Books, 1965); M. W. Daly, *British Administration and the Northern Sudan, 1917–1924: The Governor-Generalship of Sir Lee Stack in the Sudan* (Leiden: Nederlands Historisch-Archaeologisch Instituut et Istanbul, 1980); M. W. Daly, "Imperial Sudan: the Anglo-Egyptian Condominium, 1934–1956" (Cambridge: Cambridge University Press, 1991).

Anglo-German Naval Treaty

Pact, signed June 18, 1935, between Adolf HITLER and British Foreign Minister John Simon. Germany, handcuffed by the Treaty of VERSAILLES's limitations on armaments, sought to renegotiate the treaty's ship provisions with England. To these ends, Hitler met with Lord Privy Seal Anthony EDEN and Simon in Berlin on March 23, 1935, seeking a 35:100 ratio of German to British tonnage in ships. Negotiations began in London on June 4 between Simon and Hitler's ambassador-at-large, Joachim von RIBBENTROP. England agreed to the new shipping ratio, with the stipulation that Germany be allowed to expand eastward (*Drangnach Osten*).

On April 28, 1939, Germany notified Great Britain that it was abrogating the treaty after London established a mutual-assistance treaty with France.

Reference: Mathias Forster, "German-British Naval Agreement" in Christian Zentner and Friedemann Bedüftig, eds., *Encyclopedia of the Third Reich* (New York: Macmillan, 1991), 1: 325–26.

Anglo-Irish Peace Treaty

Pact, signed December 6, 1921, that established the partition of Northern Ireland from the rest of Ireland. After Ireland's civil war to expel the British, and the passage of the government's Ireland Act in 1920, the Sinn Fein faction of the Irish Republican Army and the British government finally signed the so-called Anglo-Irish Treaty. Under this pact, as historian Patrick Buckland has written, "the IRISH FREE STATE became [a] self-governing dominion within the British Empire." Members of Parliament elected from this state were required to take an oath of allegiance to the Crown, and a governor-general was appointed for the area. Six northeastern counties in Northern Ireland opted out of the plan. Further, section 11 of the treaty stated that "Northern Ireland shall not be subject to the rule of the Parliament and Government of the Free Irish State."

See also COLLINS, Michael; DE VALERA, Eamon.

References: Frank Pakenham, Earl of Longford, *Peace by Ordeal: An Account, from First-Hand Sources, of the Negotiation and Signature of the Anglo-Irish Treaty, 1921* (London: Jonathan Cape, 1935); "Irish Constitutional Crisis, 1886–1923" in Arthur Marwick, gen. ed., *The Illustrated Dictionary of British History* (London: Thames and Hudson, 1980), 152–53; Patrick Buckland, "Ireland and British Government" in Christopher Haigh, ed., *The Cambridge Historical Encyclopedia of Great Britain and Ireland* (Cambridge, England: Cambridge University Press, 1985), 307–9; Edmund Jan Osmañczyk, *The Encyclopedia of the United Nations and International Agreements* (Philadelphia: Taylor and Francis, 1985), 99.

Anglo-Italian Agreement   *See* CHAMBERLAIN, Neville.

Anschluss (Annexation)

German military and political policy of the late 1930s, used particularly for uniting Germany and Austria, either by treaty or by force. From the time of Otto von Bismarck in the 19th century some German statesmen had advocated union with Austria. Because the two countries shared a common heritage and language, it was believed by many that a German-Austrian nation would be a certainty. After World War I, Austria, which had been broken off from Hungary, passed a measure that declared itself a part of the German Republic. The TREATY OF ST. GERMAIN-EN-LAYE ended this, and Austria's admittance into the League of Nations was made contingent on the fact that the dual statehood designation would become void. Matters then stayed virtually settled until Adolf HITLER took power in Germany in 1933.

Hitler saw the policy of Anschluss as a grand part of his idea of *Lebensraum,* or the expansion of German "living space" in Europe. He had discussed Anschluss in his 1927 work *Mein Kampf,* claiming that "German-Austria must

return again to the great German Motherland." To this end, Hitler and his followers were key in the Nazi overthrow and assassination of Austrian chancellor Engelbert DOLLFUSS on July 25, 1934. By 1938, Hitler had demanded that Dollfuss's successor, Kurt von SCHUSCHNIGG, allow the German occupation of Austria. Von Schuschnigg attempted to prevent a takeover but was imprisoned by the Nazis. On March 12, 1938, the leader of the Austrian Nazis, Arthur SEYSS-INQUART, was named chancellor of Austria. That same day the German Wehrmacht crossed into Austria, which Hitler declared three days later as "the entry of my homeland into the German Reich." Under German law Austria was renamed Ostmark (East March) and absorbed into the Reich, where it remained for the rest of the war until it was liberated by the Russians. The Anschluss policy was completely voided with the signing of the Austria State Treaty in 1955.

References: Edmund Jan Osmañczyk, *The Encyclopedia of the United Nations and International Agreements* (Philadelphia: Taylor & Francis, 1985), 40; Jürgen Gehl, *Austria, Germany and the Anschluss, 1931–1938* (London: Oxford University Press, 1963); "Hitler at Linz Proclaims Austria Part of Germany as Reich Army Sweeps through Country to Brenner," New York *Herald-Tribune* (European Edition), March 13, 1938, p. 1; Gordon Brook-Shepherd, *Anschluss: The Rape of Austria* (London: Macmillan, 1963); Christian Zentner, and Friedemann Bedüftig, eds., *Encyclopedia of the Third Reich* (New York: Macmillan, 1991), 1: 24–26.

Anti-Comintern Pact, 1936   *See* LONDON NAVAL CONFERENCE TREATIES.

anti-communism   *See* RED SCARE.

anti-Semitism

Belief system of prejudice against Jews, incorporated by Adolf HITLER into his philosophy of National Socialism during the interwar period, leading to the terrorizing and eventual mass murder of 6 million Jews in the Holocaust of World War II. Prior to the 19th century, anti-Semitism in Europe was based on the belief that Jews were responsible for the crucifixion of Jesus. Its expression largely took religious and economic forms, including persecutions, expulsion, and the placement of economic and personal restrictions on Jewish people. During the 19th and early 20th centuries, however, these forms of anti-Semitism were replaced by a racial form of anti-Semitism, based on the idea that Jews were a distinct and "lesser" race.

In 20th-century Austria and Germany, rising nationalism, coupled with a struggling economy and baseless theories of Aryan racial superiority, brought feelings of anti-Semitism to a head. When the Nazi German dictator Hitler rose to power in 1933, his minions carried out the anti-Jewish policies that Hitler had incorporated into the tenets of his NAZI PARTY, outlined in his book MEIN KAMPF. As the personal liberties of Jews were gradually stripped away, many attempted to flee the region; those who did not were concentrated in ghettos and shipped to concentration camps. By the outbreak of World War II, Hitler had begun to implement his "final solution"—the extermination of Jews in all countries his armies conquered. By the end of the war, 6 million Jews had been systematically murdered.

References: Roberto Finzi, *Anti-Semitism: From Its European Roots to the Holocaust,* trans. Maud Jackson (New York: Interlink Publishing Group, 1999); John G. Gager, *The Origins of Anti-Semitism: Attitudes toward Judaism in Pagan and Christian Antiquity* (New York: Oxford University Press, 1985); Dan Cohn-Sherbok, *The Crucified Jew: Twenty Centuries of Christian Anti-Semitism* (Grand Rapids, Mich.: Wm. B. Eerdmans, 1997).

appeasement

Policy, established particularly at the Munich Conference in 1938, of satisfying or mollifying another person or party to achieve a stated end of peace. In this case *appeasement* refers to the approach used by the West to attempt to stave off war in Europe at the end of the 1930s, which failed miserably. The man for whom the policy was fashioned was one who would push the Western nations into war just to see how far they were bluffing. Starting in 1938, Adolf HITLER, chancellor of an economically ravaged Germany, saw great advantages in the policy of demanding from the small, defenseless nations surrounding Germany pieces of territory with minority German populations. After World War I the victorious Allied nations carved up the European frontiers, giving various ethnic areas to nations that had nothing in common with them. Hitler's promises were met by the acquiescence of European leaders, particularly in England and France, who hoped against hope that Hitler's apparent hunger for land could possibly be sated. Too late they realized that this policy had led the world to the brink of horrendous conflict.

The European powers cannot take sole blame for the appeasement policy, however. The leaders of the geographically isolated United States, starting in 1933, felt comfortable in allowing Germany, Italy, and Japan to break international law with few repercussions back home. Historian William Rock writes, "U.S. appeasement . . . was more a matter of procrastination and a denial of responsibility than a carefully crafted policy."

See also CHAMBERLAIN, Neville; MUNICH CRISIS; MUNICH PACT.

Adolf Hitler of Germany greets British Prime Minister Neville Chamberlain, the architect of appeasement policy. *(CORBIS/Bettmann)*

References: William R. Rock, "Appeasement" in Bruce W. Jentleson and Thomas G. Paterson, senior eds., *Encyclopedia of U.S. Foreign Relations* (New York: Oxford University Press), 1: 84–85; Arnold A. Offner, *American Appeasement: United States Foreign Policy and Germany, 1933–1938* (Cambridge, Mass.: Harvard University Press, 1969); Larry William Fuchser, *Neville Chamberlain and Appeasement: A Study in the Politics of History* (New York: W. W. Norton, 1982); Bernd-Jürgen Wendt, "Appeasement" in Christian Zentner and Friedemann Bedüftig, eds., *Encyclopedia of the Third Reich* (New York: Macmillan, 1991), 1: 34–35.

Aragon, Louis   *See* DADA; SURREALISM.

Arbuckle, Fatty (1887–1933)

American silent film actor. Born Roscoe Conkling Arbuckle in Smith Center, Kansas, on March 24, 1887, Arbuckle worked in odd jobs, particularly as a plumber's assistant, before joining carnivals and vaudeville as a performer. In 1908 he was hired by the fledgling Selig Polyscope Company to appear in short one-reel films in Hollywood. His rotund face and comic demeanor charmed audiences from the start, although for the first few years he appeared uncredited.

In 1913, Arbuckle joined Mack Sennett's Keystone Kops and appeared in several of Sennett's farcical comedies. He worked with such stars as Mabel Normand and Chester Conklin, and in 1914's *Tillie's Punctured Romance* with a young British actor named Charlie CHAPLIN. During World War I, Arbuckle became one of the most popular Hollywood stars; his screen appearances were seen by tens of thousands of fans. In 1917 he left Sennett and established his own film company, with director Joseph M. Schenck, called Comique. He hired a talented young actor, Buster KEATON, and produce such films as *The Butcher Boy* (1917), released by Famous Players Lasky. Arbuckle was making in excess of $10,000 a day at this time.

On Labor Day in 1921, Arbuckle threw a party on the 12th floor of San Francisco's St. Francis Hotel to celebrate the $3 million contract he had just signed with Paramount Studios. In attendance was Virginia Rappé, a 25-year-old actress and the fiancée of Henry Lehrman, who had directed a few of Arbuckle's films. Arbuckle had offered Rappé the opportunity to be in one of his next films. What happened next led to the end of his career, though many of the facts remain in dispute. According to the allegations leveled against him, the actor apparently took Rappé into an adjoining room, from which screams could be heard above the din of the party's loud music. When the door to the room was opened. Rappé was found on the bed exclaiming, "Roscoe has hurt me." Arbuckle, drunk, had apparently raped the young actress with a champagne bottle. When Rappé's distress continued, she was taken to a local hospital. A few days later she died of a ruptured bladder and Arbuckle was arrested for murder. The newspapers played up the story to such a degree that it became the first Hollywood scandal.

At his trial, a sensation for the era, the details of what Arbuckle had allegedly done to Rappé were passed around on pieces of paper so as not to be mentioned in open court. Arbuckle maintained that he had not raped the young woman, and in the first and second trials the juries were deadlocked. In 1923 a third jury found Arbuckle not guilty. The facts, when sorted out, showed that Rappé had not been raped, and that her ruptured bladder had most likely been caused by an illegal abortion. By the time of Arbuckle's acquittal, however, so many sordid details of the crime for which he had been wrongfully accused had reached the public that his future in film was ruined. The HAYS OFFICE, which oversaw censorship in the movie industry, banned Arbuckle from filmmaking. His $1 million a year career was over.

Except for some small directing jobs (for which Arbuckle was credited as "William B. Goodrich"), he barely worked again. By 1933, however, many had forgiven him, and he was slated to make a comeback in the new "talking pictures." On June 29, 1933, shortly before

"Fatty" Arbuckle at trial *(CORBIS/Bettmann)*

his comeback, Arbuckle was found dead from a massive heart attack at New York's Park Central Hotel. He was forty-six years old.

References: Ephraim Katz, *The Film Encyclopedia* (New York: HarperPerennial, 1994), 44; David Anthony Yallop, *The Day the Cheering Stopped: The True Story of Fatty Arbuckle* (New York: St. Martin's, 1976); Ronald J. Lilek, "The Fatty Arbuckle Scandal: the Man, the Crime, the Trials" (Master's Thesis, Arizona State University, 1976); Andy Edmonds, *Frame-up! The Untold Story of Roscoe "Fatty" Arbuckle* (New York: William Morrow and Co., 1991); "'Fatty' Arbuckle Dies Hailing His Return as Star," *New York Herald Tribune*, June 30, 1933, p. 19.

Arliss, George (1868–1946)

English actor, noted for his roles in such interwar films as *The Man Who Played God* (1921), *Green Goddess* (1923), and *Disraeli* (1929), for which he won the Best Actor Academy Award in 1930. Born in London as Augustus George Andrews on April 10, 1868, he was the son of William Joseph Arliss Andrews, a noted printer and publisher in London's Bloombury section and Rebekah (Tomkins) Andrews. Arliss was educated in London's common schools, then worked in his father's firm until 1886, when he began what became a blossoming stage career by appearing as an extra in a play at the Elephant and Castle Theatre. He toured England for the next several years, delivering performances that made him a leading actor on the English stage. In late 1901 Arliss left for the United States, and, with the support of producer David Belasco, appeared at Belasco's Theater in New York in *The Darling of the Gods,* playing the role of Zakkuri. In 1911 he starred in L. N. Parker's *Disraeli,* a biographical play about the famed British prime minister. Ten years later, Arliss made his debut on film in the silent feature *The Devil.* He returned to the stage in England in 1923 to rave reviews in the role of the Rajah in *Green Goddess.*

Six years later, Arliss began a notable career in talking pictures, reprising his roles in film versions of *Disraeli* (1929) and *Green Goddess* (1930). Directed by Alfred E. Green, *Disraeli,* in some ways a landmark work, demonstrates Arliss's acting talents at their best. For nearly another decade he appeared in almost 20 films, including roles as Alexander Hamilton and the duke of Wellington. In 1937, when he discovered that his wife, Florence Kate Arliss, was going blind, he retired to care for her. Arliss predeceased her, however. He died in London on February 5, 1946, at the age of seventy-seven. He had written two autobiographies, *Up the Years from Bloomsbury* (1927) and *My Ten Years in the Studios* (1940).

References: Gerald Lawrence, "Arliss, George" in Sir Leslie Stephen and Sir Sidney Lee et al., eds., *The Dictionary of National Biography* (Oxford, England: Oxford University Press), 5: 14–15; Ephraim Katz, *The Film Encyclopedia* (New York: HarperPerennial, 1994), 48; "[Obituary:] Mr. George Arliss," *The Times* (London), February 6, 1946, p. 7.

Armstrong Louis (1900–1971)

American jazz musician and singer, whose lyrical style and composition set the tone for U.S. jazz throughout most of the 20th century. Born in New Orleans on August 4, 1900 (he later changed his birthdate to July 4), Armstrong was orphaned at the age of 10 and reared in what was called the Waif's Home, where he learned to play the cornet, bugle, and clarinet before age fifteen. By 1920 he was working in the Fate Marable Band on riverboats in the Mississippi River. Two years later he joined Chicago's famous Joe "King" Oliver's Creole Jazz Band. It was Armstrong's cornet that bested his boss, also a cornetist. Competing with Oliver led to Armstrong's departure, and, in 1925 he formed his own ensemble, the Hot Five (and later, Seven), with such talents as Johnny Dodd on clarinet, Kid Ory on trombone, Johnny St. Cyr on banjo, and Armstrong's wife Lillian (Lil) on piano. The Hot Five sold many of its recordings—including classic renditions of "Potato Head Blues," "West End Blues," and "Heebie Jee-

bies"—to African-American and white audiences alike. It was in "Heebie Jeebies," the group's first hit, that Armstrong perfected his scat technique. The music's popularity transcended the rigid color barrier in America, and Armstrong became accepted and cherished among the mainstream. His unique figure, standing on the stage belting out solos on the cornet and then the trumpet, earned him the nickname Satchmo (short for "satchel mouth").

During the 1920s, Armstrong expanded his portfolio to include stints on Broadway (in which he played in the musical *Hot Chocolates*) and in such films as *Pennies from Heaven* (1936) and *Artists and Models* (1937). In 1929 he disbanded the Hot Five and established Louis Armstrong and His Orchestra, which included such stars as Hoagy Carmichael on vocals and Earl Hines on piano, releasing such songs as "Ain't Misbehavin'" and "Bessie Couldn't Help It." In 1937 he became the first African-American to host a radio show, with the *Fleischmann's Yeast Hour.*

The years after World War II saw a decline in Armstrong's popularity, although he continued to work steadily with his band, the All-Stars, and as an actor, appearing in some 35 films, including *High Society* (1956) and *Hello Dolly* (1969). He died from a heart attack in his home in Queens, New York, on July 6, 1971.

See also ELLINGTON, Duke; JAZZ.

References: Elizabeth Wenning, "Louis Armstrong" in Barbara Carlisle Bigelow, ed., *Contemporary Black Biography* (Detroit: Gale Research, 1992), 2: 10–13; Robert Goffin, (James F. Benzou, trans.), *Horn of Plenty: The Story of Louis Armstrong* (New York: Allen, Towne & Heath, 1947); James Lincoln Collier, *Great Jazz Artists* (New York: Four Winds, 1977); Sam Tanenhaus, *Louis Armstrong* (New York: Chelsea House, 1989); "Louis Armstrong, Jazz Trumpeter and Singer, Dies," *New York Times,* July 7, 1971, p. 1.

Arp, Jean   *See* DADA; SURREALISM.

Art Deco

Design style and artistic movement of the 1920s and 1930s characterized by straight lines and sleek forms. Although it began around 1910, the style was not formally named until 1925, when it took its named from the Exposition Internationale des Arts Décoratifs et Industriels Modernes, which was held in Paris that year. Art Deco was not limited to fine art, unlike some of the other artistic movements of the era; it encompassed jewelry, textiles, furniture, interior decor, buildings, and other structures, including billboards. Artists from various fields became part of the movement, including the fashion designer Erté; the designer Paul Poiret; the artist/jewelers H. G. Murphy, Raynmond Templier, and Wiwen Nilsson; the furniture designers Maurice Dufrène and Jacques Ruhlmann;

the architect Eliel Saarinen; glass and jewelry designer René Lalique; the figural sculptor Chiparus; and the graphic artist Edward McKnight Kauffer, among others. In the United States the movement was solidified by such public structures in New York as Rockefeller Center, the Chrysler building, and the Empire State building.

Art Deco faded after 1935 and was completely over by the start of World War II. It made a comeback in the 1960s, and today many of its remnants, particularly in Miami Beach, Florida, are tourist attractions.

References: Thomas Walters, *Art Deco* (London: Academy Editions, 1973); Alastair Duncan, *American Art Deco* (London: Thames & Hudson, 1986); Mike Darton, ed., *Art Deco: An Illustrated Guide to the Decorative Style, 1920–40* (Secaucus, N.J.: Wellfleet Press, 1989).

assassinations

Assassination—politically motivated murder—as a tool of radicals has long been used to disrupt governments as well as civil and world affairs. The period between the world wars witnessed a spate of murders of political figures across the globe, which in many ways led the world closer to the war which would engulf it starting in 1939. Such assassinations include:

Rosa Luxemburg and Karl Liebknecht, German revolutionaries (January 15, 1919)

Amir Habibullah Khan of Afghanistan (February 20, 1919).

Kurt Eisner, German Socialist politician (February 21, 1919).

Emiliano Zapata, Mexican revolutionary (April 10, 1919).

Hugo Haase, German Socialist and president of the German Social Democratic Party (October 8, 1919).

Venustiano Carranza, President of Mexico (May 20, 1920).

Eduardo Dato Iradier, Premier of Spain (March 8, 1921).

Mehmed Talat Pasha, exiled Turkish politician (March 15, 1921).

Milorad Draskoviç, Yugoslavian politician (July 21, 1921).

Matthias Erzberger, German statesman (August 26, 1921).

Dr. Antonio Granjo, Portuguese Premier, and Antonio Machado Dos Santo, Portuguese politician (both October 19, 1921).

Takashi Hara, Japanese prime minister (November 4, 1921).

Said Halim Pasha, former Turkish grand vizier (December 6, 1921).

Sir Henry Hughes Wilson, British army officer (January 22, 1922).

Walther Rathenau, German industrialist (January 24, 1922).

Michael Collins, Irish patriot (August 22, 1922).

Gabriel Narutowicz, first president of the Polish Republic (December 16, 1922).

Cardinal Soldevilla y Romero, archbishop of Saragossa, Spain (June 4, 1923).

Alexander Stambolski, former Bulgarian prime minister (June 14, 1923).

Francisco "Pancho" Villa, Mexican rebel (July 20, 1923).

Giacomo Matteotti, Italian socialist leader (about June 10, 1924).

Sir Lee Stack, British governor-general of the Sudan (November 19, 1924).

General Kosta Georgiev, Bulgarian army officer (April 15, 1925).

Kevin Christopher O'Higgins, Irish revolutionary and constitutionalist (July 10, 1927).

Stefan Radiç, leader of the Croatian Peasant Party; his nephew, Paul Radiç, and Dr. George Basaritchik (all on June 20, 1928).

Alvaro Obregón, president-elect of Mexico (July 17, 1928).

Chang Tso-lin, Chinese warlord of Manchuria (October 10, 1928).

Prince Osachi Hamaguchi, Japanese prime minister (shot November 14, 1930, he succumbed to his wounds August 10, 1931).

Junnosuke Inouye, Japanese minister of finance (February 9, 1932).

Paul Doumer, president of France (shot on May 6, 1932, he died the next day).

Ki Tsuyoshi Inukai, Japanese prime minister (May 16, 1932).

Anton Cermak, mayor of Chicago (February 15, 1933; died March 6, 1933).

Luis Sanchez Cerro, president of Peru (April 30, 1933).

Assis Khan, older brother of King Mohammed Nadir Shah of Afghanistan (June 6, 1933).

King Mohammed Nadir Shah of Afghanistan (November 8, 1933).

Ion Duca, Romanian premier (December 30, 1933).

Cesar Augusto Sandino, Nicaraguan rebel (February 21, 1934).

Ernst Roehm, Nazi leader (June 30, 1934).

Engelbert Dollfuss, chancellor of Austria (July 25, 1934).

Alexander I, king of Yugoslavia (October 9, 1934).

Jean Louis Barthou, French foreign minister (October 9, 1934).

Sergei Kirov, Soviet politician (December 1, 1934).

Huey Pierce Long, United States senator (shot September 8, 1935; died September 10, 1935).

Korekiyo Takahashi and Makoko Saito, Japanese statesmen (both February 26, 1936).

Jafar al-Askari, former Iraqi prime minister (October 30, 1936).

Ernst vom Rath, third secretary of the German Embassy in Paris (November 7, 1938).

Premier Armand Calinescu, Romanian prime minister (September 21, 1939).

Reference: Harris M. Lentz, III, "Assassinations and Executions: An Encyclopedia of Political Violence, 1865–1986" (Jefferson, N.C.: McFarland & Co., 1988), 41–77.

Astaire, Fred (1899–1987)

American dancer and actor, whose consummate moves and debonair style influenced the interwar era. Born Frederick Austerlitz on May 10, 1899, in Omaha, Nebraska, he was the son of an Austrian immigrant. A natural talent when he was a young child, Astaire entered show business at the age of five, and in 1906 formed a vaudeville (and later Broadway) act with his sister, Adele. The duo acted in such stage hits as *For Goodness Sake* (1922), *Funny Face* (1927), and *The Band Wagon* (1931). When Adele Astaire retired to marry in 1932, her brother went out on his own, moving to California to try his hand in motion pictures. Signed by Radio-Keith-Orpheum (RKO), Astaire first appeared in a small part in MGM's *Dancing Lady* (1933). That same year he appeared with Ginger Rogers in *Flying Down to Rio,* the first of nine highly successful films starring the two. Astaire's films during this period include *The Gay Divorcee* (1934), *Roberta* (1935), *Top Hat* (1935), *Swing Time* (1936), and *The Story of Vernon and Irene Castle* (1939). His sophistication, grace, and talent made him an international screen star.

Astaire opened a chain of dancing schools in the 1940s, then resumed his film career, appearing in musicals, dramas, and television programs through the 1970s. In 1949 he was presented with a special Oscar for his contributions to the silver screen. Astaire died in Los Angeles on June 22, 1987. He was universally mourned as perhaps the finest all-around entertainer of the 20th century.

References: Ephraim Katz, *The Film Encyclopedia* (New York: HarperPerennial, 1994), 56–57; Richard F. Shepard, "Fred Astaire, the Ultimate Dancer, Dies," *The New York Times,* June 23, 1987, p. A1.

Aston, Francis William (1877–1945)

English physicist, corecipient of the 1922 Nobel Prize in physics (with Niels BOHR) "for his discovery, by means of his mass spectrograph, of isotopes in a large number of non-radioactive elements, and for his enunciation of the whole-number rule." Aston was born in Harborne, Birmingham, England, on September 1, 1877, and received his bachelor's degree from Cambridge University in 1912. After working for a time at a brewery, he became a researcher at the University of Birmingham from 1903 to 1909, and at Cambridge from 1909 to 1914. During this period he worked on the study of organic compounds in brewing, then advanced to study what biographer Bernard Schlessinger calls "the phenomena in gas discharge tubes and discovered the Aston Dark Space." This work led him to identify two isotopes of neon and eventually to inventing the mass spectrograph, which he was able to use to identify further isotopes.

After working for a time for the Royal Aircraft Establishment in England, Aston returned to Cambridge, where he worked until his death on November 20, 1945.

References: Bernard S. Schlessinger, "Aston, Francis William" in Bernard S. and June H. Schlessinger, eds., *The Who's Who of Nobel Prize Winners* (Phoenix, Ariz.: Oryx, 1986), 156–57; Thomas Watson MacCallum and Stephen Taylor, eds., *The Nobel Prize-Winners and the Nobel Foundation, 1901–1937* (Zurich, Switzerland: Central European Times Publishing, 1938), 144.

Atatürk   *See* KEMAL, Mustafa.

Auden, W. H. (1907–1973)

British-American poet, playwright, and critic. Born Wystan Hugh Auden on February 21, 1907, in York, England, he was the son of a medical officer and a nurse. For a time he studied to be a mining engineer, but by 1922 Auden's talent for poetry was apparent. He attended Oxford University (1925–28) and soon published *Poems* (1930) and *The Orators* (1932), a collection of prose and verse, both of which established him as the leading voice of a new generation. He next taught at several universities throughout Europe and the United States. In 1939 he moved to the United States, where he became a naturalized U.S. citizen in 1946.

A prolific writer, Auden achieved success in a variety of styles, creating perhaps the largest, richest, and most varied body of work of any 20th-century poet. In addition to poetry, he wrote plays, sonnets, free verse, and critical essays. His interwar works include *The Dance of Death* (1933), *The Dog Beneath the Skin* (1935), *Look Stranger!* (1936), *Spain* (1937), and *On the Frontier* (1938). Known for incorporating into his literary work popular culture, current events, and vernacular speech, Auden also drew from literature, art, social theories, and scientific information to create his poetry. He examined society's moral problems and recounted the journey or quest for social and spiritual justice.

Later works include *The Double Man* (1941), the Pulitzer Prize–winning *Age of Anxiety* (1948), *The Shield of Achilles* (1955), *About the House* (1965), and *Academic Graffiti* (1971). He died in Vienna, Austria, on September 28, 1973.

References: Richard Davenport-Hines, *Auden* (New York: Pantheon, 1995); Edward Callan, *Auden: A Carnival of Intellect* (New York: Oxford University Press, 1983); Wendell Stacy Johnson, *W. H. Auden* (New York: Continuum, 1990).

B

Bailey v. Drexel Furniture Company (1922)
Landmark U.S. Supreme Court decision which held that taxes enacted by the government on companies that use child labor are unconstitutional. On February 24, 1919, Congress enacted the CHILD LABOR ACT, which used heavy taxation to discourage the use of child labor. The Drexel Furniture Company of North Carolina sued Bailey, the collector of internal revenue for the western district of North Carolina, to stop him from collecting specialized child labor taxes on the children working for them. The U.S. District Court for the western district of North Carolina held for Drexel, and Bailey appealed to the Court for relief. Arguments in the case were heard on March 7 and 8, 1922.

Nine weeks later, on May 15, 1922, the Court struck down the Child Labor Act as an unconstitutional infringement on "the conduct of regulation which is reserved by the Constitution exclusively to the States." Chief Justice William Howard Taft, a former president of the United States and the only person to occupy both the White House and the Supreme Court, spoke for an 8-1 Court (Justice John Hessin CLARKE dissented) in his opinion. Child labor was banned by federal law with the passage of the Fair Labor Standards Act of 1938.

References: Henry Steele Commager, ed., *Documents of American History* (New York: Appleton-Century-Crofts, 1949), 333–34; Harold W. Chase, and Craig R. Ducat, *Constitutional Interpretation: Cases-Essays-Materials* (St. Paul, Minn.: West Publishing Co., 1979), 538–39; *Bailey v. Drexel Furniture Company* 259 US 20 (1922).

Baker, Josephine (1906–1975)
African-American dancer and singer whose presence in Paris in the 1920s brought a dose of American culture to JAZZ AGE Europe. Born in St. Louis, Missouri, on June 3, 1906, Baker became a street performer at the age of thirteen, and at sixteen was touring the United States with the Dixie Steppers vaudeville troupe from Philadelphia. She starred in the road rendition of *Shuffle Along* (1923), where her electric energy wowed the crowds. The troupe moved to New York City, and Baker got a part in the Broadway show *Chocolate Dandies* (1924). She eventually moved on to play the floor show of the landmark Plantation Club. Dismayed at the racial prejudice endemic in the United States, Baker left for Paris in 1925. She got a part in *La Revue Nègre* at the Théâtre des Champs-Élysées, where she introduced the *danse sauvage* to stunned crowds. In 1926 she was hired by the famed Folies-Bergère, where she danced nearly nude, covered only by a semiskirt made up of bananas. She began to sing professionally in 1930, and in 1937 she became a naturalized French citizen.

During World War II and the Nazi occupation of France, Baker was active in the Resistance, the underground opposition to the Nazi rule. For her heroism she was awarded the Croix de Guerre and the Legion of Honour with rosette. In later years she became an outspoken supporter of the U.S. civil rights movement and supported numerous humanitarian activities, such as encouraging international adoption.

When Baker died in Paris on April 12, 1975, she was given a state funeral, an unprecedented honor for someone not born in France.

References: Lynn Haney, *Naked at the Feast: A Biography of Josephine Baker* (New York: Dodd, Mead, 1981); Phyllis Rose, *Jazz Cleopatra: Josephine Baker in Her Time* (New York: Doubleday, 1989); Jean-Claude Baker, and Chris Chase, *Josephine: The Hungry Heart* (New York: Random House, 1993).

Balanchine, George *See* DANCE.

Baldwin, Roger Nash (1884–1981)

American reformer and civil rights and civil liberties activist, one of the founders of the AMERICAN CIVIL LIBERTIES UNION. Born in Wellesley, Massachusetts, on January 21, 1884, the son of Unitarian parents, Baldwin received bachelor's and master's degrees from Harvard University in 1904 and 1905, respectively. He later taught sociology at Washington University in St. Louis, Missouri.

From 1907 to 1910, Baldwin served as St. Louis's chief probation officer, and from this experience he wrote, with Bernard Flexner, *Juvenile Courts and Probation* (1912), which became a standard work in that field. He then served as executive secretary of the St. Louis Civic League, which advocated reformist government. In 1917, Baldwin moved to New York City, where he became the head of the American Union Against Militarism, an antiwar group. In his last years living in St. Louis, Baldwin's politics had shifted rapidly to the left, as he embraced the writings and teachings of such anarchists as Emma Goldman and Prince Peter Kropotkin. With the start of World War I, he became an avowed pacifist and registered as a conscientious objector. When he was drafted for military service, Baldwin refused to serve and was thus sentenced to a year in prison. After his release, he joined with civil libertarians Norman Mattoon Thomas, Felix Frankfurter, and Helen Keller to found the (ACLU), which Baldwin later called "a permanent, national, nonpartisan organization with the single purpose of defending the whole Bill of Rights for everybody."

For the remainder of his life, Baldwin was in the vanguard of thousands of cases involving civil liberties issues; during his tenure as head of the ACLU, the organization championed the causes of teacher John Thomas Scopes, the man at the center of the SCOPES TRIAL; the Jehovah's Witnesses, whose children were being forced to salute the flag in public schools against their religious beliefs; the novelist James JOYCE and his U.S.-banned novel, *Ulysses;* industrialist Henry FORD, who fought for the right to distribute antiunion leaflets; and Nicola SACCO and Bartolomeo VANZETTI. Baldwin served as executive director of the ACLU from 1920 to 1950, then spent the next five years as the organization's national chair.

In 1981, President Jimmy Carter presented him with the Presidential Medal of Freedom, the highest award given to a civilian. Baldwin died of emphysema in Ridgewood, New Jersey, on August 26, 1981, at the age of 97.

References: Richard Pearson, "Roger Baldwin, a Founder of ACLU, Dies," *Washington Post,* August 27, 1981, p. C10; Peggy Lamson, "Roger Baldwin, Founder of the American Civil Liberties Union: A Portrait" (Boston: Houghton Mifflin, 1976); "The Reminiscences of Roger Nash Baldwin," two volumes, Oral History Research Office, Columbia University; "Roger Nash Baldwin" in Nancy L. Roberts, *American Peace Writers, Editors and Periodicals* (Westport, Conn.: Greenwood, 1991), 13–14.

Baldwin, Stanley (1867–1947)

English politician and statesman, prime minister (1923–24, 1924–29, 1935–37). The only child of Alfred Baldwin, an ironmaster and member of Parliament (MP) from Bewdley, and Louisa (MacDonald) Baldwin, Stanley Baldwin was born on August 3, 1867, at Lower Park House in Bewdley, Worcestershire, England. He completed his education at Trinity College, Cambridge, where he studied history and received a bachelor's degree.

After leaving school, Baldwin worked at his father's iron business in Wilden, near Stourport-on-Severn in Worcestershire. He married in 1892 and ran unsuccessfully for Parliament in 1906. But upon the 1908 death of his father, Baldwin was elected to fill his seat, representing Bewdley. He rose steadily through the parliamentary ranks until in June 1917, he was advanced to the post of financial secretary in the coalition government of Prime Minister David LLOYD GEORGE.

In 1922, Baldwin was one of the Conservative MPs who turned against Lloyd George's coalition government with the Liberals at the "Carlton Club Meeting" in London, where he demanded that the Conservatives run their own candidate for prime minister in the upcoming General Election. Faced with such insurrection in his party, Lloyd George quit and was replaced by Baldwin's choice for PM, Andrew Bonar LAW. For his support in helping Law to gain the PM slot, Baldwin was named chancellor of the exchequer. In this post he met with American leaders in Washington, D.C., to negotiate a reduction in England's war debt to the United States. In 1923, Law became seriously ill, and Baldwin replaced him as party leader in the House of Commons, calling for "salvation for this country . . . Faith, Hope, Love and Work." On May 20, 1923, Law, a dying man who would succumb to throat cancer five months later, resigned as prime minister, and Baldwin was quickly named as his replacement. In this, the first of three administrations as PM, Baldwin called for an increase in England's air defenses, and met with French premier Raymond POINCARÉ to discuss such issues as the occupation of the Ruhr Valley by French troops and war reparations. Clashing with his political opponents on tariff issues, Baldwin dissolved Parliament and called for general elections, which were held in December 1923. Baldwin's Conservatives were left with the most seats, but a combination of the Labour and Liberal parties left him a minority leader. He resigned on January 16, 1924, to be replaced by James Ramsay MACDONALD.

The issue of the so-called Campbell Prosecution (in which a Labour sympathizer and communist was not indicted for calling for resistance against the government) led MacDonald to call for another general election in

October 1924. Baldwin, having been reelected head of the Conservatives, was at the forefront of a wave that swept the party back into complete control of the House of Commons, and for the second time he became prime minister. In this second administration Baldwin dropped his tariff support, advocated an end to food taxes, and helped pass a sugar subsidy act. He signed the LOCARNO PACT in 1925; dealt with the GENERAL STRIKE in 1926; presided that same year over the THIRD IMPERIAL CONFERENCE, in which Dominion nations discussed increased sovereignty from England; and oversaw the extension of the franchise to women older than twenty-one. Whe he dissolved Parliament on May 11, 1929, Baldwin's Conservatives lost enough seats for another Labour-Liberal coalition to drive him from the prime minister's post for the second time.

In the nearly six years that his party was out of power, Baldwin remained a leading figure in British politics. Even when Conservatives won overwhelmingly in the 1931 general election, Baldwin was content to serve merely as Lord President in MacDonald's cabinet. Representing his nation at the OTTAWA ECONOMIC CONFERENCE in 1932, Baldwin spent much of the early 1930s decrying the rise of Nazism in Germany and calling for strong British rearmament. On May 16, 1935, MacDonald—feeling increasing political heat from his Conservative allies, the only support of his coalition government—resigned as prime minister. On June 7, King GEORGE V appointed Baldwin in MacDonald's place, marking a record third time one man had held the position.

In his third administration Baldwin oversaw passage of the Second GOVERNMENT OF INDIA ACT, which lent a measure of independence to India; was forced to deal with the political outrage over the Hoare-Laval Agreement (in which Foreign Minister Sir Samuel Hoare and French premier Pierre Laval agreed to end the ETHIOPIAN CRISIS by ceding that nation to Italy) by demanding Hoare's resignation; directed the buildup of British defenses as the threat from Germany became more defined; and handled matters relating to the abdication of King EDWARD VIII. Faced with the growing coercion of Adolf HITLER's Germany over Europe and the unstable economic situation in England, Baldwin, nearing seventy years of age, resigned as prime minister on May 5, 1937. He named Neville CHAMBERLAIN as his successor. On June 8, 1937, the day he retired from Parliament, Baldwin was elevated to the peerage as first earl Baldwin of Bewdley and viscount Corvedale.

Baldwin spent the last 10 years of his life in retirement and died at the age of eighty on December 14, 1947. *See also* ELECTIONS, BRITISH; Imperial Conference, Second; Imperial Conference, Fifth.

References: Helen Holden, "Stanley Baldwin" in Dermot Englefield, Janet Seaton, and Isobel White, *Facts about the British Prime Ministers: A Compilation of Biographical and Historical Information* (New York: H.W. Wilson, 1995), 253–61; John Ramsden, *The Age of Balfour and Baldwin, 1902–1940* (London: Longman, 1978); Carol A. Jackson, "Baldwin, Stanley, 1st Earl Baldwin of Bewdley" in Bruce W. Jentleson and Thomas G. Paterson, senior eds., *Encyclopedia of U.S. Foreign Relations* (New York: Oxford University Press, 1997), 1: 131; "Death of Lord Baldwin. Prime Minister Three Times. Between The Wars," *The Times* (London), December 15, 1947, 4–6.

Banking Acts of 1933 and 1935   *See* GLASS-STEAGALL ACTS.

Banting, Frederick Grant (1891–1941)

Canadian physician and medical researcher, whose landmark work during the 1920s led to the discovery of the use of insulin to combat diabetes, and who was the corecipient (with Scottish researcher John James Richard MACLEOD) of the 1923 Nobel Prize in medicine and physiology. Born in the village of Alliston, in Ontario, Canada, on November 4, 1891, Banting was the son of William Thompson Banting and Margaret (Grant) Banting. He attended Victoria College in Toronto, where he received an M.B. degree in 1916, and the University of Toronto, which awarded him an M.D. degree in 1922. He was wounded in World War I and returned to Canada before the war's end. He worked as a surgeon at the Hospital for Sick Children in Toronto and maintained a private practice in London, Ontario.

In 1921, Banting returned to the University of Toronto, where he worked with MacLeod on the secretions of the pancreas and their impact on human health. Working more closely with the American-born Canadian physiologist Charles Herbert Best, Banting succeeded in isolating the secretion of the pancreas, and discovered the hormone insulin. He began to understand how it regulated sugar levels in the body. In 1923, Banting and MacLeod were jointly awarded the Nobel Prize, even though much of Banting's work had been conducted with his colleagues Best and J. B. Collip. Banting shared half of his award money with them for their part in the discovery. The Canadian Parliament granted Banting an annual salary of $7,500 and established the Frederick Banting Research Foundation to continue study and inquiry into insulin production. Also, the Ontario legislature founded the Banting-Best chair of medicine at the University of Toronto.

Banting served as a master of the department of medicine for many years, and in 1934 was knighted by King GEORGE V. Serving as a major in the Canadian army during World War II, he worked for the Canadian and British governments on various medical techniques. On February 21, 1941, the plane that Banting was in crashed near Newfoundland, killing all on board. He was forty-nine.

References: Lloyd G. Stevenson, "Banting, Frederick Grant" in Charles Coulston Gillespie, ed. in chief, *Dictionary of Scientific Biography* (New York: Charles Scribner's Sons, 1980–90), 1: 440–43; Joel J. Schlessinger, "Banting, Frederick Grant, Sir" in Bernard S. and June H. Schlessinger, eds., *The Who's Who of Nobel Prize Winners* (Phoenix, Ariz.: Oryx, 1986), 84–85; "Banting, Sir Frederick Grant" in *The Canadian Encyclopedia* (Edmonton, Alberta: Hurtig Publishers, 1988), 1: 175–76; Michael Bliss, *Banting: A Biography* (Toronto, Ontario: McClelland and Stewart, 1984); Michael Bliss, *The Discovery of Insulin* (Chicago: University of Chicago Press, 1982); Thomas Watson MacCallum and Stephen Taylor, eds., *The Nobel Prize-Winners and the Nobel Foundation, 1901–1937* (Zurich, Switzerland: Central European Times Publishing Co. Ltd., 1938), 207.

Barrow, Clyde Champion (1909–1934) and Bonnie Parker (1911–1934)

American outlaws, killed in a shootout with police in Louisiana in 1934 after a long trail of robbery and murder. Barrow, born in Telico, Texas, and Parker, born in Rowena, Texas, were in many ways destined to be together, and to die together at a young age. Clyde was a thief and robber long before he met Parker in January 1930, but she became involved in the same life of crime. After he spent two years in prison for robbery (during which she smuggled him a gun and he escaped, only to be recaptured and sent back for the remainder of his sentence), the two became close and they began a twenty-one-month-long crime spree, working in conjunction with his brother Buck Barrow and sister-in-law Blanche, as well as William Daniel Jones and Ray Hamilton. Through Texas, Oklahoma, and Missouri, the group robbed gas stations and restaurants, netting meager funds because of the Depression. On May 20, 1933, the U.S. Commissioner in Dallas issued a warrant against the pair for taking a stolen vehicle across state lines, then a federal offense. The Federal Bureau of Investigation was brought into the case to hunt them down.

During their spree Bonnie and Clyde, as the couple became widely known, committed some thirteen murders, including the executions of two police officers who had stopped them in Grapevine, Texas. After this episode, there was an all-points warrant issued on the pair for their immediate capture. Barrow claimed that he would not be taken alive. Texas Ranger Frank Hamer, who received a tip that the two would be traveling down a certain road in Louisiana, decided to kill them rather than risk the deaths of more officers. On the morning of May 23, 1934, Hamer and his men hid along the road near Sailes, Louisiana; when the duo came down the road, the Rangers opened fire on their car before the two had a chance to respond, killing them in a barrage of gunfire rarely seen in those times. Barrow was just

Bonnie Parker and Clyde Barrow mug for the camera in one of the photographs that made them infamous. *(CORBIS/Bettmann)*

twenty-five; Parker twenty-three. The destitute children of a nationwide economic depression, the two outlaws gained legendary status. Their thrilling getaways, violent crime spree, and devoted romance (evident in their many self-portrait photographs) have been immortalized in countless films, documentaries, and books since the 1930s.

References: E. R. Milner, *The Lives and Times of Bonnie and Clyde* (Carbondale: Southern Illinois University Press, 1996); Emma Krause Parker, *Fugitives: the Story of Clyde Barrow and Bonnie Parker, as told by Bonnie's Mother (Mrs. Emma Parker) and Clyde's Sister (Nell Barrow Cowan). Compiled, arranged and edited by Jan I. Fortune* (Dallas, Texas: Ranger Press, 1934); "Posse Kills Clyde Barrow and Bonnie Parker: Elusive Desperadoes Shot to Death in Louisiana," *Dallas Morning News,* May 24, 1934, p. 1.

Barrymore, Lionel (1878–1954), Ethel (1879–1959), and John (1882–1942)

Famed American acting family, whose monumental performances in many motion pictures, particularly in the 1920s and 1930s, marked the era. The eldest, Lionel, was born Lionel Blythe on April 28, 1878; his sister, Ethel, was born Ethel Mae Blythe on August 15, 1879; the youngest, John, was born John Sidney Blythe on February 15, 1882. All were born in Philadelphia, the children of British stage actor Herbert Blythe and Georgianna Drew. Their maternal grandfather, the Irish actor John Drew (1827–62), is considered perhaps the foremost stage actor of his time, while their uncle, also John Drew (1853–1927), is considered one of the stage's best performers. His work with an obscure actor named Herbert Blythe, later to call himself Maurice Barrymore, gave rise to the greatest of acting families.

Lionel Barrymore first appeared on the stage with his uncle in 1898 in *The Mummy and the Hummingbird.* He appeared in more than 140 films in his career, from *The Paris Hat* (1908) to *Main Street to Broadway* (1953). Considered one of the finest stage and film actors of the early 20th century, he was nominated for two Academy Awards, and won the 1932 Best Actor Oscar for *A Free Soul* (1931); he consistently delivered impressive performances, from that of Count Andre Dakkar in *The Mysterious Island* (1929) to Rasputin in *Rasputin and the Empress* (1932). He died on November 15, 1954.

Ethel Barrymore first went on stage in 1896, when her uncle John Drew introduced her on the New York stage in *Rosemary.* Her lengthy stage and film career, which lasted more than forty years, makes her one of the most impressive acting talents of the century. Nominated for four Academy Awards, she was awarded the 1945 Oscar for Best Supporting Actress for her work in *None but the Lonely Heart* (1944). Her interwar film work was marked by only two performances, as the Czarina in *Rasputin and the Empress* (1932) and in *Peter Ibbetson* (1932). Her theater work during this period included *The Second Mrs. Tanqueray* (1924), *Kingdon of God* (1928), *Scarlet Sister Mary* (1931), and *Whitcoaks* (1938). With her death on June 18, 1959, the era of the three Barrymores ended.

John Barrymore, first starred on stage in 1903 with his sister Ethel in the play *Captain Jinks of the Horse Marines.* He then appeared in *The Dictator* (1905) and toured Europe and Australia starring in that production. Several plays followed, but by the end of the first decade of the 20th century he had gone to California to make movies. His first confirmed film role was in 1914's *An American Citizen,* although there are several roles he might have played previously without credit. His breakthrough role came in 1920 when he played the dual title role in *Dr. Jekyll and Mr. Hyde.* Other interwar performances that marked his career include *Sherlock Holmes* (1922), *Beau Brummel* (1924), *Don Juan* (1926), and, during the talking era, *Moby Dick* (1930) and *Svengali* (1931). For these acting roles, and for his distinctive appearance, Barrymore became known as "The Great Profile." Plagued by alcoholism, he continued to act but his films became less and less momorable. He died suddenly in Hollywood on May 29, 1942.

The three siblings appeared in only one film together, *Rasputin and the Empress* (1932). Brothers Lionel and John appeared without Ethel in three films: *Arsène Lupin* (1932), *Grand Hotel* (1932), and *Dinner at Eight* (1933).

See also ACADEMY AWARDS.

References: Montrose Jonas Moses, *Famous Actor-Families in America* (New York: T. Y. Crowell & Co., 1906); Mildred C. Kuner, "Ethel Barrymore" in Frank Magill, ed., *Great Lives From History—American Women Series* (Pasadena, Calif.: Salem Press, 1985), 1: 150–55; L. Moody Simms, Jr., "Barrymore, Ethel" in Allen Johnson and Dumas Malone et al., eds., *Dictionary of American Biography* (New York: Charles Scribner's Sons, 1930–95), 6: 38–39; Ephraim Katz, The Film Encyclopedia (New York: HarperPerennial, 1994), 90–91; "John Barrymore Dies in Hollywood; Actor, 60, in Stage and Screen; Kept the Tradition of Famous Theatre Family," *New York Times,* May 30, 1942, p. 1; "Lionel Barrymore Is Dead at 76; Actor's Career Spanned 61 Years," *New York Times,* November 16, 1954, p. 1; "Ethel Barrymore Is Dead at 79; One of Stage's 'Royal Family'," *New York Times,* June 19, 1959, p. 1.

Barthou, Jean-Louis (1862–1934)

French politician. Born in the village of Oloron-Sainte-Marie, in the Basses-Pyrénées, France, on August 25, 1862, Barthou was a young child when his country was overrun by Prussia, during the Franco-Prussian War of 1871 and so he became a French nationalist at an early age. In 1884, after he attended the University of Bordeaux, he started a law practice in the town of Pau. He entered politics soon thereafter and rose to become a deputy in 1889.

From 1894 to 1913, Barthou held a number of cabinet posts. When Aristide BRIAND's government collapsed in March 1913, Barthou was named prime minister. His ministry held together until December of that year, when he called for compulsory military conscription.

In 1917, Barthou served as minister without portfolio in the war cabinet of Paul Painlevé, and after World War I he served as a French delegate to several international conferences, including the GENOA CONFERENCE in 1922. He was also a member of the Reparations Commission, the body that determined the amount of German war reparations to be paid to the Allies. He served as minister of justice in Raymond POINCARÉ's cabinet in 1926, and held the same post in Briand's cabinet in 1929.

After serving as premier for a short period in the government of President Gaston Doumergue, Barthou was chosen as minister of foreign affairs when Doumergue was named as prime minister in 1934. In this office, he attempted to bring a reasonable peace within Europe, as well as make France a superpower on the continent.

Toward this end, he reached out to various European powers, including the new nation of Yugoslavia. In October 1934 he invited that nation's King ALEXANDER to France and met the king in Marseille on October 9. While they were driving through the city in an open car, a Macedonian terrorist, Vlada Gheorghieff, leaned into the car and fired at both men, killing Alexander instantly and mortally wounding Barthou, who died that night at a local hospital. Barthou was but another victim of the ethnic chaos that was slowly enveloping postwar Europe.

References: James Friguglietti, "Barthou, Louis" in Warren F. Kuehl, ed., *Biographical Dictionary of Internationalists* (Westport, Conn.: Greenwood, 1983), 56–58; Robert J. Young, "Cultural Politics and the Politics of Culture in the Third French Republic: The Case of Louis Barthou," *French Historical Studies,* 17: 2 (fall 1991), 343–58; John R. Jones, "The Foreign Policy of Louis Barthou, 1933–1934" (Ph.D. dissertation, University of North Carolina, 1958); "King of Yugoslavia Murdered. M. Barthou Fatally Wounded. Croat Assassin's Attack at Marseilles. Criminal Cut Down," *The Times* (London), October 10, 1934, p. 14; "M. Barthou. Loss to France," *The Times* (London), October 10, 1934, p. 19; "M. Barthou. State Funeral on Saturday," *The Times* (London), October 11, 1934, p. 14.

Bartók, Béla (1881–1945)

Hungarian composer, teacher, and pianist. Born Béla Viktor Janos Bartók in Nagyszentmiklós, Austria-Hungary (now Sinnicolaul-Mare, Romania), on March 25, 1881, he started to play the piano at the age of five with lessons from his mother. After his father's death in 1888, the family moved to Bohemia, where Bartók continued to study and made his first public appearance at age eleven. A few years later, he enrolled at the Royal Academy of Music in Budapest and became schooled in the romantics. Before World War I, he became a close associate of fellow Hungarian Zoltan Kodaly, who was working to preserve the folk songs of his native Hungary. The two men published a collection of such folk songs in 1906. In 1907, Bartók was named to the piano faculty at the academy.

As Bartók tried to make Hungarian music a world classic, in 1910 he released his First String Quartet, and a few years later produced his opera *A kékszakállú herceg vára* ("Duke Bluebeard's Castle"). His work with Hungarian composer Arnold Schoenberg produced such works as two sonatas for violin and piano in 1922 and 1923, and a ballet, *Csodálatos mandarin* ("The Miraculous Mandarin"), completed in 1918–19 and produced in 1926. Perhaps his best interwar work, however, is *Mikrokosmos* (1926–39), a six-book collection of piano pieces. These include *Music for Strings, Percussion, and Celesta* (1936), and the *Sonata for Two Pianos and Percussion* (1937).

After the start of World War II, Bartók fled to the United States, where he was able to get a teaching position at Columbia University. While there, he was commissioned by Serge Koussevitzky to create a performance for the Boston Symphony; the result was *Concerto for Orchestra* (1943), his last great piece. Bartók died in New York on September 26, 1945.

References: Peter Laki, ed., *Bartók and His World* (Princeton, N.J.: Princeton University Press, 1995); Paul Griffiths, "Bartók, Béla Viktor János" in Alan Bullock and R. B. Woodings, eds., *20th Century Culture: A Biographical Companion* (New York: Harper & Row, 1983), 46.

Baseball, Major League

The American baseball leagues produced during the interwar period perhaps some of the finest athletes ever to play the game. Among this group can be included Ty Cobb, Babe RUTH, and Walter JOHNSON.

The 1919 season was perhaps the most important in the history of the game. The Chicago White Sox, with a lineup dominated by such names as Happy Felsch, "Shoeless Joe" Jackson, and Chick Gandil, won the regular season to face the Cincinnati Reds in the World Series, but apparently fell apart in the Fall Classic to go down to defeat, 5 games to 3. By the start of the 1920 season, however, rumors began to swirl that several of the Sox's best players had been on the take to throw the series. An investigation, and the hiring by the baseball club owners of federal judge Kenesaw Mountain LANDIS as the first commissioner of baseball, led to a trial (in which all the suspected players were acquitted) and their subsequent banishment by Landis from the game forever. This BLACK SOX SCANDAL tainted the game for years to come. As the game matured through the 1920s, many credited Landis with "saving" the game.

Before the 1920 season, many sportswriters would never have predicted that the upstart Cleveland Indians would capture the American League and win the league pennant for a shot at the World Series. The Indians went on a seasonwide tear, winning a stunning 98 games (with 54 losses) and fielding such talent as second baseman Bill Wambsganss and outfielder/manager Tris Speaker. Then, tragedy struck. While playing the New York Yankees at the Polo Grounds on August 16, Indians shortstop Ray Chapman was beaned by Yankees pitcher Carl Mays and died the next day of massive head injuries. (He became the first man in baseball ever to die from a playing-related injury. (The only other man to have died on the field was umpire John McSherry, who collapsed from a heart attack on Opening Day, 1996.) The Indians rallied, winning the American League over the Yankees, and met the Brooklyn Dodgers in the World Series. Led by pitcher Stan Covelski, who won three of the five Cleveland victories, the grand slam by outfielder Elmer Smith (the first in World Series history), and the first unassisted triple play by second baseman Wambsganss, the Indians took five out of seven games and were the world champions.

1921 became the year of the "Railroad Series," when the New York Yankees faced their crosstown rivals the New York Giants in the World Series. But 1921 was not just the first World Series since 1906 (when the Chicago White Sox played the Chicago Cubs) that two teams in one city played one another; it was really the year of Babe Ruth. The rotund, 26-year-old hitter continued to amaze the baseball world. In the era when the ball was dead (not as lively as today), he had hit 54 home runs in 1920; in 1921, however, he hit a monstrous 59 homers, as well as batting 170 runs batted in, with a .378 batting average, which many baseball historians consider one of the greatest assemblages of numbers by one player in baseball history. Ruth was also joined by such talent as Bob Meusel, Wally Pipp, and pitchers Carl Mays, Waite Hoyt, and Bob Shawkey, who accumulated 68 of the Yankees's 98 victories. The National League's Giants, led by manager John McGraw, won 94 games and reached the World Series for the seventh time in McGraw's nineteen-year career in New York. The Series started with Mays and Hoyt throwing shutouts at the Polo Grounds, but the Giants took five of the next seven to win the championship. Ruth hit only one homer, and was the only Yankee to hit over .300 with a .313 average.

1922 was the year of battings, as St. Louis Browns first baseman George Sisler led the majors with a .420 average, while the St. Louis Cardinals' second baseman Rogers Hornsby won the Triple Crown with a .401 average, 42 home runs, and 152 runs batted in. For St. Louis, however, it was not enough: The world champion New York Giants won the pennant, with St. Louis tied for third. The Giants were led by Casey Stengel, whose .368 average was one of the season's best. In the American League, the Yankees fought the St. Louis Browns for most of the season for the top spot, winning the pennant by one game and 94 victories. Thus the 1922 World Series was a repeat of the 1921 games, with another "Subway Series" in New York. The result, as well, was the same: in the first best-of-seven games, the Giants won 4 games to 1, with Babe Ruth being held to a .118 batting average. The Giant attack was led by Heinie Groh, who hit .474, and Frankie Frisch, who hit a likewise spectacular .471.

1923 saw the construction of Yankee Stadium. The team had been playing in the New York Giants park, the Polo Grounds, but after two consecutive Giant victories in 1921 and 1922, the Giants told the Yankees to leave. Yankee owner Col. Jacob Ruppert then purchased some land a quarter mile from the Polo Grounds, and proceeded to build a 62,000 seat palace. Whereas all previous ball parks had been built with a team in mind, the new field was constructed for Babe Ruth, and thus became known as

"the house that Ruth built." Opening on April 18, Ruth met expectations and slammed a three-run homer to beat the Red Sox, 4–1. It was one of Ruth's 41 round trippers that year. The hitting of Ruth, Meusel, Pipp, as well as the pitching of Hoyt, Mays, and newcomer Herb Pennock saw the Yankees win the American League by sixteen games over Ty Cobb and the Detroit Tigers. McGraw's New York Giants again won the National League, beating Cincinnati by four games. The World Series opened on October 10 in New York for the third straight year, but this time in two distinct ball parks. The result was different as well. Behind the pitching of Pennock, who won two games, and the .368 hitting (and three homers) of Ruth, the Yankees won the Series in five games, earning for them their first world championship and the beginning of a dynasty which has lasted to this day.

1924 saw the New York Giants win their fourth consecutive pennant, meeting the Washington Senators in the World Series. The Senators, perennial losers, were led by righthanded pitcher Walter Johnson. Johnson was in the world championship for the first time in his eighteen-year career. With 23 wins and a 2.72 earned run average, Johnson helped the Senators defeat Ruth and the Yankees by three games. The Series opened in Washington on October 4, with Johnson losing to New York's Ray Nehf, 4–3. In fact, Johnson also was on the losing end of Game 5, 6–2. Yet it was his performance in Game 7, a twelve-inning thriller, as a reliever, saw him come in in the ninth inning and hold the Giants scoreless. In the bottom of the 12th, a hit by Earl McNeely scored the winning run, making the Senators the world champs, four games to three.

In 1925, an intestinal abscess sidelined Babe Ruth for most of the season, and although a younger player named Lou GEHRIG replaced Wally Pipp at first, the Yankees finished in seventh place, just above the last-place Boston Red Sox. The Pittsburgh Pirates, led by manager Bill Mckechnie, took the World Series over the Washington Senators in a spectacular game seven marked by two crucial errors by Senators shortstop Roger Peckinpaugh. Pittsburgh outfielder Max Carey batted 58, with the winning team hitting only four home runs in the entire seven-game series.

The 1926 St. Louis Cardinals, led by player-manager Rogers Hornsby, went to the World Series and defeated the favored New York Yankees in seven games. Babe Ruth had yet another incredible season, batting .372 with 47 home runs and 145 RBI's.

1927 was perhaps the finest year for baseball. Ruth set a record which was to last until 1961–60 home runs in a single season. But he was just a part of the Yankees' new lineup—called "Murderer's Row"—which included Gehrig, Tony Lazzeri, Mark Koenig, Earle Combs, and Bob Meusal. On top of Ruth's 60 homers, Gehrig hit 175 RBI's, leading the team to a 110–44 record and a sweep, in the World Series, of the Pittsburgh Pirates.

In 1928, Ty Cobb, one of the best all-around players to ever play the game, ended his remarkable career, finishing with 4,191 hits, a .367 career batting average, and 892 stolen bases. Babe Ruth continued to hit home runs—this year it was 54—and set a new record: from 1926 to 1928, Ruth hit 161 home runs, a record only broken by Mark McGwire of the St. Louis Cardinals from 1996–98. The Yankees again went to the World Series, and defeated Bill McKechnie and his St. Louis Cardinals, four games to none.

1929 saw the appearance of Lefty Grove, who goes 20–6 with a 2.82 ERA and 170 strikeouts, which leads the American League. The World Champion New York Yankees fade to second behind Grove's Philadelphia A's, led by manager Connie Mack, who faced the Chicago Cubs in the World Series. Backed by the pitching of Howard Ehmke, the A's took the Cubs, four games to one.

Hack Wilson of the Chicago Cubs produces one of the finest seasons in baseball history in 1930, when he hits 56 home runs (the National League record until 1998, when Mark McGwire of the St. Louis Cardinals and Sammy Sosa of the Chicago Cubs hit more), 190 RBIs (a record which remains untouched), and a batting average of .356. However, the Cubs fade at the end of the season, and finish second behind the St. Louis Cardinals. Philadelphia beats Washington for the American League crown, and in the World Series defeated St. Louis four games to two behind the hitting of Al Simmons and the pitching of Lefty Grove.

In 1931, Philadelphia's Lefty Grove goes 31–4 with a 2.06 ERA and 175 strikeouts, while the Cardinals' Frankie Frisch hits .311 and 82 RBIs—both men lead their respective teams into the World Series, where St. Louis avenges its loss the year before and defeats the A's, four games to three.

In 1932, Philadelphia's Jimmie Foxx finished with 58 home runs—two shy of Babe Ruth's record—as well as a .364 batting average and 169 RBIs. However, Foxx could not get his team into the World Series, having been beaten by 13 games by the New York Yankees, who won 107 games, led by the steady lineup of Ruth, Gehrig, and Lazzeri. The Chicago Cubs took the National League crown, and the Series was marked by Ruth's call, in game 3, of a home run against pitcher Charlie Root, leading the Yankees to a four-game sweep.

In 1933, the season was interrupted by the First All-Star Game, in which Ruth homers to lead the American League at Chicago's Comiskey Park, 4–2. The Senators beat the Yankees for the pennant, but lost to the National League champ New York Giants, four games to one.

The name of Dizzy Dean came out in 1934, when he led the St. Louis Cardinals—dubbed "The Gashouse Gang"—to a four-to-three games victory over the Detroit Tigers in the World Series.

1935 saw the first night game, held May 24, at Crosley Field, the home of the Cincinnati Reds. Led by catcher-manager Mickey Cochrane, the Detroit Tigers, losers in the 1934 Series, with Hank Greenberg, Goose Goslin, and Charlie Gehringer, defeated the Yankees for the pennant, then beat the hot Cubs from Chicago in the World Series, four games to two, for their first world championship ever.

1936 saw the first vote for the Hall of Fame in Cooperstown, New York, slated to open in 1939; inducted in the first year were Ruth, Cobb, Honus Wagner, Christy Mathewson, and Johnson. For the first time since 1923, two teams from the same city met in the World Series: the Yankees and the Giants. Playing in their first Series since Babe Ruth's departure, the Yankees added the power of Joe DiMaggio. The Giants faced the Yankees with pitcher Carl Hubbell, who won game one, but the Yankees recovered to win four of the next five to take the series and the championship.

In 1937, the Yankees repeated as American League champs, and met the Giants again in the series. This time, things were a bit different: the Yankees won the series, but in five games instead of six. Tris Speaker, Cy Young, and Nap Lajoie were inducted into the Hall of Fame.

1938 saw the last great year for Gehrig. Detroit Tiger slugger Hank Greenberg hits 58 home runs to close within two of Ruth's season record of 60. Cincinnati pitcher Johnny Vander Meer pitches two consecutive no-hitters, the first and possibly last time such a feat will ever be accomplished. The Yankees appear in the World Series again, and quickly dispatch the Chicago Cubs in four games. Game four marks Gehrig's last series appearance; he finishes the series with four hits in 14 at-bats, for a .286 average.

1939 sees Gehrig remove himself from the Yankee lineup after 2,130 consecutive games, due to fatigue; he is later diagnosed with amyotrophic lateral sclerosis, a fatal disease which will claim his life a brief two years later. The Yankees persevered, and won the American League, facing Cincinnati in the World Series. Another four game sweep followed, making Yankee manager Joe McCarthy the first manager to win four consecutive world championships.

Baseball, Negro League

Until Jackie Robinson broke in with the Brooklyn Dodgers in 1947, African Americans were segregated from playing in the professional baseball leagues in the United States. Black teams had always been prevalent in the United States, but it was not until Andrew "Rube" Foster, the owner of the Chicago American Giants, met with other owners of other black teams in Kansas City in 1920 that the Negro National League was established. Starting with eight teams—the Chicago Giants and the Chicago American Giants, the Detroit Stars, the Kansas City Monarchs, the Dayton (Ohio) Marcos, the Indianapolis

ABCs, the St. Louis Giants, and a Cuban team called the Stars—the league started play. In 1923, Nat Strong, a New York promoter, began the Eastern Colored League with six teams, including the Brooklyn Royal Giants and the Baltimore Black Sox. In 1924 the East met the Midwest in the first "Colored World Series," in which the Monarchs beat the Philadelphia Hilldales. In 1928, however, the Eastern Colored League broke up and, after Foster's death in 1930, the Negro National League went the same way.

New teams sprouted up, but they collapsed because of the GREAT DEPRESSION. In 1932, however, the second Negro National League was founded. From this league sprang some of the most famous stars of professional baseball—men who would have played in the major leagues if there had not been a color line. These men included James "Cool Papa" Bell, Josh Gibson, Satchel Paige, and Walter "Buck" Leonard. They played the same baseball as their white counterparts, except to all-black audiences. All-Star games were staged, as were World Series.

The Negro Leagues ended in the 1960s when baseball was integrated—too late for all but Paige to participate. However, their legacy is remembered in a Hall of Fame museum in Kansas City.

References: Michael L. Cooper, *Playing America's Game: The Story of Negro League Baseball* (New York: Lodestar Books, 1993); John Holway, *Blackball Stars: Negro League Pioneers* (Westport, Conn.: Meckler Books, 1988).

Basie, Count   *See* JAZZ.

The Battleship Potemkin

Classic 1925 silent film by Russian director and film theorist Sergei Mikhailovich EISENSTEIN, which defined an entire era of motion pictures, particularly Russian filmmaking. Taking a cue from the 1905 riot aboard the Russian battleship *Potemkin*, Eisenstein created a movie that fit into the vision of Soviet realism that was pushed by the government in the 1920s. In the film, when the ship's doctor verifies that rancid meat is safe to eat, the sailors go ashore and purchase their own. On their return the admiral demands that all who did so must come forward; those who do not are to be shot. When Vakulinchik (played by Aleksandr Antonov) appeals to his shipmates to rise up, he is shot and his body thrown onto the Odessa pier. The citizens of Odessa, seeing the corpse, begin a riot against the treatment meted out to the sailors, until Cossacks come and fire on them as they disperse down the steps of the Odessa pier in one of the most famed scenes in film history. After the slaughter ends, Czarist ships comes to destroy the Potemkin to end further rioting.

References: Herbert Marshall, ed., *Sergei Eisenstein's The Battleship Potemkin* (New York: Avon Books, 1978); Sergie Eisenstein, (Jay Leyda, ed.; Diana Matias, trans.), *Eisenstein: Three Films* (New York: Harper & Row, 1974); Leonard Maltin, ed., *Movie and Video Guide 1996 Edition* (New York: Plume, 1995), 1031.

Bauhaus

German school of art and architecture that lasted from 1919 to 1934, when it was ended by Adolf HITLER's Nazi government. The name was coined by German architect and Bauhaus founder Walter GROPIUS, who combined the roots of the German words *bauen* ("to build") and *haus* ("house"). The Staatliches Bauhaus Weimar was founded at Weimar in 1919. The school of art used expressionist creativity "to unite all the creative arts into architecture." The artists who worked with the Bauhaus included the Hungarian painter and designer László Moholy-Nagy; the Swiss painter and graphic artist Paul KLEE, who authored *Pedagogical Sketchbook* (1925); the cubist and expressionist Lyonel Feininger; the architect and furniture designer Marcel Breuer; and architect Ludwig MIES VAN DER ROHE.

The teaching focused on functional craftsmanship as it applied to industrial mass production. The style was characterized by severe geometric design. Josef Albers taught the *Vorkurs*, or preliminary course, which involved Bauhaus students in an absorbing process on the principles of German design and materials. Buildings were constructed that, although functional, involved intricate architectural designs.

In 1933, after Hitler rose to power, the Bauhaus was no longer to be tolerated and was closed down. Gropius and Albers went to the United States and joined the staff on Black Mountain College in North Carolina; Mies van der Rohe taught at the architectural school of the Illinois Institute of Technology; Moholy-Nagy went to Chicago, where he founded the Chicago Institute of Design. The Bauhaus influence in design, typography, architecture, and furniture found international acclaim.

References: Frank Whitford, *Bauhaus* (London: Thames & Hudson, 1995); Herbert Bayer and Walter and Ise Gropius, eds., *Bauhaus: 1919–1928* (Boston: Charles T. Branford Co., 1959), 114–21; *Reader's Digest Great Events of the 20th Century: How They Changed Our Lives* (Pleasantville, N.Y.: Reader's Digest Association, 1977), 156.

Beard, Charles Austin (1874–1948), and Mary Ritter Beard (1876–1958)

American husband and wife historians, noted for such works as, *History of the United States* (1921), *The Rise of American Civilization* (two volumes, 1927). *The Making of American Civilization* (1937), and *America in Midpassage* (two volumes, 1939). Beard was born on his family farm near Knightstown, Indiana, and attended nearby Spiceland Academy, a Quaker school. He and his brother later ran a local newspaper that had been purchased by their father. Beard entered DePauw University and, after receiving a doctorate in 1898, spent a year studying English constitutional history at Oxford University.

After he returned to the United States in 1900, Beard married Ritter, a fellow historian he had met at DePauw. A women's rights advocate as well as a historian, she was born in Indianapolis in 1876. Together, the Beards became one of the most famous husband and wife writing teams. After they married, the couple went back to England, where Charles Beard wrote articles on labor history and Mary Ritter Beard worked in the British suffragist movement. Charles Beard's first work, *The Industrial Revolution,* was published in 1901. Returning to the United States, he entered Columbia University, where he earned a master's degree and a doctorate. Mary Ritter Beard worked for the Women's Trade Union League as a union activist and edited the suffragist newspaper *The Woman Voter.* Her books during this period include *Woman's Work in Municipalities* (1915).

In 1921 the Beards began to collaborate on several works, which many consider some of the finest ever written on American history. The first, *History of the United States* (1921), is still considered a classic; the second, *The Rise of American Civilization* (1927–30), was a work that biographer Cushing Strout said was "dominated by his [argument] of a recurring conflict between province and metropolis, agriculture and business, which 'figured in every great national crisis.'" Charles Beard on his own also wrote *The Idea of National Interest* and *The Open Door at Home* (both 1934), which held that the GREAT DEPRESSION would allow the United States a chance to review its dealings and alliances with the nations of the world; he also contributed pieces to H. L. MENCKEN's literary magazine, the *American Mercury.* In one of his final works, *The Devil Theory of War* (1936), Beard asserted that Woodrow Wilson had forced the United States into war in 1917, a controversial idea. Mary Ritter Beard published widely during the 1930s including the books *Understanding Women* (1931), *America through Women's Eyes* (1933), and *Laughing Their Way: Women's Humor in America* (1934).

Charles Beard died in New Haven, Connecticut, on September 1, 1948. Mary Ritter Beard survived him by a decade, dying on August 14, 1958, in Phoenix, Arizona.

References: Ellen Nore, *Charles A. Beard: An Intellectual Biography* (Carbondale: Southern Illinois University Press, 1983); Richard Hofstadter, *The Progressive Historians: Turner, Beard, Parrington* (New York: Knopf, 1968); Marvin C. Swanson, ed., "Charles A. Beard: An Observance of the Centennial of his Birth, DePauw University, Greencastle, Indiana, October 11–12, 1974" (Greencastle, Indiana: The University,

1976; Clifton K. Yearley, "Mary Beard" in Frank Magill, ed., *Great Lives from History—American Women Series* (Pasadena, Calif.: Salem Press, 1985), 1: 170–74; Cushing Strout, "Beard, Charles Austin" in Allen Johnson and Dumas Malone et al., eds., *Dictionary of American Biography* (New York: Charles Scribner's Sons, 1930–95), 4: 63.

Beavers, Louise (1902–1962)

American actress, the first African American to receive major roles in motion pictures. Born in Cincinnati, Ohio, on March 8, 1902, she moved with her parents to Pasadena, California, when she was eleven. There she worked as a maid to silent film actress Leatrice Joy. Starting in 1923, Beavers began her own film career as the archetypal "mammy" character with roles in *Gold Diggers* (1923), *Uncle Tom's Cabin* (1927), *Coquette* (1929), *Wall Street* (1929), *She Couldn't Say No* (1930), *Imitation of Life* (1934), in which she played Aunt Delilah, *Brother Rat* (1938), and *Made for Each Other* (1939). As film historian Ephraim Katz writes, "She became one of Hollywood's most frequently employed black performers, but her considerable talent was wasted in a constant repetition of good-natured black mama roles, nearly always as a maid, housekeeper, or cook." Beavers later moved to television, where from 1952 to 1953 she played the title role in the series *Beulah.* She died in 1962; in 1976, she was named to the Black Filmmakers Hall of Fame.

References: Eleanor W. Traylor, "Beavers, Louise" in Rayford W. Logan and Michael R. Winston, eds., *Dictionary of American Negro Biography* (New York: W. W. Norton & Co., 1982), 35–36; Elizabeth R. Nelson, "Beavers, Louise" in Allen Johnson and Dumas Malone et al., eds., *Dictionary of American Biography* (New York: Charles Scribner's Sons, 1930–95), 7: 43–45; Ephraim Katz, *The Film Encyclopedia* (New York: HarperPerennial, 1994), 103.

Beck, Józef (1894–1944)

Polish soldier and politician. Born in Warsaw, Poland, on October 4, 1894, he served in Józef Klemens PILSUDSKI's Polish Legion in World War I and worked closely with Pilsudski, serving for a time as his military attaché in Paris, after the war. In 1932, Pilsudski named Beck as the Polish foreign minister, where he was forced to balance Germany's growing power to the west and the Soviet Union to the east. When Germany occupied Czechoslovakia in 1939, Beck greedily grabbed Teschen for Poland, seeing the division of the Czech nation as a Polish gain.

Too late, however, Beck came to realize that Hitler had planned the same fate for Poland. Beck worked to save his nation by signing various mutual assistance treaties in 1939, namely with Great Britain on April 6, and then with France on May 19, in a desperate attempt to head off the expected German assault. Beck's estimation that Hitler would invade was correct; his appraisal that England and France would save Poland was wrong, although the German invasion on September 2, 1939, plunged the European continent into its second major war in a generation. Beck, still serving as foreign minister of a nation being rapidly decimated, was ordered by Hitler to surrender the port of Danzig and end the invasion more quickly. Beck refused, and fled to Romania to escape capture. He spent the rest of the war there and died in exile in the Romanian city of Stânesti on June 5, 1944.

References: Christian Zentner and Friedemann Bedüftig, eds., *Encyclopedia of the Third Reich* (New York: Macmillan, 1991), 1: 73; George J. Lerski, *Historical Dictionary of Poland, 966–1945* (Westport, Conn.: Greenwood, 1996), 30–31; John Hunter Harley, *The Authentic Biography of Colonel Beck, by J. H. Harley; based on the Polish by Conrad Wrzos, introduction by Count Edward Raczynski* (London: Hutchinson & Co., 1939).

Beebe, Charles William (1877–1962)

American naturalist and explorer. Born in Brooklyn, New York, on July 29, 1877, Beebe graduated from Columbia University with a bachelor's degree in 1898. The following year he joined the New York Zoological Society as a curator in ornithology, as well as the director of scientific research. In his work at the society, where he remained until his retirement in 1952, he conducted important investigations at the Simla Research Station in Trinidad.

In 1905, Beebe's first work, *Two Bird Lovers in Mexico*, heralded his examinations of the bird world and culminated in the four-volume *Monographs of the Pheasants* (1918), which made him famous in his field. In the 1920s he conducted two distinguished expeditions: one to the Galápagos Islands, resulted in his *Galapagos: World's End* (1924), the first work on the subject in the 20th century, which brought that island's rich and diverse panorama of wildlife to the American people; the other, to the Sargasso Sea in the wooden ship *Arcturus*, became the basis of his 1926 work *The Arcturus Adventure*. One of the earliest scientists to use the bathysphere for deep-sea diving, Beebe chronicled his adventures in *Half Mile Down* (1934), in which he described his setting of a deep-sea record, 3,028 feet, which was not eclipsed until 1949. In the book he wrote, "At 11: 12 A.M. we came to rest gently at 3,000 feet, and I knew that this was my ultimate floor; the cable on the winch was very near its end. A few days ago the water had appeared blacker at 2,500 feet than could be imagined, yet now to this same imagination it seemed to show as blacker than black. It seemed as if all future nights in the upper world must be considered only relative degrees of twilight."

Beebe's narrative of his adventurous life, *Adventuring with Beebe* (1955), appeared shortly after his retirement. He was working at Simla on June 4, 1962, when he died.

See also ANDREWS, Roy Chapman.

References: Robert Henry Welker, *Natural Man: The Life of William Beebe* (Bloomington: Indiana University Press, 1975); Tim M. Berra, *William Beebe: An Annotated Bibliography* (Hamden, Conn.: Archon Books, 1977); William Beebe, *Half Mile Down, by William Beebe, director of the department of tropical research of the New York Zoological Society, with 123 illustrations and 8 colored plates. Published under the auspices of the New York Zoological Society* (New York: Harcourt, Brace, 1934); William Beebe, *The Book of Naturalists, An Anthology of the Best Natural History* (New York: Alfred A. Knopf, 1944).

Beer Hall Putsch

Revolutionary action of German militants, led by Adolf HITLER and his group of National Socialists (Nazis), in their attempt on November 8 and 9, 1923, to overthrow the Bavarian government established at Munich. The *putsch* (the German term for revolution) came after the collapse of the German economy: the rate of exchange fell from four marks to seventy-five marks to the dollar, finally reaching four hundred marks to the dollar in 1922. After Germany defaulted on reparations payments in July 1923 and the French occupied the Ruhr valley, the mark fell to 160,000 marks to the dollar. That November it dropped still further, to four million marks to the dollar. It took a wheelbarrow of currency to buy a loaf of bread. Germans lost their savings and were left destitute.

Hitler, head of the fledgling Workers' Party (which would become the National Socialist German Workers' Party, the NAZI PARTY), decided that a revolution was needed. On November 8, 1923, he and several of his forces burst into the beer hall in Munich to proclaim a revolt against the Weimar government. "The National Revolution has begun!" Hitler shouted. "No one may leave the hall. Unless there is immediate quiet I shall have a machine gun posted in the gallery. The Bavarian and Reich governments have been removed and a provisional national government formed. The barracks of the Reichswehr and police are occupied. The army and the police are marching on the city under the swastika banner!" Hitler had few troops, and the action was a bluff. Nonetheless, several government officials in the room believed his claims. They refused to submit to Hitler until General Erich Ludendorff, a military leader during World War I and a supporter of Hitler, arrived and convinced them that Hitler was in charge.

The following day, attempting to mimic Benito MUSSOLINI's march on Rome, Hitler and his three thousand followers marched to the Marienplatz in Munich; there they were met by soldiers loyal to the Weimar government

The collaborators of the Beer Hall Putsch, including General Erich Ludendorff (center) and Adolf Hitler (fourth from right), pose after their trial in 1923. (*CORBIS/Hulton-Deutsch Collection*)

who ordered the Nazis to disperse or be fired upon. In the panic that followed, sixteen Nazis and three Weimar police officers were shot and killed. Arrested, Hitler and Ludendorff were tried for treason; Ludendorff was acquitted, but Hitler was convicted and sentenced to serve five years in prison. There he composed his thoughts on his life and his goals for German society in his book, MEIN KAMPF. He was released after only eight months.

See also NAZI PARTY.

References: Harold J. Gordon, *Hitler and the Beer Hall Putsch* (Princeton, N.J.: Princeton University Press, 1972); Geoffrey Pridham, *Hitler's Rise to Power: The Nazi Movement in Bavaria, 1923–1933)* (London: Hart-Davis MacGibbon, 1973); Richard Hanser, *Putsch! How Hitler Made Revolution* (New York: P. H. Wyden, 1970).

Beiderbecke, Bix (1903–1931)

American cornetist and pianist, one of the leading musicians of the JAZZ AGE before his death at age twenty-eight

in 1931. Born Leon Bismarck on March 10, 1903, in Davenport, Iowa, his musical talent was apparent at age three, when he was playing the piano. He mastered the cornet, the instrument with which he became popular, at age fourteen. At sixteen he became a fan of his older brother's jazz records and started to play with local bands. His family enrolled him in a military academy, but instead he started a band in Chicago and began to play local venues.

In 1922, after spending some time back at home in Iowa, Beiderbecke returned to Chicago. The following year he joined a band called the Wolverines, with which he began a tour through parts of the Midwest and cut his first album. In 1924 the band moved to New York, but soon after Beiderbecke left the group and joined the Jean Goldkette Orchestra, which at the time included Tommy and Jimmy DORSEY and violinist Joe Venuti. Beiderbecke's first stint with Goldkette failed because he could not properly read music; in 1925 he worked for saxophonist Frank Trumhauer's Detroit-based band, then for the Charlie Straight Orchestra. Later in 1925, Beiderbecke went back to the Jean Goldkette Orchestra. At this time he and some of his fellow artists from that group cut an album under the group title "Bix Beiderbecke's Rhythm Jugglers." One of the hits from the album was *Davenport Blues,* named after Beiderbecke's home town. He then joined renowned orchestra conductors Paul Whiteman and Frank Trumhauer to lead one of the best big bands of the era. With Trumhauer he invented the concept of "cool jazz."

In 1929, Beiderbecke quit the band after suffering a nervous breakdown. Few knew that it was brought on by a ravenous appetite for bootleg liquor at the height of Prohibition, and that he was a full-blown alcoholic. Within two years his health had deteriorated so that he was constantly near death. On August 6, 1931, at age twenty-eight, he was found dead in his New York City apartment.

The legacy of Bix Beiderbecke may be that of a musician on the cutting edge who died too soon. He invented, with Trumhauer, the concept of "cool jazz" in 1927, and his numerous recordings, including *In a Mist, Candle Light, Flashes,* and *In the Dark,* four compositions known as "The Modern Suite," made him even bigger after his death and influenced musicians for generations to come. A motion picture based on his life story, *Young Man with a Horn,* starring Kirk Douglas and Lauren Bacall, was released in 1950.

References: Richard M. Sudhalter, and Philip R. Evans, *Bix: Man & Legend* (New Rochelle, N.Y.: Arlington House, 1974); Ralph Berton, *Remembering Bix: A Memoir of The Jazz Age* (New York: Harper & Row, 1974); John Paul Perhonis, "The Bix Beiderbecke Story: The Jazz Musician in Legend, Fiction and Fact; A Study of the Images of Jazz in the National Culture, 1930–Present" (M.A. thesis, University of Minnesota, 1978); Burnett James, *Bix Beiderbecke* (New York: Barnes, 1961).

Benavente, Jacinto (1866–1954)

Born in Madrid, Spain, Benavente was the son of a successful pediatrician. As a young man he pursued a legal career but abandoned his studies after the death of his father relieved him of the necessity of earning a living. He traveled throughout Europe and on his return to Spain, began to write and edit for several newspapers and other publications. Eventually, he succeeded in publishing a collection of poems and *Cartas de mujeres* (1892–93), a series of women's letters, for which he received critical recognition.

Benavente's career veered toward drama, and he wrote several plays—comedies and dramas dealing with all aspects of Spanish life at all social levels—that he collectively titled "The Fantastic Theater." Among these, his satires and farces, the latter consisting mostly of one-acts, are considered his finest work. The frequently performed *Los intereses creados* (1907), an allegory on the nature of evil, is regarded as Benavente's masterpiece. In 1922 Benavente was awarded the Nobel Prize in literature. His collected works were published from 1941 to 1955.

Benchley, Robert   *See* ALGONQUIN ROUND TABLE.

Benedict XV (1854–1922)

Roman Catholic leader and pope (1914–22), born Giacomo Paolo Battista della Chiesa in Genoa, Italy. He attended the University of Genoa, from which he received a doctorate in 1875, and later studied theology at the Capranica College in Rome. Ordained a priest in 1878, he went to Madrid four years later to act as secretary to the Spanish nuncio, the future cardinal Mariano Rampolla. There, della Chiesa became known as "The Curate of the Two Pesetas" for his charitable work with the poor. In 1887 he was recalled to Rome, where he was named a *minutante* (administrative secretary), and, in 1901, as a *sostituto* (undersecretary of state) of the Holy See. Six years later he was named archbishop of Bologna, and he became a cardinal in June 1914. There he remained until the death of Pius X on August 20, 1914. Shortly after World War I exploded in Europe, the cardinal attended the conclave in Rome to choose the new pope. After ten ballots the delegates turned to a tested veteran diplomat among their ranks who could deal with the world war: della Chiesa was chosen pope with 38 votes out of 57, and he took the name Benedict XV.

As World War I raged, Benedict called on all sides to exercise restraint in combat and keep the Church in a neutral state. When he stepped forward in 1917 to act as a mediator, the Germans acceded but the Allies refused. Instead, Benedict turned to aiding prisoners of war on both sides, as well as Belgian and Armenian refugees. He was criticized in the Allied nations when after the war he called for an end to the blockade of Germany, but he used his influence to call for tolerance during the negotiation of the TREATY OF VERSAILLES, from which he was excluded because of his neutral stand. Benedict may be more remembered, however, for his promulgation of the Code of Canon Law, which he credited to his predecessor, Pius X. During his pontificate he canonized Joan of Arc and Margaret Mary Alacoque, both of France, and established a diplomatic representative in Great Britain, which had broken away and formed the Anglican Church three hundred years earlier.

Papal historian Hubert Jedin says of Benedict, "[He] was small of stature, slight, and somewhat misshapen, but of an active mind, clear thinking and clever, a finished diplomat, filled with zeal for souls." The conflagration that had been the war was too much for Benedict, and soon after it ended his health declined. On January 22, 1922, suffering from the lingering effects of the influenza that was gripping the world, he died in his sleep. He is considered one of the finest popes of the 20th century and has been called "the good samaritan of humanity."

See also PIUS XI; PIUS XII.

References: John Norman Davidson Kelly, *The Oxford Dictionary of Popes* (Oxford, England: Oxford University Press, 1986), 314–16; Matthew Bunson, *The Pope Encyclopedia: An A to Z of the Holy See* (New York: Crown Trade Paperbacks, 1995), 46–47; "Pope Benedict Died at 6 O'Clock This Morning; Weakens After an Early Rally Yesterday; Cardinal Bourne Had False Report of Death," *The World* (New York), January 22, 1922, p. 1; "Funeral of the Pope. Last Scenes in St. Peter's. Traditional Ceremony," *The Times* (London), January 27, 1922, p. 10.

Beneš, Edvard (1884–1948)

Czechoslovak statesman, prime minister (1935–38). Born in the village of Kozlany, Bohemia, then a province of the Austro-Hungarian Empire (now in the Czech Republic), on May 28, 1884, he was the son of poor Moravian parents. He received his education at the universities of Prague and Dijon (France), and at the Sorbonne in Paris. For several years before the outbreak of World War I, he taught political science at the Commercial Academy in Prague and in 1922 was named as a professor of sociology at Prague University. During the war he worked closely with the philosopher and stateman Tomás MASARYK to establish a Czechoslovak nation independent of the Austro-Hungarian Empire. At the end of the war, in 1918, when this independent Czechoslovakia was formulated, Beneš was named minister of foreign affairs in the new government, serving in that position until 1935. In 1921 he was named prime minister, serving until 1922, and he served as the Czechoslovak member of the Council of the League of Nations from 1923 to 1927.

On December 18, 1935, Beneš was named president when Masaryk resigned due to ill health. He served only until October 5, 1938, when Beneš resigned to express his outrage over the sellout of his nation by the Allies in the Munich Pact, which handed Czechoslovakia's Sudetenland region over to Germany. Fleeing with the outbreak of World War II, Beneš headed the Czech government-in-exile, which he helped establish in London on July 1940. In December 1943 he signed on behalf of the exile government the Soviet-Czechoslovak Treaty of Friendship; after Germany's defeat in May 1945, he returned to Prague as the head of the postwar Czech government.

Unable to hold together a coalition government joining communist and noncommunist politicians, he resigned the presidency in 1948. Beneš soon suffered a paralyzing stroke, and on September 3, 1948, he died at Sezimovo Usti, Bohemia. He was the author of *Germany and*

Czechoslovakia (two volumes, 1937) and *Democracy Today and Tomorrow* (1939).

See also MUNICH CRISIS/MUNICH PACT.

Refer to Appendix 1 for text of the Munich Agreement.

References: Sharon L. Wolchik, "Benes, Eduard" in Bruce W. Jentleson and Thomas G. Paterson, senior eds., *Encyclopedia of U.S. Foreign Relations* (New York: Oxford University Press, 1997), 1: 143; "Bene[&hacek;]s, Eduard" in Warren F. Kuehl, ed., *Biographical Dictionary of Internationalists* (Westport, Conn.: Greenwood Press, 1983), 68–69; Crabités, Pierre, *Bene[&hacek;]s, Statesman of Central Europe* (London: G. Routledge and Sons, 1935).

Bennett, Richard Bedford (1870–1947)

Canadian lawyer and politician, prime minister (1930–35). Born at Hopewell Hill, New Brunswick, on July 3, 1870, the scion of a shipbuilding family, Bennett was educated at Dalhousie University in Nova Scotia, where he later taught. Eventually, he practiced law with the future Canadian senator James A. Lougheed. In 1897, Bennett went to Calgary, Alberta, where he became distinguished in provincial politics.

Fourteen years later he was elected to Parliament as a Conservative representing Calgary West. During World War I he served in the cabinet of Prime Minister Robert Borden as director general of national service. After Borden was replaced by Arthur MEIGHEN, Bennett was named as the minister of justice and federal attorney general and, in 1926, as minister of finance. The following year, he became the head of the Conservative Party, and saw the Conservative faction through the beginning of the GREAT DEPRESSION as the opposition to Prime Minister William Lyon Mackenzie KING. In 1930, Bennett's party was elected to a majority in Parliament, and Bennett himself was elevated to prime minister, urging a program of higher tariffs for foreign goods to protect Canadian industry. In 1930 he led the Commonwealth nations at the Fourth IMPERIAL CONFERENCE in London to demand a greater degree of independence and autonomy from Great Britain; two years later, he hosted the OTTAWA ECONOMIC CONFERENCE in the Canadian capital, where he pushed for tariff preferences among the Commonwealth nations. Influenced by the NEW DEAL program of U.S. President Franklin ROOSEVELT, Bennett attempted to end the depression in Canada by announcing a series of policy reforms on radio, including minimum wage legislation, increased government regulation over banking, and the advent of health and unemployment insurance. Most of Bennett's program to improve the financial situation failed, however, and its failure is considered the main reason for his party's overwhelming defeat in 1935. Two acts that he had championed, the minimum wage and unemployment insurance acts, were later struck down by the judicial committee of the Imperial Privy Council in London.

Bennett remained as leader of the Conservative opposition until 1938, when he stepped down to live in England. In 1941 he was made a viscount and served in the House of Lords in London until his death. Bennett died in Mickleham, Surrey, England, on June 26, 1947.

References: "Bennett, Richard Bedford, Viscount" in *The Canadian Encyclopedia* (Edmonton, Alberta: Hurtig Publishers, 1988), 1: 203–4; "Rt. Honourable Richard Bedford Bennett" in *Canada, The Founders and the Guardians: Fathers of Confederation, Governors General, Prime Ministers—A Collection of Biographical Sketches and Portraits* (Ottawa: The Queen's Printer, 1968), 140; James Henry Gray, *R. B. Bennett: The Calgary Years* (Toronto: University of Toronto Press, 1991); Peter B. Waite, *The Loner: Three Sketches of the Personal Life and Ideas of R. B. Bennett, 1870–1947* (Toronto: University of Toronto Press, 1992); Larry Arthur Glassford, *Reaction and Reform: The Politics of the Conservative Party under R. B. Bennett, 1927–1938* (Toronto: University of Toronto Press, 1992).

Benton, Thomas Hart *See* PAINTING.

Bergius, Friedrich Karl Rudolph (1884–1949)
German chemist and Nobel laureate. The son of Heinrich and Marie (Hanse) Bergius, he was born in Goldschmieden, Germany, on October 11, 1884. He received his education in chemistry from the universities of Berlin, Breslau, Leipzig, and Karlsruhe. In 1912, after being awarded his doctorate, Bergius discovered a new system to pull coal molecules apart and, after forcing hydrogen molecules into the mix, liquefied the coal into gasoline. For this discovery, he was the corecipient of the 1931 Nobel Prize in chemistry with fellow German chemist Carl BOSCH. The process he had invented was used by the German army during World War II to compensate for gasoline shortages. He survived the war, and later advised the Argentinian government on the construction of certain industries. He died in Buenos Aires on March 30, 1949, at the age of 55.

References: Günther Kerstein, "Bergius, Friedrich," in Charles Coulston Gillespie, ed. in chief, *Dictionary of Scientific Biography* (New York: Charles Scribner's Sons, 1980–90), 2: 3–4; Mary Porrett, "Bergius, Friedrich Karl Rudolph" in Bernard S. and June H. Schlessinger, eds., *The Who's Who of Nobel Prize Winners* (Phoenix, Ariz.: Oryx, 1986), 12.

Bergson, Henri-Louis (1859–1941)
French philosopher, writer, and Nobel laureate. Born in Paris on October 18, 1859, he attended the École Normale Supérieure, from which he graduated in 1881. He taught literature at the Lycée of Angers from 1881 to 1883, at the Lycée of Clermont-Ferrand from 1883 to 1888, and at the Collège Rollin and Lycée Henry IV from 1888 to 1898.

He developed a humanistic philosophy of process to counter positivism. Bergson published a series of works that biographer Pete Gunter describes as "a forum for new ideas in aesthetics, psychology, biology, and philosophy." These included *Essai sur les données immédiates de la conscience* (*Time and Free Will: An Essay on the Immediate Data of Consciousness*, 1889; English translation, 1910), *Matière et mémoire: essai sur la relation du corps avec l'esprit* (*Matter and Memory*, 1896; English translation, 1911), and *L'Évolution créatrice* (*Creative Evolution*, 1907; English translation, 1911). He was awarded the 1927 Nobel Prize in literature for his entire body of work.

Bergson wrote only one book after winning the Nobel, *Les deux sources de la morale et de la religion* (The two sources of morality and religion, 1932; English translation, 1935). He died in Paris on January 4, 1941.

References: Pete A. Gunter, "Bergson, Henri Louis" in Bernard S. and June H. Schlessinger, eds., *The Who's Who of Nobel Prize Winners* (Phoenix, Ariz.: Oryx, 1986), 56–57.

Berkeley, Busby (1895–1976)
American film director and choreographer, known for the lavish production numbers in his films made during the GREAT DEPRESSION. Born William Berkeley Enos in Los Angeles, California, on November 29, 1895, he was the son of a theatrical director and an actor. He received his nickname, "Busby," from an actor, Amy Busby, who worked with his father. The Enoses moved to New York in their son's infancy, and he attended schools there, afterward working for a time in a shoe factory in Massachusetts. In 1917, when the United States entered World War I, Enos enlisted in the army, seeing action in France with the 312th Field Artillery. Later, because of his skill at entertaining his fellow troops, he was named General John J. Pershing's entertainment officer.

After leaving the army in 1917, Enos returned to New York and joined a theatrical troupe that toured the United States. His first major acting appearance was in 1919 in the play *Irene*. But Enos soon discovered that his talent was in the production of dance numbers. Although he first worked in Boston, by 1925 he had returned to New York, where he worked for a time on the short-lived musical *Holka-Polka*. Within two years he was called by the famed playwright/composer duo of Richard RODGERS and Moss HART to coordinate the dancing in *A Connecticut Yankee*. After several years of Broadway work, in 1930 film mogul Samuel GOLDWYN brought Enos, now using the name Busby Berkeley, to Hollywood. Berkeley's first screen choreography credit came on the Florenz Ziegfeld directed *Whoopee (1930),* in which Berkeley used camera moves to capture the dancers' movement to a greater extent than ever before. After several additional films with Goldwyn, in 1932 Berkeley moved over to work with Warner Brothers. Here his name was made, starting with the smash *Forty-second Street* (1933). From 1932 until 1937, Berkeley was involved in every dance number done for any Warner Brothers picture. He won Academy Award nominations for Best Dance Direction in 1935, 1936, and 1937. In such films as *Gold Diggers of 1933* and its sequel, *Gold Diggers of 1935,* he used innovative camera shots. In *Footlight Parade* (1933), dancers in the water—dubbed as "aqua dancers"—created a dancing pyramid that had never before been seen.

By the late 1930s, however, the musical was falling from favor, and Berkeley was being pushed aside. After directing two nonmusical pictures for Warner Brothers, he moved to MGM, where he worked on such films as *Broadway Serenade* (1939) and did limited work through the 1940s. By the 1950s Berkeley had retired. There was a revival of interest in his films in the late 1960s, and once again he bathed in his fans' adulation. Berkeley, who had never had a dancing lesson, died on March 14, 1976. Today, the term *busby berkeley* refers to an elaborate musical number.

References: John Springer, *All Talking, All Singing, All Dancing* (New York: Citadel, 1966); "Berkeley, Busby" in Charles Moritz, ed., *Current Biography 1971* (New York: H.W. Wilson, 1971), 40–43; Tony Thomas and Jim Terry, *The Busby Berkeley Book* (Greenwich, Conn.: New York Graphic Society, 1973); Tony Thomas, *That's Dancing!* (New York: Abrams, 1984), 104–23.

Berle, Adolf Augustus   *See* BRAIN TRUST.

Berlin, Irving (1888–1989)

American song writer whose patriotic and popular songs, including *God Bless America* and *White Christmas,* were some of the most famous of the interwar period. Born Israel Isadore Baline in the village of Temum, Russia, on May 11, 1888, he was the sixth of eight children of Moses Baline, a poor Jewish cantor, and his wife Leah. The Balines emigrated to the United States when their son Israel was just five years old to flee the anti-Jewish pogroms and settled in New York City's Lower East Side slums. When Moses Baline died three years later, eight-year-old Israel was forced to work to help support his large family. For a time he worked as a guide for a singing beggar, but soon he worked in a saloon, where he was exposed to the world of vaudeville. In 1905 he became a singing waiter in a Chinatown restaurant, and, deciding to break into show business, went about writing songs. His

first, *Marie from Sunny Italy,* was published in 1907, but a printer's error on the record listed him as "Isreal Berlin." He changed his first name to Irving and the name stuck.

In 1911, Berlin hit gold with *Alexander's Ragtime Band,* which has become one of the most celebrated songs of the 20th century. He wrote the scores for shows, including *Watch Your Step* (1914). As a soldier in World War I, he composed *Yip, Yip, Yaphank,* which included the famed song *Oh, How I Hate to Get Up in the Morning.* Berlin later said that there are only six tunes in the world, but, as biographer Marilyn Berger explained, "from those six tunes he fashioned, according to his catalogue, 1,500 songs." He established the Irving Berlin Music Corporation in 1919 to guard the copyrights to his songs, and worked in Tin Pan Alley, the section of New York where the major popular-music publishers were based. During the 1920s, he produced some of the finest popular music ever written. For his second wife he wrote *Always,* still considered a wedding staple; he wrote tunes for the Ziegfeld Follies and for the MARX BROTHERS. In 1932 he collaborated with Moss HART on the musical *Face the Music,* which included the tunes *Let's Have Another Cup of Coffee* and *Soft Lights and Sweet Music.* Two years later his song *Heat Wave* was sung by Ethel Waters in *As Thousands Cheer.* He wrote tunes that were sung by Fred ASTAIRE, Alice Faye, and Bing Crosby, and appeared in such interwar films as *Puttin' on the Ritz* (1930), *Top Hat* (1935), and *Alexander's Ragtime Band* (1938), which featured twenty-eight of his songs. Among his hits is the classic "God Bless America" (1939), the rights to which Berlin dedicated to the Boy and Girl Scouts of America (by the time of his death, it had earned for the two groups some $700,000) and for which he was awarded the Congressional Gold Medal.

Ironically, Berlin could not read music, but he wrote songs that became classics in American musical history. The famed composer Jerome Kern once said of him, "Irving Berlin has no place in American music. He is American music."

On September 22, 1989, Berlin died in his sleep at his home in Manhattan at the age of 101. He remains the most versatile popular songwriter in American history.

References: "Berlin, Irving" in Charles Moritz, ed., *Current Biography 1963* (New York: H. W. Wilson, 1963), 33–36; Laurence Bergreen, *As Thousands Cheer: The Life of Irving Berlin* (New York: Viking, 1990); Ian Whitcomb, *Irving Berlin and Ragtime America* (London: Century, 1987); Marilyn Berger, "Irving Berlin, Nation's Songwriter, Dies," *New York Times,* September 23, 1989, p. 1.

Berlin, Treaty of

Pact, 1921, that formally ended the state of war that had existed between the United States and Germany since 1917. The final and crushing defeat of the TREATY OF VER-

SAILLES in the U.S. Senate on November 19, 1919, led to a search for a diplomatic way for the U.S. government to legally end the state of war that existed. In 1920, Representative Stephen G. Porter of Pennsylvania introduced the so-called Porter Resolution, which sought to end the state of war through legislative means. Although the bill passed the House and Senate, it was vetoed by President Woodrow WILSON. In 1921, Senator Philander C. Knox introduced the Knox Resolution, which accomplished the same ends, but this time President Warren HARDING signed it into law. The Treaty of Berlin was formally signed on August 25, 1921; its harshest stipulation allowed the United States to take the value of former German properties in America (such as the aspirin company Bayer) that had been seized during the war and apply such value to American claims against Germany.

References: John E. Findling, *Dictionary of American Diplomatic History* (Westport, Conn.: Greenwood, 1989), 57; Arnold A. Offner, *The Origins of World War II: American Foreign Policy and World Politics, 1917–1942* (New York: Praeger, 1975); Harold Tiffany Butler, "Partisan Positions on Isolationism vs. Internationalism, 1918–1933," (Ph.D. dissertation, Syracuse University, 1963).

Bethune, Mary McLeod (1875–1955)

American educator, political and civil rights leader, and presidential adviser during the interwar period. The fifteenth of seventeen children of former slaves Samuel and Patsy (McIntosh) McLeod, Bethune was born on July 10, 1875, in Mayesville, South Carolina. She grew up amid the poverty and oppression of the U.S. South during Reconstruction. Through her early experiences at missionary schools for African-Americans in South Carolina, North Carolina, and Chicago, Illinois, Bethune understood the importance of education in the emerging struggle for civil rights. After several teaching engagements throughout the South, Bethune founded the Daytona Educational and Industrial School for Negro Girls in Daytona Beach, Florida, which later merged with the Cookman Institute to become Bethune-Cookman College. She served as the school's president from 1904 until 1942.

Bethune expanded her sights beyond educational reform by joining several black women's organizations. Over the years she developed a keen understanding of the needs of African Americans, and in 1935 Bethune founded the National Council of Negro Women. She also served as an adviser on African American affairs to four presidents, including Calvin COOLIDGE and Herbert HOOVER, who appointed her head of the National Child Welfare Commission and the Commission on Home Building and Home Ownership. In 1936 president Franklin D. ROOSEVELT tapped Bethune as director of the Division of Negro Affairs from the NEW DEAL's National Youth Administration. She was the first African-American woman to hold so high an office in the federal government. During these years, Bethune worked tirelessly to expand educational and employment opportunities for African-Americans and to combat discrimination in government programs and agencies.

Throughout her life Bethune strove to influence legislation affecting African-Americans and women. For this work she was awarded the NAACP's Spingarn Medal in 1935. She was also granted honorary degrees from, among other institutions, Bennett College (1936), Tuskegee Institute (1937), Howard University (1942), Atlanta University (1943), West Virginia State College (1947), and Rollins College (1949). She demonstrated the value of education and was an important voice for human rights until her death on May 18, 1955, in Daytona Beach, Florida.

References: Malu Halasa, *Mary McLeod Bethune* (New York: Chelsea House, 1989); Bernice Anderson Poole, *Mary McLeod Bethune* (Los Angeles: Melrose Square, 1994); Margo McLoone, *Mary McLeod Bethune: A Photo-Illustrated Biography* (Mankato, Minn.: Bridgestone, 1997).

Bevin, Ernest (1881–1951)

British statesman and labor leader. Born in Winsford, Somerset, England, on March 7, 1881, his only education was at a small boys' school near his home. When Bevin left school at age 13, he wandered through a number of meaningless jobs, earning barely sustainable wages. He then became a unionist and joined the local socialist party. In 1909 he ran unsuccessfully as a socialist for a seat on the Bristol city council; the next year, however, he turned to union organizing and helped to organize the carters, who carted around materials on the Bristol docks. A carmen's branch of the Dockers' Union was formed in 1910 with Bevin as its first president.

By 1920 Bevin had become assistant general secretary of the Dockers' Union. The demise of the so-called triple alliance of the miners, railwaymen, and transport workers on April 15, 1921, called "Black Friday," led Bevin to merge his forces into a new and more powerful Transport and General Workers' Union with some 300,000 members in 1922. He was on the brink of becoming one of the most influential labor leaders in the world.

All that changed on May 4, 1926, when the Trades Union Council (TUC), of which Bevin was a leading member, called a national GENERAL STRIKE against the government in support of a strike by the coal miners. More than 3 million of Britain's 5 million trade unionists went out on strike for nine days, crippling the nation's transport, steel, and iron industries. But the government was able to keep essential services going and broke the back of the strike, for a time ending the power of the unions.

Bevin was largely unaffected by the failure of strike, however, and remained near the top of the TUC leadership, rising to become chairman in 1936. By this time he was recognized as someone the government needed and wanted to do business with.

Bevin's talent for keeping the nation at peace with its unions was called on in 1940, when Prime Minister Winston Churchill made Bevin his minister of labor and national service, where he served until 1945. He later served as foreign minister (1945–51) during the early years of the cold war. Bevin died in London on April 14, 1951.

References: Francis-Williams, "Bevin, Ernest" in Sir Leslie Stephen and Sir Sidney Lee et al., eds., *The Dictionary of National Biography* (Oxford, England: Oxford University Press, 1917–1993), 6: 102–10; Robert M. Hathaway, "Bevin, Ernest" in Bruce W. Jentleson and Thomas G. Paterson, senior eds., *Encyclopedia of U.S. Foreign Relations* (New York: Oxford University Press, 1997), 1: 153; Peter Weiler, *Ernest Bevin* (Manchester, England: Manchester University Press, 1993); Francis Williams, *Ernest Bevin: Portrait of a Great Englishman* (London: Hutchinson, 1952).

Birdseye, Clarence (1886–1956)

American businessman and inventor. Born in Brooklyn, New York, on December 9, 1886, Birdseye was the son of a lawyer. When he was a teenager, his family moved to Montclair, New Jersey, where he attended cooking classes. These led him to the discovery that ultimately earned him fame. At first, however, he moved toward different fields. After attending Amherst University, he worked as a naturalist for the U.S. Biological Survey. In 1912 he went to Labrador to work as a fur trader; while there, he saw a need to preserve food properly through freezing.

After returning to the United States, Birdseye experimented with freezing meats and vegetables to preserve them while securing their freshness. At first his investigations used ice and salt, but he quickly came upon a solution of quick-freezing. He was aided by another invention of the 1920s—the appearance of refrigerator units meant for average American homes. In 1924, Birdseye and three partners formed the General Seafoods Company to market frozen fish fillets to the consumer market. Birdseye was able to exploit his name by coming up with a perfect symbol for the company: a bird's eye. In 1928 he sold his process to the Postum Company for $22 million; several years later Postum became General Foods, which still markets a line of "Birdseye" products.

Birdseye held more than three hundred American and foreign patents, one of which was his invention of freeze-drying—the removal of water from food so it can be packaged safely and conveniently until needed. Birdseye died at his home in New York City's Gramercy Hotel on October 7, 1956.

References: Gerald Carson, "Birdseye, Clarence" in Allen Johnson and Dumas Malone et al., eds., *Dictionary of American Biography* (New York: Charles Scribner's Sons, 1930–95), 6: 60–62; Hannah Campbell, "The Father of Frozen Foods," *Country Living*, 12: 5 (May 1989), 162–64; "Clarence Birdseye is Dead at 69; Inventor of Frozen-Food Process," *New York Times*, October 9, 1956, p. 35.

Birth Control Movement   See SANGER, Margaret; STOPES, Marie Carmichael.

Black Chamber, The

Super-secret American espionage organization, started during World War I but used to great advantage by the U.S. government during the interwar years. Headed by the brilliant cryptologist Herbert O. Yardley, the office, formally called MI-8, broke the codes of several nations during the 1920s. One such code break, against Japan, gave U.S. Secretary of State Charles Evans HUGHES secret Japanese cables during the WASHINGTON NAVAL CONFERENCE in 1921 and 1922, allowing the office to thereby trump Japan's diplomatic moves. In 1929 the State Department closed down the Black Chamber, and a disappointed Yardley published *The American Black Chamber*. The book let the Japanese know that their secret codes had been known for years, and enabled them to change their encryption methods before the start of World War II.

References: Richard Deacon, *Spyclopedia: The Comprehensive Handbook of Espionage* (New York: Silver Arrow Books, 1987), 165; Herbert O. Yardley, *The American Black Chamber* (Indianapolis: Bobbs-Merrill, 1931).

Black Monday

American event, May 27, 1935, in which the U.S. Supreme Court struck down key portions of President Franklin D. ROOSEVELT's NEW DEAL economic program. On this date the court handed down three major decisions: *Louisville Bank v. Radford,* which struck down the FRAZIER-LEMKE MORTGAGE RELIEF ACT as unconstitutional; *Humphrey's Executor v. United States,* which denied the president the power to remove from office members of regulatory agencies who disagreed with his policies; and SCHECHTER POULTRY CORP. V. UNITED STATES, which held the National Industrial Recovery Act (1933) to be unconstitutional. What shook the Roosevelt administration to its core was that three of the court's most liberal justices—Louis Brandeis, Benjamin Cardozo, and Harlan Fiske Stone—voted with the majority in the three cases. Black

Monday sent a message to the administration and to Congress that the Supreme Court would strictly scrutinize all legislation meant to end the GREAT DEPRESSION, and would strike down any that tended in any way to be unconstitutional. After further defeats before the court in 1936 and 1937, Roosevelt initiated the COURT-PACKING CONTROVERSY with his plan to stack the court with more sympathetic judges, but the plan was killed by Congress.

Reference: Rayman L. Solomon, "Black Monday" in Kermit L. Hall, ed. in chief, *The Oxford Companion to the Supreme Court of the United States* (New York: Oxford University Press, 1992), 75.

Black Sox Scandal

Sports scandal involving several members of the 1919 Chicago White Sox team. That team is still considered one of the best in baseball history: it included first baseman Chick Gandil; second baseman Eddie Collins; shortstop Swede Risberg; third baseman Buck Weaver; outfielders Nemo Leibold, Shano Collins, Happy Felsch, and "Shoeless" Joe Jackson; catcher Ray Schalk; pitchers Eddie Cicotte, Grover Lowdermilk, Dickie Kerr, and Claude "Lefty" Williams; and manager "Kid" Gleason. Jackson had seven home runs, 96 runs batted in, and an impressive .351 average during the season, while Cicotte went 29-7 with a 1.82 earned run average. The club seemed headed for its first world championship after winning the American League crown over the Cleveland Indians by three and one-half games with an 88-52 record. Meeting the underdog Cincinnati Reds, led by manager Pat Moran, in the World Series, the Sox looked like champs.

However, some of these champion players were secretly conspiring with mobsters like Arnold Rothstein to throw the series that year for financial payoffs. The players, led by Cicotte, were poorly paid by the White Sox owner, Charles Comiskey, and sought to gain some revenue from another source. In game one on October 1, in Cincinnati, the Reds' Dutch Ruether pitched a masterful six-hitter on the way to a 9-1 victory. Cincinnati left-hander Slim Sallee gave up ten hits to the Sox the following day, but on the basis of shortstop Larry Kopf's two-run triple in the fourth, he was able to pull out a 4-2 victory, sending the series to Chicago. There, on October 3, Sox hurler Dickey Kerr, who was not in on the scam, threw a masterful three-hit shutout, 3-0, to bring the White Sox back into the series.

Cincinnati then responded with two shutouts, 2-0 with Jimmy Ring pitching, and then 5-0, thrown by Hod Eller. By today's rules, teams need to win four-out-of-seven to win the series; in 1919, however, the rule was best-of-eight. Chicago won game six in 10 innings, 5-4, and Cicotte brought the Sox back to 4-3 with a seven hitter, 4-1, in Cincinnati on October 8. In the eighth game, however, the Cincinnati lineup ripped into lefthander Lefty Williams, scoring four first-inning runs and adding three more in the sixth to take a 10-1 lead; the Sox replied with four in the eighth, but it was not enough: Cincinnati's Hod Eller won his second game, 10-5, and with it the series went to the Reds. Many of the Sox players had admirable numbers: Joe Jackson had led all players by batting .375; Weaver was at .324. But Cicotte had lost two of his three starts, and Williams, who had gone 23-11 during the regular season, dropped all three of his decisions.

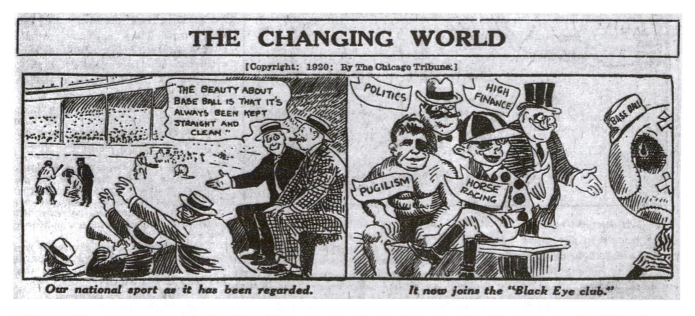

A *Chicago Tribune* cartoon laments the state of the national pastime in the wake of the Black Sox scandal. *(CORBIS)*

The unexpected Sox loss sent shockwaves through the baseball world, but it seemed as if the Reds had just turned out to be the better team. However, rumors were soon rife that a fix had been in. During the 1920 season these rumors were investigated by the attorney general. The sign that the series would be thrown was when Cicotte hit the first batter he faced in game one, Morrie Rath. The players were called before a prosecutor, where they confessed that they had thrown the series for payment by Rothstein, who in the end paid them nothing. Indicted, the men stood trial, but their confessions mysteriously disappeared from the prosecutor's office. The men were all acquitted, but the new baseball commissioner, Judge Kenesaw Mountain LANDIS, in an effort to clean up the sport, banned eight of the players from baseball for life, including Jackson and Cicotte. In banning the men, Landis pronounced, "Regardless of the verdict of juries, no player that throws a ball game, no player that entertains proposals or promises to throw a game, no player that sits in a conference with a bunch of crooked players and gamblers where the ways and means of throwing games are discussed, and does not promptly tell his club about it, will ever again play professional baseball." Baseball's most infamous moment had come to an ugly end.

References: "Sox, Quietly Confident, Await Clash With Reds Today; Cicotte and Ruether Picked to Pitch in Opening Battle," *Chicago Daily News*, October 1, 1919, p. 17; "White Sox Lose in Opener, 9-1; Reds Drive Cicotte to Dugout; Ruether Holds Foe Helpless," *Chicago Daily News*, October 2, 1919, p. 1; "White Sox Crushed Again, 4-2; Williams Wild, Passes Giving Reds Victory," *Chicago Daily News*, October 3, 1919, p. 1; "Kerr Hurls Sox to Victory, 3 to 0; Midget Holds Reds Helpless, Allowing Only Three Hits," *Chicago Daily News*, October 4, 1919, p. 1; "Sox Humbled in Fourth Game, 2-0; Cicotte's Boots Turn Slab Duel to Reds' Favor," *Chicago Daily News*, October 5, 1919, p. 1; "Sox Crumble Before Eller, 5 to 0; Gleason's Machine Goes to Pieces in Fifth of Series," *Chicago Daily News*, October 7, 1919, p. 1; "Sox Fight to Victory in Tenth, 5-4; Lead of 4 Runs Is Overcome to Bear Reds," *Chicago Daily News*, October 8, 1919, p. 1; "Sox Battle to Third Victory, 4-1," *Chicago Daily News*, October 9, 1919, p. 1; "Reds Are New World's Champions; Sox Handed Real Mauling in Final, 10-5," *Chicago Daily News*, October 10, 1919, p. 1; "White Sox Players Are Not Guilty; Charges of Conspiracy Do Not Hold," *Buffalo Express*, August 3, 1921, p. 1.

Bloomsbury Group

Influential literary and intellectual group named for its London center, Bloomsbury Square. Founded by the Scottish painter and set designer Duncan James Corrowr Grant, the group included the economist John Maynard KEYNES, biographer Lytton Strachey, and novelists Virginia WOOLF and E. M. Forster. Over the years, other writers who on occasion joined the group's discussions included T. S. ELIOT, the Irish poet William Butler YEATS, D. H. LAWRENCE, Walter Greenwood, George Orwell, and Saxon Sidney-Turner, among others. For many years they met at the London homes of Woolf and Clive and Vanessa Bell. The group's earliest years were in the decade before World War I, but until 1930 they continued to meet in the Bloomsbury section of London, near the British Museum, discussing literature and religion. Many of the members gradually moved on to the social scenes in Oxford and Cambridge. The significance of Bloomsbury lies not so much in what it did as a group, but in the members who belonged to it: their output, in the aggregate, was amazing and constitutes some of the finest works in British literary history.

References: Frances Partridge, *A Bloomsbury Album: Friends in Focus* (Boston: Little, Brown, 1987); John Keith Johnstone, *The Bloomsbury Group: A Study of E. M. Forster, Lytton Strachey, Virginia Woolf, and Their Circle* (New York: Noonday Press, 1954).

Blue Angel, The   See DIETRICH, Marlene.

Blum, Léon (1872–1950)

French politician and statesman. Born Léon-André Blum in Paris on April 9, 1872, to a French Jewish family, Blum dropped the "André" from his name soon after he received his law degree from the University of Paris in 1894. A socialist early in his life, he formally joined the French Socialist Party in 1899, was elected to the Chamber of Deputies in 1919, led the party beginning in 1925. A leader in the move to reconstruct the party after the Communists bolted at the end of World War I, he helped establish the French Socialist Party as a major political entity while at the same time establishing *Le Populaire* as the party's official journal.

During the 1920s, Blum was in the opposition against the governments of Alexandre Millerand and Raymond POINCARÉ. In the elections of 1928, although his party gained more than 100 seats in the chamber, he was defeated. He did not return to power until 1929, and he was reelected in 1932 and 1936. In 1932 he established a program to aid the unemployed, and in a coalition with Radical Socialists, the Communists, and other leftists he formed the Popular Front, which came to power in 1936. Blum thus became the first Jewish premier of France. To combat the GREAT DEPRESSION, he instituted a 40-hour workweek and paid vacations for workers. However, his failure to address the growing Nazi threat in Germany and his refusal to intervene in the SPANISH CIVIL WAR caused him to be labeled an appeaser. Blum's plans to nationalize state industries led many on the right to claim, "Better Hitler than Blum." When the assembly refused to grant him additional powers to combat the economic downturn, he resigned, serving only as vice-premier in the government of Camille Chautemps until 1938, when he again became premier. When he was succeeded by Edouard DALADIER, Blum refused to serve in his government.

When Germany invaded France in 1940, Blum was captured and put on trial by the Vichy government, and he was imprisoned until 1945. In December 1946, after arranging for a loan from the United States to rebuild his war-torn nation, Blum again became premier in a coalition "caretaker" government that lasted but a month, until January 1947. He died on March 30, 1950, at his estate at Jouy-en-Josas.

References: Neil Heyman, "Léon Blum" in Anne Commire, ed., *Historic World Leaders* (Detroit: Gale Research, 1994), 2: 118–21; Joel Colton, "Blum, Léon" in Warren F. Kuehl, ed., *Biographical Dictionary of Internationalists* (Westport, Conn.: Greenwood, 1983), 85–86; Joel Colton, *Léon Blum: Humanist in Politics* (New York: Alfred A. Knopf, 1966), 3–7.

Bohr, Niels Henrik David (1885–1962)

Danish physicist and Nobel Prize corecipient. The son of Christian Bohr, a professor of physiology, and Ellen (Adler) Bohr, he was born in Copenhagen, Denmark, on October 7, 1885. He received his bachelor's, master's, and doctorate degrees at the University of Copenhagen in 1909 and 1911. He served as a professor of physics at Cambridge University, the University of Manchester, the University of Copenhagen, and Victoria University in England in the early 1910s, and then remained at the University of Copenhagen from 1916 until his death.

During this period, Bohr conducted some of the most intensive work on the structure and behavior of atoms and their emanating radiation, spending his entire career studying the field of quantum physics. This work garnered him the 1922 Nobel Prize in physics (with Francis William ASTON). Bohr's work eventually led to the elaboration and application of atomic and nuclear science. He died on November 18, 1962.

References: Janice N. Sieburth, "Bohr, Niels Henrik David" in Bernard S. and June H. Schlessinger, eds., *The Who's Who of Nobel Prize Winners* (Phoenix, Ariz.: Oryx, 1986), 157; Leon Rosenfeld, "Bohr, Niels Henrik David" in Charles Coulston Gillespie, ed. in chief, *Dictionary of Scientific Biography* (New York: Charles Scribner's Sons, 1980–90), 2: 239–54.

Bonus March

American protest staged in Washington, D.C., in 1932, primarily by U.S. veterans of World War I, to demand a "bonus" promised to them in the 1920s by the U.S. government and which they needed at the height of the GREAT DEPRESSION. In 1925, Congress had passed the ADJUSTED COMPENSATION ACT OF 1924 over a presidential veto, establishing a bonus or endowment to be held for each individual veteran in trust until 1949 and then paid in one lump sum.

By 1931 the mood in the country had shifted. A terrible economic depression, then in its third year, had ruined the life savings of millions, including many veterans of World War I. Congress passed a bill allowing each veteran to take 50 percent of their allotted bonus. President Herbert HOOVER vetoed it, however, saying that it would "provide an enormous sum of money to a vast majority who are able to care for themselves." Congress then overrode this veto. But on May 29, 1932, the veterans came back for more. An army of veterans, their wives, and their children camped in Anacostia, on the outskirts of Washington, D.C., to ask that the remainder of the bonus be delivered. Hoover refused, and Congress did not have the votes to override him. Hoover asked for $100,000 to assist those who wanted to go home, but the amount would be deducted from their final bonus. On June 17, many of the veterans, tired and weary, began to leave.

The adjournment of Congress on July 16 stalled any opportunity for the passage of a bill that election year. Still, many marchers stayed. Secretary of War Patrick J. Hurley announced that the shanties constructed by the veterans—dubbed "HOOVERVILLES"—were to be torn down to make way for permanent structures. On July 28, U.S. Army soldiers tried to remove the veterans. A gunfire ensued, leaving two veterans dead. Hoover then ordered federal troops, under the command of General Douglas MacArthur, to use the necessary force to clear the marchers. MacArthur's men marched on the Bonus camp, burning down tents, as the marchers fled into Maryland. The march was over, but its effects were not. Newspapers across the nation condemned the assault and criticized Hoover's handling of the situation. It was the last in a series of mistakes that would cost Hoover the presidency.

The bonus was finally awarded to the marchers and their families four years after the march with the passage by Congress of the ADJUSTED COMPENSATION ACT OF 1936.

References: "National Affairs: Heroes," *Time*, August 8, 1932, p. 5; John D. Weaver, "Bonus March," *American Heritage* 14, no. 4 (June 1963): 18–23, 92–97; H. W. Blakeley, "When the Army Was Smeared," *Combat Forces Journal* 1 (February 1952): 26–30; Roger Daniels, *The Bonus March: An Episode of the Great Depression* (Westport, Conn.: Greenwood, 1971); John W. Killigrew, "The Army and the Bonus Incident," *Military Affairs* 21 (Summer 1962): 59–65; Donald J. Lisio, *The President and Protest: Hoover, Conspiracy, and the Bonus Riot* (Columbia: University of Missouri Press, 1974).

Borah, William Edgar (1865–1940)

American politician. Born in the village of Fairfield, Illinois, on June 29, 1865, the seventh of ten children, Borah attended the University of Kansas but soon left because of illness. He studied law in the office of his brother-in-law and was admitted to the Kansas bar in 1890. The following year, he moved to Idaho and immediately became involved in local politics.

In 1907, Borah ran as the Republican candidate for the U.S. Senate and was easily swept into office. Until his death, almost thirty-three years later, Borah served in that seat.

An extreme isolationist, Borah spent much of the years during and after World War I voting against U.S. interference in European affairs and advocating for disarmament. During the debate over American entry into the LEAGUE OF NATIONS, he was one of a number of senators strongly opposed. As one of these "IRRECONCILABLES" he traveled the nation, along with Senator Hiram JOHNSON of California, delivering remarks against the League to raise opposition to it as a balance to President Woodrow WILSON's pro-League speeches. In 1924, Borah became chair of the powerful Senate Foreign Relations Committee. In the 1930s he voted against the NATIONAL RECOVERY ADMINISTRATION and the Lend-Lease Bill, which sought to send material aid to Great Britain in the years before World War II.

Borah was also a strong opponent of dictatorship. On May 6, 1937, he took to the Senate floor to strongly denounce FASCISM, saying of the movement, "There is not tenet of democracy which fascism does not challenge. There is not a vital principle of free government with which this ruthless creed is not in conflict. It is built and professes to be built upon the ruins of democracy."

Borah died suddenly after suffering a stroke in Washington, D.C., on January 19, 1940, at the age of seventy-four, just months after the war that he had tried so hard to keep his nation out of erupted in Europe. Mount Borah and Borah Peak in Idaho were named in his honor.

References: Claudius O. Johnson, *Borah of Idaho* (New York: Longmans, Green and Co., 1936); Marian C. McKenna, *Borah* (Ann Arbor: University of Michigan Press, 1961); Thomas M. Robertson, Jr., "The Political Career of William E. Borah," (Master's Thesis, Princeton University, 1933); Janet M. Manson, "Borah, William Edgar" in Bruce W. Jentleson and Thomas G. Paterson, senior eds., *Encyclopedia of U.S. Foreign Relations* (New York: Oxford University Press, 1997), 1: 163; "Text of Senator Borah's Address Denouncing Fascism," *Washington Post*, May 7, 1937, p. 5.

Bordet, Jules (1870–1961)

Belgian serologist, immunologist, and Nobel laureate. Born in the village of Soignes, Belgium, on June 13, 1870, he received his medical degree from the University of Brussels in 1892. From 1894 until 1900 he worked at the prestigious Pasteur Institute in Paris, finally returning to his native country to found a similar research center, the Institut antirabique et bactériologique du Brabant (Antirabies and Bacteriological Institute of Brabant). Soon after opening the institute, Bordet developed the complement fixation test. In 1903 he renamed the center the *Institut Pasteur du Brabant*. There in 1906 he discovered, with Octave Gengou, the *Hemophilus pertussis,* or whooping cough bacillus.

From 1907 until 1935, Bordet was a bacteriology professor at the University of Brussels. While there he discovered, through investigations into blood immunity diseases, two antimicrobic sera. One, which he called alexin, he discovered in human blood prior to immunization; the other, an alexin antibody, was produced by the body after immunization. He also discovered a serum diagnosis test of the effect of syphilis on human immunity. For this and his earlier work, Bordet was awarded the 1919 Nobel Prize in medicine and physiology.

Bordet continued to work as director of the institute. He retired from the position in 1940 (his son, Paul Bordet, succeeded him in the office) but continued his research work on the human immune system. He died in Brussels on April 6, 1961.

References: Loralyn Whitney, "Bordet, Jules Jean Baptiste Vincent" in Bernard S. and June H. Schlessinger, eds., *The Who's Who of Nobel Prize Winners* (Phoenix, Ariz.: Oryx, 1986), 83–84; Thomas Watson MacCallum, and Stephen Taylor, eds., *The Nobel Prize-Winners and the Nobel Foundation, 1901–1937* (Zurich, Switzerland: Central European Times Publishing, 1938), 202.

Bosch, Carl (1874–1940)

German chemist and Nobel laureate. Born in Cologne, Germany, on August 27, 1874, Bosch received his doctorate at the University of Leipzig in 1898. He worked as a researcher and administrator at the Ludwigshafen am Rhein at Badische Anilin und Sodafabrik (BASF), still one of the largest chemical companies in the world, from 1899 to 1925, and at the I. G. Farbenindustrie from 1925 until his death. Working with the fixing of nitrogen particles, Bosch produced barium cyanide and ammonia, making the modern production of fertilizers much more efficient and improving modern farming methods. For this work he was awarded (with Friedrich BERGIUS) the 1931 Nobel Prize in chemistry.

Bosch died in Heidelberg, Germany, on April 26, 1940.

References: Günther Kerstein, "Bosch, Carl" in Charles Coulston Gillespie, ed. in chief, *Dictionary of Scientific Biography* (New York: Charles Scribner's Sons, 1980–90), 2:

323–24; Mary Porrett, "Bosch, Carl" in Bernard S. and June H. Schlessinger, eds., *The Who's Who of Nobel Prize Winners* (Phoenix, Ariz.: Oryx, 1986), 12.

Boulogne Conference

Meeting, 1920, held in the French city of Boulogne-sur-Seine. On May 15 and 16, 1920, representatives of France, Great Britain, Russia, the United States, and Canada had met at the English seaside resort of Hythe, in Hampshire, to discuss the amount and magnitude of German reparations to the former World War I allies, but no agreement had been reached, except that the members would meet again in Boulogne. The Boulogne Conference, held June 21–22, resulted in an agreement to accept indemnities from Germany until 1962. Further talks were held in the resort city of Spa later in the year.

See also HYTHE CONFERENCE; SPA CONFERENCE.

References: Edmund Jan Osmańczyk, *The Encyclopedia of the United Nations and International Agreements* (Philadelphia: Taylor & Francis, 1985), 94.

Bourgeois, Léon-Victor-Auguste (1851–1925)

French politician, diplomat, and Nobel laureate, considered the "spiritual father" of the LEAGUE OF NATIONS. Born in Paris on May 21, 1851, he received his doctorate in law from the University of Paris and practiced there for several years. In 1876 he left to hold various government positions over the next decade. In 1887, Bourgeois was named as chief commissioner of the Paris police.

The following year, he was elected as a deputy to the National Assembly from the Marne district. On November 1, 1895, he was named premier, serving until April 21, 1896, after which he headed the Radical Socialist Party, served in the French Senate from 1905 to 1923, and acted as that body's president from 1920 to 1923. In this capacity Bourgeois spoke out for a feeling of cooperation among the nations of Europe, and in 1903 he was named to the International Court of Justice at the Hague in the Netherlands. In 1919 he was an aide to French prime minister Georges Clemenceau and was active in trying to get a more conciliatory agreement against the Germans enacted, but he failed. He did support the League of Nations concept, however, and when he returned to the Senate, he began to speak out in support of the League. He was elected the first president of the League of Nations Council. For his work to bring about peace in Europe, Bourgeois was awarded the Nobel Peace Prize in 1920.

Three years later he retired from the French Senate as blindness set in, and he spent the last two years of his life at his estate at Château d'Oger, near Épernay. He died on September 29, 1925, and was honored in a state funeral.

References: Bullit Lowry, "Bourgeois, Léon-Victor Auguste" in Bernard S. and June H. Schlessinger, eds., *The Who's Who of Nobel Prize Winners* (Phoenix, Ariz.: Oryx, 1986), 131; Bernard C. Weber, "Bourgeois, Léon-Victor Auguste" in Warren F. Kuehl, ed., *Biographical Dictionary of Internationalists* (Westport, Conn.: Greenwood, 1983), 98–100; Thomas Watson MacCallum and Stephen Taylor, eds., *The Nobel Prize-Winners and the Nobel Foundation, 1901–1937* (Zurich, Switzerland: Central European Times Publishing, 1938), 358.

Bourke-White, Margaret (1904–1971)

American photographer and photojournalist. Born Margaret White on June 14, 1904, in New York City, she attended Columbia University, the University of Michigan, Western Reserve University, and Cornell University, which awarded her a bachelor's degree in 1927. She studied photography in college, and after she completed her studies, she added her mother's birth name, Bourke, to her own. She immediately began her career in industrial photography and was soon known for her spirit of individuality. In 1929 her work caught the eye of Henry Robinson LUCE, the publisher of *Time,* who hired her to do photography for his new magazine on finance, *Fortune.* Her assignments, including one on the effects of the first FIVE-YEAR PLAN in the Soviet Union, took her around the world. Luce next founded *Life* magazine, and he set Bourke-White to do the first cover in 1936. Her photo of Fort Peck Dam, Montana, was typical of her stark style. In 1935, Bourke-White met the southern writer Erskine Caldwell, and with him collaborated on three books: *You Have Seen Their Faces* (1937), on the lives of southern sharecroppers; *North of the Danube* (1939), on the Czechoslovak people before the Nazi invasion; and *Say, Is This the U.S.A.* (1941). The two married in 1939, but the marriage dissolved two years later.

Bourke-White covered World War II for *Life,* becoming the first female photographer to cover the U.S. Army. Her gritty photos captured the mood for the civilian population back home. She died in New York on August 27, 1971.

References: Vicki Goldberg, *Margaret Bourke-White: A Biography* (New York: Harper & Row, 1986); Catherine Udall Turley, "Margaret Bourke-White" in Frank Magill, ed., *Great Lives from History—American Women Series* (Pasadena, Calif.: Salem, 1985), 1: 237–41; H. H. Arnason, *History of Modern Art: Painting, Sculpture, Architecture, Photography* (New York: Harry N. Abrams, 1986), 377; Alden Whitman, "Margaret Bourke-White, Photo-Journalist, Is Dead," *New York Times,* August 28, 1971, pp. 1, 28.

Bow, Clara (1905–1965)

American film actress, known for her portrayal of flappers and noted as the "It girl." Born Clara Gordon Bow in Brooklyn, New York, on August 25, 1905, she grew up in poverty (her father was a waiter, and her mother was mentally ill). When she was sixteen, she entered a photo beauty contest for a movie fan magazine and won a small part as a girl dancing on a table in the film *Enemies of Women*, which was not released until 1923. Her career lasted 11 years, from the first visions of her in *Beyond the Rainbow* (1922) to her role as Lou in *Hoopla* (1933). Bow's enduring image is that of Betty Lou Spence in *It* (1927) and the nurse Mary Preston in *Wings* (1927), the first film to win the Best Picture Academy Award. Her role in *It* was no less than the embodiment of the Roaring Twenties. Writer Ephraim Katz explains the "It girl" phenomenon: "The Title became widely accepted as a term defining the unself-conscious attraction of the modern young woman—that 'something extra' that separated her from the ordinary crowd."

Bow's career ended with the advent of movie sound (her Brooklyn accent was not well accepted). She had also been destroyed financially by gambling debts, and other rumors dimmed her popularity. In 1931 she married cowboy star Rex Bell (who later became lieutenant governor of Nevada), and she retired from the screen two years later. She died on September 27, 1965. Film historian Norman Zierold lists her among the three greatest silent film actresses, along with Theda Bara and Pola Negri.

References: Ephraim Katz, *The Film Encyclopedia* (New York: HarperPerennial, 1994), 155–56; David Stenn, *Clara Bow: Runnin' Wild* (New York: Doubleday, 1988); Norman J. Zierold, *Sex Goddesses of the Silent Screen* (Chicago: Henry Regnery Company, 1973).

boxing

Boxing was a huge sport before the end of World War I, but it became a business during the postwar period. In 1921 in Jersey City, New Jersey, Jack Dempsey knocked out French pugilist Georges Carpentier, known as "The Orchid," in a fight which was the first to go over $1 million in gate receipts. Dempsey was the first champion of the period. He took the heavyweight championship when he knocked out Jess Willard at Toledo on July 4, 1919. Dempsey held the championship for seven years, losing it to Gene Tunney in Philadelphia on September 23, 1926. Tunney retired without losing the crown, and it was up to German champ Max Schmeling to defeat Jack Sharkey in New York City on June 12, 1930. Almost exactly two years later, on June 21, 1932, Sharkey faced Schmeling for a rematch and took the crown back from him in a fifteen-round decision. Italian fighter Primo Carnera defeated Sharkey a year later, but Carnera lost in 1934 to Jim Braddock. Braddock, in turn, was knocked out in the eight round on June 22, 1937, by black fighter Joe Louis, who would go on to hold the crown for twelve years.

Brain Trust

Influential group of academic advisors to Franklin Delano ROOSEVELT, as New York governor and later as President. This small number of academics were assembled to advise Roosevelt on issues that he wanted to stress during his presidential campaign. Members included professor Felix Frankfurter of the Harvard Law School, attorney Basil O'Connor, lawyer Adolf Augustus Berle, journalist and educator Raymond Moley, and Rexford Tugwell of Columbia University. The name of the group was coined by *New York Times* reporter James Kieran.

There is no formal history of the Brain Trust; as historian Elliot Rosen explained, "Just as Roosevelt never formally announced the existence of a brains trust, so its dissolution proceeded without fanfare as the circle of advisers enlarged in the presidential years and as Roosevelt required lawyers capable of legislative draftsmanship and administrative execution of his program."

References: Elliot A. Rosen, *Hoover, Roosevelt and the Brains Trust: From Depression to New Deal* (New York: Columbia University Press, 1977); Ronnie J. Phillips, *The Chicago Plan*

HEAVYWEIGHT BOXING CHAMPIONSHIP FIGHTS, 1919–1937				
DATE OF FIGHT	**PLACE**	**WINNER**	**LOSER**	**ROUNDS**
July 4, 1919	Toledo, Ohio	Jack Dempsey	Jess Willard	KO-3
Sept. 23, 1926	Philadelphia	Gene Tunney	Jack Dempsey	10
June 12, 1930	New York City	Max Schmeling	Jack Sharkey	4
June 21, 1932	Long Island City	Jack Sharkey	Max Schmeling	15
June 29, 1933	Long Island City	Primo Carnera	Jack Sharkey	KO-6
June 14, 1934	Long Island City	Max Baer	Primo Carnera	KO-11
June 13, 1935	Long Island City	Jim Braddock	Max Baer	15
June 22, 1937	Chicago	Joe Louis	Jim Braddock	KO-8

and New Deal Banking Reform (Armonk, N.Y.: M. E. Sharpe, 1995); Jordan A. Schwarz, *Liberal: Adolf A. Berle and the Vision of an American Era* (New York: The Free Press, 1987); Elliott A. Rosen, "Brains Trust" in Otis L. Graham, Jr. and Meghan Robinson Wander, eds., *Franklin D. Roosevelt: His Life and Times: An Encyclopedic View* (Boston: G. K. Hall, 1985), 40–41.

Branting, Karl Hjalmar (1860–1925)

Swedish Socialist leader, diplomat, and Nobel laureate. Born in Stockholm on November 12, 1860, Branting attended the University of Uppsala from 1877 to 1882 but did not receive a degree. He worked as a labor journalist for two leading labor newspapers—*Tiden* ("The Times") and *Socialdemokraten* ("Social Democrat")—but he soon turned to politics. In 1889 Branting was one of the organizers of the Swedish Social Democratic Party (SDP). The first member of the SDP elected to the *Riksdag*, the Swedish Parliament, he led the fight for universal suffrage in Sweden, which was finally accomplished in 1907. In 1905, when Norway separated from Sweden, it was the pacifist Branting who called on his fellow Swedes to avoid

Karl Branting *(CORBIS/Hulton-Deutsch Collection)*

war and settle differences between the two nations amicably. Because of his lifelong work on behalf of international peace, he was chosen as Sweden's representative at the VERSAILLES Peace Conference in 1919.

In 1920 the country turned to Branting as prime minister to form a cabinet, the first one led by Social Democrats. Although his first term lasted less than a year, in 1921 he was again named prime minister, serving from 1921 to 1923 (when he held the foreign minister portfolio as well) and again from 1924 to 1925. He was the first Swedish delegate to the LEAGUE OF NATIONS (1922–25). For lifelong commitment to pacifism and neutrality in the war, as well as for his work during the Norwegian crisis and with the League of Nations, Branting was awarded (with Christian Louis LANGE of Norway) the Nobel prize in 1921.

From 1921 until his death, Branting was a leading voice in international attempts to settle border situations that threatened to explode into war, including the Greek-Italian dispute over the Dodecanese Islands in 1923. He served as a mediator in the Turkish argument over the stationing of British troops in Istanbul in 1924, which ended with evacuation of the soldiers and Britain's recognition of Turkey.

In January 1925 he resigned as prime minister when his health began to deteriorate. He died on February 24, 1925.

References: Bernard S. Schlessinger, "Branting, Karl Hjalmar" in Bernard S. and June H. Schlessinger, eds., *The Who's Who of Nobel Prize Winners* (Phoenix, Ariz.: Oryx, 1986), 131–32; Franklin D. Scott, "Branting, Karl Hjalmar" in Warren F. Kuehl, ed., *Biographical Dictionary of Internationalists* (Westport, Conn.: Greenwood, 1983), 106–08; Thomas Watson MacCallum, and Stephen Taylor, eds., *The Nobel Prize-Winners and the Nobel Foundation, 1901–1937* (Zurich, Switzerland: Central European Times Publishing, 1938), 359; Tyler Wasson, ed., *Nobel Prize Winners: An H. W. Wilson Biographical Dictionary* (New York: H. W. Wilson, 1987), 141–43.

Brave New World   *See* HUXLEY, Aldous.

Breton, André   *See* DADA; SURREALISM.

Briand, Aristide (1862–1932)

French politician and diplomat. Briand was born in Nantes, France, on March 28, 1862, and received a law degree from the University of Paris in 1881, but decided to enter journalism instead. In 1894 he joined the French Socialist Party after hearing a speech in Nantes at a congress of workingmen. Eight years later, he was elected to the Chamber of Deputies, and, over the next three decades, held 21 different offices in various cabinets, and was 12 times premier; six separate times he held the post of prime minister.

During the years before, during, and after World War I, Briand was an outspoken advocate for a peace organization which would put a stop to war. He led France through the war, but afterward was a key player in the formation of the LEAGUE OF NATIONS, which was established at the VERSAILLES Peace Conference in 1919. During the 1920s, he worked to make peace with Germany once and for all, helping to draft the LOCARNO PACT of 1925 and the KELLOGG-BRIAND PACT of 1929, both of which were landmark treaties. This lifetime of work won him in 1926 the Nobel Peace Prize. German Foreign Minister Gustav STRESEMANN was the corecipient. Briand continued his pacifist work until his death, going so far as to propose the idea of a European Union in 1930. On March 7, 1932, he died in Paris.

See also CHAMBERLAIN, Sir Joseph Austen; KELLOGG, Frank Billings.

References: Bernard S. Schlessinger, "Briand, Aristide Pierre Henri" in Bernard S. and June H. Schlessinger, eds., *The Who's Who of Nobel Prize Winners* (Phoenix, Ariz.: Oryx, 1986), 133; Irwin Abrams, *The Nobel Peace Prize and the Laureates: An Illustrated Biographical History, 1901–1987* (Boston: G. K. Hall & Co., 1988), 103–4; Douglas W. Houston, "Briand, Arystede [sic] Pierre Henri" in Warren F. Kuehl, ed., *Biographical Dictionary of Internationalists* (Westport, Conn.: Greenwood, 1983), 111–13; Thomas Watson MacCallum and Stephen Taylor, eds., *The Nobel Prize–Winners and the Nobel Foundation, 1901–1937* (Zurich, Switzerland: Central European Times Publishing, 1938), 367–68; "Briand May Be Asked to Head New Ministry," *New York Herald* (European edition), October 30, 1929, p. 1; Richard Lamb, *The Drift to War, 1922–1939* (New York: St. Martin's Press, 1989).

British Union of Fascists   *See* MOSLEY, Oswald Ernald.

Broglie, Louis-Victor-Pierre-Raymond de (1892–1987)
French physicist and Nobel laureate. He was born in Dieppe, France, on August 15, 1892, and attended the University of Paris, where he earned licenses in history (1910) and in science (1913). He taught physics at the University of Paris from 1926 until 1962. From 1926 to 1929, he worked on the wave nature of the electron and its properties. Biographer Linda Arny writes, "He showed that both matter and radiation displayed the properties of both particles and waves, which fit the Einstein theory that matter is merely a form of energy and the two can be converted into each other." For this work and his studies of electrons, de Broglie was awarded the 1929 Nobel Prize in physics. De Broglie died in 1987.

References: Linda Arny, "Broglie, Louis-Victor Pierre Raymond de" in Bernard S. and June H. Schlessinger, eds., *The Who's Who of Nobel Prize Winners* (Phoenix, Ariz.: Oryx, 1986), 160; Thomas Watson MacCallum and Stephen Taylor, eds., *The Nobel Prize-Winners and the Nobel Foundation, 1901–1937* (Zurich, Switzerland: Central European Times Publishing, 1938), 93–94.

Brooks, Cleanth, Jr. (1906–1994)
American writer and critic, member of the FUGITIVES, an important and prominent assemblage of American poets and critics situated near Vanderbilt University in Nashville, Tennessee, during the 1920s. Born in Murray, Kentucky, on October 16, 1906, he was educated at Vanderbilt and at Tulane University in New Orleans, Louisiana. After accepting a Rhodes Scholarship, he spent time at Exeter College in Oxford, England. In 1932, he began to teach at Louisiana State University in Baton Rouge. Starting in 1935, Brooks collaborated with poet Robert Penn WARREN as editor of the literary journal *The Southern Review*. Today, the Robert Penn Warren–Cleanth Brooks Award is bestowed annually by the Advisory Group of the Center for Robert Penn Warren Studies at Western Kentucky University for outstanding literary criticism. Brooks died in 1994.

References: James J. Sosnoski, "Cleanth Brooks" in Gregory S. Jay, ed., *Modern American Critics, 1920–1955* (Detroit: Gale Research, 1988), 33–42; Mark Royden Winchell, *Cleanth Brooks and the Rise of Modern Criticism* (Charlottesville: University Press of Virginia, 1996); John M. Bradbury, *The Fugitives: A Critical Account* (Chapel Hill: University of North Carolina Press, 1958); Louise Cowan, *The Fugitive Group: A Literary History* (Baton Rouge: Louisiana State University Press, 1959).

Brooks, Louise (1906–1985)
American silent film actress, famed for her roles in German impressionist films. Brooks was born Mary Louise Brooks on November 14, 1906, in the village of Cherryvale, Kansas, one of four children of Leonard and Myra Brooks. She began dancing while a teenager and got her break by starring in Florenz Ziegfeld's Follies on Broadway in 1925. That same year, she made her debut on the screen in an uncredited role in *The Street of Forgotten Men*. Eventually she starred in *Just Another Blonde* (1926), director Howard Hawks's *A Girl In Every Port* (1928), and William Wellman's *Beggars of Life* (1928). These roles captured the attention of famed German director Georg Wilhelm PABST, and he cast her as Lulu in *Pandora's Box* (1928), considered one of the finest films of the silent era. The story of a spell-binding dancer, the film catapulted Brooks to fame. Her role as the enchant-

ing Thymiane in Pabst's follow-up *Diary of a Lost Girl* (1929) made her an icon of the 1920s with her short hairdo and JAZZ AGE look.

Following *Diary,* Brooks returned to the United States, but her career faltered. She appeared in only a few roles in the 1930s, and went into retirement soon after. Her autobiography, *Lulu in Hollywood,* was published in 1982. Brooks died on August 8, 1985, in Rochester, New York.

References: Barry Paris, *Louise Brooks* (New York: Knopf, 1989); Ephraim Katz, *The Film Encyclopedia* (New York: Harper Perennial, 1994), 180; Herbert Mitgang, "Louise Brooks, Proud Star of Silent Screen, Dead at 78," *New York Times,* August 10, 1985, p. 29.

Broun, Heywood (1888–1939)

American journalist and sportswriter, member of the famed ALGONQUIN ROUND TABLE, an unceremonial assemblage of famed literary figures in the 1920s and 1930s which met in a New York hotel. Born Matthew Heywood Campbell Broun in Brooklyn, New York on December 7, 1888, he was the son of Heywood Cox Broun, a printer, and Henriette (Bruce) Broun. He attended Harvard University but he left in 1910, joining the staffs of first the New York *Morning Telegraph* and then the *New York Tribune.* After he joined the *Tribune* in 1912, he became a sportswriter and drama critic, roles that won him wide acclaim. In 1921 he moved to the *New York World,* where he began the critically acclaimed column "It Seems to Me," making him one of the most read American journalists of his time. His support for the doomed anarchist murderers Nicola SACCO and Bartolomeo VANZETTI before their execution in 1927 led to his departure from the *World* in 1928. Thereafter, he turned out his column on a freelance basis, and it appeared until his death. An active socialist, he ran for Congress in 1930 on that party's ticket but he was defeated. In 1933, after calling in his column for the establishment of a "newspaper writers' union," he was one of the founding members of the American Newspaper Guild, and served as the organization's first president, a position he held for five terms.

Broun died suddenly in New York City on December 18, 1939. He was the author of *It Seems to Me* (1935), a compendium of his most famous columns, *Pieces of Hate* (1922), and *The Boy Grew Older* (1927).

References: Richard O'Connor, *Heywood Broun: A Biography* (New York: Putnam, 1975), 5–15; "Broun, Heywood Campbell" in Sam G. Riley, *Biographical Dictionary of American Newspaper Columnists* (Westport, Conn.: Greenwood, 1995), 42–43; Frank Scully, *Rogues' Gallery: Profiles of My Eminent Contemporaries* (Hollywood, Calif.: Murray & Gee, 1943); James W. Harper, "Broun, Heywood Campbell" in David L.

Porter, ed., *Biographical Dictionary of American Sports: Outdoor Sports* (Westport, Conn.: Greenwood Press, 1988), 53–55.

Bruce, Stanley Melbourne (1883–1967)

Australian businessman, politician, and diplomat. Born in Melbourne on April 15, 1883, he graduated from Cambridge University in England in 1908. Prior to his graduation, however, he joined the mercantile business of his family—Paterson, Lainge, and Bruce—where he served as chair of the London board from 1906 to 1914. Although he read commercial law and was called to the bar, his family's business occupied most of his time.

In 1914, Bruce changed places with an older brother and ran the Australian side of the business. Enlisting in the Australian Army, he saw heavy action during World War I and was wounded during the battle for Gallipoli. For these wounds and for bravery during battle, he was awarded the Military Cross and the Croix de Guerre avec Palme. Bruce returned to the family business in 1918, but that same year he ran for and was elected to a seat in the Australian House of Representatives, representing the area of Flinders in Victoria, as a member of the Nationalist party. Three years later, his rise in Australian politics was assured when he was named as the senior delegate of his country to the LEAGUE OF NATIONS. Bruce's stay was short, and upon his return to Australia in 1921 he was named treasurer, a post he held until 1923, and privy councillor.

In 1923, Earle Page, a leading Australian politician (and later prime minister), refused to support William Morris HUGHES's attempts to be reelected prime minister. In a deal called the National-Country Coalition, Page supported Bruce for the prime ministership (while Bruce held the minister for external affairs portfolio) in return for Page being named as deputy. Bruce served as prime minister until 1929, up until that time the longest reigning government in the history of the Commonwealth. Using the motto "Men, Money, and Markets," the Bruce government oversaw a rapid expansion in the Australian economy in the 1920s, advocated more self-government at the IMPERIAL CONFERENCES of 1923 and 1926, and directed the government's move to Canberra in 1927. By the end of the decade, as the effects of the GREAT DEPRESSION washed over Australia, Bruce was faced with worsening economic conditions and labor strife, and his refusal to instigate needed social reforms led to growing unrest among the electorate. When Bruce attempted to abolish the Commonwealth Arbitration Court as a measure to end the labor crisis, his fall from power was assured. He advanced the Maritime Industries Bill of 1929, but was tossed out of office in favor of James Henry Scullin that October, the first Australian prime minister to lose his seat. In 1931, however, when James A. Lyons came to power as prime minister, Bruce was elected to a seat in Parliament.

Bruce's voice became important during the years leading up to the outbreak of World War II. From 1933 until 1945, he was Australia's High Commissioner in London, where he spoke against condemning Japan for its attack on Manchuria and, when the League of Nations called for sanctions against Italy for invading Ethiopia, claimed that England and the Commonwealth nations must ask for a similar prohibition on Germany for its many violations of international law. In 1933 he served as an Australian representative to the World Economic Conference; as president of the Montreux Conference, where the Treaty of LAUSANNE was renegotiated; and as a delegate to the Fifth Imperial Conference. During World War II, he was an integral member of British prime minister Winston Churchill's "war cabinet" and his Pacific War Council. For his lifelong services to his nation and his people, in 1947 Bruce was knighted Viscount Bruce of Melbourne. He died in London, where he had retired, on August 25, 1967.

References: Heather Radi, "Bruce, Stanley Melbourne" in Bede Nairn and Geoffrey Serle, gen. eds., *Australian Dictionary of Biography* (Carlton, Victoria: Melbourne University Press, 1976–88), 7: 453–61; Heather Radi, "Bruce, Stanley Melbourne, Viscount Bruce" in Graeme Aplin, Stephen Glynn Foster, and Michael McKernan, eds., *Australians: A Historical Dictionary* (New South Wales: Fairfax, Syme & Weldon Associates, 1987), 60–61; "Bruce, Stanley Melbourne" in John Arnold and Deirdre Morris, gen. eds., *Monash Biographical Dictionary of 20th Century Australia* (Port Melbourne, Victoria: Reed Reference Publishing, 1994), 71–72; Malcolm Saunders, "Bruce, Stanley Melbourne" in Warren F. Kuehl, ed., *Biographical Dictionary of Internationalists* (Westport, Conn.: Greenwood, 1983), 117–19; "Viscount Bruce of Melbourne, Australian Leader, Dead at 84," *New York Times*, August 26, 1967, p. 27.

Bryan, William Jennings (1860–1925)   *See* SCOPES MONKEY TRIAL.

Bryce Report

Report, published in 1922, which examined wartime atrocities committed by the Germans during World War I officially titled "Report of the Committee on Alleged German Outrages." On December 15, 1914, British prime minister Herbert Asquith appointed several men, including James Bryce, Viscount Bryce; Sir Frederick Pollock; Sir Alfred Hopkinson; Herbert Albert Laurens Fisher, vice chancellor of the University of Sheffield; and Harold Cox, "to be a Committee to consider and advise on the evidence collected on behalf of His Majesty's Government as to outrages alleged to have been committed by German troops during the present War, cases of alleged maltreatment of civilians in the invaded territories, and breaches of the laws and established usages of war; and to prepare a report for His Majesty's Government allowing the conclusion at which they arrive on the evidence now available."

Bryce was considered one of Great Britain's preeminent historians and jurists. He had previously published several works, including *Studies in History and Jurisprudence* (1901), and had served as a member of the Schools Inquiry Commission (1864–67), which investigated school conditions in some selected English and Welsh counties. In 1916, Bryce compiled another report on alleged atrocities (the actual writing was done by historian Arnold Toynbee) documenting the treatment of Armenians in the Ottoman Empire.

The Bryce Commission set out to collect facts relating to German atrocities: the members interviewed some twelve hundred witnesses, particularly refugees fleeing from the German army and living in areas controlled by the British and French; examined documents published by the Belgian government relating to barbarities committed during the occupation of Belgium starting in 1914; and examined the captured diaries of 37 German soldiers. The Bryce Report, published in two volumes, contained the conclusions of the committee and a summary of the atrocities that were found to have some credence, as well as documents furnished by the British government, the testimony of some five hundred witnesses, and the diary excerpts. The Committee concluded that the Germans had conducted a systematic campaign against civilian populations in areas that they attacked or occupied.

After discussing each individual fact, and showing evidence as to its truthfulness, the committee reported.

(1) That there were in many parts of Belgium deliberate and systematically organised massacres of the civil population, accompanied by many isolated murders and other outrages.

(2) That in the conduct of the war generally innocent victims, both men and women, were murdered in large numbers, women violated, and children murdered.

(3) That looting, house burning, and the wanton destruction of property were ordered and countenanced by the officers of the German Army, that elaborate provisions had been made for systematic incendiarism at the very outbreak of the war, and that the burnings and destruction were frequent where no military necessity could be alleged, being indeed part of a general system of general terrorisation.

(4) That the rules and usages of war were frequently broken, particularly the using of civilians, including women and children, as a shield for advancing forces exposed to fire, to a less degree by

killing the wounded and prisoners, and in the frequent abuse of the Red Cross and the White Flag.

The Bryce Report and the commission were in some sense a forerunner of the Nuremberg War Crimes Trials that brought Nazi war criminals to justice after World War II.

References: Michael Sanders and Philip M. Taylor, *British Propaganda during World War I 1914–1918* (London: Macmillan, 1982), 143–44; Herbert A.L. Fisher, *James Bryce (Viscount Bryce of Dechmont, O.M.)* (New York: Macmillan, 1927); Hugh Tulloch, *James Bryce's American Commonwealth: The Anglo-American Background* (Woodbridge, Suffolk, England: Boydell, 1988); Keith Robbins, *Politicians, Diplomacy, and War in Modern British History* (London: Hambleton Press, 1994). For information on Bryce, see E. I. Carlyle, "Bryce, James" in Sir Leslie Stephen and Sir Sidney Lee et al., eds., *The Dictionary of National Biography* (Oxford, England: Oxford University Press, 1917–1993), 3: 127–35; Edmund S. Ions, "James Bryce and American Democracy, 1870–1920" (New York: Humanities Press, 1970); Dennis J. Mahoney, "Bryce, James" in Leonard W. Levy, ed. in chief, *Encyclopedia of the American Constitution* (New York: Macmillan, 1986–92), 1: 166.

Bucareli Agreements

Series of understandings, 1923, in which the Mexican government agreed to acknowledge the right of U.S. oil companies to exist in Mexico in exchange for American recognition of the government of Mexican president Alvaro OBREGÓN. After the Mexican government ruled that all subsoil rights belonged to the nation that they were in, U.S. President Warren G. HARDING sent American representatives to Mexico City to negotiate a deal so that U.S. oil companies could continue to operate there. These negotiations lasted from May 14 to August 15, 1923. Obregón, whose government had seized power, agreed to recognize all oil deals made with the previous government, closing off the possibility of further disputes.

References: Kenneth Grieb, "Bucareli Agreements" in Bruce W. Jentleson and Thomas G. Paterson, senior eds., *Encyclopedia of U.S. Foreign Relations* (New York: Oxford University Press, 1997), 1: 186–87; Robert J. Shafer, and Donald J. Mabry, *Neighbors—Mexico and the United States: Wetbacks and Oil* (Chicago: Nelson-Hall, 1981); Antonio Gómez Robledo (Salmón de la Selva, trans.), *The Bucareli Agreements and International Law* (Mexico City: National University of Mexico Press, 1940); Daniel Dominic Di Piazza, "The Bucareli Conference and United States–Mexican Relations" (Ph.D. dissertation, University of Missouri, 1966).

Buchman, Frank   *See* MORAL RE-ARMAMENT.

Buck, Pearl S. (1892–1973)

American novelist and Nobel laureate. Born July 26, 1892, in Hillsboro, West Virginia, she was taken by her missionary parents, Absalom and Carrie (Sydenstricker) Comfort, to China, where she lived except for a short period until 1933. She returned to the United States to attend Randolph-Macon College in Virginia, and in 1917 married fellow China missionary John Lossing Buck, whereupon the couple returned to Asia. Buck detailed life in rural China in her several novels that even today are considered classics. Her first, *East Wind, West Wind* (1930), was followed by the even more successful *The Good Earth* (1931), which earned the Pulitzer Prize and the William Dean Howells Medal of the American Academy of Arts and Letters. Some have called *The Good Earth* one of the finest novels of the 20th century. It was eventually translated into twenty languages. The lives of the novel's two main characters, Wang Lung and O-Lan, are intrinsically linked with that of the soil they work. Wang Lung venerates and worships the land, while O-Lan embraces the land as providing food and security. When famine forces them to find work in the city, O-Lan goes bravely and supports her husband; they return to the farm when they have enough money, but prosperity breeds greed and stupidity. The book was made into a film in 1937, starring Paul Muni and Luise Rainer. It received five Academy Award nominations, including Best Picture, Best Director, and Best Actress (which Rainer won).

Although Buck ended her missionary work in 1933 and divorced her husband (later marrying her publisher, Richard Walsh), she continued her writings on Chinese life, following up her success with such books as a translation of the Chinese novel *Shui-hu Chuan* (*All Men Are Brothers*, 1933); *The Exile* (1936) and *Fighting Angel* (1936), both on her parents and their missionary work in China; and *The Patriot* (1939). In 1938 for her body of work which the Nobel committee called "her rich and genuine epic pictures of Chinese life, and for her masterly biographies," Buck was awarded the Nobel Prize in literature (with Toni Morrison, she is one of only two American women to receive the prize).

Buck continued to write, producing such works as *Other Gods* (1940), *Today and Forever* (1941), *Pavilion of Women* (1946), and *One Bright Day* (1950). In 1949 she founded Welcome House, the first interracial adoption agency in the United States. She died in Danby, Vermont, on March 6, 1973.

References: Vedelia Van Meter, "Buck, Pearl Comfort Sydenstricker" in Bernard S. and June H. Schlessinger, eds., *The Who's Who of Nobel Prize Winners* (Phoenix, Ariz.: Oryx, 1986), 60; "Pearl Comfort Sydenstricker Buck" in Nancy L. Roberts, *American Peace Writers, Editors and Periodicals* (Westport, Conn.: Greenwood, 1991), 41–42; Pearl S. Buck, *My Several Worlds* (New York: John Day, 1954); Nora B. Stirling, *Pearl Buck: A Woman in Conflict* (Piscataway, N.J.: New Century, 1983); Jean McConnell, "Pearl S. Buck" in Frank Magill, ed., *Great Lives from History—American Women Series* (Pasadena, Calif.: Salem, 1985), 1: 295–99; Tyler Wasson, ed., *Nobel Prize Winners: An H. W. Wilson Biographical Dictionary* (New York: H. W. Wilson, 1987), 162–64.

Buck v. Bell (1927)

Landmark U.S. Supreme Court decision, which upheld the right of states to use compulsory sterilization on persons the state deemed "unfit." Plaintiff Carrie Buck sued the superintendent of the State Colony of Epileptics and the Feeble Minded in Virginia to enjoin him from performing a salpingectomy, an operation that leaves the patient permanently sterilized. In the case Buck was described as "a feeble minded white woman" who was committed to the state, "the daughter of a feeble minded mother, and the mother of an illegitimate feeble minded child." The Circuit Court of Amherst County, Virginia, ordered Buck to undergo the operation and, on appeal, the Virginia Supreme Court of Appeals upheld the order. The U.S. Supreme Court heard arguments on April 22, 1927.

Less than two weeks later, on May 2, 1927, Justice Oliver Wendell HOLMES spoke for an 8-1 Court (Justice Pierce Butler dissented) in holding that the operation was constitutional under the Fourteenth Amendment. In effect, the decision gave the government the right to determine which women were competent to become mothers. In what many believe to have been the most unfortunate opinion of his career, Holmes wrote, "We have seen more than once that the public welfare may call upon the best citizens for their lives. It would be strange if it could not call upon those who already sap the strength of the State for these lesser sacrifices, often not felt to be such by those concerned, in order to prevent our being swamped with incompetence. It is better for all the world, if instead of waiting to execute degenerate offspring for crime, or to let them starve for their imbecility, society can prevent those who are manifestly unfit from continuing their kind. The principle that sustains compulsory vaccination is broad enough to cover cutting the Fallopian tubes. . . . Three generations of imbeciles is enough."

Compulsory sterilization laws in the United States were not eased until the mid-1960s.

See also EUGENICS.

References: Fred D. Ragan, "Buck v. Bell" in Kermit L. Hall, ed. in chief, *The Oxford Companion to the Supreme Court of the United States* (New York: Oxford University Press, 1992), 97–98; David J. Smith, *The Sterilization of Carrie Buck* (N.J.: New Horizon Press, 1989); Paul A. Lombardo, "Three Generations, No Imbeciles: New Light on *Buck v. Bell*," *New York Law Review* 60 (April 1985): 30–62; Stephen Jay Gould,

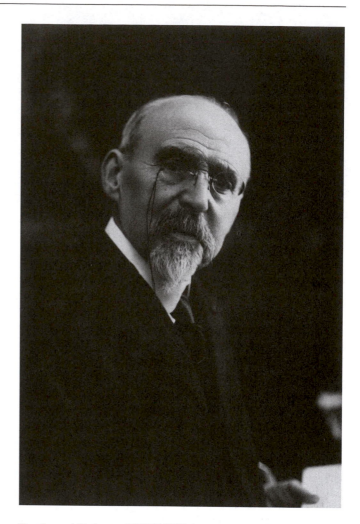

Ferdinand Buisson (*CORBIS/Hulton-Deutsch Collection*)

"Carrie Buck's Daughter," *Natural History* 93 (1997): 14–18; *Buck v. Bell* 274 US 200 (1927).

Buisson, Ferdinand-Édouard (1841–1932)

French educator and peace activist, corecipient of the 1927 Nobel Peace Prize (with German peace activist Ludwig QUIDDE) for his lifelong work to establish a climate of peace between France and Germany and for his conception of the French peace organizations, *La Ligue Internationale de la Paix et de la Liberté* (1867) and *La Ligue des Droits de l'Homme* (1898). Born in Paris on December 20, 1841, he wanted to become a teacher but refused to take the oath of loyalty required by the government of Napoleon III; instead, Buisson went to Switzerland, where he taught philosophy in Neuchâtel from 1866 to 1870. At this time he became a pacifist, attending the Geneva Peace Conference in 1867 and calling for the institution of a United States of Europe to end war once and for all on that continent.

Under France's Third Republic, Buisson was named as inspector general of the Parisian school system in 1871. When in 1896, he became a professor of pedagogy at the Sorbonne, his politics had moved directly to the left. By 1902, Buisson was elected to the Chamber of Deputies, where he served until 1914, and again from 1919 to 1924. Although he strongly supported World War I and its prosecution, he hoped that the end of the conflict would bring a new sense of peace in Europe. To this end, he dismissed the Treaty of VERSAILLES as a document meant to punish rather than absolve Germany for the war. He became a speaker on pacifism in the 1920s, and he said in one address, "A force exists which is far greater than France, far greater than Germany, far greater than any nation, and that is mankind. But above mankind itself stands justice, which finds its most perfect expression in human brotherhood." At age 86, Buisson received the Nobel, becoming the oldest Nobel laureate to date. He died in Thieuloy-Saint-Antoine, France, on February 16, 1932.

References: Charlotte B. Brown, "Buisson, Ferdinand Edouard" in Bernard S. and June H. Schlessinger, eds., *The Who's Who of Nobel Prize Winners* (Phoenix, Ariz.: Oryx, 1986), 134; Thomas Watson MacCallum, and Stephen Taylor, eds., *The Nobel Prize-Winners and the Nobel Foundation, 1901–1937* (Zurich, Switzerland: Central European Times Publishing, 1938), 371–72; Irwin Abrams, *The Nobel Peace Prize and the Laureates: An Illustrated Biographical History, 1901–1987* (Boston: G. K. Hall & Co., 1988), 109–11.

Bukharin, Nikolai Ivanovich (1888–1938)

Russian communist leader and editor. Bukharin was born in Moscow on September 27, 1888, little of his early life is known, except that he became a revolutionary while studying economics. He joined the Russian Social-Democratic Workers' Party in 1906, and within two years was a leading member of the left's Bolshevik ("majority") wing. Arrested and deported to the city of Onega near the White Sea, Bukharin escaped and fled to eastern Europe, where he joined another Russian revolutionary, Vladimir LENIN, in the Polish city of Krakow, as co-editor of the revolutionary newspaper *Pravda* ("Truth"). In 1916, Bukharin went to New York, where he worked on the Leninist newspaper *Novy Mir* (New world).

After the Russian Revolution and the overthrow of the Czar in February 1917, Bukharin returned to Russia and became a leading member of the organized workers' groups, called Soviets, which aimed to overthrow the fragile Kerensky government. In August he was elected as a member of Russia's Central Committee of the Communist Party. Following the Bolshevik takeover, that November, Lenin made Bukharin editor of *Pravda*, a post he held until 1929.

Following Lenin's death in January 1924, Bukharin was named as a full member of the Soviet Politburo, where power was shared for a time between Joseph STALIN and Leon TROTSKY. For a time, he was the chief ideological spokesperson for the government. An early supporter of Lenin's NEW ECONOMIC POLICY and Stalin's plans to rapidly industrialize the Soviet Union, Bukharin was at odds with Trotsky, Lev Kamenev, and Grigorii Zinoviev. Because of his stand, Bukharin replaced Zinoviev as the chairman of the Comintern's Central Committee in 1926. In 1929, however, Stalin reversed course and supported a program of forced collectivization that Trotsky and Zinoviev had once supported and Bukharin had opposed vociferously. That same year, amidst Stalin's attempt to center all power in one entity—himself—he used this disagreement to have Bukharin stripped of all party positions, in effect ending his career in the Communist Party.

But this was not enough. Labeling Bukharin as a danger, in January 1937 Stalin had Bukharin arrested and placed on trial in the last of the massive show trials that dominated the purges. Forced to confess to membership in a 'Trotskyist-Rightist Bloc,' Bukharin and another of his codefendants, Aleksei Rykov, confessed to being allies of the disgraced Trotsky but denied that they were wreckers or criminals. Nonetheless, they were labeled by the prosecutor as "scum and filth," found guilty, and sentenced to death.

On or about March 14, 1938, Bukharin was shot to death and buried in an unknown grave, along with countless millions of Stalin's victims. In 1988, the Soviet government posthumously rehabilitated Bukharin.

References: Stephen F. Cohen, *Bukharin and the Bolshevik Revolution: A Political Biography, 1888–1938* (New York: A. A. Knopf, 1973); Roy Aleksandrovich Medvedev (A. D. P. Briggs, trans.), *Nikolai Bukharin: The Last Years* (New York: Norton, 1980); Geoffrey Hosking, *The First Socialist Society: A History of the Soviet Union from Within* (Cambridge, Mass.: Harvard University Press, 1992), 188.

Bullitt, William Christian (1891–1967)

American diplomat. Born in Philadelphia, Pennsylvania, on January 25, 1891, Bullitt graduated from Yale University in 1912 and attended Harvard Law School. In 1917, he joined the State Department in Washington, D.C., as an assistant. Within two years he had risen sufficiently in the diplomatic ranks so that he was able to attend the talks at the VERSAILLES Peace Conference even though his boss, Secretary of State Robert Lansing, was largely kept out of the conference. After Paris, he was sent on a secret mission to Soviet Russia to interview and discover the motives of Russian leader Vladimir LENIN (becoming the first Western diplomat to interview him). On his return to the United States, he called for the recognition of the Soviet state and was essentially blacklisted from further service. Disagreeing with the policies of President WILSON, Bullitt aided enemies of the LEAGUE OF NATIONS by disclosing secret negotiations the president held at Versailles. Bullitt returned to private life when Warren G. HARDING, a Republican, won the presidency in 1920.

Thirteen years passed before Democrats again held the White House, a period in which Bullitt became an intimate of Franklin D. ROOSEVELT. When Roosevelt became president in 1933, Bullitt returned to the State Department. With U.S. recognition of the Soviet Union, he was named as the first American ambassador to that nation, serving until 1936. Bullitt returned to the United States in 1936, after which he was appointed as U.S. ambassador to France (1936–41). During these years, Bullitt had had a rare look at the growing European alarm at the militaristic rise of Nazi Germany. In 1941, he returned to the United States and served as a special assistant to Secretary of the Navy Frank Knox. In 1944, Bullitt resigned from the State Department and joined LIFE magazine as a foreign correspondent. He attempted to join the U.S. Army but was denied because of his age (he was 53), so instead he enlisted in the French army and saw action as the chief of staff of General Charles de Gaulle's psychological intelligence section, rising to the rank of major and earning the Croix de Guerre. After the war he spent much of his time warning America that the Soviet Union was a growing threat.

On February 15, 1967, Bullitt died in the American Hospital in Paris of leukemia.

References: Richard N. Billings, *So Close to Greatness: A Biography of William C. Bullitt* (New York: Macmillan, 1987); Beatrice Farnsworth, *William C. Bullitt and the Soviet Union* (Bloomington: Indiana University Press, 1967); "William Bullitt Dies in France; First U.S. Envoy to Soviet Union," *New York Times*, February 16, 1967, pp. 1, 44.

Bulwer-Lytton, Victor Alexander George Robert
See LYTTON COMMISSION; MANCHURIAN CRISIS.

Bunin, Ivan Alexeievich (1870–1953)
Russian poet and novelist, awarded the 1933 Nobel Prize in literature for "the strict artistry with which he has carried on the classical Russian traditions in prose writing." Born in Voronezh, Russia, on October 22, 1870, he was the son of Aleksej Bunin and Ljudmilla Aleksandrovna Cubarova Bunin. Bunin did not obtain a college degree; rather, he turned to writing. Little is known about his life, except that he fled his native land and settled as an exile in Paris. His works brilliantly told the stories of his Mother Russia. They included *The Village* (1923), *Mitya's Love* (1926), and *Well of Days* (1933). His best-known work remains *The Gentleman from San Francisco* (1927). He died in Paris on November 8, 1953.

References: Julian W. Connolly, *Ivan Bunin* (Boston: Twayne, 1982); Cheryl Chan and June H. Schlessinger, "Bunin, Ivan Alexeievich" in Bernard S. and June H. Schlessinger, eds., *The Who's Who of Nobel Prize Winners* (Phoenix, Ariz.: Oryx, 1986), 58; Thomas Watson MacCallum and Stephen Taylor, eds., *The Nobel Prize-Winners and the Nobel Foundation, 1901–1937* (Zurich, Switzerland: Central European Times Publishing, 1938), 320–21.

Burchfield, Charles Ephraim (1893–1967)
American painter, known during the 1920s and 1930s for his scenes of American urban and industrial life. Born in the town of Ashtabula Harbor, Ohio, on April 9, 1893, he attended the Cleveland School of Art from 1912 to 1916. After moving to Salem, Ohio, he spent his spare time painting with watercolors and sketching scenes of nature. After serving in World War I, he worked as a wallpaper designer in Buffalo, New York, until he could afford to spend more time on his art.

Burchfield's success came in the 1920s and 1930s, when his varied watercolors were exhibited in various outlets, including solo exhibitions at the Metropolitan Museum of Art and the Museum of Modern Art in New York, the Corcoran Gallery of Art in Washington, D.C., the Carnegie Museum of Art, and the Whitney Museum of American Art. In such works as *Abandoned Farmhouse* (1932), Burchfield displayed the loneliness of a deserted dwelling in its final stages of collapse. Many of his paintings have been compared to those of Edward Hopper (1882–1967), in that Burchfield's works described the harshness of American small town life. Of his art which showed the heart of middle America, he once said, "If these scenes speak of a great sorrow on the land, they also allude to the resilience of the people who lived on it." In the interwar period he was perhaps the most important watercolor artist in the United States.

Burchfield died in Gardenville, New York, on January 10, 1973. The previous year, the Charles Burchfield Center had been dedicated at Buffalo State College in New York.

References: Matthew Baigell, *Charles Burchfield* (New York: Watson-Guptill Publications, 1976); John Ireland Howe Baur, *The Inlander: Life and Work of Charles Burchfield, 1893–1967* (Newark: University of Delaware Press, 1982); "Charles Burchfield Dies at 73; Artist Known for Water-Colors," *New York Times*, January 11, 1967, p. 25.

Burroughs, Edgar Rice (1875–1950)
American writer whose Tarzan series thrilled millions during the 1920s and 1930s. Burroughs, born in Chicago, Illinois, on September 1, 1875, attended Phillips Academy in Orchard Lake, Michigan; after a short period

in the U.S. Cavalry, with which he saw action in the Spanish-American War, he entered into private business in Chicago. Until 1912, he also worked part-time as a storekeeper, a gold miner in Oregon, and a cowboy in Idaho. Returning to Chicago, he began a writing career that lasted his entire life.

In that year, 1912, he published his first work, *A Princess of Mars*, a tale of fantasy. Two years later *Tarzan of the Apes*, the story of the mythical Lord Greystoke brought up by apes after his parents were marooned in Africa, was an immediate and overwhelming success; it was followed by 24 additional Tarzan books. Soon after the first Tarzan movie, *Tarzan of the Apes* (1918), was filmed in California, Burroughs moved to a suburb of Los Angeles, which soon took the name Tarzana. *The Romance of Tarzan* (1918) and *The Adventures of Tarzan* (1921) followed soon after. He continued to write, publishing 91 novels and countless short stories and articles. During World War II, he served as a correspondent for the *Los Angeles Times*. Burroughs died in Encino, California, on March 19, 1950.

References: Richard A. Lupoff, *Edgar Rice Burroughs, Master of Adventure* (New York: Canaveral, 1965); Irwin Porges, *Edgar Rice Burroughs: The Man Who Created Tarzan* (Provo, Utah: Brigham Young University Press, 1975); George T. McWhorter, *Burroughs Dictionary: An Alphabetical List of Proper Names, Words, Phrases, and Concepts Contained in the Published Works of Edgar Rice Burroughs* (Lanham, Md.: University Press of America, 1987).

Butenandt, Adolf Friedrich Johann (1903–1995)

German chemist and Nobel laureate. Butenandt, born in the village of Bremerhaven-Lehe, Germany, on March 24, 1903, studied chemistry, biology, and physics at the universities at Marburg and Göttingen. From 1933 until 1936 he taught at the Technische Hochschule in Danzig, and from 1936 to 1945 at the Kaiser Wilhelm Institute for Biochemistry at Berlin. He conducted research on female hormones, including estrogen and progesterone, and the male hormone androsterone, which he was the first to isolate; he also made investigations into the chemical structure of progestin. For this work on sex hormones he was awarded (with Leopold RUZICKA) the 1939 Nobel Prize in chemistry. Because of a Nazi decree banning all German citizens from accepting Nobels, however, he did not receive the prize until 1949. He spent the remainder of his life in various researches, including that of other sex hormones and their relationship to human sexuality. Butenandt died in Munich on January 18, 1995.

References: Connie Dowell, "Butenandt, Adolf Friedrich Johann" in Bernard S. and June H. Schlessinger, eds., *The Who's Who of Nobel Prize Winners* (Phoenix, Ariz.: Oryx, 1986), 15, 172–74; David Binder, "Adolf Butenandt Is Dead at 91; Won Nobel for Hormone Work," *New York Times*, January 19, 1995, p. B11.

Butler, Nicholas Murray (1862–1947)

American educator, administrator, and Nobel laureate. The son of Henry Leny Butler and Mary (Murray) Butler, he was born in Elizabeth, New Jersey, on April 2, 1862, and attended Columbia University in New York (from which he received a bachelor's degree in 1882, a master's in 1883, and a doctorate in 1884). After studying in Berlin and Paris, Butler returned to the United States, and Columbia, as an assistant professor of philosophy. In 1890 he was promoted to full professor, and, when Seth Low resigned as president of Columbia in 1901, Butler became acting president; a year later, he was formally elected to the position.

During his 44-year run as president of Columbia, Butler turned the university into one of the world's leading institutions for higher learning. Before and after World War I, Butler made his name by speaking out on international issues, and several times was chosen by both Democratic and Republican presidents as an unofficial envoy to foreign leaders. In 1928, French premier Aristide BRIAND called on him to obtain the endorsement of Pope PIUS XI of the KELLOGG-BRIAND PACT, which outlawed war. With former Secretary of State Elihu Root, Butler became an advocate for world peace, founding the Carnegie Endowment for International Peace in 1910. During the 1920s and early 1930s, he called for an international body to mediate disputes. For this lifetime of peace work, Butler was awarded (with corecipient Jane ADDAMS) the 1931 Nobel Peace Prize.

A lifelong educator and activist, Butler retired as the head of Columbia in 1945 with the title of president emeritus. He died two years later, on December 7, 1947.

References: Frank L. Turner, "Butler, Nicholas Murray" in Bernard S. and June H. Schlessinger, eds., *The Who's Who of Nobel Prize Winners* (Phoenix, Ariz.: Oryx, 1986), 135; Nicholas Murray Butler, *Across the Busy Years: Recollections and Reflections* (New York: Charles Scribner's Sons, 1939), 1: 20–47; John Braeman, "Nicholas Murray Butler" in Frank N. Magill, ed., *Great Lives from History: American Series* (Pasadena, Calif.: Salem, 1987), 1: 366–72; Albert Marrin, *Nicholas Murray Butler* (Boston: Twayne Publishers, 1976), 15–56; Hugh Hawkins, "Butler, Nicholas Murray" in Allen Johnson and Dumas Malone et al., eds., *Dictionary of American Biography* (New York: Charles Scribner's Sons, 1930–95), 4: 133–38; Barbara Ruth Peltzman, "Nicholas Murray Butler" in John F. Ohles, ed., *Biographical Dictionary of American Educators* (Westport, Conn.: Greenwood, 1978), 1: 215–17; Sondra L. Herman, *Eleven against War: Studies in American Internationalist Thought, 1898–1921* (Stanford, Calif.: Hoover Institution Press, 1969), 7, 22–27; Irwin Abrams, *The Nobel*

Peace Prize and the Laureates: An Illustrated Biographical History, 1901–1987 (Boston: G. K. Hall & Co., 1988), 118; "Nicholas Murray Butler Is Dead in Hospital at 85," New York *Herald Tribune,* December 7, 1947, pp. 1, 16–20.

Byrd, Richard Evelyn (1888–1957)

American naval officer and explorer, noted for his historic voyage across the North Pole. Born on October 25, 1888, in Winchester, Virginia, he traced his descendants back to the founding of the Virginia colony; his brother Harry Flood Byrd became the governor of Virginia and a U.S. senator. As a young man, he traveled around the world, then attended the Virginia Military Institute and the University of Virginia before entering the U.S. Naval Academy at Annapolis, from which he graduated in 1912.

After injuring his foot, Byrd was forced to retire from active naval duty in 1916, but he was recalled to limited service during World War I, serving as the commander of several American naval air stations in Canada. In 1918, he became a naval air pilot with the rank of lieutenant commander, and for a time he commanded naval air stations at Halifax and North Sydney, Nova Scotia. After the war, he was an integral part of the efforts to fly an airplane nonstop across the Atlantic Ocean.

Starting in 1925, Byrd was a member of the MacMillan Expedition to Newfoundland, serving in the naval unit of the voyage. On May 8, 1926, with Floyd Bennett as a copilot, he flew from King's Bay, Spitsbergen, Norway, nonstop to the North Pole and back in a two-day trip. After Charles LINDBERGH flew to Paris from New York nonstop, Byrd tried the same journey in June 1927 with three passengers, but after 42 hours bad weather forced him to land on the French coast. In 1928, he flew to the Antarctic and landed that December. Byrd established a settlement on the Bay of Whales, dubbing it "Little America." He later used the site as the base for his second expedition (1933–35), and for the 1946–47 Navy expedition of which he was a member. In November 1929, he flew from "Little America" with Bernt Balchen, Harold June, and Capt. A. C. McKinley in the trimotored aircraft *Floyd Bennett* to the South Pole and back, making Byrd the first man to reach both Poles and travel back safely. Returning to the United States, he was awarded, by special order of Congress, the rank of rear admiral, retired. In 1926, the Geographical Society of Philadelphia awarded Byrd the Elisha Kent Kane gold medal. The 1930 film, *With Byrd at the South Pole,* chronicles the expedition. In 1933 Byrd returned to "Little America," and after setting up another camp 123 miles south of it was stricken by carbon monoxide poisoning. A rescue party saved him. In November 1939, he returned a third time to the area, to claim "Little America" officially for the United States.

Byrd died in Boston, Massachusetts, on March 11, 1957. He was the author of *Skyward* (1928), *Little America* (1930), *Discovery* (1935), and *Alone* (1938).

References: Peter J. Anderson, "Byrd, Richard Evelyn" in Allen Johnson and Dumas Malone et al., eds., *Dictionary of American Biography* (New York: Charles Scribner's Sons, 1930–95), 6: 91–94; Harry Adams, *Beyond the Barrier with Byrd: An Authentic Story of the Byrd Atlantic Exploring Expedition* (Chicago and New York: M. A. Donohue & Co., 1932); "Flew to Pole, Byrd Declares," *New York Herald* (European edition), May 10, 1926, p. 1; "Byrd Flies to North Pole and Back; Round Trip From Kings Bay in 15 Hrs. 51 Min.; Circles Top of the World Several Times," *New York Times,* May 10, 1926, p. 1; "Admiral Byrd Dies at 68; Made 5 Polar Expeditions," *New York Times,* March 12, 1957, pp. 1, 18.

The Cabinet of Dr. Caligari

German expressionist motion picture (*Das Kabinett des Dr. Caligari* in German), 1919, considered one of the greatest films to come out of Germany during the silent era. The story of Dr. Caligari, who works at a fair exhibiting the somnambulist Cesare, and how Caligari is murdered when Cesare predicts his untimely death, is told with stunning visuals for its time. Starring Werner Krauss as Dr. Caligari, and Conrad Veidt as Cesare, the film was directed by Robert Wiene, whose other expressionist films, including the silent historical drama *I.N.R.I.* (1923), were also acclaimed. Weine, working with cinematographer Willy Hameister and costume designer Walter Reimann, produced a film whose dark shadows and surreal sets came in the midst of the art revolution in WEIMAR GERMANY.

References: Mike Budd, ed., *"The Cabinet of Dr. Caligari": Texts, Contexts, Histories* (New Brunswick, N.J.: Rutgers University Press, 1990); Carl Mayer (R. V. Adkinson, trans.), *The Cabinet of Dr. Caligari: A Film by Robert Wiene, Carl Mayer and Hans Janowitz* (New York: Simon & Schuster, 1972).

Cagney, James (1899–1986)

American motion picture actor, known particularly for his screen portrayals of mobsters. Born James Francis Cagney, Jr., in New York City's Lower East Side on July 17, 1899, he was the son of a bartender and amateur boxer. Cagney began his career by following in his father's boxing shoes, and soon became one of his area's best. He later worked at Wanamaker's department store in New York to help support his family. Just after World War I, Cagney was offered an opportunity to work in a vaudeville troupe as a female impersonator for $35 a week. It was during one play, *Pitter Patter,* in 1921, that he met an actress named Frances Willard. A year later, the two married, and they remained together until his death.

Cagney worked on the stage with little notice until 1929, when he appeared with Joan Blondell in *Penny Arcade.* The performance earned Cagney an invitation to Hollywood; in 1930 he made his film debut in *Sinner's Holiday.* It was not until his fifth role, as the Prohibition-era gangster Tom Powers in the 1931 epic *Public Enemy,* that Cagney became a major star, making audiences gasp when he smashed half a grapefruit into the face of actress Mae Clarke. Throughout the 1930s, Cagney poured out several outstanding performances, as a race car driver in *The Crowd Roars* (1932), manhandling matinee idol in *Lady Killer* (1933), and a boxer in *Winner Takes All* (1933), among others. He worked with Pat O'Brien in one of the best films of the period, *Angels with Dirty Faces* (1938), and appeared with Humphrey Bogart in *The Roaring Twenties* (1939). In one of his finest performances, Cagney was awarded the Best Actor Oscar for his portrayal of George M. Cohan in *Yankee Doodle Dandy* (1942). He retired to his farm in Stanfordville, New York, in 1961, though he appeared in a few films in the 1980s.

Cagney died at his farm on March 30, 1986. According to movie reviewer Gene Siskel, "The secret of his appeal? He always seemed to be dancing, even when he was standing still. He was always the bantam rooster, rising up on his toes to stare down a taller man. He will always be thought of as a 'tough guy,' even though he considered himself 'a song-and-dance man.'"

References: Ephraim Katz, *The Film Encyclopedia* (New York: HarperPerennial, 1994), 204; Michael Freedland, *Cagney: A Biography* (New York: Stein & Day, 1975); Homer Dickens, *The Films of James Cagney* (Secaucus, N.J.: Citadel, 1972); Gene Siskel, "James Cagney Dead at 86," *Miami Herald,* March 31, 1986, p. 4A.

Capone, Al (1899–1947)

American mobster, known for his interwar criminal activity, particularly his meteoric rise during PROHIBITION and the GREAT DEPRESSION. Born in Naples, Italy, on January 17, 1899, the son of a poor barber, Capone moved with his family to New York City when he was a youngster. Quitting school after sixth grade, he joined a street gang run by hoodlum Johnny Torrio, which later became the criminal organization that inhabited New York's immigrant community before and during World War I. During these years, Capone's behavior steadily grew more violent and his criminal activities more serious. In a scuffle, he was cut across the cheek with a knife; the resulting scar left him with the nickname "Scarface."

In the early 1920s Capone moved to Chicago, where Torrio had enlisted in a Chicago crime syndicate run by Big Jim Colosimo. Torrio needed a loyal henchman and called Capone. When Colosimo was murdered, the two took over the enterprise, which controlled bootlegging, prostitution, and gambling in Chicago. When Torrio was wounded in an assassination attempt and retired, he handed his empire over to Capone, who made himself the king of all mobsters in a short period. In the next several years, Capone paid off the political element in Chicago, while using violence to eliminate his competitors in the bootlegging trade. This pattern of savagery culminated in the ST. VALENTINE'S DAY MASSACRE in 1929, when Capone had his henchmen slaughter the gang of his rival, "Bugs" Moran. Although Moran escaped the massacre, seven men were killed.

Capone's victory over Moran was short-lived; the attention brought on by the killings led to an all-out assault by the U.S. government to put Capone in prison. On April 23, 1930, the Chicago Crime Commission issued the first "Public Enemies" list with 28 names, and Capone's was at the top of the list. By this time, Capone had amassed a personal fortune and was living like a king. After several years of intense investigation by the federal government, he was indicted on income-tax evasion. Convicted in 1931, he was sentenced to serve 11 years in prison and was exiled to Alcatraz Island in California. There, the effects of untreated venereal disease ravaged his health; by 1939 he was near death. Paroled that year, he retired to his mansion in Miami, Florida, an invalid. He died on January 25, 1947, perhaps the most famous criminal boss ever to hold sway in the United States.

References: John Kobler, *Capone: The Life and World of Al Capone* (New York: Putnam, 1971); Laurence Bergreen, *Capone: The Man and the Era* (New York: Simon & Schuster, 1994); Gus Tyler, *Organized Crime in America* (Ann Arbor: University of Michigan Press, 1962); "Capone Dead at 48; Dry Era Gang Chief," *New York Times*, January 26, 1947, p. 7.

Capone, Frank   *See* MOTION PICTURES, TALKING.

Carter, Howard (1873–1939)

English archaeologist, noted for his 1922 discovery of the tomb of Tutankhamen. Born in Swaffham, Norfolk, England, on May 9, 1873, Carter was the youngest son of Samuel John Carter, a painter who specialized in animal portraits, and Martha Joyce (Sandys) Carter. Because of his ill health, the child was taught at home, and never received a secondary education. His early and enduring interest became archaeology, but he was taught to be a draftsman; however, when only 17 years old, he was able to combine these two careers when he went to Egypt to work with the English Archaeological Survey as an assistant draftsman with the Egypt Exploration Fund. In 1892, he studied archaeology for four months under Sir William Flinders Petrie at El-Amarna.

Perhaps the greatest archaeological discovery of the century was Carter's finding of the tomb of Tutankhamen (known as king Tut) in the Valley of the Kings near Luxor in November 1922. Tutankhamen, an Egyptian king of the

Howard Carter points to the opening of Tutankhamen's tomb as excavations continue in February 1923. *(CORBIS/Bettmann)*

18th Dynasty, lived about 1358 B.C. and died as a boy. Lord George Edward Stanhope Carnarvon, a British Egyptologist, had become Carter's patron in his quest to find the tombs of the other pharaohs of Egypt. Carter found Tutankhamen's tomb beneath rubble left behind from the excavation of the tomb of Ramses VI, and after revealing a series of rock steps, opened the tomb's door. As Carter peeked into Tutankhamen's tomb, Carnarvon asked him, "Well, can you see anything?" and Carter answered, "Yes, wonderful things." Inside were golden chariots, a throne, and chairs of exquisite antiquity, all surrounding a sarcophagus encapsulating the body of the young king. On February 12, 1924, over a year after its initial discovery, the sarcophagus was opened, revealing the gold-encrusted and encased body of Tutankhamen. Further chambers were found, and although the Egyptian government for a time closed down the investigation, it continued until the final chamber was revealed in 1928. In the record of the Tutankhamen expedition, Carter wrote, "Among the immense quantities of material in Tut-ankh-Amen's tomb, as also exhibited in the beautiful reliefs of his reign in the great colonade of the Temple of Luxor, we find extreme delicacy of style together with character of the utmost refinement. In the case of a painted scene, vase, or statue, the primary idea of art is obvious, but in utilitarian objects such as a walking-stick, staff, or wine-strainer, art, as we know too well to-day, is not a necessity. Here in this tomb the artistic value seems to have been always the first consideration. . . . After so many years of barren labour a sudden development of great magnitude finds one unprepared. One is, for instance, confronted by the question of adequate and competent assistance."

Carter also carried out investigations of the tombs of Hatshepsut and Amenhotep I, as well as other areas in the Valley of the Kings. His discovery of the tomb of Tutankhamen, however, ranks among the greatest of the 20th century. And although the tomb was supposedly cursed (12 of the 16 members of the party who first opened the tomb died of mysterious causes), Carter himself lived 16 years after the find, debunking the skeptics. He spent those years cataloguing and writing about the fantastic treasures that he had uncovered. He died in London on March 2, 1939.

Carter biographer Arnold Brackman noted, "Carter was not thus accepted by the archaeological establishment of his time. He lacked formal training; he was self-taught. He had no old school tie. In the class-conscious Victorian and Edwardian England in which he reached his majority, his origins worked against him—he never truly came up from downstairs." Nonetheless, Carter's legacy remains secure.

References: Percy E. Newberry, "Carter, Howard" in Sir Leslie Stephen and Sir Sidney Lee et al., eds., *The Dictionary of National Biography* (Oxford, England: Oxford University Press, 1917–1993), 4: 151–52; Thomas Garnet Henry James, *Howard Carter: The Path to Tutankhamun* (London: Kegan Paul International, 1992); Nicholas Reeves and John H. Taylor, *Howard Carter Before Tutankhamun* (London: British Museum Press, 1992); Harry Burton, *The Discovery of Tutankhamun's Tomb* (New York: The Metropolitan Museum of Art, 1977); Sir Arthur Hardinge, *The Life of Henry Howard Molyneux Herbert, Fourth Earl of Carnarvon* (London: Oxford; three volumes, 1925); Carter's descriptions of the finding of Tut's tomb can be found in Carter, *The Tomb of Tut-ankh-amen: Discovered by the late Earl of Carnarvon and Howard Carter* (London: Cassell, 1923–33), 1: xii–xiii, as well as in the report, "Sarcophagus of Pharaoh Found in Inner Chamber," *New York Herald-Tribune* (European Edition), February 17, 1923, p. 1; Arnold C. Brackman, *The Search for the Gold of Tutankhamen* (New York: Mason/Charter, 1976), 172; "Obituary: Mr. Howard Carter," *The Times* (London), March 3, 1939, p. 16.

cartoons, strip and moving

Forms of journalistic communication and entertainment that gained mass appeal in the United States during the interwar period. Although the earliest political cartoons are known to have appeared in 16th-century Germany during the Reformation, the editorial cartoon was popularized by journalists in 18th-century England and widely used in the American press by the mid-19th century. The printed comic strip, a humorous narrative applied to series of cartoons, was developed in the late 19th century as a commercial art form. One of the earliest popular strips was Rudolph Dirks's *The Katzenjammer Kids*, which appeared in the *New York Sunday Journal* in December 1897. By the interwar period editorial, political, and humorous cartoons had become regular syndicated features in newspapers, often used to boost circulation or to represent (or to sway) popular political opinion.

In the 1920s the "funnies" became a favorite entertainment source, and such humorous strips as *Barney Google, Bringing up Father, Gasoline Alley, Little Orphan Annie,* and *Winnie Winkle* appeared, drawn by such cartoonists as Harold Gray, Cliff Sterrett, Frank King, Martin Bannerman, and C. W. Kahles, among others. Illustrator John Held became known in the 1920s for his cultural cartoons of FLAPPERS with bobbed hair and short skirts that appeared on the covers of such magazines as *The New Yorker, Vanity Fair,* and *Harper's Bazaar.* In 1929, Burn Hogarth originated the *Tarzan* strip, based on Edgar Rice BURROUGHS's widely read novels. In the 1930s the influential comic artist Alex Raymond introduced the popular *Jungle Jim* and *Flash Gordon.* Chick Young's still popular *Blondie,* Al Capp's satirical *Li'l Abner,* and Chester Gould's detective strip *Dick Tracy* were also syndicated in many newspapers. Other strips developed into ongoing adventure tales (primarily those of superheroes), told through the episodic publication of comic books.

The moving or animated cartoon was first produced by Winsor McKay in 1909 with his *Gertie the Dinosaur,* which thrilled those who saw it. After that advance, Max Fleischer and Walt DISNEY dominated the scene for the next decade with the development of a series of short animated cartoons that were shown in theaters before feature films. Fleischer himself appeared in his *Out of the Inkwell* shorts with his drawing board while his drawings of the clown Koko came to animated life. Fleischer also created Betty Boop, the adorable infant Billy Boop, and Bimbo the Cat. Disney began with a series of shorts entitled *Alice in Cartoonland,* which combined the movements of a live actress with an animated one. The first speaking cartoon with synchronized sound was Disney's *Steamboat Willie* (1928), debuting the enduring character of Mickey Mouse. Disney's work culminated with the production of *Snow White and the Seven Dwarfs* (1938), the first full-length animated feature film.

References: Danny Peary and Gerald Peary, *The American Animated Cartoon: A Critical Anthology* (New York: Dutton, 1980); Danny Peary and Gerald Peary, *Anything Can Happen in a Comic Strip: Centennial Reflections on an American Art Form* (Columbus, Ohio: Ohio State University Libraries, 1995); John Geipel, *The Cartoon: A Short History of Graphic Comedy and Satire* (South Brunswick, N.J.: A.S. Barnes, 1972). Leonard Maltin, *The Disney Films* (New York: Crown, 1984), 307–14.

Cary, Joyce (1888–1957)

British novelist whose works during the 1930s explored English social change and drew on his experiences in Africa. Born Arthur Joyce Lunel Cary in Londonderry, Ireland, on December 7, 1888, Cary studied art in Edinburgh, Scotland, then went to Trinity College, Oxford, from which he graduated in 1912. That year, he went to the Balkans, where he joined a unit of Montenegrin soldiers and saw action in the Balkan Wars (1912–13). After joining the British Red Cross and then the Nigerian Political Service, a civil service corps, he went to Nigeria and was wounded in Cameroon during World War I. Cary attempted to return to Africa, but continued poor health forced him to retire in 1920.

He melded his experiences in Africa with his love of the continent's peoples and cultures in his writings, the first of which was published in 1932 as *Aissa Saved.* The tale of an African girl who is converted to Christianity but still retains portions of her original faith became Cary's most famous. He followed it up with three additional works: *An American Visitor* (1933), *The African Witch* (1936), and *Mister Johnson* (1939). His last interwar work was *Castle Corner* (1938). He died on March 29, 1957.

References: Alan Bishop, *Gentleman Rider: A Life of Joyce Cary* (London: M. Joseph, 1988); Robert Bloom, *The Indeterminate World: A Study of the Novels of Joyce Cary* (Philadelphia: University of Pennsylvania Press, 1962); Douglas Stewart, *The Ark of God: Studies in Five Modern Novelists* (London: Carey Kingsgate, 1961).

Cassel, Gustav (1866–1945)

Swedish economist. Born Karl Gustav Cassel in Stockholm on October 20, 1866, Cassel graduated from Uppsala University in 1895 and became a professor of political economy and financial science at Stockholm University.

Following World War I, Cassell became one of the world's leading economists due to his ideas on how to expand the postwar economies of both the victorious Allied nations and the defeated countries that had sided with Germany. His numerous lectures and papers, including his 1920 discourse entitled "The World's Monetary Problems," led the League of Nations to solicit his opinions on currency matters. He served as Sweden's representative at the International Chamber of Commerce meeting in London in 1921, and at the GENOA CONFERENCE in 1922. In that year he received the gold medal of the Royal Swedish Academy of Science, and four years later he became the Academy's president. In 1931, he advised the Swedish Riksbank on how to end the GREAT DEPRESSION. Cassel died in Stockholm on January 14, 1945. His works included *Fundamental Thoughts in Economics* (1925) and *The Crisis in the World's Monetary System* (1932).

References: Benny Carlson, *Staten Som Monster* (*The State as a Monster*): *Gustav Cassel and Eli Heckscher on the Role and Growth of the State* (Lanham, Md.: University Press of America, 1994); Gustav Cassel, "The Rate of Interest, the Bank Rate, and the Stabilization of Prices," *Quarterly Journal of Economics* 42 (1927–28): 511–29; "Cassel, Davidsson and Heckscher on Swedish Monetary Policy; A Confidential Report to the Riksbank in 1931," *Economy and History* 22 (1979): 2.

Cecil, Robert (1864–1958)

British diplomat, Nobel laureate, and First Viscount Cecil of Chelwood. The son of Robert Arthur Talbot Cecil and Georgiana (Alderson) Cecil, he was born in London on September 14, 1864, and attended Oxford University, where he studied law and earned his degree in 1884. After some years as an attorney, he was elected to Parliament in 1906 and served until 1923. During World War I, he was the assistant secretary of state for foreign affairs from 1918–19. After the war Cecil participated in drafting the LEAGUE OF NATIONS Covenant and wholly devoted his career to League affairs, acting as League president from 1923–45. For his work, he was awarded the Nobel Prize for Peace in 1937, the last such award given before the outbreak of World War II. Without doubt, Cecil was crushed as his beloved League was powerless to stop the advancing tide of war that swept the world. At the drafting of the United Nations after the war in 1946, Cecil said, "The League is dead; long live the United Nations." He died on November 24, 1958.

References: Bullitt Lowry, "Cecil, Edgar Algernon Robert Gascoyne, Sir" in Bernard S. and June H. Schlessinger, eds., *The Who's Who of Nobel Prize Winners* (Phoenix, Ariz.: Oryx, 1986), 137; J. A. Thompson, "Cecil, Edgar Algernon Robert Gascoyne" in Warren F. Kuehl, ed., *Biographical Dictionary of Internationalists* (Westport, Conn.: Greenwood, 1983), 147–49; Tyler Wasson, ed., *Nobel Prize Winners: An H. W. Wilson Biographical Dictionary* (New York: H. W. Wilson, 1987), 188–90; Richard Lamb, *The Drift to War, 1922–1939* (New York: St. Martin's, 1989).

Chaco Boundary War

Conflict, 1932–35, between Bolivia and Paraguay over the region known as the Chaco Boreal. Also known as the Gran Chaco or El Chaco the Chaco Boreal is an area of approximately 250,000 square miles, located north of the Pilcomayo River, which had variously been under the administrative control of Charcas (the former name of Bolivia) and Paraguay. Following Bolivia's loss of territory to Chile in the so-called War of the Pacific (1879–83) and Paraguay's territorial dispossession in the Paraguayan War of 1864–70, the Chaco Boreal became an important outlet to the sea for both nations. By 1932, Paraguay had for several decades owned the Chaco, although except for allowing some Mennonite colonies to thrive there and leaving a few nomadic Indian tribes to their own devices, it had done little to utilize the area's resources. Bolivia wanted the region to be able to open a sea-water port at the Rio Paraguay River and—with the discovery of the Chaco's oil reserves by the Standard Oil Company in the 1920s—to exploit this rich resource. Instability in the Paraguayan government during the first two decades of the 20th century allowed Bolivia to construct a number of well-armed forts inside the Chaco. A border incident erupted in 1929, but military action was put off until 1932.

When war did come, Bolivia, because of its fort construction, was far more prepared to fight a war of attrition than Paraguay. Yet by 1935, a severe drain of troops—the conflict had killed an estimated 1 million on both sides—hurt Bolivia more severely, and Paraguay gained in the region. From the outset, the LEAGUE OF NATIONS had attempted to intervene, as had several Pan-American conferences, all to no avail. Substantial negotiations were started under the auspices of Argentine foreign minister Carlos SAAVEDRA LAMAS, who was awarded the 1935 Nobel Peace Prize for his work in ending the conflict. Finally, at Buenos Aires on June 14, 1935, a truce was declared; a treaty formally ending the war was signed on July 21, 1938, by the two warring nations, Argentina, Brazil, Chile, Peru, Uruguay, and the United States. Under the pact, Paraguay received roughly three-quarters of the area and Bolivia was awarded the oil-producing strip, as well as access to the seaport of Puerto Casado, which was linked to Bolivia by a land route opened to it through Paraguayan territory.

References: Dennis M. Hanratty, and Sandra W. Meditz, eds., *Paraguay: A Country Study* (Washington, D.C.: Government Printing Office, 1990), 35–36; John Hoyt Williams, "Chaco War" in Helen Delpar, ed., *Encyclopedia of Latin America* (New York: McGraw-Hill, 1974), 130–31; "Roosevelt Agrees to Serve as Chaco Dispute Arbitrator," *Washington Post*, July 13, 1938, p. 2.

Chadwick, James (1891–1974)

English physicist and Nobel laureate, discovered the neutron. Born in Manchester, England, on October 20, 1891, he received his master's degree in science from Victoria University in Manchester, and an additional degree from the Honours School of Physics in 1911. Chadwick then worked in the Physical Laboratory in Manchester under the tutelage of Nobel laureate Ernest Rutherford, where he studied radioactivity. In 1913, he was awarded the 1851 Exhibition Scholarship and was sent to Berlin, where he worked at the Physikalisch Technische Reichsanstalt at Charlottenburg under physicist Hans Geiger. At the outbreak of World War I, Chadwick was interned by the Germans at Ruhleben, where he spent the entire war. He returned to England after the war to work with Rutherford at the Cavendish Laboratory at Cambridge University, where Chadwick was awarded his doctorate in 1921.

Rutherford and Chadwick worked on the disintegration of atoms by bombarding nitrogen with alpha particles in what was then the first test of nuclear fission. Chadwick became a lecturer and assistant director of radioactive research at Cavendish. In 1932, he bombarded beryllium with alpha particles and discovered one of the fundamental pieces of atomic theory: the neutron. For this discovery, Chadwick was awarded the Hughes Medal of the Royal Society that year. He was also awarded the 1935 Nobel Prize in physics.

In 1935, Chadwick was named the Lyon Jones Professor of Physics at the University of Liverpool. During World War II, he directed British research on atomic weaponry, and for a time worked on the American Manhattan Project at Los Alamos, New Mexico. In 1945, for his lifelong work, Chadwick was knighted. He died in Cambridge on July 24, 1974.

References: Sarah H. Spurgin, "Chadwick, James, Sir" in Bernard S. and June H. Schlessinger, eds., *The Who's Who of Nobel Prize Winners* (Phoenix, Ariz.: Oryx, 1986), 162.

Chamberlain, Austen (1863–1937)

British politician, diplomat, and Nobel laureate. Born in Birmingham, England, on October 16, 1863, he was the son of Joseph Chamberlain, who was a member of Parliament from 1876 until 1906, and a half-brother of Neville CHAMBERLAIN. He attended Cambridge University, graduating in 1885. He served for a few years as his father's personal secretary; then, in 1892, he was elected to Parliament from East Worcestershire. When his father died in 1914, he became a member from West Birmingham, a seat he held until his death.

In 1895, Chamberlain was named as civil lord of admiralty; from 1900 to 1902 he served as financial secretary to the treasury (1900–1902), as postmaster general (1902–3), and as chancellor of the exchequer (1903–6). During the coalition government with the Unionists formed by then prime minister Herbert Asquith in 1915, Chamberlain served as Secretary of State for India. He resigned in 1917, but a year later accepted the position as chancellor of the exchequer in the coalition government of the new prime minister, David LLOYD GEORGE. When Andrew Bonar LAW retired from the leadership of the Conservative Party in 1921, Chamberlain succeeded him. In the government of Prime Minister Stanley BALDWIN in 1924, Chamberlain was named foreign minister. Perhaps his most important contribution in this position was his work with German foreign minister Gustav STRESEMANN and French foreign minister Aristide BRIAND to secure passage of the LOCARNO PACT, which secured the borders of Europe after the end of World War I in an attempt to end the possibility of future war. For this, Chamberlain was the corecipient (with Charles G. DAWES) of the Nobel Prize for Peace in 1925.

Chamberlain served as foreign minister until 1929, when he retired. He died in London on March 16, 1937. His published works include *The League of Nations* (1926), *Peace in Our Time: Addresses on Europe and the Empire* (1928), *Down the Years* (1935), and *Politics from Inside: An Epistolary Chronicle, 1906–1914* (1936).

References: Frank L. Turner, "Chamberlain, Joseph Austen, Sir" in Bernard S. and June H. Schlessinger, eds., *The Who's Who of Nobel Prize Winners* (Phoenix, Ariz.: Oryx, 1986), 132–33; Charles Petrie, "Chamberlain, Sir (Joseph) Austen" in Sir Leslie Stephen and Sir Sidney Lee et al., eds., *The Dictionary of National Biography* (Oxford, England: Oxford University Press, 1917–1993), 4: 163–68; Irwin Abrams, *The Nobel Peace Prize and the Laureates: An Illustrated Biographical History, 1901–1987* (Boston: G. K. Hall, 1988), 103; Thomas Watson MacCallum and Stephen Taylor, eds., *The Nobel Prize–Winners and the Nobel Foundation, 1901–1937* (Zurich, Switzerland: Central European Times Publishing, 1938), 364–65; Richard Lamb, *The Drift to War, 1922–1939* (New York: St. Martin's, 1989); Gordon A. Craig, "The British Foreign Office from Grey to Austen Chamberlain" in Gordon A. Craig and Felix Gilbert, eds., *The Diplomats, 1919–1939* (Princeton, N.J.: Princeton University Press, 1994), 15–48.

Chamberlain, Neville (1869–1940)

British politician and diplomat, known for his attempt as prime minister to stave off war in Europe by appeasing Adolf HITLER with the Czech Sudetenland. The youngest son of politician and reformer Joseph Chamberlain and his second wife, Florence (Kenrick) Chamberlain, and the half-brother of Austen CHAMBERLAIN, Neville Chamberlain was born in Edgbaston, Birmingham, on March 18, 1869. He attended Mason College (now the University of Birmingham), and worked as an accountant after graduation. In 1890 his father purchased an island in the Bahamas and sent Neville there to raise sisal. Neville spent seven years trying to raise the crop, but the soil was too thin and the enterprise failed. He returned to Birmingham in 1897 to enter business, and gradually achieved financial success.

In 1911 Chamberlain entered the political arena when he was elected to the Birmingham City Council. In 1915, he was named Lord Mayor of Birmingham. In 1918 he was elected to Parliament, as a Coalition Conservative for the district of Birmingham.

Four years later Chamberlain supported Prime Minister Andrew Bonar LAW's withdrawal from the coalition government, and for his support Chamberlain was named postmaster-general in the new cabinet. In 1923 he was named minister of health and was promoted to chancellor of the exchequer. But that November the Labour Party won the national elections, James Ramsey MACDONALD was named prime minister, and Chamberlain returned to his seat in Parliament. In October 1924, when Stanley BALDWIN once again became prime minister, he named Chamberlain as his minister of health.

In 1929, MacDonald and the Labour Party were returned to office, and Chamberlain again returned to his seat as an opposition member of Parliament. Named Conservative Party chair in June 1930, he became in effect the number two person in the party behind Baldwin. In 1931, when the Labour government collapsed, the three main parties (Labour, Conservative, and Liberal) all agreed to a national government headed by MacDonald, who named Chamberlain his chancellor of the exchequer. Chamberlain served in this position for the next five and half years. During this period, he attempted to solve the worsening economic situation that was then gripping the world. He attended a monetary conference in Lausanne, Switzerland, in June 1932, where the question of German reparations was discussed. In 1935, the Conservatives won a majority in Parliament, and Baldwin once again became prime minister. However, within two years, he was beset by major domestic and international problems, including growing militarism by Germany and the abdication of King EDWARD VIII. On May 28, 1937, he retired, naming Chamberlain as his successor.

Almost from the start, Chamberlain seemed more willing to use APPEASEMENT in his dealings with Germany and Italy than to negotiate from a position of power. On February 20, 1938, Foreign Secretary Anthony EDEN resigned, citing his opposition to Chamberlain's attempts to negotiate with Italian leader Benito MUSSOLINI. Chamberlain replaced Eden with Edward Wood, Lord Halifax. Even after Hitler's Germany invaded Austria on March 12, 1938, Chamberlain continued talks with Italy; the result was the Anglo-Italian Agreement, signed in Rome on April 16, 1938, in which Great Britain agreed not to challenge Italian gains in Ethiopia.

On September 15, 1938, Chamberlain met with Hitler at the German leader's residence at Berchtesgaden, in Bavaria. While these talks were initially unsuccessful (they resumed at the German village of Godesberg on September 22, and on September 29 in Munich), after Mussolini and French premier Édouard DALADIER were included, Chamberlain agreed to allow Hitler to occupy the Sudetenland, the German-speaking area of Czechoslovakia. Believing that he had staved off war in Europe, Chamberlain returned to England and proclaimed his deal with the German leader. In a speech from the prime minister's residence at 10 Downing Street, he said on radio, "This is the second time in our history that there has come back from Germany to Downing Street peace with honour. I believe it is peace for our time."

Emboldened by his perception that France and England were eager to avoid another war on the European continent at any cost, however, Hitler decided to push for more land after he had promised not to. On March 10, 1939, German tanks rolled into the remainder of Czechoslovakia, and Chamberlain realized that he had been duped. After being pushed into action by numerous members of his government, he signed a treaty of alliance with France, claiming that if Poland, Romania, or Greece were invaded, Britain would come to their rescue. When Germany attacked Poland on September 1, 1939, Chamberlain's government declared war.

Within a year, the failure of the British army against Germany caused a weakening in Chamberlain's support in Parliament among his fellow Conservatives. On May 10, 1940, after a vote of no confidence was taken, he resigned, taking the seat of Lord President in the cabinet of Winston Churchill. On September 30, 1940, however, Chamberlain resigned due to ill health. He was, in fact, close to death. Retiring to his home at Highfield Park, near Reading, he died on November 9, 1940.

See also MUNICH CRISIS; MUNICH PACT.

References: Sir Keith Grahame Feiling, *The Life of Neville Chamberlain* (London: Macmillan, 1946); Justus D. Doenecke, "Neville Chamberlain" in Anne Commire, ed., *Historic World Leaders* (Detroit: Gale Research, 1994), 2: 195–200; W. W. Hadley, "Chamberlain, (Arthur) Neville" in Sir Leslie Stephen and Sir Sidney Lee et al., eds., *The Dictionary of National Biography* (Oxford, England: Oxford University Press, 1917–1993), 4: 155–63; Helen Holden, "Neville Chamberlain" in Dermot Englefield, Janet Seaton, and Isobel White, *Facts about the British Prime Ministers: A Compilation of Biographical and Historical Information* (New York: H. W. Wilson, 1995), 270–75; Bernard V. Burke, "Chamberlain, Arthur Neville" in Bruce W. Jentleson and Thomas G. Paterson, senior eds., *Encyclopedia of U.S. Foreign Relations* (New York: Oxford University Press, 1997), 1: 235; "Mr. Chamberlain. Death on Saturday Evening. A Peaceful End," *The Times* (London), November 11, 1940, p. 4.

Chanel, Coco (1883–1971)

French fashion and perfume magnate. Born Gabrielle Bonheur Chanel in the Auvergne region of France on (or about) August 19, 1883, Chanel's mother died of tuberculosis when she was six and her father then abandoned her and her three sisters. Gabrielle grew up with her two aunts. She opened a millinery shop in Deauville in 1913, where she began to build what eventually became an empire. Selling sweaters and hats, Chanel became a noted and innovative fashion leader by the end of World War I, admired for her modern and elegant fashions. A *Vogue* magazine article in 1917 cemented her position as a leading style-setter. In 1921, she released a perfume called Chanel No. 5 (her favorite number) which became the first fragrance to be commercially successful. During the 1920s, Chanel designed costumes for film director Jean Renoir, artist Jean COCTEAU, and dance impresario Serge Diaghilev, and established Parfums Chanel in 1924. In the 1930s, she solidified her reputation as a couturier designing costumes for Renoir's film *La Marseillaise* and for Spanish painter Salvador Dalí's *Baccanale* by the Ballets Russes. She embodied the Parisian art and culture scene just before the start of World War II.

When the war broke out, Chanel closed her couture house. After the war, she returned to her business, soon introducing a new style of women's clothing based on casual elegance that once again made her the leader in women's fashion. On January 10, 1971, Chanel died at her apartment in the Ritz Hotel in Paris. A businesswoman with a magical grasp of the future of fashion and culture, she remains an admired figure.

References: Edmonde Charles-Roux, *Chanel and Her World* (New York: Vendome, 1979); Alex Madsen, *Chanel: A Woman of Her Own* (New York: Henry Holt and Co., 1990); "Chanel, the Couturier, Dead in Paris," *New York Times*, January 11, 1971, p. 1.

Chaney, Lon (1883–1930)

American silent film actor, whose classic roles in such films as *The Hunchback of Notre Dame* (1923) and *The Phantom of the Opera* (1927) are considered masterpieces of the interwar era. Born Alonso Chaney on April 1, 1883, in Colorado Springs, Colorado, he was the son of deaf parents, from whom he learned through sign language and facial expressions the fine art of pantomime, which he later used in his numerous acting roles. He attended school only until the fifth grade, then left to become a tour guide on Colorado's Pike's Peak. Later, he worked at the opera house in Colorado Springs. With his older brother, John, a theater owner, he cowrote a script for a play entitled *The Little Tycoon*, in which he starred in his stage debut. His lack of success on the stage pushed Chaney in 1912 to go to California, and try to break in to the new entertainment medium of motion pictures.

From 1913 (when he starred in *The Trap*) until his death in 1930, Chaney starred in more than 150 shorts and features that range from the strange to the macabre. His first acting role, although uncredited, was in 1912's *Poor Jake's Demise*. He also directed six films for Universal Studios in 1915. In almost all of his performances he exhibited such talent that even today he is considered one of the finest actors ever to grace the screen. His work in 1919's *The Miracle Man*, of which only a few frames exist today, is considered by some film historians as one of the finest performances on film. His role in *The* HUNCHBACK OF NOTRE DAME (1923) is also considered some of the greatest acting in motion picture history. In the film, he wore a painful 40-pound rubber device to create the illusion of a hump on his back. His offering in the 1925 thriller *The Phantom of the Opera* is also stirring. Chaney also made famous his roles in such films as *Road to Mandalay* (1926), *Mr. Wu* (1927), and *Laugh, Clown, Laugh* (1928). In 1925, he starred in MGM's *The Unholy Three*. Acting as the ventriloquist Echo, Chaney's performance earned the film a rating as one of the *New York Times* "Top 25" of that year. The film was so well received that it was remade five years later, Chaney's first and only talking picture. The remake was the start of Chaney's second career, his transformation from a silent to a talking star. Yet a month later, Chaney died of bronchial cancer.

Chaney's life story was told in *Man of a Thousand Faces* (1957). His son, Lon Chaney Jr., also made his name in several film horror roles.

References: Ephraim Katz, *The Film Encyclopedia* (New York: HarperPerennial, 1994), 238–39; Michael F. Blake, *Lon Chaney: The Man Behind the Thousand Faces* (Vestal, N.Y.: Vestal Press, 1993); Robert Gordon Anderson, *Faces, Forms, Films: The Artistry of Lon Chaney* (South Brunswick, N.J.: A. S. Barnes, 1971).

Chaplin, Charlie (1889–1977)

English comedian and actor whose classic character "the tramp" thrilled audiences of silent films for much of the interwar period. Born Charles Spencer Chaplin on April 16, 1889, in a poor section of London, he was the son of an English vaudeville actor. In 1910, Chaplin left for the United States, where he became a leading actor in Fred Karno's vaudeville troupe, which ran shows across the nation. In November 1913 he was in California, where at that time a growing cadre of small studios were producing short silent films of varying quality. Chaplin joined Mack Sennett, producer of the famed Keystone Kops films. His first film with Sennett, *Making a Living* (1913), was a disappointment, but after a series of other films Chaplin honed his part as an evil character in *Tillie's Punctured Romance* (1914) opposite Mabel Normand and Marie DRESSLER. His breakout role came in *Kid Auto Races at Venice* (1914), in which, donning baggy pants and the strange mustache, he first defined his persona as "the tramp."

In 1915, Chaplin signed with the Essanay Film Company and produced a series of films, including *The Tramp*, that made him a screen star. Film historian Ephraim Katz wrote, "The Essanay period saw the full bloom of Charlie's screen character, the invincible vagabond, the resilient little fellow with an eye for beauty and a pretense of elegance who stood up heroically and pathetically against overwhelming odds and somehow triumphed." In 1916 Chaplin moved to the Mutual Film Company, where he starred in such early classics as *The Rink* (1916), *Easy Street* (1917), *The Cure* (1917), and *The Adventurer* (1917). He moved to the First National Film Company in 1918, starring in the war parody *Shoulder Arms* (1918) before he headlined in *The Kid* (1921) with Jackie Coogan playing his innocent son. *The Kid* came in second only to *Birth of a Nation* at the box office. In 1919, Chaplin founded, with Mary Pickford, D. W. Griffith, and Douglas FAIRBANKS, the United Artists corporation to produce original motion pictures.

After a period in Europe, Chaplin returned to the United States to star in *The Gold Rush* (1925), considered by many film historians to be his finest performance ever. And although the advent of sound in motion pictures seemed to put an end to the silent film era, Chaplin adapted to the new technology and starred and directed CITY LIGHTS (1931), in which he was cast as a downtrodden figure, forever capturing Chaplin's sad-sack image. Convinced that silent films would survive, he plunged ahead with another success: *Modern Times* (1936), a satirical look at modern technology and society's adaptation to it. In 1940, as war spread across Europe, Chaplin directed and starred in his most criticized work: *The Great Dictator,* in which he played the dual roles of a Jewish barber and Adenoid Hynkel, the strange dictator of "Tomania," in what was an obvious slap at Adolf HITLER. Audiences did not understand the film, however, and it was a box-office disappointment.

A pacifist with strong leftist leanings, Chaplin's ideology came to the fore in his films and his private life during the postwar years, leading to a loss in popularity and his self-imposed exile to Switzerland in 1952.

In 1972, he was coaxed back to the United States for what became his last trip there to accept a special Academy Award for "the incalculable effect he has had on making motion pictures the art form of the century." Three years later, he was knighted by Queen Elizabeth II of Great Britain, and spent his remaining years as "Sir Charles," Chaplin died on December 25, 1977, at his home in Switzerland.

Chaplin's image on the screen in his 80 or more films continues to fascinate and captivate many. His acting, a kind of pantomime that few if any have mastered, is perhaps one of the greatest legacies of film.

References: Ephraim Katz, *The Film Encyclopedia* (New York: HarperPerennial, 1994), 240–41; Harry M. Geduld, *Chapliniana: A Commentary on Charlie Chaplin's 81 Movies* (Bloomington: Indiana University Press, 1987); "Chaplin Film Pandemonium; Stars Mobbed at Broadway Premiere," *Daily Telegraph* (London), February 7, 1936, p. 10; Raoul Sobel and David Francis, *Chaplin: Genesis of a Clown* (London: Quartet Books, 1977); "Charlie Chaplin Dead at 88; Made the Film an Art Form," *New York Times,* December 26, 1977, p. 1; Alden Whitman, "Chaplin's Little Tramp, an Everyman Trying to Gild Cage of Life, Enthralled World," *New York Times,* December 26, 1977, p. 28.

Chauri Chaura affair

Demonstration, February 4, 1922, in which nationalists agitating for Indian independence murdered 23 local police officers. Little is written in Indian history of this event; it is surmised to have been a response to Mohandas K. GANDHI's call for noncooperation with the British authorities in India, a program called *asahyog.* The riot took place in the district of Gorakhpur, in the province of Uttar Pradesh, when a crowd assembled to protest the sale of British items by vendors in the area. The protest was covered by a number of *chaukidars,* or rural police. A confrontation developed, and one of the officers fired into the

Charlie Chaplin as the "little tramp" *(CORBIS/Bettmann)*

air. A riot started, and three demonstrators were killed. Nationalists then rushed the police station in Chauri Chaura, forcing the small number of officers to retreat into the station. The crowd locked them inside and doused the building with kerosene, burning to death all 23 men inside. When Gandhi learned that members of the Nationalist Party were responsible for the incident, he called off the movement.

References: Shahid Amin, *Event, Metaphor, Memory: Chauri Chaura, 1922–1992* (Berkeley: University of California Press, 1995); Francis Watson, *The Trial of Mr. Gandhi* (London: Macmillan, 1969), 49.

Chesterton, G. K. (Gilbert Keith)   *See* MENCKEN, H. L.

Chiang Kai-shek   (1887–1975)

Chinese general and politician, last leader of a noncommunist China (1927–1949) and leader of the Chinese Nationalists on Taiwan (Formosa) until his death. Born in Fenghwa, in Chekiang Province, China, on October 31, 1887, he received his military training at Paoting and at the Tokyo Military College. While in Tokyo, he met and befriended Sun Yat-sen, and upon his return joined the Chinese People's Party (the Nationalists), also known as the Kuomintang. Chiang was a leader in the revolution of 1911 in which Sun and his followers overthrew the old Chinese dynastic order and established the Chinese Republic. Chiang fought at Sun's side until 1916, when the civil wars subsided, after which Chiang went into private business.

In 1923 Chiang visited Soviet Russia to study military methodology. As commander, he developed the Kuomintang army from 1923 to 1925, and upon Sun's death in 1925 he took over. His first move was to purge all of the communists from the ranks of the military. While in Russia, Chiang had seen the Soviet system as a threat to China, and now he intended to stop it at all costs. Chiang's purge began a long period of civil strife, and the leading communist, MAO TSE-TUNG, started a new government in Wuhan. Chiang set up an alternate government in Nanking. In the first few months, he dealt with an abortive uprising in Canton, and he resigned. The following year, however, he was called back into service, marching northward to take over the ancient Chinese capital of Peking. Serving as head of the Chinese Nationalist government from 1928 to 1931, Chiang tried to stabilize the regime. He resigned in favor of Lin Sen, but was reappointed in 1932 to conduct an all-out war against Mao and the communists. His war against the Reds led to the LONG MARCH of Mao's forces from 1934 to 1936 to escape their destruction. In 1936 disaffection among the northern armies on Chiang's side led to his kidnapping by General Chang Hsueh-liang (Chiang was held prisoner for two weeks).

The outbreak of the SINO-JAPANESE WAR in 1937 caused Chiang to broker a peace with Mao in an effort to present a united front against the Japanese invaders. During World War II, Chiang was an integral leader in the Allied attack. Again president of the Nationalist government, he met with U.S. president Franklin D. ROOSEVELT and British prime minister Winston Churchill at Cairo in 1943. His strategy of keeping the Japanese bogged down in China worked, and helped to draw off troops and supplies needed elsewhere.

With the end of the war in 1945, however, Chiang returned to Nanking with the expressed intent of destroying the communists once and for all. But the communists had spent the war building themselves into a massive fighting force. City after city was forfeited by the Nationalists, until on January 21, 1949, Chiang fled to the island of Taiwan, where he resumed his presidency and established the Republic of China as a last bastion against the communist Chinese. Chiang served as president of Taiwan until his death on April 6, 1975.

References: Justus D. Doenecke, "Chiang Kai-Shek" in Anne Commire, ed., *Historic World Leaders* (Detroit: Gale Research, 1994), 1: 90–96; "Chiang Kai-shek" in Howard L. Boorman, ed., *Biographical Dictionary of Republican China* (New York: Columbia University Press, 1967–79), 1: 319–38; "Chiang Kai-shek Is Dead in Taipei at 87; Last of Big Four of World War II," *New York Times,* April 6, 1975, pp. 1, 47.

Child Labor Act

U.S. congressional legislation, enacted February 24, 1919, which in effect prohibited all workers under the age of 14. In 1916, the U.S. Congress passed the Keating-Owen Act, banning child labor; however, in 1918, in *Hammer v. Dagenhart et al.,* the U.S. Supreme Court struck the act down as an unconstitutional burden on interstate commerce. The Congress then attempted to tax such labor until it became prohibitively expensive to use it, thus making child labor illegal through a back door. The product of this effort, the Child Labor Act, was enacted as part of "an Act to provide revenue and for other purposes." The relevant portion of the act reads:

> Every person (other than a bona fide boys' or girls' canning club recognized by the Agricultural Department of a State and of the United States) operating (a) any mine or quarry situated in the United States in which children under the age of sixteen years have been employed or permitted to work during any portion of the taxable year; or (b) any mill, cannery, workshop, factory, or manufacturing establishment situated in the United States in which children

under the age of fourteen years have been employed or permitted to work, or children between the ages of fourteen and sixteen have been employed or permitted to work more than eight hours in any day or more than six days in any week, or after the hour of seven o'clock post meridian, or before the hour of six o'clock ante meridian, during any portion of the taxable year, shall pay for each taxable year, in addition to all other taxes imposed by law, an excise tax equivalent to 10 per centum of the entire net profits or accrued for such year from the sale or disposition of the product of such mine, quarry, mill, cannery, workshop, factory, or manufacturing establishment.

The law was quickly challenged. In 1922 the Drexel Furniture Company in North Carolina sued Bailey, the collector of internal revenue for the western district of North Carolina, to strike down the law as an unconstitutional regulation of labor in the states, an action reserved for the states only and not the federal government. On May 15, the Supreme Court, in BAILEY V. DREXEL FURNITURE COMPANY, struck down the Child Labor Act. In 1924, the Congress passed a constitutional amendment to end child labor, but it did not receive enough support in the states and was never ratified. Child labor was finally barred by federal law in 1938 with the enactment of the Fair Labor Standards Act.

References: Henry Steele Commager, ed., *Documents of American History* (New York: Appleton-Century-Crofts, 1949), 332; Harold W. Chase and Craig R. Ducat, *Constitutional Interpretation: Cases-Essays-Materials* (St. Paul, Minn.: West Publishing Co., 1979), 435–36; Stanley I. Kutler, "Child Labor Amendment" in Leonard W. Levy, ed. in chief, *Encyclopedia of the American Constitution* (New York: Macmillan, 1986–92), 1: 246.

Chinese Exclusion Act   *See* IMMIGRATION ACT OF 1924.

Christie, Agatha   (1890–1976)

English writer, famed for her interwar mystery stories. Born Agatha Mary Clarissa Miller in Torquay, Devon, England, on September 15, 1890, she was educated at home by her mother. While working as a nurse during World War I, she began to compose short stories. Christie's first published work, *The Mysterious Affair at Styles* (1920), introduced the Belgian detective Hercule Poirot, for whom she became famous. She continued the line of surprising plot twists with Poirot in *The Murder of Roger Ackroyd* (1926). In 1930, Christie introduced a new character: Miss Jane Marple, the older woman who solves mysteries, in *Murder at the Vicarage*.

Christie's first marriage, to Archibald Christie, ended in divorce in 1928. While in the Middle East in 1930, she met archaeology professor Max Edgar Lucien Mallowan, and the two were married that same year. Traveling with Mallowan, Christie used the scenes in Iraq and Syria for novels, including *Murder in Mesopotamia* (1930), *Murder on the Orient Express* (1934), *Death on the Nile* (1937), and *Appointment with Death* (1938). In all, she published more than a hundred works, including six books under the pen name of Mary Westmacott, and 14 plays. Her repeated use of characters such as Poirot and Marple made her a beloved and entertaining author.

In 1971 Christie was made a Dame Commander of the Order of the British Empire. She died on January 12, 1976, in Wallingford, Oxfordshire. In an obituary, Max Lowenthal noted, "The sheer volume of Dame Agatha's writing since 1920 . . . was enough to stagger even the most incurable addict of detective fiction."

References: Janet P. Morgan, *Agatha Christie: A Biography* (New York: Knopf, 1985); Henry Reymond Fitzwalter, ed., *Agatha Christie: First Lady of Crime* (New York: Holt, Rinehart & Winston, 1977); Dawn B. Sova, *Agatha Christie A to Z: The Essential Reference to Her Life and Writings* (New York: Facts On File, 1996); Max Lowenthal, "Agatha Christie, Creator of Poirot, Dies," *New York Times,* January 13, 1976, pp. 1, 40.

Ciano, Galeazzo   (1903–1944)

Italian politician. Ciano was born in Livorno, Italy, on March 18, 1903. He marched with his father in Benito MUSSOLINI's March on Rome in 1922, then studied law at the University of Rome before beginning a career as a journalist. In 1925, however, he joined the Italian diplomatic corps, seeing service at Rio de Janeiro, Buenos Aires, and at the Vatican. In 1930, he married Edda, Mussolini's eldest daughter.

Now a part of the Fascist dictator's family, Ciano was named consul general in Shanghai, rising to become the Italian Minister to China. In 1933, he returned to Italy, and in 1934 was named Minister of Press and Propaganda in his father-in-law's government. An aviator, he commanded several bombing missions during the Italian invasion of Ethiopia from 1935 to 1936. That June, at age 33, he was named Mussolini's foreign minister, even though he lacked the experience and the credentials such an office required—especially during a time when Italy was melding its interests with Nazi Germany in a power grab across Europe that would eventually erupt into world war. Ciano was not a friend of Germany, however, and relations between him and German foreign minister Joachim von RIBBENTROP went from a lack of cordiality to a refusal to speak together. After the German ANSCHLUSS of Austria in March 1938, Ciano warned Mussolini of the danger

Germany was posing to both Italy and itself, but he was ignored. Mussolini signed the Tripartite Treaty in May 1939, assuring Italy's cooperation with the foreign policy interests of Germany and Japan.

With the start of World War II in Europe in September 1939, Ciano began a secret diary in which he detailed his attempts to convince Mussolini that Germany and Japan were leading the world toward war, and the humiliation Ciano felt at being left out of the negotiations that were sealing his nation's fate. His repeated attempts to persuade Mussolini led to his removal as foreign minister on February 5, 1943, when he was given the now-token position as Italian ambassador to the Vatican. There, however, he secretly joined with dissidents within Mussolini's Fascist Grand Council who were pushing for Mussolini's removal from power. Captured by the Germans, Ciano was delivered into the hands of Fascists loyal to Mussolini at Verona, where he was tried for treason, found guilty, and executed by firing squad on January 11, 1944.

References: Marcia F. Lavine, "Ciano, Galeazzo" in Frank J. Coppa, ed. in chief, *Dictionary of Modern Italian History* (Westport, Conn.: Greenwood, 1985), 81–82; Howard McGaw Smyth, *Secrets of the Fascist Era: How Uncle Sam Obtained Some of the Top-Level Documents of Mussolini's Period* (Carbondale: Southern Illinois University Press, 1975); Malcolm Muggeridge, ed., *Ciano's Diary, 1939–1943* (London: Heinemann, 1948).

City Lights

1931 film, considered one of the classics of all time, starring Charlie CHAPLIN. In this love story, "the tramp," played by Chaplin, falls in love with a beautiful blind woman (Virginia Cherill), and helps her to raise money for an operation to cure her blindness. In the end, her sight is restored, but Chaplin has by then become a worthless tramp again and she does not recognize him when she sees him in front of her flower stand. In the final scene of the film, conceived on the spot by Chaplin, the woman realizes that Chaplin, whom she had been laughing at moments before, is in fact the man who helped her regain her sight. Although it was filmed four years after the advent of sound pictures, Chaplin did *City Lights* as silent in tribute to that medium. The film was a success.

References: Gerard Molyneaux, *Charles Chaplin's City Lights: Its Production and Dialectical Structure* (New York: Garland Publishing, 1983); Leonard Maltin, ed., *Movie and Video Guide, 1996 Edition* (New York: Plume, 1995), 235.

Civil Aeronautics Act

U.S. congressional legislation, enacted on June 23, 1938, which coordinated all nonmilitary American aviation under a federal entity, the Civil Aeronautics Authority. The first Congressional action to foster and regulate U.S. air commerce was the Air Commerce Act, enacted May 20, 1926, putting the nation's fledgling airways and aircraft system under the direction of the Secretary of Commerce and the Aeronautics Branch of that department. In 1934, the branch was renamed the Bureau of Air Commerce. On August 22, 1938, President Franklin D. ROOSEVELT signed the act into law. Two years later he split the Civil Aeronautics Authority into the Civil Aeronautics Board and the Civil Aeronautics Administration.

Reference: James Stuart Olson, *Historical Dictionary of the New Deal: From Inauguration to Preparation for War* (Westport, Conn.: Greenwood, 1985), 81.

Civilian Conservation Corps

U.S. federal agency, established under the NEW DEAL of President Franklin Delano ROOSEVELT. As one of his goals for putting people back to work in the midst of the horrendous GREAT DEPRESSION, Roosevelt also conceived of the plan to help conserve the nation's natural resources, including its water, timber, and soil. He asked Congress on March 21, 1933, to establish such a program. Congress enacted the Civilian Conservation Corps (CCC), as part of the Unemployment Relief Act of March 31, 1933. Originally called "Emergency Conservation Work," the agency was first headed by labor official Robert Fechner until his death in 1939, and thereafter by James J. McEntee.

During its existence, the CCC provided for the employment of some 3 million men between the ages of 17 and 23, whose work some historians have concluded added some $1.5 billion to $2 billion of value to the national domain. The total lifetime cost of the program was approximately $3 billion. For this price tag, some 2.25 million trees were planted, 4,000 fire observation towers were constructed, 6 million erosion dams were built, and state parks were either augmented or initiated. In June 1942, the program considered to have succeeded in its aims, Congress voted to abolish it within ten months, at which time it was officially closed.

References: Mark Grossman, *The ABC-Clio Companion to the Environmental Movement* (Santa Barbara, Calif.: ABC-Clio, 1995), 50–51; John A. Salmond, *The Civilian Conservation Corps, 1933–1942: A New Deal Case Study* (Durham, N.C.: Duke University Press, 1967).

Clark Memorandum

Important diplomatic document, prepared in 1930 by U.S. Undersecretary of State J. Reuben Clark, outlining foreign policy during the interwar period. In September 1928,

President Calvin COOLIDGE instructed Secretary of State Frank Billings KELLOGG to prepare a report on the Monroe Doctrine's usefulness in current American foreign policy. Formulated in 1823 by President James Monroe, the doctrine called for the use of American military power to keep Europe out of the Western Hemisphere's affairs (in effect declaring that the American continents were no longer open for colonization by European powers). Kellogg gave the assignment to Undersecretary Clark, who delivered his memorandum on December 17 of that year. Most of the document (which was not formally published until 1930) deals with the articulation of the Monroe Doctrine and various political and diplomatic correspondence relating to it at the time it was formulated. Clark came to the conclusion that the doctrine and its Roosevelt Corollary (enunciated by President Theodore Roosevelt in 1902) did not legally allow for American intervention in hemispheric concerns.

Clark wrote, "It is not believed that this corollary is justified by the terms of the Monroe Doctrine, however much it may be justified by the application of self-preservation." And although he noted that "so far as Latin America is concerned, the doctrine is now, and always has been, not an instrument of violence and oppression, but an unbought, freely bestowed, and wholly effective guaranty of their freedom, independence, and territorial integrity against the imperialistic designs of Europe," Clark explained that a new policy, one allowing for more sovereignty for Latin American nations in regard to their own affairs, should be established by the United States. Although Kellogg and Coolidge's successor, Herbert HOOVER, did not accept Clark's recommendation, Hoover's successor, Franklin Delano ROOSEVELT, used the memorandum as the basis for his GOOD NEIGHBOR POLICY toward Latin America in the 1930s.

References: Reuben J. Clark, *Memorandum on the Monroe Doctrine, 17 December 1928* (Washington, D.C.: Government Printing Office, 1930), ix–xxv; Gaddis Smith, "Clark Memorandum" in Bruce W. Jentleson and Thomas G. Paterson, senior eds., *Encyclopedia of U.S. Foreign Relations* (New York: Oxford University Press, 1977), 1: 262; Bryce Wood, *The Making of the Good Neighbor Policy* (New York: Columbia University Press, 1961).

Clarke, John Hessin (1857–1945)

American jurist, promoter of world peace. Born in New Lisbon, Ohio, on September 18, 1857, Clarke was the son of Irish Protestants who had fled from their native land. They settled in New Lisbon in 1830, where his father became a successful attorney. Clarke received his bachelor's and master's degrees from Western Reserve College (now Western Reserve University) in Cleveland in 1877 and 1879, respectively. He read the law in his father's office, then passed the Ohio bar in 1878. Although he practiced law for a brief time with his father, he soon moved to Youngstown, where he represented corporations and the railroads.

Buying a stake in a local newspaper, the *Vindicator,* Clarke began a reform drive in the pages of the publication. Later, he moved to Cleveland, where he joined the prestigious law firm of Williamson and Cushing, continuing his representation of the nation's railroads. Although he was involved in civic affairs, for many years he turned down nominations for the U.S. Senate and governor. Later in life he ran for office: in 1903 and again in 1914, he was the unsuccessful Democratic candidate for the U.S. Senate.

Shortly after this second loss, President Woodrow WILSON named Clarke to the federal court for the northern district of Ohio. In 1916 Wilson named Clarke to the U.S. Supreme Court to replace Charles Evans HUGHES, who had resigned to run for president. In his six years on the high court, Clarke wrote several important majority opinions, most notably that in ABRAMS V. UNITED STATES (1919) as well as decisions that struck down the use of "yellow dog" contracts and monopolies.

On September 1, 1922, Clarke announced his retirement to the court, effective on his 65th birthday, September 18. He used the time to lobby for American participation in the LEAGUE OF NATIONS and for world peace. For the next several years, Clarke spoke forcefully on the issue of peace. He had written of his ideas in a 1918 article, "A Call To Service," in the *American Bar Association Journal.* In 1922, he established the League of Nations Non-Partisan Committee, a lobbying group on behalf of the League, which he headed until 1928. Although for the first years of his campaign he seemed to be gaining attention for his views, by 1928 his was a forgotten crusade. He resigned in 1928 and faded from the public eye. Clarke died in San Diego, California, on March 22, 1945.

References: Hoyt Landon Warner, *The Life of Mr. Justice Clarke: A Testament to the Power of Liberal Dissent in America* (Cleveland: Western Reserve University Press, 1959); "John Hessin Clarke" in Nancy L. Roberts, *American Peace Writers, Editors and Periodicals* (Westport, Conn.: Greenwood, 1991), 58; Clare Cushman, "John H. Clarke" in Clare Cushman, ed., *The Supreme Court Justices: Illustrated Biographies, 1789–1995* (Washington, D.C.: Congressional Quarterly, 1995), 336; Hoyt Landon Warner, "Clarke, John Hessin" in Warren F. Kuehl, ed., *Biographical Dictionary of Internationalists* (Westport, Conn.: Greenwood, 1983), 157–59; John Hessin Clarke, "A Call to Service: The Duty of the Bench and Bar to Aid in Securing a League of Nations to Enforce the Peace of the World," *ABA Journal* 4 (4) (October 1918): 567–82.

Cobb, Ty   See BASEBALL, MAJOR LEAGUE.

Cochin China   *See* HO CHI MINH.

Cocteau, Jean (1889–1963)
French writer, artist, and dramatist, recognized as the embodiment of the French artistic avant-garde during the 1920s and 1930s. Born on July 5, 1889, into a rich middle-class family in Maisons-Laffitte, near Paris, Cocteau was educated at the Lycée Condorcet. His star began to rise after World War I, when his *Le Potomak,* a medley of prose, verse, and cartoons, was published in 1919. The following year his pantomime-ballet *Le Boeuf sur le toit* was staged. One of the most versatile artists of the 20th century, he went on to write plays (*Orphée,* 1926), novels (*Les Enfants Terribles,* 1929), and poetry (*Vocabulaire,* 1922); he also painted, created ballets (*Les Biches,* 1924), and even produced and directed films (*The Blood of a Poet,* 1932). His surrealistic work was infused with personal symbolism and self-examination.

Cocteau was a member of an extraordinarily creative group of artists who gathered in Paris during the interwar period. He pursued the friendship of other artistic leaders, including the photographer Man Ray and the painter Pablo PICASSO. Cocteau also championed American JAZZ and the actor and comedian Charlie CHAPLIN. In 1955 he was admitted to the prestigious Académie Française. Cocteau died on October 11, 1963.

See also SURREALISM.

References: Wallace Fowlie, *Jean Cocteau: The History of a Poet's Age* (Bloomington: Indiana University Press, 1966); Renbe Gilson, *Jean Cocteau,* trans. Ciba Vaughan (New York: Crown, 1969); Elizabeth Sprigge and Jean-Jacques Kihm, *Jean Cocteau: The Man and the Mirror* (New York: Coward-McCann, 1968).

collective security
Policy, particularly of the United States, during the interwar period that held that the major Allies who had fought together in World War I would stand as one to prevent another world war from breaking out, using force if necessary. The LEAGUE OF NATIONS and later the United Nations were both founded on this principle. Under Article 10 of the League Covenant, "The Members of the League undertake to respect and preserve as against external aggression the territorial integrity and existing political independence of all Members of the League. In case of any such aggression or in case of any threat or danger of such aggression, the Council shall advise upon the means by which this obligation shall be fulfilled." Under Article 27 of the United Nations Covenant (established immediately after World War II), any permanent members of the Security Council may veto collective security measures if they are not in the member's interest.

References: Richard N. Current, "The United States and 'Collective Security': Notes on the History of an Idea" in Alexander DeConde, ed., *Isolation and Security: Ideas and Interests in Twentieth-Century American Foreign Policy* (Durham, N.C.: Duke University Press, 1957), 33–55; Miroslav Nincic, "Collective Security" in Bruce W. Jentleson and Thomas G. Paterson, senior eds., *Encyclopedia of U.S. Foreign Relations* (New York: Oxford University Press, 1997), 1: 288–89; Robert Alexander Divine, "Franklin D. Roosevelt and Collective Security, 1933," *Mississippi Valley Historical Review* 48, no. 1 (1961–1962): 42–59; Ostrower, Gary B., *Collective Insecurity: The United States and the League of Nations during the Early Thirties* (Cranbury, N.J.: Bucknell University Press, 1979); Howard Jablon, "The State Department and Collective Security, 1933–34," *The Historian* 23, no. 2 (February 1971): 248–63.

Collins, Michael (1890–1922)
Irish nationalist leader. Born in Clonakilty, in County Cork, Ireland, on October 16, 1890, Collins was employed as a civil servant in Britain from 1906 until he went back to Ireland in 1916. As a nationalist who desired to see an end to the British rule over the southern (or Catholic) section of Ireland, Collins fought in the Easter Rebellion. He was arrested and held prisoner at Frongoch, Marioneth, before being released in December 1916. He rose to leadership in the Sinn Féin movement (the political wing of the Irish Republican Army) for Irish independence along with Arthur GRIFFITH and Eamon DE VALERA, who were both imprisoned. In December 1918, Collins was elected to the Dail Eireann, the Irish assembly that convened in Dublin, as one of 27 assembly members to call for an Irish Republic. Collins was named as the Sinn Féin minister of home affairs and, after he aided in De Valera's escape from prison, as minister of finance. Collins was one of the Irish revolutionaries most sought-after by the British, and a bounty of ten thousand pounds was placed on his head.

After a truce was arranged with London in July 1921, Collins and Griffith went to the British seeking a lasting peace. They signed the ANGLO-IRISH PEACE TREATY, which established British rule in Northern Ireland but gave the Irish Free State a measure of independence. Collins knew that the measure would be hated by his fellow IRA nationalists, and he may have known that by his agreement to it he was signing his own death warrant. However, he returned to Ireland and told his people that the accord was the best they could do under the circumstances. De Valera, once his friend, cursed Collins and the treaty, calling for its destruction. The Dail passed the treaty, and Griffith was named as president of the Irish Free State, with Collins as chair. The antitreaty nationalists started a civil war, and Collins was forced to take up arms against his former allies. Griffith's death on August 12, 1922, left Collins as head of the provisional government. Ten days later, Collins was assassinated while on a military inspection at Beal-na-

Michael Collins and Arthur Griffith, December 1921
(CORBIS/Bettmann)

Blath, in County Cork. He was only 31 years old and was mourned by many as an Irish patriot.

References: "Collins, Michael" in D. J. Hickey and J. E. Doherty, *A Dictionary of Irish History since 1800* (Dublin: Gill & Macmillan, 1980), 22; "Terms of Anglo-Irish Pact Foreshadow Lasting Peace," New York *Herald* (European Edition), December 7, 1921, p. 1; "General Collins Dead. Killed in Ambush. Chief of Staff's Message to Army. Calm Discipline and No Reprisal," *Irish Times*, August 23, 1922, p. 5.

comic strips   *See* CARTOONS, STRIP AND MOVING.

Committee of Responsibilities (Committee of 15)

See VERSAILLES, Treaty of.

Commodity Credit Corporation

U.S. government agency established by Executive Order 6340, signed October 17, 1933, by President Franklin D. ROOSEVELT, which aided farmers with price supports for their crops during the GREAT DEPRESSION. At the height of the Depression, average crop prices fell about 65 percent, driving many farms out of business and endangering America's ability to feed itself.

The Commodity Credit Corporation was established to "support prices of agricultural commodities through loans, purchases, payments, and other operations; make available materials and facilities required in the production and marketing of agricultural commodities; procure agricultural commodities for sale to other government agencies, foreign governments, and domestic, foreign, or international relief or rehabilitation agencies, and to meet domestic requirements; dispose of surplus agricultural commodities; and increase domestic and foreign consumption of agricultural commodities through [the] development of new markets."

After its creation, Congress established through a series of laws a list of "floor prices" at which farmers could sell their crops to individuals, to companies, or to the government. The agency operated in association with the Reconstruction Finance Corporation until July 1, 1939, when its powers were transferred to the Department of Agriculture.

References: Theodore Saloutos, *The American Farmer and the New Deal* (Ames: Iowa State University Press, 1982); David E. Hamilton, *From New Day to New Deal: American Farm Policy from Hoover to Roosevelt, 1928–1933* (Chapel Hill: University of North Carolina Press, 1991).

communism

Forms of communism have existed throughout the centuries, but a new strain was theorized in the mid-19th century in response to the rise of capitalism, reinforced by the industrial revolution, which had created a new class of impoverished workers. Utopian socialists, anarchists, and other revolutionaries sought a communal solution to this poverty. In 1848 the social philosophers Karl Marx and Friedrich Engels published the *Communist Manifesto*, which posited the inevitability of communism arising from a class war. They embraced collective ownership and control of the means of production and predicted the overthrow of capitalism and the creation of a classless society—all of which came to be known as *marxism*. Marxism greatly influenced the development of late 19th- and early 20th-century socialism in Europe and the United States.

In Russia the communist political movement began when the Social Democratic Labor Party split in 1903 into two factions, known as Bolshevism and Menshevism. The Bolsheviks, led by Vladimir LENIN, called for armed revolution and triumphed in the Russian Revolution of 1917. The Communist Party, formed in 1918, established a dictatorship. Lenin founded the Communist International (known as Comintern), which claimed Communist leadership of the world socialist movement. Its effort to incite revolution failed, however, and in 1935 the Comintern began to form coalitions. In the 1930s, as leader of the USSR, Joseph STALIN instituted forcible agricultural collectivization as part of his policy of "socialism in one country." During World War II the Comintern dissolved in 1943 as a show of support for the Allied war effort.

In the United States, after the Soviet revolution of 1917 and the end of World War I, anticommunism set in. This fear of radicals infiltrating the country led to the RED SCARE—mass deportations of people (often recent immigrants from Eastern European countries) who were suspected of being communists. Support for the Communist Party grew in small but vocal numbers during the 1930s, as these forces joined with other leftist organizations to work for black civil rights, labor and unions, and relief for the unemployed. These activists, many of them women and working-class people, argued that political and economic equality was not possible without a socialist transformation of the prevailing capitalist system.

References: John Rees, *The Algebra of Revolution: The Dialectic and the Classical Marxist Tradition* (New York: Routledge, 1999); M. J. Heale, *American Anticommunism; Combating the Enemy Within, 1830–1970* (Baltimore, Md.: Johns Hopkins University Press, 1990); Earl Ofari Hutchinson, *Blacks and Reds: Race and Class in Conflict, 1919–1990* (Ann Arbor: Michigan State University Press, 1994); Jeremy Smith, *The Bolsheviks and the National Question, 1917–23* (New York: St. Martin's, 1999).

Compton, Arthur Holly (1892–1962)

American physicist and Nobel laureate. Born in Wooster, Ohio, on September 10, 1892, he received his bachelor's degree in science from the College of Wooster, and his doctorate from Princeton University. He served as a professor at the University of Minnesota, Cambridge University, and the University of Chicago, among other institutions. During these years he worked on the theory of radiation, inventing the Compton effect, used to measure the wavelengths of X rays. For this work he was awarded (with Charles T. R. WILSON) the Nobel Prize in physics in 1927. Writes biographer I. Helen Gross, "The Compton effect referred to the increase of the wavelength of X-rays caused by the scattering of the incident radia-

tion by electrons. It was important in the developing theories of quantum versus wave nature."

In his later years, Compton worked on other methods for studying X-ray scattering, and he investigated cosmic rays. From 1942 until 1945, he was the director of the Metallurgical Project, which developed the first nuclear reactor. He died in Berkeley, California, on March 15, 1962.

References: "Compton, Arthur Holly" in Charles Moritz, ed., *Current Biography 1940* (New York: H. W. Wilson, 1940), 184–86; Helen I. Gross, "Compton, Arthur Holly" in Bernard S. and June H. Schlessinger, eds., *The Who's Who of Nobel Prize Winners* (Phoenix, Ariz.: Oryx, 1986), 159.

Confessing Church

German evangelical movement that openly opposed the NAZI regime. Organized by Lutheran minister Martin Niemöeller, the Confessing Church (*Bekennende Kirche*), also known as the Confession Movement or the Confession Front, emanated from the Pastors' Emergency League to Resist Hitlerism, which Niemöeller had also established. The Confessing Church, which sought to represent all Germans who opposed Hitler and his Nazi government, met at Barmen from May 21 to 31, 1934, and then issued what was called the Barmen Confessional Synod, or the Barmen Declaration, in which the church stated that unity "can come only from the word of God in faith through the Holy Spirit." (The statement did not cover crimes against Jews, and historians have faulted the church for its lack of a stand in this area.) On October 19, 1945, the Church released the Stuttgart Declaration of [German] Guilt over crimes committed by the Nazi regime and apologized for the Church's silence regarding the brutal genocide of the Jews.

References: Christian Zentner and Friedemann Bedüftig, eds., *Encyclopedia of the Third Reich* (New York: Macmillan, 1991), 1: 63–65; Martin Niemöeller (Renee Spodheim, trans.), *Of Guilt and Hope* (New York: Philosophical Library, 1947); James Bentley, *Martin Niemöeller* (Oxford: Oxford University Press, 1984).

Connelly, Marc (1890–1980)

Pulitzer Prize-winning American playwright. Born Marcus Cook Connelly in McKeesport, Pennsylvania, on December 13, 1890, he left school in 1902, when his father died, so that he could support his mother. His first job was as a reporter with the Associated Press and then with the Pittsburgh *Gazette Times*—experiences he later used in some of his plays.

Connelly began writing plays while working as a reporter, and in 1914 he moved to New York. He survived by writing and selling song lyrics. In 1917, he was hired by the *New York Telegraph* as a drama critic, and it was in that position that he met George S. Kaufman, then the drama critic for the *New York Times*. After writing their respective columns, the two men would meet and compare ideas for their own plays. In 1921 their first collaboration, *Dulcy*, opened on Broadway, starring Lynn Fontanne. The lead character was based on one created by columnist Franklin Pierce ADAMS.

Connelly was also an active member of the ALGONQUIN ROUND TABLE meeting regularly with such literary peers as Dorothy PARKER, Heywood BROUN, and Robert Benchley.

During these years, although Kaufman and Connelly worked together on several other plays in the 1920s, Connelly's greatest success came while working on his own. In 1930, he wrote *The Green Pastures* (based on Roark Bradford's 1929 work, *Ol' Man Adam an' His Chillun*), a folk version of the Old Testament told through the lives of black Americans in the southern United States. It was staged in New York's Mansfield Theater on February 26, 1930, and was made into a motion picture in 1936. Connelly received the Pulitzer Prize in 1930 for the work. One critic called the play "the divine comedy of the modern theatre."

Alden Whitman, in an obituary of Connelly, wrote, "Nothing in Mr. Connelly's subsequent career surpassed that moment." When the rest of his plays in the 1930s did not fare as well, Connelly turned to writing for films, teaching, and writing books, including his memoirs, which appeared in 1968. On December 21, 1980, Connelly died in New York City.

References: "Connelly, Marc" in Charles Moritz, ed., *Current Biography 1969* (New York: H. W. Wilson, 1969), 104–107; Paul T. Nolan, *Marc Connelly* (New York: Twayne Publishers, 1969); Walter C. Daniel, *"De Lawd": Richard B. Harrison and The Green Pastures* (New York: Greenwood, 1986); Bennett Cerf and Van H. Cartmell, eds., *Sixteen Famous American Plays* (New York: Garden City Publishing Co., 1941); Alden Whitman, "Marc Connelly, Playwright, Dies; Won Fame With 'Green Pastures,'" *New York Times*, December 22, 1980, p. A1.

consumer movement
U.S. social movement that stressed improved consumer information and protection, arising out of the Progressive movement of the early 20th century. The years following the passage of the Food and Drug Act of 1906 (better known as the Pure Food and Drug Act) were a period of reform of laws that had failed in previous years to protect consumers from bad food, drugs, and other day-to-day products. Yet this action failed to address other fundamental problems in the American consumer market.

The leading figure of the interwar period who led the way in disclosing and examining the way Americans purchase consumer items was Frederick John Schlink, whose 1924 work, *Your Money's Worth: A Study in the Waste of the Consumer's Dollar* (cowritten with Stuart Chase) was the first summary of brand-name products and their effectiveness. The book's popularity led Schlink to form a "consumer's club" in his hometown of White Plains, New York, and in 1929 to establish Consumer's Research, Inc., the forerunner of today's product-testing companies. In 1933, he and Arthur Kallet released *100,000,000 Guinea Pigs: Dangers in Everyday Foods, Drugs, and Cosmetics*, an exposé of the U.S. government's failure to safeguard the food the American people ate. The *New York Times* said of his 1935 work, *Eat, Drink, and Be Wary*, "Mr. Schlink is perhaps a bit too venomous in his excoriations of practically all scientific pronouncements with regard to diet . . . but in essentials there is so much truth in his book, truth that needed badly to be said, loudly and spectacularly, that the public owes him a debt of gratitude for writing it."

Schlink and his company were not the only alarms warning the American people about product safety. For example, Mary Catherine Phillips's 1934 work, *Skin Deep: The Truth about Beauty Aids*, uncovered secrets in the cosmetics industry; Bissel B. Palmer's *Paying through the Teeth*, and Ruth de Forest Lamb's *The American Chamber of Horrors* disclosed widespread fraud in the federal government's control of drugs and other medicines. These works led to the establishment of the Consumers Union, Inc., in 1936, and the passage of the Food, Drug, and Cosmetic Act in 1938, which required all pharmaceuticals to be tested before being sold.

In other areas of consumer affairs, in 1938 the U.S. Congress enacted the Wheeler-Lea Amendment to the Federal Trade Commission (FTC) Act, which allowed the FTC to control false and deceptive ads, including false advertising on radio (later extended to television). To protect air travelers, the Civil Aeronautics Board was established to examine and oversee issues of safety in civilian air traffic in the United States.

The consumer movement attained complete recognition with the establishment of the Consumers' Advisory Board, part of the NATIONAL RECOVERY ADMINISTRATION, in 1935. By the start of World War II, the government had become an integral part of the effort to protect consumers' rights.

References: Frederick John Schlink and Stuart Chase, *Your Money's Worth: A Study in the Waste of the Consumer's Dollar* (New York: Macmillan, 1927); Mary Catherine Phillips, "Skin Deep: The Truth about Beauty Aids . . . Safe and Harmful" (New York: Vanguard, 1934); Bissell Barbour Palmer, *Paying through the Teeth* (New York: Vanguard, 1935).

Coolidge, Archibald Cary (1866–1928)
American historian and editor. Born in Boston, Massachusetts, on March 6, 1866, into a family which biogra-

pher Lawrence Gelfand called "an old family of Boston Brahmins" (his paternal grandmother was a granddaughter of Thomas Jefferson), Coolidge received his bachelor's degree from Harvard College in 1887 and a doctorate from the University of Freiburg in Germany in 1892. During this period he worked for the U.S. Minister to St. Petersburg and was private secretary to his uncle, Thomas J. Coolidge, the U.S. Minister to France. When he returned to the United States in 1893, he became a history instructor at Harvard.

In 1908, Coolidge began a series of works that defined him as an important scholar of American history: *The United States as a World Power* (1908), *Origins of the Triple Alliance* (1917), and *Ten Years of War and Peace* (1927). During the VERSAILLES Peace Conference in Paris in 1919, he acted as the head of the U.S. mission in Paris and Vienna. In 1922, then Secretary of Commerce Herbert HOOVER asked Coolidge to head the U.S. team to help the Red Cross bring foodstuffs and medical supplies into Russia during the famine. When he returned to the United States in 1922, Coolidge was instrumental in the establishment of *Foreign Affairs* magazine, serving as editor-in-chief during the first five years of the magazine's existence and publishing many of his own articles, unsigned, on topics important to the formation of foreign policy.

Coolidge died suddenly in Boston on January 14, 1928.

References: Ephraim Emerton, "Coolidge, Archibald Cary" in Allen Johnson and Dumas Malone et al., eds., *Dictionary of American Biography* (New York: Charles Scribner's Sons, 1930–95), 2: 393–95; Lawrence E. Gelfand, "Coolidge, Archibald Cary" in Warren F. Kuehl, ed., *Biographical Dictionary of Internationalists* (Westport, Conn.: Greenwood, 1983), 167–69; Robert F. Byrnes, *Awakening American Education to the World: The Role of Archibald Cary Coolidge, 1866–1928* (Notre Dame: University of Notre Dame Press, 1982); Harold Jefferson Coolidge and Robert H. Lord, "Archibald Cary Coolidge: Life and Letters" (Boston: Houghton Mifflin, 1932).

Coolidge, Calvin (1872–1933)

American politician, 30th president of the United States. The only American president to have been born on the Fourth of July, Coolidge, born in the small Vermont village of Plymouth Notch in 1872, was educated at the Ludlow Academy in Vermont, moving on to Amherst College in 1891. He studied law in Northampton, Massachusetts, and was admitted to the state bar. He was elected to the Northampton city council, and later served as mayor of the city. In 1911, Coolidge was elected to the state senate, and two years later rose to become president of that body. In 1915, he was elected lieutenant governor and remained a cautious party leader, a stand that got him elected gover-

Calvin Coolidge *(CORBIS/Bettmann)*

nor in 1918. As governor, he authored a work showing off his state, entitled *Have Faith in Massachusetts* (1919).

Coolidge may well have remained the governor had not the Boston police handed him a labor conflict that he used to his full political advantage. To protest low wages, the police force unionized and went on strike. After seeing the situation head down the path of violence, Coolidge said, "There is no right to strike against the public safety by anybody, anywhere, any time." Calling in the state National Guard, he crushed the strike, earning the enmity of labor. From others, however, he received accolades for this stand, including a telegram of congratulations from President Woodrow WILSON. Many urged Coolidge to seek higher office, something he was reluctant to do. But at the 1920 Republican National Convention, when Senator Hiram Warren JOHNSON of California declined to run with Senator Warren G. HARDING, Coolidge was selected in his stead. That November, he was elected vice president of the United States. His tenure as vice president was without controversy. On August 2, 1923, Harding died unexpectedly. Coolidge was vacationing at his father's home in Vermont; his father, a justice of the peace, swore him in as president on the family bible. He finished out Harding's term and was elected in 1924, serving his full term through 1929.

In his nearly six years as chief executive, Coolidge did little to change the course of the nation. He made some tax cuts and believed in laissez-faire business. His January 25, 1925, speech outlined his doctrine on American commerce: "The Business of America is Business." The motto has become synonymous with the do-it-all 1920s. However, Coolidge left the nation unprepared for the economic collapse that would soon follow.

In 1928, when many speculated that he would run for a second term, Coolidge gave reporters a one-line note: "I do not choose to run for president in 1928." It was simple and to the point, reflecting Coolidge's most appealing qualities as U.S. president: his new England simplicity and his personal honesty. In March 1929, when his successor, Herbert HOOVER, was sworn in, Coolidge retired to his farm in Northampton, Massachusetts, where he wrote his autobiography. He died there on January 5, 1933, four years after leaving the White House.

References: Calvin Coolidge, *The Autobiography of Calvin Coolidge* (New York: Cosmopolitan Book Corp., 1929); Francis Russell, "The Strike That Made a President," *American Heritage,* 14, no. 6 (October 1963): 44–47; Charles Morrow Wilson, "Lamplight Inauguration," *American Heritage* 15, no. 1 (December 1963): 80–86; Donald R. McCoy, *Calvin Coolidge: The Quiet President* (New York: Macmillan, 1967); Howard H. Quint and Robert H. Ferrell, eds., *The Talkative President: The Off-the-Record Press Conferences of Calvin Coolidge* (Amherst, Mass.: University of Massachusetts Press, 1964).

Coolidge Conference

International conference on arms limitations, also known as the Geneva Naval Conference. In 1927, U.S. President Calvin Coolidge invited leaders of the nations that had participated in the WASHINGTON NAVAL CONFERENCE of 1921–22 to assemble in Geneva, Switzerland, to disuss further reductions in their naval armaments. France and Italy did not send delegates, but the United States, the United Kingdom, and Japan discussed limitations of submarines and cruisers. The meeting failed miserably, however, because of an Anglo-Japanese naval agreement that was unacceptable to the United States. In retrospect, the conference was just another diplomatic failure on the road to World War II.

References: John E. Findling, *Dictionary of American Diplomatic History* (Westport, Conn.: Greenwood, 1989), 204; Lewis Ethan Ellis, *Republican Foreign Policy, 1921–1933* (New Brunswick, N.J.: Rutgers University Press, 1968); Stephen Roskill, *Naval Policy between the Wars,* vol. 1 (New York: Walker and Co., 1968), 59; Gordon A. Craig, "The British Foreign Office from Grey to Austen Chamberlain," in Gordon A. Craig and Felix Gilbert, eds., *The Diplomats, 1919–1939*

(Princeton, N.J.: Princeton University Press, 1994), 44; perhaps the two most important articles on this conference and its failure are Sir Arthur Salter, "The Technique of Open Diplomacy," *The Political Quarterly* 3 (1932): 64–65, and David Carlton, "Great Britain and the Coolidge Naval Disarmament Conference of 1927," *Political Science Quarterly* 83, no. 4 (1968): 573–98.

Coughlin, Charles Edward (1891–1979)

Canadian-American clergyman, known as the "radio priest." Born in Hamilton, Ontario, Canada, on October 25, 1891, he attended St. Michael's College in Toronto. He entered the priesthood and was ordained a Roman Catholic priest in 1916. He became the pastor of the Shrine of the Little Flower in Royal Oak, Michigan, in 1926, and within four years he was broadcasting his sermons over the new medium of radio, gaining millions of listeners.

Coughlin threw his support behind Franklin D. ROOSEVELT for president in 1932, calling on his supporters to vote for the Democrat. After Roosevelt was elected, however, Coughlin began to view the new president's programs as attacks on the poor, and he began to lace his sermons with populist rhetoric and exclamations against Jews. In 1936, he joined with elements of assassinated senator Huey LONG's supporters and founded the National Union for Social Justice. In one speech, he said of the president, "The great betrayer and liar, Franklin D. Roosevelt, who promised to drive the money changers from the temple, had succeeded [only] in driving the farmers from their homesteads and the citizens from their homes in the cities. . . . I ask you to purge the man who claims to be a Democrat, from the Democratic Party, and I mean Franklin Double-Crossing Roosevelt."

Coughlin's Magazine, *Social Justice* (published from 1936 until 1942), was banned from the mail during World War II, at the same time that the Catholic Church ordered him to cease broadcasting his hate-filled sermons. Coughlin, denied his platform, remained at his pastorate until he retired in 1966. He died in Bloomfield Hills, Michigan, on October 27, 1979.

References: J. Gordon Melton, *Religious Leaders of America: A Biographical Guide to Founders and Leaders of Religious Bodies, Churches, and Spiritual Groups in North America* (Detroit: Gale Research, 1991), 223; Alan Brinkley, *Voices of Protest* (New York: Vintage Books, 1983); Bernard V. Burke, "Coughlin, Charles Edward" in Bruce W. Jentleson and Thomas G. Paterson, senior eds., *Encyclopedia of U.S. Foreign Relations* (New York: Oxford University Press, 1997), 1: 367.

court-packing controversy

American governmental and political conflict, in which President Franklin D. ROOSEVELT attempted to "stack" the

U.S. Supreme Court with justices who sympathized with his NEW DEAL program after the Court struck down key measures as unconstitutional.

On May 27, 1935, known as BLACK MONDAY, in three separate cases the Court held several portions of the New Deal economic program to be unconstitutional. Court decisions in 1936 and 1937 served to further erode the constitutionality of Roosevelt's program. The President's sneak attack on the Court began on January 6, 1937, when he delivered before Congress his State of the Union address. In it he remarked, "Even at the present time, the Supreme Court is laboring under a heavy burden. Its difficulties in this respect were superficially lightened some years ago by authorizing the Court, in its discretion, to refuse to hear appeals in many classes of cases. This discretion was so freely exercised that in the last fiscal year, although 867 petitions for review were presented to the Court, it declined to hear 717 cases." Roosevelt intended to increase the number of justices on the Court to gain a majority that would rule in his favor.

His plan, which was shepherded through Congress by Senate Majority Leader Joseph Taylor ROBINSON of Arkansas, seemed headed for easy passage, especially in a Congress controlled by the Democrats. Nonetheless, several Democrats were uneasy. Senator Burton K. Wheeler of Montana asked Chief Justice Charles Evans HUGHES to write a letter to Congress claiming that there was no need for further justices to relieve any burden. Hughes wrote such a letter, and it set off a firestorm. Congressional Republicans, in the minority, could do little to stop the action; instead, they allowed the Democrats to defend it at their peril. Once Hughes's letter was released, the air seemed to go out of the Democrats' will to tinker with the Court. Further erosion came when the Court upheld several pieces of New Deal legislation in different decisions, and Justice Willis van Devanter announced his retirement, allowing Roosevelt to name a new justice, a total of five for him. After the proposed legislation got out of the Judiciary Committee, Democrats led by Wheeler filibustered it on the Senate floor, eventually voting to table it back to committee. Robinson's death ended all hopes for passage of the act.

Historians Joseph Alsop Jr. and Turner Catledge catalog the controversy in their book, *The 168 Days* (named after the period of time the issue raged). They write, "Court Packing, as Roosevelt's forces saw it, went straight to the heart of the trouble: the personnel of the Court. It was simple; it involved no long-term alteration in the government structure, and it was clearly constitutional."

References: Barry Cushman, "The Hughes Court and Constitutional Consultation," 1997 discourse, copy provided to the author by Professor Cushman; "Roosevelt Appoints Two Foes of Anti-Court Bill Democrats, Starts Tour Aiding 'Liberals'," *The Washington Post*, July 8, 1938, p. 1; Joseph Alsop Jr. and Turner Catledge, *The 168 Days* (Garden City, N.Y.: Doubleday and Co., 1971), 29, 71.

Cox, James Middleton   (1870–1957)

American newspaper publisher and politician. Born in Jacksonburg, Ohio, on March 31, 1870, he worked during his early years as a reporter for several Ohio newspapers. Cox had careers in a considerable number of fields—teaching, reporting, and, with his considerable wealth, editing several Ohio newspapers. He also served as a private secretary to Congressman Paul Sorg.

Cox was elected as a U.S. representative from Ohio's Third Congressional District in 1908 and served two terms, leaving the House in 1913. During this service, he spoke out against tariffs. He did not run for a third term in 1912, instead turning to run for the governorship. With the support of Democratic presidential candidate Woodrow WILSON, Cox won. He served a single term as governor but was defeated in 1914; two years later, however, he ran again, and was reelected, serving this time for four years, until 1921.

Cox was still the sitting governor when in 1920 he was nominated for president by the Democrats meeting in convention in San Francisco. Unfortunately for Cox, he ran for president in a year in which the leader of his party, Woodrow WILSON, was a dying man whose plans for U.S. inclusion in the LEAGUE OF NATIONS had destroyed much of his remaining credibility with the American people. The League was unpopular, but the Democrats, with Cox's firm backing, inserted a pro-League plank into the party platform: "The Democratic Party favors the League of Nations as the surest, if not the only, practicable means of maintaining the permanent peace of the world and terminating the insufferable burden of great military and naval establishments." When Republican presidential nominee Warren G. HARDING accepted the Democrat call to make the election a referendum on the League, Cox, replied, in his speech accepting the Democrat ticket, "Senator Harding, as the Republican candidate for the Presidency, proposes in plain words that we remain out of it. As the Democratic candidate I favor going in." Cox advocated American entry into the League, and at one point called those on the opposite side "League Liars." Burdened with Wilson's failed policies, Cox was defeated in a landslide, 404 electoral votes to 127.

After the election, he retired from public life and never held office again. His memoirs, *Journey Through My Years*, appeared in 1946. Cox died on July 15, 1957.

See also ELECTIONS, U.S.

References: James M. Cox, *Journey Through My Years* (New York: Simon & Schuster, 1946); Daniel M. Smith, "Cox, James Middleton" in Allen Johnson and Dumas Malone et al., eds., *Dictionary of American Biography* (New York: Charles

Scribner's Sons, 1930–95), 6: 128–30; James E. Cebula, "Cox, James Middleton" in Warren F. Kuehl, ed., *Biographical Dictionary of Internationalists* (Westport, Conn.: Greenwood, 1983), 175–76; James E. Cebula, "James M. Cox, Journalist and Politician" (Ph.D. dissertation, University of Cincinnati, 1972).

Crater, Joseph Force (1889–1937?)

American jurist, whose bizarre disappearance in 1930 has continued to mystify followers of his case. Born in Easton, Pennsylvania, Crater earned his bachelor's degree from Lafayette College and his law degree from Columbia University. He started a law practice in New York City and rose to become president of the Cayuga Democratic Club, a part of the city's Tammany Hall dominant political machine. In April 1930, he was named to the New York State Supreme Court by then governor Franklin D. ROOSEVELT.

On August 6, 1930, after sitting on the court just four months, Crater vanished. He had just returned from a vacation in Maine to take care of some business at his office. He cashed two checks with a value of $5,130, a tremendous amount of money at the time. He then left his office, hailed a cab, and disappeared. The police investigation found no evidence of foul play. A grand jury found evidence of corruption in the Cayuga Club, however, which eventually led to Judge Samuel Seabury's investigation of corruption in New York City's government and the downfall of Major Jimmy Walker.

To this day, no one knows what became of Crater. He was declared legally dead in 1937.

References: Stella Wheeler Crater, *The Empty Robe* (Garden City, N.Y.: Doubleday, 1961); Murray Teigh Bloom, "Is It Judge Crater's Body?" *Harper's* (November 1959), 41–47; Sam Roberts, "Happy 50th Anniversary, Judge Crater; Will You Please Call Your Office?" *Sunday [Daily] News Magazine* (New York), August 3, 1980, 20–21, 24.

Crosby, Bing   *See* JAZZ.

Cullen, Countee (1903–1946)

American poet, an integral player in the HARLEM RENAISSANCE. Born in New York City on May 30, 1903, Cullen attended New York City schools, then received a bachelor's degree from New York University in 1925 and a master's degree from Harvard University the following year. As a teenager, influenced by the poetry of Alfred, Lord Tennyson and John Keats, Cullen began to write his own. He won an award in a poetry contest when he was 15, and in 1924 another poem, *The Ballad of the Brown Girl*, came in second in another contest. In 1925, Cullen's first publication, *Color,*

Countee Cullen *(CORBIS/Bettmann)*

was released, eventually followed by *Copper Sun* (1927), *The Black Christ* (1929), *The Medea and some Poems* (1935), and his only novel, *One Way to Heaven* (1932). His work applied traditional verse forms to African-American themes. A major figure of the Harlem Renaissance, Cullen's poetry complemented the thriving intellectual and cultural contributions of other African-American writers, artists, and musicians in Harlem at this time.

From 1926 to 1928 Cullen was the assistant editor of *Opportunity: A Journal of American Negro Life,* and from 1935 until his death he taught French in the New York schools. He died on January 9, 1946.

References: Margaret Perry, *A Bio-Bibliography of Countée P. Cullen, 1903–1946* (Westport, Conn.: Greenwood, 1971); Blanche E. Ferguson, *Countee Cullen and the Negro Renaissance* (New York: Dodd, Mead, 1966); Houston A. Baker, *A Many-Colored Coat of Dreams: The Poetry of Countee Cullen* (Detroit: Broadside, 1974).

Cummings, E(dward) E(stlin) (1894–1962)

American poet, writer, and painter self-styled as e. e. cummings. Born Edward Estlin Cummings in Cambridge, Massachusetts, on October 14, 1894, he received his bachelor's and master's degree's from Harvard University in 1914 and 1916, respectively. During World War I, he served in the ambulance corps. Captured by the Germans, he was imprisoned for several months on espionage charges. Upon his release, Cummings studied painting in Paris. In 1922 he published *The Enormous Room,* prose based on his experiences as a prisoner of war. He returned to the United States in 1924.

In 1931, Cummings published a series of drawings and paintings called *CIOPW,* which stood for charcoal, ink, oil, pencil, and watercolor. He is best known, however, for his numerous books of poetry, many of which were published in the interwar years. His signature style of experimental language and typography was first seen in *Tulips and Chimneys* (1923). He was noted for writing all things in lower-case letters; even his name appeared in that fashion. Other works during this period include *XLI Poems* (1925), *Is 5* (1926), *Christmas Tree* (1928), *No Thanks* (1935), and *Collected Poems* (1938). His 1927 play, *him,* is also considered an important work. In *Eimi* (1933), another work of prose, Cummings reviewed a trip he took to Soviet Russia and attacked the subjugation of the Russian people.

Cummings died at his farm in North Conway, New Hampshire.

References: e. e. Cummings, (George James Firmage, ed.), *The Enormous Room* (New York: Liveright, 1978); Richard S. Kennedy, *Dreams in the Mirror: A Biography of e. e. cummings* (New York: Liveright, 1980); Charles Norman, *e. e. cummings: The Magic-maker* (Indianapolis: Bobbs-Merrill, 1972).

Curzon Line

Suggested Polish-Soviet boundary. On December 8, 1919, George Nathaniel Curzon, first Baron and first Marquis Curzon of Kedleston (1859–1925), the English undersecretary of state for foreign affairs, proposed to the Supreme Council of the Allied Powers at VERSAILLES that an ethnic and line be drawn between Soviet Russia to the east and Poland to the west, running from the southern point of Lithuania south to the Bug River near Brest-Litovsk, southward along the Bug to Sokal, where it would curve west toward the Czechoslovakia border. Neither nation went for the plan, although a line of demarcation was established by them under the Treaty of RIGA in 1921. When Germany and the Soviet Union secretly divided Poland in a 1939 agreement (the so-called Molotov-Ribbentrop Line), the two parties used the points of the Curzon Line as a base. After World War II, the border between Poland and the U.S.S.R. was re-established at the Curzon Line by agreement among the Allied leaders.

References: Nayana Goradia, *Lord Curzon: The Last of the British Moghuls* (New York: Oxford University Press, 1993); G. H. Bennett, *British Foreign Policy during the Curzon Period, 1919–24* (New York: St. Martin's, 1995); Max M. Laserson, *The Curzon Line: A Historical and Critical Analysis* (New York: Carnegie Endowment for International Peace, 1944).

Dada

International artistic movement initiated by French poet Tristan Tzara in 1916. During World War I, pacifists met at Hugo Ball's Cabaret Voltaire in Zurich, Switzerland, then an outpost of neutrality, to condemn the war and what they believed to be the end of civilization. To this end, Tzara and other artists founded an artistic movement based on absurdity and nonsense, reflecting the senselessness and futility of modern life. Calling the movement "dada" ("hobby-horse" in French), which he and his friends casually picked out of a French-German dictionary, Tzara said, "We spit on humanity. Dada is the abolition of the logic. . . . There is a great negative work of destruction to be done. We must sweep everything away and sweep clean." Artists involved in the movement included, among others, French writers Louis Aragon, Pierre Chapka-Bonnière, and André Breton, German poet and writer Richard Hüelsenbeck, Romanian nonfigurative painter Marcel Janco, American painter, photographer, and filmmaker Man Ray, Russian abstract painter Wassily Kandinsky, and French painter Francis Picabia. French artists Jean Arp and Marcel Duchamp and German painter and sculptor Max Ernst carried the movement to New York, where Dadaist art was shown at Alfred Stieglitz's 291 gallery as well as in the extensive collections of Walter Arensberg.

The European and American artists showcased their various techniques in such journals as *391, The Blind Man, The New York Dada,* and *Rongwrong.* The viewing public was confounded by Duchamp's "ready-mades" and his complex, nonfunctional machines; by Arp's abstract, organic works in various media; and by Ernst's experiments in collage and photomontage. The literary manifestations of Dada were most often characterized by nonsense poems and random language combinations.

In 1917, during World War I, Dada came to Berlin, where German Dadaists put on exhibitions of their works and displayed them in such magazines as *Club Dada* and *Jedermann sein eigner Fussball* (Everyman his own football). In 1919 the Dada poets, essayists, and critics Tzara, Aragon, and Breton founded the Dadaist magazine *Littérature,* which featured their own writings as well as those by Paul Éluard and Philippe Soupault.

The end of the war brought a mood change in the art world, however, and by 1922 many of the Dada artists had moved on to SURREALISM. One offshoot of Dada was Merz, an artistic movement initiated by German artist Kurt Schwitters in 1920 (he had used the letters MERZ in one of his collages).

References: Annabelle Melzer, *Dada and Surrealist Performance* (Baltimore: Johns Hopkins University Press, 1996); Allan Carl Greenberg, *Artists and Revolution: Dada and the Bauhaus, 1917–1925* (Ann Arbor, Mich.: UMI Research Press, 1979); *Reader's Digest Great Events of the 20th Century: How They Changed Our Lives* (Pleasantville, N.Y.: Reader's Digest Association, 1977), 186–88.

Daladier, Édouard (1884–1970)

French politician and stateman, prime minister (1933–34, 1936, 1938–40). Born in the village of Carpentras, in Vaucluse, France, on June 18, 1884, he studied at the Lycée Duparc in Lyon, where his history instructor was Édouard HERRIOT. Under Herriot's direction, Daladier earned his degree in history at the University of Lyon and taught at Nîmes; later, he worked in Grenoble, Marseille, and then at the prestigious Lycée Condorcet in Paris. While teaching at Grenoble, Daladier was elected mayor of Carpentras, where he served until the start of World War I.

When the war broke out, Daladier volunteered for service, rising from the rank of private to that of captain, eventually earning the Legion of Honor and the Croix de Guerre. In 1919, he returned to his position at the Lycée

Condorcet, but Herriot persuaded him to run for the French Chamber of Deputies as a Radical Socialist from the *département* of Vaucluse. Elected in that year, he would serve until the German invasion of France in 1940. Although he was not a legislative master, he became an expert in military affairs—so much so that by 1924 Herriot, now prime minister, named Daladier as minister to the colonies. He served as minister of public works and minister of war until 1933, when he was named prime minister.

From 1933 until 1940, Daladier served three terms as prime minister, during which his nation and the rest of Europe slipped closer to war. He attempted to manage the continent's deteriorating military and diplomatic position and the growing economic crisis resulting from the GREAT DEPRESSION. During his third term, he bowed to the demands of German chancellor Adolf HITLER and agreed, with British prime minister Neville CHAMBERLAIN, to allow Germany to occupy the Sudetenland of Czechoslovakia. This policy, called APPEASEMENT, led to further land grabs by Germany and Europe's 1939 slide toward war. Daladier led France in declaring was against Germany when that nation invaded Poland on September 1, 1939. In an address before the Chamber of Deputies the following day, Daladier explained this action: "The Government yesterday decreed general mobilization. . . . The whole nation is answering the call with serious and resolute calm. The young men have rejoined their regiments. They are now defending our frontiers. The example of dignified courage which they have just set to the world must provide inspiration for our debates. In a great impulse of national brotherliness they have forgotten everything which only yesterday could divide them. They no longer acknowledge any service but the service of France. As we send them the grateful greeting of the nation let us all pledge ourselves together to be worthy of them. . . . Thus has the Government put France into a position to act in accordance with our vital interests and with national honor . . . Peace had been endangered for several days. The demands of Germany on Poland were threatening to provoke a conflict. I shall show you in a moment how—perhaps for the first time in history—all the peaceful forces of the world, moral and material, were leagued together during those days and during those nights to save the world's peace. But just when it could still be hoped that all those repeated efforts were going to be crowned with success, Germany abruptly brought them to naught."

The nation rallied around its leader; however, on March 20, 1940, Daladier was forced to resign when a vote of no confidence was taken against him. He served for a period in the succeeding cabinet as minister of war, then was named foreign minister. On June 6, 1940, he resigned this post, and on November 17, 1940, the Vichy government, in collaboration with the occupying Germans, arrested him. His trial took place in February 1942; the charges were dropped but he remained imprisoned, first in France and then in Germany. He was rescued by American troops from the Itter Castle in Austria on May 5, 1945. After the war, he served in the Chamber of Deputies from 1946 until 1958, becoming president of the Radical Party in 1953 and retiring in 1958. Daladier died in Paris on October 10, 1970.

References: Stanton B. Leeds, *These Rule France: The Story of Édouard Daladier and the Men around Daladier* (Indianapolis: Bobbs-Merrill, 1940); André Géraud, *The Gravediggers of France: Gamelin, Daladier, Reynaud, Pétain, and Laval; Military Defeat, Armistice, Counter-Revolution* (Garden City, N. Y.: Doubleday, Doran & Co., 1944).

Dale, Henry Hallett (1875–1968)

English researcher and Nobel laureate. Born in London on June 9, 1875, he graduated from Trinity College at Cambridge, afterward studying medicine at St. Bartholomew's Hospital in London. In 1904, he was named director of the Wellstone Physiological Research Laboratories, where he served until 1914. During this period he worked on ways to treat typhoid, malaria, and enteric fever; he also discovered two chemical substances that form the basis of all nervous system function in the human body. He was knighted in 1932 for this work. Dale then served as director of the National Institute for Medical Research at Hampstead, London, and from 1942 until he retired, he served as the Fullerian Professor of Chemistry at the Royal Institution in England and the director of the Davy-Faraday Research Laboratory. While in these positions, Dale worked on the chemicals adrenaline and acetylcholine, studying their reactions in the stimulation of nerve impulses and how histamine works in tissues. For this work, he was the corecipient, with Otto LOEWI of Germany, of the 1936 Nobel Prize in medicine and physiology.

Dale worked at the Royal Institution of Great Britain as the director from 1942 until he retired in 1946. He died in Cambridge on July 23, 1968.

References: Rashelle Karp, "Dale, Henry Hallett, Sir" in Bernard S. and June H. Schlessinger, eds., *The Who's Who of Nobel Prize Winners* (Phoenix, Ariz.: Oryx, 1986), 90; William F. Bynum, "Dale, Henry Hallett" in Charles Coulston Gillespie, ed. in chief, *Dictionary of Scientific Biography* (New York: Charles Scribner's Sons, 1980–90), 1: 104–107; Thomas Watson MacCallum and Stephen Taylor, eds., *The Nobel Prize–Winners and the Nobel Foundation, 1901–1937* (Zurich, Switzerland: Central European Times Publishing, 1938), 239–40.

Dali, Salvador   *See* SURREALISM.

dance

Form of artistic expression and theatrical performance combining human movement and musical accompaniment that flourished during the interwar period, as choreographers explored innovative new styles. In the early 20th century, modern dance became part of the world's theatrical tradition with the introduction of Sergei Diaghilev's Ballets Russes to the Paris scene in 1909. Diaghilev used asymmetry and perpetual motion to revolutionize traditional ballet. Over the next two decades the exciting Russian style, coupled with the influences of the first generation of American modern-dance innovators (such as Isadora DUNCAN and Ruth St. Denis), brought a ballet renaissance to Europe and the United States. Paris, London, and New York became major cultural centers for the art form. One of the most influential figures in modern ballet was Russian-born dancer George Balanchine, who had been a member of Diaghilev's company. Balanchine moved to the United States in 1933 and founded the School of American Ballet in 1934. His choreography emphasized abstract form and simple design. After World War II, Balanchine became the artistic director and principal choreographer of the groundbreaking New York City Ballet.

The second generation of modern-dance innovators included the choreographers Martha Graham, Doris Humphrey, and Charles Weidman, who had all studied dance in the 1920s at the Denishawn school, founded by St. Denis and her husband Ted Shawn. Graham launched her own dance company in 1929, and her works concentrated on deliberate, intellectual, and dramatic movement. She was among the first choreographers to employ a racially integrated group of dancers. Together Humphrey and Weidman formed their school and dance company in 1927. Weidman's work combined comic satire, abstract movement, and mime techniques.

Modern dance also appeared in musical film during the interwar period at the hands of such choreographers as Busby BERKELEY and Agnes De Mille. Popular DANCING crazes, such as ragtime, SWING, tap, and other forms of individual JAZZ dance, also came into vogue during the interwar period.

See also MUSICALS.

References: Terri A. Mester, *Movement and Modernism: Yeats, Eliot, Lawrence, Williams, and Early Twentieth-Century Dance* (Fayetteville: University of Arkansas Press, 1997); Agnes De Mille, *Martha: The Life and Work of Martha Graham* (New York: Vintage Books, 1992); Anna Halprin, *Moving toward Life: Five Decades of Transformational Dance,* ed. Rachel Kaplan (Hanover, Conn.: Wesleyan University Press, 1995); Ruth St. Denis, *An Unfinished Life: An Autobiography* (1939; reprint, Brooklyn, N.Y.: Dance Horizons, 1969).

dancing

Americans found new ways to express themselves through dance in the interwar period. The twenties have in fact been called the Dance Age, or the JAZZ AGE. In 1920 the dance that opened the era was the "modern" waltz. The main dance step of the era was the jitterbug, a jazz variation of the two-step in which couples danced athletically in 4/4 time. Among the dances derived from the jitterbug are the Charleston, the Black Bottom, the shag, and the lindy hop. Ragtime, JAZZ, and SWING music allowed for the creation of such dance crazes as the Turkey Trot and the Texas Tommy. Followers of swing became known as "jitterbugs" for their rapid shuffling dance steps. In 1937 the era of "group participation" dances opened, with such moves as the Suzy-Q, the Big Apple, and the step known as Peelin' the Peach. Ballroom dancing became popular when instructor Arthur Murray introduced the five-step approach in 1925, and, five years later, the Westchester move.

References: Lawrence R. Broer and John D. Walter, eds., *Dancing Fools and Weary Blues: The Great Escape of the Twenties* (Bowling Green, Ohio: Bowling Green State University Popular Press, 1990); Christy Lane, *All That Jazz and More:*

Two flappers do the Charleston on a Chicago rooftop at the height of the dance craze, December 1926. *(CORBIS/Underwood & Underwood)*

The Complete Book of Jazz Dancing (New York: Leisure Press, 1983).

D'Annunzio, Gabriel   *See* FIUME.

Danzig Corridor

Strip of territory established by the Treaty of VERSAILLES that gave the Polish city of Danzig (Gdansk) direct access to the Baltic Sea through what had been German lands. An effort to repossess the Danzig Corridor was the ostensible reason for Germany's September 1, 1939, attack on Poland, which set off World War II.

Danzig has historically been an important trading and seaport, and Germany's lack of such a port on its border with Eastern Europe made it of extreme strategic importance. In the 13th century, Danzig was part of the Hanseatic League, an association of German cities banded together to conduct commerce in northern Europe. Conquered by the Teutonic Knights in 1308, it was made a part of a free and autonomous Polish state in 1466. It was ceded to Prussia during the second partition of Poland in 1793, but was a free city from 1807 to 1814 and again in 1919 following World War I, when the city's disposition was specified in the VERSAILLES Treaty. Hitler's demand for Danzig in 1939 and his subsequent invasion of Poland began World War II. It was held by Germans until its liberation by Soviet troops on March 30, 1945. The scene of massive labor strikes by dockworkers in 1970 and 1980, it has in the intervening years become a symbol of Poland's freedom from domination.

References: Alan John Percivale Taylor, "The Outbreak of War" in Alan John Percivale Taylor and John Morris Roberts, eds., *Purnell's History of the 20th Century* (New York: Purnell, 1979), 6: 1655–67; "Nazi Rule in Danzig. Complaints to the League," *The Times* (London), January 21, 1936, p. 11.

Darling, Jay Norwood (1876–1962)

American cartoonist, writer, and environmentalist known as "Ding" Darling. Born October 21, 1876, in Norwood, Michigan, Darling attended Beloit College in Wisconsin, from which he received his doctorate in 1900 in biology. Soon after, he began his journalistic career as a political cartoonist for the Sioux City, Iowa, *Tribune*. In 1906, he started to work for the renowned *Des Moines Register*, where he remained for the rest of his life. His satirical political cartoons eventually appeared in 130 American newspapers. For this work, he won the Pulitzer prize for cartooning in both 1923 and 1942.

Darling was also an ardent environmentalist, years before such a stance was popular. His interest in wildlife and waterfowl preservation led him to take a leave of absence from his job to become the chief of the U.S. Biological Survey, the precursor of the U.S. Fish and Wildlife Service, from 1934 to 1935. During this period, Darling founded and served as the first president of the National Wildlife Federation, one of the largest environmental protection groups in the United States. His J. N. "Ding" Darling Foundation aided in the establishment of the Lewis and Clark Trail Commission to set aside areas for recreational purposes. Darling was still active in the environmental movement when he suddenly died on February 12, 1962. A wildlife sanctuary on Sanibel Island on the western coast of Florida was named in his honor.

Reference: James D. Davis, "Darling, Jay Norwood" in Richard H. Stroud, ed., *National Leaders of American Conservation* (Washington, D.C.: Smithsonian Institution Press, 1985), 117–18.

Darrow, Clarence Seward (1857–1938)

American attorney, defender of John T. Scopes in the infamous SCOPES "MONKEY TRIAL" as well as teenage killers LEOPOLD AND LOEB. Born in Kinsman, Ohio, on April 18, 1857, he was admitted to the Ohio bar in 1878, and began a practice in Ashtabula before moving to Chicago, the city in which he became famous as one of the nation's leading criminal attorneys. In 1894, in sympathy with a strike being conducted against the Chicago and Northwestern Railroad, Darrow resigned as the railroad's counsel, then acted as a member of the defense team for Eugene V. DEBS, the head of the strikers' union, who was tried for conspiracy. In 1902, Darrow defended coal miners striking against anthracite mines in Scranton and Philadelphia, Pennsylvania. Other famous cases before the interwar period were in defense of "Big Bill" Haywood (head of the Western Federation of Miners, who had been accused of helping to assassinate Idaho Governor Frank Steunenberg) and the McNamara brothers (who had been accused of dynamiting the *Los Angeles Times* building).

In 1924, Darrow was called to defend Nathan Leopold and Richard Loeb, accused of kidnapping and murdering their cousin, Bobby Franks, heir to the Sears Roebuck fortune. Darrow took on the case not because he condoned the crime, to which they had confessed, but because he believed that they should be saved from capital punishment, which he opposed. In a brilliant closing argument which lasted several hours, Darrow appealed to the judge to spare the two young men from the electric chair. In the end, Darrow's argument worked, and the two were handed sentences of life imprisonment.

Perhaps the capstone of Darrow's career came in 1925, when he defended teacher Scopes from a charge of violating Tennessee state law by teaching evolution in the schools. In a brawl with former U.S. Secretary of State Williams Jennings Bryan, the prosecutor in the case, Darrow "cross-examined" Bryan on biblical teachings, challenging his belief in the literal truth of the Bible. Darrow lost the case but proved his point of freedom of thought, inspiring people throughout the United States.

Although he retired in 1927 from practicing law, Darrow was a consultant to the defense at the SCOTTSBORO CASE trial in Alabama in 1932. Darrow died in Chicago on March 13, 1938. His published writings include *Crime, Its Cause and Treatment* (1925), *The Story of My Life* (1932), and *Infidels and Heretics* (1933), written with Wallace Rice.

References: Clarence Darrow (Arthur Weinberg, ed.), *Attorney for the Damned* (New York: Simon & Schuster, 1957); Charles Yale Harrison, *Clarence Darrow* (New York: J. Cape & H. Smith, 1931); Willard D. Hunsberger, *Clarence Darrow: A Bibliography* (Metuchen, N.J.: Scarecrow, 1981).

Daugherty, Harry Micajah (1860–1941)
American politician and U.S. attorney general, implicated in and tried for massive corruption in the Justice Department. Born in Washington Court House, Ohio, on January 26, 1860, Daugherty received a law degree from the University of Michigan in 1891, and practiced law in his hometown. He became a noted attorney in the area, and used his name to get political favors. He served as a township clerk, then two terms in the Ohio legislature (1890–94). In 1893, Daugherty moved to Columbus, set up another law practice, and soon made a fortune. He ran two unsuccessful political campaigns during this time— for state attorney general in 1895 and for governor in 1897—and discovered that he would be a better campaign manager than politician.

In 1902, Daugherty first met Warren G. HARDING, a Ohio native who was running that year for lieutenant governor. They became close friends, and Daugherty was soon running Harding's campaigns, including his successful bid for the U.S. Senate in 1914. In 1920, Daugherty was telling reporters that the Republican National Convention that year would be deadlocked, and that in desperation the leaders of the party would turn to Harding as a compromise candidate. Sure enough, the backbenchers in the Republican Party turned to Harding, who accepted the presidential nod, with Daugherty running his successful campaign that year. When Harding was assembling his cabinet, he rewarded his friend with the post of attorney general, a move that was met with criticism. By 1922, however, Daugherty was facing trouble: rumors had surfaced that there was massive corruption in the Justice Department. After Harding's death, Daugherty could not hide any longer, and in 1924 President Calvin COOLIDGE ordered him to hand over his files to Congress. Coolidge asked for and received Daugherty's resignation in March 1924.

In 1927 Daugherty was indicted and tried and acquitted on charges of conspiracy to defraud the U.S. government. Daugherty was neither convicted nor exonerated, however. He went back to Ohio to practice law, and wrote *The Inside Story of the Harding Tragedy* (1932), which he claimed vindicated him in the scandal. Daugherty died in Columbus on October 12, 1941.

References: James N. Giglio, *H. M. Daugherty and the Politics of Expediency* (Kent, Ohio: Kent State University Press, 1978); Eugene Trani and David L. Wilson, *The Presidency of Warren G. Harding* (Lawrence: University Press of Kansas, 1977).

Davis, Bette (1908–1989)
Academy Award–winning U.S. actress. Born in Lowell, Massachusetts, on April 5, 1908, as Ruth Elizabeth Davis, she studied drama in New York, and started on her stage work in 1926. In 1931, she went to Hollywood, where she got her first film role in *Way Back Home* (1931). Her big break came when she played Mildred Rogers, a waitress, in *Of Human Bondage* (1934), opposite Leslie Howard. The following year, Davis won the Academy Award for Best Actress for her performance as Joyce Leath in *Dangerous*. She won her second Oscar in 1938 for her role in JEZEBEL. Other major roles in the 1930s include *Petrified Forest* (1936), *Dark Victory* (1939), and *The Private Lives of Elizabeth and Essex* (1939). Davis is known for her portrayals of strong-willed independent women. Her later film and television work earned her great praise. In 1940, she was elected president of the Academy of Motion Picture Arts and Sciences, the first woman to hold that post.

References: Ephraim Katz, *The Film Encyclopedia* (New York: HarperPerennial, 1994), 332–33; Barbara Leaming, *Bette Davis: A Biography* (New York: Simon & Schuster, 1992); Gene Ringgold, *Bette Davis: Her Films and Career* (Secaucus, N.J.: Citadel, 1985).

Davis, John William (1873–1955)
American attorney and politician, presidential candidate of the Democratic Party in 1924. He was born in Clarksburg, West Virginia, on April 13, 1873, the son of U.S. Congressman John James Davis. He graduated from Washington and Lee University in Virginia in 1892, and was admitted to the West Virginia state bar shortly thereafter. Like his father, Davis served in the West Virginia House of Delegates (1899), as well as in the U.S. House of Representatives (1911–13). His terms in these two institutions were not noteworthy, but apparently they gained the attention of now President Woodrow WILSON. After his inauguration, Wilson asked Davis to become his administration's solicitor general (in effect, the deputy attorney

general), in which capacity Davis argued the administration's position before the U.S. Supreme Court. Serving until 1918 (he also was the chief counselor of the American Red Cross during this period), Davis is considered one of the finest solicitors general ever to serve since the position was established in 1871. In 1918, upon Wilson's urging, he accepted the post of U.S. ambassador to Great Britain, where he worked with the Germans at the end of the war to gain fair treatment for Allied prisoners of war before their exchange. He served in this post until 1921, and, the following year, was named president of the American Bar Association.

In 1924, the little-known Davis, through an interesting turn of events, surprisingly won the Democratic nomination for president of the United States. Davis had not even been considered a candidate for the presidential nomination when the Democratic Convention opened in New York's Madison Square Garden. However, as ballot after ballot was taken, the established candidates, William Gibbs McAdoo, a former secretary of the treasury, and New York Governor Al Smith, were deadlocked. Davis, whose only political experience had been in the House and as the envoy to England, soon became the compromise candidate of these competing forces. After a record 103 ballots, he was nominated. His running mate, Governor Charles Wayland Bryan of Nebraska, was quickly nominated, and the ticket moved outward to gather support among the American people.

Historians agree that when Davis entered the political arena, he was woefully unprepared and too disorganized to campaign against a popular president in the midst of unrestrained prosperity. On November 4, election day, Davis was swept by a tide of Republicanism, capturing only 8.3 million votes to President Calvin COOLIDGE's 15.7 million, with the electoral votes being 382 to 136. (A third candidate in the race, independent Robert LA FOLLETTE, received 4.8 million votes.) After the bitter loss, Davis returned to his law practice. In 1932, he supported then New York Governor Franklin D. ROOSEVELT for the presidency, but soon after Roosevelt's election, Davis conflicted with many of Roosevelt's more liberal policies. At first his criticism was muted; however, as the 1936 election approached, he and other like-minded Democrats formed the Liberty League coalition to oppose the NEW DEAL. He denounced the Wagner Labor Relations Act as illegal and condemned other New Deal legislation. In 1940, he backed Republican Wendell Wilkie for the presidency, marking a complete break with his party. He never supported a Democratic presidential candidate again.

In 1952 Davis defended several school districts against a lawsuit by the NAACP in the early stages of the famous case *Brown v. Board of Education of Topeka, Kansas*. Davis died on March 24, 1955. He remains one of the most prominent American attorneys in the chronicle of the nation's law record. He argued before the U.S. Supreme Court 140 times—more than any other person in the history of the Court.

See also ELECTIONS, U.S.

References: William H. Harbaugh, *Lawyer's Lawyer: The Life of John W. Davis* (New York: Oxford University Press, 1973); William H. Harbaugh, "Davis, John William" in Kermit L. Hall, ed. in chief, *The Oxford Companion to the Supreme Court of the United States* (New York: Oxford University Press, 1992), 219; William H. Harbaugh, "Davis, John William" in Warren F. Kuehl, ed., *Biographical Dictionary of Internationalists* (Westport, Conn.: Greenwood, 1983), 198–99; "John W. Davis Dies at 81; Lost to Coolidge in 1924; Former Envoy to Britain, Constitutional Lawyer, Succumbs in South," *New York Times*, March 25, 1955, pp. 1, 24.

Davis, Norman Hezekiah (1878–1944)

American financier, diplomat, and editor. Born in Bedford County, Tennessee, on August 9, 1878, he attended Vanderbilt and Stanford Universities but never received a degree. He returned to Tennessee and purchased a farm and a factory that manufactured overalls. From 1902 to 1917, Davis lived in Cuba, where he served as president of the Trust Company of Cuba while amassing a considerable fortune. During the administration of U.S. President Woodrow WILSON, he volunteered advice on foreign policy matters, and in doing so became an intimate of the president. In 1919, Davis was named as an assistant secretary in the U.S. Treasury Department before being named by Wilson as part of the American delegation to the VERSAILLES Peace Conference. After returning to the United States, Davis served as undersecretary of state, leaving office in March 1921. After he left the federal government, Davis founded the Council on Foreign Relations—a nonprofit interest group that continues today to examine and discuss foreign policy questions—as well as the council's influential journal, *Foreign Affairs*.

Although connected to a Democratic administration, Davis was chosen by Republican presidents during the 1920s and 1930s to serve as a delegate to several international parleys, including the LONDON NAVAL CONFERENCE and the GENEVA DISARMAMENT CONFERENCE. In 1924, he was also the head of the LEAGUE OF NATIONS commission investigating the final disposition of the Lithuanian city of Memel or, Klaip'eda. The commission concluded that the disputed city should belong under Lithuanian control. Davis later served as president of the board of the International Red Cross from 1938 until his death on July 1, 1944, in Hot Springs, Virginia.

References: Harold B. Whiteman, Jr., "Davis, Norman Hezekiah" in Warren F. Kuehl, ed., *Biographical Dictionary of Internationalists* (Westport, Conn.: Greenwood, 1983), 200–2; Kenneth J. Grieb, "Davis, Norman Hezekiah" in

Bruce W. Jentleson and Thomas G. Paterson, senior eds., *Encyclopedia of U.S. Foreign Relations* (New York: Oxford University Press, 1997), 1: 411–12; Harold B. Whiteman, Jr., "Norman H. Davis and the Search for International Peace and Security, 1917–1944" (Ph.D. dissertation, Yale University, 1958); Peter Grose, *Continuing the Inquiry: The Council on Foreign Relations from 1921 to 1996* (New York: Council on Foreign Relations, 1996); Robert D. Schulzinger, *The Wise Men of Foreign Affairs: The History of the Council on Foreign Relations* (New York: Columbia University Press, 1984).

Davisson, Clinton Joseph (1881–1958)

American physicist and Nobel laureate. Born in Bloomington, Illinois, on October 22, 1881, he received his Bachelor of Science degree from the University of Chicago in 1908 and his doctorate from Princeton University in 1911. Davisson worked as a professor of physics at the Carnegie Institute of Technology in Pittsburgh from 1911 to 1917, and as a physicist at the Bell Telephone Laboratories from 1917 to 1946. At Bell he conducted, in conjunction with George Paget THOMSON, experiments into the diffraction of electrons with the use of crystals. For this work, they shared the 1937 Nobel Prize in physics.

After leaving Bell Laboratories, Davisson spent his final years as a professor of physics at the University of Virginia at Charlottesville. He died on February 1, 1958.

References: Bernard S. Schlessinger, "Davisson, Clinton Joseph" in Bernard S. and June H. Schlessinger, eds., *The Who's Who of Nobel Prize Winners* (Phoenix, Ariz.: Oryx, 1986), 163; Thomas Watson MacCallum and Stephen Taylor, eds., *The Nobel Prize–Winners and the Nobel Foundation, 1901–1937* (Zurich, Switzerland: Central European Times Publishing, 1938), 104–05.

Dawes, Charles Gates (1865–1951)

American lawyer, financier, and politician, noted architect of the DAWES PLAN. Dawes was born in Marietta, Ohio, on August 27, 1865, the son of General Rufus Dawes, a Civil War veteran and politician in his own right (he served in the U.S. Congress from 1881 to 1883) and Mary Beman (Gates) Dawes. He attended Marietta College and the Cincinnati Law School, the latter awarding him a law degree in 1886. He was admitted to the Nebraska bar that year, and began a practice in railroad law in the capital, Lincoln, which lasted until 1894. He then went into the business of manufactured gas, eventually becoming the president of the LaCrosse Gas Light Company (Wisconsin) and of the Northwestern Gas Light and Coke Company in Evanston, Illinois.

A Republican, Dawes started his political career as the Illinois manager for the successful presidential campaign of William McKinley in 1896. For his work, the new pres-

ident appointed Dawes the comptroller of the currency in the Treasury Department, a post he held from 1897 until 1902. A reformer, he helped launch numerous bank improvements. In 1902, Dawes left his post to run unsuccessfully for the U.S. Senate. Returning to civilian life, he entered banking, helping to organize the Central Trust Company of Illinois at Chicago (later renamed the Central Republic Bank and Trust Company), which he served as president (1902–21) and board chairman (1921–25). During that World War I, Dawes was commissioned a major, and spent 1917 and 1918 in France as U.S. General John J. Pershing's personal agent purchasing supplies for the American Expeditionary Force, the U.S. contingent fighting in Europe. For work as the American delegate on the military board of Allied supply, in which he purchased items at low cost for the Allied army as a whole, he was promoted to brigadier general at the end of the war. For the rest of his life he would be addressed as "General Dawes." His experiences during the war are chronicled in his memoir, *A Journal of the Great War* (1921).

After returning to the United States, Dawes became an important voice in the push to institute national budget reform in the U.S. government. In 1921, President Warren G. HARDING named him as the nation's first director of the budget. His prior work in the military, holding down costs while eliminating waste and duplication, served him well in this new post, where he instituted several reforms leading to fiscal restraint. At this time, the REPARATIONS crisis in Europe was beginning. After the war, the Allies had demanded payments, or reparations, from the defeated nations Germany and Austria. A depression had hit both of these countries hard, and they fell behind on these massive and crippling payments. In December 1923 President Calvin COOLIDGE named Dawes chair of the Expert Commission on German Finances and Reparations. Dawes immediately went to work on what became known as the DAWES PLAN: by obtaining a loan of 800 million gold marks abroad, he stabilized the plummeting German currency; then, by mortgaging the German railroads and industrial plants, he raised more than 16 billion gold marks to lay down payments on the reparations debt. For this work, and for resolving a crisis that might have led to a war, Dawes shared the 1925 Nobel Prize in Peace with Sir Austen CHAMBERLAIN.

Dawes's loyalty to the Republican Party, his reformist mind, and his outstanding work to stave off war in Europe led many to consider him as a possible president of the United States. When the Republicans met in Cleveland, June 10–12, 1924, President Calvin COOLIDGE picked Dawes as his running mate. That November, in a landslide, the Republicans returned to power, and Dawes became the thirtieth vice president of the United States. As vice president, he was a strong supporter of Coolidge's moves toward establishing world peace. As president of the U.S. Senate, he lent important support toward the passage of the KELLOGG-BRIAND PACT. In 1928, when Coolidge refused to run for a second full term, Dawes, the loyal follower, acceded to his wishes and declined to run for president, a nomination that surely would have been his had he wanted it. When Herbert HOOVER was elected president, one of his first appointments was that of Dawes as the U.S. ambassador to Great Britain, where he served until 1932. In 1930, he was a delegate to the LONDON NAVAL CONFERENCE. Hoover named Dawes chair of the Reconstruction Finance Corporation in 1932, but he only served a few months, resigning on June 6, 1932, to establish the City National Bank and Trust Company in Chicago, of which he was chair until his death. Dawes published *The Banking System of the United States* (1892), *A Journal of the Great War* (1921), *Notes as Vice-President* (1935), *How Long Prosperity?* (1937), *Journal as Ambassador to Great Britain* (1939), and *A Journal of Reparations* (1939). Dawes died in Evanston, Illinois, on April 23, 1951.

See also YOUNG, Owen D.; YOUNG PLAN.

References: Donald R. McCoy, "Dawes, Charles Gates" in Allen Johnson and Dumas Malone et al., eds., *Dictionary of American Biography* (New York: Charles Scribner's Sons, 1930–95), 5: 159–60; Steve Wood, "Dawes, Charles Gates" in Bernard S. and June H. Schlessinger, eds., *The Who's Who of Nobel Prize Winners* (Phoenix, Ariz.: Oryx, 1986), 133; Edward A. Goedeken, "Charles G. Dawes in War and Peace, 1917–1922," (Ph.D. dissertation, University of Kansas, 1984); Bascom N. Timmons, *Portrait of an American: Charles G. Dawes* (New York: Henry Holt & Co., 1953); George P. Auld, *The Dawes Plan and the New Economics* (London: Allen & Unwin, 1927); Melvyn P. Leffler, *The Elusive Quest: America's Pursuit of European Stability and French Security, 1919–1933* (Chapel Hill: University of North Carolina Press, 1979); Paul Roscoe Leach, *That Man Dawes: The Story of a Man Who Has Placed His Name High among the Great of the World in This Generation Because He Ruled His Life by Common Sense* (Chicago: Reilly & Lee Co., 1930).

Dawes Plan

Economic formula devised in 1924 by American politician Charles Gates DAWES for the payment of war REPARATIONS by Germany to the Allied nations as laid out in the Treaty of VERSAILLES. The Reparation Commission, established on January 14, 1924, was composed of Dawes as chair and Owen D. YOUNG, both of the United States; Robert M. Kindersley and J. C. Stamp of Great Britain; J. Parmentier and Edgard Allix of France; Alberto Pirelli and Federico Flora of Italy; and E. Francqui and Maurice Houtart of Belgium. Historian George Finch wrote of the plan at the time, "On the whole, it seems hopeful that the universal conscience, to which Chairman Dawes appeals in his letter of April 9th transmitting the plan of his com-

mittee to the Reparation Commission, will agree with him that it is based 'upon those principles of justice, fairness, and mutual interest, in the supremacy of which not only the creditors of Germany and Germany herself, but the world, has a vital and enduring concern." However, problems returned with the GREAT DEPRESSION. The terms were reworked in 1929 with the YOUNG PLAN.

References: Charles Gates Dawes, *A Journal of Reparations* (London: Macmillan, 1939); George P. Auld, *The Dawes Plan and the New Economics* (London: Allen ä Unwin, 1927); George A. Finch, *The Dawes Report on German Reparation Payments*, American Journal of International Law 18 (1924): 434–35.

Debs, Eugene Victor (1855–1926)

American socialist and labor leader, jailed by the United States during World War I for violating the Espionage Act. Born in Terre Haute, Indiana, on November 5, 1855, he left at age 14 to work on the railroads, rising to become a locomotive fireman. A unionist, in 1875 he helped to organize the Brotherhood of Locomotive Fireman, to which he was elected as national secretary and treasurer in 1880. In 1885, Debs served a single term in the Indiana legislature.

Starting in the early 1890s, Debs attempted to organize railroad workers into a single union. In 1893 he became president of the American Railway Union, and he led it during a massive strike against the Great Northern Railroad in 1894. In the wake of the strike against the Chicago Pullman Palace Car Company in 1895, Debs was sentenced to six months in prison for violating a federal injunction. During his prison term, Debs read Marx's *Communist Manifesto* and became a Socialist, although he campaigned for Democrat William Jennings BRYAN for the presidency in 1896. Two years later, however, he helped form the Social Democratic Party, and he ran as the party's presidential candidate in 1900. In 1901 the name was changed to the Socialist Party of America, and, in 1904, 1908, and 1912, Debs ran again as the party's candidate, each time gaining more votes but getting nowhere near to influencing the election's outcome.

In 1917, after the Congress enacted the Sedition Act (known as the Espionage Act), which prohibited criticism of the government during wartime, Debs publicly opposed U.S. involvement in World War I and was put on trial for sedition. Found guilty and imprisoned (his case, DEBS V. UNITED STATES, went to the U.S. Supreme Court in 1919), he nonetheless was nominated by the Socialists in 1920 as their presidential candidate. He remains the only candidate to run for the nation's highest office while in jail. Debs was viewed sympathetically by many Americans, and he captured more than 900,000 votes in the 1920 election—more than he ever had before. In 1921,

President Warren G. HARDING pardoned him, and Debs went back to Indiana unbroken in spirit and conviction. His time in prison had broken him physically, however, and he slowly slid toward death. He died in Elmhurst, Illinois, on October 20, 1926. His U.S. citizenship, which was stripped when he was convicted of sedition, was restored posthumously in 1976. Debs remains the only person to run for president five times.

References: Ray Ginger, *The Bending Cross: A Biography of Eugene Victor Debs* (New York: Russell & Russell, 1949); Scott Molloy, "Debs, Eugene Victor" in Mari Jo Buhle, Paul Buhle, and Dan Georgakas, eds., *Encyclopedia of the American Left* (New York: Garland Publishing, 1990), 184–87; "Debs Is Nominated by the Socialists: Atlanta Prisoner Is Made Party's Presidential Candidate for Fifth Time," *New York Times*, May 14, 1920, p. 3.

Debs v. United States (1919)

U.S. Supreme Court decision that upheld the lower ruling that Socialist leader Eugene V. DEBS had violated the Espionage Act of 1917. According to the lower court's decision, Debs had "caused and incited and attempted to cause and incite insubordination, disloyalty, mutiny and refusal of duty in the military and naval forces of the United States and with intent so to do delivered, to an assembly of people, a public speech, set forth. [One of the counts of the indictment] alleges that he obstructed and attempted to obstruct the recruiting and enlistment service of the United States and to that end and with that intent delivered the same speech." Debs was sentenced to 10 years in prison on each count, with the sentences to run concurrently. Debs appealed his conviction directly to the U.S. Supreme Court, on the grounds that the act was a violation of the First Amendment to the U.S. Constitution. Arguments were heard on January 27 and 28, 1919.

Justice Oliver Wendell HOLMES delivered the unanimous Court opinion on March 10, less than seven weeks later. He wrote, "We are of opinion that the verdict on the fourth count, for obstructing and attempting to obstruct the recruiting service of the United States, must be sustained. . . . We see no sufficient reason for differing from the conclusion but think it unnecessary to discuss the question in detail." This case was the third in a series of six cases heard by the Supreme Court from 1919 to 1920 regarding sedition and the First Amendment to the U.S. Constitution.

References: The papers regarding Debs's trial and conviction in 1918 are located in the Department of Justice Control Files, file #77175, RG 60, National Archives, Washington, D.C.; Elder Witt, ed., *Congressional Quarterly's Guide to the U.S. Supreme Court* (Washington, D.C.: Congressional Quarterly, 1979), 397–98; Michael E. Parrish, "Debs v. United States" in Leonard W. Levy, ed. in chief, *Encyclopedia of the American Constitution* (New York: Macmillan, 1986–92), 2: 544–45; *Debs v. United States* 249 US 211 (1919).

Debye, Peter Joseph William (1884–1966)

Dutch-American physicist and Nobel laureate. Born Petrus Josephus Wilhelmus Debye in Maastricht, the Netherlands, on March 24, 1884, he was trained as an electrical engineer and received his doctorate at the University of Munich. In 1911, he was named a professor of theoretical physics at the University of Zurich in Switzerland. He also taught intermittently at the universities at Utrecht and Göttingen, and eventually was named director of the Physical Institute at Leipzig in 1927.

In his researches, Debye had investigated the dipole moments and the diffraction of X rays and electrons in gases—landmark work which was to be used in the study of the human anatomy. Biographer Bernard Schlessinger writes, "By utilizing [these] techniques. . . . Debye established invaluable tools for structure determination. Debye also made significant contributions in the areas of specific heats of bodies at various temperatures, magnetic cooling, crystal structure determination, the theory of solutions, and polymer size determinations." For this work, Debye was awarded the 1936 Nobel Prize in chemistry.

After fleeing from the Netherlands in 1939, Debye spent the remainder of his career at Cornell University in New York, later becoming a naturalized American citizen. He retired in 1952. His publications include *The Dipole Moment and Chemical Structure* (1932). Debye died in Ithaca, New York, on November 2, 1966.

References: Bernard S. Schlessinger, "Debye, Peter Josephus Wilhelmus" in Bernard S. and June H. Schlessinger, eds., *The Who's Who of Nobel Prize Winners* (Phoenix, Ariz.: Oryx, 1986), 14; Thomas Watson MacCallum and Stephen Taylor, eds., *The Nobel Prize–Winners and the Nobel Foundation, 1901–1937* (Zurich, Switzerland: Central European Times Publishing 1938), 166.

Decline of the West, The

Controversial book published in the interwar years by German philosopher Oswald Spengler, which espoused theories of the future of humanity in the 21st century and beyond. Originally published in Germany in two volumes as *Der Untergang des Abendlandes* from 1918 to 1922 (the English translation appeared from 1926 to 1928), the work examines eight major empires and cultures throughout history: the Egyptian, Mesopotamian, Indian, Chinese, so-called "Classical," "Magian" (Spengler's term for Near Eastern), Mexican, and "Faustian" or Western. In examining several indicators of what Spengler felt contributed to the decline of each individual civilization, he predicted, using these same gauges, the decline of American and European culture. Historian Robert Wistrich writes of the work, it "was originally conceived in 1911 as a critique of German foreign policy in the late Wilhelminian era. Spengler expanded the scope of the book to create a new cyclical philosophy of history . . . a morphology of culture whose inspiration derived from Goethe and Nietzsche. Combining dazzling erudition in the fields of history, politics, art, mathematics and the physical sciences, Spengler prophesied the drying up of western cultural productivity and the emergence of a new age of Caesarism, dominated by the ruthless competition of power politics, high technology and social organization."

References: Stuart H. Hughes, *Oswald Spengler: A Critical Estimate* (Cambridge, Mass.: Harvard University Press, 1953); Robert S. Wistrich, *Who's Who in Nazi Germany* (London: Routledge, 1995), 239–40.

De Forest, Lee (1873–1961)

American inventor, creator of such technical innovations as radiotelephony (1919), a communication system for trains (1924), the photoelectric cell (1929), and the television apparatus (1936). Born in Council Bluffs, Iowa, on August 26, 1873, he moved with his family at an early age to Talladega, Alabama, where he attended local schools. After finishing his public education at the Mt. Hernon School for Boys in Massachusetts, De Forest received a bachelor's degree in science from the Sheffield Scientific School at Yale University. He earned a doctorate in 1899 at Yale with his thesis, "Reflection of the Hertzian Waves from the Ends of Parallel Wires." From an early age, De Forest was interested in wireless communications. After graduation he worked for the Western Electric Company in Chicago until 1900, but soon after began to work on developing a system that mated audio and video, at the time an unknown concept. Working with engineer Edwin W. Smythe, the two men developed, in 1902, a radio receiver which worked with the use of an electrolytic detector. That same year, De Forest founded the American De Forest Wireless Telegraph Company, which was used during the Russo-Japanese War of 1904 to send press reports from the battlefield with a wireless telegraph.

During the next two decades, De Forest worked to both perfect and expand the uses of his technology. During the 1920s, he developed sound for previously silent MOTION PICTURES, and in 1923 he demonstrated this new technology at the Rivoli Theater in New York City, where the first talking shorts were shown. During the 1920s and 1930s, he developed numerous innovations in the area of radio and television, including radiotelephony (1919), a radio signaling system (1923), a communication system for trains (1924), a loudspeaker system (1925), the photoelectric cell (1929), and a rough mechanism for broad-

casting photographs into people's homes, which eventually became television (1936). De Forest later supplemented these experiments by establishing color television pictures. During his life he held more than three hundred patents. In 1950 he published his autobiography, *Father of Radio*. He died June 30, 1961.

References: Tom Lewis, *Empire of the Air: The Men Who Made Radio* (New York: Edward Burlingame Books, 1991); James A. Hijiya, *Lee de Forest and the Fatherhood of Radio* (Bethlehem, Penn.: Lehigh University Press, 1992); Lee de Forest, *Father of Radio: The Autobiography of Lee de Forest* (Chicago: Wilcox & Follett, 1950).

Deledda, Grazia (1871–1936)

Italian writer and Nobel laureate. Born in the small village of Nuoro on the island of Sardinia on September 27, 1871, she was the daughter of Giovantonio Deledda and his wife Chrisceda (Cambosu) Deledda. She did not receive much formal education, but she was writing short stories and articles, and contributing them to magazines, before she was 18. By 1895, she had published three books on Sardinian life—*Fior di Sardegna* (Flower of Sardinia, 1891), *Racconti sardi* (Sardinian tales, 1894), and *Anime oneste* (Honest souls, 1895). Although she married Palmerino Madesani, a civil servant, in 1897 and moved to Rome, she continued to write on the spirit of her homeland as she saw it.

Deledda's next series of works were novels dealing with all facets of human existence—*Dopo il divorzio* (After the divorce, 1902), *Elias Portolu* (1903), *Cenere* (Ashes, 1904), and *La via del male* (The path of evil, 1906). Her novel *L'edera* (The ivy, 1908) is considered one of her finest. She followed these with *Colombi e sparvieri* (Doves and sparrowhawks, 1912) and *Canne al vento* (Reeds in the wind, 1913). In the years during and after World War I she wrote *L'incendio nell'oliveto* (Fire in the olive grove, 1918) and *La Madre* (The mother, 1920). In 1927, Deledda was awarded the 1926 Nobel Prize in literature for her "idealistically inspired writings which with plastic clarity picture the life of her native island and with depth and sympathy deal with human problems in general."

Deledda's last novels did not explore Sardinian life; they include *La fuga in Egitto* (Flight into Egypt, 1925) and *Il paese del vento* (Land of the wind, 1931), her last work. Several months after winning the Nobel, she was diagnosed with early symptoms of breast cancer; she continued to work for nine more years before dying of the disease in Rome on August 16, 1936.

References: Tyler Wasson, ed., *Nobel Prize Winners: An H. W. Wilson Biographical Dictionary* (New York: H. W. Wilson, 1987), 257–59; Mario Aste, *Grazia Deledda: Ethnic Novelist* (Potomac, Md.: Scripta Humanistica, 1990); Stanley Kunitz and Howard Haycraft, eds., "Twentieth Century Authors: A Biographical Dictionary of Modern Literature" (New York: H. W. Wilson, 1942); Bernard S. and June H. Schlessinger, eds., *The Who's Who of Nobel Prize Winners* (Phoenix, Ariz.: Oryx, 1986), 56.

della Chiesa, Giacomo   *See* BENEDICT XV.

DeMille, Cecil B. (1881–1959)

American motion picture producer and director, noted for his box-office hits of the interwar period. Born in Ashfield, Massachusetts, on August 12, 1881, DeMille studied at the Pennsylvania Military College and at the American Academy of Dramatic Arts before becoming a stage actor in 1900, working with his brother, the playwright William Churchill DeMille. In 1913 DeMille, Jesse Lasky, Arthur Freed, and Samuel GOLDWYN established the Jesse Lasky Feature Play Company, which evolved into Paramount Pictures. DeMille appeared in the Studio's first feature, *The Straw Man* (1914), but soon realized that he was more talented behind the camera than in front of it. In 1919 he began directing. His pictures in the 1920s made his name: *The Ten Commandments* (1923) and *The King of Kings* (1927) were two of the more popular silent MOTION PICTURES. His films of the 1930s were not noteworthy; he finished his career with a second version of *The Ten Commandments* (1956). De Mille died in Hollywood on January 21, 1959.

References: Cecil B. DeMille (Donald Hayne, ed.), *The Autobiography of Cecil B. DeMille* (London: W. H. Allen, 1960); Sumiko Higashi, *Cecil B. DeMille and American Culture: The Silent Era* (Berkeley: University of California Press, 1994); Gene Ringgold and DeWitt Bodeen, *The Films of Cecil B. DeMille* (New York: Citadel, 1969).

Denby, Edwin   *See* TEAPOT DOME SCANDAL.

Dennis, Lawrence   *See* MENCKEN, H. L.

De Stijl

Dutch artistic movement, 1917–28, founded by the Dutch architect Theo von Doesburg to obtain from observers a general response to the movement's abstract art. Dutch for "the style," the movement included Gerrit Thomas Rietveld, whose Schröder House, built in Utrecht in the Netherlands in 1924, was a system of glass and masonry; and Dutch painter Piet Mondrian, who founded *De Stijl* magazine with van Doesburg in 1917, working on it until 1932. Using only flat fields, straight lines, and primary colors Mondrian's *Composition with Red, Yellow, and Blue* (1937) typifies the nonobjective, geometric style of the movement.

References: Mildred Friedman, ed., *De Stijl, 1917–1931; Visions of Utopia* (New York: Abbeville, 1982); Alfred H. Barr, Jr., *De Stijl: 1917–1928* (New York: Museum of Modern Art, 1961); Nancy J. Troy, *The De Stijl Environment* (Cambridge, Mass.: MIT Press, 1983).

De Valéra, Éamon (1882–1975)

Irish political leader and diplomat, president of the Dáil Eireann (1919–21), president of the Irish Republic (1921–22), president of the Republic of Ireland (1959–73). Born Edward de Valéra in New York on October 14, 1882, he was the son of a Spanish father and an Irish mother who had emigrated to America. When de Valéra's father died in 1884, his mother sent their son to live with her family in County Limerick in her native Ireland. De Valéra attended Blackrock College and the Royal University, both in Dublin, and graduated from the latter in 1904. For a time he taught mathematics at several Irish colleges before turning to politics in 1913.

The history of "the Troubles," as they are called in Ireland, is long and bloody. There has long been in Ireland, which unlike England is largely Catholic, a movement to break away from British rule and influence. De Valéra was but one of the young men who in the years around World War I joined the group initially called the Irish Volunteers, which used violence to agitate for Irish independence. The Volunteers eventually became the Irish Republican Army (IRA), and their fight carried over into what is called the Easter Rebellion of 1916. De Valéra led a group of Volunteer insurgents during this nationalist uprising, and they eventually surrendered. De Valéra was initially sentenced to death for these activities, but the sentence was commuted and he remained in prison until a general amnesty was issued on June 15, 1917. He was arrested again for similar activities in 1918 and was deported to England.

That same year De Valéra was elected president of Sinn Féin, the political wing of the IRA (a position he held until 1926), and although he was elected to the British Parliament from East Clare, in protest he did not take his seat. Instead, with the aid of fellow IRA member Michael COLLINS, De Valéra escaped to the United States to gather financial aid for Irish independence. He returned to Ireland in 1921, following the passage of the ANGLO-IRISH PEACE TREATY. However, when he realized the pact established continual British rule over Northern Ireland, he denounced it and began a heated political battle with Collins. Collins's assassination on August 22, 1922, did not end the controversy, however. A civil war broke out between pro- and anti-treaty activists, which lasted until

1923. De Valéra was imprisoned by William Thomas Cosgrave, head of the new Irish Republic, until 1924, when he refused to sit in the Dáil Éireann, Ireland's national assembly. De Valéra then began in 1927 his party Fianna Fáil (literally, "Warriors of Ireland"), which in 1932 defeated Cosgrave's government, and De Valéra was elected the Irish prime minister. He instituted several changes in the government to separate Ireland from Great Britain, including the withholding of land annuities, which led to concessions from the London government by conceding control over the naval bases at Berehaven, Cobh, and Lough Swilly. De Valéra served as president of the Council of the LEAGUE OF NATIONS in 1932. During World War II, he declared Ireland's neutrality.

During the postwar era, de Valéra served two additional terms as prime minister and, starting in 1959, two terms as president, thus becoming one of the longest serving leaders of the century. He retired in 1973 and died on August 29, 1975.

References: "De Valéra, Eamon" in D. J. Hickey and J. E. Doherty, *A Dictionary of Irish History since 1800* (Dublin: Gill & Macmillan, 1980), 121–26; John P. O'Carroll, and John A. Murphy, eds., *De Valera and His Times* (Cork: Cork University Press, 1983); John Bowman, *De Valera and the Ulster Question, 1917–1973* (Oxford: Clarendon Press, 1982).

Dietrich, Marlene (1904–1992)

German-American actress and singer, noted for her important film work during the 1920s and 1930s. Dietrich was born Maria Magdalene von Losch just outside of Berlin, Germany, on December 27, 1901, the daughter of a police lieutenant. She began singing in the German cabaret scene in the first years of WEIMAR GERMANY, entrancing audiences with her figure and voice. In 1924 she married Rudolf Sieber, with whom she had one daughter; although they only lived together for five years, they never divorced and remained legally a couple until his death in 1976. Dietrich's first role was in the 1923 German silent film *Der Kleine Napoleon* (The little napoleon), and she starred in a number of silent dramas during the remainder of the decade. Dietrich's last silent film was *Ship of Lost Men* (1929), starring Dietrich as an aviator aboard a ship of murderers who must disguise her sex to avoid being killed.

In 1929, Dietrich met German director Josef von Sternberg, who cast her as the cabaret singer Lola-Lola in *Der Blaue Engel* (*The Blue Angel*, 1930). Sternberg then took her to Hollywood, where he cast her in *Morocco* (1930), the film that made her an international star. Subsequent films included *Shanghai Express* (1932), *Blonde Venus* (1932), *The Song of Songs* (1933), *The Devil is a Woman* (1935), and *I Loved a Soldier* (1936), the successes of which made her one of the highest-paid actresses in

Marlene Dietrich *(CORBIS/Bettmann)*

Hollywood at the time. But by the end of the decade, after some failures, she had retreated back to Europe.

In 1939, Dietrich was lured back to Hollywood to make a comeback in a western, *Destry Rides Again,* starring James Stewart. The film was a huge success, showing her talent in a whole new genre. During World War II, she remained in the United States, became a U.S. citizen, and toured her adopted country in support of the war effort against her native land. After the war, she performed in Las Vegas and on Broadway and appeared in such films as *A Foreign Affair* (1948), *Jigsaw* (1949), *Montecarlo* (1956), *Around the World in 80 Days* (1956), and *Witness for the Prosecution* (1957). Her biographer, Alexander Walker, notes that "a brief appearance as a heavily veiled Prussian baroness in *Just a Gigolo* (1978) was her last work on the big screen. Her last greatest acting role was as Madame Bertholt in *Judgment at Nuremberg* (1961)."

Dietrich spent the last 13 years of her life in her Paris apartment, the last 12 in bed in complete seclusion from the world. When she died on May 6, 1992, she was best remembered for her earliest work.

References: Alexander Walker, *Dietrich* (New York: Harper & Row, 1984); Donald Spoto, *Blue Angel: The Life of Marlene*

Dietrich (Garden City, N.Y.: Doubleday, 1992); Maria Riva, *Marlene Dietrich* (New York: Alfred A. Knopf, 1992).

Dirac, Paul Adrien Maurice (1902–1984)

English physicist and Nobel laureate. Born in Bristol, England, on August 8, 1902, he received his bachelor's degree from Bristol University in 1921. During a career at Cambridge University (1927–68) and Florida State University (1971–84), Dirac worked in the field of quantum dynamics, which deals with atomic particles. Biographer Virginia Hooten explains, "[Dirac's] mathematical treatment of electronic properties predicted the existence of positrons, previously unobserved, at an early stage in his career. Dirac continued to develop the new field of quantum mechanics, his great contribution being the Dirac wave equations which included special relativity in the Schrödinger equation." For this work in atomic theory, Dirac was co-awarded (with Erwin SCHRÖDINGER) the 1933 Nobel Prize in physics.

Dirac worked on atomic theory for the remainder of his life. In 1971 he came to the United States to teach physics at Florida State University in Tallahassee. He died on October 20, 1984.

References: Virginia A. Hooton, "Dirac, Paul Adrien Maurice" in Bernard S. and June H. Schlessinger, eds., *The Who's Who of Nobel Prize Winners* (Phoenix, Ariz.: Oryx, 1986), 161; Thomas Watson MacCallum and Stephen Taylor, eds., *The Nobel Prize–Winners and the Nobel Foundation, 1901–1937* (Zurich, Switzerland: Central European Times Publishing, 1938), 98.

dirigibles *See* ZEPPELINS AND DIRIGIBLES.

Disney, Walt (1901–1966)

American film producer and animation pioneer. Born on December 5, 1901, in Chicago, Illinois, he spent much of his childhood on a Missouri farm before moving to Kansas City at age eight. He studied art and in 1919 became a commercial illustrator. Disney began his career in the early 1920s with a series of shorts entitled *Alice in Cartoonland,* which combined the movements of a living actress with an animated one. But he was soon forced to shut down his studio and went to work for animator Charles Minz in New York, where he created the character of Oswald the Rabbit.

Disney left Minz in 1927 and, with the advent of MOTION PICTURE sound in 1928, delivered a succession of delightful family films, many featuring a mouse who started out with the name of Mortimer, made his debut in *Steamboat Willie* on November 18, 1928, and evolved into Mickey Mouse. That same year, Disney released the first of his *Silly Symphonies,* a series of whimsical cartoons. He created a coterie of characters destined to be ingrained in the minds of people all over the world, including Mickey's friend Donald Duck, his dog Pluto, and his girlfriend Minnie Mouse. In 1937 Disney produced the first full-length animated cartoon motion picture, *Snow White and the Seven Dwarfs.* His last interwar film was *Pinocchio* (1939). His other classic animated films include *Fantasia* (1940) and *Alice in Wonderland* (1951).

After the 1950s, Walt Disney Productions began making wildlife documentaries, soon producing its first live-action film with a human cast. Disney continued to focus on the "family market," bringing his exuberant imagination to appreciative audiences worldwide. The most honored filmmaker to date, Disney won 31 Academy Awards during his career. He died on December 15, 1966.

See also CARTOONS, STRIP AND MOVING.

References: Diane Disney Miller, *The Story of Walt Disney* (New York: Holt, 1957); Bob Thomas, *Walt Disney* (New York: Simon & Schuster, 1976); Robert Durant Feild, *The Art of Walt Disney* (London: Collins, 1947).

Dodd, William Edward (1869–1940)

American historian and diplomat, U.S. ambassador to Germany (1933–37). Born to a farming family on October 21, 1869, near Clayton, North Carolina, Dodd attended local schools and the Oak Ridge Military Academy. After failing to get into the United States Military Academy at West Point, he instead studied at the Virginia Polytechnic Institute, from which he graduated in 1895 and where he later taught a class in history. After borrowing some money from relatives, he attended the University of Leipzig, which awarded him a Ph.D. magna cum laude in 1900.

After he returned to the United States, Dodd worked for a short time at the Library of Congress in Washington, D.C., before he obtained a position as a professor of history at Randolph-Macon Woman's College in Lynchburg, Virginia. Aside from publishing numerous articles on history, he also penned biographies of southern politicians Nathaniel Macon (1903) and Jefferson Davis (1907). In 1908, he moved to the University of Chicago, where he remained for the rest of his life.

While at Chicago, Dodd continued his research into major American figures, publishing such works as *The Cotton Kingdom: A Chronicle of the Old South* (1919), *Woodrow Wilson and His Work* (1920), and *Lincoln or Lee: Comparison and Contrast of the Two Greatest Leaders in the War between the States* (1928), and he edited, with historian Ray Stannard Baker, six volumes of *The Public Papers of Woodrow Wilson* (1925–27). During World War I, he was a close adviser to WILSON, and was active in Democratic party circles during the 1920s. Then, according to Louis R. Smith Jr., a Dodd biographer, "In 1933 President

Franklin D. ROOSEVELT hoped to capitalize on Dodd's German ties and appointed him ambassador to Germany." During his tenure as ambassador, Dodd repeatedly warned Roosevelt that Adolf HITLER was slowly moving Germany toward war, and that rapid militarization of the German state would plunge Europe into another conflict. Instead of accepting Dodd's advice, however, Roosevelt and the U.S. State Department saw their ambassador as a barrier to improved relations with the NAZI regime. Left to slowly twist in the wind in Berlin, Dodd was finally recalled to the United States in 1937 and removed from his position.

Crushed because of the criticism of his work in Berlin, Dodd retired to his farm in Round Hill, Virginia, to work on new books. His health, however, soon began to fail, and on February 9, 1940, Dodd died.

References: Avery Craven, "Dodd, William Edward" in Allen Johnson and Dumas Malone et al., eds., *Dictionary of American Biography* (New York: Charles Scribner's Sons, 1930–95), 2: 152–54; Louis R. Smith, Jr., "Dodd, William Edward" in Bruce W. Jentleson and Thomas G. Paterson, senior eds., *Encyclopedia of U.S. Foreign Relations* (New York: Oxford University Press, 1997), 2: 27; John E. Findling, *Dictionary of American Diplomatic History* (Westport, Conn.: Greenwood, 1989), 159–60; Robert Dallek, *Democrat and Diplomat: The Life of William E. Dodd* (New York: Oxford University Press, 1968); Robert Dallek, "Beyond Tradition: The Diplomatic Careers of William E. Dodd and George S. Messersmith, 1933–1939," *South Atlantic Quarterly* 66 (Spring 1967): 233–44; Douglas Little, "Claude Bowers and His Mission to Spain: The Diplomacy of a Jeffersonian Democrat" in Kenneth Paul Jones, ed., *U.S. Diplomats in Europe, 1919–1941* (Santa Barbara, Calif.: ABC-Clio, 1981), 144; L. F. Gittler, "Scholar among Nazis: Former Ambassador Dodd," *Washington Post*, July 7, 1938, p. 7.

Dollfuss, Engelbert (1892–1934)

Austrian politician and chancellor (1932–34), murdered by Nazi sympathizers in their attempt to take over the government. Born in the village of Texing, in lower Austria, on October 4, 1892, Dollfuss studied law at the University of Vienna and economics at the University of Berlin, where he received a degree. During World War I, he saw action as a member of a Tyrolean regiment. A member of the Christian Socialist Party, he entered politics in 1931, when he was named president of the Federal Railways. That same year he was named as the minister of agriculture and forestry. In 1932, the government installed him as chancellor of Austria.

When Dollfuss took over the Austrian government, he was considered a lightweight, but he emphasized his leadership with strong defiance against German intervention in his nation. This stance earned him the nickname "Millimetternich," due to his small size and ability to stand up against the Germans like another Austrian diplomat, Count Clemens von Metternich. To combat the Nazis' growing influence in Austria, he ordered on March 7, 1933, the institution of new laws that ended freedom of speech and the press, and the right to assemble. He also used the power of the state to crush all political opposition, having declared illegal the Communist Party and the *Schutzbund* (the armed defense group of the Social Democratic Party), as well as the small Austrian Nazi Party. Dollfuss then dissolved Parliament and called a new Parliament that soon enacted a new constitution which established the "Christian German Federal State on a cooperative basis" in an attempt to head off a German invasion.

It was, however, too late. On July 25, 1934, Nazi sympathizers in Austria struck at Dollfuss's government. As part of the secret group called SS Standarte 89, they wore Austrian army uniforms and seized government buildings. Dollfuss was confronted in his office by one of the coup leaders, Otto Planetta, who shot the chancellor in the throat. The Austrian leader lay on the ground for hours, begging for medical aid, before he died from loss of blood. The coup then collapsed, and thirteen of the plotters were eventually hanged for Dollfuss's murder. Former German chancellor Franz von Papen accepted the position of minister to Austria on July 26, 1934, the day after Dollfuss had been assassinated.

At the Nuremberg War Crimes trials at the end of World War II, it was shown that "the evidence . . . [was presented] of the preparations for the seizure of Austria showed the part played by the SS Standarte 89 in the murder of Dollfuss and described the memorial plaque which was erected as a tribute to the SS men who participated in that murder." Von Papen was found guilty for his role in Dollfuss's murder.

See also SCHUSCHNIGG, KURT VON.

References: Gordon Brook-Shepherd, *Dollfuss* (London: Macmillan 1961); R. John Rath, "The Molding of Engelbert Dollfuss as an Agrarian Reformer," *Austrian History Yearbook* 28 (1997): 173–215; "Herr Dollfuss Killed By Nazis. Attempted Rising in Vienna. Ministers Held Prisoners in Chancery. Sharp Fighting and Truce," *The Times* (London), July 26, 1934, p. 12; "Herr Dollfuss Dead," *The Times* (London), July 26, 1934, p. 13; "Austrian Nazis Kill Dollfuss, Revolt Fails; 147 Plotters Held; Martial Law in Effect; Italian Army, Navy, Planes Ready to Act," *New York Times*, July 26, 1934, p. 1; Carl Sifakis, *Encyclopedia of Assassinations* (New York: Facts On File, 1991), 45.

Domagk, Gerhard (1895–1964)

German bacteriologist who was awarded but refused the 1939 Nobel Prize in medicine and physiology. Born in Lagow, in Brandenburg, Germany, on October 30, 1895, he served in the German army during World War I, then received his medical degree from the University of Kiel in 1921. He served as a professor at the University of Muenster from 1925 to 1964, and worked at the I.G. Farbenindustrie research institute as director of research from 1928 to 1964. During these years, he synthesized the effects of prontosil rubrum, a sulfonamide compound used in fighting diseases. His later work included research into cures for tuberculosis and cancer. For his discovery of prontosil, he was awarded the 1939 Nobel prize, but because of an edict passed by the HITLER regime, German Nobel winners could not accept the award.

Domagk continued to work on antibacterial compounds until his death in Beirberg, Brandenburg, Germany, on April 24, 1964.

References: Carlyle Edwards, "Domagk, Gerhard" in Bernard S. and June H. Schlessinger, eds., *The Who's Who of Nobel Prize Winners* (Phoenix, Ariz.: Oryx, 1986), 91; Tyler Wasson, ed., *Nobel Prize Winners: An H. W. Wilson Biographical Dictionary* (New York: The H. W. Wilson Company, 1987), 266–68.

Dominican Republic, U.S. Occupation of

Following the assassination of Dominican president Ramón Cáceres (1868–1911), the country was plunged into chaos. A succession of ephemeral presidents bankrupted the republic to pay off their supporters.

U.S. president Woodrow Wilson believed that American intervention would promote democracy and prevent the collapse of the Dominican economy and staunch political anarchy. In November 1915 Wilson insisted that U.S. officials take control of the Dominican government's finances and begin to train a police force that would replace the army and militia. The Dominican national assembly refused to cede control to the United States, and in May 1916 U.S. Marines were dispatched to Santo Domingo and began an eight-year occupation.

The occupiers imposed martial law in the face of strong anti-American feeling. Despite this antipathy, reforms of Dominican financial and legal institutions were undertaken, as well as efforts to improve conditions for the rural population. Roads, public schools, and sanitation facilities were built; medical services were provided.

Improvements in the standard of living, however, did not prevent armed resistance to the occupation forces in rural areas. By the 1920 U.S. presidential campaign, Republicans were criticizing American involvement in the Dominican Republic. This led to negotiations to end the American occupation. In 1924 the marines withdrew, although U.S. supervision of Dominican customs continued until 1940.

Dorsey, Jimmy (1904–1957) and Tommy (1905–1956)

American band-leader brothers, famed during the 1920s and 1930s for their SWING or "big band" sound. James Francis, born on February 29, 1904, and Thomas, born on November 19, 1905, grew up in a musical family in Shenandoah, Pennsylvania. At an early age, they became interested in JAZZ, Jimmy became an expert in the clarinet and alto saxophone and had a solo act by 1927. Tommy, who became skilled in the trombone and trumpet, joined Jimmy in 1930, and together they played in bands with Paul Whiteman, Bix BEIDERBECKE, and orchestra leader Jean Goldkette. They also began to front their own bands, calling themselves the Dorseys Novelty Six and, later, Dorsey's Wild Canaries. In 1933 they formed the Dorsey Brothers Orchestra, which included such famed talent as Ray McKinley, Glenn Miller, and Bob Crosby. Their major hit was "I'm Getting Sentimental Over You," recorded in 1932. The Dorsey Brothers Orchestra lasted until 1935, when they broke up over a disagreement, and reunited in the postwar period. Their sound captured the times and the imagination of the audiences that swooned to their incredible melodies in such hits as "The Breeze and 1," "Green Eyes," and "Amapola."

Tommy Dorsey choked to death in his sleep on November 26, 1956. Jimmy lived but a year longer, dying in New York City on June 12, 1957.

Reference: Herb Sanford, *Tommy and Jimmy: The Dorsey Years* (New Rochelle, N.Y.: Arlington House, 1972).

Dos Passos, John Roderigo (1896–1970)

American writer, whose trilogy, *U.S.A.,* which consisted of the works *The 42nd Parallel* (1930), *1919* (1932), and *The Big Money* (1936), made him one of the leading writers of the post–World War I era. Historian Virginia Carr called him "a passionate polemicist on America's injustices." Dos Passos was born in Chicago and educated at Harvard University. Starting in 1920, he began to publish a series of novels, including *One Man's Initiation—1917* (1920), *Three Soldiers* (1921), and *Manhattan Transfer* (1925). In the latter, he introduced the method of disrupting the story with biographies, newspaper headlines and the lyrics of popular songs to help describe life in New York leading up to and including the PROHIBITION era. He used the same methods in later works, which were focused on the theme of human corruption by society—including the *U.S.A.* trilogy and *Adventures of a Young Man* (1939).

Dos Passos, who passed from a leftist to a rightist ideology in his lifetime, died in Baltimore, Maryland, on August 28, 1970.

References: Virginia Spencer Carr, *Dos Passos: A Life* (Garden City, N.Y.: Doubleday, 1984); Michael Clark, *Dos Passos' Early Fiction, 1912–1938* (Selinsgrove, Pa.: Susquehanna University Press, 1987); Jack Potter, *A Bibliography of John Dos Passos* (Folcroft, Pa.: Folcroft Library Editions, 1976).

Doumer, Paul (1857–1932)

French politician and president (1931–32). Born in the French village of Aurillac, in the *département* of Cantal (formerly part of the province of Auvergne), on March 22, 1857, Doumer was elected as a Radical to the Chamber of Deputies from the *département* of Yonne, and his interest in finance and fiscal matters led to his appointment in 1895 as the minister of finance in the cabinet of Léon BOURGEOIS, where he served until being named as governor-general of the French colony in Indochina the following year.

Doumer spent more time (1897–1902) in Indochina than any previous French administrator of the colony and tried to put the economy in a self-sufficient mode by imposing heavy taxes on the local people, which led to bitter feelings against the French populace. Doumer returned to France in 1902 when he was elected again to the Chamber of Deputies, moving to the Senate in 1912. From 1927 to 1931 he was president of the Senate, and, from 1921 to 1922, was minister of finance in the cabinet of Aristide BRIAND, serving in that same position from December 1925 to March 1926.

On May 31, 1931, Doumer was elected the 13th president of the French Republic, a number that perhaps foretold his bad luck. He served only a year, from May 1931 until May 1932. On May 7, 1932, he was assassinated by a White Russian sympathizer, Paul Gorgoulov, who claimed to the police that he was both a physician and the kidnapper of the LINDBERGH baby. Doumer was the author of *L'Indochine française* (1904).

References: "Outrage in France. The President Shot. Serious Condition. Message from the King," *The Times* (London), May 7, 1932, p. 12; "French President Dies of His Wounds 14 Hours After Being Shot By Russians; Two Others Wounded Defending Him," *New York Times*, May 7, 1932, p. 1.

Dracula

1931 film, based on Bram Stoker's 1897 novel, which starred Hungarian-American actor Bela Lugosi, who had played the role on the New York stage. The studio wanted Lon CHANEY for the role, but he died before filming could start. Instead, Lugosi was selected to play Dracula, the owner of a castle in the Carpathian Mountains in eastern Europe who travels to London in search of new victims. There he is confronted by Professor Van Helsing (played by Edward Van Sloan), who tries to protect those around him from Dracula's thirst for blood. Directed by Tod Browning, the film became one of the most popular movies of the early sound years, and propelled Lugosi to international fame.

References: Arthur Lennig, *The Count: The Life and Films of Bela "Dracula" Lugosi* (New York: Putnam, 1974).

Dressler, Marie (1869–1934)

Canadian-American actress in silent films and early talking pictures. Born Leila Marie Koerber on November 8, 1869, in Couburg, Ontario, Canada, she achieved early success on the stage in New York and London. In 1914, she went to Hollywood, and starred in Mack Sennett's *Tillie's Punctured Romance,* the first film of rising comedie actor Charlie CHAPLIN. An accomplished comic and character actress, she appeared in such pictures as *Anna Christie* (1930) with Greta GARBO; *Min and Bill* (1931), for which she won the Academy Award for Best Actress; *Tugboat Annie* (1933), and *Dinner at Eight* (1933). Suffering from cancer, she died in Santa Barbara, California, on July 28, 1934.

Reference: Ephraim Katz, *The Film Encyclopedia* (New York: HarperPerennial, 1994), 359.

DuBois, W. E. B. (1868–1963)

American educator, writer, and civil rights activist. Born William Edward Burghardt DuBois in Great Barrington, Massachusetts, he was of African, Dutch, and French heritage. DuBois earned a bachelor's degree from Fisk University and became the first African American to receive a doctorate from Harvard University (1895). He then taught economics, history, and sociology at Atlanta University (1898–1910, 1932–44).

DuBois advocated full and immediate racial equality for African Americans, and in 1905 helped found the Niagara civil rights movement. In 1909 he organized the National Negro Committee, which became the National Association for the Advancement of Colored People (NAACP) in 1910. He edited the NAACP magazine, *The Crisis,* until 1932. Frustrated that the association was not taking a more intellectual and aggressive stance, DuBois left the NAACP in 1934. His lively disagreements and debates with civil rights leader Booker T. Washington—who believed that black Americans should build technical rather than intellectual skills to earn social equality—gained the national attention of African Americans and whites alike.

DuBois's classic works include *The Souls of Black Folk* (1903), *The Negro* (1915), *Darkwater* (1920), *Black Reconstruction* (1935), *Dusk of Dawn* (1940), *Color and Democracy* (1945), and *The World and Africa* (1947). Later in life he advocated pan-Africanism and promoted worldwide liberation for black people. He joined the Communist Party in 1961 and, discouraged by ongoing racism in the United States, moved to Ghana shortly before his death in 1963. His autobiography, *A Soliloquy on Viewing My Life from the Last Decade of Its First Century,* was published posthumously, in 1968.

Reference: Keith E. Byerman, *Seizing the Word: History, Art, and Self in the Work of W. E. B. DuBois* (Athens: University of Georgia Press, 1994).

Duchamp, Marcel   See DADA; SURREALISM.

Duncan, Isadora (1877–1927)

American ballet dancer and dance pioneer, active in the socialist movement of the 1920s. Born Dora Angela Duncan in San Francisco, California, on May 26, 1877, she was the daughter of Joseph Duncan, a San Francisco banker, and Mary Dora (Grey) Duncan, a member of a wealthy Irish Catholic family. Enrolled in ballet lessons as a child, she dismissed the rigid rules of her teachers and made up her own moves, creating personal interpretations of the music of such classical composers as Beethoven and Wagner. She made debuts in Chicago and New York City but was not especially successful there, and in 1898 she left the United States for Europe. In London, Duncan found wealthy patrons who enjoyed her radical dances. A leftist who sympathized with the aims of socialists in Russia, she visited that nation in 1905 and became interested in the dances of Sergei Diaghilev.

Duncan led an existence far ahead of her times: unmarried, she bore two children, one with the Singer sewing machine heir Patrick Singer. In 1913, both children and their nanny drowned in the Seine in Paris, a tragedy from which Duncan never recovered. During World War I she planned to open dance schools around the world, but these dreams failed. In 1920, she returned to Russia, then in the throes of a revolution that Duncan supported. There she met the eccentric Russian poet Sergei Yesenin, 17 years her junior. Two years later, they were married and toured Europe and the United States, where Duncan was often booed, called a communist, and, in Boston, harassed. She then left her native land, never to see it again. Back in Paris, her marriage to Yesenin dissolved; he returned to the Soviet Union, where in 1925 he took his own life at age 30. On September 14, 1927, while riding in her car in Paris, Duncan was killed when the long, trailing scarf with which she was identified became caught in the wheel; she was decapitated.

Duncan wrote two books, the autobiographical *My Life* (1927) and *The Art of Dance* (1928). In the former, she mused, "How strange and terrible to approach a human being through the envelope of flesh and find a soul."

References: Franklin Rosemont, "Duncan, Isadora" in Mari Jo Buhle, Paul Buhle, and Dan Georgakas, eds., *Encyclopedia of the American Left* (New York: Garland Publishing, 1990), 206–207; Isadora Duncan, *My Life* (New York: Boni & Liveright, 1927).

Durant, Will (1885–1981) and
Ariel (1898–1981)

American historians, famed for such interwar works as *The Story of Philosophy* (1926) and the landmark series *The Story of Civilization*. Born William James Durant in North Adams, Massachusetts, on November 5, 1885, Will Durant graduated from St. Peter's Jesuit College in Jersey City, New Jersey, and Columbia University. In 1907, he served for a time as reporter on William Randolph Hearst's *New York Journal,* but eventually turned to teaching. In 1913, while working at the Ferrer Modern School in New York City, Durant married one of his pupils, Russian-born Ida Kaufman, whom he called Ariel (she later legally adopted the name).

In 1917, Durant wrote *Philosophy and the Social Problem,* following it up with *The Story of Philosophy* (1926), which became one of the most famous history books of the decade. However, his greatest accomplishment is the 11-part series *The Story of Civilization,* of which Ariel Durant was the unnamed coauthor. Starting in 1935 with *Our Oriental Heritage,* the duo explored history through art, literature, sculpture, and other forms of the humanities. It was not until the seventh volume, *The Age of Reason Begins* (1961), that Ariel Durant received credit as the coauthor. The two concluded the series with the tenth volume, *Rousseau and Revolution* (1967), which won them the Pulitzer Prize for history, and the 11th volume, *The Age of Napoleon* (1975).

Ariel Durant died in Los Angeles, California, on October 25, 1981. Broken-hearted at the loss, Will Durant died two weeks later, on November 5, 1981.

References: Will and Ariel Durant, *A Dual Autobiography* (New York: Simon & Schuster, 1977); Raymond Frey, *William James Durant: An Intellectual Biography* (Lewiston, N.Y.: E. Mellen Press, 1991).

Dust Bowl

The Great Plains section of the United States that suffered a horrendous drought, turning the soil into dust in the 1930s. In the years before World War I, much of the area encompassing the Great Plains, the middle section of the United States embracing Texas, Oklahoma, Kansas, and parts of Colorado and New Mexico, was used for cattle grazing. After the war, to feed the American people and others around the world, the farmers who occupied these lands turned to growing wheat and other grains. In their mad rush for higher yields, they overused the land. A drought fell upon the region in the early 1930s and exacerbated a troubling environmental situation. When winds came, they literally created clouds of soil turned dust. Tens of thousands fled their farms, adding to the ranks of the unemployed in those worst years of the GREAT DEPRESSION. Governor Ernest W. Marland of Oklahoma said in 1936 that more federal aid

Oklahoma dust storm, 1937 *(CORBIS/Bettmann)*

to the farmers was needed, that "forty or fifty thousand of these people . . . haven't anything, they are just burned out."

President Franklin D. ROOSEVELT'S NEW DEAL sought to alleviate the conditions of the Dust Bowl. In addition to the establishment of the SOIL CONSERVATION SERVICE, which helped farmers apply new techniques to avoid soil erosion and provide for the enrichment of the soil, the Congress passed the Taylor Conservation Act, which regulated the grazing of cattle on overused lands.

References: Donald Worster, *Dust Bowl: The Southern Plains in the 1930s* (New York: Oxford University Press, 1982); R. Douglas Hurt, *The Dust Bowl: An Agricultural and Social History* (Chicago: Nelson-Hall, 1981); "Conservation" in Otis L. Graham, Jr., and Meghan Robinson Wander, eds., *Franklin D. Roosevelt: His Life and Times: An Encyclopedic View* (Boston: G. K. Hall, 1985), 78.

Earhart, Amelia (1898–1937)

American aviator, the first woman to cross the Atlantic Ocean in an airplane. Born in Atchison, Kansas, on July 24, 1898, she became interested in watching planes take off as a child. She attended the prestigious Ogontz School for Girls in Rydal, Pennsylvania. In 1918, after just ten hours of flight instruction, Earhart made her first solo flight at Los Angeles, California. She then attended Columbia University and went to summer school at Harvard University before doing some social work at the Denison House in Boston.

In 1928, after getting her pilot's license, she was asked to join pilot Wilmer Stutz and mechanic Lou Gordon on a transatlantic flight. They set out in the *Friendship* from Trepassey Bay, Newfoundland, and landed in Wales 20 hours and 40 minutes later, making her the first woman to fly across that ocean. On May 20, 1932, the fifth anniversary of Charles LINDBERGH's historic solo flight across the Atlantic, Earhart accomplished the same feat in 13 hours and 30 minutes—a new record. For her effort, she was awarded the Distinguished Flying Cross, the first woman to be so honored. This trip was part of a publicity stunt conducted by New York publisher George Palmer Putnam, who had married Earhart on February 7, 1931. Earhart had worked for Putnam when she served as the aviation editor for *Cosmopolitan* magazine from 1928 to 1930. In January 1935, Earhart became the first woman to fly from Hawaii to Oakland, California, and, that May, she flew from Mexico City to New York City in 14 hours.

In March 1937, Earhart attempted an around-the-world trip. Accompanied by a navigator, she took off from California but crashed in Honolulu, forcing her to cancel their plans. She returned to the United States mainland and had the plane repaired. On June 1, she again left on the flight, this time with Fred Noonan as her navigator, and going from Miami, Florida, eastward. Their trip went well until they reached one of its last legs, from Lae, New Guinea, to Honolulu. On July 2, the two circled around Howland Island in the Pacific, trying to land. They were never heard from again. American ships in the area sought to find wreckage or bodies, but no trace of the two aviators was found.

In the more than half a century since her disappearance, Earhart has become more myth than reality. In 1997, on the 50th anniversary of her doomed flight, American Linda Finch completed the Earhart trip in another plane of the same model, an Electra.

References: Doris L. Rich, *Amelia Earhart: A Biography* (Washington, D.C.: Smithsonian Institution Press, 1989); Vincent V. Loomis, *Amelia Earhart: The Final Story* (New York: Random House, 1985); "Hear Amelia's Faint Calls: Searchers' Hopes Revived by Signals; 57 Planes on Way" *Chicago Herald and Examiner,* July 5, 1937, p. 1.

Ebert, Friedrich (1871–1925)

German politician, first president of the postwar German republic (1919–25). Born in Heidelberg, Germany, on February 4, 1871, Ebert had little formal education. He was apprenticed as a saddle maker, but soon joined a trade union and advanced promptly in the ranks. Joining the socialist party, he became the managing editor of the party newspaper *Bremer Volkszeitung* in 1893, and labor secretary for the city of Bremen seven years later. In 1905, he became the leader of the German Social Democratic Party, and, in 1913, succeeded August Bebel as party chair. When World War I exploded in August 1914, he reluctantly backed appropriations for it to be properly fought.

At the end of the war, Ebert supported the attempts of Prince Max Baden to enact a new constitution at the city of Weimar and establish democracy in Germany. When revolution broke out in November 1919, Baden resigned as German chancellor and asked Ebert to replace him. He held office for only a day, establishing a socialist government. In January 1919, elections made Socialist Philipp Scheidemann the new chancellor, and Ebert was elected the first president of WEIMAR GERMANY. He served until his death in 1925, during which he was forced to deal with the burgeoning postwar economic crisis in Germany, the REPARATIONS demanded by the Allies, and the occupation by French troops of the Ruhr Valley. In 1925, a German court ruled that his support of a munitions workers' strike during the war amounted to high treason. He died suddenly on February 28, 1925. The Germany he sought to preserve through the ballot box disintegrated just a few years later.

References: Barbara Sapinsley, *From Kaiser to Hitler: The Life and Death of a Democracy, 1919–1933* (New York: Grosset & Dunlap, 1968); Jürgen Baron, Von Kruedener, ed., *Economic Crisis and Political Collapse: The Weimar Republic, 1924–1933* (New York: Oxford University Press, 1990); David Abraham, *The Collapse of the Weimar Republic: Political Economy and Crisis* (New York: Holmes & Meier, 1986).

Eden, Anthony (1897–1977)

English politician and statesman. Born to a distinguished English family at Windlestone Hall in Durham, England, on June 12, 1897. Robert Anthony Eden, known to the world as Anthony Eden, attended the prestigious Eton school, then saw service in World War I, where he was advanced to captain in the King's Royal Rifle Corps. Following the war, he attended Christ Church at Oxford University, where in 1922 he was awarded a degree with honors in Oriental languages. The next year he was elected to Parliament, representing the area of Warwick and Leamington; from 1926 to 1929, however, he also served as the private secretary to Austen CHAMBERLAIN, at the time foreign secretary.

In 1931, Eden was named undersecretary of state for foreign affairs; three years later, he was advanced to Lord Privy Seal and asked to apply his talents to international monetary relations. In 1935, when Stanley BALDWIN once again became prime minister, Eden was appointed as minister without portfolio for the LEAGUE OF NATIONS, where he attempted to rescue that slowly dying organization. After just six months, in December 1935, Eden was named foreign minister, a post he held until he resigned in February 1938 to protest Prime Minister Neville CHAMBERLAIN's APPEASEMENT policy toward NAZI Germany. In 1937 he concluded the "gentlemen's agreement" with count CIANO regarding the Mediterranean. When Germany invaded Poland in September 1939 and England declared war, Chamberlain was able to convince Eden to return to the government as dominions secretary. On May 10, 1940, when Winston Churchill succeeded to the prime ministership, Eden was named secretary of state for

war. During this period, he also served as foreign secretary. He left office when the Conservatives were thrown out of power in 1945, but returned as foreign secretary in 1951.

On April 6, 1955, Eden became prime minister, serving until 1957. On October 20, 1954, Eden was dubbed Knight of the Garter by Queen Elizabeth II, and made the first earl of Avon, as well as viscount Eden of Royal Leamington Spa.

Eden died in Alvediston, Wiltshire, England, on January 14, 1977.

References: David Carlton, "Anthony Eden: A Biography" (London: A. Lane, 1981); C. Lewis Broad, "Anthony Eden: The Chronicle of a Career" (New York: Thomas Y. Crowell, 1955); Anthony R. Peters, "Anthony Eden at the Foreign Office, 1931–1938" (New York: St. Martin's, 1986).

Edward VIII (1894–1972)

British monarch, ruled January 20–December 11, 1936, who abdicated in favor of his brother, GEORGE VI, so that he could marry American Wallis Warfield Simpson. The eldest son of King GEORGE V and his wife, Queen Mary of Teck, Edward was born at White Lodge in Richmond Park, Surrey, on June 23, 1894, and was christened Edward Albert Christian George Andrew Patrick David. The Czar of Russia, Nicholas II, and his then-fiancée, Alexandra, were the godparents at his baptism. Edward prepared for a naval career at the Osborne school and at the Royal Naval College at Dartmouth. In 1911, at Carnarvon Castle in Wales, he was named Prince of Wales, and was thus officially designated the heir to the throne of England. Edward attended Magdalen College at Oxford, but his academic career was cut short by World War I, during which he served as an aide-de-camp to the commander of the British contingent in France, and later served in Egypt and Italy. In February 1918 Edward left the front to take a seat in the House of Lords. He spent the postwar years in an ambassadorial stance, visiting foreign nations as well as British possessions and dominions. On January 20, 1936 his father, George V, died, and Edward assumed the throne as King Edward VIII.

Almost immediately, he became embroiled in a grave and disturbing crisis that challenged his right to remain on the throne. As Prince of Wales, Edward, who was unmarried, had been privately seeing an American, Wallis Warfield Simpson, who had been twice divorced. They wished to marry, but because with marriage Simpson would become Queen, Prime Minister Stanley BALDWIN refused to sanction her union with the king. According to the unwritten British constitution, without sanction from the minister, the king must choose between the throne and the woman he loved. On December 11, 1936, after almost a year of indecision,

Edward abdicated the throne to his brother Albert (who took the name George VI) on a radio broadcast heard by almost every British citizen, as well as many others throughout the world. Edward said:

> "A few hours ago I discharged my last duty as King and Emperor. And now that I have been succeeded by my brother, the Duke of York, my first words must be to declare my allegiance to him. This I do with all my heart.
>
> You know the reasons which have impelled me to renounce the throne, but I want you to understand that in making up my mind I did not forget the country or the empire which, as Prince of Wales and lately as King, I have for twenty-five years tried to serve.
>
> But you must believe me when I tell you that I have found it impossible to carry the heavy burden of responsibility and to discharge my duties as King as I would wish to do without the help and support of the woman I love."

By a patent signed by his brother, George VI, on March 3, 1937, Edward was named duke of Windsor. On June 3, 1937, at the Château de Candé in Monts, France, he married Simpson, and although she officially became the duchess of Windsor, she never held a formal royal rank. In the years leading up to World War II, the couple lived in Paris. When the Nazis invaded France, Edward and his wife fled to Lisbon, Portugal. His brother then named him the royal governor of the Bahamas, where he served until 1945. Never at home in the nation he ruled over for only 325 days, he spent much of the rest of his life overseas. In 1951, he published his autobiography, *A King's Story*, which was also the name of a 1965 documentary of his life. In February 1952, at his brother George's funeral, Edward appeared at a royal event for the first time in nearly 20 years.

On May 28, 1972, Edward died in Paris. His niece, now Queen Elizabeth II, allowed him to be buried at Frogmore, Windsor, in Berkshire, and the duchess was finally received by the Windsor family. She died in Paris on April 24, 1986, and was laid to rest next to her husband.

References: M. E. Hudson and Mary Clark, *Crown of a Thousand Years: A Millennium of British History presented as a pageant of Kings and Queens* (New York: Crown Publishers, 1978), 142–44; Bamber Gascoigne, *Encyclopedia of Britain* (New York: Macmillan, 1993), 207; "The New King. Ambassador of Empire. Fitted for a Great Task," *The Times* (London), January 21, 1936, p. 16; "King Abdicates in Favor of Duke of York; George VI to Be Proclaimed Tomorrow After Speedy Formality," New York *Herald-Tribune* (European Edition), December 11, 1936, p. 1.

Eijkman, Christiaan (1858–1930)

Dutch physician and pathologist, Nobel laureate. Born in Nijkerk, the Netherlands, on August 11, 1858, he received his M.D. from the University of Amsterdam in 1883. After serving in the Dutch army from 1886 to 1887, he worked as the director of the *Geneeskundig Laboratorium* (Medical Laboratory) in Java, Indonesia, from 1888 to 1896, and taught at the University of Utrecht from 1898 until 1928. Throughout this period, he investigated ways to cure beriberi and other diseases of vitamin deficiency. Writes biographer Rashelle Karp, "He also studied the physiology of tropical residents and conducted fermentation tests and testing for the colon bacillus in water." For finding the antineuritic principle in food, Eijkman was the corecipient (with Frederick HOPKINS) of the 1929 Nobel Prize in medicine and physiology.

Eijkman died less than a year after the bestowal of the Nobel, in Utrecht on November 5, 1930.

References: Rashelle Karp, "Eijkman, Christiaan" in Bernard S. and June H. Schlessinger, eds., *The Who's Who of Nobel Prize Winners* (Phoenix, Arizona: Oryx, 1986), 86; Thomas Watson MacCallum and Stephen Taylor, eds., *The Nobel Prize-Winners and the Nobel Foundation, 1901–1937* (Zurich, Switzerland: Central European Times Publishing, 1938), 217–19.

Einstein, Albert (1879–1955)

German-American physicist and Nobel laureate. Born in Ulm, Germany, on March 14, 1879, the son of German Jews, he received his doctorate from the University of Zurich in 1905. He served as a professor of physics at the University of Zurich from 1909 to 1911, at the German University in Prague from 1911 to 1912, as the director of the Kaiser Wilhelm Institute (now the Max Planck Institute) in Berlin from 1914 to 1933, and at Princeton University from 1933 until his retirement in 1945. For Einstein's work on the photoelectric effects of atoms, which he described in a 1905 paper in *Annalen der Physik* ("The Quantum Law of the Emission and Absorption of Light"), he was awarded the 1921 Nobel Prize in physics. As biographer John Smith explains, "Einstein's Law of the Photoelectric Effect became the basis of quantitative photochemistry. He was nominated for the Nobel Prize every year from 1910 to 1922 except for 1911 and 1915, and the Nobel Prize in 1921 notes his contributions to theoretical physics in the area of quantum theory. Einstein's work changed contemporary thinking and formed the basis for the modern science of physics." Einstein remains most famous for his theory of relativity, however.

In 1933, Einstein fled his native Germany because of the takeover of the government by Adolf HITLER and the NAZIS; he spent some time in Switzerland before going to the United States to become a professor of theoretical physics at Princeton. In 1939, he wrote an impassioned letter to U.S. president Franklin D. ROOSEVELT, asking him to start a government investigation into the possibility of constructing an atomic weapon. Einstein's correspondence led to the establishment of the Manhattan Project, which built the first atomic weapon, used on Japan twice in August 1945. In 1940, Einstein became an American citizen. He was active in the World Government Movement during World War II. In 1948, three years after he retired, he was invited to become the first president of the state of Israel, an honor which he declined. He was integral in helping to establish the Hebrew University in Jerusalem, however.

Einstein died in Princeton, New Jersey, on April 18, 1955. His numerous interwar scientific and nonscientific works include *Relativity* (1920), *Investigations on Theory of Brownian Movement* (1926), *About Zionism* (1930), *Why War?* (1933), *My Philosophy* (1934), *and The Evolution of Physics* (1938). Einstein's name is one of the most well known in the history of physics. In 1999, *Time* magazine named Einstein as its man of the 20th century.

References: John Smith, "Einstein, Albert" in Bernard S. and June H. Schlessinger, eds., *The Who's Who of Nobel Prize Winners* (Phoenix, Arizona: Oryx, 1986), 156; Thomas Watson MacCallum and Stephen Taylor, eds., *The Nobel Prize-Winners and the Nobel Foundation, 1901–1937* (Zurich, Switzerland: Central European Times Publishing, 1938), 73–75.

Einthoven, Willem (1860–1927)

Dutch physiologist and Nobel laureate. Born in Samarang, Java, the Dutch East Indies (now Indonesia), on May 22, 1860, he received his doctorate at the University of Utrecht in 1855, and served as a professor of physiology at the University of Leiden from 1885 until his death. Einthoven's early work involved the bronchial system; in 1892 he published *Über die Wirkung der Bronchialmuskeln nach einer neuen Methode untersucht, und über Asthma nervosum* (On the function of the bronchial muscles investigated by a new method, and on nervous asthma). Starting in 1908, however, he began to study the properties of the electrocardiogram, first investigated by British physiologist Augustus D. Waller of St. Mary's Medical School in London. Einthoven also demonstrated the first use of the string galvanometer and other medical equipment on human beings. For this landmark work, he was awarded the 1924 Nobel Prize in medicine and physiology.

Einthoven died in Leiden on September 29, 1927.

References: Rashelle Karp, "Einthoven, Willem" in Bernard S. and June H. Schlessinger, eds., *The Who's Who of Nobel Prize Winners* (Phoenix, Ariz.: Oryx, 1986), 85; Thomas Watson MacCallum and Stephen Taylor, eds., *The Nobel Prize-Winners* *and the Nobel Foundation, 1901–1937* (Zurich, Switzerland: Central European Times Publishing, 1938), 210.

Eisenstein, Sergei Mikhailovich (1898–1948)

Russian film director, famed for such interwar silent masterpieces as *The BATTLESHIP POTEMKIN* (1924), *October* (*Oktjabr,* 1928), and *Alexander Nevsky* (1938). Born in Riga, Latvia, on January 23, 1898, Eisenstein was the son of an affluent German Jewish architect and a Russian mother. He attended the Institute of Civil Engineering in Petrograd; when the czar was overthrown in 1917, he joined the Red Army. When he returned to Moscow in the early 1920s, he worked at the Proletkult Theater as a set designer for director Vsevolod Meyerhold. Drawing from Meyerhold's innovative set design ideas, Eisenstein developed a new film editing technique called the "montage of attractions," which employed a series of conflicting shots and abbreviated time spans to overlap and enhance the meaning of various images. He left Meyerhold to work for the Peredvizhaniya Theater, producing his first film, *Statschka* ("Strike") in 1924. His second film, the enormously influential *The Battleship Potemkin*, assured Eisenstein's name as one of the true masters of silent imagery. Later films, including *October* (based on John Reed's book *Ten Days That Shook the World*) further exhibited Eisenstein's famed montage technique, although the Stalin regime ordered Eisenstein to make some adjustments to his editing style.

In 1929 Eisenstein investigated sound-recording techniques throughout Europe and the United States, where he was embraced by such figures as Charlie CHAPLIN, Walt DISNEY, and D. W. GRIFFITH. Perhaps the Soviet Union's greatest filmmaker, Eisenstein was certainly one of the most talented directors of the silent era. He died in Moscow on February 11, 1948. In 1998, the 100th anniversary of his birth, the Bank of Russia issued two two-ruble coins with his likeness.

References: Ephraim Katz, *The Film Encyclopedia* (New York: HarperPerennial, 1994), 379–84; Herbert Marshall, ed., *Sergei Eisenstein's The Battleship Potemkin* (New York: Avon Books, 1978); Sergei Eisenstein (Jay Leyda, ed.; Diana Matias, trans.), *Eisenstein: Three Films* (New York: Harper & Row, 1974).

elections, German

Starting in 1932, German elections of representatives to the Reichstag slowly drew the NAZI PARTY, or National Socialists, into power. The Reichstag, the lower house of the German Parliament (the upper house was called the Reichsrat), had existed from the time of the German Empire, through the WEIMAR REPUBLIC, until 1933, when under the orders of Chancellor Adolf HITLER it invalidated the Weimar Constitution and gave absolute power to Hitler and his cabinet. The Reichstag's power thus became that of a rubber stamp. Hitler's rise had been quick: in the September 14, 1930, election, the Nazis won over six million votes to become the second largest party in Germany. In March and April 1932, Germany held a contest for president: Paul von HINDENBURG received 50 percent of the vote, with Hitler in second with 30 percent and Communist Ernst Thälmann third with 13 percent. In the runoff held in April, Hindenburg received 53 percent, Hitler 37 percent, and Thälmann 10 percent. This set the stage for the Reichstag elections in November 1932, which occurred in the midst of a horrendous economic crisis.

In that race, the Nazis received 17,264,323 votes and 288 seats in the Reichstag, versus 7,176,226 votes and 119 seats for the Socialists and 4,746,034 votes and 79 seats for the Communists, thus leaving the 22 million Germans who had voted for parties other than the Nazis effectively in the minority. Chancellor Kurt von Schleicher asked President von Hindenburg to dissolve the Reichstag and call for new elections to save the country from the Nazis and Hitler. Instead, on January 30, the aged von Hindenburg named Hitler as the new chancellor. In 1934 voters approved the combining of the presidency and the chancellorship in Hitler's person. He remained in charge until the Third Reich's collapse at the end of World War II.

References: Henry Ashby Turner, Jr. *Hitler's Thirty Days to Power: January 1933* (Reading, Mass.: Addison-Wesley, 1996); "Hitler Wins by Close Margin in Quiet Election; Nationalist Coalition Gets 52 p.c. of Total as 39,289,854 Ballot," New York *Herald* (European edition), March 6, 1933, p. 1.

elections, United Kingdom

From 1922 until 1935, Great Britain held six elections, in which power swung between the right (Conservatives) and the left (Labour) and culminated, from 1931–40, in coalition government.

1922: On October 19, 1922, Conservative Member of Parliament Austen CHAMBERLAIN called for a party meeting at London's Carlton Club due to overwhelming dissatisfaction with Prime Minister David LLOYD GEORGE's handling of the government. The members voted, 187 to 87, to ask for Lloyd George's resignation and an end to the coalition government with the Labourites. Lloyd George promptly resigned; former Conservative Party head Andrew Bonar LAW was then asked by King GEORGE V to form a government. Law formed the first exclusively Conservative government since 1886, and then called elections to confirm his power. On November 17, Law's party won 38.2 percent of the vote, picking up 345 seats in Parliament; Labour came in second with 29.5 percent and

142 seats; and the Liberals finished in third, with 29.1 percent and 116 seats. Law was named prime minister but served only until May 20, 1923, when he resigned due to illness and was replaced by Stanley BALDWIN.

1923: Prime Minister Baldwin called for early elections just a year after he took office as a mandate on the Conservatives' stand on tariff reform. On October 29, the Conservatives won 38.1 percent and 258 seats; Labour came in second with 30.5 percent and 191 seats; and the Liberals came in third with 29.6 percent and 159 seats. The loss of 87 seats by the Conservatives led to Baldwin's resignation on January 22, 1924, and allowed Labour leader James Ramsay MACDONALD to form a minority government the following day. Historian Peter Clarke writes, "MacDonald looked the part of prime minister, and though his short-lived administration had meager legislative achievements, this could easily be blamed upon its minority position."

1924: Prime Minister MacDonald's minority Labour government lost a vote of censure in Parliament, so he was forced to call for elections, to be held on October 29. A few days before the crucial vote, however, the so-called Zinoviev Letter—supposedly written by Soviet revolutionary Gregori Zinoviev, chair of the Comintern in the Soviet Union—emerged. The letter urged British communists to promote revolution through acts of sedition and implied that MacDonald's government was close to the infant Soviet regime in Moscow. It had been agreed that the letter would be kept secret, but it was leaked to the press, leading to the Labour party's and MacDonald's certain defeat. After the crucial election, it was claimed that the letter had been a forgery. The allegation stunned the electorate, and led to one of the worst defeats for any party in modern British history. The Conservatives won 419 seats, a 161-seat gain from 1923, with 48.3 percent of the vote; MacDonald's Labourites received 33 percent of the vote but lost 40 seats; the Liberals received only 17.6 percent of the vote and 40 seats, down 119 seats. MacDonald resigned as prime minister and was replaced by Baldwin, his predecessor.

1929: The worldwide GREAT DEPRESSION, and massive unemployment were the issues that pushed the Baldwin government to call for elections after five years in power. Labour leader and former prime minister MacDonald stood for election on a platform of government intervention to remedy the situation, with a blueprint influenced by economist John Maynard KEYNES. On this basis, Labour won the election, gaining 37.1 percent of the vote and capturing 288 seats; the Conservatives came in second with 38.2 percent, receiving 260 seats (a loss of 159 seats from the 1924 election); the liberals came in a distant third, with 23.4 percent, while gaining 19 seats for a

BRITISH GENERAL ELECTION RESULTS, 1922–1935

Great Britain held general elections for Parliament in 1922, 1923, 1924, 1929, 1931, and 1935. The following is a breakdown of the results of these elections, with votes listed by party:

1922 (November 15)

PARTY	TOTAL VOTES	MPs ELECTED	PERCENT SHARE OF TOTAL VOTE
Conservative	5,500,382	345	38.2
National Liberal	1,673,240	62	11.6
Liberal	2,516,240	54	17.5
Labour	4,241,383	142	29.5
Others	462,340	12	3.2
Totals	14,393,632	615	100.0
Turnout:	71.3 percent		

1923 (December 6)

PARTY	TOTAL VOTES	MPs ELECTED	PERCENT SHARE OF TOTAL VOTE
Conservative	5,538,824	258	38.1
Liberal	4,311,147	159	29.6
Labour	4,438,508	191	30.5
Others	260,042	7	1.8
Totals	14,548,521	615	100.0
Turnout:	70.8 percent		

1924 (October 29)

PARTY	TOTAL VOTES	MPs ELECTED	PERCENT SHARE OF TOTAL VOTE
Conservative	8,039,598	419	48.3
Liberal	2,928,747	40	17.6
Labour	5,489,077	151	33.0
Communist	55,346	1	.3
Others	126,511	4	.8
Totals	16,639,279	615	100.0
Turnout:	76.6 percent		

1929 (May 30)

PARTY	TOTAL VOTES	MPs ELECTED	PERCENT SHARE OF TOTAL VOTE
Conservative	8,656,473	260	38.2
Liberal	5,308,510	59	23.4
Labour	8,389,512	288	37.1
Communist	50,614	–	.3
Others	243,266	8	1.0
Totals	22,648,375	615	100.0
Turnout:	76.1 percent		

1931 (October 27)

PARTY	TOTAL VOTES	MPs ELECTED	PERCENT SHARE OF TOTAL VOTE
Conservative[1]	11,978,745	473	55.2
National Labour[1]	341,370	13	1.6
Liberal National[1]	809,302	35	3.7

PARTY	TOTAL VOTES	MPs ELECTED	PERCENT SHARE OF TOTAL VOTE
Liberal	1,403,102	33	6.5
Independent Liberal	106,106	4	.5
Labour	6,649,630	52	30.6
Communist	78,824	–	.3
New Party	36,377	–	.2
Others	256,917	5	1.2
Totals	21,656,373	615	100.0
Turnout:	76.3 percent		

1935 (November 14)

PARTY	TOTAL VOTES	MPs ELECTED	PERCENT SHARE OF TOTAL VOTE
Conservative	11,810,158	432	53.7
Liberal	1,422,116	20	6.4
Labor	8,325,491	154	37.9
Independent Labor	139,577	4	.7
Communist	27,117	1	.1
Others	272,595	4	1.2
Totals	21,997,054	615	100.0
Turnout:	71.2 percent		

[1]The Conservatives joined with members from the National Labour and Liberal National parties to form a "National Unity Government," with a total of 554 seats.

A "–" signifies no seats attained.

Source: David and Gareth Butler, *British Political Facts, 1900–1994* (New York: St. Martin's, 1994), 215–16.

total of 59. Baldwin resigned, and for the second time in six years MacDonald formed a government.

1931: During a political crisis that formed as a result of the MacDonald government's inability to end the Depression, several Labour members of Parliament left the party; to avoid having to call new elections, MacDonald formed a coalition government in August after his cabinet resigned. To confirm this new "National Government," however, he called elections for October. The National Government won 67 percent of the vote and 554 seats in Parliament, with the Conservatives taking 473 of these seats; the opposition, composed mainly of Labour members, won only 56 seats, of which Labour held 52. It confirmed MacDonald's continuance in power within the coalition.

1935: The power sharing of MacDonald and the Conservatives in Parliament was tested when MacDonald called for a general election. The lingering issue of unemployment was also a concern. Although the National Government won 432 seats (a decline of 41 from 1931) and 53.7 percent of the vote, Labour increased its total to 158 seats (up 102) and 38 percent of the vote. MacDonald, whose own Labour party was outnumbered 10 to 1 in Parliament, resigned as prime minister to be replaced again by Baldwin. Within two years, however, continued economic distress as well as a growing international crisis led Baldwin to hand over the reins of government to Neville CHAMBERLAIN on May 28, 1937.

References: Peter Clarke, "Government and Politics in England: Realignment and Readjustment" in Christopher Haigh, ed., *The Cambridge Historical Encyclopedia of Great Britain and Ireland* (Cambridge, England: Cambridge University Press, 1985), 294–96; David and Gareth Butler, *British Political Facts, 1900–1994* (New York: St. Martin's, 1994), 215–16.

elections, United States

Between 1919 and 1939, the United States held five presidential elections and 10 congressional elections.

1920: This was the first postwar election (the Congressional elections of 1918 came the same week that the war ended), and the impact of Woodrow WILSON's Treaty of VERSAILLES, as well as its disastrous defeat in the U.S. Senate, was before the voters for the first time. Wilson, slowly dying of a massive stroke he had suffered during the League fight (he would succumb on February 3, 1923), was not up for reelection, but any Democratic candidate, unless an outright opponent of U.S. participation in the LEAGUE OF NATIONS, would be saddled with its unpopularity by the Republican candidate. Not that the Republicans were without troubles: with the death in January 1919 of party leader Theodore Roosevelt, the party was essentially headless and leaderless. Such diverse figures as Senator Hiram JOHNSON of California, one of the Senate "IRRECONCILABLES" who helped to torpedo the League; General Leonard Wood, famed for his exploits during the Spanish-American War; and Governor Frank O. Lowden of Illinois were vying for the presidential nomination.

Following the end of World War I, Americans as a whole were in a testy and unpredictable mood. The war had taken its toll on the economy and the people. The political shakeup over the Versailles Treaty fight and the incapacitation of the president made the electorate desire a presidential candidate who promised them the return to stability. For the first time, following passage of the Nineteenth Amendment to the Constitution, women would be voting. The campaign season started on May 10, when, after a five-day convention, the Socialist-Labor Party, which had been beset by internal strife since breaking up in 1900 when the more moderate Socialists started their own party, nominated William Wesley Cox of St. Louis, Missouri, for president, and August Gilhaus of Brooklyn, New York, for vice president. At the same time, the Socialists named Eugene V. DEBS, their four-time (1900, 1904, 1908, and 1912) candidate for president, at that moment imprisoned for violating the Espionage Act of 1917, as their Presidential candidate, and Debs's little-known personal attorney, Seymour Stedman of Chicago, as his running mate. (Historians note that the delegates, in a temperament to name an "all inmate" ticket, wanted to select Kate Richards O'Hare, then also in prison for violating the Sedition Act, but party leaders who feared a devastating vote and the lack of a campaign by imprisoned candidates went with Stedman.)

On June 8 the Republicans convened in Chicago, with a number of eminent party leaders jockeying for the presidential nomination, among them Lowden and Wood. Women were added for the first time as delegates to demonstrate their new voting power under the Nineteenth Amendment, which was being passed by the states and would be added to the Constitution in August. As the balloting got under way, it was apparent that neither Lowden nor Wood had sufficient support to win the nomination. On June 11, as the convention deadlocked, party leaders met late at night and undertook to find a third candidate who could get the nod quickly: they found that

man in Senator Warren G. HARDING, a colorless former newspaperman from Ohio famed in the Senate for making friends and playing cards. Harding's name had never been attached to any legislation, nor was he a considerable speaker, but he was without enemies and he was in Chicago. At 2 A.M. on June 12, Senator Frank Brandegee of Connecticut approached Harding and asked him if there were any skeletons in his closet; Harding retired for a period, then returned and answered that there were none. Brandegee returned to the party leaders, meeting in a back room, and called Harding fit and ready. They selected Governor Calvin COOLIDGE of Massachusetts, famed for breaking the Boston Police strike the previous year, as his running mate, and submitted the names to the convention. Hot and weary, the delegates approved the choices, and Harding, a man who in 1914 was the editor of a newspaper in Marion, Ohio, was one step away from becoming president of the United States.

On June 28 the Democrats assembled in San Francisco and spent 38 ballots fighting over former secretary of the treasury William Gibbs McAdoo, President Wilson's son-in-law, and Attorney General Alexander Mitchell Palmer, a Quaker who had cracked down on suspected Communists with widespread arrests during the PALMER RAID the previous year. As with the Republicans, there was no consensus behind one candidate; in a repeat, party leaders met and chose Governor James Middleton COX of Ohio, like Harding a bland newspaperman with little name recognition outside his home state. Assistant Secretary of the Navy Franklin Delano ROOSEVELT, a distant cousin of the former president Theodore Roosevelt, was selected as Cox's running mate, and a platform was constructed endorsing the League of Nations and U.S. entry into the organization.

For the Republicans, the League was the paramount issue. In his keynote speech at the Republican convention, Senator Henry Cabot LODGE of Massachusetts said, "Mr. Wilson and his dynasty, his heirs and assigns, or anybody that is his, anybody who with bent knee has served his purpose, must be driven from all control of the government and all influence in it." Harding conducted a porchfront campaign from his home in Marion, where crowds flocked to hear him speak. Much of his platform was based on his "Return to Normalcy" speech, in which he called for a return to the way of life seen in America before World War I. Cox and Roosevelt both criss-crossed the nation (Cox alone traveled 22,000 miles), calling on the voters to reward Wilson for his work to secure peace in Paris. The nation, however, was tired of war and entanglements overseas, and wanted nothing more than Harding's promised "Return to Normalcy." The influential *Literary Digest,* in a nationwide survey, predicted an overwhelming Republican victory.

On November 2 Harding was elected president over Cox, 404 electoral votes to 127, and a popular vote of

Floor scene at the 1920 Democratic National Convention in San Francisco *(CORBIS)*

16,152,200 to 9,147,353. Socialist Debs received 919,799 (a record vote for a Socialist, as well as for an imprisoned candidate), Prohibitionist Watkins polled 189,408, Socialist-Labor candidate Cox got 31,175, and Farmer-Labor nominee Christenson only tallied 25,541. Harding swept all of the United States save the Deep South (he did capture the lone southern state of Tennessee); Cox took all the southern states, including Florida and Texas. Voter turnout was the lowest it would be for the *entire* century, however— a minuscule 43 percent, despite the increase in eligible voters due to women's suffrage. (The record year for American voter turnout, incidentally, is 1876, with 83 percent.) In Congress, although the Republicans had held a small majority in the Sixty-sixth Congress (1919–21) in the House (237 seats to 191) and Senate (48 seats to 47), the 1920 elections gave them a solid hold on both houses, as they picked up 63 seats in the House to give them a 300–132 advantage (with twelve third-party seats), and eleven seats in the Senate to give them a 59–37 dominance.

The election of 1920 was a direct repudiation by the American people of Wilsonism and Wilsonian foreign policy, which had earned the nation an unsettled peace at the end of World War I. Journalist William Allen White said that the American people were "tired of issues, sick at heart of ideals, and weary of being noble."

1922: The congressional midterm election of the Harding administration was a complete reversal of the 1920 contest: Democrats picked up six seats in the Senate, and, with two additional seats going to third parties, cut the Republican edge from 59–37 to 51–43–2. In the House, the Democrats won an astounding 75 seats, changing the House from a 300–132–12 Republican advantage to a slim 225–207–2 majority.

1924: With President Harding's death the previous year, and with scandals floating around his administration over questions of ethics involving chiefly the TEAPOT DOME SCANDAL, the reelection of Harding's successor, Calvin COOLIDGE, did not seem secure at all. In fact, it seemed that if the Democrats could nominate a popular enough person for president, they would capture the White House. Prior to the meetings of the two major parties, several minor parties nominated candidates. On May 13, the Socialist-Laborites named Frank T. Johns of Michigan for president and Verne Reynolds of Maryland for vice president; on June 5 the Prohibitionists named Herman P. Faris of Missouri for president and Marie Caroline Brehm for vice president, the first female ever to be named to the ticket of a party destined to get more than a few votes. (Several women candidates had run on other minor tickets, but had received only a smattering of ballots). After the Democrats and Republicans named their respective tickets, the Farmer-Labor Progressives, meeting for the first time on June 19, named Duncan McDonald of Illinois for president and William Bouck of Washington for vice president; on July 10 these two men stepped down, however, and were replaced by William Z. Foster of Illinois for president, and Benjamin Gitlow of New York for vice president. (The Workers' Party, the leading Communist-affiliated political party in the United States at the time, formally nominated Foster and Gitlow as their candidates on July 10 as well.) On July 4 the Conference for Progressive Political Action, also known as the Progressive Party, met and named Senator Robert M. LA FOLLETTE, Republican of Wisconsin, for president and, two weeks later, Senator Burton K. Wheeler, Democrat of Montana, for vice president. These minor parties stood little chance of capturing the White House, however.

The Republicans met in Cleveland June 10–12, and nominated Coolidge on the first ballot, adding financier Charles G. DAWES, who had served honorably in the Harding administration as budget director, for vice president. Of Coolidge, one nominating speaker said, he "never wasted any time, never wasted any words, and never wasted any public money." The meeting was covered on radio stations in 12 cities, including WEAF in New York and WCAP in Washington, D.C. Famed sports announcer Graham McNamee covered the convention activities, bringing the work of the delegates into the homes of the American people for the first time.

For the Democrats, however, the prospects of a return to power brightened as they convened in New York City's Madison Square Garden on June 24, with the possible nominees, Governor Al SMITH of New York and former secretary of the treasury William G. McAdoo, who was also Wilson's son-in-law, close in the numbers of delegates pledged to them. The Democrats began their convention with more acrimony than at any time in their party history since the destructive Charleston Convention of 1860, where divided over the slavery question, Northern and Southern Democrats walked out and formed their own parties. In 1924, however, the issue was not race but religion: the power of the Ku Klux Klan and its anti-Catholic ideology was bitterly discussed as the nomination swung between Smith, a Roman Catholic, and McAdoo, a Protestant. The convention voted to denounce the Klan, 542 votes to 541, and the watered-down platform denounced "any effort to arouse religious or racial dissension." The fight then turned to the nomination. For days the race swung between Smith's anti-Klan forces and McAdoo's supporters, who wished not to discuss the issue of religion. After a record 103 ballots, the delegates, exhausted, turned to attorney and long-time Democratic party activist John William DAVIS as their presidential nominee, and former Nebraska governor Charles Wayland Bryan, the brother of three-time presidential nominee William

Jennings BRYAN, as his running mate. The convention lasted so long that humorist Will ROGERS complained that New York City had invited the delegates to visit the place, not live there!

The campaign was bitter, and the two major parties virtually shut out any mention of the third-party nominees. From the start, most insiders predicted a Coolidge victory, the size of which was a matter of debate. The Teapot Dome scandal, which had cost the Republicans in credibility, did not seem to hurt Coolidge; the American people seemed to be pleased with the nation's economic health. The motto of the Republicans, "Keep Cool with Coolidge," seemed to urge a referendum on the economy. On these grounds, Davis and Bryan had little chance. Managing Davis's campaign was Frank Lyon Polk, a lawyer and former undersecretary of state under Woodrow Wilson (1919–20). Historian William Harbaugh writes, "The Ku Klux Klan issue apparently cut both ways. Charles Bryan's presence on the ticket seems to have encouraged many Eastern Catholics to sit out the election. On the other hand, Davis ran better among rural Protestants in Maryland and Missouri and better in the Klan-ridden South as a whole than Cox had done in 1920, when there was no Klan. He carried Oklahoma despite the election of a Klan-supported Republican senatorial candidate, and in West Virginia, where the head of the Klan called him 'the best man' even after he had denounced the organization, resentment of his anglophobia and postwar labor record was reportedly decisive."

On November 4, Coolidge was elected to a full term of his own, capturing 15,725,016 popular votes to Davis's 8,385,503 and La Follette's 4,822,856; the electoral vote was 382 for Coolidge, 136 for Davis, and 13 for La Follette. The Republicans, as they did four years earlier, swept the nation except in the South, where Davis ran strong; La Follette's electoral votes came solely from his home state, Wisconsin. The minor parties tallied thus: Faris, 57,520; Johns, 36,429; Foster, 36,386. For the incoming Sixty-ninth Congress, the Republicans increased their majority by three seats in the Senate to 54–40 (with two third-party seats); in the House, there would be 247 Republicans to 183 Democrats and five of a third party, an increase of 22 Republican seats from the Sixty-eighth Congress.

1926: The congressional midterm election hurt the Republicans: the Democrats picked up seven seats in the Senate to make the majority 49–47; in the House, they took 12 seats to lessen the Republican majority to 237–195, with three independents.

1928: The Republicans, having won two straight presidential elections, seemed on the brink of capturing a third if Coolidge, whose popularity was still high because of his matter-of-fact administration and the bustling economy, would consent to run for a second full term. Yet when Coolidge passed a note to reporters, saying simply, "I do not choose to run for President in 1928," his exit from the race blew it wide open for both parties, which rushed to name candidates.

The Republicans met in Kansas City on June 12 with the question on their lips, "Who but HOOVER?" Herbert Hoover was "the Great Engineer" who had served as War Relief Administrator in Russia during World War I, and as the loyal and honorable secretary of commerce in the Harding and Coolidge administrations; he was seen as a bloodless but efficient administrator. Hoover was quickly nominated, and Senator Charles Curtis of Kansas, a Kaw Indian and the first Native American to sit in the U.S. Senate, became his running mate. Hoover called for the status quo: the enforcement of PROHIBITION, a high tariff on foreign goods, and the cutting of income taxes.

The Democrats met in Houston with far less acrimony than in their last two races. Roosevelt, the 1920 vice presidential candidate, nominated Smith, "the Happy Warrior," who wanted to end Prohibition; on the first ballot he was nominated. The delegates named Senator Joseph Taylor ROBINSON of Arkansas, a southern Democrat and Prohibition champion. They were an odd couple: a northern "wet" and a southern "dry." But that was hardly their greatest hurdle. Smith's Roman Catholicism scared many who saw him as a tool of the Vatican. He was called a devil, and many said that the Pope was "packing his bags to move to Washington." Protestants also feared Smith's attempts to curtail Prohibition, which Hoover labeled "a noble experiment."

In the end, however, it was probably the sound economy that enticed the nation to stick with the Republicans. On November 6, Hoover was elected president, with 21,392,190 popular votes to Smith's 15,016,443; the electoral vote was 444 to 87. By way of the latter tally, Hoover's election was more convincing than Harding's had been in 1920 or Coolidge's in 1924: the former commerce secretary took formerly Democratic states, such as Florida, North Carolina, Texas, and Virginia, while Smith took the smaller traditionally Democratic states of the South, as well as Massachusetts and Rhode Island. Socialist Norman Thomas captured 267,835 votes, the largest count for any left-leaning party in the history of the United States up to that time. Workers' Party candidate William Z. Foster increased his vote some twelve thousand fron 1924 to 48,228; other parties, including the Prohibitionists and Farmer-Laborites, finished with but a handful of votes. For the incoming Seventy-first Congress, the Republicans gained eight seats in the Senate, where 56 Republicans, 39 Democrats, and one third-party senator, and a pickup of 30 seats allowed the Republicans to strengthen their hold in the House with 267 Republicans, 167 Democrats, and one third-party seat.

Historian Paul Boller Jr. writes, "Smith was convinced that religion had done him in. He was partly right; unquestionably bigotry cost him many votes. So did his wetness and his association with Tammany. But Hoover himself was probably closer to the mark when he said: 'General Prosperity was on my side.' The Republican party was still the majority party in 1928, the times were still relatively good, and millions of voters believed Republican orators when they identified the GOP with economic advance. 'You can't lick this prosperity thing,' cried Will Rogers after the election. One of the Republican slogans was: 'Hoover and Happiness or Smith and Soup Houses! Which Shall It Be?' The voters chose Hoover. As it turned out, they got soup houses also."

1930: The congressional midterm elections were a disaster for the Republicans, primarily fallout from the STOCK MARKET CRASH of the previous year. They lost the House, as the Democrats won 53 seats to take a 220–214 (with one Independent) advantage, and they came within one vote (48 to 47, with one independent) of losing the Senate.

1932: The nation was mired deep in the GREAT DEPRESSION in the election year of 1932, and President Hoover, who had strained mightily both domestically and internationally to fight the Depression without massive new government programs, was blamed for the worsening situation. The Republicans gathered in a dark mood in Chicago on June 14, while Washington, D.C., was ringed by participants in the BONUS MARCH, World War I veterans demanding their promised bonuses from the government. There was little stomach in the party for a nomination fight, and quietly, without rancor, Hoover and Curtis were quickly renominated. Just 11 days after the Republicans left Chicago, the Democrats assembled in the same hall on June 27. Then New York Governor Roosevelt, whose programs in his home state had been considered landmark in trying to reduce the Depression's effects, was the leading candidate for the presidential nomination, but he was opposed by former governor and presidential candidate Smith (whom Roosevelt had nominated in 1928) and Speaker of the House of Representatives John Nance GARNER. On the first and second ballots, Roosevelt led, with Smith trailing and Garner far behind, but Roosevelt could not muster enough votes to capture the nomination outright. The third ballot continued the deadlock. At this point, Roosevelt's managers panicked, seeing another 1924 debacle in the making. They then approached Garner with a deal: if he released his delegates to Roosevelt, he would get second place on the ticket. A conservative southern Democrat from Texas, Garner found himself more in sympathy with Roosevelt than with Smith, and agreed. Smith, who had become a political enemy of Roosevelt, refused to make the nomination unanimous, but Roosevelt won on the fourth ballot, and Garner received the vice-presidential nod. Roosevelt decided to show that his handicap—polio-stricken legs—was no impediment to the presidency, flying to Chicago and accepting the nomination in person for the first time in U.S. political history. (Up to this time, the nominees were usually informed of their selections by telegram and a greeting party sent by the convention.) Roosevelt explained his platform and then said to the assembled delegates, "I pledge you, I pledge myself, to a new deal for the American people. Let us all here assembled constitute ourselves prophets of a new order of competence and of courage. This is more than a political campaign; it is a call to arms. Give me your help, not to win votes alone, but to win in this crusade to restore America to its own people."

POPULAR AND ELECTORAL VOTES IN AMERICAN PRESIDENTIAL ELECTIONS, 1920–1936

The following tables illustrate the candidates, popular votes, percentage of the total vote for each candidate, and electoral vote, in the American presidential elections from 1920 to 1936. Total percentages may not add up to 100 percent because smaller parties that are not listed here registered some votes.

1920

PARTY	CANDIDATES	POPULAR VOTE	PERCENT	ELECTORAL VOTE
Republican	Warren G. Harding			
	Calvin Coolidge	16,133,314	60.30	404
Democrat	James M. Cox			
	Franklin D. Roosevelt	9,140,884	34.17	127
Socialist	Eugene V. Debs			
	Seymour Stedman	913,664	3.42	—
Farmer-Labor	Parley P. Christensen			
	Max S. Hayes	264,540	.99	—
Others		301,384	1.13	—
Total Vote:		26,753,786		
Harding Plurality:		6,992,430		

1924

PARTY	CANDIDATES	POPULAR VOTE	PERCENT	ELECTORAL VOTE
Republican	Calvin Coolidge			
	Charles G. Dawes	15,717,553	54.00	382
Democrat	John W. Davis			
	Charles W. Bryan	8,386,169	28.84	136
Progressive/				
Socialist	Robert La Follette			
	Burton K. Wheeler	4,814,050	16.56	13
Others		158,187	.55	—
Total Vote:		29,075,959		
Coolidge Plurality:		7,331,384		

1928

PARTY	CANDIDATES	POPULAR VOTE	PERCENT	ELECTORAL VOTE
Republican	Herbert Hoover			
	Charles Curtis	21,411,911	58.20	444
Democrat	Alfred E. Smith			
	Joseph T. Robinson	15,000,185	40.77	87
Socialist	Norman Thomas			
	James H. Maurer	266,453	.72	—

PARTY	CANDIDATES	POPULAR VOTE	PERCENT	ELECTORAL VOTE
Workers'	William Z. Foster			
	Benjamin Gitlow	48,170	.13	—
Others		63,565	.17	—
Total Vote:		36,790,364		
Hoover Plurality:		6,411,806		

1932

PARTY	CANDIDATES	POPULAR VOTE	PERCENT	ELECTORAL VOTE
Democrat	Franklin D. Roosevelt			
	John Nance Garner	22,825,016	57.42	472
Republican	Herbert Hoover			
	Charles Curtis	15,758,397	39.64	59
Socialist	Norman Thomas			
	James H. Maurer	883,990	2.22	—
Communist	William Z. Foster			
	James W. Ford	102,221	.26	—
Others		179,758	.45	—
Total Vote:		39,749,382		
Roosevelt Plurality:		7,066,619		

1936

PARTY	CANDIDATES	POPULAR VOTE	PERCENT	ELECTORAL VOTE
Democrat	Franklin D. Roosevelt			
	John Nance Garner	27,747,636	60.79	523
Republican	Alf M. Landon			
	Frank Knox	16,679,543	36.54	8
Union	William Lemke			
	Thomas O'Brien	892,492	1.96	—
Socialist	Norman Thomas			
	James H. Maurer	187,785	.41	—
Others		134,847	.30	—
Total Vote:		45,642,303		
Roosevelt Plurality:		11,068,093		

Other tickets in the field included Norman Thomas and James H. Maurer on the Socialist ticket and Communist William Z. Foster and James W. Ford, the first black man to be nominated for vice president and to receive actual votes. The race was between Hoover and Roosevelt, however. Hoover spent much of his time in the White House, trying to solve the economic crisis, but Roosevelt was traveling across America and winning the support of Republicans George Norris and Hiram Johnson. By the end of the campaign, Hoover called Roosevelt's program "dangerous" and "the same philosophy of government which has poisoned all of Europe." Americans, scared of the worsening depression, cast their lot with the New York governor. On November 8, 1932, the Roosevelt landslide many had predicted was magnified by 10 times: Roosevelt won 472 electoral votes to Hoover's 59 (he won only six states); Roosevelt's edge in the popular vote margin was 22,821,857 to 15,761,845. Socialist Thomas won 881,951 votes, the most since Debs had taken in 1920; Communist Foster tallied 102,785, with Prohibitionist William Upshaw attaining 81,869 votes. As well as taking the White House, the Democrats swept the Senate, taking 13 seats and making their total there 59–36 (with one third-party seat); in the House they won an unprecedented 90 seats to increase their majority to 313–117 (with five third-party seats).

The election of 1932 was a landmark event, in which most of the old order was overthrown for a new, revolutionary, and untried economic formula to battle national economic distress.

1934: The Democrats were again victorious in the congressional midterm election, as they increased their majorities in both the Senate (69–25, with one Farmer-Laborite and one Progressive) and the House (319–103, with 10 or a third party).

1936: After four years of Roosevelt in office, however, the voters were worse off economically than they had been four years earlier, when they elected him on his promise of "a NEW DEAL." Although prosperity was not in evidence, many Americans praised Roosevelt for attempting to solve the crisis. Still, many in both parties despised him: Democrat Al Smith, once Roosevelt's friend, said of Roosevelt's advisers, the BRAIN TRUST: "The young brain-trusters caught the Socialists in swimming and they ran away with their clothes." On January 25, 1936, Smith called Roosevelt "a socialist" who was patterning the nation after the Soviet Union. Further erosions to Roosevelt's stance on issues came when the U.S. Supreme Court struck down key portions of the president's program in 1935, on the day known as BLACK MONDAY, and in 1936.

In this atmosphere of uncertainty and distrust, the Republicans saw a golden opportunity to recapture the White House. Meeting in Cleveland June 9–12, the party selected on the first ballot Governor Alf LANDON of Kansas, a party man who was praised by conservatives for his tight fiscal policy and by liberals for his innovative programs to help the unemployed and farmers in his agricultural state. For vice president, Col. Frank Knox, publisher of the *Chicago Daily News* and a conservative critic of Roosevelt, was chosen. Both men were longtime Republican activists, having supported Theodore Roosevelt's "Bull Moose" party in 1912. The Democrats, convening in Philadelphia June 23–27, renominated Roosevelt and Garner to wild adulation and jubilation. Fringe parties like the Socialists, which nominated Norman Thomas for a third time; the Communists, which fronted Earl Browder; and the Union Party, founded by radio "hate priest" Father Charles COUGHLIN and pushing the candidacy of Republican Congressman William Lemke of North Dakota for president, entered national tickets as well. Their influence was nominal at best, however.

The election, like the one held four years earlier, became a referendum on the current occupant of the White House. Landon steered a cautious line by attacking Roosevelt's policies as "strangling . . . free enterprise," while calling the president "a fine and charming gentleman." Landon also stressed his progressive credentials while calling attention to his budgetary conservatism in

managing the Kansas economy. But the flat Landon had little chance to beat Roosevelt, whose popularity was evident in the huge crowds attracted to his few campaign stops. What seemed to take everyone by surprise was a poll released at the end of October, compiled by the respected *Literary Digest,* which had correctly predicted presidential winners since 1912. The magazine reported that it believed Landon would pull off a stunning upset by more than 300,000 votes.

But on election day, November 3, Roosevelt carried every state in the Union except Maine and Vermont, giving him 523 electoral votes to Landon's eight—he won 27,751,597 votes (60.8 percent) to Landon's 16,679,583. It was, since the days of James Monroe in the early 19th century, the most lopsided electoral vote margin. Third-party candidates did poorly: Thomas won 187,720 votes, and Browder received 80,150. Lemke's Union ticket embraced 882,479 votes, but that was far fewer than was expected, and the movement died out soon after the election. The contest also swept Democrats into office across the nation, particularly in Congress, where again the Democrats picked up seats in the Senate (increasing their total to 76, with 16 Republicans and four from a third party), as well as the House (up to 331-89, with 13 third-party seats). The verdict on Roosevelt and the New Deal was in: the nation liked the direction it was headed in, even though it had not yet seen any results of that change. The *Literary Digest* poll was flawed because it was based on telephone interviews, and in those days of the Depression, only the rich could afford telephones; the results were therefore skewed. The magazine went out of business shortly after the election.

1938: The COURT-PACKING CONTROVERSY, as well as Roosevelt's refusal to campaign for conservative Democrats (particularly in the South), cost the president's party dearly: the election marked a watershed for Democratic power in the Congress. While the party lost only seven seats in the Senate, allowing its majority to remain 69-23 with four independents, in the House it was devastated, losing 70 seats to remain in the majority, but at a 261-164 count (with four independents), which emboldened the Republicans to join with the remaining conservative Democrats to challenge Roosevelt's economic and social programs.

References: For **presidential elections,** Donald R. McCoy, "Election of 1920" in Arthur M. Schlesinger, Jr., ed., *History of American Presidential Elections, 1789–1968* (New York: Chelsea House Publishers, 1985), 3: 2349–69; James T. Havel, *U.S. Presidential Candidates and the Elections: A Biographical and Historical Guide* (New York: Macmillan Library Reference USA, 1996), 2: 106–43; Colleen McGuiness, ed., *National Party Conventions, 1831–1988* (Washington, D.C.: Congressional Quarterly, 1991), 79–92; Edmund H. Harvey,

Jr., *Reader's Digest: Our Glorious Century* (Pleasantville, N.Y.: Reader's Digest, 1994), 108; Wesley M. Bagby, *The Road to Normalcy: The Presidential Campaign and Election of 1920* (Baltimore: The Johns Hopkins University Press, 1962); Jeffrey L. Swanson, "That Smoke-Filled Room: A Utahn's Role in the 1920 GOP Convention," *Utah Historical Quarterly* 45 (1977): 369–79; "Socialist Nominee to Test Kentucky Sedition Law," *St. Louis Post-Dispatch,* September 29, 1920, p. 1; Robert K. Murray, *The 103rd Ballot: Democrats and the Disaster in Madison Square Garden* (New York: Harper & Row, 1976); William H. Harbaugh, *Lawyer's Lawyer: The Life of John W. Davis* (New York: Oxford University Press, 1973), 248; Peter John Baker, "The Presidential Election of 1928" (Ph.D. dissertation, Georgetown University, 1950); Ruth Caridad Silva, *Rum, Religion and Votes: 1928 Re-examined* (University Park: Pennsylvania State University Press, 1962); "Republicans Name Landon Unanimously; He Accepts Platform, Adding Own Ideas," *New York Times,* June 12, 1936, p. 1; Paul F. Boller, Jr., *Presidential Campaigns* (New York: Oxford University Press, 1985), 212–49. For **congressional elections,** Congressional Quarterly, *Congress A to Z* (Washington, D.C.: Congressional Quarterly, 1993), Congressional Quarterly, *Congressional Quarterly's Guide to Congress* (Washington, D.C.: Congressional Quarterly, 1991); Congressional Quarterly, *Congressional Quarterly's Guide to U.S. Elections* (Washington, D.C.: Congressional Quarterly, 1994), 815–1355; David W. Brady, *Critical Elections and Congressional Policymaking* (Stanford, Calif.: Stanford University Press, 1988).

Eliot, T. S. (1888–1965)

American-born British poet and Nobel laureate, noted for his postwar poem *The Waste Land* (1922), which became a touchstone for the generation of postwar writers. The scion of a distinguished New England family, Thomas Stearns Eliot was born in St. Louis, Missouri, on September 26, 1888, the grandson of William Greenleaf Eliot, who founded Washington University in St. Louis. Eliot earned bachelor's and master's degrees at Harvard College before attending the Sorbonne and Oxford University.

Afterward, he remained in England and for a short time taught in a boys' school near London. During World War I, he worked as a clerk at Lloyd's Bank and began to write in 1917—the year he published his first book of poems, *Prufrock and Other Observations.* He came under the influence of his contemporary Ezra POUND, who encouraged Eliot and assisted in the publication of his work in a number of magazines. Eliot edited the British literary magazine *The Egoist* (1917–19), and in 1922 founded the quarterly literary review *Criterion.* He edited the quarterly until the start of World War II. In 1927 he became a British citizen. During the interwar period, Eliot published a body of work that would make his name, including *Gerontion* (1919) and *The Waste Land* (1922), both expressing the

barrenness of modern life; *Ash Wednesday* (1930), a religious drama; and the drama *Murder in the Cathedral* (1935), about the assassination of Thomas à Becket. Works completed during and after World War II, including *The Family Reunion* (1939) and *Four Quartets* (1943), helped him win the 1948 Nobel Prize in literature.

After winning the Nobel, Eliot published *The Cocktail Party* (1950), *The Confidential Clerk* (1954), *The Elder Statesman* (1959), and other pieces of poetry, criticism, and drama. He died in London on January 4, 1965.

References: Stephen Spender, *Eliot* (London: Fontana, 1975); Bernard Bergonzi, "Eliot, Thomas Stearns" in Alan Bullock and R. B. Woodings, eds., *20th Century Culture: A Biographical Companion* (New York: Harper & Row, 1983), 211; Dame Helen Louise Gardner, *The Art of T. S. Eliot* (New York: Dutton, 1950).

Ellington, Duke (1899–1974)

American jazz pianist, composer, and bandleader considered, along with Louis ARMSTRONG, to be one of the finest musicians in the JAZZ world. Born Edward Kennedy Ellington in Washington, D.C., on April 29, 1899, he was raised in a middle-class home. He left high school in his senior year to join a series of jazz bands in the D.C. area. After serving in the U.S. Navy during World War I, Ellington returned to the United States in 1918 and formed his first band, the Washingtonians, which featured Sonny Greer, Otto Hardwicke, and Arthur Whetsol. The group played Ellington's first composition, "Soda Fountain Rag," written when he worked in a soda fountain as a youth. The band played jazz at local clubs and bars, and in the early 1920s moved to New York City, where they got work at the prestigious Kentucky Club and, within three years, the famed Cotton Club. During this period Ellington's band, which had added trumpeter Bubber Miley, performed such works as "Creole Love Call," "Choo Choo," "Rainy Nights," and "Black and Tan Fantasy," almost all of which became major hits of the era. In 1926 Ellington established the Duke Ellington Orchestra, which featured trombonist Tricky Sam Nanton and introduced such songs as "East St. Louis Toodleoo" and "Birmingham Breakdown."

In 1928 Ellington added to the orchestra alto saxophonist Johnny Hodges and clarinetist Barney Bigard, and in 1929 Coolie Williams replaced Miley. After the group left the Cotton Club in 1931, they toured Europe twice and became one of the major bands of the decade. In 1935 they added Rex Stewart on cornet and Ivie Anderson as lead singer. They released such numbers as "It Don't Mean a Thing If It Ain't Got That Swing," "Sophisticated Lady," "Mood Indigo," "Tiger Rag," "Rockin' in Rhythm," "I Let a Song Go Out of My Heart," and "Solitude." The three-minute-long "Daybreak Express" and other compositions

Duke Ellington *(CORBIS/Bettmann)*

charmed both black and white audiences, despite the prevalent racism of the era.

In the 1940s, the collapse of the big band era did not end Ellington's work. In fact, he and his orchestra adopted the new jazz form of bebop and became even more popular. In 1969, Ellington received the Presidential Medal of Freedom. He died on May 24, 1974.

References: Elizabeth Wenning and Barbara Carlisle Bigelow, "Duke Ellington" in Barbara Carlisle Bigelow, ed., *Contemporary Black Biography* (Detroit: Gale Research, 1992), 5: 91–95; John J. Chilton, "Ellington, Edward Kennedy (Duke)" in Alan Bullock and R. B. Woodings, eds., *20th Century Culture: A Biographical Companion* (New York: Harper & Row, 1983), 212.

Ernst, Max   *See* DADA; SURREALISM.

Esch-Cummins (Transportation) Act

U.S. congressional legislation, enacted February 28, 1920, in which the Congress released railroads from government controls established during World War I, enabling them to raise rates, while at the same time creating a railway labor board to deal with union difficulties.

The Congress had placed the railroads under federal authority for the entire wartime period. Under this law, this command ceased to exist at 12:01 A.M., March 1, 1920, at which time the president was authorized to "adjust, settle, liquidate, and wind up all matters, including compensation, and all questions and disputes of whatsoever nature, arising out of or incident to Federal

control." Section 302 of the act established "Railroad Boards of Labor Adjustment" to "receive for hearing . . . any dispute involving only grievances, rules, or working conditions . . . between the carrier and its employees or subordinate officials." Also established was a Railway Labor Board, consisting of nine members (three named by the labor union, three by railroad management, and three by the president pending confirmation by the U.S. Senate), which would "hear . . . and decide any dispute" that a board of labor adjustment had failed to settle.

In 1922 and again in 1924, the U.S. Supreme Court looked into whether certain sections of the act were constitutional in the cases of *Railroad Commission of Wisconsin v. Chicago, Burlington & Quincy Railroad Company,* and *Dayton-Goose Creek Railway Company v. United States.*

References: Text of legislation at U.S. Statutes at Large, XLI: 456–57; Henry Steele Commager, ed., *Documents of American History* (New York: Appleton-Century-Crofts, 1949), 345–46; Rogers MacVeagh, *The Transportation Act, 1920* (New York: Henry Holt, 1923).

Ethiopian War

Invasion and occupation of Ethiopia by the Italian army, which dragged the world closer to unrestrained warfare. Ethiopia was an independent African empire that had never been colonized by Europeans. Italian fascist dictator Benito MUSSOLINI ordered the invasion to consolidate Italy's empire in the Horn of Africa and to avenge an earlier humiliating defeat at the Battle of Adowa in 1896, when some 25,000 Italians were routed.

All had seemed well when an Italo-Ethiopian Friendship Pact was signed in 1928. This was done only to lower Ethiopia's guard, however. On December 5, 1934, a series of border clashes took place between Ethiopian and Italian troops in ITALIAN SOMALILAND. On October 2, 1935, more than a hundred thousand Italian troops invaded, as the Italians crossed the Mareb River, separating Italian Eritrea from Ethiopia. Under the leadership of Emperor HAILE SELASSIE, the Ethiopian armies resisted the conquest for seven months before the Italians stormed the capital at Addis Ababa in May 1936. Haile Selassie had appeared before the LEAGUE OF NATIONS on January 3, 1936, to ask for support. The League urged its members to apply sanctions, but the call was ignored. On July 16, 1936, the League canceled its call for sanctions. The Italian occupation of Ethiopia, a step toward the APPEASEMENT of the dictators of Germany and Italy, did not end until Allied troops defeated Italian forces in 1941 during World War II and restored Haile Selassie to power.

References: *The Abyssinian Dispute* (New York: Carnegie Endowment for International Peace, 1935); Pietro Badoglio, *The War in Abyssinia* (London: Metheun, 1937); Brice Harris,

The United States and the Italo-Ethiopian Crisis (Stanford, Calif.: Hoover Institution Press, 1964); "3 Ethiopian Towns Bombed as War Starts; Hundreds Killed, Negus Protests to League; Adowa, Adigrat, Agame Bombed as Mussolini's Airplanes Follow Troops Across Frontier at Dawn," New York *Herald-Tribune* (European Edition), October 4, 1935, p. 1.

eugenics

Scientific theory proposed in 1883 by British statistician Francis Galton and further developed in the United States and England during the interwar period. Eugenics is the idea that the human species can and should be improved through control of hereditary factors. A distant cousin of Charles Darwin, Galton believed that a systematic, government-enacted program of eugenics could augment the evolutionary process of natural selection. He postulated that such selective breeding would "hasten racial progress" by removing so-called inferior genes from the gene pool.

In the United States a eugenics movement developed in the early 20th century in a nation of growing ethnic and racial diversity. A number of white social reformers were drawn to the possibility of eugenics as a means of enhancing the human race, even though the theory legitimized elitism and racism. The proponents offered two forms: "positive eugenics" encouraged reproduction among the "fit"; "negative eugenics" discouraged reproduction among the "unfit," who were often defined as the impoverished in general and as immigrant women from non-northern European and non-western European countries in particular. Other eugenicists sponsored laws to restrict immigration, which the U.S. Congress enacted with the IMMIGRATION ACT OF 1921 and the IMMIGRATION ACT OF 1924.

Eugenics was also important to the birth-control movement because it provided a scientific language with which to discuss sexual reproduction. It also supported the argument for women's right to contraception. For these reasons the birth-control pioneers Margaret SANGER and Marie STOPES somewhat embraced the theory, and in 1921 the American Eugenics Society was founded. Despite their intentions, the fear of unrestrained population growth among the poor and the ethnic masses dominated the discussions. Other eugenicists called for compulsory sterilization of insane, criminal, and mentally retarded people. These eugenicists were encouraged by the 1927 U.S. Supreme Court landmark decision in BUCK V. BELL, which held that states could sterilize persons they deemed unfit or "feeble-minded."

The eugenics movement was eventually discredited by the full disclosure of Adolf HITLER's racial policies in Nazi Germany, during which tens of thousands of disabled persons were incarcerated, sterilized, and in many cases experimented on. In 1973 the American Eugenics Society changed its name to the Society for the Study of Social Biology.

References: Judith K. Grether, "Sterilization and Eugenics: An Examination of Early Twentieth-Century Population Control in the United States" (Ph.D. diss., University of Oregon, 1980); Linda Gordon, "The Politics of Population: Birth Control and the Eugenics Movement," *Radical America* 8 (1974): 61–97; Barry Mehler, "A History of the American Eugenics Society, 1921–1941" (Ph.D. diss., University of Illinois at Urbana-Champaign, 1988).

Euler-Chelpin, Hans Karl August Simon von
(1873–1964)

German chemist and Nobel laureate. Born in Augsberg, Germany, on February 15, 1873, he received a doctorate from the University of Berlin in 1895, and he served as a professor of chemistry (1900–41) and director of the Institute of Biochemistry (1929–41) at the University of Stockholm until his retirement. During this period, Euler-Chelpin examined the fermentation of sugars in plants and fungi and coenzyme action, and how vitamins worked in the synthesis of nutrition. For his lifelong work, he was the corecipient (with Arthur HARDEN) the 1929 Nobel Prize in chemistry.

Euler-Chelpin served in both world wars for his native Germany, and he spent his final years at his home there. He died in Stockholm on November 6, 1964.

References: Linda C. Bradley, "Euler-Chelpin, Hans Karl August Simon von" in Bernard S. and June H. Schlessinger, eds., *The Who's Who of Nobel Prize Winners* (Phoenix, Ariz.: Oryx, 1986), 11; Thomas Watson MacCallum and Stephen Taylor, eds., *The Nobel Prize-Winners and the Nobel Foundation, 1901–1937* (Zurich, Switzerland: Central European Times Publishing, 1938), 155.

Everest expedition   *See* MALLORY AND IRVINE EXPEDITION.

Évian Conference

Meeting, July 6–15, 1938, in the French city of Évian-les-Bains, to discuss the pending fate of European Jews and their potential emigration from Nazi Germany after Hitler had annexed Austria, trapping tens of thousands of Jews behind the Nazi veil of power. Within 11 days of the annexation, U.S. President Franklin D. ROOSEVELT proposed a conference. Delegates from 32 nations—including Australia, Canada, England, France, New Zealand, the United States, and some Latin American countries—convened. The chief of the American delegation, Myron C. Taylor, said in his opening statement that the United

States was prepared to accept 27,370 Jewish refugees. The British and Australian delegates could not accept more refugees, and the British refused to allow any of the Jews to go to its protectorate of Palestine. This attitude permeated the entire conference and led to its ultimate failure.

With the close of the conference after just nine days, the Nazis concluded that the world did not care what happened to the European Jews, and in effect changed their plan from one of persecution and harassment to mass murder. Historian David S. Wyman writes, "The Evian Conference stands in historical perspective as a critical turning point. At the conference the Western democracies made it clear that they were willing to do next to nothing for the Jews of Europe. Soon afterward, *Kristallnacht,* which took place in the autumn of 1938, signaled to the world that Jews could no longer live where the Nazis ruled. At Evian, the world had shown that it would not make room for the Jews. Thus 1938 became the crucial year for the coming of the Holocaust."

See KRISTALLNACHT.

References: John Mendelsohn, ed., *The Holocaust: Selected Documents in Eighteen Volumes* (New York: Garland Publishing, 1982), 5: 228–64; "3 Democracies Lead at Parley Over Refugees," *Washington Post,* July 7, 1938, p. 1; "Taylor Heads Committee on Refugee Help; Most of Nations Frankly Inhospitable; America Urged for Settlers," *Washington Post,* July 8, 1938, p. 5; "U.S. Accepts Compromise on Refugees; Agrees to Postpone Decision of Giving Aid to All Nations," *Washington Post,* July 12, 1938, p. 1; "'Big Three' Plan for Refugees of Reich Endorsed; Small Nations, Except Colombia, Accept Provisions for Permanent Body," *The Washington Post,* July 14, 1938, p. 9; David S. Wyman, "Evian Conference" in Israel Gutman, ed. in chief, *Encyclopedia of the Holocaust* (New York: Macmillan, 1990) 2: 454–57.

Ex Parte Grossman (1925)

U.S. Supreme Court decision which held that the U.S. president possessed the constitutional power to pardon. On November 24, 1920, Philip Grossman was charged by the District Court of the United States for the Northern District of Illinois with violating the National PROHIBITION Act by selling liquor at his place of business in Chicago. A restraining order was filed against Grossman, but the court had him arrested again after he was found still selling liquor. Grossman was tried, convicted of the offense, and sentenced to a year in the Chicago House of Detention and a $1,000 fine. The Court of Appeals for the Fourth Circuit affirmed the ruling.

In December 1923, for an unknown reason, U.S. President Calvin COOLIDGE pardoned Grossman from the jail time on the condition that the fine be paid. The defendant paid the fine and was released. In May 1924, however, the District Court decided that the president's pardon was invalid and ordered Grossman returned to jail. Grossman then filed a writ of habeas corpus against Ritchie Graham, the Superintendent of the House of Correction, to let him out of prison. Graham was forced to show the court why he continued to jail the defendant. The District Court held that the pardon was not proper in a case involving a local injunction that was violated. Grossman appealed to the U.S. Supreme Court. Special counsel of the U.S. Justice Department appeared during arguments on December 1, 1924, to argue that the detention was valid; in an amicus curiae brief, the U.S. Attorney General, Harlan Fiske Stone (later to sit on the Supreme Court himself), asked the Court to uphold the president's right to pardon.

Three full months later, on March 2, 1925, the Court unanimously held that the president's power to pardon was absolute and ordered Grossman released immediately. In the decision, written by Chief Justice William Howard Taft, the Court held that since the violation of the Prohibition law was an "offense against the United States," Coolidge had been well within his bounds to pardon the offender. "Executive clemency exists to afford relief from undue harshness or evident mistake in the operation or enforcement of the criminal law," Taft wrote. "The administration of justice by the courts is not necessarily wise or certainly considerate of circumstances which may properly mitigate guilt. To afford a remedy, it has always been thought essential in popular governments, as well as in monarchies, to vest in some other authority than the courts power to ameliorate or avoid particular criminal judgments. It is a check entrusted to the executive for special cases. To exercise it to the extent of destroying the deterrent effect of judicial punishment would be to pervert it; but whoever is to make it useful must have full discretion to exercise it."

References: Harold W. Chase and Craig R. Ducat, *Constitutional Interpretation: Cases-Essays-Materials* (St. Paul, Minn.: West Publishing Co., 1979), 260–61; text of decision at 267 U.S. 87 (1925).

Fairbanks, Douglas (1883–1939)

American silent film actor, famed for his interwar performances in such films as *The Mark of Zorro* (1920), *The Three Musketeers* (1921), *Robin Hood* (1922), *The Thief of Baghdad* (1924), *The Black Pirate* (1926), *The Gaucho* (1927), and *The Iron Mask* (1929). Born Douglas Elton Ulman in Denver, Colorado, on May 23, 1883, he was raised by his mother after his parents separated. After he attended college, he played small parts on the stage; in 1915 he went to Hollywood, where his first role was in Triangle Pictures' *The Lamb* (1915). In 1917, with the assistance of director D. W. Griffith, he formed his own production company.

Starting in 1920, Fairbanks appeared in several of the most popular films of the silent era, cementing his image as the swashbuckling screen hero. In 1919 he founded, with Griffith, Charlie CHAPLIN, and Mary Pickford, the United Artists Corporation. The following year he married Pickford; the two divorced in 1935. In all, he acted in 43 films, including five "talkies."

The advent of talking MOTION PICTURES was the end for Fairbanks, although he continued to work in small films. His high-pitched voice was his undoing, and in 1936 he announced his retirement from acting, although he continued to produce pictures. His last role was in United Artists' 1934 film *The Private Life of Don Juan*. On December 21, 1939, Fairbanks died in Santa Monica, California, leaving a legacy of incredible silent film roles. He was one of the 36 founders of the Academy of Motion Picture Arts and Sciences, an association dedicated to preserving and celebrating the motion picture, and he served as its first president.

References: Ephraim Katz, *The Film Encyclopedia* (New York: HarperPerennial, 1994), 399; John C. Tibbetts and James M. Walsh, *His Majesty the American: The Films of Douglas Fairbanks, Sr.* (New Brunswick, N.J.: A. S. Barnes, 1977).

Fall, Albert Bacon (1861–1944)

American politician, implicated in the TEAPOT DOME SCANDAL. Born in Frankfort, Kentucky, on November 26, 1861, he studied the law there and then moved to New Mexico Territory, where he practiced law in Las Cruces in 1889. From 1890 until 1912, Fall held a series of territorial political posts, including positions as a member of the territorial house and territorial council, as an associate justice of the New Mexico Territorial Supreme Court, and twice as territorial attorney general. In 1912, when New Mexico was admitted to the Union, Fall was elected by the state legislature as one of two U.S. Senators. A close friend of Senator Warren G. HARDING of Ohio, he advocated for a strong American response to the incursions of Mexican insurgent Pancho Villa in 1916. Fall was a stern critic of President Woodrow WILSON and opposed the Treaty of VERSAILLES.

In 1920, Harding was elected president, and although he wanted Fall as his secretary of state, he was persuaded by party leaders to offer Fall the far less glamorous position of secretary of the interior. Within three months of taking office, Fall and Secretary of the Navy Edwin Denby were conspiring to sell leases to the U.S. oil reserves at Teapot Dome, Wyoming, as well as a similar supply at Elk Hills, California, to oilmen Harry F. Sinclair and Edward L. Doheny for bribes. By 1923, Fall was shut out of most cabinet meetings and, dissatisfied with his position, resigned from the government and retired to New Mexico.

That October, however, after Harding's death, Senator Thomas J. Walsh, Democrat of Montana, held hearings into the lease of Teapot Dome and Elk Hills, which exposed Fall as a bribe taker. When Fall tried to explain the Doheny and Sinclair payoffs as the settlement of a loan from a friend, he was implicated in lying. In 1929, he was convicted (Doheny was acquitted of actually making the bribe), and became the first cabinet officer in U.S. history to be sent to prison. Sentenced to one year, Fall served nine months before being paroled and returning to New Mexico, where he spent the remainder of his life. He died in El Paso, Texas, on November 30, 1944.

References: Eugene P. Trani, "The Secretaries of the Department of the Interior, 1849–1969," unpublished manuscript, National Anthropological Archives (Washington, D.C.), 170–76; Burl Noggle, *Teapot Dome: Oil and Politics in the 1920s* (Baton Rouge: Louisiana State University Press, 1962); "Ex-Secretary Fall Dies in El Paso, 83," *New York Times,* December 1, 1944, p. 23.

Farm Security Administration

U.S. agency, established in 1937, under the Resettlement Administration as a NEW DEAL program created by U.S. President Franklin D. ROOSEVELT to assist poverty-stricken farmers battered by the GREAT DEPRESSION and the DUST BOWL.

The onset of the Great Depression in 1929 found farmers already suffering in the wake of a steady drop in agricultural product prices that had begun in 1920. Little was done on a national scale until the election of Roosevelt as president in 1932; when he took office the following year, one of the numerous ALPHABET AGENCIES he established was the Agricultural Adjustment Administration (AAA), which in fact made matters worse for small family farms. Well-off farmers were rewarded with price supports, while poorer farmers and sharecroppers were forced to leave the land and find jobs as migrant workers. After two years of continuing disaster, the Roosevelt administration turned to creating the Resettlement administration, which provided low-cost loans and other forms of assistance to poor farmers who had hung onto their land.

This program was slightly more successful than the AAA, but by 1937 the situation demanded still further action, and the AAA was folded into the Department of Agriculture and renamed the Farm Security Administration (FSA). During its existence, the FSA helped more than four thousand displaced tenant farmers become landowners, organized collective farms in several states, and developed camps where migrant farm workers and their families could find housing and medical treatment.

By 1942 the FSA's budget had been slashed drastically, however, and much of its workload, including its historic photographs section, was transferred to the Office of War Information. Photographer Dorothea Lange hauntingly captured the plight of the rural poor for the FSA in her striking collection of images from the camps.

References: Sidney Baldwin, "The Farm Security Administration: A Study in Politics and Administration" (Master's thesis, Syracuse University, 1956); James Stuart Olson, *Historical Dictionary of the New Deal: From Inauguration to Preparation for War* (Westport, Conn.: Greenwood, 1985), 165–66.

fascism

Political ideology and form of government, practiced especially in Italy during the regime of Benito MUSSOLINI. Defined by Martin Kitchen as "any program for setting up a centralized autocratic regime with severely nationalistic policies, exercising regimentation of industry, commerce, and finance, rigid censorship, and forcible suppression of opposition," fascism had its roots in Italy with the March on Rome in 1922, an insurrection that led to the formation of a new government, at the request of the king, under Mussolini. Once Mussolini had his hand on power, he and his "Blackshirts" ruled Italy with a totalitarian hand that was not broken until he was executed in 1945. The Nazi state in Germany, built by the NAZI PARTY and its dictator ADOLF HITLER, is also considered by political theorists to be fascist, as is Francisco FRANCO's Spain (1939–1975). Franco's regime was the longest-lasting of the three, largely because he kept Spain nonbelligerent during World War II and thus avoided the destructive defeat that befell the leaders of Germany and Italy.

References: Martin Kitchen, *Fascism* (London: Macmillan, 1976); John Louis Spivak, *Europe under the Terror* (New York: Simon and Schuster, 1936).

Faulkner, William Harrison (1897–1962)

American novelist, considered one of the greatest writers of the 20th century for his numerous books. Faulkner was born in New Albany, Mississippi, on September 25, 1897, and lived most of his life in Oxford, Mississippi, which explains the essential "Southernness" he displayed. He so wished to fight in World War I that in 1918, after being rejected by the U.S. Army Corps as a pilot, he joined the Royal Air Force in Canada. He returned to the United States after the war and attended the University of Mississippi for two years.

After working for two years as the postmaster at the University of Mississippi, Faulkner published his first work, *The Marble Faun* (1924), a book of poetry. He then worked on a newspaper in New Orleans. After working closely with the writer Sherwood Anderson, Faulkner released *Soldier's Pay* (1926), which was followed by *Mosquitoes* (1927), *Sartoris* (1929), and *The Sound and the Fury* (1929). Many of his novels explored rural and small-town life, the tales of southern families coming to terms with their history of slave ownership. Next came *Sanctuary* (1931), considered one of his best works; *Light in August* (1932); *Pylon* (1935); *Absalom! Absalom!* (1936); and *The Unvanquished* (1938). Utilizing satire and historical irony, Faulkner encapsulated the southern way of life and point of view. His works—all of which appeared just before, during, and after World War II including *The Wild Palms* (1939), *The Hamlet* (1940), and *Intruder in the Dust* (1948)—increased his reputation as the definitive chroni-

William Faulkner *(CORBIS/Bettmann)*

cler of the struggle with family history with a southern backdrop, but the stories carried universal themes as well.

Faulkner was awarded the Nobel Prize in literature in 1949 for his body of work. After winning the Nobel, he spent several years touring the world on behalf of the U.S. State Department, then served as a writer-in-residence at the University of Virginia in Charlottesville. He won two Pulitzer Prizes—for *A Fable* (1954) and *The Reivers* (1962). Faulkner died in Byhalia, Mississippi, on July 6, 1962.

References: Joseph Leo Blotner, *Faulkner: A Biography* (New York: Random House, 1974); Michael Millgate, *The Achievement of William Faulkner* (Athens, Georgia: University of Georgia Press, 1989); Doreen Fowler and Ann J. Abadie, eds., *Faulkner and Popular Culture: Faulkner and Yoknapatawpha, 1988* (Jackson: University Press of Mississippi, 1990).

Federal Arts Project   *See* WORKS PROGRESS ADMINISTRATION.

Federal Communications Commission

U.S. federal agency, established June 19, 1934, to oversee radio and other communications in the United States. The Communications Act of 1934 unified, for the first time, federal authority over communications via radio, wire, and telegraph (later expanded to include television and cellular communications) in one independent office. The agency was granted the power to license radio stations and regulate communications for aeronautical (planes and airports), marine (ship to shore), land transportation (railroad and other forms), and other purposes.

References: Robert L. Hilliard, *The Federal Communications Commission: A Primer* (Boston: Focal Press, 1991); James Stuart Olson, *Historical Dictionary of the New Deal: From*

Inauguration to Preparation for War (Westport, Conn.: Greenwood, 1985), 171–72.

Federal Deposit Insurance Corporation   *See* GLASS-STEAGALL ACTS.

Federal Emergency Relief Administration   *See* HOPKINS, HARRY LLOYD.

Federal Theatre Project   *See* WORKS PROGRESS ADMINISTRATION.

Federal Writers' Project   *See* WORKS PROGRESS ADMINISTRATION.

feminism

Belief in the economic, political, and social equality of women and men, which was furthered by women's rights advocates in the United States, Europe, and elsewhere during the interwar period. The 20th-century quest for women's equality in the United States traces its roots to the abolitionist, civil rights, and working-class labor movements of the 19th century. Thanks to more than seventy years of effort by such suffragists as Elizabeth Cady Stanton and Susan B. Anthony, U.S. women finally received the vote in 1920 with the passage of the NINETEENTH AMENDMENT. Noting the crucial contributions made by women during World War I, President Woodrow WILSON in early 1919 actually declared women's suffrage to be an emergency war measure. The League of Women Voters was created in 1920 to educate the new voters about the issues of political representation. Electoral feminists learned during this decade that women did not vote as a bloc; in fact, there was no such thing as the "women's vote." Disparate elements of the feminist movement were no longer held together by the struggle for suffrage.

There was no moderate retreat in activism after World War I, in part because the goal of suffrage had been achieved and in part because younger women were enjoying new economic and social freedoms in the postwar years of prosperity. But there were also many kinds of feminists, working toward myriad social and political causes. Alice Paul, leader of the National Woman's Party, proposed an Equal Rights Amendment in 1923 to the U.S. Congress (passed by Congress in 1972, the amendment was never ratified). The ERA created a philosophical divide among feminists, as they struggled to define their various understandings of the roots of women's subordination as well as the strategies for overcoming it. The primarily white, middle-class women of the League worked for good government and for laws protecting working women and children. These feminists worked for social reform and for improving the conditions facing the poor (mostly immigrant women and their children) in such urban environments as Chicago and New York. They worked to protect, nurture, and assimilate other women, calling on the federal government's obligation to support poor and working-class mothers. Through this maternalism, these feminists won protective labor policies, pensions for widowed mothers, maternity and infancy services, and educational initiatives to speed the process of AMERICANIZATION, which the reformers believed would mitigate the effects of poverty.

Other women found that although they had been welcomed in the work force during World War I, when their labor was needed, they were expected to return to their domestic realms now that there was peace. Some so-called NEW WOMEN—educated, self-supporting, often unmarried—held jobs outside of the home. As leaders of various social, political, and educational reform movements, these feminists helped revolutionize U.S. women's notions of themselves. African-American feminists worked during these years to improve social and political problems that affected black communities and black women specifically. This feminism focused primarily on challenging racism and the demoralizing social and economic problems that it bred.

Women's movements blossomed throughout the world during the interwar period. For example, feminists in Great Britain campaigned for equal pay in the civil service, which culminated in a parliamentary vote for reform. In Mexico, in the years leading up to the Mexican Revolution, an unprecedented amount of women's organizing and vocational and educational training influenced a generation of women for the coming feminism of the 1920s and 1930s. In Australia women campaigned for indigenous rights. In postwar Germany, feminist activism grew out of that country's leftist traditions of Marxism, communism, and socialism.

References: Christine Bolt, *The Women's Movements in the United States and Britain from the 1790s to the 1920s* (Amherst: University of Massachusetts Press, 1993); J. Stanley Lemons, *The Woman Citizen: Social Feminism in the 1920's* (Charlottesville: University Press of Virginia, 1990); Patricia Hill Collins, *Black Feminist Thought* (Boston: Unwin Hyman, 1990); Marta Cotera, *Chicana Feminism* (Austin, Tex.: Information System Development, 1977); Margaret Randall, *Gathering Rage: The Failure of Twentieth-Century Revolutions to Develop a Feminist Agenda* (New York: Monthly Review Press, 1992).

Fermi, Enrico (1901–1954)

Italian-American physicist and Nobel laureate. Born in Rome, Italy, on September 29, 1901, he studied at the University of Pisa, from which he received his doctorate in physics in 1922, and several other schools in Leiden and Rome. He taught at universities in Florence (1924–26) and Rome (1926–38). In 1938, Fermi was awarded the Nobel Prize in physics for his work on neutrons and radioactivity; his years of research in this area have influenced other branches of science, including artificial radioactivity and nuclear fission.

Soon after winning his Nobel, Fermi fled to the United States because of the increasing oppression of the Italian Fascist regime and went to work at Columbia University (1939–45). On December 2, 1942, he helped engineer the first nuclear chain reaction at the University of Chicago, and during World War II he worked on the construction of an atomic weapon. In 1944, he became a naturalized American citizen; two years later, he became a professor of physics at the Institute for Nuclear Studies of the University of Chicago. Fermi died suddenly on November 28, 1954.

References: Al Nicosia and Bernard S. Schlessinger, "Fermi, Enrico" in Bernard S. and June H. Schlessinger, eds., *The Who's Who of Nobel Prize Winners* (Phoenix, Ariz.: Oryx, 1986), 163–64.

Fibiger, Johannes Andreas Grib (1867–1928)

Danish pathologist and Nobel laureate. Born in Silkeborg, Denmark, on April 23, 1867, he received his baccalaureate (1883) and his M.D. (1890) from the University of Copenhagen. He worked at that college as a researcher from 1891 to 1894, at the Bleghams Hospital for Contagious Diseases in Copenhagen from 1894 to 1897, and as a professor of Pathological Anatomy at the University of Copenhagen from 1897 to 1928. Fibiger spent his life researching cancer, most notably the *Spiroptera* carcinoma and artificially produced cancers in rats. For this work, he was awarded the 1926 Nobel Prize in medicine and physiology.

Ironically, Fibiger died of colon cancer on January 30, 1928.

References: Barbara I. McNutt, "Fibiger, Johannes Andreas Grib" in Bernard S. and June H. Schlessinger, eds., *The Who's Who of Nobel Prize Winners* (Phoenix, Ariz.: Oryx, 1986), 85–86; Thomas Watson MacCallum and Stephen Taylor, eds., *The Nobel Prize-Winners and the Nobel Foundation, 1901–1937* (Zurich, Switzerland: Central European Times Publishing, 1938), 211–12.

Film   *See* MOTION PICTURES, SILENT; MOTION PICTURES, TALKING.

Film Noir   *See* MOTION PICTURES, TALKING.

Fireside Chats

Series of weekly radio broadcasts delivered by U.S. President Franklin Delano ROOSEVELT on his plans to combat the GREAT DEPRESSION, so called because many Americans sat by their hearths to hear the president on their home radios. These talks contributed to FDR's popularity and gained support for his programs. Roosevelt first took to the airwaves at 10 P.M. eastern time on March 12, 1933, to address the nation on the impending bank crisis. Roosevelt said, "I want to talk for a few minutes with the people of the United States about banking—with the comparatively few who understand the mechanics of banking but more particularly with the overwhelming majority who use banks for the making of deposits and the drawing of checks." He added, "I want to tell you what has been done in the last few days, why it was done, and what the next steps are going to be. I recognize that the many proclamations from State Capitols and from Washington, the legislation, the Treasury regulations, etc., couched for the most part in banking and legal terms should be explained for the benefit of the average citizen. I owe this in particular because of the fortitude and good temper with which everybody has accepted the inconvenience and hardships of the banking holiday. I know that when you understand what we in Washington have been about I shall continue to have your cooperation as fully as I have had your sympathy and help during the past week."

One of the "fireside chats," which were given irregularly throughout the mid-1930s, was delivered from Roosevelt's home at Hyde Park, New York; the rest were from the White House. In the presidential papers at F.D.R.'s library, there are 30 speeches listed as "fireside chats," while an additional three speeches were delivered in the same mode but not designated as such.

Reference: Russell D. Buhite and David W. Levy, eds., *FDR's Fireside Chats* (Norman, Okla.: University of Oklahoma Press, 1992).

Fischer, Hans (1881–1945)

German chemist and Nobel laureate. Born in Hochstam-Main, Germany, on July 27, 1881, he received his doctorate from the University of Marburg in Germany in 1904 and his M.D. from the University of Munich in 1908. He served as a professor of chemistry at a number of German universities, including the University of Munich and the University of Berlin, as well as the University of Innsbruck and the University of Vienna, both in Austria. During this period, he worked on the structural composition of blood to discover the properties of the crystalline salt hemin obtained from hemoglobin. For his landmark work on blood properties, Fischer was awarded the 1930 Nobel Prize in chemistry.

After winning the Nobel, writes biographer Kay Harvey, "[Fischer] worked out the structural formulas for both biliverdin and bilirubin, and in 1942 he synthesized biliverdin, with the synthesis of bilirubin following in 1944. He also worked out the complete structure of chlorophylls, demonstrating that chlorophylls were substituted porphins with an atom of magnesium at the center, thus paving the way for their synthesis by his pupils." Fischer died suddenly in Munich on March 31, 1945.

References: Kay Harvey, "Fischer, Hans" in Bernard S. and June H. Schlessinger, eds., *The Who's Who of Nobel Prize Winners* (Phoenix, Ariz.: Oryx, 1986), 11–12; Thomas Watson MacCallum and Stephen Taylor, eds., *The Nobel Prize-Winners and the Nobel Foundation, 1901–1937* (Zurich, Switzerland: Central European Times Publishing, 1938), 154.

Fitzgerald, F. Scott (1896–1940)

American novelist, whose works both shaped and epitomized the "roaring" 1920s. A distant relative of Francis Scott Key, who wrote "The Star Spangled Banner" in 1814, Francis Scott Key Fitzgerald was born on September 24, 1896, in St. Paul, Minnesota. He attended Princeton University until he volunteered for service during World War I. He never served in a combat, instead spending his time abroad as a general's aide. After the war, he lived in New York City, and wrote for an advertising agency. His own first writings, a series of short stories, were submitted to *The Smart Set* magazine, and, after they were published, Fitzgerald decided to make writing his profession. The short stories were also published in book form in *Flappers and Philosophers* (1920).

In his first published novel, *This Side of Paradise* (1920), Fitzgerald described his era with accuracy and biting satire. He continued this trend with *The Beautiful and the Damned* (1921), *Tales of the Jazz Age* (1922)—from which the era gets its name—the play *The Vegetable* (1923), and in 1925, what many consider his greatest and most important work, *The Great Gatsby*. A member of the "LOST GENERATION" of writers, Fitzgerald lived an extravagant life, perhaps reflected in *Gatsby*. Centering on the ambitious Gatsby, a wealthy young man fleeing a murky past, the novel deals with those who surround him: a rich, fast crowd that parties day and night in the days of PROHIBITION.

For many, Fitzgerald's novels perfectly captures the spirit of the JAZZ AGE. After *Gatsby*, however, Fitzgerald met with limited success. His *All the Sad Young Men* (1926) was a series of short stories; it was followed by *Tender Is the Night* (1934), and *Taps at Reveille* (1935). Their failures contributed to his bouts with depression and alcoholism. In his last three years Fitzgerald wrote screenplays for Hollywood motion pictures, but his ideas never caught on. It seems that the death of the Jazz Age in the grips of the GREAT DEPRESSION in 1929 was Fitzgerald's undoing as well. When he died of a heart attack on December 21,

1940, at the age of 44, the *New York Herald-Tribune* called him "a chronicler of the Lost Generation."

References: Henry Dan Piper, *F. Scott Fitzgerald: A Critical Portrait* (New York: Holt, Rinehart and Winston, 1965); Alfred Kazin, *F. Scott Fitzgerald: The Man and His Work* (Cleveland: World Publishing Company, 1951); Richard Daniel Lehan, *F. Scott Fitzgerald and the Craft of Fiction* (Carbondale: Southern Illinois University Press, 1966); "F. Scott Fitzgerald Dies at 44; Chronicler of 'Lost Generation,'" *New York Herald-Tribune*, December 23, 1940, p. 14.

Fiume

Major port city on the Adriatic Sea, subject of a significant crisis between Italy and Yugoslavia in 1919. Located about 40 miles southeast of the Italian city of Trieste at the headwaters of the Gulf of Kvarnero (or Quarnero), Fiume was in the 19th century considered a part of the Austro-Hungarian Empire, but in 1918 after the end of World War I was given to Croatia, a part of the nation that was to become Yugoslavia.

At the VERSAILLES Peace Conference in 1919, Fiume became a point of great dispute between the Italian delegation, which sought to have the city declared as part of Italy so that it could have an Adriatic port, and the United States, which backed Yugoslavian claims on it. When the conference refused to back Italy's desires, an Italian nationalist, war hero Gabriele d'Annunzio, led a ragtag army of soldiers (called the *Arditi*, or "Children of God") to Fiume and occupied it in the name of Italy on September 11, 1919, igniting the first crisis of postwar Europe. To avoid war, Italy and Yugoslavia established Fiume as a free state under the RAPALLO Treaty of 1920. In December 1920, Italian prime minister Giovanni Giolitti sent General Enrico Caviglia to forcibly remove d'Annunzio and cohorts from the city, and on January 27, 1924, under the Treaty of Rome, most of the city, with the port of Rijeka, was given to Italy. During World War II, Yugoslavia occupied the city, and, after the war, Fiume was eventually assigned to Yugoslavia by the Treaty of Paris in 1947 and renamed Rijeka.

References: Salvatore Saladino, "Fiume (Rijeka)" in Frank J. Coppa, ed. in chief, *Dictionary of Modern Italian History* (Westport, Conn.: Greenwood, 1985), 159–60; Paul Johnson, *Modern Times: The World from the Twenties to the Eighties* (New York: Harper & Row, 1983), 95; Edmund Jan Osmańczyk, *The Encyclopedia of the United Nations and International Agreements* (Philadelphia: Taylor & Francis, 1985), 670.

five-year-plan

Series of economic blueprints, first established by the Soviet Union in 1928, to expand that nation's industrial output. In 1921, Vladimir LENIN, the head of the Soviet Union, instituted the NEW ECONOMIC POLICY, which oversaw the rapid government takeover of industry and the collectivization of farms and factories. By 1928, Lenin's successor, Joseph STALIN, instituted the Five-Year-Plan, an economic program with a timed agenda. The first plan covered the period from October 1, 1928, until September 30, 1933, but because of the changing economy the first plan was ended in December 1932. The period ended with 61.5 percent of peasant farms collectivized, and 93.7 percent of the industrial output that had been projected was realized. In the second Five-Year Plan (1933–37), better defense and increased industrial output were stressed. Industrial output rose by only 4 percent in this period, and collectivization only rose to 74 percent. The third Five-Year Plan (1938–42) was interrupted by the German invasion, and the entire Soviet economy was put on a firm footing not to increase consumer goods or collectivize farms, but to rapidly build up the Soviet military.

References: Grigorii Fedorovich Grinko, *Piatiletnii plan narodnogo khoziaistva* (The five-year plan of the Soviet Union: a political interpretation) (London: M. Lawrence, 1930); Robert William Davies, *Crisis and Progress in the Soviet Economy, 1931–1933* (Basingstoke, England: Macmillan, 1996).

Flanagan, Hallie   *See* WORKS PROGRESS ADMINISTRATION.

flappers

Descriptive term for U.S. women who embraced the "flapper style" in the 1920s. The flapper style—characterized by bobbed hair, knee-length skirts or straight dresses, stockings rolled at the knees, and heeled shoes—was associated with female independence and unconventional behavior. The heroines of the JAZZ AGE, these women were rebels when compared with the demure Gibson girl of the past generation. No longer confined to the domestic realm, the flappers symbolized a revolution in fashion as well as mores.

Silent film star Louise BROOKS typified the flapper style of sleek looks as well as the flappers' perceived lifestyle of exuberant socializing. Brooks's social circle included the very figures who defined the Jazz Age: the composer George GERSHWIN, the novelist F. Scott FITZGERALD, and the critic H. L. MENCKEN, among others. The writer Dorothy PARKER wrote of this persona in her poem "The Flapper":

> The playful flapper here we see
> The fairest of the fair.
> She's not what Grandma used to be.
> You might say, au contraire.
> Her girlish ways may make a stir.

Her manners cause a scene,
But there is no more harm in her
Than in a submarine.

References: Paula S. Fass, *The Beautiful and the Damned: American Youth in the 1920s* (New York: Oxford University Press, 1977); Elizabeth Stevenson, *Babbits and Bohemians: The American 1920s* (New York: Macmillan, 1967).

Fleischer, Max   *See* CARTOONS, STRIP AND MOVING.

football, collegiate

Intercollegiate team sport that soared to popularity in the United States during the interwar period. Evolving from England's soccer and rugby games, American football had developed its modern rules by the mid-19th century, with the help of Yale University's Walter Camp. American football had become the most popular intercollegiate sport by the turn of the century, as thousands of college students and alumni turned out to cheer their teams to victory. The "football weekend" became a way of life on college campuses throughout the country. To systematize the rules of the game (and to lessen the often extreme violence that the competition incited), the National Collegiate Athletic Association was formed in 1906.

Devoted fans followed various teams and players throughout the seasons. During the interwar period the three-time All-American halfback Harold "Red" Grange—also called the "Galloping Ghost" for his elusive maneuvers on the field—rose to hero status. In his years playing for the University of Illinois (1923–25), Grange gained 3,637 yards and scored 31 touchdowns in only 20 games. He went on to play professionally for the Chicago Bears (1925–26, 1929–34). The American Professional Football Association (later renamed the National Football League) was founded in 1920, headed by the legendary Olympic athlete Jim Thorpe, but the professional sport did not attract much attention until after World War II, when the owners decided to end racial segregation within teams.

References: Benjamin G. Rader, *American Sports: From the Age of Folk Games to the Age of Televised Sports* (Englewood Cliffs, N.J.: Prentice Hall, 1996); Mark Stewart, *Football: A History of the Gridiron Game* (Danbury, Conn.: Franklin Watts, 1999); Ted Yanak and Pam Cornelison, "Red Grange," in *The Great American History Fact-Finder* (Boston: Houghton Mifflin, 1993), 183.

Forbes Commission

Committee, headed by former Philippines governor-general William Cameron Forbes, sent to that nation in 1921 by U.S. President Warren G. HARDING to determine whether "the Philippine Government is now in a position to warrant its total separation from the U.S. Government." The co-chair of the mission was General Leonard Wood, who had fought in the Spanish-American War and was the military governor of Cuba, who would later serve as governor-general of the islands himself. Forbes was against independence, and many pro-independence Filipinos criticized his selection. The mission arrived in the Philippines on May 14, 1921, and their final report was released on October 8 of that same year. The commission concluded:

"The great bulk of the Christian Filipinos have a very natural desire for independence; most of them desire independence under the protection of the United States; a very small percentage desire immediate independence with separation from the United States; a very substantial element is opposed to independence, especially at this time. The Moros [members of the Moro Province of the islands] are a unit against independence and are united for continuance of American control and, in case of separation of the Philippines from the United States, desire their portion of the islands to be retained as American territory under American control. The pagans and non-Christians, constituting about 10 percent of the population, are for continued American control."

With this conclusion, the committee proposed that "the present general status of the Philippine Islands continue until the people have had time to absorb and thoroughly master powers already in their hands." Independence did not come to the Philippines until 1946.

References: The Forbes-Wood report can be found in its entirety in William Cameron Forbes, *The Philippine Islands* (Boston and New York: Houghton Mifflin, 1928), 2: 520–44; Teodoro A. Agoncillo and Oscar M. Alfonso, *History of the Filipino People* (Quezon City: Malaya Books, 1967), 364–67.

Ford, Henry (1863–1947)

American industrial revolutionary and innovator of automobile manufacturing. Born on a farm near Dearborn, Michigan, as a child Ford enjoyed working with machinery. In the 1890s he began experimenting with the internal combustion engine, and by 1896 Ford had produced his first car, built by hand. He established the Ford Motor Company in 1903, which skyrocketed to success with the 1908 introduction of the Model T. He introduced the principles of the assembly line and standardized parts in 1913, which made automobiles for the first time affordable to the average family; by 1917 the cars sold for $360 each.

Ford became one of the richest people in the United States, and for a time he considered a political career. In 1918 he ran, unsuccessfully, for the U.S. Senate. Also a philanthropist, Ford established the Ford Foundation with his son Edsel in 1936. The company developed problems in the late 1920s and early 1930s, however, and Ford refused to make the necessary changes in his production system, his automobiles, even his labor policies. He released the Model A in 1933, but by the mid-1930s the company was deeply divided. In 1945, two years before his death, Ford handed over control to his grandson, Henry Ford II.

Reference: Ray Batchelor, *Henry Ford: Mass Production, Modernism, and Design* (New York: Manchester University Press; distributed by St. Martin's, 1994).

Fordney-McCumber Act

U.S. congressional legislation, September 21, 1922, which raised duties on manufactured and farm products and introduced the principle of the flexible tariff for the first time. Writes historian Michael E. Parrish, "The Fordney-McCumber Act, boosting tariff rates back to late nineteenth-century levels, retained . . . prohibitive rates for foreign farm products. But in the long run it probably took more money out of the pockets of farmers than it returned. The new duties all but barred foreign raw wool from the American market, for example, but the rates on both the woolen and cotton textiles were high enough to price all but the cheapest of foreign goods out of the country . . . farmers and other consumers paid the bill. By erecting an impenetrable wall around the domestic market, the Fordney-McCumber tariff gave windfall profits to American chemical, dye, steel, and aluminum producers. Except for farmers who raised very special crops such as almonds, olives, dates, and citrus fruits, the measure proved to be an empty victory for agriculture." One of the leading Democrats to oppose Fordney-McCumber was Furnifold M. Simmons of North Carolina, the ranking Democrat on the Senate Finance Committee. The action was sponsored in the House by Joseph W. Fordney, Republican of Michigan, and in the Senate by Porter J. McCumber, Republican of North Dakota.

References: Robert K. Murray, *The Politics of Normalcy: Governmental Theory and Practice in the Harding-Coolidge Era* (New York: Norton, 1973); Frank William Taussig, *The Tariff History of the United States, Including a Consideration of the Tariff of 1930* (New York: G. P. Putnam, 1931); Michael E. Parrish, *Anxious Decades: America in Prosperity and Depression, 1920–1941* (New York: W. W. Norton, 1992), 86.

Foreign Service, U.S.   *See* GREW, JOSEPH CLARK; ROGERS ACT.

Four-Power Treaty

Pact, 1921, which was the main achievement of the WASHINGTON NAVAL CONFERENCE. During the conference, which lasted from November 1921 until February 1922, the conferees agreed on several pacts, including the Four-

Power Treaty and the NINE-POWER TREATY. In the former agreement—which historian J. Chal Vinson writes "abrogated the Anglo-Japanese alliance, [and] bound the signatories—Great Britain, the United States, France, and Japan—to respect each other's possessions 'in the region of the Pacific Ocean' for ten years, and to settle any mutual controversy by conference, if negotiations through regular diplomatic channels broke down"—the four main powers seemed to come to some agreement on the disposition of certain territories in the Pacific. U.S. Secretary of State Charles Evans HUGHES, foreseeing possible Senate reaction against the treaty, enlisted the aid of Senator Henry Cabot LODGE, who had been so instrumental in the destruction of the Treaty of VERSAILLES. Lodge was able to muster enough support to get the treaty heard in the Senate. On March 11, 1922, sensing that there might be trouble gathering the two-thirds vote needed for passage, Hughes wrote to Senator Oscar W. Underwood of Alabama that the failure of the Senate to ratify the agreement "would be nothing short of a national calamity." On March 24, after Lodge allowed the Senate to vote on various additions and amendments, however, the treaty passed, 67 to 27, with two abstentions. Historian Thomas Buckley writes, "The Four-Power Treaty . . . achieved the main hope of the American government—abrogation of the Anglo-Japanese alliance. Whether the alliance had been a threat to the United States is a moot point. General feeling at the time was that there was little chance the British would fight the Americans in the event the latter should clash with the Japanese. As Hughes and the American government realized, the danger was that the Japanese would continue the alliance to further their interests on the Chinese mainland and in the Pacific."

References: J. Chal Vinson, "The Parchment Peace: The Senate Defense of the Four-Power Treaty of the Washington Conference," *Mississippi Valley Historical Review* 39, 2 (September 1952): 303–14; Department of State, "Papers Relating to the Foreign Relations of the United States, 1922" (Washington, D.C.: Government Printing Office, 1938), 1: 48–50; Thomas H. Buckley, *The United States and the Washington Conference, 1921–1922* (Knoxville: University of Tennessee Press, 1970), 143.

France, Anatole (1844–1924)

French writer and Nobel laureate. Born Jacques Anatole-François Thibault in Paris, France, on April 16, 1844, he received his baccalaureate from the Collège Stanislas in Nice, France, in 1864. He worked as a freelance journalist from 1862 to 1877, and as a librarian at the Bibliothèque du Sénat from 1876 to 1890. In 1868 he published *Alfred de Vigny,* and in 1881 he began work on a series of publications with French life as a background, starting with *Le Crime de Sylvestre Bonnard, membre de l'institut* (The crime

Delegates to the Washington Naval Conference during negotiations for the Four-Power Treaty (*CORBIS/Bettmann*)

of Sylvester Bonnard). He continued with *Thaïs* (1890), *L'Étui de nacre* (Mother of pearl, 1892), and *La Rotisserie de la reine pedauque* (At the sign of the Reine Pedauque, 1893). By this time he was a leading French literary figure, and he continued to write until the end of his life. In 1896 he was elected to the Academie Française.

For his body of work, France was awarded the 1921 Nobel Prize in literature. E. A. Karlfeldt, the permanent Secretary of the Swedish Academy, said on presenting the Nobel, "Mr. Anatole France, you have inherited that admirable tool, the French language, the language of a noble and classical nation, which is reverently guarded by the famous academy you adorn and is maintained by it in an enviable condition of purity. You have that brilliant tool of piercing sharpness, and in your hand it acquires a scintillating beauty. You have used it masterfully to cut out *chefs-d'oeuvre* very French in their style and refinement. But it is not your art alone that charms us: we revere your creative genius as well, and we have been enticed by the generous, compassionate heart which so many exalted pages of your works reveal."

France died on October 12, 1924.

References: Gerald Kirk, "France, Anatole" in Bernard S. and June H. Schlessinger, eds., *The Who's Who of Nobel Prize Winners* (Phoenix, Ariz.: Oryx, 1986), 54; Thomas Watson MacCallum and Stephen Taylor, eds., *The Nobel Prize-Winners and the Nobel Foundation, 1901–1937* (Zurich, Switzerland: Central European Times Publishing, 1938), 294–95.

Franck, James (1882–1964)

German-American physicist and Nobel laureate. Born in Hamburg, Germany, on August 26, 1882, Franck attended the University of Berlin, which awarded him a doctorate in 1906. He began his career as a physics professor at the University of Berlin soon after graduating, and remained there until 1918, when he moved to the Kaiser Wilhelm Institute for a two-year stint. In 1920, he moved to the

University of Göttingen, where he worked until 1933. In 1925, Franck was the corecipient (with Gustav HERTZ) of the Nobel Prize in physics for his work in the "discovery of the laws governing the impact of an electron upon an atom."

After working at the University of Copenhagen, Franck criticized the HITLER regime in Germany and emigrated to the United States, where he worked at Johns Hopkins University from 1935 to 1938, and at the University of Chicago from 1938 to 1947. While at Chicago, he prepared the Franck Report, which asked that any atomic device constructed by the United States be demonstrated to the world in an open display rather than in a surprise attack on Japan—advice that was ignored. When Franck retired in 1947, he returned to his native Germany. He died in Göttingen on May 21, 1964.

References: Frank Kellerman, "Franck, James" in Bernard S. and June H. Schlessinger, eds., *The Who's Who of Nobel Prize Winners* (Phoenix, Ariz.: Oryx, 1986), 158; Thomas Watson MacCallum and Stephen Taylor, eds., *The Nobel Prize-Winners and the Nobel Foundation, 1901–1937* (Zurich: Central European Times Publishing, 1938), 83–84.

Franco, Francisco (1892–1975)

Spanish generalissimo ("general"), head of the nationalist forces that conquered Spain during its bloody civil war (1937–38) and president (1938–75). Born Francisco Paulino Hermenegildo Teódulo Franco-Bahamonde in El Ferrol, Galicia, Spain, on December 4, 1892, he hoped to serve in the Spanish navy, but instead was sent to the army, entering the infantry Academy at Toledo when he was 14 and graduating three years later. His first service came during the Spanish campaign in Morocco in 1909, and in 1912 he was transferred there. Promoted the following year to the rank of first lieutenant of cavalry, Franco was soon praised for his professional abilities in handling combat and troops under his command. In 1915 he was again promoted, to captain, but in 1916 he was seriously wounded and returned to Spain to recover. In 1920, he was named as second-in-command of the Spanish Foreign Legion, rising to commander three years later. He was instrumental in helping to put down the Rif rebellion of ABD EL-KRIM in Morocco, and he became a national hero. In 1926, at age 33, Franco was made a brigadier general in the Spanish army. Two years later he was named director of the General Military Academy at Saragossa.

After the fall of King ALFONSO XIII in 1931, Franco was dismissed from his post by the moderate government that took Alfonso's place. When conservatives took over the government in 1933, Franco was reinstated, and promoted the following year to major general. In 1935, he was named chief of the Spanish Army General Staff to assemble a program to quell violence and to reinforce the military after it was decimated by the leftists who had succeeded Alfonso. In 1936 the government collapsed, and new elections were called. Franco sided with the rightist National Bloc, but the leftist Popular Front won the election and formed a government. Still, because of cultural and economic concerns, the country spiraled out of control. Franco asked the government to call for a state of emergency, but his appeal was refused. On July 18, 1936, Franco issued a manifesto from the Canary Islands, where he had exiled himself, demanding the end of the government and the transfer of its power to him. After traveling to Morocco to confirm his control of the military, he and his men landed in Spain and marched to Madrid to take over. Stopped outside of Madrid, the rightists, or Falangists (the Spanish Fascist Party was known as the Falange), declared Franco their generalissimo and established a Nationalist government on October 1, 1936, with Franco at its head. Franco then launched the SPANISH CIVIL WAR, in which, with German and Italian help, he was able to defeat the forces of the Republic government, which was backed by the Soviets and an army of leftists from around the world. The war ended, after tens of thousands of deaths, on April 1, 1939, after Franco took Madrid and was generally recognized as the leader of Spain.

Franco was forced to deal with a nation wracked by three years of devastating civil war and an economy destroyed by the war and global depression. For these reasons, he remained nonbelligerent during World War II, and after the war was one of the few leaders who was not thrown from office or put on trial for war crimes. He remained in power until his death in Madrid on November 20, 1975.

See also FASCISM.

References: John William Donald Trythall, *El Caudillo: A Political Biography of Franco* (New York: McGraw-Hill, 1970); Paul Preston, *Franco: A Biography* (London: Harper-Collins, 1993); Laurence Ernest Snellgrove, *Franco and the Spanish Civil War* (New York: McGraw-Hill, 1968).

Frank, Hans (1900–1946)

German lawyer and intimate of Adolf HITLER, governor-general of Poland during World War II. Frank was born in the village of Karlsruhe, a village in southwest Germany, on May 23, 1900. Little is known of his early life; he served in the German army only in 1918, the last year of World War I. After the war he joined the police units called *Freikorps,* which fought the communists in the streets in 1919. Joining the NAZI PARTY (National Socialist) in 1921, he became a member of the *Schutzstaffel* or SS.

During the 1920s Frank defended Brownshirt rogues who attacked communists in the streets. As Hitler's personal attorney, he became the head of the Nazi party's legal division. Hitler also named him as Bavarian minister of justice, Reich minister of justice, and, in the 1930s, *Reichsleiter* (Reich leader) of the Nazi party. After Poland was conquered in October 1939, Hitler named his friend governor-general of occupied Poland. Frank declared German to be Poland's new official language, confiscated on a mass scale Polish and Jewish property, and by 1942 had transported 85 percent of Poland's Jews to concentration camps. In a speech that Frank delivered before his fellow Nazis on December 16, 1941, he said, "One way or another—I will tell you that quite openly—*we must finish off the Jews* [Frank's emphasis]. The Führer put it into words once: 'Should united Jewry again succeed in setting off a world war, then the blood sacrifice shall not be made only by the peoples driven into war, but then the Jew of Europe will have met his end.' I know that there is criticism of many of the measures now applied to the Jews in the Reich. There are always deliberate attempts to speak again and again of cruelty, harshness, etc.: this emerges from the reports on the popular mood. I appeal to you, before now I continue speaking: first, agree with me on one formula: we will have pity, on principle, only for the German people, and for nobody else in the world. The others had no pity for us either. As an old National Socialist, I must also say that if the pack of Jews were to survive the war in Europe while we sacrifice the best of our blood for the preservation of Europe, then this war would still be only a partial success. I will therefore, on principle, approach Jewish affairs in the expectation that the Jews will disappear. They must go."

At the end of the war, Frank was captured by the Allies and put on trial with other high-ranking Nazis at Nuremberg starting in November 1945. On October 1, 1946, he was found guilty of committing war crimes and crimes against humanity, and sentenced to death. On October 16, he walked from his cell in the Nuremberg Prison to the gallows, where he was hanged. Frank's *Diary*, edited by Polish author Stanislaw Piotrowski, was published in Warsaw in 1961.

References: Christian Zentner and Friedemann Bedüftig, eds., *Encyclopedia of the Third Reich* (New York: Macmillan; two volumes, 1991); Louis L. Snyder, *Encyclopedia of the Third Reich* (New York: MacGraw-Hill Book Company, 1976), 97–98; Ann and John Tusa, *The Nuremberg Trial* (New York: Atheneum, 1986); Telford Taylor, *The Anatomy of the Nuremberg Trials: A Personal Memoir* (New York: Alfred A. Knopf, 1992).

Frankenstein

Famed horror film, 1931, which set the standard for motion pictures of the genre. This was not the first filmed version of the British novel, written by Mary Shelley in 1818. The first rendition was the 1910 silent film *Franken-*

stein, produced by Thomas Edison. A second but lesser known version was 1915's *Life Without Soul*, starring Percy Standing as "the Creation." A third version was produced in Italy in 1920.

For the 1931 film, several actors were considered for the role of the monster, but director James Wade plucked an obscure actor named Boris KARLOFF from the British stage for the part. Karloff went on to deliver one of the finest performances in film history.

In the much-ballyhooed sequel, *Bride of Frankenstein* (1935), considered by many film historians to have been one of the greatest horror films of all time, Karloff reprised his role as the monster, with English actress Elsa Lanchester playing the bride.

See also MOTION PICTURES, SILENT; MOTION PICTURES, TALKING.

References: George Levine and U. C. Knoepflmacher, *The Endurance of Frankenstein: Essays on Mary Shelley's Novel* (Berkeley: University of California Press, 1979); Richard J. Anobile, ed., *Frankenstein* (New York: Universe Books, 1974).

Frazier-Lemke Mortgage Relief Act

U.S. congressional legislation enacted June 28, 1934, also known as the Federal Farm Bankruptcy Act or Federal Farm Mortgage Act, which established a moratorium on farm foreclosures during the height of the GREAT DEPRESSION. Sponsored by Senator Lynn Joseph Frazier of North Dakota and Representative William Lemke of the same state, the legislation was intended to force a halt to farm foreclosures and stop the loss of U.S. farms to banks. However, the rate of foreclosures continued; so much so, that by 1934, 25 percent of all U.S. farmers had lost their land to foreclosure alone.

On May 27, 1935, "BLACK MONDAY," the U.S. Supreme Court struck down Frazier-Lemke by holding, in *Louisville Joint Stock Land Bank v. Radford*, that "valid liens obtained before bankruptcy [was declared] could be enforced on exempt property." On August 28, 1935, Congress enacted a similar act, called the "new Frazier-Lemke Act," and that action was upheld by the Court as constitutional in the 1937 decision *Wright v. Vinton Branch of Mountain Trust Bank of Roanoke, Virginia.*

References: Leonard W. Levy, "Louisville Joint Stock Land Bank v. Radford" in Leonard W. Levy, ed. in chief, *Encyclopedia of the American Constitution* (New York: Macmillan, 1986–92), 3: 1180.

Frick, Wilhelm (1877–1946)

German politician, architect of the Nazi system of concentration camps that claimed more than 20 million people. Born the son of a schoolteacher in Alsenz, in the area known as the German Palatinate, on March 12, 1877, Frick studied law in Munich and Berlin before being awarded a doctorate at Heidenberg. From 1912 he practiced law in Berlin; because of a lung condition he did not fight in World War I. A bureaucrat in the postwar WEIMAR REPUBLIC, Frick was one of the first major German politicians to openly declare his sympathy for the NAZI PARTY (the National Socialists) in 1919. Adolf HITLER wrote in his memoirs, MEIN KAMPF, that Frick was one of two Germans he knew "who had the courage to be Germans first and then officials."

After the BEER-HALL PUTSCH, the Nazis' unsuccessful attempt to grab power in 1923, Frick saw to it that Hitler received a light sentence and, when he was released, aided him in financing Nazi presses and publications. In 1933, when Hitler was elected chancellor, he rewarded Frick with the office of minister of the interior. Under his leadership the Gestapo (the secret police who used terrorist methods against those suspected of disloyalty) was created, the Nuremberg Race Laws (which deprived German Jews of their rights of citizenship) were promulgated (Frick is credited with writing them himself), concentration camps for Jews and dissidents were established, and churches were repressed. Further, Frick helped Hitler plan the 1939 invasion of Poland. In 1943, Frick was removed as interior minister and appointed "Protector" of Bohemia and Moravia in Czechoslovakia; there, he established the SS unit that brutalized tens of thousands of Czech citizens.

At the end of the war, Frick was charged with committing crimes against peace, committing war crimes, and committing crimes against humanity at the Nuremberg War Crimes trials in November 1945. Unlike Hans FRANK, FRICK was unrepentant for his Nazi service. On October 1, 1946, Frick was found guilty on all three counts, and sentenced to death; on October 16, he and the other convicted Nazis were hanged inside Nuremberg Prison. According to witnesses, Frick's last words were, "Long live eternal Germany!"

References: Christian Zentner and Friedemann Bedüftig, eds., *Encyclopedia of the Third Reich* (New York: Macmillan, 1991), 1: 299–300; Ann and John Tusa, *The Nuremberg Trial* (New York: Atheneum, 1986); Telford Taylor, *The Anatomy of the Nuremberg Trials: A Personal Memoir* (New York: Alfred A. Knopf, 1992); James Taylor and Warren Shaw, *The Third Reich Almanac* (New York: World Almanac, 1987), 122; Louis L. Snyder, *Encyclopedia of the Third Reich* (New York: McGraw-Hill Book Co., 1976), 100–101.

Fugitives, The

Influential group of U.S. poets and critics, associated with Vanderbilt University in Nashville, Tennessee, during the 1920s. Deriving their writing from the history and culture of the American South, this informal group, which included Cleanth BROOKS, Walter Clyde Curry, Donald Davidson, William Yandell Elliott, James M. Frank, William Frierson, Stanley Johnson, Merrill Moore, John Crowe Ransom, Laura Riding, Alfred Starr, Alec Brock Stevenson, Allen Tate, Robert Penn WARREN, Jesse Wills, and Ridley Wills, among others, helped introduce the so-called "southern style" of writing to a national audience. As part of their program, they published 19 issues of the magazine *The Fugitive* from 1922 until 1925, which contained verse and articles relating to southern literature. The group disbanded in 1925, when many of the members went their separate ways.

References: James J. Sosnoski, "Cleanth Brooks" in Gregory S. Jay, ed., *Modern American Critics, 1920–1955* (Detroit: Gale Research, 1988), 33–42; Louise Cowan, *The Fugitive Group: A Literary History* (Baton Rouge: Louisiana State University Press, 1959); John M. Bradbury, *The Fugitives: A Critical Account* (Chapel Hill: University of North Carolina Press, 1958).

Gable, Clark (1901–1960)

American motion picture actor, known for his leading romantic roles in several Hollywood films of the 1930s. William Clark Gable was born on February 1, 1901, in Cadiz, Ohio, and lost his mother when he was just seven months old. He never finished high school, but held various odd jobs, including working in a tire factory in Akron. After he saw the play *The Bird of Paradise,* he decided on a career in acting and starred in a number of plays while touring with several companies. In 1924, he was taken to Hollywood by Josephine Dillon, the manager of a Portland, Oregon, theater where he had worked. Dillon, 12 years older than the 23-year-old Gable, married the young actor, and got him parts in several films as an extra, starting with *The Forbidden Paradise* (1924). Gable returned to the theater when his career did not advance.

After seeing Gable in the play *The Last Mile* an excited Lionel BARRYMORE got the young actor a screen test before the producer Irving Thalberg, but Gable's oversized ears scared Thalberg and he turned Gable down. Instead, Gable was hired by MGM, and, with the addition of a mustache, appeared with Joan Crawford in *Dance, Fools, Dance* (1931), and, that same year, with Norma Shearer in *A Free Soul.* When he refused to do a certain film for the studio, he was loaned out to Columbia Studios for the 1934 picture *It Happened One Night,* for which he won a Best Actor Oscar, and he returned to MGM a star. From the time of his screen debut until 1939, he starred in 47 films, including *Manhattan Melodrama* (1934), *Mutiny on the Bounty* (1935), which garnered him another Best Actor Academy Award nomination for his role as Fletcher Christian, and GONE WITH THE WIND (1939), for which he received yet another nomination for the Best Actor Oscar for his classic role as Rhett Butler.

Gable's life took a horrible turn on January 16, 1942, when his 33-year-old wife, actress Carole Lombard, was killed in a plane crash during a War Bond drive. Gable, grief-stricken, joined the U.S. Army Air Corps and saw action in Europe during World War II. Not until *The Misfits* (1961) with Marilyn Monroe, did Gable seem to regain his old form. But its filming took a toll on him, and Gable suffered a fatal heart attack shortly after its completion.

See also MOTION PICTURES, TALKING.

References: Charles Samuels, *The King: a Biography of Clark Gable* (New York: Coward-McCann, 1962); Lyn Tornabene, *Long Live the King: a Biography of Clark Gable* (New York: Putnam, 1976); Gabe Essoe, *The Films of Clark Gable* (Secaucus, N.J.: Citadel, 1974).

Galsworthy, John (1867–1933)

English novelist, playwright, and Nobel laureate. The son of John Galsworthy and Blanche Bailey (Bartleet) Galsworthy, he was born in the village of Kingson Hill, Surrey, England, on August 14, 1867. He was educated at Harrow, one of the most respected of English boarding schools, and later studied law at New College, Oxford. For a time, he traveled, then began to write at the age of 28, publishing his first stories under the *nom de plume* of John Sinjohn. Although he published two books before the turn of the century, his first major work was *The Island Pharisees* (1904).

Two years later, Galsworthy wrote *The Man of Property* (1906), the first in the series of novels called *The Forsyte Saga,* all dealing with an English family in the Victorian and Edwardian eras. While the work was immediately successful, he did not continue the series until *In Chancery* appeared in 1920 and *To Let* in 1921. He then published the *Modern Comedy* trilogy: *The White Monkey* (1924), *The Silver Spoon* (1926), and *Swan Song* (1928).

In 1932, Galsworthy was awarded the Nobel Prize in literature, and *The Forsyte Saga* was named as the reason behind the award.

Galsworthy lived but a few weeks after his Nobel bestowal; he died at Grove Lodge, in Hampstead, England, on January 31, 1933.

References: H. V. Marrot, *The Life and Letters of John Galsworthy* (London: Heinemann, 1935); Howard L. Ford, "Galsworthy, John" in Bernard S. and June H. Schlessinger, eds., *The Who's Who of Nobel Prize Winners* (Phoenix, Ariz.: Oryx, 1986), 58; Thomas Watson MacCallum and Stephen Taylor, eds., *The Nobel Prize-Winners and the Nobel Foundation, 1901–1937* (Zurich, Switzerland: Central European Times Publishing, 1938), 318–19.

Gance, Abel (1889–1981)

French silent MOTION PICTURE director, noted for his monumental antiwar documentary, *J'Accuse* (1919), containing vivid scenes from the front during World War I, as well as for his majestic masterpiece, *Napoléon* (1927). Born in Paris on October 25, 1889, he began to work in the French cinema in 1909. Two years later, he established a film company in Paris. During World War I he was excused from military service because of bad health. However, he set to work to document the horrors and atrocities of that appalling conflict. Filming at the front, Gance put together what many today would consider a radical antiwar film, *J'Accuse*. In one scene, he goes so far as to call upon the ghosts of war to rise from their graves.

Perhaps Gance's greatest work is the monumental *Napoléon vu par Abel Gance*, or, as it is simply called, *Napoléon*. In the film, which starred the French actor Albert Dieudonné as Napoleon, Gance used hand-colored scenes and four wide screens (he filmed the movie with cameras in three distinct positions) to document this massive drama of Napoleon's reign in France; it is considered by many film historians to have been the finest film of the silent era. Gance designed *Napoléon* to be the first part in a D. W. Griffith-type epic of historic proportions. The film ran disastrously over budget, however, and soon after its release became so obscure that it was thought for many years to have been lost. But a single copy was rediscovered in the 1970s; it was cleaned up and re-released in 1980 to amazed and cheering crowds. Gance, at this time 90 years old, basked in the limelight of rediscovered fame. This was his final triumph; he died in Paris on November 10, 1981.

References: Steven Philip Kramer, *Abel Gance* (Boston: Twayne Publishers, 1978); Leonard Maltin, ed., *Movie and Video Guide 1996 Edition* (New York: Plume, 1995), 660.

Gandhi-Irwin Pact

Agreement, 1931, between Indian nationalist Mohandas K. GANDHI and Lord Irwin, governor-general of India.

When the civil disobedience campaign initiated by Gandhi to protest inhumane treatment of the Indian people by British colonial administrators seemed to be at a stalemate, Gandhi wrote a letter to Governor-General Edward Frederick Lindley, then Lord Irwin (later Lord Halifax), asking for a meeting. The two men met several times in February and March 1931. Both understood that they were limited in what they could do, but agreed to meet one another as gentlemen, not as a British administrator and an Indian protester. On March 5, they announced the Gandhi-Irwin Pact, an agreement designed to curb tensions in India. As historian Surjit Mansingh writes, "What came to be known as the Gandhi-Irwin pact was agreement on a limited list of items . . . [the Indian National] Congress agreed to withdraw the special powers and punitive police detailed for it but ruled out inquiry into police misconduct. The government agreed to release all prisoners taken during the civil disobedience movement, restore forfeited lands if not sold, treat village officials applying for their old posts with liberality, and not prosecute persons collecting salt for home consumption; the government monopoly on salt remained."

Reference: Surjit Mansingh, *Historical Dictionary of India* (Lanham, Md.: Scarecrow, 1996), 150–51.

Gandhi, Mohandas Karamchand (1869–1948)

Indian nationalist, diplomat, and spiritual leader, known as the "Mahatma" (in Sanskrit, "great-souled one"), who led his country from colonial British rule to nationhood. He was born in Porbandar, in the Kathiawar state of western India, then a British province, on October 2, 1869; his father was the *dewan,* or prime minister, of the city. Gandhi was married at the age of 13—a marriage that lasted for 60 years, until the death of his wife, Kasturbai, in 1944. At 19, he went to London, where he studied law at University College and was called to the bar of the Inner Temple, one of the inns of court of England, in 1889. He practiced law in Bombay for a short time, but he soon moved to South Africa, where he became a leading local barrister. During the Boer War and the 1906 conflict with the Zulus, he served the British forces as a member of the Indian ambulance corps, which he himself had established.

In 1908, Gandhi decided to stand for equal rights for the Indian minority in South Africa, which was treated with disdain. Three times he was jailed for civil disobedience, but in 1914 General Jan Smuts concluded an agreement with Gandhi to remove some of the most detested laws against Indians. When World War I broke out, Gandhi was in London, and while there he established a corps of Indian students to serve in the British ambulance corps. He returned to India in 1915, where he became a leader in the *Swaraj* ("home rule") movement. Gandhi began at the same time the *Satyagraha* ("truth seeking")

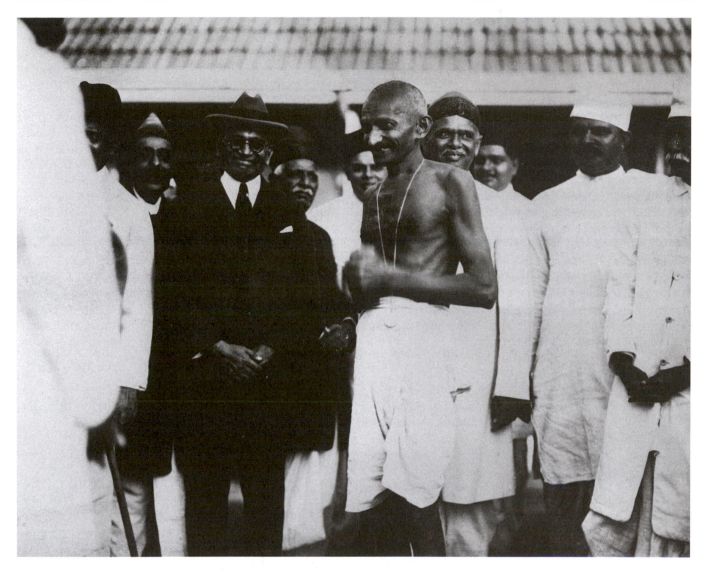

Mohandas K. Gandhi smiles during a 1928 interview. *(CORBIS/Bettmann)*

movement to end the British rule of his land. In 1917, after long pressing the English government, Gandhi got his first reform victory when the British abolished indentured emigration.

In 1919, the British enacted the ROWLATT ACTS, which extended wartime restraints on the freedom of speech. In response, Gandhi called for a national *hartal*, or general strike. On April 6, 1919, the Indian people responded with a massive work stoppage that brought the nation to a halt. A week later, on April 13, 23 Indian police officers were slaughtered in the JALLIANWALA BAGH MASSACRE. For his nonviolent response to these developments, Gandhi became popularly known as Mahatma. He became a leading figure in the Indian National Congress, composed of Hindus, and led a series of boycotts of products controlled by the British government. In 1925, he led a movement to improve the lives of so-called "untouchables," those in the lowest caste, people he

called *Harijans,* or "Children of God." In 1930, after Gandhi had launched the SALT SATYAGRAHA, or Salt March, to protest taxes on salt, he was invited by the British viceroy, Lord Irwin, to discuss ways to change the laws. The result was the GANDHI-IRWIN PACT, a landmark in British-Indian relations, which temporarily ended Gandhi's campaign of nonviolence.

In 1931, Gandhi was a representative of the Indian National Congress at the Round Table Conference held in London for a full discussion of the constitutional issues, but when he returned to India he resumed his campaign of civil disobedience and was arrested. While in prison he began a "fast unto death" to protest the treatment of the *Harijans,* but broke it after seven days; a subsequent fast in 1933 ended only when he was released from prison. The following year, at the age of 65, Gandhi retired as the head of the Indian National Congress, but he remained a major force in the drive to attain Indian independence.

With the start of World War II, Gandhi told Britain that the price for Indian cooperation against Nazi Germany was the promise of Indian independence. In 1942, however, Gandhi was jailed again; there he demanded that "either we get freedom or we die." Released only for the funeral of his wife, Gandhi was imprisoned for 21 months. To protect the Muslim minority, Gandhi went along with the plan proposed by Mohammed Ali Jinnah that the northern portion of India would be partitioned into a separate Muslim state, which became Pakistan in 1948.

Following the end of the war, Gandhi was an integral part of the talks to end British rule. On August 15, 1947, the British turned control over civil government to Indians; Viscount Mountbatten, the last viceroy, said that Gandhi was "the architect of India's freedom through nonviolence." But on January 30, 1948, as he moved to deliver his morning prayer, a Hindu radical opposed to the partition of India shot Gandhi to death. Gandhi was mourned for being one of the most important spiritual and political leaders of the 20th century.

See also NEHRU, Jawaharlal.

References: Paul Dickson, "Mohandas Gandhi" in Anne Commire, ed., *Historic World Leaders* (Detroit: Gale Research, 1994), 1: 171–76; James D. Hunt, "Gandhi, Mohandas Karamchand" in Harold Josephson, ed. in chief, *Biographical Dictionary of Modern Peace Leaders* (Westport, Conn.: Greenwood, 1985), 312–15; "Mohandas K. Gandhi Leads the Nonviolent Indian Reform Movement" in Frank M. Magill, ed., *Great Events from History: Worldwide Twentieth Century Series* (Englewood Cliffs, N.J.: Salem, 1980), 1: 175–80; S. R. Bakshi, "The Dandi March of Gandhi," *The Modern Review* 134, 4 (April 1974): 250–58; Parshotam Mehra, *A Dictionary of Modern Indian History, 1707–1947* (Delhi, India: Oxford University Press, 1985), 253–59; "Gandhi Is Assassinated by Hindu," New York *Herald-Tribune* (European Edition), January 31, 1948, p. 1.

Garbo, Greta (1905–1990)

Swedish-American actress, famed for numerous interwar motion picture roles, including *Anna Christie* (1930), *Queen Christina* (1933), *Anna Karenina* (1935), *Camille* (1936), and *Ninotchka* (1939). Born Greta Louisa Gustafsson in Stockholm, Sweden, on September 18, 1905, she studied acting for three years at the dramatic school of the Stockholm Royal Theater, afterward becoming the protégée of Swedish film director Mauritz Stiller. She joined Stiller's film *Gösta Berling's Saga* in 1924, and to bill his new star, Stiller changed her name to Garbo. Her success in that vehicle led to a flurry of international offers; she signed with the Metro-Goldwyn-Mayer studio in the United States and went to America to star in *The Torrent* (1926). Her performance in the silent film *Love* (1927),

based on Tolstoy's *Anna Karenina,* is considered a classic. The picture was made with two endings—one happy for U.S. audiences, and another with the novel's tragic ending for the European public. She repeated the performance in *Anna Karenina* with Frederic March.

From 1926 until 1941, Garbo starred in 26 pictures, and when she appeared in her first sound feature, *Anna Christie,* the film was billed as "Garbo Talks!" The embodiment of the *femme fatale,* she played strong characters in *Mata Hari* (1931), *Grand Hotel* (1932), *As You Desire Me* (1932), *Queen Christina, Camille,* and *Ninotchka* (1939). Her performance in *Camille,* based on the 1848 Alexandre Dumas *fils* novel *The Lady of the Camellias,* was considered one of her finest. She retired from acting altogether after the failure of her 1941 film *Two-Faced Woman,* and went into a seclusion that lasted until her death. Garbo died in New York on April 15, 1990, setting off a flurry of remembrances of her long-distant career. Film historian Ephraim Katz wrote shortly before her death, "Clarence Brown, her erstwhile director, said it all in 1963: 'Today, without having made a film since 1940, she is still the greatest. She is the prototype of all stars.'"

References: Frederick Sands, *The Divine Garbo* (New York: Grosset & Dunlap, 1979); Fritiof Billquist, *Garbo: A Biography* (New York: Putnam, 1960); Michael Conway, *The Films of Greta Garbo* (New York: Citadel, 1963); Ephraim Katz, *The Film Encyclopedia* (New York: HarperPerennial, 1994), 464–65.

Garner, John Nance (1868–1967)

American politician and the 32nd vice president of the United States (1933–41). Born in Red Rive County, Texas, on November 22, 1868, the son of a Confederate cavalry officer, he studied law in Clarksville, Texas, and was admitted to the state bar in 1890. That same year, he opened a law office in the town of Uvalde, where he served as a county judge from 1893 to 1896. In 1898, Garner was elected to the state legislature and, in 1902, to the first of 15 terms in the U.S. House of Representatives. Garner said later, "When I entered Congress, the autocratic leaders of the [Democratic] party thought I was just another cow thief from Texas."

Rising through the House's seniority system, in 1928 Garner was elected minority leader. In 1930, when the Republicans won a majority of the House by only a few seats, Garner shortly became Speaker of the House (1931–33). He was elected by his Democratic colleagues as Speaker by three votes, and he held sway as one of the most powerful politicians in America.

In 1932, Garner sought the Democratic presidential nomination. As a Texan and Speaker with conservative and isolationist views, he was Texas's favorite son for the nomination and was backed by the California delegation as well. On the first vote at the Democratic National Convention in Chicago, then Governor Franklin D. ROOSEVELT led, with former governor and 1928 presidential nominee Al SMITH second, and Garner a distant third. After another ballot, Roosevelt edged closer to the nomination, but his adviser, James A. Farley, feared that on a third ballot delegates pledged to Roosevelt would slip toward Smith or a potential fourth candidate, former secretary of war Newton D. Baker. After consultations with publisher William Randolph Hearst, who backed Garner, Garner decided to ask his delegates to vote for Roosevelt; in exchange, Garner would receive second place on the ticket—a final bargain that, although alleged, was never announced. When Roosevelt was nominated on the fourth ballot, Garner received the vice presidential nomination without a dissenting vote.

That November, Roosevelt and Garner swept to victory based on American's fears over the burgeoning GREAT DEPRESSION, bringing the Democrats to power for the first time since 1921. As the presiding officer of the Senate, Garner oversaw the passage in the Congress of Roosevelt's NEW DEAL program, although he opposed much of what Roosevelt was proposing. Still, Garner worked as a loyal Democrat and vice president. During his two terms, he came to regret that he had left his job as Speaker. Garner is perhaps more famous for his axiom on the office of the vice president: "[The office] isn't worth a bucket of warm spit." He also said later, "Worst damn-fool mistake I ever made was letting myself be elected Vice President of the United States. . . . Should have stuck with my old chores as Speaker of the House. I gave up the second most important job in the Government for one that didn't amount to a hill of beans."

In 1940, when Roosevelt decided to run for an unprecedented third term, Garner—increasingly distressed over the direction of Roosevelt's policies—was dismissed from the ticket and replaced by former secretary of agriculture Henry Wallace. Garner returned to Uvalde, where he lived the rest of his life in retirement. On November 7, 1967, he died at his home.

References: Bascom Nolly Timmons, *Garner of Texas: A Personal History* (New York: Harper, 1948); Marquis James, *Mr. Garner of Texas* (Indianapolis: Bobbs-Merrill, 1939); George Rothwell Brown, *Speaker of the House: The Romantic Story of John N. Garner* (New York: Brewer, Warren & Putnam, 1932); Alden Whitman, "John Nance Garner, 98, Is Dead; Vice President under Roosevelt," *New York Times*, November 8, 1967, p. 1.

Garvey, Marcus (1887–1940)
Jamaican-American revolutionary, founder of the pan-Africanist Universal Negro Improvement Association, which during the 1920s and 1930s sought to improve the lives of blacks around the world. Born in St. Ann's Bay, Jamaica, on August 17, 1887, he educated himself after leaving school at age 14. An activist for the rights of black people around the world, he took some meager savings and traveled to Central America and London (1912–14), after which he returned home and founded the Universal Negro Improvement and Conservation Association and African Communities League, later shortened to the Universal Negro Improvement Association (UNIA), whose key goal was to unite all blacks in a spiritual journey to a homeland in Africa.

Because he was not taken seriously in Jamaica, in 1916 Garvey went to the United States and started branches of UNIA in several American cities with large black populations, including New York City, his headquarters. By 1919 Garvey, known to his followers as "the Black Moses," claimed more than two million adherents. Through the official publication of UNIA, *Negro World*, Garvey claimed that only through economic independence could blacks expect to establish an African homeland. To this end, he created a chain of restaurants and laundries, and to help transport blacks to Africa, started the Black Star shipping line in 1919. In 1920, he held a convention in New York City with delegates from all over the world.

Garvey's message challenged mainstream black leaders in the United States, however, who preached integration rather than abandonment of America. Further, slipshod business practices opened Garvey up to an investigation by the U.S. government, and in 1922 he and some of his UNIA directors were indicted for fraud in connection with a ship purchase for the Black Star Line. Garvey was found guilty and sentenced to five years in prison, but served only two when his sentence was commuted by President Calvin COOLIDGE, who ordered him deported from the United States. Garvey returned to Jamaica and then England, but he was never able to bring together his "back to Africa" movement again. He died in relative obscurity in London on June 10, 1940.

References: Barbara Bair, "Garveyism" in Mari Jo Buhle, Paul Buhle, and Dan Georgakas, eds., *Encyclopedia of the American Left* (New York: Garland Publishing, 1990), 253–55; Donald Spivey and Joyce Hanson, "Garvey, Marcus Moziah" in Bruce W. Jentleson and Thomas G. Paterson, senior eds., *Encyclopedia of U.S. Foreign Relations* (New York: Oxford University Press, 1997), 2: 202.

Gehrig, Lou (1903–1941)
American baseball player, holder of many major league records, including the most consecutive games played (2,130), a record broken in 1996. Gehrig, born in New York City on June 19, 1903, attended Columbia University, where he became an expert ball player, before joining the New York Yankee organization in 1923. Starting in

1925, when he replaced Wally Pipp at first base, Gehrig had one of the finest careers in the history of major league baseball. Known as "the Iron Horse," he hit .313 in 1926 and continued to hit over .300 for the next 12 seasons. In 1927, batting fourth behind the immortal Babe RUTH, Gehrig was an integral part of a Yankee team that went 100–44 that year; Gehrig finished the season with 47 home runs (second only to Ruth's record-breaking 60), a batting average of .373, and 175 runs batted in, making Ruth and Gehrig the most lethal one-two combination in baseball history, the heart of a lineup known as "Murderers' Row."

In 1928, Gehrig hit .374 and led the Yankees in a sweep of the St. Louis Cardinals in the World Series that year, in which he batted .345. In 1934 he won the Triple Crown (the most homers, hits, and runs batted in) with a .363 average, 210 hits (including 49 home runs), and 165 R.B.I. In 1935, he hit his two-thousandth hit, a record at that time. Gehrig won the Most Valuable Player award in 1936, hit his four-hundredth career home run, and led the Yankees to another World Series championship.

In 1938, the season in which he passed 2,000 consecutive games played, Gehrig was slower than usual, and batted only .295, the first time he had batted below the .300 mark in 13 years. After playing only eight games of the 1939 season, he decided to remove himself from the lineup, ending his streak at 2,130 games. (On September 6, 1995, Baltimore Orioles shortstop Cal Ripken played in his 2,131st consecutive game, breaking Gehrig's 56-year-old record.) Then Gehrig was diagnosed with amyotrophic lateral sclerosis (ALS), a rare and fatal disease that attacks the nervous system. On July 4, 1939, Gehrig was honored by the Yankees as he retired. In a speech before the crowd, he said, "Fans, for the past two weeks you have been reading about the bad break I got. Yet today I consider myself the luckiest man on the face of this earth. I have been in ballparks for seventeen years and have never received anything but kindness and encouragement from you fans. Look at these grand men. Which of you wouldn't consider it the highlight of his career just to associate with them for even one day? Sure, I'm lucky." Two years later, on June 2, 1941, Gehrig died of ALS in New York City.

See also BASEBALL, MAJOR LEAGUE.

References: David A. Adler, *Lou Gehrig: The Luckiest Man* (San Diego: Harcourt Brace, 1997); Ray Robinson, *Iron Horse: Lou Gehrig in His Time* (New York: W. W. Norton, 1990).

General Strike

National stoppage of work, May 4–13, 1926, by members of Great Britain's major industries. The General Strike began when the Trades Union Council (TUC), led by trade unionist Ernest BEVIN, ordered its members to strike in support of miners. The strike extended to all forms of transport, the iron and steel industries, and many other trades, including electricity workers and printing workers. Bevin thought that by bringing into the strike transport workers, the unions could force the government to deal with the issues from which the strike first emanated: wage cuts and longer hours. However, the government of Prime Minister Stanley BALDWIN was able to marshal the resources to continue delivering essential services to the people, and within nine days the strike collapsed. Nothing was gained by the unions, and labor unions in general found themselves worse off after the retaliatory Trade Union Act was passed in 1927. This legislation outlawed general strikes and sympathetic strikes and banned civil servants from joining unions affiliated with the TUC.

See also LLOYD GEORGE, David.

References: Peter Clarke, "Government and Politics in England: Realignment and Readjustment" in Christopher Haigh, ed., *The Cambridge Historical Encyclopedia of Great Britain and Ireland* (Cambridge, England: Cambridge University Press, 1985), 296; "[Editorial:] Rally Round the Government!" *The Daily Mirror,* March 4, 1926, p. 7; "This Is a Peril to Freedom of Constitution: Prime Minister's Speech in Parliament Condemning the General Strike," *The Daily Mirror,* March 4, 1926, p. 8.

Geneva Disarmament Conference

Meeting, 1932–34, held in the Swiss city, which dissolved in disharmony because of Germany's defiance. Officially called the Conference for the Reduction and Limitation of Armaments, the parley opened on February 2, 1932. Almost immediately, Germany demanded to be allowed "military equality" with the other conference powers or its delegation would withdraw from the meeting. After several months of negotiations, on December 12, 1932, France, Great Britain, and Italy issued a communiqué that read, "Germany and the other States disarmed by the VERSAILLES Treaty should be ensured equality in a system which gives security to all nations." In effect, this was a complete surrender to Germany, which just a few weeks later elected Adolf HITLER as chancellor.

References: Lewis Ethan Ellis, *Republican Foreign Policy, 1921–1933* (New Brunswick, N.J.: Rutgers University Press, 1968); Edmund Jan Osmańczyk, *The Encyclopedia of the United Nations and International Agreements* (Philadelphia: Taylor & Francis, 1985), 307; Philip Noel-Baker, *The First World Disarmament Conference, 1932–1933, And Why It Failed* (Oxford and New York: Pergamon, 1979).

Geneva Naval Conference   *See* COOLIDGE CONFERENCE.

Geneva Protocol

Series of rules, enacted 1925, by a number of leading international powers, to prohibit the use of chemical weapons during wartime. Officially called the Protocol for the Prohibition of the Use in War of Asphyxiating Poisonous or Other Gases, and of Bacteriological Methods of Warfare, the treaty was signed at Geneva, Switzerland, on June 17, 1925.

During World War I, both sides in the conflict used poisonous gases against their opponents, with frighteningly effective results. After the war, the heads of state from several powers—including Great Britain, the United States, and France—held talks to formulate a treaty to end the use of such weapons. Starting in 1925, delegates from these nations met in Geneva, Switzerland, to draw up the protocol. In the document the signatories declared their intention to prohibit the use of all poisonous gases during war. Further, the pact avowed, "The High Contracting Parties will exert every effort to induce other States to accede to the present Protocol."

The Geneva Protocol's effectiveness has been limited at best, violated by such nations as Iran, Iraq, and the Soviet Union. A new treaty, the Chemical Weapons Convention, was ratified by the United States and other nations in 1997.

References: David Hunter Miller, *The Geneva Protocol* (New York: Macmillan, 1925); Arms Control and Disarmament Agency, *Arms Control and Disarmament Agreements: Texts and Histories of the Negotiations* (Washington, D.C.: Government Printing Office, 1990); Michael Eisenstadt, "Chemical Weapons" in Bruce W. Jentleson and Thomas G. Paterson, senior eds., *Encyclopedia of U.S. Foreign Relations* (New York: Oxford University Press, 1997), 1: 237; Edmund Jan Osmañczyk, *The Encyclopedia of the United Nations and International Agreements* (Philadelphia: Taylor & Francis, 1985), 293.

Genoa Conference

Meeting, April 1922, in the Italian city of Genoa, called by British Prime Minister David LLOYD GEORGE to unite the nations of Europe. Held April 10–16, it had been preceded in January of that year by a similar conference in Cannes, France, between the British and French. Set to discuss REPARATIONS and the global economic situation, the conference, considered by many historians to have been one of the largest peace conferences held in the interwar period, broke up over a single issue: the possible recognition by the major powers of Soviet Russia and its Bolshevik government. However, Germany did set the stage for future talks by working with the Soviet delegates to prepare a treaty of cooperation, which was signed later that year at RAPALLO. In 1926, the GERMAN-SOVIET NEUTRALITY TREATY, which set in motion the establishment of an "economic League of Nations"—the forerunner of the modern European Economic Union—was signed.

References: Stephen White, *The Origins of Détente: The Genoa Conference and Soviet-Western Relations, 1921–1922* (Cambridge: Cambridge University Press, 1985); Carole Fink, *The Genoa Conference: European Diplomacy, 1921–1922* (Chapel Hill: University of North Carolina Press, 1984); Dean Elizabeth Traynor, *International Monetary and Financial Conferences in the Interwar Period* (Washington, D.C.: Catholic University of America Press, 1949); "Harding to Decide This Week on Genoa," *New York Times*, January 25, 1922, p. 1; "Against Genoa. Strong American Feeling. No Recognition of Soviet," *The Times* (London), January 25, 1922, p. 10; "Genoa Rumours. Postponement Suggested. America's Decided Attitude," *The Times* (London), January 26, 1922, p. 10; "Genoa Conference. Statement by Italian Delegate," *The Times* (London), January 27, 1922, p. 9; "German Hopes of Genoa. Dr. Wirth's Reply to M. Poincaré. Payments and the Taxation Plan," *The Times* (London), January 27, 1922, p. 10.

George V (1865–1936)

British monarch, ruled Great Britain and Ireland (1910–1936). The second son of King Edward VII (ruled 1901–1910) and his wife Alexandra, George was born at Marlborough House in London on June 3, 1865, and christened George Frederick Ernest Albert. He was a first cousin, through his father, of Wilhelm II, the last kaiser of Germany; he was also a first cousin, through his mother, of Czar Nicholas II of Russia, the last czarist ruler of that nation. His older brother, Prince Edward Albert Victor, was the Duke of Clarence, and heir presumptive to the throne, but he died in 1892. Shortly thereafter, George—whose father, then the Prince of Wales, was now the heir to the throne—was named as the Duke of York and Earl of Inverness.

In 1893, George married his second cousin, Princess Victoria Mary of Teck, and they had six children—two of whom, Edward and Albert, would one day serve as king of England. George's father Edward was crowned king in 1901, upon the death of his mother, Queen Victoria. However, he only ruled until May 6, 1910, when he died suddenly, and on that same day his son succeeded him. King George V was crowned in Westminster Abbey on June 22, 1911. George ruled over Great Britain and the dominions for 26 years, and in that time he was forced to deal with the growing European crisis that ultimately exploded into World War I. In 1917, responding to anti-German sentiment in his nation, George changed the official name of his royal house from the German Saxe-Coburg and Gotha to the more English-sounding Windsor, which is still used today. During the early 1920s, he immersed himself in the Irish crisis; in June 1921 he helped institute the Parliament of Northern Ireland, and he is credited by most historians with having helped to establish the peace treaty there that created the IRISH FREE STATE in 1922. George also pushed for limited autonomy for the dominions, and this was finally accomplished in the STATUTE OF WESTMINSTER, enacted by Parliament in 1931.

George celebrated the 25th anniversary of his ascendance to the crown in May 1936, but he was by then in poor health. On the evening of January 20, 1936, while he was in a coma, the royal physician apparently injected him with a fatal solution that quickly ended his life.

See also EDWARD VIII; GEORGE VI.

References: M. E. Hudson and Mary Clark, *Crown of a Thousand Years: A Millennium of British History Presented as a Pageant of Kings and Queens* (New York: Crown Publishers, 1978), 139–41; Bamber Gascoigne, *Encyclopedia of Britain* (New York: Macmillan, 1993), 254; "Death of The King: A Peaceful Ending at Midnight. Royal Family's Long Vigil. Parliament to Meet This Evening," *The Times* (London), January 21, 1936, p. 12.

George VI (1895–1952)

British monarch, ruled Great Britain and Ireland (1936–1952). The second son of King GEORGE V and his wife Queen Mary of Teck, he was born at the royal residence Sandringham, on December 14, 1895, and christened Albert Frederick Arthur George. Like his brother Edward Albert was educated at the Osborne and Dartmouth naval colleges, and in 1913, as per his royal duties to serve his nation, was made a midshipman on the H.M.S. *Collingwood*. He saw service on that ship during the early years of World War I, and was at the famed Battle of Jutland in 1916. In 1918, Albert was transferred to the Royal Naval Air Service, where he was trained as a pilot. In 1920, while he was at Trinity College at Cambridge University, his father named him duke of York, and he became second in line to the throne. He met and fell in love with Elizabeth Bowes-Lyon, the daughter of the 14th earl of Strathmore, and the two were married in Westminster Abbey on April 26, 1923.

Prince Albert would probably have remained duke of York had events in 1936 not taken a strange turn. After the death of his father on January 20, 1936, his older brother, Edward, then prince of Wales, advanced to the throne as King EDWARD VIII. However, Edward had been in a longstanding relationship with American divorcée Wallis Warfield Simpson. When Prime Minister Stanley BALDWIN refused to sanction a marriage between the two (because of Simpson's previous divorce), Edward abdicated on December 11, 1936, and on that day Albert became king, taking the name George as his official name. He and his wife were crowned in Westminster Abbey on May 12, 1936. In 1938 they toured France, and a year

later visited Canada and the United States, welcomed by officials and crowds wherever they went.

During World War II, George and his wife refused to leave London during the worst days of the blitzkrieg launched by German planes against the city, and at times they went about to give support to the multitudes suffering under the attacks. On June 16, 1944, just 10 days after the Allied landings there, George visited the beachhead at Normandy.

On February 6, 1952, George died in his sleep. His daughter, Elizabeth, was crowned queen upon his death.

References: Mildred E. Hudson and Mary Clark, *Crown of a Thousand Years: A Millennium of British History Presented as a Pageant of Kings and Queens* (New York: Crown Publishers, 1978), 146–47; Bamber Gascoigne, *Encyclopedia of Britain* (New York: Macmillan, 1993), 254–55.

German-Japanese Anti-Comintern Pact

Treaty, signed in Berlin on November 25, 1936, between Germany and Japan, designed in large part to counter the growing power of the Soviet Union. From the time of Adolf HITLER's ascension in Germany, Hitler had sought to sign declarations of friendship with other nations that wished to oppose the Soviet Union. Hitler initiated talks with Imperial Japan starting in 1936. The signatories to this historic pact were German Foreign Minister Joachim von RIBBENTROP and Viscount Kintomo Mushakoji, the Imperial Japanese ambassador to Germany. The propaganda effect of the pact was greater than its political substance—it paved the way for future German-Japanese collaboration.

References: Otto D. Tolischus, "Berlin-Tokyo Pact Signed; London, Paris Call It Blind to Conceal New Aggression," *New York Times,* November 26, 1936, p. 1; "Text of Berlin-Tokyo Pact," *New York Times,* November 26, 1936, p. 26; "[Opinion:] The Japanese-German Pact," *New York Times,* November 26, 1936, p. 30.

German-Soviet Neutrality Treaty

Pact, 1926, negotiated between the government of WEIMAR GERMANY and the Bolshevik Soviet government to settle numerous border and security differences developed after the end of World War I. The treaty confirmed "friendly relations" between the two governments. Minister of Foreign Affairs Gustav STRESEMANN (for the German government) and Ambassador Nicholas Nicolaievich Krestinsky (for the Soviet government) agreed in the pact to "settle amicably" all future political and economic matters between the two parties.

Reference: "Neutrality Agreement between Germany and the U.S.S.R., 1926" in Louis L. Snyder, ed., *Documents of German*

History (New Brunswick, N.J.: Rutgers University Press, 1958), 402–403.

Gershwin, George (1898–1937)

American composer, famed for his numerous compositions during the interwar era, including *Rhapsody in Blue* (1924) and the opera *Porgy and Bess* (1935). Born Jacob Gershvin in Brooklyn, New York, on September 26, 1898, he was the son of Russian-Jewish immigrants. He listened to JAZZ as a child, and studied the piano from age 12. In 1914, he began to play for the Jerome Remick Music Publishing Company. Within two years, he had published his first song, "When You Want 'Em You Can't Get 'Em." However, it was the success of his 1918 song "Swanee" (later sung by Al JOLSON) that made him popular on Tin Pan Alley. With his brother, Ira (born Israel Gershvin in 1896), who wrote the lyrics, Gershwin composed a long list of popular songs, including "I Got Rhythm," "Someone to Watch Over Me," and "The Man I Love." In 1922, the Gershwins wrote *Blue Monday* (later called *135th Street*), a jazz opera, for the *George White Scandals* of

George Gershwin *(CORBIS/Bettmann)*

1922. Impressed by their work, orchestra leader Paul Whiteman asked Gershwin to write a piece for his opera; Gershwin then wrote *Rhapsody in Blue,* his most famous piece. Throughout the 1920s, Gershwin produced such Broadway hits as *Lady Be Good* (1924), *Funny Face* (1927), *An American in Paris* (1928) and *Of Thee I Sing* (1931), which became the first musical to win the Pulitzer Prize for drama. His concert works include *Piano Concerto in F Major* (1925) and *Second Rhapsody* (1931).

In 1935, the Gershwins wrote the music and words for the opera *Porgy and Bess,* based on the novel *Porgy* by DuBose Heyward. To lend authenticity to the music, George Gershwin spent the time writing the opera on Folly Island near Charleston, South Carolina, where he immersed himself in the language and culture of the black population. The opera remains perhaps his greatest accomplishment; more than half a century later, it is firmly established in the opera repertory.

The Gershwins also wrote film scores in Hollywood. George Gershwin returned to New York, but soon after he began to have serious headaches. On July 9, 1937, Gershwin slipped into a coma. He underwent a brain operation, and a tumor was found and removed, but it was too late. Five hours after the surgery, on July 11, Gershwin died at age 38. In 1998, on the centennial of his birth, he was awarded a posthumous Pulitzer Prize for, as the Pulitzer committee stated, "his distinguished and enduring contributions to American music."

References: Alan Kendall, *George Gershwin: A Biography* (New York: Universe Books, 1987); Barbara Mitchell, *"America, I Hear You": A Story about George Gershwin* (Minneapolis: Carolrhoda Books, 1987); Deena Rosenberg, *Fascinating Rhythm: The Collaboration of George and Ira Gershwin* (New York: Dutton, 1991); John S. Wilson, "Ira Gershwin, Lyricist, Dies; Songs Embodied Broadway," *New York Times,* August 18, 1983, pp. A1, D19.

Gish, Lillian (1893–1993) and Dorothy (1898–1968)

American actresses, famed for their work particularly during the silent film era. Lillian Diana Gish was born in Springfield, Ohio, on October 14, 1893, while her sister Dorothy Elizabeth was born in Massillon, Ohio, on March 11, 1898. Their father was frequently absent from the home, leaving their mother, Mary, to support the family through acting. When both girls were old enough, they joined their mother onstage and, to supplement the family income, posed for photographs, a novelty at the time. In 1912, the sisters met Mary Pickford, a Canadian-American actress who was just beginning a career in silent films. MOTION PICTURES at that time were short, clumsy vehicles, lasting no more than several minutes with a thin plot. Pickford introduced the sisters to D. W. Griffith, a leading director with a company called Biograph.

Impressed with the Gish sisters' acting abilities, Griffith cast them in 1912's *An Unseen Enemy,* their first picture. In her career, Dorothy would star in more than a hundred features, while her sister Lillian would become the grande dame of the screen, appearing in 86 films over the next eight decades.

Dorothy's acting was confined to silent films, including *Romola* (1924), *Nell Gwyn* (1926), and *Madame Pompadour* (1927). She moved to England in 1926, and retired from the screen two years later, remaining a fixture of the English stage. She died on June 4, 1968, in Rapallo, Italy.

Lillian starred in a number of D. W. Griffith's films, including *Birth of a Nation* (1915), *Intolerance* (1916), and *Hearts of the World* (1918), as well as *Broken Blossoms* (1919), *Way Down East* (1921), and *Orphans of the Storm* (1921). Later in the decade, she took lead roles in *The Scarlet Letter* (1926) and *The Wind* (1928). She also appeared on stage in a series of roles.

In 1970, Lillian received a special Academy Award "for superlative artistry and distinguished contributions to the progress of motion pictures"; she was also awarded the Life Achievement Award in 1984 from the American Film Institute. She died in her sleep on February 27, 1993, in New York City.

References: Lillian Gish, (James E. Frasher, ed.), *Dorothy and Lillian Gish* (New York: Scribner, 1973); Albert Bigelow Paine, *Life and Lillian Gish* (New York: Macmillan, 1932); Lillian Gish (with Ann Pinchot), *Lillian Gish: The Movies, Mr. Griffith, and Me* (Englewood Cliffs, N.J.: Prentice-Hall, 1969).

Gitlow v. New York (1925)

Landmark U.S. Supreme Court decision, in which it was held that certain utterances "advocating the overthrow of organized government by force, violence and unlawful means" could constitutionally be banned. Benjamin Gitlow was a founding member of the left wing section of the Communist Labor Party of the United States, founded at a conference in New York City in June 1919. The conference elected a National Council, of which Gitlow was a member, and asked this council to adopt a party manifesto of its program. Under Gitlow's leadership and penmanship, the proposed decree was published in the July 5, 1919, edition of *The Revolutionary Age,* the official journal of the party. In the publication, Gitlow wrote, "The world is in crisis. Capitalism, the prevailing system of society, is in [the] process of disintegration and collapse. . . . Humanity can be saved from its excesses only by the Communist Revolution. There can now be only the Socialism which is one in temper and purpose with the proletarian revolutionary struggle. . . . The class struggle is the heart of Socialism. Without strict conformity to the class struggle, in its revolutionary implications, Socialism

becomes either sheer Utopianism, or a method of reaction . . . the dominant Socialism united with the capitalist governments to prevent a revolution." For this publication, Gitlow, along with three others, was indicted in the Supreme Court of New York for the "statutory crime of criminal anarchy." The law defined "criminal anarchy" as "the doctrine that organized government should be overthrown by force or violence, or by [the] assassination of the executive head or of any of the executive officials of government, or by any lawful means," of which the advocacy "by word or mouth or writing is a felony." Gitlow was tried, convicted, and sentenced to a term of five to 10 years in prison. On appeal, the conviction was affirmed by the Appellate Division and the New York State Court of Appeals, and the Supreme Court agreed to hear the case. Arguments were heard on April 12, 1923, but the Court asked for re-argument, which was heard on November 23 of that same year.

It was not until June 8, 1925, a full two years since the Court first heard the issues in the case, that it handed down a decision. Justice Edward Sanford held for the 7–2 majority upholding Gitlow's conviction. Sanford wrote, "It was not necessary, within the meaning of the [New York] statute, that the defendant should have advocated 'some definite or immediate act or acts' of force, violence or unlawfulness. It was sufficient if such acts were advocated in general terms, and it was essential that their immediate execution should have been advocated. Nor was it necessary that the language should have been 'reasonably and ordinarily calculated to incite certain persons' to acts of force, violence or unlawfulness. The advocacy need not be addressed to specific persons. Thus the publication and circulation of a newspaper article may be an encouragement to endeavor to persuade to murder, although not addressed to any person in particular." In their dissent, Justices Oliver Wendell HOLMES and Louis Brandeis held that "the general principle of free speech . . . must be taken to be included in the Fourteenth Amendment."

References: Paul L. Murphy, "Gitlow v. New York" in Kermit L. Hall, ed. in chief, *The Oxford Companion to the Supreme Court of the United States* (New York: Oxford University Press, 1992), 339–40; Harold Josephson, "Political Justice during the Red Scare: The Trial of Benjamin Gitlow" in Michael Belknap, ed., *American Political Trials* (Westport, Conn.: Greenwood, 1981); 153–75; *Gitlow v. New York* 268 US 652 (1925).

Glass-Steagall Acts

Two sets of U.S. congressional legislation enacted within little more than a single year to reform banking laws to alleviate the effects of the GREAT DEPRESSION. The first act was enacted June 16, 1932, to combat with government action the bank closing crisis that had enveloped the country following the STOCK MARKET CRASH of October

29, 1929. Introduced by Representative Henry Bascom Steagall of Alabama and Senator Carter Glass of Virginia, the act created the Federal Deposit Insurance Corporation (FDIC), which established a three-member board of directors to oversee the operations of banks. Under the act, the depositors' holdings were initially insured up to $2,500. National and state banks in the Federal Reserve system joined the FDIC.

The second Glass-Steagall Act was enacted August 22, 1933. In the action, the government loaned funds to Federal Reserve member banks in an attempt to shore up deposits and instill confidence in the banking system as a whole.

Historian Michael E. Parrish writes, "Except for underwriting state and local government securities, the Glass-Steagall Act prohibited commercial banks from engaging in investment banking, a practice that had encouraged speculation in the previous decade. The act also raised the capital requirements of national banks. Their officers were given two years to divest themselves of all personal loans from their own institutions. Most important of all . . . despite Roosevelt's initial opposition, the law included a momentous amendment offered by Republican Senator Arthur Vandenberg of Michigan—a state hit very hard by bank failures—that insured national bank deposits up to $2,500. The insurance fund, subsidized by the federal government and the banks, was to be administered by a new agency, the Federal Deposit Insurance Corporation (FDIC)."

References: Francis G. Awalt, "Recollections of the Banking Crisis of 1993," *Business History Review* 43 (Autumn 1969): 347–71; John Augustus Lapp, *The First Chapter of the New Deal* (Chicago: J. A. Prescott & Son, 1933); George J. Benston, *The Separation of Commercial and Investment Banking: the Glass-Steagall Act Revisited and Reconsidered* (Houndmills, Basingstoke, Hampshire: Macmillan in association with Dept. of Banking and Finance, City University Business School, London, 1990); Michael E. Parrish, *Anxious Decades: America in Prosperity and Depression, 1920–1941* (New York: W. W. Norton, 1992), 292.

Goddard, Robert Hutchings (1882–1945)

American physicist and rocket scientist, considered the father of modern rocketry and space flight, whose investigations into rocket science in the 1920s paved the way for the space race of the 1960s. Born in Worcester, Massachusetts, on October 5, 1882, he took an early interest in rocketry. He earned his bachelor's degree at the Worcester Polytechnic Institute, then studied rocketry for several years. In 1917, while teaching at Worcester, he received a grant from the Smithsonian Institution to continue his studies into the dynamics of rocket-based travel.

In 1920, Goddard published *A Method of Reaching Extreme Altitudes,* considered one of the three greatest works written on the subject of space flight in that period. In 1923, Romanian-German mathematician Hermann Oberth published his work on rockets, *Die Rakete zu den Planetenräumen* (The rocket into interplanetary space), which followed Goddard's thesis on whether a motor utilizing liquid fuels could be constructed. Although Goddard himself had already done it, he did not publish his results for nearly 20 years; his report, *Liquid Propellant Rocket Development,* which reviewed his rocket research from 1919 to 1936, was published by the Smithsonian in 1936. On November 1, 1923, his first liquid-fueled rocket was carried aloft; three years later, a liquid-propelled rocket was also fired. On July 17, 1929, he sent into the sky his first rocket with a camera on board. On March 28, 1935, the first rocket with instruments aboard for steering was fired.

Goddard continued his research during World War II and up until his sudden death on August 10, 1945. Most of his work was duplicated by his contemporaries, who saw after his death the true value of his hypotheses: in 1969, the liquid-fueled Saturn V rocket carrying three men went to the moon. The National Air and Space Administration's Goddard Space Flight Center in Maryland is named in his honor.

References: Robert Hutchings Goddard, *The Autobiography of Robert Hutchings Goddard, Father of the Space Age* (Worcester, Mass.: A. J. St. Onge, 1966); Milton Lehman, *This High Man: The Life of Robert H. Goddard* (New York: Farrar, Straus & Giroux, 1963); *Robert H. Goddard: American Rocket Pioneer* (Greenbelt, Md.: Goddard Space Flight Center, 1989); "Goddard, Robert Hutchings" in Roy Porter, cons. ed., *The Biographical Dictionary of Scientists* (New York: Oxford University Press, 1994), 278–79.

Goebbels, Josef (1897–1945)

German politician and NAZI PARTY member and propagandist. Born in the village of Rheydt, Germany, on October 29, 1897, he was club-footed, and because of this abnormality he was exempt from military service in World War I. In 1921, he was awarded a doctorate in philosophy from the University of Heidelberg, and, the following year, joined the burgeoning National Socialist (Nazi) party, led by Adolf HITLER. For a time, Goebbels worked as a Nazi Party organizer in the Rhineland, then occupied by the French, until his activities became obvious and he was expelled in 1924. Two years later, he was named as the *Gauleiter* (district leader) for Berlin, and was soon named to head all of the Nazi organization in the Brandenburg province.

In 1927, Goebbels, with an eye toward spreading the Nazi message, founded and edited the journal *Der Angriff*

(The attack), which became the official organ of the Nazi Party. Elected in 1928 to the Reichstag, the German parliament, Goebbels in 1929 was elevated to become Hitler's chief propaganda minister. Four years later, when Hitler became chancellor, he named Goebbels the minister of popular enlightenment and propaganda. Seeing how the use of films and newspapers spread the Nazis' message, Goebbels became the first to use these media with precision. Under his direction, all free press was banned, and newspapers became a government-only function. He established the National Culture Chamber, in which only newspapers, literature, music, and art sanctioned by the government could be displayed. As he stated, "Propaganda is a means to an end . . . if that end is attained, the means are good; whether they satisfy exigent esthetic requirements in immaterial." During the military build-up that preceded World War II, Goebbels encouraged the German nation to believe that it could conquer the world. As the war went on, and Germany began to lose the conflict, Goebbels used propaganda to urge the nation to fight on. Even as the Russian troops were marching across Germany to Berlin toward victory, Goebbels removed several divisions—at least 187,000 men—from the front lines to film his great epic, *Kolberg,* named for the German city that survived an invasion by Napoleon, in a bizarre attempt to rally the German people against another invasion. When the film was finally shown, it was in near-empty Berlin theaters, with Soviet guns pounding the outskirts of the city.

As the end of the war neared, Hitler named Goebbels "president of the Reich capital," with orders to mobilize all Germans in a last-ditch attempt to stave off defeat. When Soviet troops entered Berlin, Goebbels and his family joined Hitler in the chancellery bunker. There, on or about May 1, 1945, he and his wife poisoned their children, then took their own lives. Goebbels's burnt body was later found by Soviet officers.

References: Roger Manvell, *Dr. Goebbels: His Life and Death* (New York: Simon & Schuster, 1960); Joseph Goebbels (Oliver Watson, trans.), *Das Tagebuch von Joseph Goebbels, 1925/26* (The early Goebbels diaries, 1925–1926) (New York: Praeger, 1963); Ernest Kohn Bramsted, *Goebbels and National Socialist Propaganda, 1925–1945* (East Lansing: Michigan State University Press, 1965).

Goldkette, Jean   *See* BEIDERBECKE, BIX; DORSEY, JIMMY AND TOMMY; JAZZ.

Goldwyn, Samuel (1882–1974)

American MOTION PICTURE producer, a leader in the U.S. movie industry during the interwar period. He was born with the name Shmuel or Schmuel Gelbfisz in the Jewish ghetto of Warsaw, Poland, in 1882, the son of a used-furniture merchant. In 1895, he emigrated to England and then to America, where, according to him, an immigration clerk changed the name Gelbfisz to Goldfish; Goldwyn, refusing to use the name, changed it himself to Goldwyn. He moved to the upstate New York town of Gloversville, and there became a successful leather glove salesman.

In 1913, Goldwyn moved his glove trade to Manhattan and met the sister of Jesse Lasky, a theatrical producer and head of the Jesse Lasky Feature Photoplay Company, which made motion pictures. Lasky made Goldwyn a partner in his company, and they produced *The Squaw Man* (1914), but the arrangement (as well as Goldwyn's marriage to Lasky's sister) did not last. Goldwyn then founded in 1916 the Goldwyn Pictures Corporation, and in the next several years he brought such stars as Madge Kennedy and Mabel Normand to the screen. In 1924, Goldwyn merged his company into Metro-Goldwyn-Mayer (MGM), where he produced such films as *Dodsworth* (1936), *Wuthering Heights* (1939), and *The Little Foxes* (1941). In his later years at MGM, he produced *The Best Years of Our Lives* (1946), *Guys and Dolls* (1955), and the film version of the stage play *Porgy and Bess* (1959).

Goldwyn died in Los Angeles on January 31, 1974, one of the last of the early Hollywood producers.

See also HOLLYWOOD.

References: Andrew Scott Berg, *Goldwyn: A Biography* (New York: Knopf, 1989); Arthur Marx, *Goldwyn: A Biography of the Man Behind the Myth* (New York: Norton, 1976); Carol Easton, *The Search for Sam Goldwyn: A Biography* (New York: Morrow, 1976).

Gondra Doctrine

Statement of principles, enunciated by Paraguayan diplomat and President Manuel Gondra at the Fifth Inter-American Conference, held in Santiago, Chile, in 1923, to have the states of the Americas renounce the use of force when one of the parties asked to establish an "investigating commission" to study a potential conflict. Writes Gondra biographer Daniel Masterson, "The treaty's seven articles detail procedures for the settlement of disputes between the American republics through an impartial investigation of the facts relating to the controversy. Disputes that couldn't be resolved through normal diplomatic means would be submitted to a commission of inquiry composed of five members, all nationals of American states, who would then render a final report within one year. The report would not have the force of arbitral awards and would be binding on the parties involved for only six months after its issuance." Gondra called for commissions to be established in Washington, D.C., and Montevideo, Uruguay, which would sit in judgment of disputes. This statement of principles led to the establishment of the peacekeeping force within the Organization of

American States, and was the first real opportunity for peace in Latin America.

References: Daniel M. Masterson, "Gondra Treaty (1923)" in Barbara A. Tenenbaum, ed. in chief, *Encyclopedia of Latin American History and Culture* (New York: Charles Scribner's Sons, 1996), 3: 80–81; Samuel Inman, Guy, *Inter-American Conferences, 1826–1954: History and Problems* (Washington, D.C.: University Press of America, 1965), 88–106.

Gone with the Wind

Landmark novel by American author Margaret MITCHELL, and motion picture. Mitchell's work—a sprawling, expansive saga set against the backdrop of the pre– and post–Civil War American South—is an epic tale of one family's struggle to stay together during war, mixing both moving character drama and intense action to portray the period like no other work before or since. The book sold some one million copies in ten years after its original publication in 1936. It follows the life of Scarlett O'Hara, a southern belle who pursues the man she wants, plantation owner Ashley Wilkes, even to the point of marrying another man, Rhett Butler, a brutish Confederate blockade-runner whom she professes to hate but in fact desires.

In 1939, a film based directly on the book starred Clark GABLE and Vivien Leigh in the starring roles. The film garnered 13 Academy Award nominations, eventually winning eight, including Best Picture, Best Director (Victor Fleming, one of three directors to have worked on the film), Best Actress (Leigh), Best Screenplay, and Best Supporting Actress (Hattie McDaniel, the first African-American actor to win an Oscar).

References: Richard Harwell, *Gone With the Wind as Book and Film* (Columbia, S.C.: University of South Carolina Press, 1983); Margaret Mitchell (Richard Harwell, ed.), *Margaret Mitchell's Gone With the Wind Letters, 1936–1949* (London: Sidgwick & Jackson, 1987); Sidney Coe Howard (Richard Harwell, ed.), *GWTW: The Screenplay, by Sidney Howard* (New York: Macmillan, 1980).

Good Earth, The   *See* BUCK, PEARL S.

Goodman, Benny   *See* SWING.

Good Neighbor Policy

Statement of principles of the U.S. government during the years 1933 to 1945, used to foster political and economic cooperation between the United States and the Latin American nations. The doctrine was enunciated in a speech by U.S. President Franklin Delano ROOSEVELT before the Chautauqua Institute in New York on August 14, 1936.

In the first two decades of the 20th century, several American leaders, such as Herbert HOOVER and Elihu Root, attempted to modify the Monroe Doctrine of the 19th century with a policy that treated all of the neighbors of Central and South America with diplomatic equality. Even after the Roosevelt Corollary to the Monroe Doctrine emphasized American power in the area, attempts were made to make the United States a better hemispheric partner. But Roosevelt's Good Neighbor Policy was not the first diplomatic attempt at implementing this approach. In 1929, near the end of the Calvin COOLIDGE administration, the president asked Secretary of State Frank KELLOGG to draft a new policy toward the Americas. The statement, prepared by Undersecretary of State J. Reuben Clark and called the CLARK MEMORANDUM, did just that, and was used by President Herbert HOOVER during his single term to conclude a series of diplomatic efforts with Latin America and extend American friendship there as never before.

When he came into office on March 4, 1933, Roosevelt decided to implement this course as part of his NEW DEAL program. In his inaugural address, he said, "In the field of world policy I would dedicate this Nation to the policy of the good neighbor—the neighbor who resolutely respects himself and, because he does so, respects the rights of others—the neighbor who respects his obligations and respects the sanctity of his agreements in and with a world of neighbors."

The policy was not a signal to the Americas that U.S. influence would end completely, however. Writes historian Stephen J. Randall, "The administration went further than any of its predecessors in formally accepting the principle of nonintervention in the internal affairs of other American states. Secretary of State Cordell HULL signed the Convention on the Rights and Duties of States concluded at the Montevideo Conference in 1933, as well as the protocol on nonintervention drafted at the 1936 Inter-American Conference in Buenos Aires. The official U.S. interpretation of these conventions is critical to an understanding of what the Roosevelt administration meant by the 'good neighbor' and intervention. At no time did the administration yield its right to protect its nationals and U.S. corporations operating in Latin America, and that dimension was as important to Latin Americans as direct military intervention."

References: Ruhl J. Bartlett, ed., *The Record of American Diplomacy: Documents and Readings in the History of American Foreign Relations* (New York: Alfred A. Knopf, 1950), 551–52; Stephen J. Randall, "Good Neighbor Policy" in Bruce W. Jentleson and Thomas G. Paterson, senior eds., *Encyclopedia of U.S. Foreign Relations* (New York: Oxford University Press, 1997), 2: 226–29.

Government of India Acts

Set of British Parliamentary legislation. The first act, enacted 1919, allowed a greater degree of, but not full and complete, independence for the then-British colony of India. Sponsored by Secretary of State for India Edwin Montagu and the viceroy of India, Lord Chelmsford, the law was enacted to allow the Indians a greater say in how their government was run. While such ministries as local government, agriculture, and education were transferred to the control of Indians, other areas of life, including revenue collection and police, were reserved to the governor-general's discretion. Also known as the Montagu-Chelmsford Reforms, the action established a chamber of princes, merely a consultative committee; conferred on the Indians nearly half of the seats on the governor general's executive council; and allowed almost complete jurisdiction of Indian ministers over their departments.

The second Government of India Act, enacted in 1935, supplemented the first act and continued the "Indianization" of the Indian government. After five years of heated and tense negotiations, the British government signed the act into law to appease a growing restlessness in India. The act was to create an "All-India Federation," to be split into eleven provinces which were to have a higher degree of self-rule than ever before. Following provincial elections to be held in 1937, the action called "provincial autonomy" was inaugurated, which brought this sense of independence. Burma, which had been a part of India, also became a separate entity at this time.

References: "Montagu-Chelmsford Reforms" in Surjit Mansingh, *Historical Dictionary of India* (Lanham, Md.: Scarecrow, 1996), 160–61; 261–62.

Graf Zeppelin   See ZEPPELINS AND DIRIGIBLES.

Grange, Red   See FOOTBALL, COLLEGIATE.

Great Depression

Period of rapid economic decline and crisis in the United States, 1929–39, characterized by immense unemployment and starvation, the effects of which were experienced globally. This interval of business degeneration was not the first in American history to carry the name "Great Depression"; the period from 1873 until 1897 was also so named and was marked by increases in unemployment. In many ways, the depression began years before the U.S. stock market crashed in October 1929; agricultural prices had been going steadily downhill for the entire decade (except for a slight uptick from 1924–25), making an already bad situation worse on America's farms and culminating in the

UNEMPLOYMENT IN THE UNITED STATES, 1925–39			
YEAR	TOTAL EMPLOYED	TOTAL UNEMPLOYED	PERCENT
1925	44,192,000	817,000	1.8
1926	45,498,000	464,000	1.0
1927	45,319,000	1,620,000	3.6
1928	46,057,000	1,857,000	4.0
1929	47,925,000	1,429,000	3.0
1930	46,081,000	2,896,000	6.3
1931	42,530,000	7,037,000	16.5
1932	38,727,000	11,385,000	29.4
1933	38,827,000	11,842,000	30.5
1934	41,474,000	9,761,000	23.5
1935	42,653,000	9,092,000	21.3
1936	44,830,000	7,386,000	16.5
1937	46,279,000	6,403,000	13.8
1938	43,416,000	9,796,000	22.6
1939	44,993,000	8,786,000	19.5

Source: Otis L. Graham, Jr., and Meghan Robinson Wander, eds., *Franklin D. Roosevelt: His Life and Times: An Encyclopedic View* (Boston: G. K. Hall, 1985), 163.

DUST BOWL of the 1930s. During the free-spending 1920s, the U.S. government started down the protectionist road by enacting several tariffs, including the FORDNEY-MCCUMBER ACT and, in the 1930s, the SMOOT-HAWLEY TARIFF. Spending by the American people, without a comparable rise in wages, also led to a recession. But what may have really been the circumstance that caused the whole house of cards to fall was rampant speculation in the stock market. The STOCK MARKET CRASH, which came on October 24, followed by several days of frenzied selling, shocked the world. The U.S. government seemed frozen by the crisis; President Herbert HOOVER refused to intervene, believing the fundamentals of the economy to be sound.

As the emergency worsened, unemployment shot up, the gross national product collapsed, and the electorate's mood darkened. The passage of Smoot-Hawley, and the decision by the British to withdraw from gold backing for the pound, seemed to push the world deeper into depression. The end of REPARATIONS payments and the failure of banks in the United States and Europe exacerbated the distress. Industrial output in the United States alone shrank 10 percent a year from 1929 to 1932.

By 1932, industrial stocks had lost 80 percent of their value from just two years earlier. That year, New York Governor Franklin D. ROOSEVELT ran for president. Roosevelt had tackled the depression in New York with a series of measures intending to aid the unemployed and restart the economy. On his platform of giving the Ameri-

Unemployment and inflation tumbled millions of Americans into the depths of poverty and hunger in the early years of the Great Depression. Social support was in short supply. In New York City, a breadline winds around one of the towers of the Brooklyn Bridge. *(CORBIS)*

can people a NEW DEAL, Roosevelt was elected as president in 1932. He went to work right away, calling in his inaugural address for emergency powers to combat the depression. He closed banks and forced Congress to enact the National Recovery Act to halt price slides, and employment programs to put the nation back to work. And although the Supreme Court struck down key parts of this program as unconstitutional on BLACK MONDAY, Congress enacted legislation tailored to fit the Court's narrow definition of constitutionality. The depression did not end until 1941, when prices and wages were back to their pre-1929 levels.

See also NATIONAL RECOVERY ADMINISTRATION; WORKS PROGRESS ADMINISTRATION.

References: George D. Green, "Great Depression" in Otis L. Graham, Jr., and Meghan Robinson Wander, eds., *Franklin D.*

Roosevelt: His Life and Times: An Encyclopedic View (Boston: G. K. Hall, 1985), 162–66; Dixon Wecter, *The Age of the Great Depression, 1929–1941* (New York: Macmillan, 1948).

Great Gatsby, The   *See* FITZGERALD, F. SCOTT.

Great Terror   *See* STALIN, JOSEPH.

Grew, Joseph Clark (1880–1965)
American diplomat, ambassador to Japan (1932–41). Born the scion of a wealthy Boston family on May 27, 1880, he attended the prestigious Groton School and Harvard University, from which he graduated in 1902. After spending some time overseas, he began work as a clerk in the U.S.

AGRICULTURAL PRICES IN THE UNITED STATES FOR VARIOUS COMMODITIES, 1919–32

YEAR	WHEAT	CORN (CENTS PER BUSHEL)	OATS (CENTS PER POUND)	POTATOES	PEANUTS
1919	216.3	150.7	76.7	191.1	9.33
1920	182.6	61.0	53.8	133.2	5.26
1921	103.0	52.7	32.2	113.5	3.99
1922	96.6	75.2	37.4	68.6	4.68
1923	92.6	83.5	40.7	91.5	6.78
1924	124.7	105.3	47.8	71.5	5.68
1925	143.7	69.9	38.8	166.3	4.56
1926	121.7	75.3	40.1	136.3	4.97
1927	119.0	84.9	47.1	108.9	5.04
1928	99.8	84.3	40.7	57.2	4.90
1929	103.4	79.8	41.9	131.5	3.83
1930	67.0	59.4	32.2	91.5	3.54
1931	39.0	32.1	21.3	46.4	2.09
1932	37.9	31.8	15.7	38.8	1.53

Source: U.S. Department of Agriculture, *Yearbook of Agriculture, 1934* (Washington, D.C.: Government Printing Office, 1935).

State Department, first being stationed in Cairo, then moving to Mexico City, St. Petersburg, Berlin, and Vienna. Returning to Berlin in 1912, Grew was given the rank of counselor of embassy. He spent much of 1913 and 1914 trying, with Ambassador James W. Gerard, to avoid war in Europe, which Grew foresaw as a disaster. After the United States became involved in the war in 1917, Grew was recalled to Washington, D.C., where he served as chief of the State Department's Division of Western Affairs.

From 1924 to 1927, Grew served as undersecretary of state in the COOLIDGE administration, where he was responsible for helping to establish the U.S. Foreign Service in 1924. In 1932, President Herbert HOOVER named him as U.S. ambassador to Japan, where he served until the start of World War II. During the 1930s, Grew was a staunch critic of the rise of Japanese militarism, but he also warned the U.S. government that imposing sanctions on Tokyo would not only anger the Japanese but increase the possibility that the Japanese military would strike at the United States. In early 1941, as tensions rose to a fever pitch, Grew privately warned that the U.S. naval base at Pearl Harbor, Hawaii, was a possible target for such retaliation. After the start of the war between the United States and Japan, he was exchanged, along with other American diplomats, for Japanese representatives in America. He returned to the State Department, serving as undersecretary of state for a second time (1944–45).

When Grew retired from the State Department in September 1945, the *New York Times* said of him, "As Ambassador to Tokyo for 10 years preceding Pearl Harbor he fought valiantly to preserve the peace while warning the American government of the possibility of Japanese treachery . . . Japanese treachery won out, and Mr. Grew felt that his life-work had crashed all about him. It must, therefore, have given him special satisfaction to preside over the liquidation of Japanese ambitions, and his counsel contributed much to the speedy end of the Pacific war through [the] utilization of the Japanese Emperor." Grew wrote his memoirs, *Turbulent Era: A Diplomatic Record of Forty Years, 1904–1945* (1952), as well as *Ten Years in Japan: A Contemporary Record Drawn from the Diaries and Private and Official Papers of Joseph C. Grew, United States Ambassador to Japan* (1944). He died on May 25, 1965.

References: Waldo H. Heinrichs, *American Ambassador: Joseph C. Grew and the Development of the United States Diplomatic Tradition* (Boston: Little, Brown, 1966); Barney J. Rickman, III, "Grew, Joseph Clark" in Bruce W. Jentleson and Thomas G. Paterson, senior eds., *Encyclopedia of U.S. Foreign Relations* (New York: Oxford University Press, 1997), 2: 255; "Joseph C. Grew, 84, Ex-Envoy, Is Dead," *New York Times*, May 27, 1965, pp. 1, 37.

Griffith, Arthur (1872–1922)

Irish political leader. As a young man, Griffith published a newspaper, the *United Irishmen*, which advocated the creation of an Irish assembly. He was also a member of the

Irish Republican Brotherhood, but he withdrew in 1902 to form Sinn Féin, the political arm of the Irish Republican Army. Sinn Féin advocated for an economically and politically self-sufficient Ireland and adopted passive resistance to the British, but it gained little support before World War I.

This changed in 1916, however, when the Irish Volunteers (the military wing of the IRA) achieved home rule for 26 of 32 Irish counties in the Dublin Uprising or Easter Rebellion. From 1916 through 1918, Griffith was imprisoned and his newspaper suppressed. While in prison, however, he was elected vice president of a new "Irish Republic." Sinn Féin was reorganized under Éamon DE VALÉRA and established an Irish assembly called the Dáil Éireann. But at this point the independence movement was divided. The Volunteers accepted an agreement that had been forged between London and Dublin (signed by Griffith and independence leader Michael COLLINS), but a breakaway group was bitterly opposed to it.

There was continued resistance against the British until December 1921, when a peace treaty was signed between representatives of the Dáil Éireann and the British government. The treaty was ratified on January 15, 1922, by a vote of 64 to 57, which brought into being the IRISH FREE STATE, of which Griffith was the first president and Collins was chair of the provisional government. In August of that year, however, Griffith unexpectedly died.

Reference: Calton Younger, *A State of Disunion: Arthur Griffith, Michael Collins, James Craig, Eamon de Valera* (London: Fontana, 1972).

Gropius, Walter (1883–1969)

German-American architect, founder of the BAUHAUS school of German architecture before he fled Nazi Germany and spent the rest of his life in the United States. Born in Berlin on May 18, 1883, he was the son of an architect. Gropius studied architecture at technical institutes at Munich and in Berlin, where for a short time he worked in an architecture firm. After brief service in the German army, Gropius finished school and began to construct numerous buildings in the German area of Pomerania. He then spent time in Italy and England before returning to Berlin to work in the architectural firm of Peter Behrens. From Behrens he received lessons in progressive architecture, which he carried on when he went to work in the years before World War I for the *Deutscher Werkbund* ("German Labour League"), a school of design creation. Afterward, he collaborated with Alfred Meyer to build the Fagus Shoe-Last Factory at Alfeld-an-der-Leine, in which he demonstrated the use of glass walls.

Gropius served in the German army during World War I as a cavalry officer on the eastern front, where he was wounded and received the Iron Cross for bravery in

battle. He emerged from the war with a longing to change European architecture and thus the future of the continent. To this end, in 1919 he went to WEIMAR and became the director of two schools of art, which merged into the *Staatliches Bauhaus Weimar,* or Weimar Bauhaus School. He then assembled a team of avant-garde artists, including the Swiss painter and graphic artist Johannes Itten, the Swiss painter Paul KLEE, the German designer Oskar Schlemmer, and the Russian abstract painter Wassily Kandinsky, in an effort to establish a school of art at the forefront of culture during the postwar rebuilding. Art historian Alan Windsor writes, "The Bauhaus was organized to train artists and designers so that they might cooperate, on an international basis if necessary, to create a new environment in which beauty, imagination and economy were instinct in all common artifacts and in a 'total' architecture." In 1925, Gropius moved Bauhaus to Dessau, where he designed the school building. During the late 1920s and early 1930s, however, his ideas and that of the Bauhaus came under increasing scrutiny from the German authorities. When Adolf HITLER came to power in 1933, Gropius was forced to close the school. With his second wife, he fled his homeland for the United States.

At the Harvard University School of Design, Gropius headed the department of architecture from 1938 to 1952, and in 1944 he became a naturalized U.S. citizen. He was active in the architecture firm known as The Architects' Collaborative (TAC), which he founded in 1946, until his death. As part of TAC, he helped to design the U.S. Embassy in Athens, Greece, as well as the Harvard University Graduate Center. Gropius died in Boston, Massachusetts, on July 5, 1969.

References: Reginald R. Isaacs, *Gropius: An Illustrated Biography of the Creator of the Bauhaus* (Boston: Little, Brown, 1991); Dennis Sharp, *Bauhaus, Dessau: Walter Gropius* (London: Phaidon, 1993); Alan Windsor, "Gropius, Walter Adolph" in Alan Bullock and R. B. Woodings, eds., *20th Century Culture: A Biographical Companion* (New York: Harper & Row, 1983), 291.

Group of Seven

Canadian artistic movement, founded around 1920 by seven original artists but expanded to include others until it was disbanded in 1933. The original members of the Group—Franklin Carmichael, Lawren Harris, A. Y. Jackson, Franz Johnston, Arthur Lismer, J. E. H. MacDonald, and F. H. Varley—were all friends in Toronto prior to World War I.

The Group was initiated after they exhibited their works individually at the Art Gallery of Toronto in 1920. As they developed into a school of landscape artists who captured the feel of the panorama of the Ontario countryside, they were noticed by the arts community. Eric Brown, director of the National Gallery of Canada, began to purchase their works, and made sure that these were exhibited at the Wembley Art Show in England in 1924 and 1925. As Group biographer Christopher Varley explains,

> Like the European *fin de siècle* symbolists and postimpressionists from whom their aesthetic largely derived, the Group rebelled against the constraints of 19th century naturalism and tried to establish a more equitable and independent relationship between art and nature . . . In 1922, MacDonald began using thinner paint and more stylized designs, and Harris, Carmichael and Varley soon began heading in the same direction. Harris went further than the others, however, and by the mid-1920s he had reduced his paintings to a few simplified and nearly monochromatic forms. Ten years later he became the only member of the Group, and one of the first Canadian artists, to turn to abstraction.

After Johnston left in 1926, he was replaced by A. J. Casson. In 1930, and again in 1932, other artists were invited to join the Group to expand its talent base. When its members disbanded in 1933, however, it was because their art had begun to take on the appearance of the paintings that through the earlier works the artists had sought to distance themselves from.

References: Peter Mellen, *The Group of Seven* (Toronto: McClelland and Stewart, 1970); Christopher Varley, "Group of Seven" in *The Canadian Encyclopedia* (Edmonton, Alberta: Hurtig Publishers, 1988), 2: 942–43.

Grovey v. Townsend (295 U.S. 45 {1935})

Landmark United States Supreme Court decision, which held that state political parties could exclude blacks from voting if they did not act with the use of "state action." Grovey was the third in a series of cases historians call "the white primary cases." Starting in 1927, with *Nixon v. Herndon,* and continuing in 1932 in *Nixon v. Condon,* the Court held that states could not exclude black voters from participating in primaries to decide candidates for a general election. However, after *Condon,* the Texas state legislature allowed the parties to control who voted in their particular primaries, and the Democratic Party, meeting in convention, decided to ban all blacks from voting in party primaries. When R. R. Grovey, a black voter, asked for a ballot to vote in the Democratic primary in 1932 under so-called "Condon rules," he was denied a ballot by the county clerk, Townsend. Grovey then sued Townsend, claiming that the exclusion was a violation of his rights under the U.S. Constitution. The Court heard arguments on March 11, 1935.

Three weeks later, on April 1, the Court held unanimously (Justice Owen Roberts delivering the opinion of the Court) that Townsend had no standing to sue because there was no "state action" involved in any possible discrimination. Justice Roberts remarked: "We find no ground for holding that the respondent has in obedience to the mandate of the law of Texas discriminated against the petitioner or denied him any right guaranteed by the Fourteenth and Fifteenth Amendments."

The holding in *Grovey* was later overruled in *Smith v. Allwright* (1944).

References: Kenneth L. Karst, "Grovey v. Townsend" in Leonard W. Levy, ed. in chief, *Encyclopedia of the American Constitution* (New York: Macmillan Publishing Company; four volumes and one supplement, 1986–92), II: 874; Paul Finkelman, "Grovey v. Townsend" in Kermit L. Hall, ed. in chief, *The Oxford Companion to the Supreme Court of the United States* (New York: Oxford University Press, 1992), 355.

Guillaume, Charles-Édouard (1861–1938)

Swiss physicist and Nobel laureate. Born in Fleurier, Switzerland, on February 15, 1861, he received his doctorate from the Zurich Polytechnic in 1883. Guillaume served as the administrator of, and a researcher at, the International Bureau of Weights and Measures in Paris from 1883 until 1936. There, while working on increasing the standard of weights and measures, he discovered invar, an iron and nickel alloy used in weights. He also found anomalies in the composition of such alloys. Little noticed for many years, in 1920 Guillaume was awarded the Nobel Prize in physics for these discoveries.

Guillaume died in Paris on June 13, 1938.

References: Barbara N. List, "Guillaume, Charles Edouard" in Bernard S. and June H. Schlessinger, eds., *The Who's Who of Nobel Prize Winners* (Phoenix, Ariz.: Oryx, 1986), 155–56; Thomas Watson MacCallum and Stephen Taylor, eds., *The Nobel Prize–Winners and the Nobel Foundation, 1901–1937* (Zurich, Switzerland: Central European Times Publishing, 1938), 72.

Guthrie, Woody (1912–1967)

American folksinger and composer, famed during the 1930s as the voice of the "DUST BOWL refugees" fleeing economic despair in the American Midwest. Born Woodrow Wilson Guthrie in the town of Okemah, Oklahoma, on July 14, 1912, he was named after the Democrat who was elected U.S. president later that year. Endowed with some musical ability, Guthrie left home at age 15 to travel around the United States by train. During the GREAT DEPRESSION, carrying a guitar and harmonica, he was a welcome voice delivering entertainment to hoboes and other victims of the economic downturn. Reflecting his own and others' experiences, he wrote and played such tunes as "Do Re Mi," "Pastures of Plenty," "Hard Traveling," "Blowing Down This Old Dusty Road," "Tom Joad," and "Union Maid." Perhaps the most famous of his more than a thousand songs is "This Land Is Your Land." He joined with folksinger Pete Seeger to form the Almanac Singers. A union sympathizer who flirted with communism, he wrote a column for the American Communist Party newspaper *The Daily Worker.* When asked about his political affiliation, Guthrie reportedly answered, "I ain't a communist necessarily, but I been in the red all my life." During the 1930s, he toured with Seeger, Huddie William Ledbetter (known as "Leadbelly"), Lee Hays, Cisco Houston, and other folksingers.

In the 1940s and 1950s, after serving in the Merchant Marines during the war, he continued to tour and sing.

Guthrie's final years were marked by a fight against Huntington's disease; on October 3, 1967, he died in New York City.

References: Henrietta Yurchenco, *A Mighty Hard Road: The Woody Guthrie Story* (New York: McGraw-Hill, 1970): Janelle Yates, *Woody Guthrie: American Balladeer* (Staten Island, N.Y.: Ward Hill, 1995); "Woody Guthrie, Folk Singer and Composer, Dies; Rambler and Balladeer of the American Scene was 55," *New York Times,* October 4, 1967, p. 47.

Haile Selassie (1892–1975)

Emperor of Ethiopia (1930–75). Born Ras (or Prince) Tafari Makonnen in Ejarsa Gora, Harar, in what is now eastern Ethiopia, on July 23, 1892, he was the great-grandson of Haile Malekot, King of Shoa, and the son of Ras Makonnen, an adviser to King Menelik II of Ethiopia. He married Menelik's daughter in 1911. He was named regent in 1917 but was forced to wait until the death of the Empress Zauditu before he could be crowned *negus,* or king. On April 3, 1930, he was crowned as Haile Selassie, meaning "Might of the Trinity."

In 1921, Haile Selassie enacted the first Ethiopian constitution, which sought to modernize the nation. Many of the tribes in Ethiopia saw his modernization program as a threat to their way of life, however, and undertook a series of revolts to overthrow him. These all failed, and by 1934, Haile Selassie had become the undisputed leader. But outside pressures began to grow. Italy had colonized the province of Eritrea, to the north of Ethiopia, and intended to use the province as a power base for future aggression in Africa. In December 1934 a series of border clashes led to a LEAGUE OF NATIONS castigation of both sides, but no further action was taken. On October 3, 1935, the Italian leader Benito MUSSOLINI unleashed an invasion of Ethiopia, initiating the ETHIOPIAN WAR, which was quickly condemned by the League. The Italians used chemical weapons on the Ethiopian troops and slowly advanced to the capital of Addis Ababa. On May 2, 1936, Haile Selassie went into exile, and although he pleaded his case before the League, Italy annexed his nation, a move that was recognized by Britain and France.

In 1935 he was named by *Time* magazine Man of the Year. Haile Selassie, now a king without a land, established a government-in-exile, which existed until he and other African and Allied forces entered Addis Ababa on May 5, 1941. After World War II, Haile Selassie continued to be an important world leader, making his nation one of the founding members of the United Nations and the Organization of African Unity. His various social reforms led to numerous coups, however, and in 1974 a mutiny by the army led to his removal. Haile Selassie died under house arrest on August 27, 1975.

See also ITALIAN SOMALILAND.

References: George L. Simpson, Jr., "Haile Selassie I" in Anne Commire, ed., *Historic World Leaders* (Detroit: Gale Research, 1994), 1: 192–96; Harold G. Marcus, *Haile Selassie I: The Formative Years, 1892–1936* (Los Angeles: University of California Press, 1987); Chris Prouty and Eugene Rosenfield, *Historical Dictionary of Ethiopia* (London: Scarecrow, 1982).

Haiti, U.S. Occupation of

In February 1915 Vilbrun Guillaume Sam took control of the government of Haiti, a country in the throes of revolutionary turmoil. By July 1915 Sam's tenuous hold over the country ended abruptly and violently when he was forcibly removed from the French embassy where he had sought asylum and was subsequently torn apart by a mob. The violation of the French legation provided a pretext for intervention, and with U.S. Marines having already landed in the Haitian capital of Port-au-Prince, President Woodrow Wilson ordered that American forces protect foreign assets and supervise a new national election. Philippe Sudre Dartiguenave became president and saw to it that the reluctant Haitian senate ratified a treaty rendering Haiti a protectorate of the United States. Haiti's customs and *gendarmerie* (police corps) yielded to American control.

A new Haitian constitution, adopted by a questionable vote, was adopted in 1918. Dartiguenave remained president—no provisions for a new election having been made—and American officers were in de facto control of the government. The *corvée* (conscripted labor) was revived by the *gendarmerie* to force Haitian peasants to work on public works projects. This highly unpopular action exacerbated hostilities and late in 1918, a revolt, led by Charlemagne Péralte and Benoit Batraville, against the *corvée* and the U.S. presence in Haiti commenced. The rebels were defeated by 1920 by U.S. Marines, who for the first time used airplane power to support combat troops.

In 1922 President Dartiguenave was replaced by the more compliant Louis Borno. The new U.S. administration appointed General John H. Russell high commissioner in Haiti. Russell and Borno constituted a joint dictatorship that controlled activities in the country until 1930. Good coffee harvests during these years of high prices ensured relative prosperity, and the Russell-Borno regime initiated much-needed public works. However, against popular support, Russell increased American control, which eventually led to protests and, later, riots. Martial law was declared.

The 1929 riots were an international embarrassment to the Hoover administration, which was trying to pursue a "good neighbor" policy in Latin America. Wanting out of Haiti, Hoover sent two special commissions to the island. Borno was ousted and Sténio Vincent was elected president. In August 1933 Vincent and U.S. president Franklin D. Roosevelt signed an executive agreement to end the U.S. occupation of Haiti in August of 1934, when all American troops later withdrew.

References: Robert Debs Heinl, Jr., Nancy Gordon Heinl, and Michael Heinl. *Written in Blood: The Story of the Haitian People 1492–1995.* Revised and expanded ed. (Lanham, Md.: University Press of America, 1996); Jan Rogozínski, *A Brief History of the Caribbean.* Revised ed. (New York: Facts On File, Inc., 1999).

Hammerstein, Oscar (1895–1960)

American lyricist and librettist, whose collaboration with Jerome KERN produced the classic interwar Broadway musical, *Show Boat,* as well as other popular shows of the period. Born in New York City on July 12, 1895, Hammerstein was the grandson of Oscar Hammerstein, a noted theater producer and director, and the nephew of Arthur Hammerstein, a Broadway producer. Intending to be an attorney, Oscar II, as he was known, attended the Hamilton Institute, a semimilitary academy in New York, before entering Columbia University in 1912. At Columbia he was exposed to the stage, and while attending Columbia Law School he wrote plays. When his job as a process server did not work out, Hammerstein quit the legal profession altogether and concentrated on his stage work.

In 1917, Hammerstein wrote a play that was produced by his uncle Arthur, serving as the assistant stage manager. After stage managing another show in 1918, he wrote the musical comedy *Always You,* which opened in 1920. In

1921, he collaborated with Otto Harbach and Frank Mandel on the lyrics for *Tickle Me,* which was successful. Starting in 1923, after a string of failures, he began a series of productions that became some of the biggest hits of the 1920s, including *Wildflower* (1923), *Rose Marie* (1924), and *Sunny* (1925), the latter a collaboration with Kern. The work with Kern led the producer to enlist Hammerstein's assistance in bringing novelist Edna Ferber's *Show Boat* to the stage. Using a myriad of characters (including, for the first time, a mix of blacks and whites) and dynamic lyrics, Hammerstein brought the world of the Mississippi River and riverboat life to the stage.

Biographer David Ewen explains, "Hammerstein conceived with his composer-collaborator a new type of musical production that was unconventional in its treatment of American backgrounds, characters, social problems, and local color. Discarding the paraphernalia and ritual that had so long burdened the American theater (the line of chorus girls, synthetic humor and dances, big production numbers, contrived songs), Hammerstein and Kern realized in *Show Boat* a folk play with music in which all the elements of musical theater were subservient to the aesthetic and dramatic demands of the play, and in which the songs, humor, and stage play were basic to the text." The play, which first appeared on Broadway in 1927, became one of the most successful productions of the era.

After *Show Boat,* Hammerstein drafted the lyrics for such plays as *The New Moon* (1928) and Kern's *Music in the Air* (1932). During and after World War II, Hammerstein began a collaboration with composer Richard RODGERS from which emerged such classics as *Oklahoma!* (1943), *Carousel* (1945), *South Pacific* (1949), *The King and I* (1951), and *The Sound of Music* (1959). Hammerstein died in Doylestown, Pennsylvania, on August 23, 1960.

References: Hugh Fordin, *Getting to Know Him: A Biography of Oscar Hammerstein II* (New York: Random House, 1977); Miles Kreuger, *Showboat: The Story of a Classic American Musical* (New York: Oxford University Press, 1977); David Ewen, "Hammerstein, Oscar, II" in Allen Johnson and Dumas Malone et al., eds., *Dictionary of American Biography* (New York: Charles Scribner's Sons, 1930–95), 6: 273–74; Ethan Mordden, *Rodgers & Hammerstein* (New York: Abrams, 1992); "Oscar Hammerstein 2d Is Dead; Librettist and Producer Was 65," *New York Times,* August 23, 1960, pp. 1, 25.

Hamsun, Knut (1859–1952)

Norwegian novelist and Nobel laureate. Born Knud Pederson Hamsund on August 4, 1859, in Lom, Norway, he attended local schools but never received a college degree. Starting in 1890, with the publication of *Sult* (Hunger), Hamsun established himself as a chronicler of Norwegian stories dealing with the theme of humankind and nature.

Yet it was *Markens grøde* (Growth of the Soil, 1917), that became his most famous novel, for which Hamsun won the 1920 Nobel Prize in literature. Harald Hjärne, Chairman of the Nobel Committee of the Swedish Academy, said of Hamsun, "Hamsun's work is an epic of labour to which the author has given monumental lines. It is not a question of disparate labour which divides men within and among themselves; it is a question of the concentrated toil which in its purest form shapes men entirely, which mollifies and brings together divided spirits, which protects and increases their fruits with a regular and uninterrupted progress. The labour of the pioneer and the first farmer with all its difficulties, under the poet's pen, thus takes on the character of a heroic struggle that yields nothing to the grandeur of the manly sacrifice for one's country and companions in arms. Just as the peasant poet Hesiod described the labours of the field, so Hamsun has put in the foreground of his work the ideal labourer who dedicates his whole life and all his powers to clearing the land and to triumphing over the obstacles with which men and the forces of nature confront him. If Hamsun has cast behind him all the weighty memories of civilization, he has by his own work contributed to a precise understanding of the new culture that our era expects to arise from the progress of physical labour as a continuation of ancient civilization."

Hamsun loved everything German, and the rise of Adolf HITLER seemed to inspire something in him to turn his back on his own nation. When Germany invaded Norway, Hamsun applauded the action, earning the eternal enmity of his fellow Norwegians. After Norway was liberated in 1945, Hamsun was arrested and examined by psychiatrists, who concluded that he suffered from a mental disease. He was then sued by the government, which forced him to pay a fine that sapped him of most of his fortune. His only work following the war, which he hoped would re-establish his reputation, was *Paa gjengrodde Stier* (On Overgrown Paths, 1949), which is considered his memoir. Hamsun died at Nørholm, near Grimstad, Norway, on February 19, 1952.

References: Harald Næss, *Knut Hamsun* (Boston: Twayne Publishers, 1984); Dolores Buttry, "Knut Hamsun: A Scandinavian Rousseau" (Ph.D. diss., University of Illinois at Urbana-Champaign, 1978); Solveig Olsen, "Hamsun, Knut Pedersen" in Bernard S. and June H. Schlessinger, eds., *The Who's Who of Nobel Prize Winners* (Phoenix, Ariz.: Oryx, 1986), 53–54; Thomas Watson MacCallum and Stephen Taylor, eds., *The Nobel Prize–Winners and the Nobel Foundation, 1901–1937* (Zurich, Switzerland: Central European Times Publishing, 1938), 291–93.

Harden, Arthur (1865–1940)

British chemist and Nobel laureate. Born in Manchester, England, on October 12, 1865, he earned his bachelor of science degree from the University of Manchester in 1885, and his doctorate from the University of Erlangen in Germany in 1888. Harden spent his career as a professor of chemistry at the University of Manchester from 1888 to 1897, and at the British Institute of Preventative Medicine from 1897 until his retirement in 1930. While at these two institutions, he investigated the fermentation of sugars and fermentative enzymes. For this work, Harden was the corecipient (with Hans EULER-CHELPIN) of the 1929 Nobel Prize in chemistry.

In 1936, Harden was knighted. He died four years later, on June 17, 1940.

References: Lisa Kammerlocher, "Harden, Arthur, Sir" in Bernard S. and June H. Schlessinger, eds., *The Who's Who of Nobel Prize Winners* (Phoenix, Ariz.: Oryx, 1986), 11; Aaron J. Ihde, "Harden, Arthur" in Charles Coulston Gillespie, ed. in chief, *Dictionary of Scientific Biography* (New York: Charles Scribner's Sons, 1980–90), 5: 110–12; Thomas Watson MacCallum and Stephen Taylor, eds., *The Nobel Prize–Winners and the Nobel Foundation, 1901–1937* (Zurich, Switzerland: Central European Times Publishing, 1938), 151–52.

Harding, Warren G. (1865–1923)

American politician, U.S. senator from Ohio (1914–21), 29th president of the United States (1921–23). Born Warren Gamaliel Harding in Marion, Ohio, on November 2, 1865, he attended Ohio Central College in Iberia before studying the law. In 1884, he bought the Marion, Ohio, *Star*, which was a weekly newspaper until Harding made it a daily. His Republican politics brought him to the attention of Ohio politician Senator Joseph Foraker, and Harding became his protégé. Determined to become a politician himself, Harding was elected to the Ohio State Senate in 1900, serving four years, and, in 1904, he was elected lieutenant governor, but was defeated for governor in 1910. Instead, in 1914 his close friend Harry M. DAUGHERTY convinced him to run for the Senate. Elected to a single six-year term, Harding did not sponsor any significant legislation; however, he was characterized by his strong support for the stand of the "IRRECONCILABLES," a group of senators strongly opposed to the VERSAILLES Treaty and led by Henry Cabot LODGE of Massachusetts, as well as for PROHIBITION and the passage of the Eighteenth Amendment in 1919.

Harding was a party loyalist, but not seen as anyone who could advance further than the Senate. That all changed in 1920, when the Republican National Convention deadlocked over several candidates for president and, in a back room, party leaders selected him as a compromise candidate. Harding was nominated, and Governor Calvin COOLIDGE of Massachusetts was named as his running mate. Labeling his election as "a return to normalcy." Harding was easily elected as the 29th president over his

Florence and Warren G. Harding examine the poll results that would make him president on election night in 1920. *(CORBIS/Bettmann)*

Democratic opponent, Governor James M. COX of Ohio, to become the first Republican president since 1913.

In his two and a half years as president, Harding's major achievement was the WASHINGTON NAVAL CONFERENCE, which significantly cut naval armaments following World War I. While two of his choices for his cabinet, Charles Evans HUGHES at State and Herbert HOOVER at Commerce, have withstood the test of time and have duly earned their places in history, Harding's other picks were considerably worse: he named his friend Daugherty as attorney general, and fellow senator Albert B. FALL as secretary of the interior. Although Harding himself was not corrupt, these men took advantage of their high government positions: Daugherty was implicated in corruption in the Justice Department, and Fall was involved in the selling of government oil leases to cronies for bribes in the TEAPOT DOME SCANDAL. By the summer of 1923, there were rumors that the Harding administration was up to its ears in corruption.

Harding sought to escape both the heat of the Washington, D.C., summer and that of the investigations swirling around his advisers. He vacationed in Alaska in July, but on his return to the U.S. mainland he became ill. On August 2, 1923, Harding died in Room 8064 of the Palace Hotel in San Francisco and rumors about the cause of death flurried. In his 1996 work on the president's last illness, historian Robert H. Ferrell states flatly that tainted shellfish brought on a massive coronary, not apoplexy as the newspapers reported.

References: Samuel Hopkins Adams, *Incredible Era: The Life and Times of Warren Gamaliel Harding* (Boston: Houghton Mifflin, 1939), 80–81; Kenneth J. Grieb, "Harding, Warren" in Bruce W. Jentleson and Thomas G. Paterson, senior eds., *Encyclopedia of U.S. Foreign Relations* (New York: Oxford University Press, 1997), 2: 282–83; Robert H. Ferrell, *The Strange Deaths of President Harding* (Columbia: University of Missouri Press, 1996); "President Harding Is Dead of Apoplexy; End Comes Instantly as Wife Is Reading to Him; Coolidge Takes Oath of Office" *Washington Post,* August 3, 1923, p. 1.

Hare-Hawes-Cutting Act

U.S. congressional legislation, enacted January 17, 1933, which provided for the orderly transition of power from the U.S. government to the people of the Philippines, with set rights to military and naval bases in the Philippines established for the U.S. military, and with a tariff on all Filipino goods imported into the United States. Named after its sponsors, Senators Harry B. Hawes and Bronson Cutting, and Representative Butler B. Hare, the legislation was originally vetoed by President Herbert HOOVER in January 1933, shortly before he left office, on the grounds that the bill failed to live up to the "triple responsibility" that the United States had to the Filipino people. On that same day, however, the House overturned the veto, 274 to 94, and on January 17 the Senate did likewise, 66 to 26. A provision of the law required the Philippine legislature to vote in favor of the law, or to establish a convention that would do the same thing. President of the Philippine Senate Manuel Luis Quezon y Molina was the leading Filipino behind the measure (he was in the camp called the "Pros," while the opposition was labeled the "Antis"). In the end, however, the legislature turned down the act in October 1933 because of the trade provisions, which many feared would wreck the island's economy; objections to restrictions on Filipino immigration into the United States; and the desire of the United States to maintain a "military presence" in the island even after independence.

In 1934, the U.S. Congress sent to the Philippine legislature a new action, the TYDINGS-MCDUFFIE ACT.

References: José P. Melencio, *Arguments against Philippine Independence and Their Answers* (Washington, D.C.: Philippine Press Bureau, 1919); Teodoro A. Agoncillo and Oscar M. Alfonso, *History of the Filipino People* (Quezon City: Malaya Books, 1967), 382–86; Norman G. Owen, ed., *Compadre Colonialism: Studies on the Philippines under American Rule* (Ann Arbor, Mich.: Center for South and Southeast Asian Studies, 1971).

Harlem Renaissance

Period of extraordinary artistic, literary, musical, and intellectual activity among African Americans during the interwar period. The movement began in 1910 in the upper section of Manhattan known as Harlem, then primarily a white middle-class neighborhodd. As the JAZZ AGE dawned in white America in the early 1920s, Harlem was transformed by the mass migration of African Americans from the U.S. South to northern cities such as New York. Although many of these migrants were poor, a large number of them were ambitious and talented artists, writers, and musicians, and their output during the 1920s and early 1930s produced what is known as the Harlem Renaissance.

Harlem became a center for fashion, entertainment, and nightlife for African Americans who had escaped the segregation, racial persecution, and economic deprivation of the Deep South. Through Harlem's flourishing black-owned theaters, clubs, magazines, and newspapers, the movement sought to demonstrate and call attention to the heritage and culture of black Americans through art, literature, music, and other forms of expression. Taking their inspiration from Harlem's thriving political, artistic, and

cultural milieu, the following people are part of this rich legacy: the writers Zora Neale HURSTON (*Their Eyes Were Watching God,* 1937) and James Weldon JOHNSON (*God's Trombones,* 1927); the poets Langston HUGHES (*The Weary Blues,* 1926, and *Not Without Laughter,* 1930), Claude McKay (*Harlem's Shadows,* 1922, and *Home to Harlem,* 1928), and Countee CULLEN (*An Anthology of Verse by Negro Poets,* 1927); and the musicians and singers Duke ELLINGTON, Lil Hardin, Earl Hines, Billie HOLIDAY, Huddie "Leadbelly" Ledbetter, Bill "Bojangles" Robinson, Bessie SMITH, and Ethel Waters. African-American painters and sculptors such as Aaron Douglas, Jacob Lawrence, and Augusta Savage created art that affirmed their identity and introduced black themes into American modernism. Photographers such as Walker Evans, Richard S. Roberts, Doris Ulmann, James VanDerZee, and Carl Van Vechten (a white photographer of the renaissance and also a generous patron of the movement's music, literature, and journalism) captured Harlem's celebrities, dancers, street life, families, and fashions.

Although the movement faded during the 1930s with the onset of the GREAT DEPRESSION, it influenced countless subsequent artists and thinkers. Similar artistic phenomena occurred in a number of other urban centers during these years, including the formation of African-American artistic, literary, and musical enclaves in Baltimore, Boston, Chicago, Detroit, Philadelphia, San Francisco, and Washington, D.C. Repercussions of this cultural revolution, which embraced white as well as black artists, were felt around the world, as the Harlem Renaissance extended its sphere of influence from the United States to Europe (most notably Paris), Africa, and the Caribbean.

References: Jervis Anderson, *This Was Harlem: A Cultural Portrait, 1900–1950* (New York: Farrar, Straus & Giroux, 1981); Cary D. Wintz, *Black Culture and the Harlem Renaissance* (Houston: Rice University Press, 1988); Nathan Irvin Huggins, *Harlem Renaissance* (New York: Oxford University Press, 1971).

Harris, Abram Lincoln (1899–1963)

American economist and writer on the economic issues of African-Americans, particularly during the 1930s in such writings as his landmark *The Black Worker* (1931), *The Negro and the Labor Movement* (1931), and *The Negro as Capitalist* (1936). Born in 1899, he was a graduate of Virginia Union University, and served on the faculties of Virginia State College and Howard University in Washington, D.C., from 1927 to 1945. Later, he taught at the University of Chicago (1946–63). Harris's early views were based on a marxist perspective, but he was later influenced by the liberalism of John Stuart Mill. He concluded that a unified working class offered the best option for African Americans. He died in Chicago on November 16, 1963.

References: Roger Weiss, "Harris, Abram Lincoln" in Rayford W. Logan and Michael R. Winston, eds., *Dictionary of American Negro Biography* (New York: W. W. Norton, 1982), 291–92; "Dr. A.L. Harris, Professor at U. of C., Is Dead; Economist, 64, Wrote Several Books," *Chicago Tribune,* November 17, 1963, p. 26.

Hart, Moss (1904–1961)

American playwright, known for his delightful comedies and musicals of the 1930s and beyond. Born in New York City, Hart studied at Columbia University and began his theatrical career as an office boy in a New York agency. His first successful play, *Once in a Lifetime* (1930), was the beginning of a 10-year collaboration with the playwright GEORGE S. KAUFMAN. Among their other plays are *You Can't Take It with You* (1936), which won a Pulitzer Prize; *I'd Rather Be Right* (1937); *The Man Who Came to Dinner* (1939); and *George Washington Slept Here* (1940). Hart also collaborated on MUSICALS with composers Irving BERLIN (*Face the Music,* 1932), Cole PORTER (*Jubilee,* 1935), and Kurt Weill and Ira Gershwin (*Lady in the Dark,* 1941).

After World War II, Hart wrote *Winged Victory* (1943) and *Light up the Sky* (1948), among other plays. He also wrote movie scripts, including *Gentleman's Agreement* (1947), which won an Academy Award, and *Hans Christian Anderson* (1952). In 1956 he directed the long-running Broadway hit *My Fair Lady,* for which he won a Tony award, and followed this up with directing *Camelot* (1960), just a year before his death.

Reference: Moss Hart, *Act One: An Autobiography* (New York: Vintage Books, 1976, ©1959).

Haworth, Walter Norman (1883–1950)

British chemist and Nobel laureate. Born in the village of Chorley, England, on March 19, 1883, Haworth attended school only until the age of 14, when he went to work in his father's linoleum factory. He later attended the universities of Manchester and Göttingen, Germany, and then taught chemistry at the Imperial College in South Kensington, London.

From 1920 until 1925, Haworth was a professor of organic chemistry at Armstrong College (now King's College) at the University of Durham, then occupied the chair as Mason Professor of Chemistry at the University of Birmingham from 1925 until his retirement in 1949. At Birmingham, writes editor Tyler Wasson, "Haworth directed research into the structure of monosaccharides (simple sugars) and oligosaccharides, the somewhat more complex sugars built from a small number of simple sugars." During the 1920s and 1930s, he investigated vitamin C and, in similar work, synthesized ascorbic acid. For this work, he received the 1937 Nobel Prize in chemistry which he shared with Paul KARRER, who had accomplished similar work on vitamins A and B_2. In the award presentation, Haworth's investigations into vitamin C were said to have "open[ed] the way to the artificial production of the compound, a thing of very great importance in the case of vitamins which do occur in nature only in a state of very great dilution."

During World War II, even though he suffered from ill health, Haworth worked on British research into the atomic bomb, while simultaneously trying to find vaccines for tuberculosis and pneumonia. For the former work, he was knighted in 1947. On March 18, 1950, Haworth died at his home. He had been presented with several major honors in his field, including the Longstaff Medal of the British Chemical Society in 1933 and the Royal Medal of the Royal Society in 1942.

References: Barbara Edmanson, "Haworth, Walter Norman, Sir" in Bernard S. and June H. Schlessinger, eds., *The Who's Who of Nobel Prize Winners* (Phoenix, Ariz.: Oryx, 1986), 14; Sheldon J. Kopperl, "Haworth, Walter Norman" in Charles Coulston Gillespie, ed. in chief, *Dictionary of Scientific Biography* (New York: Charles Scribner's Sons, 1980–90), 5: 184–86; Thomas Watson MacCallum and Stephen Taylor, eds., *The Nobel Prize-Winners and the Nobel Foundation, 1901–1937* (Zurich, Switzerland: Central European Times Publishing, 1938), 167; Tyler Wasson, ed., *Nobel Prize Winners: An H. W. Wilson Biographical Dictionary* (New York: H. W. Wilson, 1987), 422–23.

Hays Office

Organization, founded in 1922, which oversaw production and quality standards in the making of MOTION PICTURES. In the midst of such scandals as the suicide of actress Peg Entwhistle and the drug-induced death of actor Wallace Reid, as well as the rampant use of drugs in HOLLYWOOD, in 1922 Louis B. MAYER, the head of Metro-Goldwyn-Mayer, feared that the government would step in and try to regulate filmmaking. With the support of other studio heads, he formed the Motion Picture Producers and Distributors of America (MPPDA), to clean up the image of films. When the media questioned Mayer's reign over the group, the MPPDA decided to hire an outsider reputable enough to establish a code of conduct among filmmakers without being questioned. The first, and only, man to be approached for the position was Will Hays, postmaster general in the HARDING administration. Hays was directed to establish a code that would produce "human, heart-warming pictures" that were not sensational and did not appeal to Americans' prurient interests.

Hays would have remained an obscure lawyer in Indiana had he not been chosen as chair of the Republican National Committee in 1918 to help the Republicans win back the White House, which had been in Democratic hands since 1913. For his work during the 1920 election, which helped elect Senator Warren G. Harding of Ohio to the presidency, Hays was awarded the prize most coveted by persons wanting to "dole out" the patronage in the new administration—that of postmaster general. He had barely begun in this new job when he was tapped by the movie studio heads in Hollywood. On March 4, 1922, Hays officially became the head of the MPPDA, and served for the next 23 years. Perhaps his most famous decision came when he banned comedian Fatty ARBUCKLE, who had been accused (but later acquitted) of raping a girl who died, from making further pictures.

In his code of standards, Hays directed that filmmakers could not show the inside of a woman's thigh, and that drinking and other vices could not be displayed. Blood and dead bodies would be excluded as well. Any films that did not adhere to the code did not get the Hays Office seal of approval, in effect banning it from public display. Yet, although most of the directors in Hollywood were intimidated by Hays and his code, some stood against it. Cecil B. DE MILLE, dismissing the code as unenforceable, turned out one of the most violent pictures of the period, *The Ten Commandments,* in 1923. German director Ernst Lubitsch, afraid that he would be banned if he tried anything overt, instead peppered his films with sexual innuendoes. When Hays demanded that David O. Selznick change the famous line in GONE WITH THE WIND—replacing "Frankly my dear, I don't give a damn" with "Frankly my dear, I don't care"—Selznick left the expletive in and later paid a stiff fine.

In 1945, Hays was succeeded as head of the office that bore his name by Eric A. Johnston, an industrialist, who changed the name of the MPPDA to the Motion Picture Association of America (MPAA).

References: Gerald C. Gardner, *The Censorship Papers: Movie Censorship Letters from the Hays Office, 1934–1968* (New York: Dodd, Mead, 1987); Raymond Moley, *The Hays Office* (Indianapolis: Bobbs-Merrill, 1945).

Heisenberg, Werner Karl (1901–1976)

German physicist and Nobel laureate "for the creation of quantum mechanics, the application of which has, among other things, led to the discovery of the allotropic forms of hydrogen." Born in Würzburg, Germany, on December 5, 1901, he received his doctorate at the University of Göttingen in 1923. From 1924 to 1970 he worked as a professor of physics at the University of Copenhagen, the University of Leipzig, the University of Berlin, the University of Göttingen, and the University of Munich. During his early career, Heisenberg worked on quantum mechanics. Writes biographer Linda Arny, "He is probably better known for his formulation in 1927 of the uncertainty principle that bears his name, which states that it is

impossible *simultaneously* to determine both the position and the momentum of a particle." For this work, Heisenberg was awarded the 1932 Nobel Prize in physics. He accepted his prize in 1933.

Heisenberg continued to work on the problems of the atom for the remainder of his career. He died on February 1, 1976.

References: Linda Arny, "Heisenberg, Werner Karl" in Bernard S. and June H. Schlessinger, eds., *The Who's Who of Nobel Prize Winners* (Phoenix, Ariz.: Oryx, 1986), 161; Thomas Watson MacCallum and Stephen Taylor, eds., *The Nobel Prize-Winners and the Nobel Foundation, 1901–1937* (Zurich, Switzerland: Central European Times Publishing, 1938), 97.

Hemingway, Ernest (1895–1961)

American writer Pulitzer Prize winner, and Nobel laureate, noted for his many works of fiction based on subjects of major concern in the interwar years, during which he was a leading member of the American expatriate community in Paris. Born on July 21, 1895, in Oak Park, Illinois, he was the son of Clarence Hemingway, a physician who suffered from longtime depression and took his own life in 1928. After graduating from high school in 1917, Hemingway took a job as a reporter on the *Kansas City Star.* The following May, he was sent by the American Red Cross to serve as an ambulance driver for wounded soldiers. He was wounded that July, and while in hospital he fell in love with an older American nurse, who dismissed his advances, breaking Hemingway's heart.

Hemingway returned to the United States and married his first wife, Elizabeth Hardley Richard. They moved to Paris, where for a time Hemingway worked as a reporter for the *Toronto Star.* While in Paris, he joined the American expatriate community there, which consisted of such writers as Ezra POUND, F. Scott FITZGERALD, and Gertrude STEIN, among others. After some years of inactivity, he published a small work, *In Our Time* (1925), and, the following year, his first major novel, *The Sun Also Rises* (1926). In 1927, he published a book of short stories, *Men without Women,* which included the famed short story "Hills Like White Elephants," dealing with the controversial subject of abortion. Richardson and Hemingway divorced in 1927, after which he married Pauline Marie Pfeiffer (divorced in 1940). In 1928, he returned to the United States, settling in Key West, Florida. Hemingway divorced and married again: Martha Ellis Gellhorn (married 1940; divorced 1945) and Mary Welsh (married 1946; widowed 1961).

Perhaps his most famous work is *A Farewell to Arms* (1929), a novel of love and war based on Hemingway's experiences as an ambulance driver in World War I. During the interwar years, he also published *Death in the*

Afternoon (1932), a work on bullfighting in Spain; a series of short stories in *Winner Take Nothing* (1933); as well as the short stories "The Snows of Kilimanjaro" (1936) and "The Short Happy Life of Francis Macomber" (1936), both based on his experiences during a safari hunt in Africa. In 1937, Hemingway went to Spain to cover the SPANISH CIVIL WAR as a correspondent. While there, he took notes that led to some of his most famous novels and short stories: *The Fifth Column* (1939), *First Forty-Nine Stories* (1938), and *For Whom the Bell Tolls* (1940).

During World War II, Hemingway served again as a war correspondent and covered the D-Day landings in June 1944. In 1953 he won the Pulitzer Prize for his novella *The Old Man and the Sea* (1952). In 1954, he was awarded the Nobel Prize for Literature for his "powerful, stylemaking mastery of the art of modern narration . . . and for his influence on contemporary style."

In the last years of his life, Hemingway battled severe depression; on May 2, 1961, he killed himself with a shotgun blast to the head.

References: Charles A. Fenton, *The Apprenticeship of Ernest Hemingway: The Early Years* (New York: Farrar, Straus & Young, 1954); Linda Wagner-Martin, *Ernest Hemingway: A Reference Guide* (Boston: G. K. Hall, 1976); Earl H. Rovit, *Ernest Hemingway* (New York: Twayne Publishers, 1963); Peter L. Hays, *Ernest Hemingway* (New York: Continuum, 1990); "Hemingway Dead of Shotgun Wound; Wife Says He Was Cleaning Weapon," *New York Times*, July 3, 1961, p. 1.

Henderson, Arthur (1863–1935)

British politician, peace advocate, and Nobel laureate. Biographer Irwin Abrams calls Henderson "one of the most tragic figures among the peace laureates." Born in Glasgow, Scotland, on September 13, 1863, Henderson was educated briefly at St. Mary's School in Newcastle. A laborer for much of his early life, he was involved in trade unionism until 1903, when he entered Parliament in London. Eight years later, at the age of 48, he became the secretary of the Labour Party, serving until 1934. During World War I, he served briefly in Prime Minister David LLOYD GEORGE's War Cabinet. He was instrumental in influencing the majority of the Labour Party to support the government's war policies.

In 1924, Henderson was named home secretary in the first Labour government under Ramsay MACDONALD. Five years later, Henderson was selected as secretary for foreign affairs in MacDonald's second government, which held office until 1935, and it was during this period that he cultivated many of the contacts he had made during the early 1920s, when as a leader in the Labour Party he advocated European reconciliation and peace. He called on the Allies to lessen REPARATIONS demands against the Germans, advocated the faster evacuation of Allied troops

from German soil, and personally attended sessions of the LEAGUE OF NATIONS, serving as president of the League Council itself in 1931. Biographer David Lukowitz writes, "[Henderson] envisaged the League becoming a sort of superstate, armed with coercive powers of a financial and even military character, the very threat of which would probably deter aggression but could also in the final analysis be used to punish an aggressor." In 1934, he was awarded the Nobel Peace Prize, in the words of biographer Elizabeth Gwyn, "in recognition of the role he played as president of the League of Nations' World Disarmament Conference." Abrams writes, "When the Nobel Committee first placed him on its short list early in 1931, he was the British foreign secretary with a record of solid accomplishment in peaceful policies. . . . When Henderson came to Oslo to receive the Nobel Peace Prize in December 1934, however, Germany under HITLER had withdrawn from both the League and the [disarmament] conference, rearming rather than disarming was the order of the day, and the conference, although still formally in existence, was generally regarded as moribund."

In presenting the Nobel to him, Norwegian premier Johan Mowinckel called Henderson "a man who stands firm and faithful . . . of indestructible endurance and never-ending patience." Henderson accepted the Nobel in ill health; he died on October 20, 1935.

References: Elizabeth Gwyn, "Henderson, Arthur" in Bernard S. and June H. Schlessinger, eds., *The Who's Who of Nobel Prize Winners* (Phoenix, Ariz.: Oryx, 1986), 136; Irwin Abrams, *The Nobel Peace Prize and the Laureates: An Illustrated Biographical History, 1901–1987* (Boston: G. K. Hall & Co., 1988), 123–25; Mary Agnes Hamilton, "Henderson, Arthur" in Sir Leslie Stephen and Sir Sidney Lee et al., eds., *The Dictionary of National Biography* (Oxford: Oxford University Press, 1917–1993), 4: 417–20; David C. Lukowitz, "Henderson, Arthur" in Warren F. Kuehl, ed., *Biographical Dictionary of Internationalists* (Westport, Conn.: Greenwood, 1983), 326–28; Thomas Watson MacCallum and Stephen Taylor, eds., *The Nobel Prize-Winners and the Nobel Foundation, 1901–1937* (Zurich: Central European Times Publishing, 1938), 383; Peter Clarke, "Government and Politics in England: Realignment and Readjustment" in Christopher Haigh, ed., *The Cambridge Historical Encyclopedia of Great Britain and Ireland* (Cambridge: Cambridge University Press, 1985), 294.

Henie, Sonja (1912–1969)

Norwegian figure skater and motion picture actress, famed particularly during the interwar years. Born in Oslo, Norway, on April 18, 1912, she was trained to be a ballet dancer, but soon turned to the ice. Skating was a formulaic sport at the time in which new moves were frowned upon; Henie changed it radically by incorporating exciting and fanciful movements. She was the world women's amateur skating champion from 1927 to 1936; starting at the 1924 Winter Olympics at Chamonix, France, and continuing through the 1936 winter games at Garmisch-Partenkirchen in Germany—where she performed a Nazi salute that dogged her throughout her career—she won three gold medals. In 1936, Henie turned professional; she appeared in numerous films with an ice-skating theme, including *One in a Million* (1936), *Thin Ice* (1937), *My Lucky Star* (1938), and, her most famous, *Sun Valley Serenade* (1941)—all of which made her a popular star. Married three times, she became an American citizen in 1941. Her third husband, Norwegian shipowner Niels Onstad, founded with her the Henie and Onstad Foundation and Centre for Modern Art in Blommenholm, near Oslo, Norway.

Henie was on an airplane returning to Oslo on October 12, 1969, when she died of a heart attack.

See also OLYMPIC GAMES—1924: Chamonix Winter Games; 1928: St. Moritz Winter Games; 1932: Lake Placid Winter Games.

References: Sonja Henie, *Wings on My Feet* (New York: Prentice-Hall, 1940); Raymond Strait, with Leif Henie, *Queen of Ice, Queen of Shadows: The Unsuspected Life of Sonja Henie* (New York: Stein & Day, 1985).

Herriot, Édouard (1872–1957)

Premier of France (1924–25, 1932). Born in the village of Troyes, France, on July 5, 1872, he was educated at the École Normale Supérieure and the Lycée Louis le Grand. In 1904, he entered French political life when he was elected mayor of Lyon, he served his nation's government from 1905 until his death, except for the period from 1942 to 1945, when he was imprisoned by the German occupiers of France. A Radical Socialist, he served in the national Senate (1912–19), and in the Chamber of Deputies from 1919. After serving as premier, he was president of the Chamber of Deputies (1936–40). However, his most important work may have been as foreign minister (June–December 1932), when he attempted to deal with the GREAT DEPRESSION in Europe. His ministry, which included a dual role as premier, fell when the Chamber of Deputies refused to pay the December installment of war REPARATIONS to the United States.

When France was invaded by Germany, Herriot refused to vote in the Chamber to allow Marshal Philippe Pétain to take over as head of the German-backed Vichy government. When Herriot protested Pétain's 1942 decision to dissolve the Chamber and the Senate, he was arrested and deported to Germany, where he spent the remainder of the war until freed by Allied troops in April 1945. He then resumed his public life until his retirement in 1954.

Herriot died in Lyon on March 26, 1957.

Édouard Herriot *(CORBIS/Bettmann)*

References: Sabine Jessner, *Édouard Herriot: Patriarch of the Republic* (New York: Haskell House Publishers, 1974); Sabine Jessner, "Herriot, Édouard" in Warren F. Kuehl, ed., *Biographical Dictionary of Internationalists* (Westport, Conn.: Greenwood, 1983), 328–30.

Hertz, Gustav Ludwig (1887–1975)

German physicist and Nobel laureate. Born in Hamburg, Germany, on July 22, 1887, he was educated at the Universities of Göttingen, Berlin, and Munich, and received his doctorate from the University of Berlin in 1911. During the 1920s, he worked as a researcher at the University of Berlin, at the Philips Incandescent Lamp Factory in the Netherlands, and at the University of Halle in Germany. During this decade, he investigated the atomic structure, some of the earliest work on this subject. Writes biographer Frank Kellerman, "Hertz, in his earliest research, worked on the infrared absorption of CO_2 and the ionization potentials of several gases. His study of the relationships between electron energy losses in collisions and spectral lines provided needed data for [Niels] BOHR to develop his theory of atomic structure and for [Max] Planck to develop his ideas on quantum theory." For this work, which eventually led to the understanding of the structure of the atom, Hertz was the corecipient (with James FRANCK) of the 1925 Nobel Prize in physics.

After the Nazis came to power, Hertz, though a German Jew, was allowed to become the director of the research laboratory at the Seimens and Halske Company in Berlin until the end of World War II. After the war, he remained on the eastern side of the German division, and went to the Soviet Union to work at a research institution in Sukhumi on the Black Sea until 1954. In 1955, he returned to Germany, and went to work at the Karl Marx University in Leipzig until his retirement in 1961. Hertz died in Berlin on October 30, 1975.

References: Frank Kellerman, "Hertz, Gustav Ludwig" in Bernard S. and June H. Schlessinger, eds., *The Who's Who of Nobel Prize Winners* (Phoenix, Ariz.: Oryx, 1986), 158; Thomas Watson MacCallum and Stephen Taylor, eds., *The Nobel Prize-Winners and the Nobel Foundation, 1901–1937* (Zurich: Central European Times Publishing, 1938), 85.

Hertzog, James Barry Munnik (1866–1942)

Boer general and South African prime minister (1924–39). Born near Wellington, in the Cape Colony (now South Africa), on April 3, 1866, Hertzog, known throughout his life as J. B. M. Hertzog, studied law at Victoria College and Amsterdam University, then practiced in Pretoria from 1892 to 1895. In the latter year he was named to the Supreme Court of the Orange Free State, rising to the post of assistant chief commandant of the Orange Free State troops, leading the fight against British forces during the Boer War. Although Hertzog wished to fight on when the war was clearly lost, he eventually capitulated and signed the Treaty of Vereeniging in May 1902.

Hertzog led the struggle in trying to establish a nation-state as the Orangia-Unie (Orange Union); when the state became independent in 1907, he was named a cabinet member. In 1910, when the Union of South Africa was formed, Hertzog was taken into the national cabinet by General Louis Botha, the first prime minister, but differences with Botha soon caused a split between the two men. Hertzog then founded the National Party, which advocated a break with the British Commonwealth. Botha's death in 1919 left a leadership vacuum, and in 1924 Hertzog formed the first Nationalist government. After Hertzog took power in 1924, there were fears that he would sever all ties to Great Britain. Although he ordered that the South African flag contain no symbols of British identity, he served as South Africa's representative to the IMPERIAL CONFERENCE in London in 1926. There, he was a leading spokesman for the Commonwealth nations that desired some form of independence, and his stand led to the enactment by the British Parliament of the STATUTE OF WESTMINSTER in 1931. An avowed racist, as prime minister Hertzog instituted various methods of racial segregation, demanding that all black South Africans be separated from the rest of South African society. This policy of *apartheid* ("apartness"), while not formally put into place until after World War II, would later serve to isolate South Africa from the family of nations. Under Hertzog's leadership in 1930, white women were granted the right to vote.

Hertzog served as prime minister until 1939, when he argued for neutrality in World War II, but Jan Christiaan SMUTS, the leader of the opposition, called for alignment with Great Britain. When Hertzog's motion to remain neutral was defeated by Parliament, he resigned, and was replaced by Smuts. He then joined the opposition, but broke from them when Smuts called for equal rights between Afrikaners and the British South Africans. Retiring in 1940, he spent his remaining years in Pretoria. He died there on November 21, 1942.

References: Dr. D. W. Kruger, "Hertzog, James Barry Munnik" in W. J. De Kock, ed. in chief, *Dictionary of South African Biography* (Pretoria: Published for the National Council for Social Research, Department of Higher Education, by Nasionale Boekhandel BPK, 1968–77), 1: 366–79; Christiaan Maurits Van den Heever, *General J. B. M. Hertzog* (Johannesburg: A. P. B. Bookstore, 1946); Oswald Pirow, *James Barry Munnik Hertzog* (London: Allen, 1958).

Hess, Victor Franz (1883–1964)

Austrian-American physicist and Nobel laureate. Born in Waldstein, Austria, on June 24, 1883, Hess received his doctorate from the University of Graz in Austria in 1906, then served as a professor at the University of Graz, at the Vienna Veterinary College, and as director of research at the U.S. Radium Corporation in New York. During his early researches, he investigated radiation in the earth's atmosphere, which he called cosmic radiation. For this discovery, he was the corecipient (with Carl David ANDERSON) of the 1936 Nobel Prize in physics.

After winning the Nobel, Hess continued his research at the universities of Innsbruck and Graz in Austria, wrapping up his career at Fordham University in New York before he retired in 1958. Hess died in Mount Vernon, New York, on December 17, 1964.

References: Ralph Johnson, "Hess, Victor Franz" in Bernard S. and June H. Schlessinger, eds., *The Who's Who of Nobel Prize Winners* (Phoenix, Ariz.: Oryx, 1986), 162–63; Thomas Watson MacCallum and Stephen Taylor, eds., *The Nobel Prize–Winners and the Nobel Foundation, 1901–1937* (Zurich: Central European Times Publishing, 1938), 101–102; Tyler Wasson, ed., *Nobel Prize Winners: An H. W. Wilson Biographical*

Dictionary (New York: H. W. Wilson Company, 1987), 445–47; "Victor F. Hess, Physicist, Dies; Shared the Nobel Prize in 1936," *New York Times*, December 19, 1964, p. 29.

Heymans, Corneille-Jean-François (1892–1968)

Belgian physiologist and Nobel laureate "for his discovery of the role played by the sinus and aortic mechanisms in the regulation of respiration." Born in Ghent, Belgium, on March 28, 1892, he received his doctorate from the University of Ghent in 1920. From 1923 until his death, Heymans worked as a professor of pharmacology at the University of Ghent's J. F. Heymans School of Pharmacology, which had been founded by his father, Jean-François Heymans. From 1923 until 1938, Heymans worked on the cross-circulation of blood vessels, as well as other facets of animal and human anatomy. For this work, he was awarded the 1938 Nobel Prize in physiology and medicine. As Heymans was unable to attend the ceremonies, Professor G. Liljestrand, a member of the Staff of Professors of the Royal Caroline Institute, explained, in a statement on Heymans's accomplishments, "Heymans not only discovered the role, hitherto quite unknown, of certain organs (glomus caroticum and glomus aorticum), he also greatly enlarged our field of knowledge concerning the regulation of respiration. He showed that the various methods used for stimulating respiration had quite different mechanisms. . . . It seems likely that this increase in our knowledge of the chemo-regulation of respiration will also be of great use in research on a number of diseases."

Heymans continued to work on anatomy at the University of Ghent until his death on July 18, 1968.

References: Marlene Latuch and Carlyle Edwards, "Heymans, Corneille Jean François" in Bernard S. and June H. Schlessinger, eds., *The Who's Who of Nobel Prize Winners* (Phoenix, Ariz.: Oryx, 1986), 91; Tyler Wasson, ed., *Nobel Prize Winners: An H. W. Wilson Biographical Dictionary* (New York: H. W. Wilson Co., 1987).

Hill, Archibald Vivian (1886–1977)

English physiologist and Nobel laureate. Born in Bristol, England, on September 26, 1886, he received his master's degree from Cambridge University in 1906. He served in the British army during World War I, then worked at the University of Manchester from 1920 to 1923 and the University of London from 1923 until he retired in 1951. During these years, he investigated how muscles and nerve impulses function within the human body and how heat is produced in the muscles. For this groundbreaking work he was the corecipient (with Otto MEYERHOF) of the 1922 Nobel Prize in medicine and physiology.

From 1940 to 1945, Hill served in Parliament as a Conservative, representing Cambridge. He continued to

work on muscle research until his retirement in 1951. Hill died in Cambridge on June 3, 1977.

Reference: Barbara I. McNutt, "Hill, Archibald Vivian" in Bernard S. and June H. Schlessinger, eds., *The Who's Who of Nobel Prize Winners* (Phoenix, Ariz.: Oryx, 1986), 84.

Himmler, Heinrich (1900–1945)

German NAZI PARTY official, head of the Gestapo (1936–45). Born in Munich on October 7, 1900, he was the son of a teacher. He volunteered for duty during World War I but never served at the front or saw action. He received a degree in agriculture and got a job as an agricultural assistant. Himmler began to move toward a paramilitary ideology, however, and when the infant Workers' Party formed in Germany in 1922, he joined and was with party leader Adolf HITLER at the BEER HALL PUTSCH in 1923 (from this event he escaped serving any prison time).

In 1925, Himmler joined the reincarnation of the Workers' Party, known as the National Socialist or Nazi Party, and the following year was named the party's director of propaganda, serving in that post until 1930. He was then elected to the Reichstag and was named as chief of the Schutzstaffeln, or SS. In 1933, when Hitler rose to power, Himmler was only advanced to police chief of Munich. Yet as a loyal Nazi party member and insider in Hitler's circle, he gradually consolidated the police squads of the entire German nation under his command. He convinced Hitler that SA (Sturmabteilung) leader Ernst ROEHM was a danger to the Reich, and Hitler had Roehm (and hundreds of others) exterminated in the affair known as the Night of the Long Knives.

After the 1936 takeover of Austria in the ANSCHLUSS, Hitler placed the SS in charge of all Jewish affairs in areas controlled by the Reich. Once Himmler had established the Office of Jewish Emigration in Vienna to document all Jews, he himself set up the Mauthausen concentration camp near Linz, Austria, for Jews and other "undesirables." Under his command, the SS constituted *Junker* schools for teaching future generations in the goals of the Nazi Party and also monitored a vast network of concentration camps that stretched across Europe. After the start of World War II, Himmler was responsible for the rounding up, incarceration, and mass execution of millions of Jews, gypsies, and homosexuals. Yet as the war started going badly for Germany, he launched into secret negotiations with the Allies to surrender. Hitler discovered this treachery and had him expelled from the Nazi Party. After the war, Himmler tried to surrender to the government of Admiral Karl Doenitz, who headed Germany after Hitler's suicide. Doenitz refused to see Himmler. When the SS leader was discovered trying to slip into the British lines in disguise; he committed suicide on May 23, 1945.

References: Bradley F. Smith, *Heinrich Himmler: A Nazi in the Making, 1900–1926* (Stanford, Calif.: Hoover Institution Press, 1971); "Himmler, Heinrich" in Christian Zentner and Friedemann Bedürftig, eds., *Encyclopedia of the Third Reich* (New York: Macmillan, 1991), 1: 410–12; Richard Breitman, *The Architect of Genocide: Himmler and the Final Solution* (London: Bodley Head, 1991).

Hindenburg

German ZEPPELIN, whose spectacular destruction before a crowd at the Lakehurst Naval Station in New Jersey on May 6, 1937, ended the era of civilian travel by dirigible and terrorized the NAZI PARTY propaganda machine. The *Hindenburg* was the largest rigid airship ever constructed, at 804 feet (245 meters), and had a cost of $3.5 million. First launched at Friedrichshafen, Germany, in March 1936, the airship boasted a maximum speed of 84 mph (135 km/h) and a cruising speed of 78 mph (126 km/h), with a range of 8,000 miles, carrying up to 97 passengers and 61 crew. Because of a ban by the United States on the sale of helium to Nazi Germany, however, the blimp was lofted by highly flammable hydrogen gas. It was a recipe for a disaster.

On the Hindenburg's first flight of 1937, it left Germany carrying 97 passengers and crew. It was delayed in its docking at Lakehurst Naval Air Station for several hours because of a storm. After a few hours, the ship was cleared for landing, and at nearly 7:30 P.M. it made its way to Lakehurst. Several hundred spectators were in attendance, as was Herb Morrison, an announcer for WLS radio in Chicago. As Morrison described the landing to radio listeners, a spark flashed across the back of the blimp, and it exploded into a huge ball of flame, crumpling into a fiery mass. As passengers and crew jumped out of the gondola for their lives, heroic rescuers ran into the burning mass to save others. After just a few seconds, the burning white skeleton that had supported the *Hindenburg* came to the ground, consumed. Miraculously, of the 97 aboard only 35 were killed. One ground crewman also died.

In an investigation held in the United States, it was found that an atmospheric spark was responsible for the initial explosion. To this day, however, many speculate that a device designed to sabotage the ship was set off by anti-Nazi saboteurs.

References: Shelley Tanaka, *The Disaster of the Hindenburg* (New York: Scholastic/Madison Press, 1993); Jay Robert Nash, *Darkest Hours: A Narrative Encyclopedia of Worldwide Disasters from Ancient Times to the Present* (New York: Wallaby Books, 1977), 238–43; "33 Reported Killed as Hindenburg Explodes and Crashes to Earth in Flames at Lakehurst," *New York Herald-Tribune* (European edition), May 7, 1937, p. 1; Mariette DiChristina, "What Really Downed the Hindenburg," *Popular Science* 251, 5 (November 1997): 70–76.

Hindenburg, Paul von (1847–1934)

German military officer and politician, president (1925–34) during the rise and fall of the WEIMAR REPUBLIC. Born Paul Ludwig Hans Anton von Beckendorff und von Hindenburg in the village of Posen, Prussia, on October 2, 1847, he was the son of a military officer. He became a cadet at age 11 and later served in the Seven Weeks' War (the Austro-Prussian War of 1866) and in the Franco-Prussian War of 1870–71. He was eventually promoted to general and served on the German General Staff until his retirement in 1911. In 1914, however, he was reactivated to lead the German army in the East Prussian campaign in World War I, immediately helping to drive the Russians into horrendous losses on the eastern front. In 1916, when Kaiser Wilhelm II made Hindenburg a field marshal general, in charge of all German land forces, Hindenburg became one of the most powerful military commanders in history. When the war ended suddenly, Hindenburg's inferior officer, General Erich Ludendorff, was blamed for the defeat. With the collapse of the German government, Hindenburg supported the rightist government against the rise of the left. In June 1919, however, he retired again. From 1919 to 1925 he took no part in the Reich's politics.

Six years later, with the death of Friedrich EBERT (the German republic's first president), Hindenburg was asked by rightist parties to run for president. At age 77, he consented, and was narrowly elected over centrist Wilhelm Marx in 1925. When the GREAT DEPRESSION hit Germany hard in 1929, Hindenburg called for the Reichstag to deliver to him unconditional powers to combat it, and threatened to dissolve the body if it did not accede to his wishes. In July 1930 he dismissed the Reichstag, but the subsequent elections left the National Socialists with more power than before.

When Hindenburg's term expired in March 1932, he ran for a second term only because Adolf HITLER, the NAZI PARTY candidate, was running. Hindenburg billed himself as the only man who could stop a Nazi takeover. In the balloting, Hindenburg won 50 percent of the vote, with Hitler in second place with 30 percent and Communist candidate Ernst Thälmann in third with 13 percent. In the runoff, held the following month, Hindenburg won 53 percent, Hitler 37 percent, and Thälmann 10 percent. Hindenburg had stopped Hitler's rise to power, but not for long. In Reichstag elections that November, the Nazis won an overwhelming majority of seats, and Hindenburg was forced to deal with Hitler. Government paralysis left Hindenburg with only one choice: he yielded to the Nazi Party and named Hitler chancellor on January 30, 1933.

In the following months, Hitler shut the aged Hindenburg out of the government, and Hindenburg slowly descended into obscurity. On August 2, 1934, he died. Within days of his death, Hitler took over sole control of the government.

References: Rudolph Weterstetten, *The Biography of President von Hindenburg* (New York: Macmillan, 1930); Emil Ludwig (Eden and Cedar Paul, trans.), *Hindenburg* (Philadelphia: John C. Winston Co., 1935); Andreas Dorpalen, *Hindenburg and the Weimar Republic* (Princeton, N.J.: Princeton University Press, 1964); "Hindenburg Death Near; Hitler to Be Sole Ruler," *New York World-Telegram,* August 1, 1934, p. 1.

Hirohito (1901–1989)

Japanese emperor (1926–89), holds the distinction of being the modern national leader ruling the longest number of consecutive years. His reign oversaw Japan's turbulent interwar history, and he was the last of the World War II–era leaders to die. Born in Tokyo on April 29, 1901, Hirohito was the son of Crown Prince Yoshihito, whose reign name as Japanese emperor was Taisho (ruled 1912–26), and Princess Sadako. Emperor Taisho joined the Allies in World War I and brought Japan to world power status. In 1921 Hirohito became prince regent because of Taisho's mental illness. In 1926, Taisho died, and Hirohito assumed the throne. He called his reign *showa,* or "bright peace," an ironic name for this most turbulent period in Japan's history.

The first two decades of Hirohito's imperial reign were marked particularly by the rising militarism of the Japanese right, which was responsible for expansionist policies that led to the invasion of China and the establishment of the puppet state of Manchukuo in 1934, the outbreak of the Sino-Japanese War in 1937, and the eventual Japanese attack on the United States at Pearl Harbor on December 7, 1941.

On August 15, 1945, after the United States had dropped the atomic bombs on the Japanese cities of Hiroshima and Nagasaki, Hirohito's radio address to his subjects broadcast Japan's unconditional surrender in World War II. On September 2 he ordered all Japanese troops to lay down their arms. The new constitution of May 3, 1947, limited the emperor's powers to that of a constitutional monarch, making Hirohito a figurehead.

Hirohito died of old age on January 7, 1989, after serving as emperor for 73 years.

References: David A. Titus, "Taisho, Emperor" in Gen Itasaka, gen. ed., *Kodansha Encyclopedia of Japan* (Tokyo: Kodansha, 1983), 7: 305; Justus D. Doenecke, "Hirohito" in Anne Commire, ed., *Historic World Leaders* (Detroit: Gale Research, 1994), 1: 235–40; David Bergamini, *Japan's Imperial Conspiracy* (New York: Pocket Books, 1972); "Showa Era" in Dorothy Perkins, *Encyclopedia of Japan: Japanese History and Culture, From Abacus to Zori* (New York: Facts On File, 1991), 317; Nathaniel Thayer, "Hirohito" in Bruce W. Jentleson and Thomas G. Paterson, senior eds., *Encyclopedia of U.S. Foreign Relations* (New York: Oxford University Press, 1997), 2: 296.

Hitchcock, Alfred (1899–1980)

English film director, famed for several landmark and introspective films during the interwar period. Born in Leytonstone, England, on August 13, 1899, he was the son of a greengrocer. After receiving his education from St. Ignatius College in London, Hitchcock embarked on a career in show business by drawing advertising layouts for theaters. In 1919 he worked as a title card artist for the Famous Lasky Studios when it opened its London studio (title cards were used in silent films to display the actors' dialogue). Watching several directors produce motion pictures, Hitchcock learned how to edit and write scripts; by 1922 he was named assistant director at Lasky Studios. That same year, he directed a film that was never finished, *No. 13* (also known as *Mrs. Peabody*). Hitchcock moved to Gainsborough Pictures in 1923, and two years later directed *The Pleasure Garden* in Munich. He then directed *The Mountain Eagle* (also known as *Fear o'God,* 1926).

In 1927, Hitchcock directed what turned out to be one of the greatest and darkest thrillers of the silent era: *The Lodger* (also known as *The Case of Jonathan Drew* and *The Lodger: A Story of the London Fog*). In this psychotic and mesmerizing tale, based on the book by Marie Belloc-Lowndes, Hitchcock wove the story of a lodger in a London hotel who is accused of being Jack the Ripper and chased by a British police officer. Here, and in his subsequent films, including *Blackmail* (1929), his first talking film, *Murder!* (1930), and *The Man Who Knew Too Much* (1934), Hitchcock used dark shadows and the subtle link between sex and violence to illustrate his grim view of the world. Starting with *The Lodger,* he used his unique technique of inserting himself with small cameos into his pictures. (In *The Lodger,* he is seen at a desk in a newsroom and later in a crowd scene).

After directing the thrillers *The 39 Steps* (1935) and *The Lady Vanishes* (1938), Hitchcock went to Hollywood in 1938 to direct his first American feature, *Rebecca* (1939), which won the Best Picture Academy Award in 1940. Over the next four decades he directed such motion picture classics as *Saboteur* (1942), *Lifeboat* (1943), *Spellbound* (1943), *The Paradine Case* (1947), *Rope* (1948), *Dial M for Murder* (1954), *Rear Window* (1954), a "talking" version of *The Man Who Knew Too Much* (1956), *The Wrong Man* (1956), *Vertigo* (1958), *North by Northwest* (1959), *Psycho* (1960), *The Birds* (1963), and *Torn Curtain* (1966). He is known as a master of suspense and one of the greatest directors in film history. From 1955 to 1965 he hosted a popular television mystery program. Hitchcock's last film, *Family Plot,* appeared in 1976. He worked on a script for a film that was to be known as *The Short Night* from 1977 until his death. Named a Knight Commander of the British Empire in January 1980, Hitchcock died in Los Angeles, California, on April 29, 1980.

See also MOTION PICTURES, SILENT.

References: Gene D. Phillips, *Alfred Hitchcock* (Boston: Twayne Publishers, 1984); Donald Spoto, *The Art of Alfred Hitchcock: Fifty Years of His Motion Pictures* (New York: Hopkinson & Blake, 1976); Robert A. Harris and Michael S. Lasky, *The Films of Alfred Hitchcock* (Secaucus, N.J.: Citadel, 1976); Leonard Maltin, ed., *Movie and Video Guide 1996 Edition* (New York: Plume, 1995), 1022–23.

Hitler, Adolf (1889–1945)

Austrian-German dictator whose territorial aggressions pushed the world into World War II, which claimed some 60 million lives from 1939 to 1945. Born in the village of Branau, in Upper Austria, on April 20, 1889, Hitler was the son of a minor customs official. Although Hitler was a student of art and music, he never did well in school, and he ultimately failed in his secondary school education. Because of this failure, his application to the Vienna Academy of Arts, where he intended to study painting, was rejected. Hitler painted and sold postcards in Vienna from 1906 until 1913, and he even accepted charity from the state during this time.

Hitler believed that Germany was the most powerful military power on the European continent; this idea bred in him a strong sense of German nationalism. In 1913, to quench this thirst for Germanic culture, he migrated to Munich, then the center of German artistic life. When World War I exploded in August 1914, Hitler enlisted in a Bavarian regiment that saw extended action on the Western Front. He was twice decorated for bravery, receiving the Iron Cross, and was promoted to *Gefreiter* (the equivalent of lance corporal, with the same rank as a private first class in the U.S. Army). He was wounded in November 1918.

Returning to a defeated Germany, Hitler came to believe that Jews were most responsible for Germany's defeat at the hands of the Allies. On this belief he joined the ultranationalist German Workers' Party, which developed into the National Socialist German Workers' Party, known as the NAZI PARTY. A strong orator who synthesized the group's words into action, Hitler rose quickly to become party president in 1921. After the party released a manifesto of their beliefs, they organized themselves as a veterans' group, with brown-shirted regulars to harass people not embracing party tenets. They believed that a coup against the WEIMAR government was needed, and to these ends in November 1923, with the aid of German General Eric Ludendorff, attempted the BEER HALL PUTSCH in Munich. The Weimar government fought the takeover

attempt, and for the time being beat back Hitler and his minions. Hitler was captured, tried, found guilty of conspiring against the state, and sentenced to five years in prison. There, he dictated to his secretary Rudolf Hess the manuscript that ultimately became MEIN KAMPF (My struggle). In 1924, after only nine months, Hitler was released on parole.

By this time the German economy had stabilized, and the German Workers' Party was on the fringe. When the GREAT DEPRESSION hit Germany in 1929 and 1930, however, the discontent it caused helped ensure the success of Hitler and his comrades. In 1928 the party sponsored candidates for the German Reichstag and won seven seats; in 1932 this number rose to 230, just 74 short of a majority, although Hitler himself was defeated in that year's election by Paul von HINDENBURG. To check the power of the Nazis in the Reichstag, moderates Franz von Papen and Kurt von Schleicher were named as chancellors during this period. But the worsening depression, coupled with riots between the Nazis and the Communists, led von Hindenburg, on January 30, 1933, to accede to the Nazis by naming Hitler as chancellor. In this new government, the Nazis were the minority in the Reichstag. Von Hindenburg hoped that the more conservative majority would be a check on Hitler's authority. Soon after Hitler came to power, however, he forced the Reichstag to enact a series of laws that he claimed would be used to address growing national emergencies. Hitler then used these new powers to outlaw opposition parties and to suppress the right to free speech. When some Nazis criticized Hitler's economic policies, they were liquidated in the so-called Night of the Long Knives. With the death of von Hindenburg in 1934, Hitler consolidated the offices of Reichpresident and chancellor in the all-powerful position of *Führer,* or leader.

As outlined in Hitler's *Mein Kampf,* his ultimate goal was to avenge the humiliation of Germany that the Allies

Adolf Hitler gives the Nazi salute, 1932.
(CORBIS/Bettmann)

had pursued in the TREATY OF VERSAILLES. Determined to build Germany into a military machine and to exact revenge over the European powers that had delineated Versailles, Hitler was able to use the cover of rearmament to help gradually rebuild the German economy. In 1933, at Hitler's command, German representatives at the GENEVA DISARMAMENT CONFERENCE declared that Germany would no longer abide by Versailles's arms-limitation provision. After reinstituting universal military training and establishing youth corps based on early Nazi group cells, Hitler demanded in 1936 that areas once belonging to Germany be returned. He first occupied the Rhineland; then, in a bold move, he gave an ultimatum that Austria be taken over. In October 1938 Hitler initiated a crisis when he called for the German occupation of the Sudetenland, the German-speaking areas of Czechoslovakia. British prime minister Neville CHAMBERLAIN bargained for peace with his APPEASEMENT offer: Germany would be allowed to occupy the Sudetenland in exchange for a promise that no further territory would be demanded. Hitler signed the deal, knowing full well that he would not keep his word. A crisis had been averted, but only for the time being.

After Hitler's foreign minister Joachim von RIBBENTROP signed a pact with the Soviet Union, Hitler decided to invade Poland and split that nation into two parts: the western half for Germany (as well as the port of Danzig), the eastern half for the Soviet Union. On September 1, 1939, German troops invaded Poland, setting off World War II; England and France declared war against Nazi Germany. German forces attacked and occupied France in 1940, in effect taking over much of the European continent. The only object now in Hitler's way was his archenemy the Soviet Union. On his command, in June 1941, Germany launched Operation Barbarossa, the invasion of the Soviet Union, setting off one of the most significant and expansive military struggles in world history. Like Napoleon a century and a half before, however, the German army became bogged down in the Russian winter and took enormous losses. This operation represents a turning point in World War II, and slowly the tide of the war began to turn against Nazi Germany.

Attempting to head off the creation of a western front, German troops defended the French coast against an Allied attack. The assault came on June 6, 1944, D-Day, at Normandy; that beachhead soon grew to threaten Hitler's troops. About this time, a group of former Nazi sympathizers failed in their attempt to assassinate Hitler; he was merely wounded, however, and the conspirators were arrested and executed. Hitler became besieged with this two-front war: As the Red Army from the east and the Allied armies from the west closed in, he became more isolated in his bunker in Berlin.

On April 30, 1945, as Soviet troops battled to the outskirts of Berlin, Hitler married his longtime companion Eva Braun. The two then committed suicide; Hitler with a shot to the head and Braun with poison. They were carried outside the chancellery building, where aides poured gasoline on their corpses and immolated them. When Soviet troops eclipsed the compound, they found a hole with two burned skeletons. Hitler's death and the collapse of Nazi Germany ended one of the most treacherous periods in human history. Hitler's henchmen were put on trial at Nuremberg, but Hitler himself has been convicted of starting a war in which some 60 million people were killed, including six million Jews and others who were slaughtered in the Nazi concentration camps. Perhaps there is no other figure in the 20th century so reviled and condemned.

See also GOEBBELS, Josef; RIBBENTROP, Joachim von; ROEHM, Ernst.

References: John Toland, *Adolf Hitler* (Garden City, N.Y.: Doubleday, 1976); Wyndham Lewis, *Hitler* (London: Chatto & Windus, 1931); Joachim C. Fest (Richard and Clara Winston, trans.), *Hitler* (New York: Harcourt Brace Jovanovich, 1974); Harry Trimhorn, "Golden Anniversary of Horror," *Newsday* (New York), January 30, 1983, pp. 4, 13; William Lawrence Shirer, *Berlin Diary: The Journal of a Foreign Correspondent, 1934–1941* (New York: A. A. Knopf, 1941); Robert Edwin Herzstein, comp., *Adolf Hitler and the Third Reich, 1933–1945* (Boston: Houghton Mifflin, 1971); Ada Petrova and Peter Watson, *The Death of Hitler: The Full Story with New Evidence from Secret Russian Archives* (New York: Norton, 1995).

Ho Chi Minh (1890–1969)

Vietnamese political leader, revolutionary, and nationalist, founder of the movement for Vietnamese independence from France. Born Nguyen Sinh Cang in the central Vietnamese village of Kim Lien in Nghe An province on May 19, 1890, he was the son of Nguyen Sinh Cungon Sac, a nationalist devoted to ending France's influence in Indochina who later changed his son's name to Nguyen That Thanh. Ho received a common education and attended secondary school before working on a French passenger liner as a kitchen helper beginning in 1911. After touring the world for several years, in 1917 he settled in Paris and changed his name to Nguyen Ai Quoc (Nguyen the Patriot), becoming a noted agitator to end the French colonial hold on Vietnam.

After World War I, Ho traveled to VERSAILLES in 1919, where he begged for an audience with U.S. President Woodrow WILSON. He implored Wilson to apply his own Fourteen Points, which called for the right of self-determination for colonized peoples, to the question of the French occupation of Vietnam. But Ho was barred from the conference, and his anger against both the French and the Americans grew. Moscow's Bolshevik government, looking for allies at this time, approved of Ho's call for independence if he would help them bring communism to Vietnam. Ho agreed and while in Paris, he founded the French Communist Party. In 1924 the Soviets sent him to Canton, China, where another marxist nationalist, MAO TSE-TUNG, was openly fighting the American-backed government. Ho attempted to organize a Communist party among the Vietnamese nationalist exiles in Canton, but he was arrested and deported. Six years later, however, he returned to China to found the Indochinese Communist Party (ICP), and he opened a branch office in Hong Kong, where he served as a local representative of the Communist International (Comintern). For several years Ho moved between Moscow and China, eventually returning to Vietnam in 1941 to found the League for the Independence of Vietnam, also known as the Vietminh. In 1942 he was arrested, but was released after a year. At this time he changed his name to Ho Chi Minh ("He who enlightens").

In August 1945, as the Japanese were surrendering after the brutal U.S. assault of two atomic weapons and Japanese control over Southeast Asia was evaporating, Ho quickly moved into the power vacuum. With his followers, he occupied the northern city of Hanoi and declared Vietnamese independence standing in a Hanoi square on September 2, 1945. As the first words of this declaration, however, Ho quoted the Declaration of Independence of the United States: "All men are created equal. They are endowed by their Creator with certain inalienable rights; that among these are Life, Liberty, and the Pursuit of Happiness."

Ho's government, of which he was president (1945–69), had the support of the United States. It was threatened from the start by China, which occupied the northern reaches of Vietnam under conditions of the Potsdam Agreement, and the French, who desired to pick up the threads of their colonial empire where they had left it in 1941. Recognizing this latter threat, Ho in March 1946 signed an agreement with the French recognizing the Democratic Republic of Vietnam as a free state within the colony of Indochina. Within a year, however, the relationship between the two parties had disintegrated and an eight-year war against the French colonial forces ensued. The French were ultimately defeated and the subsequent peace treaty split the area into North Vietnam, controlled by Ho, and South Vietnam, a non-Communist entity. Ho's efforts to destabilize the south led to U.S. intervention and the start of the 10-year Vietnam War in the late 1950s.

Ho spent much of his final 25 years almost hidden from the outside world. On September 3, 1969, he died in his Hanoi home. The Vietnamese city of Saigon was renamed Ho Chi Minh City in his honor.

References: Mark Bradley, "Ho Chi Minh" in Anne Commire, ed., *Historic World Leaders* (Detroit: Gale Research, 1994), 1: 241–44; Thomas E. Hachey and Ralph E. Weber, eds., *The Awakening of a Sleeping Giant: Third World Leaders and National Liberation* (Huntington, N.Y.: R. E. Kriger Publishing Co., 1981); David Halberstam, *Ho* (New York: McGraw-Hill, 1987).

Holiday, Billie (1915–1959)

American singer, known as "Lady Day," who dominated the American JAZZ vocal from the 1930s through the early 1950s. Holiday was born Eleanora Fagan in Baltimore, Maryland, on April 7, 1915; her parents divorced soon after. At age six she worked at a Baltimore "house of ill repute," where she first heard the music of Louis ARMSTRONG and Bessie SMITH. After a difficult childhood, Holiday moved with her mother to New York City, where in 1930 she began singing in local bars.

Soon discovered for her lyrical voice, Holiday (by now called "Billie") made recordings in the mid-1930s with bandleaders Benny Goodman, Teddy Wilson, and Count Basie. These early performances included such hits as "Riffin' the Scotch" and "Your Mother's Son-in-law." In 1937 she toured with Count Basie's and Artie Shaw's orchestras. Holiday appeared in such New York clubs as the Onyx, where her dramatic style and personal approach to song wowed the crowds.

Throughout the 1940s and 1950s, Holiday performed in clubs and cabarets across the United States. She embarked on a widely praised European tour in 1956, but the frenzied pace of her career coupled with ill health caused by drug addiction led to her untimely decline. Holiday's autobiography, *Lady Sings the Blues*, was published in 1956. Her final performance was at New York's Phoenix Theater in May 1959. She died on July 17 of that year at age 44.

References: Helen Oakley Dance, "Holiday, Billie" in Allen Johnson and Dumas Malone et al., eds., *Dictionary of American Biography* (New York: Charles Scribner's Sons, 1930–95), 6: 299–300; John White, *Billie Holiday: Her Life & Times* (Tunbridge Wells, England: Spellmount, 1987); John Chilton, *Billie's Blues: A Survey of Billie Holiday's Career, 1933–1959* (London: Quartet Books, 1975).

Hollywood

U.S. city in southern California that became the heart of the motion picture industry during the interwar period. Hollywood's economic organization and the giant studio system that would rule the film industry for the next 50 years was established in the 1920s. By the mid-1920s the United States had become the world's most prolific producer of films, and the major studios were incorporated in these years: Warner Brothers Pictures, MGM (after the merger of Metro Pictures, Samuel GOLDWYN Pictures, and the Louis B. MAYER Pictures Company), Columbia Pictures, MCA (the Music Corporation of America), and

RKO Pictures. The Academy of Motion Picture Arts and Sciences was founded in 1927.

During the interwar period the Hollywood studios exerted their influence over actors, writers, directors, and producers, introducing the star system and the making of Hollywood royalty. In the silent film era of the 1920s and the lavish glamour of the 1930s, movies were made with specific stars in mind. They included, among others, Clara BOW, Lon CHANEY, Charlie CHAPLIN, Maurice Chevalier, Claudette Colbert, Gary Cooper, Joan Crawford, Marlene DIETRICH, Marie DRESSLER, Douglas FAIRBANKS, Clark GABLE, Greta GARBO, Jean Harlow, Al JOLSON, Buster KEATON, Stan LAUREL and Oliver HARDY, Myrna Loy, Bela Lugosi, Robert Montgomery, Mary Pickford, William Powell, Norma Shearer, Gloria Swanson, Norma Talmadge, Spencer Tracy, and Rudolph VALENTINO. Such legendary directors as Frank Capra, Cecil B. DEMILLE, John Ford, D. W. Griffith, Josef von Sternberg, and William Wyler flourished in Hollywood during these years. They brought to life such popular genres as the Western, science fiction, mysteries, and MUSICALS.

With the advent of "talkies" in the late 1920s, all the studios were forced to follow suit, and the 1930s became the decade of the sound revolution. In this "Golden Age," five major studios dominated the Hollywood film industry: Twentieth Century-Fox (formed from the merger of Twentieth Century Pictures and the Fox Film Corporation), MGM, Paramount, Warner Bros., and RKO. Two smaller studios, Columbia (headed by Harry Cohn) and Universal, also held their own. So-called "B studios," such as Republic Pictures and Monogram, also existed. Each studio developed its own particular style. For example, Warner Bros. produced "social problem" and gangster pictures, introducing such major stars as Humphrey Bogart, James CAGNEY, and Bette DAVIS. Universal launched the modern horror movie, with *DRACULA* (1931), *FRANKENSTEIN* (1931), and *Bride of Frankenstein* (1935). Columbia was known for its homespun tales with grassroots heroes, such as *Mr. Smith Goes to Washington* (1939) and *You Can't Take It With You* (1938). Walt DISNEY Studios introduced the first of many sophisticated feature-length animated films, *Snow White and the Seven Dwarfs* (1937).

Most of the studio chiefs relied on their production heads for story decisions: Irving Thalberg at MGM, David O. Selznick at RKO and later MGM, and Darryl Zanuck at Fox. Selznick resigned from MGM in 1935 and established his own independent company, Selznick International Pictures, which produced the enormously successful *GONE WITH THE WIND* (1939). During the GREAT DEPRESSION, Hollywood responded with optimistic, escapist entertainments to boost the public's morale. Twentieth Century Fox introduced the peppy child star Shirley Temple in these years.

References: Scott Eyman, *The Speed of Sound: Hollywood and the Talkie Revolution 1926–1930* (New York: Simon & Schuster, 1997); Jeremy Pascall, ed., *Hollywood and the Great Stars: The Stars, the Sex Symbols, the Legends, the Movies and How It All Began* (London: Phoebus, 1976); Ethan Mordden, *The Hollywood Studios: House Style in the Golden Age of the Movies* (New York: Simon & Schuster, 1989); Thomas Schatz, *The Genius of the System: Hollywood Filmmaking in the Studio Era* (New York: Pantheon, 1988).

Holmes, Oliver Wendell (1841–1935)

American jurist, associate justice of the U.S. Supreme Court. Born in Boston into an intellectual and literary family, Holmes graduated from Harvard University in 1861, after which he served with distinction as a captain in the Union army during the U.S. Civil War. After the war he practiced law in Boston and taught at the Harvard Law School. He was a Massachusetts supreme court justice (1882–1902) before being tapped by President Theodore Roosevelt to serve on the U.S. Supreme Court (1902–32).

Earning the nickname "the Great Dissenter," Holmes advocated judicial restraint throughout his service, frequently disagreeing with his more conservative colleagues on the Court. He also worked to protect freedom of expression as guaranteed under the Fourteenth Amendment of the U.S. Constitution. He delivered passionate landmark decisions (often in dissent) in many interwar cases, including SCHENCK V. UNITED STATES (1919), ABRAMS V. UNITED STATES (1919), and ADKINS V. CHILDREN'S HOSPITAL (1923).

Reference: Bernard Schwartz, *A History of the Supreme Court* (New York: Oxford University Press, 1993).

Hoover, Herbert (1874–1964)

American statesman, secretary of commerce (1921–29) and president of the United States (1929–33). The son of Quaker parents, Hoover was born in West Branch, Iowa, on August 10, 1874, and received his bachelor's degree in mining from Stanford University in 1895. After working as an engineer for some 20 years, he retire a millionaire from private business before World War I.

During the 1914 German invasion of Belgium, Hoover worked to evacuate Americans, as chair of the American Relief Commission. He then served as head of the Commission for Relief in Belgium (1915–19) to distribute food to refugees. He was appointed U.S. food administrator (1917–19). After the war Hoover was named by President Woodrow WILSON as head of the American Relief Association, which helped to alleviate hunger in postwar Europe. Hoover also used his power to distribute food and other aid to starving millions in Soviet Russia during the immense 1921–23 famine.

In 1921, President Warren G. HARDING named Hoover as U.S. secretary of commerce. Serving in this capacity through both the HARDING and COOLIDGE administrations, Hoover oversaw one of the strongest U.S. economic buildups in history. Because of this leadership, in 1928 he was nominated by the Republican Party to run for president. He was elected, the only sitting cabinet member ever to be elected to the position. His tenure was marked almost immediately by economic decline, however. In October 1929, just seven months into Hoover's administration, the STOCK MARKET CRASH occurred, heralding the worldwide financial GREAT DEPRESSION. Hoover's small attempts to alleviate the crisis through government plans did little to curb the emergency or even to slow its devastating effects. His efforts to put off German war REPARATIONS payments to slow Europe's depression failed miserably; the passage of the SMOOT-HAWLEY TARIFF in

1930 only compounded matters. Perhaps the final straw was Hoover's calling out of army troops to quell the riots involved in the BONUS MARCH in Washington, D.C., in which several World War I veterans were shot and killed.

Walter Trattner wrote about Hoover's complexities as leader:

> [Historians] have argued that he was a complex, thoughtful, intelligent and able leader who led the way into the policies and programs of the New Deal. It is true that in 1921, as Secretary of Commerce, Hoover had convened a conference on unemployment relief to deal with the problems of the postwar recession and in 1927 he had organized a major flood relief effort in the Mississippi valley. It is also true that as a result of these and other things, . . . Hoover had a great deal of support among social workers throughout the nation when he ran for President in 1928. Nevertheless, when he

Herbert Hoover *(CORBIS/Bettmann)*

was in the White House and the economy collapsed, Hoover's response to America's deep depression was less than adequate, to put it kindly—and most of the social work community turned away from him.

In 1932, beset by the strife of the depression and his failure to end it, Hoover was swept from office in a landslide election that catapulted Franklin Delano ROOSEVELT to the presidency, ending 12 years of Republican power in the White House.

Hoover spent his remaining years writing about his administration. He also served as the chair of a presidential commission in the 1950s that examined ways to make the federal government more efficient. He died on August 20, 1965. Hoover is remembered with the Hoover Presidential Library in West Branch, Iowa, and the Hoover Institution on War, Revolution, and Peace at Stanford University.

See also ELECTIONS, U.S.; HOOVER DOCTRINE; HOOVERVILLES.

References: J. Garry Clifford and Robert H. Ferrell, "Hoover, Herbert" in Bruce W. Jentleson and Thomas G. Paterson, senior eds., *Encyclopedia of U.S. Foreign Relations* (New York: Oxford University Press, 1997), 2: 309–12; John Whiteclay Chambers, II, "Hoover, Herbert Clark" in Warren F. Kuehl, ed., *Biographical Dictionary of Internationalists* (Westport, Conn.: Greenwood, 1983), 349–51; Walter I. Trattner, *From Poor Law to Welfare State: A History of Social Welfare in America* (New York: Free Press, 1994), 277.

Hoover Doctrine

Statement of principles enunciated by U.S. President Herbert HOOVER in 1931 calling for a moratorium on war REPARATIONS payments from both Allied and defeated nations in World War I, in an attempt to forestall a financial panic. During the 1920s, Germany paid reparations to the victorious Allied nations as long as American money flowed into German industry; the YOUNG PLAN of 1929 lessened these payments to a moderate level. A series of events threatened this situation, however. A 1928 move by American investors leaving Europe to return to the U.S. market, the onset of the GREAT DEPRESSION in 1929, and the paralyzing effects of the SMOOT-HAWLEY TARIFF, which was enacted the following year, propelled a dagger into the heart of European financial stability. Even France and Great Britain, paying America back for monies loaned during the war, were hard-pressed to continue payments.

By 1931, Hoover had decided to call for such a one-year moratorium. On June 20 of that year he announced the Hoover Doctrine, also called the "Hoover Moratorium." In a speech the president said, "The worldwide depression has affected the countries of Europe more severely than our own. Some of these countries are feeling to a serious extent the drain of the depression on [their] national economy. The fabric of intergovernmental debts, supportable in normal times, weighs heavily in the midst of this depression."

Although Hoover's call was accepted, the moratorium did not work; after one year, with the depression worsening, only Finland could afford to resume reparations payments. Other debtors defaulted, Germany refused to pay any further reparations under Adolf HITLER's regime, and the United States was forced to write off all remaining unpaid debts.

References: Walter Lippmann and William Oscar Scroggs, eds., *The United States in World Affairs, 1931* (New York: Harper & Row, 1932), 336–39; J. Garry Clifford and Robert H. Ferrell, "Hoover, Herbert" in Bruce W. Jentleson and Thomas G. Paterson, senior eds., *Encyclopedia of U.S. Foreign Relations* (New York: Oxford University Press, 1997), 2: 311; Lester H. Brune, *Chronological History of United States Foreign Relations, 1776 to January 20, 1981* (New York: Garland Publishing, 1985), 2: 682.

Hoovervilles

Expressive name for shantytowns, established by American veterans of World War I protesting in Washington, D.C., during the BONUS MARCH in 1932, named mockingly after U.S. President Herbert HOOVER, who declined to offer the bonuses promised by Congress after the war. Interwar period social commentator and writer John DOS PASSOS wrote of these shantytowns: "Anacostia Flats is a ghost of an army camp. . . . Instead of the tents and the long tarpaper barracks, the men are sleeping in little lean-tos built out of old newspapers, cardboard boxes, packing crates, every kind of cockeyed makeshift shelter from the rain, scraped together out of the city dump. The doughboys have changed too; there's the same goulash of faces and dialects, foreigner's pidgin English, lingo from industrial towns and farming towns, but we were all youngsters then . . . now we are getting on to middle life: sunken eyes, hollow cheeks, soft bread lines . . . in these mens' faces as in the Pharoah's dream the lean years have eaten up the fat years already."

The Bonus March was quickly crushed by the U.S. Army, and the Hooverville shanties were destroyed.

See also ADJUSTED COMPENSATION ACT OF 1924; ADJUSTED COMPENSATION ACT OF 1936.

References: Michael E. Parrish, *Anxious Decades: America in Prosperity and Depression, 1920–1941* (New York: W. W. Norton, 1992), 258–61; John D. Weaver, "Bonus March," *American Heritage* 14, 4 (June 1963): 18–23, 92–97; Walter W. Waters, *B.E.F.: The Whole Story of the Bonus Army* (New York: Arno, 1969).

Hopkins, Frederick Gowland (1861–1947)

English biochemist and Nobel laureate. Born in Eastborne, Sussex, England, on June 30, 1861, he received his bachelor's and master's degrees from the University of London in 1890 and 1894, respectively. After working at Guy's Hospital in London as a researcher from 1894 to 1897, he served as a professor of biochemistry at Cambridge University from 1898 until his death. His work on nutrition, and the vitamins that sustain it, led to the discovery of such growth-stimulating vitamins as tryptophan and xanthine oxidase as well as the properties of uric acid. For this work Hopkins was knighted in 1925, and he shared the 1929 Nobel Prize in medicine and physiology with Christiaan EIJKMAN. Hopkins died in Cambridge on May 16, 1947.

References: Rashelle Karp, "Hopkins, Frederick Gowland, Sir" in Bernard S. and June H. Schlessinger, eds., *The Who's Who of Nobel Prize Winners* (Phoenix, Ariz.: Oryx, 1986), 86–87; Ernest Baldwin, "Hopkins, Frederick Gowland" in Charles Coulston Gillespie, ed. in chief, *Dictionary of Scientific Biography* (New York: Charles Scribner's Sons, 1980–90), 5: 498–502.

Hopkins, Harry Lloyd (1890–1946)

American administrator and politician. Born in Sioux City, Iowa, on August 17, 1890, he served as a social worker in New York City in the 1920s and during the GREAT DEPRESSION. Hopkins came to the attention of then New York Governor Franklin Delano ROOSEVELT, who in 1931 appointed him director of the New York State Temporary Relief Administration. When Roosevelt became U.S. president in 1933, he named Hopkins as director of the Federal Emergency Relief Administration (1933–34) and as head of the WORKS PROGRESS ADMINISTRATION (1933–1938). In this period he oversaw the distribution of some $8.5 billion dollars to the unemployed.

In 1938 Roosevelt named Hopkins as secretary of commerce. During Roosevelt's second term, Hopkins was his chief adviser, shuttling between Washington, D.C., and Moscow to conduct diplomacy with Stalin and the Soviet government. By the end of World War II, although he continued to be an integral member of Roosevelt's inner circle, Hopkins was sick with stomach cancer. After Roosevelt's death in April 1945, Hopkins was part of President Harry S Truman's entourage at the Potsdam Conference, but he resigned his post soon after. Hopkins died in New York City on January 29, 1946. Robert E. Sherwood edited Hopkins's collections of writings in *The White House Papers of Harry L. Hopkins* (1949).

References: Henry H. Adams, *Harry Hopkins: A Biography* (New York: Putnam, 1977); Paul A. Kurzman, *Harry Hopkins and the New Deal* (Fair Lawn, N.J.: R. E. Burdick, 1974).

Horse Racing

The first horse to win the three major horse racing events in a single year—the Kentucky Derby, the Preakness near Baltimore, and the Belmont Stakes in New York (all of them being run within a span of five weeks)—was Sir Barton, ridden by jockey John Loftus. Foaled in 1916, Sir Barton, a chestnut colt whose parents were Star Shoot and Lady Sterling, won the Derby easily and captured the Belmont Stakes in a new American record of 2:17 2/5 for the mile and three-eights race. The name "Triple Crown" was not used until 1930, when sportswriter Charles Hatton of the *Daily Racing Form* coined the phrase in writing about that year's multiple-race winner, Gallant Fox. It was Gallant Fox's offspring, the chestnut colt Omaha, which followed his famed father in winning the Triple Crown in 1935, beating the favorite, Nellie Flag, at the Kentucky Derby and winning the Preakness (six lengths) and at Belmont (a length and a half). War Admiral, sired from the famed thoroughbred Man O'War, won the Triple Crown in 1937 by fighting a leg injury at the Belmont Stakes and defeating Pompoon at the Preakness by a head to win the coveted prize. In the interwar years, there were several horses that won two of the three main races but could not complete the famed trio. The first of these was Man O'War, who in 1920 won the Preakness and the Belmont but did not start the Kentucky Derby. Other "near winners" of the crown include Pillory in 1922, Zev in 1923, Twenty Grand in 1931, Burgoo King in 1932, Bold Venture in 1936, and Johnstown in 1939.

Reference: Roger Longrigg, *The History of Horse Racing* (London: Macmillan, 1972).

Horthy, Miklós (1868–1957)

Hungarian diplomat, admiral, and regent (1920–44). Born Miklós Horthy de Nagybánya in the village of Kenderes in eastern Hungary, he was educated at the naval academy in FIUME. During World War I, Horthy was advanced to the rank of admiral in the Austro-Hungarian navy. He returned to Hungary, which was split by the Allies from Austria, after the war. Inspired, he led a revolution that overthrew the Bolshevik-supported government of Communist Béla KÚN. In return for his work in deposing Kún, Horthy was named commander in chief of the Hungarian armed forces in 1919. The following year, he was named by the Hungarian National Assembly as regent, in effect becoming the royal leader of Hungary, replacing the former King Charles IV.

Horthy named several important premiers, including Stephen Bethen, under which Hungary achieved a period of financial and political stability. By 1929, however, the impact of the Treaty of TRIANON, which had brutally punished Hungary after World War I, as well as the nation's depressed financial situation, led to Bethen's resignation in 1931. To avoid Charles IV's son Archduke Otto being enthroned as king, Horthy named the fascist Gyula von Gömbös as premier. The situation went from bad to worse: Gömbös suppressed political opposition and persecuted the Jews. During this period Horthy's allegiance moved closer to the Axis powers of Germany and Italy. In 1939 his nation officially joined that power bloc by signing the Anti-Comintern Pact.

During World War II, Hungary sided again with the Axis powers, but when the war turned against Nazi Germany, Horthy tried (but failed) to make a separate peace with the Allies. Deposed, he disappeared for a time, abducted by the Germans in 1944 and held in Bavaria for a year. Arrested by American troops, Horthy was released because he had not committed any war crimes. He lived in Portugal for the remainder of his life, writing his memoirs, which were published posthumously in 1965. Horthy died in 1957.

References: Asher Cohen, "Horthy, Miklós" in Israel Gutman, ed. in chief, Encyclopedia of the Holocaust (New York: Macmillan, 1990) 2: 688–89; Thomas L. Sakmyster, Hungary's Admiral on Horseback: Miklós Horthy, 1918–1944 (Boulder, Colo.: East European Monographs, 1994); Mario D. Fenyo, Hitler, Horthy, and Hungary: German-Hungarian Relations, 1941–1944 (New Haven, Conn.: Yale University Press, 1972).

Hubble, Edwin Powell (1889–1953)

American astronomer, recognized for his unique observations of the universe particularly during the interwar period. Born in Marshfield, Missouri, on November 20, 1889, he earned a master's degree in astronomy at the University of Chicago, where he was a protégé of George E. Hale, one of the noted astronomers of the era. For a time, Hubble studied law as a Rhodes Scholar at Oxford University, where he earned a bachelor's degree in laws in 1912. He moved to Kentucky, where he opened a law practice, but he was soon bored with the law and returned to the University of Chicago to take up astronomy.

After earning a doctorate in astronomy in 1917, and serving in World War I, Hubble worked at the Mount Wilson Observatory in Pasadena, California, where he worked on 60-inch and 100-inch Hooker reflector mirrors. Before Hubble's research, it was thought that all nebulae were inside the Milky Way, but Hubble found that other nebulae, which he called Cepheid variables, were thousands of light years beyond the Milky Way. He categorized nebulae into two classifications: galactic and extragalactic. His 1929 paper A Relation between Distance and Radial Velocity among Extra-Galactic Nebulae, which appeared in the "Proceedings of the National Academy of Sciences," is considered a landmark in astronomical research, as is his 1934 work Red Shifts in the Spectra of Nebulae.

Among Hubble's other discoveries was that the universe was expanding, although the rate at which he computed it was incorrect. Although he was honored during his lifetime, Hubble was not as well known until after his death, which occurred in San Marino, California, on September 28, 1953. On April 24, 1990, the United States launched the Hubble Space Telescope, the largest device of its kind placed into earth's orbit to examine the universe.

References: Alexandr S. Sharov et al., Edwin Hubble: The Discoverer of the Big Bang Universe (Cambridge: Cambridge University Press, 1993); Edwin Powell Hubble (Norris S. Hetherington, ed.), The Edwin Hubble Papers: Previously Unpublished Manuscripts on the Extragalactic Nature of Spiral Nebulae (Tucson, Ariz.: Pachart Publishing House, 1990); Gale E. Christianson, Edwin Hubble: Mariner of the Nebulae (New York: Farrar, Straus & Giroux, 1995).

Hughes, Charles Evans (1862–1948)

American diplomat and jurist. He was born in Glens Falls, in the foothills of New York's Adirondack Mountains, on April 11, 1862. He earned a law degree from the Columbia University Law School in 1884, became a noted attorney in New York City in the late 1890s, and served as dean of the Cornell University School of Law from 1891 to 1893. Just after the turn of the century, Hughes was named as counsel for the New York state legislature, investigating potential corruption in the electric power and gas industries and life insurance industries. In 1906 he ran as a Republican for governor of New York and, backed by U.S. President Theodore ROOSEVELT, he defeated newspaper publisher William Randolph Hearst.

Re-elected in 1908, Hughes resigned from the governorship in 1910 to accept President William Howard Taft's appointment of Hughes as an associate justice of the U.S. Supreme Court, serving until 1916. That year, he was nominated for president by the Republicans, and he resigned from the Court to run the campaign. He was beaten by Woodrow WILSON, however, and returned to law, serving as a special counsel to the U.S. government in an investigation of the aircraft industry.

In 1921, after Senator Warren G. HARDING was elected president, Harding selected Hughes as his secretary of state. Hughes, who had had no diplomatic experience at the time, became Harding's most successful appointment. Hughes's tenure, which lasted through Harding's administration and part of Calvin COOLIDGE's administration, consisted of numerous diplomatic advances in the areas of disarmament. His work at the WASHINGTON NAVAL CONFERENCE in 1921–22, for example, is considered one of the finest stands of an American secretary of state. In 1925 Hughes resigned, returning to his law practice. In 1926 New York governor Al SMITH named him to a commission to investigate the state administration, and in 1928

Coolidge named Hughes to a two-year term as a judge on the Permanent Court of International Justice.

In 1930, after the death of Supreme Court Chief Justice William Howard Taft, President Herbert HOOVER named Hughes Taft's successor. Hughes served as chief justice from 1930 until his retirement in 1941. During those years, he was a conservative leader in helping to strike down several key provisions of President Franklin D. ROOSEVELT's NEW DEAL economic program. When Roosevelt tried to initiate a plan to pack the court in 1937, known as the COURT-PACKING CONTROVERSY, Hughes aided Senator Burton K. WHEELER in writing a heartfelt letter to the Senate, a move that killed Roosevelt's plan.

Hughes died in Osterville, Massachusetts, on August 27, 1948. He remains one of the few men in U.S. history to serve in the cabinet, as his party's presidential candidate, and on the U.S. Supreme Court.

References: David J. Danelski and Joseph S. Tulchin, eds., *The Autobiographical Notes of Charles Evans Hughes* (Cambridge: Harvard University Press, 1973); Mari J. Matsuda, "Hughes, Charles Evans" in Kermit L. Hall, ed. in chief, *The Oxford Companion to the Supreme Court of the United States* (New York: Oxford University Press, 1992), 414–16; Barry Cushman, "The Hughes Court and Constitutional Consultation," 1997 discourse, copy provided to the author by Professor Cushman; Burton J. Hendrick, "Governor Hughes" McClure's Magazine, 30, 5 (March 1908): 529; "Think Hughes Done With Office: Friend Say Governor Will Retire at End of Term and Devote His Time to Practice of Law," *New York Herald,* June 20, 1908, p. 7; The Charles Evans Hughes Papers, New York Public Library, contain mostly speeches from his gubernatorial campaigns of 1908; the unidentified fragment from his inaugural address, 1907, is from the Hughes Papers, Box 3, folder 4; also see the Hughes Papers in the Library of Congress for more on his career, including his work during the interwar years as secretary of state and chief justice of the U.S. Supreme Court; Betty Glad, *Charles Evans Hughes and the Illusions of Innocence: A Study in American Diplomacy* (Urbana: University of Illinois Press, 1966); John H. Fenton, "Justice Hughes Dead at 86; Served the State and Nation," *New York Times,* August 28, 1948, p. 1; "Hughes' Life: Long Career of Public Service," *New York Herald-Tribune,* August 28, 1948, p. 3.

Hughes, Langston (1902–1967)

American writer and poet, whose vivid descriptions of African-American urban life in the United States marked the HARLEM RENAISSANCE era. Born in Joplin, Missouri, on February 1, 1902, he was educated at Columbia University and Lincoln University (Pennsylvania). During his high school years in Cleveland, Ohio, Hughes was introduced to the world of poetry by an English teacher. His poems were so extraordinary that W. E. B. DUBOIS pub-

lished the young Hughes's work in *The Crisis,* the magazine of the NAACP.

Hughes worked a series of odd jobs before devoting himself in 1924 to writing. During these years he became a key figure in the Harlem Renaissance, joining the large number of black artists, writers, and singers who were collectively part of the movement. Hughes's interwar works—such as *Weary Blues* (1926), *Fine Clothes to the Jew* (1927), *Not Without Laughter* (1930), *The Ways of White Folks* (1934), and *Mulatto* (1935)—spoke out against poverty and discrimination. His autobiography, *The Big Sea,* appeared in 1940.

During the McCarthy era, Hughes was harassed for his liberal views, but despite this pressure he continued to write illuminating poetry throughout his life. He died on May 22, 1967, and is remembered as one of the earliest African-American writers to infuse black speech and music in literature to express his works' overarching theme: freedom.

References: Milton Meltzer, *Langston Hughes: A Biography* (New York: Crowell, 1968); Faith Berry, *Langston Hughes: Before and Beyond Harlem* (Westport, Conn.: L. Hill, 1983); Donald C. Dickinson, *A Bio-bibliography of Langston Hughes, 1902–1967* (Hamden, Conn.: Archon Books, 1972).

Hughes, William Morris (1864–1952)

Australian politician, prime minister (1915–23) during World War I and the postwar years, and participant at the VERSAILLES Peace Conference in 1919. Born in Pimlico, London, England, on September 25, 1864, Hughes was the son of a Welsh carpenter. After being educated at St. Stephen's School in Westminster, he emigrated to Australia when he was 20 and held a series of odd jobs. He settled in Sydney and in 1894 was elected to the provincial parliament of New South Wales. With the establishment of the Australian federation in 1901, Hughes was elected to the first House of Representatives, where he supported the Immigration Restriction Act on the grounds that immigrants were driving down wages.

In 1903, Hughes was admitted to the bar. In 1908, Andrew Fisher became prime minister and offered Hughes the position of attorney general, a position he held three times: 1908–1909, 1910–13, and 1914–21.

On October 27, 1915, Fisher resigned to become the high commissioner to Great Britain. Hughes replaced Fisher the same day, becoming the 11th prime minister of Australia. In his eight years in office (1915–23), Hughes established a firm immigration policy. Under his leadership, however, migration to Australia increased by more than 180,000 from 1921 to 1925. Hughes also guided his nation through the torrid years of World War I and its aftermath, including the Versailles Peace Conference. Biographer Lawrence Fitzhardinge writes of Hughes: "In the conference Hughes concentrated on three questions which he considered vital to Australia and likely to go against her by default." Although he had demanded that all of the Allies share in REPARATIONS, in the end he gave in to but a small share. He also asked for, in the name of the 60,000 Australians who had perished in the war, a portion of German possessions in the Pacific, finally agreeing to a system of mandates. Last, Hughes demanded and won the decision to exclude a statement in the LEAGUE OF NATIONS covenant guaranteeing the "equality of nations and of equal treatment of their nationals," a phrase in which Hughes saw a threat to "White Australia." A majority of conference members agreed with Hughes, and the clause was ultimately voted down.

In the last two years of his tenure, "Billy" Hughes, as he was known, was considered a hero for these stands. At the IMPERIAL CONFERENCE in London in 1921, he called for the development among the Allied nations of a conference on Pacific security, an issue that was included in the WASHINGTON NAVAL CONFERENCE of 1921–22. His ideas on security issues were detailed in his 1929 work, *The Splendid Adventures: A Review of Empire Relations.*

In the 1922 election, however, Hughes's old Labour allies abandoned him for "prewar" thinking regarding the Australian economy, which had virtually collapsed after the war. He was forced to resign when the Country Party, headed by Earle Christmas Page, narrowly won the election and refused to consider a coalition with Hughes. The nation turned to Hughes's treasurer, Stanley Melbourne BRUCE, to pick up the reins as prime minister.

Hughes continued to hold his seat in Parliament, and after 1934 he served in several ministerial posts, including minister for external affairs (1937–39). When Labour returned to power in 1939, even though Hughes was the elder statesman of the party, he was passed over for the prime ministership for Robert Menzies (and, for a short time, Joseph Lyons). Menzies turned to Hughes to serve as minister for industry (1939–40), attorney general (1939–41), and minister of the navy (1940–41).

In his final years, Hughes joined the Liberal Party (formed from the remnants of the United Australia Party) and wrote treatises on national and international issues, including *Crusts and Crusades* (1947) and *Politicians and Potentates* (1950). On October 28, 1952, Hughes died at his home in Lindfield.

References: W. Farmer Whyte, *William Morris Hughes: His Life and Times* (Sydney: Angus & Robertson, 1957); Lawrence Frederic Fitzhardinge, *William Morris Hughes* (Melbourne: Oxford University Press, 1973); Lawrence Frederic Fitzhardinge, *William Morris Hughes: A Political Biography* (Sydney: Angus & Robertson; two volumes, 1964–79); "Hughes, Billy (William) Morris" in John Arnold and Deirdre Morris, gen. eds., *Monash Biographical Dictionary of 20th Century Australia* (Port Melbourne, Victoria: Reed Reference Publishing, 1994), 262–63; Lawrence Frederic Fitzhardinge, "Hughes, William Morris" in Bede Nairn and Geoffrey Serle, gen. eds., *Australian Dictionary of Biography* (Carlton, Victoria: Melbourne University Press, 1976–88), 9: 393–400.

Hull, Cordell (1871–1955)

American politician and Nobel laureate. Born in Overton County, Tennessee, on October 2, 1871, he attended college in Kentucky and Ohio before returning to Tennessee to study law. Hull was admitted to the bar in 1891 and was elected to the Tennessee House of Representatives in 1892, where he served until 1897. A year later he volunteered for duty during the Spanish-American War, rising to the rank of captain. In 1903 he was named a circuit judge for the Middle Tennessee circuit, and three years later won a seat in the U.S. House of Representatives. He was reelected 12 times (except for the Republican landslide of 1920), and in 1931 Hull was elected to the U.S. Senate.

In 1933 U.S. president Franklin D. ROOSEVELT selected Hull as his secretary of state. Although Hull had no previous diplomatic experience, he took on several areas of controversy during his 11 years in the position, the longest tenure in that office in American history. Among the various peace measures Hull initiated, he advocated the lowering of tariffs worldwide to lessen the global effects of the GREAT DEPRESSION, helped settle the CHACO BOUNDARY WAR between Bolivia and Paraguay, and pushed the GOOD NEIGHBOR POLICY in the Americas by holding the Inter-American Conference in Montevideo, Uruguay.

In 1940, after war had broken out in Europe but the United States still retained its neutrality, Hull cautioned that the United States was "creating a stable and enduring world order under law." When Japan demanded neutrality in the Pacific, Hull demanded the Japanese withdrawal from China. After the United States entered World War II in December 1941, Hull and his State Department colleagues began to work for the establishment of a postwar peace organization, modeled on the League of Nations. In 1944, however, shortly after Roosevelt won a fourth term, the aged and sickly Hull resigned. He was awarded the Nobel Prize for Peace in 1945 for his "long and indefatigable work for understanding between nations." He died in Bethesda, Maryland, on July 23, 1955. His *Memoirs of Cordell Hull* were published in 1950.

References: "Hull, Cordell" in Bernard S. and June H. Schlessinger, eds., *The Who's Who of Nobel Prize Winners* (Phoenix, Ariz.: Oryx, 1986), 137; Jonathan G. Utley, "Hull, Cordell" in Bruce W. Jentleson and Thomas G. Paterson, senior eds., *Encyclopedia of U.S. Foreign Relations* (New York: Oxford University Press, 1997), 2: 319–21; Edward T. Folliard, "Hull Resigns, Stettinius to Head State Dept.; Speedy Approval of New Secretary Seen as Name Goes to Senate," *Washington Post*, November 28, 1944, p. 1.

Hull House   *See* ABBOTT, Edith; ABBOTT, Grace;
ADDAMS, Jane.

The Hunchback of Notre Dame
These 1929 and 1939 films, starring, respectively, American actor Lon CHANEY (1883–1930) and British-American actor Charles LAUGHTON (1899–1962), concerned a grotesque but kind-hearted man with a hunchback who comes to the rescue of a young woman he loves but can never have. Based on the book by Victor Hugo, the original film starred Chaney as the hunchback Quasimodo and Ruth Miller as Esmeralda, and was directed by Wallace Worsely. Chaney's acting is considered one of the best performances ever captured on film. His makeup for the role was also groundbreaking. In the second production, Laughton played Quasimodo, while Esmeralda was played by Irish actress Maureen O'Hara in her first American film. The two films are considered by film historians to be of the best of the interwar period.

Reference: Leonard Maltin, ed., *Movie and Video Guide 1996 Edition* (New York: Plume, 1995), 611.

Hurston, Zora Neale   (1891, 1901, or 1903–1960)
American novelist, anthropologist, and folklorist. Although her exact year of birth is unknown, Hurston grew up near the turn of the century in Eatonville, Florida, an African-American community where she did not experience the prevailing racial prejudice of the time. She studied at Howard University, Barnard College, and Columbia University, where the renowned anthropologist Franz Boas became her mentor. She was a major literary figure in the HARLEM RENAISSANCE, the rebirth of black artistic and racial consciousness in the 1920s and 1930s.

During this outpouring of artistic creativity in the African-American community, Hurston was awarded a Guggenheim fellowship in 1936 and conducted folklore research in the American South, the Bahamas, Haiti, and Jamaica. Although she won several literary contests and prizes sponsored by such groups as the NAACP and the Urban League, Hurston died before her literary talent was widely recognized. She wrote two pioneering folklore collections, *Mules and Men* (1935) and *Tell My Horse* (1938), as well as the novels *Jonah's Gourd Vine* (1934), *Their Eyes Were Watching God* (1937), *Moses, Man of the Mountain* (1939), and *Seraph on the Suwanee* (1948). She coauthored one play, *Mule Bone* (1931, but not performed until 1990), with the poet Langston HUGHES. Hurston's autobiography, *Dust Tracks on a Road,* was published in 1942.

Reference: Bernard Bell, "Zora Neale Hurston," in *Young Reader's Companion to American History,* ed. John A. Garraty (Boston: Houghton Mifflin, 1994), 414.

Huxley, Aldous   (1894–1963)
British novelist, essayist, and critic. Born on July 26, 1894, into a distinguished scientific and literary upper-class English family, Huxley was a student at the prestigious Eton School. He then attended Oxford University, where he entered the literary world, meeting such writers as Lytton Strachey, Bertrand Russell, and D. H. LAWRENCE. A childhood eye injury kept him out of World War I.

Huxley initially wrote only essays and poetry, but in 1921 he turned to the novel. Tackling themes of social decadence, he published *Crome Yellow* (1921), *Antic Hay* (1923), and *Point Counter Point* (1928). His 1932 *Brave New World,* a satirical novel about a scientific dystopia, explored a hopeless future. Set in the year 632 "A.F." (or "after HENRY FORD," the icon of assembly-line capitalism), the story includes embryos that are bred in bottles and human emotions that are dulled by drugs, entertainment, and conspicuous consumption. Huxley held that the uniqueness of the individual was essential to freedom.

In 1938 he moved to Hollywood, where he became a screenwriter; among his films was an adaptation of Jane Austen's *Pride and Prejudice,* which starred a young Laurence Olivier. In later years Huxley embraced mysticism and Eastern philosophies. His post–World War II works include *Ape and Essence* (1948) and *Doors of Perception* (1954). In 1958 he wrote *Brave New World Revisited,* a collection of essays exploring real-life problems of the day. He died November 22, 1963.

Reference: Jocelyn Brooks, "Aldous Huxley," in *British Writers,* ed. Ian Scott-Kilvert (New York: Charles Scribner's Sons, 1979–87), 7: 204.

Hythe Conference
Meeting, 1920, in which war REPARATIONS from World War I were discussed. French and British delegations assembled in the English resort town of Hythe on May 15, 1920. The meeting, which did not make any concrete headway, lasted until the next day. The parties adjourned and agreed to meet again in a more comprehensive conference in the French city of Boulogne and later at the Belgian city of Spa.
See also BOULOGNE CONFERENCE; SPA CONFERENCE.

References: Edmund Jan Osmańczyk, *The Encyclopedia of the United Nations and International Agreements* (Philadelphia: Taylor & Francis, 1985), 364.

Ibn Saud, Abdul-Aziz (c.1880–1953)

Muslim leader and founder of the modern state of Saudi Arabia (1932). Born in Riyadh, Arabia (now the capital of Saudi Arabia), he was a member of the Ibn Saud family, which had ruled Arabia since 1780. When Ibn Saud was a child, however, he and his family were driven from their home by their rivals for power, the Rashids; they fled to what is now Kuwait. In 1901, when he was about 21, Ibn Saud assembled an army of 40 men to go to Arabia and take his family land back. He killed the Rashidi governor and established an insurrection, seizing Riyadh. Over a two-year period, Ibn Saud conquered various parts of Arabia, and by 1903 he had taken back what had been his family's kingdom. In 1904, Ibn Rashid appealed to the Ottoman Empire for aid, and they sent troops, defeating Ibn Saud's forces on June 15, 1904. But Ibn Saud held on and after several years the Ottomans, unable to dislodge him from the area, dispersed.

During World War I, Ibn Saud allied himself with the British, offering to fight the Turkish-allied Ibn Rashid. Ibn Saud did not fight the Rashidis until 1920, but within two years he had wiped them out as a threat to his reign. In 1924, he moved against Sharif Hussein, king of the Hejaz, which encompassed the holy site of Mecca, and forced Hussein to flee. In 1926, Ibn Saud proclaimed himself king of the Hejaz; a year later he expanded the title to king of the Hejaz and of Najd and its dependencies. Five years later, he consolidated all of his territories across the Arabian Peninsula into the kingdom of Saudi Arabia. By 1933 he had signed a deal with an American oil company. The company found oil in 1938 but ceased drilling during World War II.

After the war the world was looking for new energy resources, and the possibility of millions of gallons of oil lying untapped in Saudi Arabia made that country a popular target. Ibn Saud, who had been penniless all of his life, was paid $200,000 in 1950 for the rights to oil fields. Three years later, he and his family were making $2.5 mil-

lion a week in royalties, making them one of the richest dynasties in the world. Ibn Saud's death on November 9, 1953 did not end his family's reign over the Saudi Peninsula. He was succeeded by his sons Saud and Faisal (who was assassinated in 1975), and his son Fahd Ibn Abdul Aziz (b.1923) serves as the king of Saudi Arabia today.

References: Leslie J. McLoughlin, *Ibn Saud: Founder of a Kingdom* (Houndmills, Basingstoke, Hampshire: Macmillan in association with St. Antony's College, Oxford, 1993); Roy Lebkicher, George Rentz, and Max Steineke, *The Arabia of Ibn Saud* (New York, R. F. Moore Co., 1952).

Ickes, Harold LeClaire (1874–1952)

American administrator and politician. Born in Frankstown Township, Pennsylvania, on March 15, 1874, he was admitted to the Illinois bar in 1907 and worked for several social causes. Although Ickes was a Republican, in 1912 he fled the party and joined with Theodore Roosevelt in the so-called "Bull Moose" Progressive movement. Ickes later returned to the party fold, but he was forever changed by his brush with the left. In 1932 he enticed other Republicans to vote for or support Democrat Franklin D. ROOSEVELT for the presidency. When Roosevelt formed his cabinet, he turned to Ickes, still considered a Republican, as secretary of the interior. Ickes served from 1933 until 1946, the longest tenure at that department in its history. He was largely responsible for the conservationist measures that were a key component of the NEW DEAL years in the 1930s. As head of the Public Works Administration from 1933 to 1939, he launched programs to build dams, highways, and other construction to provide employment and to change the look of conservation, spending some $5 billion during his tenure.

In 1946, after a disagreement with President Harry S Truman, Ickes resigned. He died in Washington, D.C., on February 3, 1952. His *Autobiography of a Curmudgeon* was published in 1943 and his memoirs, *Secret Diaries*, were published in three volumes from 1953–54.

References: Graham J. White, *Harold Ickes of the New Deal: His Private Life and Public Career* (Cambridge: Harvard University Press, 1985); Linda J. Lear, *Harold L. Ickes: The Aggressive Progressive, 1874–1933* (New York: Garland Publishing, 1981).

immigration

Government sanction of the lawful movement of persons from one country to another to change their permanent residence. From 1890 until just before World War II, the United States became the world's largest recipient of immigrants, from almost every corner of the world. Many immigrants at this time were eastern European, poor, and mostly uneducated who could speak little or no English. Until 1924 they were processed in large numbers at New York Harbor's Ellis Island and, if healthy, they were allowed to enter the United States.

After World War I, however, the U.S. Congress began to see a threat in some of these newly arrived immigrants. Some had turned to the leftist ideologies of anarchism and Bolshevism and had spoken out against World War I, in support of the Russian Revolution. The IMMIGRATION ACT OF 1921 was thus passed, designed to limit the numbers of immigrants to 3 percent of those who had been in the United States in 1910. When that did not work, the IMMIGRATION ACT OF 1924 limited a nation's immigration to 2 percent of that group found in the 1890 U.S. census. During the GREAT DEPRESSION, immigration was further limited; the ROOSEVELT administration deported some 500,000 Mexican workers because it was thought they were taking jobs away from Americans.

See also EVIAN CONFERENCE.

References: Virginia Yans-McLaughlin and Marjorie Lightman, *Ellis Island and the Peopling of America* (New York: New Press, 1997); Edmund Jan Osmańczyk, *The Encyclopedia of the United Nations and International Agreements* (Philadelphia: Taylor & Francis, 1985), 478; John Mendelsohn, ed., *The Holocaust: Selected Documents in Eighteen Volumes* (New York: Garland Publishing, 1982), 5: 228–64; John Bodnar, "Immigration" in Eric Foner and John A. Garraty, eds., *The Reader's Companion to American History* (Boston: Houghton Mifflin Co., 1991), 536.

Immigration Act of 1921

American congressional legislation, enacted May 19, 1921, also known as the Congressional Quota Act. After World War I the perceived threat of a wave of foreigners, particularly from eastern Europe, and of the perceived rise of anarchism, socialism, and communism among these

immigrants, led the Congress to question how to restrict the surge of legal immigration. In February 1921 both houses of Congress passed immediate legislation that imposed a temporary moratorium on all immigration into the United States. A conference committee then drafted a law that restricted future admission of certain nationalities (particularly those from Italy, Russia, and other countries of southern and eastern Europe, as well as from Africa) to 3 percent of their population in the United States in 1910. Historian Lester Brune writes, "Disillusionment with World War I, fears that larger numbers of East Europeans with socialist-communistic beliefs would arrive, and a general xenophobic view held by '100% Americans' caused Congress to pass a law that generally restricted immigration for the first time in the nation's history."

The act was extended in 1922 and was replaced by the even more restrictive IMMIGRATION ACT IN 1924, which lowered the percentage of immigrants from 3 percent of 1910 numbers to 2 percent.

References: Harold Tiffany Butler, "Partisan Positions on Isolationism vs. Internationalism, 1918–1933," (Ph.D. dissertation, Syracuse University, 1963), 203; Lester H. Brune, *Chronological History of United States Foreign Relations, 1776 to January 20, 1981* (New York: Garland Publishing, 1985), 2: 631.

Immigration Act of 1924

American congressional legislation, enacted May 26, 1924, also called the National Origins Act or the Johnson-Reed Act, which established a quota on certain groups in the United States. After a number of years of high immigration rates (mostly of eastern Europeans, many of whom were perceived to be anarchists or to hold other leftist ideologies), the U.S. Congress set an annual quota of 2 percent of a nationality's population as determined in the 1890 U.S. census, with a minimum of one hundred people for each nationality. The act placed severe limits on emigration from Italy, Russia, and other countries of southern and eastern Europe, as well as from Africa. In addition, historian Harold Butler writes, "A very controversial amendment to the Johnson Bill had the effect of excluding the Japanese although they were not specifically named." The Senate vote on this amendment came on April 16, 1924, two days before the bill was voted on. Republican Senator Le Baron B. Colt of Rhode Island, chair of the Senate Committee on Immigration, opposed the amendment. The enactment also established the U.S. Border Patrol. The legislation was highly controversial and is now widely condemned by historians and legal scholars as racist.

References: Harold Tiffany Butler, "Partisan Positions on Isolationism vs. Internationalism, 1918–1933," (Ph.D. dissertation, Syracuse University, 1963), 204; Immigration Act of 1924, 43 Stat. 153.

Imperial Conference, First

Meeting, 1921, in which the postwar situation of the English Commonwealth nations was discussed. Officially known as the Conference of the Prime Minister and Representatives of the United Kingdom, the Dominions, and India, the gathering assembled in London in June, July, and August 1921. Heading the delegation of Great Britain was Prime Minister David LLOYD GEORGE; for Canada it was Prime Minister Arthur MEIGHEN; Australia, Prime Minister William Morris HUGHES; New Zealand, Prime Minister William Ferguson Massey; South Africa, Prime Minister Jan Christiaan SMUTS; and for India, Secretary of State Edwin Samuel Montagu.

In his opening speech on June 20, host Lloyd George addressed the atmosphere: "The Conference falls at a time of great stress in this country and of serious trouble in many parts of the world. . . . It was inevitable that the nations which had put forth such colossal efforts and sustained such unparalleled losses of life, limb and treasure during the War, should feel all the consequences of overstrain and exhaustion. The systems which perplex the statesmen of all the belligerent countries at the present time are due to the condition in which the nations of the world have been left by the great War." Then Lloyd George discussed the leading issues: German REPARATIONS and disarmament, the peace treaties signed in the wake of the war's end, the British Empire's relations with the United States and Japan, and the need for friendly relations with the United States. A less conspicuous issue, but one that would soon become quite contentious, was the status of the "dominion nations" under English law. Lloyd George posed the questions: "Is it that the Dominions are seeking new powers, or are desirous of using powers they already have, or is the Conference to draw up a declaration of rights, to set down in black and white the relations between Britain and the Dominions?"

Before the conference closed, several other matters were discussed: Meighen argued that Britain should back him and his government in arguments with the United States on every issue, and the lack of U.S. and Russian participation in the LEAGUE OF NATIONS was debated. The conference agreed that the British Empire should be represented by one delegate at the future WASHINGTON NAVAL CONFERENCE on the limitation of armaments (although at that meeting Australia, Canada, India, New Zealand, and South Africa sent representatives to attend only), that new rules on air communication among the overseas territories should be instituted, and that the issues of settlement and nationality would be further discussed and studied.

References: Robert Burgess Stewart, *Treaty Relations of the British Commonwealth of Nations* (New York: Macmillan, 1939), 152–53; Arthur Berriedale Keith, *The Sovereignty of the British Dominions* (London: Macmillan, 1929), 4–5; Maurice Ollivier, comp. and ed., *The Colonial and Imperial Conferences from 1887 to 1937* (Ottawa: E. Cloutier, Queen's Printer, 1954), 1: 391–425.

Imperial Conference, Second

Meeting, 1923, during which foreign policy issues among the British Empire and its overseas territories were discussed, including the French occupation of the Ruhr Basin in western Germany, the Treaty of LAUSANNE, monetary debt to the United States, imperial defense, the recently concluded WASHINGTON NAVAL CONFERENCE, and air defense. The conference lasted from October 1 until November 8, 1923. The host was British Prime Minister Stanley BALDWIN. Representing Canada was Prime Minister William Lyon Mackenzie KING; New Zealand, Prime Minister William Ferguson Massey; South Africa, Prime Minister Jan Christiaan SMUTS; the IRISH FREE STATE, Minister of Education John MacNeill; Newfoundland, Prime Minister W. R. Warren; India, William Robert Wellesley Peel.

Opening the conference, Baldwin read a message from the British government regarding the recent death of former Prime Minister Andrew Bonar LAW. Baldwin also welcomed the inclusion of the Irish Free State under its new 1922 constitution. In his speech before the group, Lord Robert Cecil, Lord Privy Seal and the British representative on the Council of the LEAGUE OF NATIONS, related the League's recent work. The primary discussion involved allowing the "dominion nations" greater say over their foreign policies and greater autonomy in general. As Arthur Berriedale Keith wrote about the conference, "It was . . . made clear that no Dominion could be bound by any treaty which was not signed by delegates empowered to act for it, and any treaty to bind a Dominion must be ratified at its request." The text of the final communiqué read: "It is desirable that no treaty should be negotiated by any of the Governments of the Empire without due consideration of its possible effects on other parts of the Empire, or, if circumstances so demand, on the Empire as a whole." With this statement, the independence of the overseas territories became stronger.

References: Maurice Ollivier, comp. and ed., *The Colonial and Imperial Conferences From 1887 to 1937* (Ottawa: E. Cloutier, Queen's Printer, 1954), 2: 1–134; Arthur Berriedale Keith, *Dominion Autonomy in Practice* (London: Oxford University Press, 1929); Arthur Berriedale Keith, *The Governments of the British Empire* (London: Macmillan, 1936), 94.

Imperial Conference, Third

Meeting, 1926, at which the "dominion nations" under the British Empire came closer to demanding complete sovereignty from London. Meeting from October 19 to November 23, 1926, the leaders including host British Prime Minister Stanley BALDWIN and Canadian prime minister William Lyon Mackenzie KING, discussed the possibility of granting the dominion countries independence. An Inter-Imperial Relations Committee, under the direction of Arthur James Balfour, was established and concluded (in the so-called "Balfour Report") that enacting a single constitution of the British Empire, which would bring all of the overseas territories under the rule of English law, was unfeasible. The report endorsed the concept that the "self-governing communities composed of Great Britain and the Dominions" were "autonomous . . . within the British Empire, equal in status, in no way subordinate to another in any aspect of their domestic or external affairs, although united by a common allegiance to the Crown." This statement made the statute possible just five years later. One important move made at the meeting was the definition of the assemblage of nations as a "Commonwealth," as being "autonomous communities . . . and freely associated as members of the British Commonwealth of Nations."

References: Robert Burgess Stewart, *Treaty Relations of the British Commonwealth of Nations* (New York: Macmillan, 1939), 152–53; John Grieg Latham, *Australia and the British Commonwealth* (London: Macmillan, 1929), 12–14, 131–33; Maurice Ollivier, comp. and ed., *The Colonial and Imperial Conferences from 1887 to 1937* (Ottawa: E. Cloutier, Queen's Printer, 1954), 2: 135–227; Edmund Jan Osmańczyk, *The Encyclopedia of the United Nations and International Agreements* (Philadelphia: Taylor & Francis, 1985), 162; Arthur Berriedale Keith, *The Governments of the British Empire* (London: Macmillan, 1936), 254.

Imperial Conference, Fourth
Meeting, 1930, during which "inter-Imperial relations and economic questions were the two main themes." Under the supervision of British Prime Minister James Ramsay MACDONALD, such leaders as Canadian prime minister Richard Bedford BENNETT examined the reports of several committees, including the Conference on the Operation of Dominion Legislation and Shipping, to discuss the growing move among the "dominion nations" to have the British Parliament assert their independence from London. This movement received a boost when Isaac Isaacs was appointed by King GEORGE V as the first Australian-born governor-general of Australia. The conferees at the 1930 meeting voted that herewith the king would accept the advice of the overseas territory in appointing a leader, instead of unilaterally appointing someone of his choice.

In closing the conference, MacDonald said, "We meet at a time when the world is undergoing very rapid change, rapid change politically, rapid change economically, and it would have been sheer folly on our part if we had felt that we could make arrangements for the next generation in an Imperial Conference that has lasted not quite six weeks. I am of the opinion and I still believe that the British Commonwealth of Nations has got to be kept together by other things than material interests. By all means, let us provide for them, and you know that we have done our best to do it under very difficult circumstances; but, my

friends, I still believe in the spirit; I still believe in the imagination; I still believe in the homage paid to what is good and true and beautiful, and I decline to believe that those magnificent bonds of human cooperation and sympathy—those bonds are keeping us together—are going to be alienated."

Another subject before the delegates was the OTTAWA ECONOMIC CONFERENCE, held in 1932 in the Canadian capital city. Bennett had called for that conference to discuss ways to combat the growing worldwide depression.

References: Stephen Leacock, *Back to Prosperity: The Great Opportunity of the Empire Conference* (New York: Macmillan, 1932); Maurice Ollivier, comp. and ed., *The Colonial and Imperial Conferences from 1887 to 1937* (Ottawa: E. Cloutier, Queen's Printer, 1954), 2: 229–43; Arthur Berriedale Keith, *The Constitutional Law of the British Dominions* (London: Macmillan, 1933), 13.

Imperial Conference, Fifth
Meeting, 1937, in which the "dominion nations" of the United Kingdom met for the last time because they achieved a degree of independence several years earlier under the STATUTE OF WESTMINSTER. Held in London from May 14 to June 15, 1937, the conference was presided over first by British prime minister Stanley BALDWIN and then by Prime Minister Neville CHAMBERLAIN, after Baldwin's Conservative Party lost the 1937 elections.

The conference dealt with foreign affairs and defense issues. Canadian Prime Minister William Lyon Mackenzie KING and South African Prime Minister James Barry Munnik HERTZOG were in attendance. When Australia and New Zealand asked for a mutual defense in case of war, King advocated that the Canadian Parliament be allowed to vote on whether to participate in a war. Hertzog promoted the stand of neutrality. The delegates voted to allow each dominion nation to decide its own future. They also agreed "that each Member takes part in a multilateral treaty as an individual entity, and, in the absence of express provision in the treaty to the contrary, is in no way responsible for the obligations by any other Member." At the start of the conference, although the members knew it was the last of its kind, King asked for "continuity through change; progress through development of proved courses and innate tendencies; permanence and flexibility are the distinctive mark of the political institutions which are our common heritage." The Canadian constitution was "repatriated" in 1982, but Canada remains in Commonwealth .

References: Maurice Ollivier, comp. and ed., *The Colonial and Imperial Conferences from 1887 to 1937* (Ottawa: E. Cloutier, Queen's Printer, 1954), 2: 425–35; Robert Burgess Stewart, *Treaty Relations of the British Commonwealth of Nations* (New York: Macmillan, 1939).

Imperial Economic Conference   *See* OTTAWA
ECONOMIC CONFERENCE.

International Labour Organization

Specialized trade association, established under the Treaty
of VERSAILLES, June 28, 1919, to deal with labor conditions
around the world. Constituted under part 13 of the Versailles agreement, the preamble of the organization reads:

> "Whereas the LEAGUE OF NATIONS has for its object
> the establishment of universal peace, and such a
> peace can be established only if it is based upon
> social justice;
>
> And whereas conditions of labour exist involv-
> ing such injustice, hardship, and privation to large
> numbers of people as to produce unrest so great
> that the peace and harmony of the world are imper-
> illed; and an improvement of those conditions is
> urgently required: as, for example, by the regulation
> of the hours of work, including the establishment of
> a maximum working day and week, the regulation
> of the labour supply, the prevention of unemploy-
> ment, the provision of an adequate living wage, the
> protection of the worker against sickness, disease
> and injury arising out of his employment, the pro-
> tection of children, young persons and women, pro-
> vision for old age and injury, protection of the
> interests of workers when employed in countries
> other than their own, recognition of the principle of
> freedom of association, the organisation of voca-
> tional and technical education and other measures;
>
> Whereas also the failure of any nation to adopt
> humane conditions of labour is an obstacle in the
> way of other nations which desire to improve the
> conditions in their own countries; The high con-
> tracting parties, moved by sentiments of justice and
> humanity as well as by the desire to secure the per-
> manent peace of the world, agree to the following: A
> Permanent organisation is hereby established for the
> promotion of the objects set forth in the Preamble."

The organization was awarded the 1967 Nobel Prize
for Peace "in recognition of its 50 years of service in promoting international brotherhood."

References: *International Labour Conference Record of Proceedings* (Geneva: International Labour Office, 1919–);
Charles Noble Gregory, "The International Labour Organization of the League of Nations," *The American Journal of International Law,* 15 (1921): 42–50.

International Style

Innovative school of design, particularly during the 1920s,
of buildings and other architectural construction. Known

International Style row houses in Berlin, 1928
(CORBIS/Underwood & Underwood)

as "international" because the style transgressed national
borders in the years following World War I; it sprang up
simultaneously in western Europe and the United States
and was advanced by such artists and architects as Walter
GROPIUS, Ludwig MIES VAN DER ROHE, Henry-Russell Hitchcock, Le Corbusier, and Philip Johnson, among others.
The movement's characteristics included the use of new
metals and concrete that had been formulated by the
Industrial Revolution. The movement faded after World
War II and by the 1970s was known as postmodernism.

Reference: Henry Russell Hitchcock and Philip Johnson, *The
International Style* (New York: W. W. Norton, 1966).

Irish Free State

Area of complete Irish control, established by a law of the
British Parliament, December 23, 1920. After Michael
COLLINS, then a member of the Irish Republican Army
(IRA), signed the Anglo-Irish Peace Treaty of December
6, 1921, the Irish Free State was established, which com-

pleted the partition of Ireland into two states. A dissident group inside the IRA, led by Éamon DE VALÉRA, called the Fianna Fáil, refused to accept the treaty and called for elections to the Irish Dáil, or parliament. The pro-treaty Republicans won the most seats, and thus began a civil war in which Collins was murdered and thousands were killed. William Thomas Cosgrave, a member of the Sinn Féin (the political wing of the IRA), became prime minister of the Irish Free State in 1922. Cosgrave drafted a constitution that provided for a bicameral legislature made up of the Dáil (the lower house) and Saenad (Senate, the upper house). After the British Parliament agreed to this constitution, it went into effect on December 6, 1922. The Fianna Fáil called a truce so that it could participate in new elections; no party won a majority of seats, but when the Fianna Fáil boycotted the session of the Dáil, Cosgrave was able to form a government.

In 1925 the boundary between the Catholic (southern) Ireland and the heavily Protestant Northern Ireland was fixed. In 1932, Cosgrave's party lost control of the Dáil, and De Valéra took power as the Irish Free State's second prime minister. That year, the prince of Wales opened the new home of the Dáil at Stormont Castle, in east Belfast. De Valéra attempted to end the relationship between Northern Ireland and England by introducing several pieces of legislation, all of which led to a tariff fight that injured the Irish economy during the early depression years. In the 1930s, De Valéra's government enacted programs that provided for a self-sustained Irish economy, including taxing the rich.

In 1937 the Dáil's term expired, and in new elections the anti-British Republicans won a majority of the seats. De Valéra drafted a new constitution that abolished the Irish Free State and created a new entity called Éire, which would be wholly independent from London. Irish voters approved the measure, and in 1937 the Irish Free State was abolished. De Valéra was named as the prime minister of Éire, with Irish writer Douglas Hyde becoming the first president of the new state.

References: Joseph M. Curran, *The Birth of the Irish Free State, 1921–1923* (University, Alabama: University of Alabama Press, 1980); Frank Pakenham, Earl of Longford, *Peace by Ordeal: An Account, from First-Hand Sources, of the Negotiation and Signature of the Anglo-Irish Treaty, 1921* (London, G. Chapman, 1962); Padraic Colum, *Ourselves Alone! The Story of Arthur Griffith and the Origin of the Irish Free State* (New York: Crown Publishers, 1959).

Irreconcilables

Select group of U.S. senators, so named for their hostile and belligerent opposition to the passage of the Treaty of VERSAILLES in the U.S. Senate. Among this group were Republicans Henry Cabot LODGE of Massachusetts; Hiram Warren JOHNSON of California; Frank Bosworth Brandegee

of Connecticut; William Edgar BORAH of Idaho; and James A. Reed of Missouri. The men fought all attempts to enact the Versailles Treaty into law; they also resisted American participation in the LEAGUE OF NATIONS. Speeches from the Senate floor bear witness to their passionate arguments for the defeat of the League and all that it stood for.

See also LEAGUE OF NATIONS CONTROVERSY.

Reference: Ralph A. Stone, *The Irreconcilables: The Fight against the League of Nations* (Lexington: University Press of Kentucky, 1970).

Iskenderun

Turkish village, also known as Alexandretta, that played an integral role in the shaping of modern Turkey in the years after World War I. A seaport, Iskenderun is part of the *vilayet,* or village, of Antakiya (Antioch). During World War I it belonged to the Ottoman Empire, but at the end of the war French forces occupied the village. On October 20, 1918, the Mundros Truce was signed, which allowed the Allies to occupy several provinces of the Ottoman Empire, including Antep, Marash, Merzifon, Samsun, Urfa by the British, Adana by the French, and Antalya and Konya by the Italians. On May 19, 1919, troops led by Mustafa KEMAL (later known as Ataturk) landed at Samsun, beginning what is called the Turkish national struggle. Ataturk then launched a war against the Allies for control of this city. His country was far too weak to control the contest, however, and the Allies ultimately had their way; Iskenderun was consolidated into the French mandate of Syria and renamed Alexandretta. In 1937 it was granted increased autonomy, and in 1939 it was returned to Turkish authority and renamed Iskenderun.

Reference: David Fromkin, *A Peace to End All Peace: The Fall of the Ottoman Empire and the Creation of the Modern Middle East* (New York: Avon Books, 1989), 140–41.

Italian Somaliland

Controversial colony that figured prominently in Italian affairs on the continent of Africa in the 1930s. One of four of Italy's possessions in Africa (the others being Abyssinia [now Ethiopia], Libya, and Eritrea), this colony came under the umbrella name of Italian East Africa. In October 1935, Italian troops invaded the area, located on the eastern coast of Africa, and within seven months they had conquered the region. On May 9, 1936, during the ETHIOPIAN CRISIS, Italian fascist leader Benito MUSSOLINI proclaimed that Ethiopia had been annexed and replaced Ethiopian leader HAILE SALASSIE with the king of Italy, Victor Emmanuel III, as Ethiopia's new emperor. On June 1, 1936, the king annexed Somaliland as an Italian province by royal decree, making the city of Mogadiscio (now Mogadishu) the colony's capital.

After the beginning of World War II, British troops concentrated on liberating the area. Early in 1941, they cleared Italian troops out of Italian Somaliland and Eritrea; Addis Ababa, the former Ethiopian capital, was taken in April, and on May 5, Haile Salassie was restored to his throne.

References: Estelle Sylvia Pankhurst, *Ex-Italian Somaliland* (New York: Philosophical Library, 1951); I. M. Lewis, *The Modern History of Somaliland, from Nation to State* (New York: F. A. Praeger, 1965).

Izmir

Turkish *vilayet* (village), that after being occupied by Greek forces after World War I, was restored to Turkey under the Treaty of LAUSANNE. The third largest city in Turkey (followed by Istanbul and Ankara), Izmir was settled in the third millennium B.C. as Smyrna and is known as the birthplace of the poet Homer. Over the years Izmir became one of the most important seaports in Asia Minor. In 1415, Sultan Mehmet Celebi made the village part of the Ottoman Empire, to which it belonged until 1919. In May of that year, the Greeks, taking advantage of the Ottomans' defeat, took control of the city. Under the provisions of the Lausanne Treaty, however, the city was restored to Turkish rule on September 9, 1922, and the large Greek population was evacuated. Three days later, a destructive fire engulfed the area, killing some thousand people. In 1928 and 1939 further tragedy befell the city as earthquakes ravaged the land.

References: Lysimachos Oeconomos, "The Martyrdom of Smyrna and Eastern Christendom; a file of Overwhelming Evidence, Denouncing the Misdeeds of the Turks in Asia Minor and Showing Their Responsibility for the Horrors of Smyrna" (London: G. Allen & Unwin, 1922); Marjorie Housepian, *Smyrna 1922: The Destruction of a City* (London: Faber, 1972); Edmund Jan Osmañczyk, *The Encyclopedia of the United Nations and International Agreements* (Philadelphia: Taylor & Francis, 1985), 429.

Jallianwala Bagh Massacre

Slaughter, April 13, 1919, in which British colonial troops fired on a mass of unarmed Indians celebrating a Sikh festival, killing nearly four hundred men, women, and children and wounding more than twelve hundred. On that day a crowd of some twenty thousand assembled in Jallianwala Bagh, an eight-acre parcel of land surrounded on three sides by buildings and on a fourth by a wall some 15 feet tall, to call for India's independence from Britain.

Crowds had gathered in the Amritsar area of northern India to celebrate the festival of *Baisakhi,* the Hindu Solar New Year, in which Hindus go to temples to *puja* (worship). Brigadier General Reginald Dyer, head of English troops in India, moved against the crowd with only 50 soldiers. Without warning, Dyer ordered the Gurkhas (the Indian soldiers under command of England) to ring the area and open fire. For 10 minutes the troops fired into the crowd.

Dyer later told an investigating committee that he had ordered his men to open fire to "produce the necessary moral and widespread effect." The massacre was determined in the landmark Hunter Report to have been "an error in judgment." Denounced in the British House of Commons, Dyer was forced into retirement, although many of his supporters, particularly in the House of Lords, raised a fund of some thirty thousand pounds for his severance. He died in Bristol on July 23, 1927.

The Jallianwala Bagh massacre marked a turning point for India's independence movement. Just four months later, nationalist and spiritual leader Mohandas Karamchand GANDHI began his first *Satyagraha* (literally, "truth seeking") in opposition to English rule in India. On October 12, 1997, Queen Elizabeth II visited the Punjab state and the site of the Jallianwala massacre. Although protesters demanded that she officially apologize for the killings, she merely visited a monument to the event.

See also ROWLATT ACTS.

References: "Jallianwala Bagh Massacre" in Surjit Mansingh, *Historical Dictionary of India* (Lanham, Md.: Scarecrow, 1996), 201; Helen Fein, *Imperial Crime and Punishment: The Massacre at Jallianwala Bagh and British Judgment, 1919–1920* (Honolulu: University Press of Hawaii, 1977); Alfred Draper, *The Amritsar Massacre: Twilight of the Raj* (London: Buchan & Enright, 1985).

Jannings, Emil (1884–1950)

Swiss-German actor, known for the tragic roles he portrayed in silent films during the interwar period. Born Theodor Friedrich Emil Janenz in Rorschach, Switzerland, on July 23, 1884, he was brought up in the village of Goritz, Austria, where he began his stage career. In 1906 he joined a theatrical group headed by Max Reinhardt, a leading German stage director. Within a few years Jannings became skilled at his craft. His acting career began in 1914 with *Passionels Tagebuch* and ended 74 films later with 1945's *Wo ist Herr Belling?* ("Where is Mr. Belling?"). His early career, in small German films, was not particularly noteworthy; it was not until he appeared in *Passion* (1919), as Louis XV, that Jannings received the acclaim that was long in coming. He then starred in a number of productions produced by the German film company UFA, playing such characters as Henry VIII and Peter the Great and working with close friend and famed director Ernst Lubitsch.

In 1924 the German director Friedrich Wilhelm MURNAU directed *The Last Laugh,* in which Jannings played a hotel porter, and in 1925 Jannings played Boss Huller in *Variety*—both roles earned him enormous popularity. In 1930, when he appeared in a lead talking role with Marlene DIETRICH in *The Blue Angel,* Jannings was hailed as one of the finest actors in the world. In 1929 he won the

179

first Academy Award for Best Actor for his performances as August Schilling, the angry and cynical family man, in *The Way of All Flesh* (1928). He also played the dual roles of General Dolgorucki and Grand Duke Sergius Alexander in *The Last Command* (1928).

In 1933 Jannings was recruited by Joseph GOEBBELS, the minister of propaganda for the NAZI PARTY, to make films in Germany. A Nazi sympathizer who never formally joined the party, Jannings accepted, participating in several films between 1933 and 1944. As the war was ending in 1945 he began to film *Where is Mr. Belling?*, but because of the war it was never completed. Although Jannings was not arrested by the Allies after the war, he was blacklisted from returning to the United States; he settled in Austria, embittered, and died near Salzburg on January 2, 1950.

See also MOTION PICTURES, SILENT.

Reference: Ephraim Katz, *The Film Encyclopedia* (New York: HarperPerennial, 1994), 612–13.

jazz

Distinctly American form of music, developed by African-Americans before World War I and popularized in the 1920s and 1930s. Born in the southern United States, where the gospel of African-Americans merged with African chants and blues music, the new art form was embraced and expanded by black and white musicians alike. One of the first contributors to the art form was Ferdinand "Jelly Roll" Morton, who took the 1890s ragtime tunes of Scott Joplin and added a stomping beat. Morton became identified with this "stomp," evident in such tunes as "The King Porter Stomp" and "Wild Man Blues."

In the early 20th century, jazz came out of New Orleans, Louisiana, perfected by the harmonious sounds of King Joe Oliver and his Creole Jazz Band, Bunk Johnson, Alphonse Picou, Wingy Manone, and Nick LaRocca and his Original Dixieland Band. During World War I that sound was further fine-tuned by Louis ARMSTRONG. Throughout the 1920s some of the most creative jazz was developed in Chicago cabarets and New York clubs. Although he started with a small band in 1918, bandleader Paul Whiteman, known as the "King of Jazz," amassed over the years quite a collection of talented jazz musicians, including Bix BEIDER-BECKE, guitarist Eddie Long, brothers Jimmy and Tommy DORSEY (who later became bandleaders in their own right), cornetist Red Nichols, singer Bing Crosby, and pianist Hoagy Carmichael. It was Whiteman who commissioned a then young George GERSHWIN to compose the piece that later became Gershwin's well-known "Rhapsody in Blue."

Jazz developed many styles during the interwar period. Whiteman and other famed bandleaders, such as Jean Goldkette, experimented with what became known as "symphonic jazz." Other styles included the rural blues and the urban blues, typified by such female singers as Ma RAINEY, Bessie SMITH, and Billie HOLIDAY, who infused raw emotion into their songs. The innovation of "Chicago-style" jazz led to the development of such acts as Count Basie, Artie Shaw, Duke ELLINGTON, and Benny Goodman and to the advent of swing music, which was wildly popular in the 1930s and 1940s.

References: Paul Whiteman and Mary Margaret McBride, *Jazz* (New York: J. H. Sears, 1926); L. Allen Pyke, "Jazz, 1920–1927: An Analytical Study" (Ph.D. dissertation, State University of Iowa, 1962); *Reader's Digest Great Events of the 20th Century: How They Changed Our Lives* (Pleasantville, N.Y.: The Reader's Digest Association, 1977), 174–79.

Jazz Age

Post–World War I era of escapism, isolationism, and excess in the United States, also called the Roaring Twenties. Americans enjoyed a period of prosperity from 1921 to 1929, under presidents Warren G. HARDING, Calvin COOLIDGE, and Herbert HOOVER, and many seemed to experience a rising standard of living. In this era of PROHIBITION, liquor was bootlegged, organized crime escalated, the fashion of the FLAPPER was all the rage, and new forms of entertainment flourished, such as JAZZ music, HOLLYWOOD, and the Broadway MUSICALS of Irving BERLIN, Jerome KERN, Cole PORTER, and George GERSHWIN. For those who could afford it, the Jazz Age was a time of "random hedonism."

Artists and writers of the era declared a new sophisticated and sexually liberated modernism. Novelist F. Scott FITZGERALD and his wife Zelda epitomized the Jazz Age; they led an extravagant, ostentatious life filled with parties and drink. Fitzgerald's masterpiece *The Great Gatsby* (1925) beautifully captured the excesses of the Roaring Twenties. The STOCK MARKET CRASH of 1929 and the GREAT DEPRESSION that followed brought the era to a sudden halt.

References: Douglas Brinkley, *History of the United States* (New York: Viking, 1998), 378–79; Ted Yanak and Pam Cornelison, *The Great American History Fact-Finder* (Boston: Houghton Mifflin, 1993), 332.

The Jazz Singer

American MOTION PICTURE, considered the first "talkie." Efforts to establish talking dialogue within the confines of motion pictures had been under way for a number of years before American actor Al JOLSON was chosen to play the role of a sympathetic rabbi's son in the historic remake of the stage play by the same name. The play was originally based on Samson Samuelson's story "The Day of Atonement," which appeared in *Everybody's Magazine* in January 1922. On stage, American actor George Jessel had played the lead role. Jolson plays Jakie Rabinowitz, who rebels against his religious upbringing and intends to go into show business despite his father's wishes. Conflict with his father forces Jakie to strike out on his own, changing his name to Jack Robin and working small shows in Chicago before hitting it big in his native New York. The hostility the rabbi has toward Jakie's profession makes Jakie work even harder. In two small scenes Jakie talks with and sings to his mother. A loud "Stop!" is heard when his father enters the room, and the film returns to silence. Jakie pleads for acceptance, but his father asks him to leave. Days later, after forgiving his only child, the rabbi dies.

English critic and writer Cedric Belfrage said of the film, "After seeing *The Jazz Singer* I went home feeling very sad, really. And I made my contribution by predicting that the talkies wouldn't last long." But that was actually the beginning of the end for silent films. *The Jazz Singer* may have been the first film to use dialogue, but because the dialogue is limited to only two scenes, many film historians do not consider it the first "talkie." That distinction belongs to the 1928 Prohibition crime drama *Lights of New York*.

References: Samson Raphaelson, "The Jazz Singer, by Samson Raphaelson (Based on His Story, *The Day of Atonement*, in *Everybody's Magazine*, January, 1922)" (New York: Brentano's, 1925); Robert L. Carringer, ed., *The Jazz Singer* (Madison: Published for the Wisconsin Center for Film and Theater Research by the University of Wisconsin Press, 1979).

Jeffers, Robinson (1887–1962)

American poet, famed for his classic works produced during the interwar years, including *Roan Stallion, Tamar, and other Poems* (1924), *The Women at Point Sur* (1927), *Dear Judas, and other Poems* (1929), and *Thurso's Landing, and other Poems* (1932). Born John Robinson Jeffers in the town of Allegheny, now part of Pittsburgh, Pennsylvania, on January 10, 1887, Jeffers attended private schools, then graduated from Occidental College in 1905 before studying forestry and medicine at the University of Washington and the University of Zurich. He studied medicine at the University of Southern California but turned to writing poetry after receiving a large inheritance. In June 1904 the magazine *Youth's Companion* published his first work, a poem entitled "The Condor." His work is characterized by intense, virile lyrics that express the difficult realities of love, humanity, and nature.

Jeffers wrote almost up until his death. His translation of Euripides's *Medea* appeared on Broadway in 1947; he also wrote *Be Angry at the Sun* (1941), *The Double Axe* (1948), and *Hungerfeld* (1954). Jeffers died in Carmel, California, on January 20, 1962. His home, Tor House, is now a national landmark.

References: Robert Zaller, ed., *Centennial Essays for Robinson Jeffers* (Newark: University of Delaware Press, 1991); Alex A. Vardamis, *The Critical Reputation of Robinson Jeffers: A Biblio-*graphical Study (Hamden, Conn.: Archon Books, 1972); *Time* 39, 14 (April 4, 1932), 63–64.

Jinnah, Mohammed Ali (1876–1948)

Indian politician, considered the father of Pakistan. Jinnah was born on December 25, 1876, in Karachi, in what was then the British colony of India (later the capital of an independent Pakistan). He studied the law in England before returning to India to practice law in Bombay. A Muslim, he became interested in politics and joined the 1906 session of the Indian National Congress, which sought independence for India from Great Britain. In 1910 he was elected to the Imperial Legislative Council and became a nationalist, not for Indian independence but for a separate Muslim nation from India. In 1913 he joined the All-India Muslim League.

During the 1920s Jinnah and his Muslim movement were overshadowed by the figure of Mohandas K. GANDHI, who desired independence from Great Britain with Muslims and Hindus living under one government. Jinnah left the Congress for a period but rejoined when Hindu-Muslim tensions rose. In 1930 he joined the Round Table Conferences in London for a full discussion of constitutional issues, which lasted until 1932. Here he advocated his 14 points, which included a representational government, protections for minorities, and one-third of the legislature's seats set aside for Muslims; these positions were rejected, however. Many Muslims did not believe Jinnah was radical enough, and he was repudiated by the Punjab Muslim League. He settled in London to work before the Privy Council from 1930 until 1935.

Jinnah returned to India when the British government passed the second GOVERNMENT OF INDIA ACT in 1935, which allowed for more Indian representation in their government. In elections two years later, however, the Hindus won an overwhelming majority of seats in the legislature, and they decided not to include the Muslims in the formation of a government. Jinnah picked up the idea first advocated by Indian poet and philosopher Muhammad Iqbal that a separate Muslim state, in northern India, was the only solution for Muslims. Jinnah became the leader of this cause. After World War II, Jinnah faced down Gandhi and Jawaharlal NEHRU, both Indian nationalist leaders, and demanded a separate Indian state. The British acceded to his demand to avoid bloodshed, and on August 15, 1947, the British turned over control to the Indians. At Karachi a new state of Pakistan, ruled and dominated by Muslims, was founded. Jinnah, called *Qaid-e-Azam* ("the Great Leader"), was named as the first governor general of the new nation. He established a government and a working legislature, but died soon after, on September 11, 1948.

References: Stanley Wolpert, *Jinnah of Pakistan* (New York: Oxford University Press, 1984); Hector Bolitho, *Jinnah: Creator of Pakistan* (London: J. Murray, 1954).

Johnson, Hiram Warren (1867–1945)

U.S. politician, whose stance as one of the IRRECONCILABLES made him one of the leading voices in foreign affairs in the 1920s. Johnson was born on September 2, 1866, in Sacramento, California. After working in his father's law office, he studied the law (but later dropped out) at the University of California at Berkeley. He began to practice law after studying on his own in Sacramento and San Francisco.

As the prosecuting attorney for San Francisco, Johnson became known for cracking down on local corruption. In 1910 he was elected governor on a platform of reforming campaign laws. During his six years as California governor (1911–17), Johnson submitted the first unified state budget by a state executive in U.S. history. In 1912 he broke from the Republican Party and served as the vice presidential candidate of the Progressive, or "Bull Moose," Party, led by former president Theodore ROOSEVELT; the ticket came in second behind Democrat Woodrow WILSON, and outpolled the regular Republican ticket. In 1916, Johnson ran for a seat in the U.S. Senate and was elected to the first of five six-year terms (1917–45). As one of the "Irreconcilables," a group of mostly conservative Republicans in the Senate, he opposed American entry into the LEAGUE OF NATIONS in 1919 at all costs. He became an isolationist in world affairs and a protectionist at home. He sponsored the Johnson-Reed Immigration Act (the IMMIGRATION ACT OF 1924) and the NEUTRALITY ACTS of the 1930s. Later in the decade he voted to support farm legislation and, in the 1930s, various NEW DEAL measures to end the GREAT DEPRESSION. He also refused to vote for American participation in the PERMANENT COURT OF INTERNATIONAL JUSTICE, showing his staunch isolationist streak.

Johnson died on August 6, 1945, the same day the United States dropped an atomic bomb on the Japanese city of Hiroshima.

References: Michael A. Weatherson and Hal W. Bochin, *Hiram Johnson: Political Revivalist* (Lanham, Md.: University Press of America, 1995); Richard Coke Lower, *A Bloc of One: The Political Career of Hiram W. Johnson* (Stanford, Calif.: Stanford University Press, 1993); Spencer C. Olin, *California's Prodigal Sons: Hiram Johnson and the Progressives, 1911–1917* (Berkeley: University of California Press, 1968).

Johnson, James Weldon (1871–1938)

American educator and author whose books during the interwar period contributed to the revival of African-American literary and artistic spirit known as the HARLEM RENAISSANCE. Born on June 17, 1871, in Jacksonville, Florida, Johnson was the son of James Johnson and Helen Louise (Dillet) Johnson. In researching his autobiography, *Along This Way* (1933), Johnson ascertained that his maternal great grandfather was a white slave trader who married an African slave in Nassau. Johnson was taught music by his mother; he then graduated from Atlanta University with bachelor's (1894) and master's (1904) degrees. After he attended Columbia University, he served as a principal in a school in Jacksonville, Florida. He studied the law during this time and in 1897 was admitted to the Florida bar.

In 1899 Johnson and his brother John Rosamond Johnson composed the inspirational piece "Lift Every Voice and Sing," which many have called the Negro national anthem, one of more than two hundred songs he wrote in his lifetime. The lyrics include:

> Lift every voice and sing
> Till earth and heaven ring,
> Ring with the harmonies of Liberty;
> Let our rejoicing rise
> High as the listening skies,
> Let it resound loud as the rolling sea.

Johnson joined the NAACP staff in 1916, serving as executive secretary from 1920 to 1930. In 1930 he became a professor of creative literature at Fisk University. His most important works include *The Book of American Negro Poetry* (1922), *God's Trombones* (1927), and *Negro Americans, What Now* (1934).

On June 26, 1938, Johnson was killed in an automobile accident near Wiscasset, Maine.

References: James Weldon Johnson, *Along This Way: The Autobiography of James Weldon Johnson* (New York: Viking, 1933), 3–13; Sterling A. Brown, "Johnson, James Weldon" in Allen Johnson and Dumas Malone et al., eds., *Dictionary of American Biography* (New York: Charles Scribner's Sons, 1930–95), 2: 345–47; Lynn Adelman, "A Study of James Weldon Johnson," *Journal of Negro History* 52 (April 1967): 126–45.

Johnson, Robert (1911–1938)

American musical pioneer, whose JAZZ recordings remained unknown until several decades after his mysterious death at age 27. Born to a family of poor sharecroppers in the small town of Hazelhurst, Mississippi, on May 8, 1911, Johnson was raised in Memphis, Tennessee, and Robinsonville, Mississippi. At an early age he learned how to play the guitar and harmonica and began to travel to see and hear performances of the blues, that uniquely American type of music that originated in the southern United States. For several years Johnson himself played at clubs and parties in New York and Chicago. During this time he wrote such classic early blues compositions as "Dust My Broom," "Crossroads," "Sweet Home Chicago," "Ramblin' on My Mind," "Love in Vain," and "Me and the Devil Blues." Starting in 1936, Johnson recorded all of his songs—a total of only 29. These have become classic blues masterpieces, and many artists who followed his style and artistry claim Johnson as their inspiration.

Johnson died a mysterious death near Greenwood, Mississippi, in August 1937; some claim that he was poisoned by the jealous husband of his girlfriend, others that he just got sick and died. His grave has never been found. Johnson was inducted into the Rock and Roll Hall of Fame in Cleveland, Ohio, in 1986.

References: Peter Guralnick, *Searching for Robert Johnson* (New York: Dutton, 1989); Tony Russell, *The Blues: From Robert Johnson to Robert Cray* (New York: Schirmer Books, 1997).

Johnson, Walter Perry (1887–1946)

American baseball player, considered one of the finest pitchers of the 20th century. Born in Humboldt, Kansas, on November 6, 1887, he joined the Washington Senators baseball team in 1907 and remained with them throughout his 21-year career. Known as "the Big Train" for his sweeping underhanded pitches, he is second in career wins (417, second to Cy Young's 511), seventh in strikeouts (3,509), first in shutout victories (either 110 or 113), fifth all time in complete games (531), and third in innings pitched (5923 2/3). In 1924, although he lost two of the three games he pitched, he won the crucial game seven in the World Series, giving the Senators their only world championship. Johnson's other World Series appearance happened in 1925, when the Senators lost four games to three to the Pittsburgh Pirates. In 1929 he became the manager of the Senators, serving until 1932, and then from 1933 until his retirement in 1935 he was the manager of the Cleveland Indians. In 1936 he was elected to the Baseball Hall of Fame. Johnson died on December 10, 1946.

References: Steven Michael Bailey, "Walter Perry Johnson: A Biography" (Master's thesis, Arizona State University, 1990); Roger L. Treat, *Walter Johnson: King of the Pitchers* (New York: J. Messner, 1948).

Joint Plan Red

1931 American war plan devised to defeat Great Britain if necessary. From 1921 until 1945 the United States military establishment developed several "color plans" for how it would conduct war in several areas of the world. For example, War Plan Orange was a blueprint to defeat Japan. Joint Plan Red, perhaps the strangest of the color plans, was a strategy to defeat Great Britain.

References: Edward S. Miller, *War Plan Orange: The U.S. Strategy to Defeat Japan, 1897–1945* (Annapolis, Md.: Naval Institute Press, 1991); Thaddeus Holt, "Joint Plan Red," *Military History Quarterly* 1 (Autumn 1988): 48–55.

Joliot-Curie, Frédéric (1900–1958) and Irène Curie (1897–1956)

Husband and wife physicists, awarded the 1935 Nobel Prize in physics "for their jointly performed synthesis of the new radioactive elements." Irène Curie, the daughter of the noted physicist team of Pierre and Marie Curie, was born in Paris on September 12, 1897. With her parents as role models, she was educated privately, receiving her doctorate at the institute that bore her mother's name in 1925. Frédéric Joliot, born in 1900, received his education at the Paris Institute for Physics and Chemistry and later at the Paris Radium Institute, where he worked as an assistant to Marie Curie. He and Irène Curie married in 1926. Irène Curie succeeded her mother as director of the institute in 1932.

She and her husband worked on the theories of radioactivity, furthering researches that had won Marie Curie two Nobel prizes. In 1935 the Joliot-Curies were likewise awarded the Nobel. Irène Curie later split the atom.

During World War II, Frédéric Joliot-Curie was a member of the French Underground; after the war he served as a French member of the United Nation's Atomic Energy Commission. He joined the French Communist Party, and in 1950 he was dismissed from his position with the commission. In 1951 he was awarded the Stalin Prize from the Soviet Union. That same year Irène Curie was dismissed from the French Atomic Energy Commission. Disgraced by their leftist ties in their final years, Irène Curie died on March 17, 1956; her husband died on August 14, 1958.

References: Dorothy Riemenschneider, "Joliot-Curie, Irène," and L. B. Woods, "Joliot-Curie, Frédéric" in Bernard S. and June H. Schlessinger, eds., *The Who's Who of Nobel Prize Winners* (Phoenix, Ariz.: Oryx, 1986), 13–14; Thomas Watson MacCallum and Stephen Taylor, eds., *The Nobel Prize-Winners and the Nobel Foundation, 1901–1937* (Zurich: Central European Times Publishing, 1938), 164–65.

Jolson, Al (1886–1950)

American entertainer, famed for his 1927 performance in the film version of THE JAZZ SINGER, considered by many film historians to have been the first talking MOTION PICTURE. Born Asa Yoelson in the village of Srednike, Russia (now in Lithuania), on May 25, 1886, he was the son of cantor Moses Yoelson, an Orthodox Jew. Little is known of his early life, except that in 1892 his father was appointed as the cantor of a synagogue in Washington, D.C., and the family moved to the United States. As a

Irène Joliot-Curie and Frédéric Joliot-Curie *(CORBIS)*

teenager, he appeared in a stage play, *Children of the Ghetto*, at the National Theater in Washington, D.C.

Soon after starting his stage career, Jolson—now billed as Al Yoelson (in 1903 he changed it permanently to Jolson)—appeared in New York's vaudeville with his brother Harry. In 1904 he began to use the technique of blackface, in which a performer masks his face with dark makeup to hide his face from the crowd (a practice that offended many African-Americans in later years). Over the years Jolson perfected his act to include singing on one knee, belting out such tunes as "My Mammy" and "April Showers." His favorite phrase to call out to the crowd was "You ain't heard nothin' yet!"

In 1923, Jolson went to Hollywood to perform in motion pictures. He starred in a D. W. GRIFFITH vehicle, *Mammy's Boy*, but was so upset that his singing would not be heard in a silent film that he asked that all copies be destroyed. He eventually did star in a silent film, *A Planta-*

tion Act (1926) as himself, before Warner Brothers decided to place Jolson in the first picture with actual spoken dialogue, *The Jazz Singer*. The film was a sensation and marked the end of the silent era. Hollywood, so enamored of the picture, bestowed it and Jolson a special award, the first Academy Award. Jolson's second film, *The Singing Fool* (1928), was the highest-grossing picture until *Gone With the Wind* (1939).

Jolson appeared in several films in the 1930s, including *Hallelujah, I'm a Bum* (1933), *Wonder Bar* (1934), and *Go into Your Dance* (1935), but it was that initial hit that had made him a star. During World War II, Jolson sang overseas for American soldiers. After the war, with the re-release of *The Jazz Singer*, his popularity surged, and Hollywood capitalized on it by releasing *The Al Jolson Story* in 1946. What few people knew at the time was that Jolson himself sang the songs in that movie. Three years later, *Al Jolson Sings Again* came out, but Jolson was too ill to enjoy this newfound popularity. Upon his return from Korea, he collapsed in San Francisco from a heart attack and died on October 23, 1950.

References: Michael Freedland, *Jolie: The Al Jolson Story* (London: W. H. Allen, 1985); Robert Oberfirst, *Al Jolson: You Ain't Heard Nothin' Yet* (San Diego, Calif.: A. S. Barnes, 1982); Harry M. Geduld, *The Birth of the Talkies: From Edison to Jolson* (Bloomington: Indiana University Press, 1975); "Al Jolson Dead After Korea Tour; Noted Singer of Stage, Screen Has Heart Attack as He Plays Cards—Was 64," *New York Times,* October 24, 1950, p. 1.

Jones, Bobby (1902–1971)

American golfer, considered one of the greatest sports legends of the 20th century. The son of Robert Tyre Jones Sr., he was born in Atlanta, Georgia, on March 17, 1902. Although he studied the law and practiced for a time in Atlanta, Jones decided to become an amateur golfer in 1920. In a career that spanned only a decade, Jones became one of the best golf players in history. Between 1923 and 1930, he won four U.S. Open championships, three British Open championships, five U.S. amateur championships, and one British amateur championship. In 1930 he took four major tournaments (the U.S. Open, the British Open, and the amateur opens in both countries), then retired from the game. In Walker Cup competition between American and British players, he won nine of 10 matches. In 1934, four years after his retirement, Jones helped establish the Master's Tournament at the Augusta, Georgia, National Golf Club.

Jones died in Atlanta on December 18, 1971.

References: Davis, Martin, "The Greatest of Them All: The Legend of Bobby Jones" (Chicago: Triumph Books, 1996); Smith, Red, "Four!" *American Heritage,* 31: 5 (August/September 1980), 76–85.

Journey's End

Landmark interwar drama produced in 1929, by writer and playwright Robert Cedric Sherriff, which dealt with the experiences of four British soldiers in the trenches of World War I. Under the command of Captain Stanhope, the four men, including one who is killed at the start of the play and one who is paralyzed by a German shell, must deal with war and its horrendous effect on their lives. The action revolves around how the men cope with war and accept their circumstances. Sherriff's drama was one of the first to demonstrate war's ultimate price.

See also ALL QUIET ON THE WESTERN FRONT.

References: Robert Cedric Sherriff, *Journey's End: A Play in Three Acts* (London: Victor Gollancz, 1929); Rosa Maria Bracco, *Merchants of Hope: British Middlebrow Writers and the First World War, 1919–1939* (Providence, R.I.: Berg, 1993).

Joyce, James (1882–1941)

Irish poet and novelist, noted for his landmark interwar works, *Ulysses* (1922) and *Finnegans Wake* (1939). Born James Augustine Joyce in the Dublin suburb of Rathgar, on February 2, 1882, he was educated at Clongowes Wood College, Belvedere College, and University College in Dublin. His first work, *Chamber Music* (1907), a manuscript of song lyrics, was followed by *Dubliners* (1914), stories of the Irish city and its citizens plagued by moral uncertainty, the novel *A Portrait of the Artist as a Young Man* (1916), and a play, *The Exiles* (1918).

Joyce developed the techniques of the interior monologue and the stream-of-consciousness narrative. Of Joyce's interwar classic novels, Professor Charles H. Peake writes, "[Ulysses] is chiefly concerned with the experiences in Dublin on June 16, 1904 of two men—Leopold Bloom, a Jewish advertisement canvasser, who, though often absurd and frequently humiliated, remains, unlike the citizens of *Dubliners,* morally active, resilient and resourceful, and Stephen Dedalus, now bitter, defeated and dispirited. Though the events of the day are among the most commonplace recorded in literature, the brief meeting of the two men is significant for each of them, and their mental processes are verbalized with unprecedented invention and daring." Although *Ulysses* was published in Europe and was distributed widely there, it was banned from the United States as indecent material. After many years of litigation, in 1933 U.S. Federal Judge John Munro Woolsey held that *Ulysses* was not indecent and could not be banned. In 1924, Joyce began work on a novel that for a time was called "Work in Progress." Released in portions, it was not completed and released as *Finnegans Wake* until 1939.

Joyce spent much of his life in a self-imposed exile from his Irish homeland. He died in Zurich, Switzerland, on January 13, 1941. In 1944 an autobiographical work that Joyce had labored on since 1904 was released as *Stephen Hero.*

References: Richard Ellmann, "James Joyce" (New York: Oxford University Press, 1959); Thomas F. Staley, *An Annotated Critical Bibliography of James Joyce* (New York: Harvester Wheatsheaf, 1989); Harry Blamires, *The Bloomsday Book: A Guide through Joyce's "Ulysses"* (London: Methuen, 1966); Charles H. Peake, "Joyce, James Augustine Aloysius" in Alan Bullock and R. B. Woodings, eds., *20th Century Culture: A Biographical Companion* (New York: Harper & Row, 1983), 372–73.

Kahlo, Frieda *See* PAINTING.

Kaltenbrunner, Ernst (1903–1946)
NAZI PARTY official, instrumental in his role during the
ANSCHLUSS of Austria and head of the German secret police
during World War II. Born in Reid (now Innkreis), Austria,
on October 4, 1903, he obtained a doctorate in philosophy
from the University of Prague in 1926. He studied the law
and opened his own practice in the Austrian city of Linz in
1929. That same year, he was named assistant judge in
Salzburg. In 1932 he joined the Austrian Nazi Party and
was jailed in 1934 for a year for treason in trying to bring
Nazism to Austria. After his release, Kaltenbrunner was
named as the head of the Schutzstaffeln (known as the SS,
the defense and protection squads of the Reich) in Austria.

Nazi field marshal Hermann Goering recommended
that Kaltenbrunner be placed in the Nazi cabinet as state
secretary for public security, a promotion that took place
on March 11, 1938. In this role he assisted during the
German army's "annexation" of Austria. He began the
buildup of the massive system of concentration camps,
particularly the one at Mauthausen, and oversaw the capture and imprisonment of millions of Jews. On January
30, 1943, Kaltenbrunner was named as the head of the
German secret police, the Gestapo. With his chief aide,
Adolf Eichmann, Kaltenbrunner began to put the Nazi
plan known as the Final Solution—the scheme to wipe
out all of Europe's Jews—into effect.

As the war turned against Germany, however, Kaltenbrunner approached the Allies in 1944 to sign for a separate peace; he was rebuffed. As Germany fell, he was
captured by American troops and put on trial for war
crimes committed against humanity with other Nazis at
Nuremberg in 1946. Found guilty, Kaltenbrunner was
sentenced to death and hanged in Nuremberg Prison on
October 16, 1946.

References: James Taylor and Warren Shaw, *The Third Reich
Almanac* (New York: World Almanac, 1987), 186; Christian
Zentner and Friedemann Bedüftig, eds., *Encyclopedia of the
Third Reich* (New York: Macmillan, 1991), 1: 487–88; Ann
and John Tusa, *The Nuremberg Trial* (New York: Atheneum,
1986); Telford Taylor, *The Anatomy of the Nuremberg Trials: A
Personal Memoir* (New York: Alfred A. Knopf, 1992); Louis L.
Snyder, *Encyclopedia of the Third Reich* (New York: McGraw-
Hill Book Co., 1976), 190.

Kandinsky, Wassily *See* DADA; GROPIUS, WALTER.

Kapp, Wolfgang (1868–1922)
German politician and revolutionist, leader of the 1920
revolt against the republican government. He was the
son of German historian and writer Friedrich Kapp,
who had fled his native Germany during the Revolution
of 1848 and settled in New York, where his son was
born 20 years later. Little is known of Wolfgang Kapp's
early life, except that he had found his way to Germany
by the World War I. He founded the German Fatherland
Party in 1917 and served as a member of the German
Reichstag in 1918. On March 13, 1920, following a
short period of near anarchy in the streets of Berlin,
Kapp and his small band of followers initiated the so-
called "Kapp Putsch" to topple the republican government at WEIMAR of President Friedrich EBERT. When a
labor strike called by Ebert thwarted Kapp's efforts,
Kapp fled Germany just four days after his revolution
began. He spent the next two years in Sweden. Kapp
then returned to Germany but was captured and imprisoned in April 1922 to stand trial for treason against the
government. He died there on June 12, 1922, before
standing before the court.

References: Curzio Malaparte (Sylvia Saunders, trans.), *Coup d'Etat: The Technique of Revolution* (New York: E. P. Dutton & Co., 1932); Erich Eyck, *A History of the Weimar Republic* (Cambridge: Harvard University Press, 1962); "Many Killed in Berlin Rioting; Public Trial for Socialists Next Tuesday or Wednesday," *The World* (New York), January 14, 1920, p. 1.

Karlfeldt, Erik Axel (1864–1931)

Swedish writer and Nobel laureate, the only man to win two Nobel literature prizes. Born in Folkärna, Dalarna, also known as Dalecarlia, Sweden, on July 20, 1864, he graduated from the University of Uppsala. For several years he was a teacher, then a newspaper reporter for a Stockholm newspaper, then a librarian at the Royal Academy in Stockholm. In 1904 he was named a member of the Swedish Academy, he was later secretary of the Academy from 1912 until his death. His volumes of pastoral poems include *Wildmarks-och kärleksvisor* (Ballads of the woodlands and of love, 1895) *Fridolins visor* (Fridolin's ballads, 1898), *Fridolins lustgrd och dalmlningar p rim* (Fridolin's pleasure garden and Dalecarlian frescoes in rhyme, 1901), *Flora och Pomona* (Flora of Pomona, 1906), *Flora och Bellona* (Flora of Bellona, 1918), and *Hörsthorn* (Autumn cornucopia, 1927).

In 1918, Karlfeldt was awarded the Nobel Prize in literature for his body of work, but he refused to accept it. When he died on April 8, 1931, he had not yet been recognized formally for his work; that year the Nobel committee awarded him a second Nobel Prize. His work was praised as representing "our character with a style and a genuineness that we should like to be ours."

References: Parvin Kujoory, "Karlfeldt, Erik Alex" in Bernard S. and June H. Schlessinger, eds., *The Who's Who of Nobel Prize Winners* (Phoenix, Ariz.: Oryx, 1986), 53; Thomas Watson MacCallum and Stephen Taylor, eds., *The Nobel Prize-Winners and the Nobel Foundation, 1901–1937* (Zurich: Central European Times Publishing, 1938), 316–17.

Karloff, Boris (1887–1969)

British-American actor, famed for his monstrous or villainous roles in interwar classic MOTION PICTURES. Born William Henry Pratt in London on November 23, 1887, he attended King's College in London to prepare for the diplomatic service but changed his mind and instead emigrated to Canada in 1909. While there, he became an actor in small theater productions, making his debut in Molnar's *The Devil*. For the next several years he toured western Canada and the western United States, starring in several small productions. He was among the original New York cast of the Joseph Kesselring comedy *Arsenic and Old Lace*.

In 1916, Pratt landed in Hollywood, where motion pictures were still in their infancy; he landed his first role as an extra in the 1916 film *The Dumb Girl of Portici*. After a series of secondary roles, he was cast in 1932 to play the monster in FRANKENSTEIN, modeled on the creature conceived by English writer Mary Wollstonecraft Shelley. With large bolts in his neck and a flat head, Karloff's put in a performance that catapulted him to international Fame. After *Frankenstein,* however, he was typecast for a time in dark melodramas, playing in the classic *Scarface* (1932), as Imhotep in *The Mummy* (1932), as the dead Egyptologist in *The Ghoul* (1933), a repeat of the role of the monster in *The Bride of Frankenstein* (1936), and as the evil doctor in *Juggernaut* (1936). In 1938 he broke out of this rigid formula to play the devious but brilliant investigator in *Mr. Wong, Detective* (1938), the first of several films with Karloff portraying the Asian investigator.

Karloff died on February 2, 1969.

References: Peter Underwood, *Karloff: The Life of Boris Karloff, with an Appendix of the Films in which he Appeared* (New York: Drake Publishers, 1972); Scott Allen Nollen, *Boris Karloff: A Critical Account of His Screen, Stage, Radio, Television and Recording Work* (Jefferson, N.C.: McFarland & Co., 1991); Richard Bojarski and Kenneth Beale, *The Films of Boris Karloff* (Secaucus, N.J.: Citadel, 1974).

Karrer, Paul (1889–1971)

Russian-Swiss chemist and Nobel laureate. Born in Moscow in 1889, he was educated at the University of Zurich in Switzerland, where he later became an assistant at the Chemical Institute (1911), professor of chemistry (1918), and director of the institute (1919). Karrer spent his years researching the vitamin riboflavin, synthesizing the important nutrient in 1935. For this work, and for investigating the compounds and makeup of the vitamins A and B^2 and carotenoids and flavins—all-important vitamin compounds necessary for human development and life—he was the corecipient (with Walter Norman HAWORTH) of the 1937 Nobel Prize in chemistry.

Karrer retired from teaching in 1959. He died in Zurich on June 18, 1971.

Reference: Kay Harvey, "Karrer, Paul" in Bernard S. and June H. Schlessinger, eds., *The Who's Who of Nobel Prize Winners* (Phoenix, Ariz.: Oryx, 1986), 14–15.

Keaton, Buster (1895–1966)

American comedian and silent film actor, whose film work, particularly in the 1920s, marked the interwar era. Born Joseph Francis Keaton in Piqua, Kansas, on October 4, 1895, he was the son of medicine show performers and he joined the family act. When he was just six months old, magician Harry Houdini saw him fall down a flight of stairs as part of the act, and nicknamed him "Buster." As he grew up, Keaton perfected his act, eventually appearing on vaudeville after the family act split up. His unique style was demonstrated from the beginning of his MOTION PICTURE career. In *One Week* (1920), where he played a man trying to build a house Keaton used props to illustrate farce and slapstick. He followed that moderate success with *Neighbors* (1920), *The Boat* (1921), *The Balloonatic* (1923), and *The Love Nest* (1923). Following this, he worked for a time with Joseph M. Schenck in such films as *The Three Ages* (1923). He then turned out such classic silent films as *Our Hospitality* (1923), *Sherlock, Jr.* (1924), *The Navigator* (1924), *Seven Chances* (1925), and *The General* (1927), the latter of which many film historians consider one of the finest silent motion pictures ever made. After 1928, however, his output declined. He abandoned his own studio, in which he had had artistic control over his projects, and joined MGM, where he became an unhappy bit player. With the advent of sound, his farcical silent mimicry became old hat. He disappeared from the public stage for the next three decades.

In 1959, his films and image having been long forgotten and neglected by HOLLYWOOD, he was granted a special Academy Award for his body of work. Keaton was invited to Paris in 1962 to participate in a revival of his films at the Cinémathèque Française, where he soon discovered that the world was once again ready for his display of silent vaudeville. Shining again in the limelight of a rediscovered genius, he worked on two small films in 1965; he published his memoirs, *My Wonderful World of Slapstick,* in 1962. On February 1, 1966, Keaton died.

In the years since Keaton's death, his films and his deadpan character have become part of the American cinematic pantheon.

References: Rudi Blesh, *Keaton* (New York: Macmillan, 1966); Tom Dardis, *Keaton: The Man Who Wouldn't Lie Down* (New York: Scribner, 1979); George Wead and George Lellis, *The Film Career of Buster Keaton* (Boston: G. K. Hall, 1977).

Kellogg, Frank Billings (1856–1937)

American politician and Nobel laureate. As one author noted, "the biography of Frank B. Kellogg reads like a classic Horatio Alger story. A poor farm boy who received little formal education, he taught himself the law and became not only one of the nation's foremost corporate lawyers but also one of its leading trust-busters." The eldest of three children of Asa Farnsworth Kellogg and Abigail (Billings) Kellogg, he was born in Potsdam, St. Lawrence County, New York, on December 22, 1856. He moved with his family to Minnesota when he was nine and worked his parents' farm. After studying the law, he was admitted to the state bar in 1877. For three years, Kellogg served as city attorney of Rochester, Minnesota, and for five years as county attorney for Olmstead County, Minnesota.

In 1887, Kellogg joined a prestigious St. Paul law firm, where he became a corporation attorney defending the interests of major national railroad lines, later serving as special counsel to the United States in the national lawsuit to break up the Standard Oil Monopoly. Chosen president of the American Bar Association in 1912, he was elected to the U.S. Senate four years later, and served there until 1923. Named as U.S. ambassador to Great Britain in 1924 by President Calvin COOLIDGE, he was recalled the following year to replace Charles Evans HUGHES as secretary of state. During his tenure, Kellogg attempted to mediate several disputes, including that of the Tacna-Arica territorial problem between Chile and Peru. His most important accomplishment was his work to outlaw war among nations as a tool of foreign policy. Working closely with French foreign minister Aristide BRIAND, the two conceived the KELLOGG-BRIAND PACT, which was signed by 62 nations, including the United States, England, and France in Paris on August 27, 1928. For this work, Kellogg was awarded the 1929 Nobel Peace Prize, making him one of the few Americans to win this coveted prize.

After Kellogg left the State Department in 1929, he was named by President Herbert HOOVER a member of the PERMANENT COURT OF INTERNATIONAL JUSTICE at the Hague, the Netherlands, where he served from 1930 until 1935. Kellogg died in St. Paul, Minnesota, on December 21, 1937.

References: William Kamman, "Kellogg, Frank Billings" in Bernard S. and June H. Schlessinger, eds., *The Who's Who of Nobel Prize Winners* (Phoenix, Ariz.: Oryx, 1986), 134; Thomas Watson MacCallum and Stephen Taylor, eds., *The Nobel Prize–Winners and the Nobel Foundation, 1901–1937* (Zurich: Central European Times Publishing, 1938), 375; Garry J. Clifford, "Kellogg, Frank Billings" in Bruce W. Jentleson and Thomas G. Paterson, senior eds., *Encyclopedia of U.S. Foreign Relations* (New York: Oxford University Press, 3: 2–3.

Kellogg-Briand Pact

Treaty, 1929, signed by 62 nations, which aimed to end the use of war as a tool of national foreign policy, arranged by U.S. Secretary of State Frank B. KELLOGG and French prime minister Aristide BRIAND.

According to historian Harold T. Butler, the origin of the proposal for this all-encompassing treaty came from a Chicago attorney, Salmon O. Levinson, who argued that because war was considered legal by most nations, outlawing war was the only solution. The leading proponents of such an international pact were Kellogg and Briand, who wanted to curb the possibility of another war in Europe by future conflict resolution and arbitration. Signed in Paris on August 27, 1928, it asserted that the signatories were "persuaded that the time has come when a frank renunciation of war as an instrument of national policy should be made to the end that the peaceful and friendly relations now existing between their peoples" should be established. The treaty did not specify what actions could be taken to avert war, however. In the U.S. Senate vote, held on January 15, 1929, the only person to vote against the treaty's passage was Republican Senator John J. Blaine of Wisconsin. The final vote was 85–1. The House of Representatives passed it two days later, and on July 24, President Herbert HOOVER signed the pact into law.

Kellogg-Briand was probably doomed from its very inception, however. With such powers as Nazi Germany, Japan, and Soviet Russia clamoring for land expansion and augmenting their militaries, the possibility that war could be averted diminished as the optimism of the 1920s dimmed with the rise of militarism in the 1930s. In that decade many powers mentioned Kellogg-Briand as a way to avoid war, but none did anything to stop the world in its mad dash to World War II.

See also LITVINOV PROTOCOL.

References: Harold Tiffany Butler, "Partisan Positions on Isolationism vs. Internationalism, 1918–1933," (Ph.D. dissertation, Syracuse University, 1963), 137–38; Robert H. Ferrell, "The United States and the Origins of Kellogg-Briand Pact," (Ph.D. dissertation, Yale University, 1951); Robert H. Ferrell, *Peace in Their Time: The Origins of the Kellogg-Briand Pact* (New Haven, Conn.: Yale University Press, 1952); Stephen John Kneeshaw, "The Kellogg-Briand Pact: The American Reaction," (Ph.D. dissertation, University of Colorado, 1971); Harriet Hyman Alonso, "Kellogg-Briand Pact" in Bruce W. Jentleson and Thomas G. Paterson, senior eds., *Encyclopedia of U.S. Foreign Relations* (New York: Oxford University Press, 1997) 3: 3; text of pact at U.S. Statutes at Large, XXXXVI:2343.

Kemal, Mustafa (1881–1938)

Turkish politician and statesman, known as Ataturk, founder of modern state of Turkey after World War I.

Mustafa Kemal talks with Hallide Hannum, a female officer in the Turkish army, in 1923. *(CORBIS/Bettmann)*

Born in Salonika (now Thessaloniki, Greece), on March 11, 1881, he attended the Military Academy at Istanbul and graduated in 1902. Promoted through the Ottoman military ranks, he became a member of the Young Turks movement, which sought to take power from the moribund Ottoman government. In 1909, Kemal was an active leader in the coup that overthrew the regime of Ottoman sultan Abd al-Hamid II. During World War I he distinguished himself by holding off the British invasion at Gallipoli in 1915. He opposed the surrender of the Ottoman government in 1918 and its decision to sign the Treaty of Sèvres in 1920, in which the Ottoman government relinquished control of eastern Thrace to Greece. Kemal took the opportunity to resist Allied pressure on his homeland, and in 1919 he founded the Turkish National Congress. When the Treaty of Sèvres was signed and the Allies occupied Ankara, Kemal dissolved the Chamber of Deputies and formed the Grand National Assembly of Turkey.

In 1922 he started a war against Greece and won back eastern Thrace, and his troops forcibly deposed the Turkish leader Mohammed VI and sent him into exile to Italy. In 1923 he abolished the sultanate and formed the Republic of Turkey, with himself as president and prime minister. For his actions, his loyal supporters called him Ataturk ("Father of Turkey"). Ataturk started a program of moving away from the promotion of Islam as a state religion; he advocated universal education and the right to vote for women, and pushed his nation closer to Western values. He promoted private enterprise as a way of assisting the economy, but when the depression hit, he instituted numerous reforms that evolved into the state control of the means of production.

In the years before his death, Ataturk wisely foresaw the threat posed by Germany and Italy to Europe, and he moved closer to the West, becoming more friendly with Great Britain and France. He died on November 10, 1938.

See also ISKENDERUN.

References: Lord John Patrick Douglas Balfour Kinross, *Ataturk* (London: Weidenfeld & Nicolson, 1964); Homer H. Blass, "Mustafa Kemal Atatürk" in Anne Commire, ed., *Historic World Leaders* (Detroit: Gale Research, 1994), 1: 319–23; "Allies Concede Turkish Claims; Adrianople and Eastern Thrace Yielded; British Reverse Policy," *Washington Post*, September 24, 1922, p. 1; "Turk Force Retires From Neutral Zone," *Washington Post*, September 25, 1922, p. 1; "Turks Accept Armistice Plan and Stop Military Movements in Both Thrace and Chanak Area," *Washington Post*, October 2, 1922, p. 1.

Kennedy, Joseph Patrick (1888–1969)

American businessman and Kennedy family patriarch, head of the Securities and Exchange Commission (1934–35). One of four children of Irish Catholics Patrick Joseph Kennedy and Mary Augusta (Hickey) Kennedy, he was born in East Boston on September 9, 1888. He graduated from Harvard University in 1912. After marrying Rose Fitzgerald, the daughter of the mayor of Boston, Kennedy became a bank president at age 25, and within five years he had earned $1 million. In the late 1920s he became even more wealthy when he used his riches to bankroll bootlegging operations along the East Coast during Prohibition. He also speculated on the stock market, using what are now considered illegal practices, to earn millions of dollars.

Active in Democratic Party politics, Kennedy was appointed by his good friend President Franklin ROOSEVELT to the Securities and Exchange Commission in 1934, where he cracked down on the speculation that had fueled the STOCK MARKET CRASH in 1929. In 1937, Roosevelt named him as the first Irish American to serve as the U.S. ambassador to Great Britain at a time when tensions were growing in Europe over German rearmament and territorial expansion. When he resigned in 1940, Kennedy believed that England would be invaded and conquered by the Nazis.

Kennedy bred his sons for high office; his eldest, Joseph, was killed during World War II, so the elder Kennedy leaned on his second oldest son, John, to run for a political career. After serving in the House and the Senate, John was elected in 1960 the thirty-fifth president of the United States. He served only 1,037 days before being assassinated on November 22, 1963.

Kennedy spent his final days as an invalid at his home in Hyannisport, Massachusetts, where he died on November 18, 1969.

References: James N. Giglio, "Kennedy, Joseph Patrick" in Bruce W. Jentleson and Thomas G. Paterson, senior eds., *Encyclopedia of U.S. Foreign Relations* (New York: Oxford University Press, 1997), 3: 11–12; David E. Koskoff, *Joseph P. Kennedy: A Life and Time* (Englewood Cliffs, N.J.: Prentice-Hall, 1974); "Joseph P. Kennedy Dead; Forged a Political Dynasty," *New York Times*, November 19, 1969, p. 1.

Kern, Jerome (1885–1945)

American composer known for his scores in MUSICAL comedies during the interwar period. Born in New York City, Kern studied composition in New Jersey and New York, then in Germany and England. He first achieved success with the operetta *The Red Petticoat* (1912) and the musical *Very Good, Eddie* (1915). Among the numerous musicals that followed were *Leave It to Jane* (1917), *Sally* (1920), *Sunny* (1925), *The Cat and the Fiddle* (1931), and *Roberta* (1933). Collaborating with the lyricist Oscar HAMMERSTEIN and the theatrical producer Florenz Ziegfeld, Kern composed *Show Boat* (1927), which forever cemented his name in the pantheon of great composers.

Kern also created film scores, often elaborating on earlier versions of his songs for the stage, including "Ol'-Man River," "Smoke Gets in Your Eyes," and "A Fine Romance." Before his death in 1945, he composed an orchestral work, *A Portrait of Mark Twain* (1942).

Reference: Gerald Bordman, *Jerome Kern: His Life and Music* (New York: Oxford University Press, 1980).

Keynes, John Maynard (1883–1946)

British economist, principal representative of the English Treasury at the VERSAILLES Peace Conference (1919) and enunciator of "Keynesian economics." Born on June 5, 1883, in Cambridge, England, he was the son of an economics scholar. Keynes entered Trinity College at Cambridge in 1902, where he became a leading member in the early years of the BLOOMSBURY GROUP, which at times met in Cambridge. After graduating, he served for a time in the India Office at the Foreign Ministry. He also taught economics at Cambridge. During World War I he worked at the treasury, where he oversaw the audit of foreign currencies in England.

In 1919, Prime Minister David LLOYD GEORGE asked Keynes to accompany him to Versailles as an economic adviser. There he argued vociferously with Lloyd George that the REPARATIONS scheme established by the Allies against Germany would cause the outbreak of a second conflict in Europe. His pleas were ignored; he thus resigned, returned to England, and angrily wrote *The Economic Consequences of the Peace* (1919), in which he denounced the treaty's harsh reparations against Germany and its allies. During the 1920s, Keynes also wrote that continued unemployment, especially among English miners, could cause a recession or a depression.

In 1936, Keynes published what many consider to be his best work, the classic economic text *General Theory of Employment, Interest, and Money*, in which he advocated liberal government spending to lift the British economy out of the GREAT DEPRESSION. Although Keynes called this thesis "The New Economics," it has since been labeled "Keynesian economics." He believed that consumer spending was directly related to the health of a nation's economy and its level of unemployment. This monumental work was his last. During World War II he worked for the British government merely as an adviser on war finance matters. In 1944 he was chosen as the British representative to the Bretton Woods Conference in New Hampshire, where the International Monetary Fund was established. In this last role Keynes negotiated for the English treasury a multibillion dollar loan from the United States to help England with postwar reconstruction. On April 21, 1946, Keynes died.

References: Mark Blaug, *John Maynard Keynes: Life, Ideas, Legacy* (London: Macmillan in Association with the Institute of Economic Affairs, 1990); Robert Lekachman, *The Age of Keynes* (New York: Random House, 1966); "Reparation Expert Urges Modifying Payment Terms," *Washington Post*, December 4, 1921, p. 1.

Khilafat movement

Social movement, 1920–22, among Islamic Indians protesting Allied treatment of the Ottoman Empire after World War I. Following significant events that had occurred in 1919 in India (the ruthless ROWLATT ACTS and the savage JALLIANWALA BAGH MASSACRE) revolution was in the air. The movement took its name from the Indian word for caliph, KHILAFA, the title for the religious leader of Islam. Mohandas K. GANDHI, the Hindu leader of the Indian independence movement, sympathized with the aims of the movement and joined Muslim leader Maulana Muhammad Ali. Gandhi initiated the noncooperation movement, which stirred his many supporters to embrace his methods of civil disobedience. Maulana's stirring speeches helped cause a political awakening among Indian's masses. Followers of the movement boycotted British goods and institutions. Within two years, however, the movement collapsed, primarily because Mustafa KEMAL abolished the caliphate in Turkey and instituted a republic there. Gandhi also began to feel that the movement was too limited in its focus, and he thus called off the noncooperation with the British. The collapse was followed by a bitter period of Hindu–Muslim antagonism.

References: "Khilafet Movement" in Surjit Mansingh, *Historical Dictionary of India* (Lanham, Md.: Scarecrow, 1996), 217–28; Gail Minault, *The Khilafat Movement: Religious Symbolism and Political Mobilization in India* (New York: Columbia University Press, 1982).

King-Crane Commission Report

Landmark report, issues by the U.S. government on August 28, 1919, which dealt with the issue of whether Turkey (or selected parts of it) should be made into a mandate of the LEAGUE OF NATIONS. Named to the commission were Henry Churchill King, president of Oberlin College in Ohio, and Charles R. Crane, who had served as a member of President Woodrow WILSON's Special Diplomatic Commission to Russia (1917), as a member of the American section of the Peace Conference Inter-Allied Commission on Mandates in Turkey (1919), and as U.S. ambassador to China (1920–21). After an exhaustive tour of Turkey, the men issued their report, known as the King-Crane Commission Report. Among other recommendations, the report called for the formation of Armenian, Constantinopolitan, and Turkish states, under the oversight of an international and interreligious body. It also called for further study to define the boundaries of these states.

King and Crane summarized the "considerations on which America would be justified in taking a composite general mandate for Asia Minor." They recommended that the United States not take the mandate for Asia Minor unless these considerations were met. Their efforts at constructing a U.S. peace policy for the Middle East were unsuccessful, however, as their report was largely ignored at the Paris Peace Conference.

Reference: "The King-Crane Report on the Near East," *Editor & Publisher* 55 (December 2, 1922): 22–30.

King, William Lyon Mackenzie (1874–1950)

Canadian diplomat and politician, prime minister (1921–26, 1926–30, 1935–48). Born in Berlin (now Kitchener), Ontario, on December 17, 1874, King received degrees from the University of Toronto in 1895 (bachelor's), 1896 (law), and 1897 (master's), and from Harvard University in 1898 (master's) and 1909 (doctorate). He served as deputy minister of labor in the government of Charles Tupper in 1900, a post King held until being elected to Parliament in 1908. There he was chosen by Prime Minister Wilfred Laurier as minister of labor, a post which he held until 1911.

In 1919, King was chosen as the Liberal Party leader. Two years later, when Prime Minister Arthur MEIGHEN's Conservative Party lost its majority, King became prime minister. In this, the first of two terms as the Canadian leader, King attempted to move his nation further away from Great Britain and "dominion" status. When London asked him to contribute troops to a possible war over the Turkish region of Chanak in 1922, King refused. At the IMPERIAL CONFERENCE in London in 1923, King led the opposition to a uniform imperial commonwealth policy. He also advocated the establishment of a national old-age pension in 1926, and appointed Cairine Wilson as the first female senator in 1930. In that year the Liberals lost their majority, and King's office gave way to Richard Bedford BENNETT.

In 1935 the GREAT DEPRESSION drove the Conservatives out of power, however, and King, as the Liberal opposition leader, became prime minister once again. In this second tenure, he saw his nation through the worst of the depression and World War II, until 1948. King spent more time in office than any other Canadian prime minister. He instituted unemployment insurance and signed the Hyde Park Agreement, in which loans from the United States brought the two countries closer economically, with U.S. President Franklin D. ROOSEVELT in 1941. King's success in this second term was confirmed when he stepped down and his self-appointed successor, Louis Stephen St. Laurent, won election in 1948.

King had been physically drained by his tenure, however, and his retirement was short. He died in Kingsmere, Quebec, July 22, 1950.

References: Bruce Hutchinson, *The Incredible Canadian: A Candid Portrait of Mackenzie King, His Works, His Times, and His Nation* (New York: Longmans, Green, 1953); Joy E. Esberey, *Knight of the Holy Spirit: A Study of William Lyon Mackenzie King* (Toronto: University of Toronto Press, 1980); J. L. Granatstein, "King, William Lyon Mackenzie" in Bruce W. Jentleson and Thomas G. Paterson, senior eds., *Encyclopedia of U.S. Foreign Relations* (New York: Oxford University Press, 1997), 3: 18; Douglas W. Houston, "King, William Lyon Mackenzie" in Warren F. Kuehl, ed., *Biographical Dictionary of Internationalists* (Westport, Conn.: Greenwood, 1983), 401–02; Fred A. McGregor, *The Fall and Rise of Mackenzie King, 1911–1919* (Toronto: Macmillan of Canada, 1962); "Rt. Honourable William Lyon Mackenzie King" in *Canada, the Founders and the Guardians: Fathers of Confederation, Governors General, Prime Ministers—A Collection of Biographical Sketches and Portraits* (Ottawa: Queen's Printer, 1968), 138.

Konoe, Prince Fumimaro (1891–1945)

Japanese politician, prime minister (1937–39, 1940–41). A member of the distinguished Fujiwara family, which had been connected to the Japanese imperial family in some way since the beginning of Japanese imperial history, Konoye was born in Tokyo in October 1891. He graduated from the Kyoto Imperial University with a law degree in 1917, after which he became a member of the Home Ministry. In this capacity he attended the Paris Peace Conference after World War I as a secretary to ambassador Prince Kimmochi Saionji. Upon his return to Japan, Konoe took his hereditary seat in the Japanese House of Peers, the upper house of the Diet (parliament). In 1931 he was named vice president of that body; he served as its president from 1933 until 1937.

On June 3, 1937, he accepted the post of prime minister. A month later the Japanese army attacked in China, setting off a crisis that consumed the government. In an article he wrote for the *Washington Post* on July 7, 1938, Konoe said, "One year ago today Japan was forced against her will into a conflict with China. Every possible effort was made to localize the incident. Peaceful settlement was agreed to but never effected due to the failure of [the] Chinese authorities to carry it out. To avoid further possible complications the Japanese government went to great pains to evacuate her nationals from various treaty ports, including Chungking, Changsha, Yehang, Hankow and even Tsingtao, removing thousands of Japanese."

On January 4, 1939, amidst calls that the Japanese army have more control of the national economy, Konoe resigned, taking the post as minister of state without portfolio and president of the Privy Council. On July 23, 1940, he was again named prime minister, a position he held until July 16, 1941, when his cabinet resigned. Named leader for a third time, Konoe's government held only until October 16, 1941, when he resigned over disagreements with his cabinet "concerning the manner of executing national policy." Two months later the Japanese attacked the American base at Pearl Harbor, setting off World War II in the Pacific.

After the war, Konoe came forward to aid in the writing of a new constitution for then occupied Japan. He was named as a war criminal by the Allied authorities, however, before he could be arrested, Konoe poisoned himself on December 15, 1945. He explained in a suicide note, "I have been most gravely concerned with the fact that I have committed certain errors in the handling of state affairs since the outbreak of the China incident. I cannot, however, stand the humiliation of being apprehended and tried by an American court."

References: Gordon M. Berger, "Konoe Fumimaro" in Gen Itasaka, gen. ed., *Kodansha Encyclopedia of Japan* (Tokyo: Kodansha, 1983), 4: 272–73; "Japan Forced to War, Konoe Asserts," *Washington Post*, July 7, 1938, p. 1.

Kristallnacht

Translated from the German as "Night of Broken Glass," this event marks the beginning of the terror against Jews in Germany. The hatred of Adolf HITLER and his NAZI PARTY was evident from the publication of *Mein Kampf*, yet Jews and Jewish culture had been a part of German life for a thousand years. As soon as Hitler became chancellor of Germany in 1933, however, he began to enact laws to punish Germany's Jewish population. At first, this merely took the form of a one-day boycott against Jewish shops; but it soon grew to include restrictions on Jewish children attending German schools. In 1935 a series of decrees known as the Nuremberg Laws was passed by the Reichstag, which in effect stripped Jews of their German citizenship and basic human rights. Until November 1938 these laws were used mainly to harass or depress Jews. There had been little violence inflicted, although many Jews had felt the need to flee Germany.

On November 9, 1938, however, that all changed. At this time thousands of Jewish refugees lived in other parts of Europe; one of these was Herschel Grynszpan, the 17-year-old of a Polish Jew. Having fled to France, Grynszpan went to the German Embassy in Paris to inquire about his family, who had gone from Poland to Germany. When he discovered that they had been expelled back to Poland and their possessions seized by the Germans, he sought to assassinate the German ambassador to France. Instead, another diplomat, Third Secretary Ernst Vom Rath, passed by him. Grynszpan shot him to death. In Berlin, Minister of Popular Enlightenment and Propaganda Josef GOEBBELS viewed the assassination as a perfect excuse for the fury he unleashed on the night of November 9. He ordered hundreds of SS and SA officers to selected targets in Germany, Austria (which had been swallowed up that same year in the ANSCHLUSS), and the German Sudetenland. Hundreds of plain clothes SS soldiers smashed Jewish stores, looted Jewish homes, burned Jewish synagogues, and arrested hundreds of Jews. In many Germans cities, smashed glass from window fronts lay strewn in the streets. Germans called the event *Kristallnacht*, or "Night of Broken Glass." American newspapers dubbed it "Black Thursday."

Within a few days, Reichminister Herman Goering claimed that the Jews had rioted and caused all the damage, and assessed a fine of one billion marks ($400 million dollars) against the Jewish community in Germany. For Jews who wished to leave, they were assessed a tax on any property they wished to take out of the country. Of the 560,000 Jews in Germany at the time of Kristallnacht, only 160,000 ever escaped. Kristallnacht was the beginning of Hitler's reign of terror on the German Jews, who were almost completely exterminated during the Holocaust.

References: *Night of Pogroms: Kristallnacht, November 9–10, 1938*, a publication of the U.S. Holocaust Memorial Council, Washington, D.C.; Louis L. Snyder, *Encyclopedia of the Third*

A Berlin synagogue burns the morning after Kristallnacht, November 9–10, 1938. A German mob had set fire to the building, killing its caretaker and his wife. *(CORBIS/Hulton-Deutsch Collection)*

Reich (New York: Paragon House, 1989), 201; Edmund Jan Osmańczyk, *The Encyclopedia of the United Nations and International Agreements* (Philadelphia: Taylor & Francis, 1985), 447.

Krogh, August (1874–1949)

Danish physiologist and Nobel laureate. Born Schack August Steenberg Krogh in Gren, Jutland, Denmark, on November 15, 1874, he attended the University of Copenhagen, where he studied zoology, physiology, and medicine. Before receiving his science degree in 1899, Krogh worked on the functions of the air bladders of certain larvae. Starting in 1903, he researched the respiration system of the frog, and over the next two decades he was awarded several prizes for his research. In 1908 a special professorship of zoology-physiology was established for him at the University of Copenhagen. Biographer E. Snorrason writes, "From these studies Krogh early concluded that the capillaries of the muscles were partially closed during rest and, for the most part, open during work; using intensive microscopial and histological methods, he was able to demonstrate the truth of his ideas and in 1920 was awarded the Nobel Prize in physiology or medicine."

Krogh died in Copenhagen on September 13, 1949.

References: Barbara I. McNutt, "Krogh, Schack August Steenberg" in Bernard S. and June H. Schlessinger, eds., *The Who's Who of Nobel Prize Winners* (Phoenix, Ariz.: Oryx, 1986), 84; Thomas Watson MacCallum and Stephen Taylor, eds., *The Nobel Prize-Winners and the Nobel Foundation, 1901–1937* (Zurich: Central European Times Publishing, 1938), 203–204; E. Snorrason, "Krogh, Schack August Steenberg" in Charles Coulston Gillespie, ed. in chief, *Dictionary of Scientific Biography* (New York: Charles Scribner's Sons, 1980–90), 7: 501–504.

Kronstadt Revolt

Insurrection, 1921, by Russian sailors on Kronstadt, on Kotlin Island in the Gulf of Finland about 20 miles from St. Petersburg. The sailors at Kronstadt, who had once supported the Bolshevik revolution, grew restless when the government could no longer pay their salaries or feed them. On March 1, 1921, some of these sailors developed a program calling for political and economic reform in opposition to the Soviet government. The men also published *Pravda o Kronshtadte* (The truth about Kronstadt), which became a rebel newspaper; these issues were published as a book in Prague later that year.

The Bolsheviks denounced the 15 points drafted by the sailors as a plot led by the Whites, a group of czarist officers who were at that moment fighting against the Bolsheviks in the Russian Civil War. When citizens near the naval base began to strike and support the sailors, the Bol-

shevik government stepped in. Led by Leon TROTSKY and Mikhail Tukhachevsky, the Soviet forces launched an attack on the sailors and killed many; those who survived were imprisoned.

The first challenge to the Soviet authorities showed them that unless there was radical reform, more strikes would result. The rebellion at Kronstadt led to the Soviet government's drafting of the NEW ECONOMIC POLICY in 1921.

References: Israel Getzler, "The Kronstadt Revolt: 1921" in Harold Shukman, ed., *The Blackwell Encyclopedia of the Russian Revolution* (Oxford, England: Basil Blackwell, 1988), 157–60; Emanuel Pollack, *The Kronstadt Rebellion: The First Armed Revolt against the Soviets* (New York: Philosophical Library, 1959).

Kuhn, Richard (1900–1967)

Austrian-German chemist and Nobel laureate. Born in Vienna on December 3, 1900, he received his doctorate degree from the University of Munich in 1922. Working at the University of Munich (1925–26), at the Eidgenössische Technische Hochschule (Federal Institute of Technology) in Zurich as a professor of General and Analytical Chemistry (1926–29), and as the principal of the Institute of Chemistry at the Kaiser-Wilhelm-Institut (later renamed the Max Planck Institut) in Berlin, Kuhn worked on enzymes, carotenoids, vitamins, and other formulations that could be effective against infection in the human body. For this work he was awarded the 1938 Nobel Prize in chemistry.

In accordance with the policies of the German government, Kuhn declined the award; he received his diploma and medal in 1949, when the monetary reward had already been forfeited.

Kuhn worked at the University of Heidelberg from 1928 until his death on August 1, 1967.

References: Maurice Fortin, "Kuhn, Richard" in Bernard S. and June H. Schlessinger, eds., *The Who's Who of Nobel Prize Winners* (Phoenix, Ariz.: Oryx, 1986), 15; Tyler Wasson, ed., *Nobel Prize Winners: An H. W. Wilson Biographical Dictionary* (New York: H. W. Wilson Co., 1987), 577–79.

Ku Klux Klan

Secret racist organization, which flourished in the United States during the 1920s and 1930s. The first manifestation of the Klan occurred in 1866, when several former Confederate military figures in Pulaski, Tennessee, founded a secret society that terrorized freed slaves to prevent them from exercising their newly won voting and civil rights. The name of the group was a play on the Greek word *kuklos,* meaning "circle." For years after the Civil War, the Klan was infamous, until the group was investigated by the U.S. government and was finally broken up by the passage of tough federal laws in the 1870s.

The second incarnation of the Klan was organized in 1915, fueled by the militant patriotism of World War I. Until its disorganization in 1944, the Klan was a force in U.S. politics. War veteran and salesman William Joseph Simmons recreated the Klan to protest the killing of a pencil factory worker named Mary Phagan and the arrest of her alleged murdered, a Jewish merchant named Leo Frank. (Although Frank was convicted and sentenced to death, the governor of Georgia commuted the sentence; a contingent of Simmons's followers kidnapped Frank and lynched him. This group, called the Knights of Mary Phagan, evolved into the second coming of the Klan.) By 1920 this new Klan numbered only a few thousand at best. To increase membership, Simmons hired two publicists, Edward Young Clarke and Elizabeth Tyler, and offered them 80 per cent of any dues they could get recruiting members. Embracing anti-Catholic, anti-Jew, nativist, and Fundamentalist impulses, the Klan message quickly spread; by 1921 more than a hundred thousand people were members, and by 1924 this number had swelled to 3 million. The Klan's primary goal was to attack African Americans, non-Protestants, Jews, trade unionists, and the foreign-born in general. Although some of the Klan's members were nonviolent, many others committed barbarous acts in the organization's name, actions which slowly served to destroy the organization. In September 1921 the New York World did a series of exposés on the Klan's inner workings; a number of scandals inside the Klan served to tarnish the group further. A march of some forty thousand Klansmen down Pennsylvania Avenue in Washington, D.C., in August 1925 did not stave off rapid declines in membership. By the end of the decade, membership had dropped back to a hundred thousand.

Throughout the 1930s this incarnation of the Klan became less of a threat. In 1944 it was formally disbanded, when the U.S. government sued the organization for failure to pay taxes. The third birth of the Klan occurred with the start of the civil rights movement in the 1960s, as Klan members again embraced the use of violence and terrorist tactics against African Americans and civil rights workers in the South.

References: Wyn Craig, Wade The Fiery Cross: The Ku Klux Klan in America (New York: Simon & Schuster, 1987); David Mark Chalmers, Hooded Americanism: The History of the Ku Klux Klan (New York: Franklin Watts, 1981); "Secrets of the Ku Klux Klan Exposed by the 'World;' Menace of This Growing Law-Defying Organization Proved by Its Ritual and the Record of Its Activities," The World (New York), September 6, 1921, p. 1; "Ku Klux Klan's Invisible Empire of Hate Scorned by Army Officer Who Abandons It; Department of Justice to Make Inquiry," The World (New York), September 7, 1921, p. 1; "The World Exposes Roster of Ku Klux Force Peddling Klan Membership on Fee Basis, Despite Organizer's Boast They Work In Dark," The World (New York), September 9, 1921, p. 1.

Kún, Béla (1886–1937)

Hungarian communist politician, leader of the revolt to bring Soviet rule to his nation, eventually liquidated by the Soviet regime in Moscow that he wished to imitate in Budapest. Born near Györ, Hungary, he was of Jewish heritage and parentage. Kún graduated from the University of Kolozsvar with a degree in law, after which he turned to journalism and politics. When World War I broke out in August 1914, he joined the Austrian army; a year later he was captured on the eastern front and spent the remainder of the war in a Russian prisoner-of-war camp.

While imprisoned, Kún embraced Bolshevism; when he returned to Hungary after the war, he was a committed communist and hoped to bring that form of government to Hungary. He published the communist newspaper *Vörös Ujsag* ("Red News"). In November 1918, Count Bela Károlyi founded the Hungarian National Council with the intent of establishing a constitutional government in postwar Hungary. Károlyi was named prime minister, and Hungary was proclaimed a republic. The economy soon went sour, however, and on March 22, 1919, Károlyi was forced to resign in favor of Kún and a Bolshevist-Socialist government. This government instituted radical land reform, but opposition by the Hungarian peasants quickly made bad matters worse for Kún. On July 31, 1919, after just 133 days in power, Kún was forced from power by a revolution aided by the Romanian army; he fled to Vienna. There, he was arrested and confined to a mental hospital; after his release, he went to Russia. In April 1928 he again appeared in Vienna, only to be rearrested and deported to Moscow.

Kún's ultimate fate has been mired in mystery for years. Officially, it is claimed that he died in the Russian camps, but the government has never fully explained his demise.

See also TRIANON, TREATY OF.

References: Rudolf L. Tokes, *Béla Kún and the Hungarian Soviet Republic: the Origins and Role of the Communist Party of Hungary in the Revolutions of 1918–1919* (New York: Published for the Hoover Institution on War, Revolution, and Peace, by Frederick A. Praeger, 1967); Bennett Kovrig, *Communism in Hungary from Kun to Kadar* (Stanford, Calif.: Hoover Institution Press, 1979).

La Follette, Robert Marion (1855–1925)

American politician, U.S. senator from Wisconsin. La Follette was born in Primrose, Wisconsin, on June 14, 1855. After graduating from the University of Wisconsin in 1879, he was admitted to the state bar the following year and was named as the district attorney of Dane County, Wisconsin, where he served until 1884. That year, he was elected to the U.S. House of Representatives, where he served until 1891. Being a progressive, however, La Follette opposed his party leadership and did not run for reelection in 1890. He returned to Wisconsin to practice law.

La Follette served as governor of Wisconsin from 1900 to 1906, during which time he championed tax reform, the regulation of the railroads, and direct primaries in state elections. He resigned his post to take a seat in the U.S. Senate. While in the Senate, where he sat until his death, La Follette was a member of the progressive wing of the Republican Party, championing the direct election of Senators. His most spectacular break with his party came when he voted against U.S. intervention in World War I. He remained a strict isolationist, fighting American participation in the LEAGUE OF NATIONS and the World Court after the war. He continued to call for a progressive income tax system, the public ownership of all utilities, including railroads, and the repeal of the U.S. Supreme Court's power to rule certain laws of Congress to be null and void.

In the 1920s, La Follette turned against his party; he was the Senate sponsor who backed the senatorial investigation of Secretary of the Interior Albert B. FALL's dealings with the government oil reserves at TEAPOT DOME. After the Republican Party refused to consider any of La Follette's proposals for their national platform at the 1924 Republican National Convention, La Follette stormed from the convention and established the League for Progressive Political Action, with the intention of forming a third political party. With the backing of progressive, labor, and agrarian interests, this group formed into the Progressive Party, modeled in some ways after Theodore Roosevelt's Progressive "Bull Moose" Party. Choosing Senator Burton K. WHEELER, a Democrat, as his running mate, La Follette barnstormed the nation seeking the presidency. From the start, however, his chances were slim. On election day he garnered 4.8 million popular votes but only the electoral votes of his home state of Wisconsin. He returned, broken, to his Senate seat.

La Follette lived less than a year after his electoral defeat. He died suddenly in Washington on June 18, 1925. His son, Robert La Follette Jr. was elected to his father's Senate seat, where he served until 1947.

See also ELECTIONS, U.S.

References: Fred Greenbaum, *Robert Marion La Follette* (Boston: Twayne Publishers, 1975); Robert S. Maxwell, comp., *La Follette* (Englewood Cliffs, N.J.: Prentice Hall, 1969).

La Guardia, Fiorello Henry (1882–1947)

American politician, member, U.S. House of Representatives, and mayor of New York City. The second of three children of Achille Luigi Carlo La Guardia, an Italian émigré, and Irene (Coen) La Guardia, a Jewish emigrant from Austria, La Guardia was born in New York's Greenwich Village, then the Italian area of the city, on December 11, 1882. His father, a military bandmaster, traveled across the United States, and Fiorello attended school in Prescott, Arizona, until the eighth grade. When the Spanish-American War broke out in 1898, La Guardia went with his father to Florida, where all the troops were assembling. There, the young La Guardia served as a journalist for a St. Louis newspaper. When his father died in Florida, La Guardia went with his mother and siblings to live with her family in Budapest, Hungary.

While there, La Guardia worked for the American consulate, eventually rising to become the acting consul at FIUME in Italy. In 1907 he returned to the United States, serving for the next three years as a translator for new immigrants at Ellis Island. At night he studied law at New York University. After being admitted to the bar, La Guardia entered local politics as a Republican. In 1914 he was named deputy attorney general of New York State, serving until 1917, when he was elected to a seat in the U.S. House of Representatives. He became a member of the Progressive Republican bloc. La Guardia voted for U.S. entry into World War I, but when he tried to enlist himself he was rejected for being too short. Instead he learned to fly in the U.S. Air Corps and served with a squadron of American fighters in Italy. After the war he returned to New York (and to Congress); a hero, he served a total of seven two-year terms (1917–33). In Congress, La Guardia opposed the espionage acts passed at the end of the war, was a foe of PROHIBITION, and sponsored the controversial prolabor enactment, the Norris-LaGuardia Act. He was supported by Republicans, Democrats, and even Socialists.

In 1929, La Guardia ran for mayor of New York City against the popular James J. "Jimmy" Walker, and lost. By 1933, however, Walker had been removed from office after a financial scandal, and La Guardia was easily elected. Reelected in 1937 and again in 1941, he became one of the most popular mayors in the New York history, the first to be elected to three terms. Biographer Michael Ebner called him "perhaps the most outstanding mayor in U.S. history." He was a reformist mayor, helping to adopt a new city charter and reducing the power of the crooked Tammany Hall organization, which had run the city for a century. Known as the "Little Flower," La Guardia was also known to read aloud the Sunday morning comics on the radio. On December 31, 1945, he retired as mayor to take the position of director of the United Nations Relief and Rehabilitation Administration. He died on September 20, 1947.

References: Arthur Mann, "LaGuardia, Fiorello Henry" in Allen Johnson and Dumas Malone, et al., eds., *Dictionary of American Biography* (New York: Charles Scribner's Sons, 1930–95), 4: 464–67; Lawrence Elliott, *Little Flower: The Life and Times of Fiorello La Guardia* (New York: William Morrow & Co., 1983), 206; Michael H. Ebner, "LaGuardia, Fiorello" in Melvin G. Holli and Peter d'Alroy Jones, eds., *Biographical Dictionary of American Mayors, 1820–1980: Big City Mayors* (Westport, Conn.: Greenwood, 1981), 205–206; "La Guardia Is Dead; City Pays Homage to 3-Time Mayor," *New York Times,* September 21, 1947, pp. 1, 36.

Landis, Kenesaw Mountain (1866–1944)

American jurist, first commissioner of American Major League BASEBALL (1920–44). Born in Logansport, Indiana, on November 20, 1866, he was the son of Abraham Hoch Landis, a U.S. Army surgeon who had lost a leg in the Civil War at the battle at Kennesaw Mountain, Georgia, and decided to name his sixth or seventh children after the site. Landis attended the University of Cincinnati, and graduated from Chicago's Union College of Law in 1891. He practiced law there for the next 14 years, until 1905, when U.S. President Theodore Roosevelt named Landis a U.S. district judge for the northern district of Illinois. Landis remained on that bench for 15 years.

Landis was known as a hard-nosed judge who dealt decisively with cases that came before his court. The most noted of his cases are the Standard Oil Case, in which he fined the company more than $29 million for illegal freight rates; a number of sedition trials during World War I; and a suit by the American and National Leagues of major league BASEBALL, who sued the start-up Federal League in 1915 (it went out of business soon after). During this BLACK SOX SCANDAL of 1919 several Chicago White Sox players were found to have taken bribes to throw the World Series. The national baseball commission refused to deal with the accused players, who were eventually tried and acquitted in a court of law. After the case, some of the baseball team owners asked Landis to accept the position of commissioner of baseball. Landis agreed on the condition that he could have a firm hand in dealing with corruption in the sport. He took office in January 1920, and his first action was to ban all of the players involved in the scandal. He applied the strict standards from the bench to baseball, becoming one of the most authoritative commissioners in baseball history. He served 24 terms as commissioner until his death, dying in office on November 25, 1944. Soon after Landis's death he was elected to the Baseball Hall of Fame.

References: John George Taylor Spink, *Judge Landis and Twenty-Five Years of Baseball* (New York: Thomas Y. Crowell, 1947); David S. Neft and Richard M. Cohen, *The Sports Encyclopedia: Baseball* (New York: St. Martin's, 1991), 124; Jay Robert Nash, *Encyclopedia of World Crime* (Wilmette, Ill.: CrimeBooks, 1990), 3: 1884–85.

Landon, Alfred Mossman (1887–1987)

American politician. Born in West Middlesex, Pennsylvania, on September 9, 1887, Landon moved with his parents to Independence, Kansas, in 1904. He received his law degree at the University of Kansas in 1908. A Republican, he was part of the Progressive or "Bull Moose" wing of the party, led by former U.S. President Theodore Roosevelt. Although he returned to the party fold after the Bull Moosers were disbanded, he remained a progressive. During World War I, Landon served in the U.S. Army's chemical warfare service.

After the war Landon entered private business, but he wanted to join state politics. In 1932, in the midst of the

GREAT DEPRESSION, he was elected governor of Kansas. Faced with mounting budget pressures and growing unemployment, he passed a series of reformist measures through the state legislature, which alleviated the situation and allowed Landon to balance the budget.

Reelected governor in 1934, he was widely considered the frontrunner as the Republican nominee for the 1936 presidential race. At the Republican National Convention in Cleveland, Landon was indeed nominated to take on President Franklin D. ROOSEVELT. The following election was in essence a referendum on whether the American people wanted to take a chance with four more years of the New Deal (which at this time had shown few tangible results) or go in another direction. On election day, however, Landon was buried in a Democratic landslide: although he captured nearly 17 million votes, he won only the electoral votes of Maine and Vermont. Humbled but not disgraced, Landon returned to Kansas and state politics, but never held another elected office. He died on October 12, 1987. His daughter, Nancy Landon Kassebaum, has served in the U.S. Senate.

See also ELECTIONS, U.S.

References: Willis Thornton, *The Life of Alfred M. Landon* (New York: Grosset & Dunlap, 1936); Richard B. Fowler, *Deeds, Not Deficits: The Story of Alfred M. Landon* (Boston: L. C. Page & Company, 1936), 22–27.

Landsteiner, Karl (1868–1943)

Austrian-American immunologist and Nobel laureate. Born in Vienna, Austria, on June 14, 1868, he received his medical degree in 1891 from the University of Vienna, where he became interested in the impact of diet on the composition of blood. In Vienna he worked at the University Department of Pathological Anatomy and at the Wilhelmina Hospital; he later practiced as a physician at R. K. Zickenhuis Hospital in the Hague, the Netherlands. In 1922, he was offered a position at the Rockefeller Institute for Medical Research in New York, where he moved and remained for the rest of his life. For his body of research, most notably his work on human blood groupings, Landsteiner was awarded the 1930 Nobel Prize in medicine and physiology. Landsteiner died on June 26, 1943.

References: Rashelle Karp, "Landsteiner, Karl" in Bernard S. and June H. Schlessinger, eds., *The Who's Who of Nobel Prize Winners* (Phoenix, Ariz.: Oryx, 1986), 87; Thomas Watson MacCallum and Stephen Taylor, eds., *The Nobel Prize-Winners and the Nobel Foundation, 1901–1937* (Zurich: Central European Times Publishing, 1938), 222–23.

Lang, Fritz (1890–1976)

Austrian-American film director, famed for horror film and crime productions. Born Friedrich Christian Anton Lang in Vienna, Austria, on December 5, 1890, Lang studied to be an architect but had left that field to study art in Paris when World War I broke out in 1914. Fighting for the Austrian army, Lang was injured and permanently lost the sight in his right eye. After the war, he wrote short stories and plays, later directing one story as a film, *Halbblut* (Half-breed, 1919). The commercial success of his film *Die Spinnen* (The spiders, led to the landmark German silent film *Das Kabinett des Dr. Caligari* (The CABINET OF DR. CALIGARI, 1919). Lang produced other impressive films throughout the 1920s and early 1930s. *Metropolis* (1927), a wild and fanciful look at labor relations in a futuristic world, is considered by many one of the greatest foreign films made during the silent era. His other films include *Spione* (Spies, 1928) and *Die Frau Im Mond* (The girl in the moon, 1929). For his first major sound film, *M* (1931), Lang used dark scenes and sound effects to highlight the first psychological thriller of the sound age, capturing the true-life story of Peter Kürten, a German serial killer. *Das Testament des Dr. Mabuse* (The last will of Dr. Mabuse, 1933) was a slap at Germany's NAZI government; when Lang feared that his Jewish background would be exposed, he fled Germany and went first to Paris, then to the United States, where he was naturalized in 1939. In Hollywood he directed *Fury* (1936), *Western Union* (1941), and *Scarlet Street* (1945), among others. His later films, produced through the mid-1950s, never captured his earlier success. He died on August 2, 1976.

See also THE CABINET OF DR. CALIGARI.

Reference: Ephraim Katz, *The Film Encyclopedia* (New York: HarperPerennial, 1994), 686–88.

Lange, Christian Louis (1869–1938)

Norwegian writer, pacifist, and Nobel laureate. Born in Stavanger, Norway, on September 17, 1869, Lange graduated from the University of Christiana (now the University of Oslo) in 1893, then returned to earn a doctorate in 1919. From 1893 until his death, he was a writer and journalist in Norway, yet his fame rested on his renown as an internationalist. In 1890 Lange was named as secretary to the Norwegian Parliament's Nobel Committee, which he served until 1909 and again from 1934 until his death. In 1899 he served as a leading member, with founders William Randal Cremer of Great Britain and Frédéric Passy of France, of the International Parliamentary Union (IPU), of which we served as Secretary General from 1909 until 1933. The IPU "fosters contacts, co-ordination, and the exchange of experience among parliaments and parliamentarians of all countries, considers questions of international interest and concern and expresses its views on such issues in order to bring about action by parliaments and parliamentarians, contributes to the defence and promotion of human rights—an essential factor of parliamentary democracy and development, [and] contributes to better knowledge of the working of representative institutions and to the strengthening and development of their means of action."

He was the Norwegian delegate at the 1907 International Peace Conference at the Hague and the representative to the LEAGUE OF NATIONS from 1920 until 1938.

For his work toward international peace, Lange was the corecipient (with Swedish peace activist Karl Hjalmar BRANTING) of the 1921 Nobel Peace Prize.

His works include *History of Internationalism* (1919), *International Politics* (1924), and *Imperialism and Peace* (1938). He died in Oslo on December 11, 1938.

References: Bernard S. Schlessinger, "Lange, Christian Louis" in Bernard S. and June H. Schlessinger, eds., *The Who's Who of Nobel Prize Winners* (Phoenix, Ariz.: Oryx, 1986), 132; Fredrick Aandahl, "Lange, Christian Louis" in Warren F. Kuehl, ed., *Biographical Dictionary of Internationalists* (Westport, Conn.: Greenwood, 1983), 417–19.

Langmuir, Irving (1881–1957)

American chemist and Nobel laureate. Born in Brooklyn, New York, on January 31, 1881, Langmuir attended Columbia University's School of Mines and Göttingen University in Germany, from which he was awarded a doctorate in chemistry. He taught at the Stevens Institute of Technology in Hoboken, New Jersey, from 1906 to 1909. In 1909 he joined the staff of the General Electric Research Laboratory, advancing to associate director by 1932.

During his tenure at GE, Langmuir pioneered many advances in chemistry and physics, for which he became regarded as one of the finest chemists in the world. In 1913 he invented the nitrogen- and argon-filled incandescent light bulb. Working with fellow chemist Gilbert N. Lewis, he developed the Lewis-Langmuir atomic theory. Other advances include the invention of the atomic hydrogen welding torch and the development in 1918, with William D. Coolidge, of acoustic devices to detect submarines. Writes one biographer, "His contributions to the chemistry of surface processes were of great importance in many technical fields: in biology, for the study of complex viruses; in chemistry, for the study of giant molecules; and in optics, for the study of the transmission of light." For this body of work, Langmuir received the 1932 Nobel Prize in chemistry, the first American to receive the prize. Until his retirement in 1950, Langmuir continued to investigate chemistry theory. In 1941 he developed a method for optically detecting viruses that previously could not be detected through microscopic study. With Vincent J. Schaefer, Langmuir invented silver iodide crystals, which are used to seed clouds to make rain. The author of *Phenomena, Atoms, and Molecules* (1950), a compendium of his research papers, Langmuir died in Falmouth, Massachusetts, on August 16, 1957.

References: Albert Rosenfeld, "Langmuir, Irving" in Allen Johnson and Dumas Malone et al., eds., *Dictionary of American Biography* (New York: Charles Scribner's Sons, 1930–95), 6: 363–65; Linda C. Bradley, "Langmuir, Irving" in Bernard S. and June H. Schlessinger, eds., *The Who's Who of Nobel Prize Winners* (Phoenix, Ariz.: Oryx, 1986), 12; Thomas Watson MacCallum and Stephen Taylor, eds., *The Nobel Prize–Winners and the Nobel Foundation, 1901–1937* (Zurich: Central European Times Publishing, 1938), 160–61; Tyler Wasson, ed., *Nobel Prize Winners: An H. W. Wilson Biographical Dictionary* (New York: H. W. Wilson Co., 1987), 597–99.

Lateran Treaties or Concordats

Three separate pacts signed, February 11, 1929, between the Vatican and the fascist government of Italy in the Lateran Palace in Rome to recognize relations between the two states, to consider the Vatican as an extraterritoriality of Italy, and to establish Roman Catholicism as the state religion of Italy. Signing on behalf of the Vatican was Pope PIUS XI, for Italy, Benito MUSSOLINI. The agreements allowed the Vatican access through the clergy to minister to Italians, while at the same time guaranteeing that Roman Catholicism would be the nation's sole religion. Rome guaranteed that the Holy See would be considered "neutral and inviolable territory" independent from Italy. A separate treaty, called the Financial Convention, called for Italian compensation of 750 million lire in cash and an additional 1 billion lire in government bonds to pay for former papal lands taken from the church during the unification of Italy.

References: Elisa Carrillo, "Lateran Accords" in Frank J. Coppa, ed. in chief, *Dictionary of Modern Italian History* (Westport, Conn.: Greenwood, 1985), 232–33; Daniel Binchy, *Church and State in Fascist Italy* (New York: Oxford University Press, 1941).

Laughton, Charles (1899–1962)

British-American actor, famed for his roles in such interwar films as *The Private Life of Henry VIII* (1933) and *Mutiny on the Bounty* (1935). Born in Scarborough, Yorkshire, England, on July 1, 1899, the son of hotelkeepers, Laughton attended the prestigious Stonyhurst School. After serving with the British army in World War I, he attended London's Royal Academy of Dramatic Arts. From 1926 until 1931 he appeared in various stage productions, finally appearing in New York in 1931 in *Payment Deferred*.

In 1932, Laughton began a lifelong career in Hollywood. In 1932 he played Nero in *The Sign of the Cross*, and the following year he starred in *The Private Life of Henry VIII*; this presentation as the slovenly king won Laughton an Academy Award for best actor. Returning for a time to his old stomping grounds in London, he appeared at London's Old Vic theater. Back in Hollywood, Laughton appeared in such interwar pieces as *The Barretts of Wimpole Street* (1934) and *Ruggles of Red Gap* (1935); as Inspector Javert in *Les Misérables* (1935), and in the momentous roles of Captain Bligh in *Mutiny on the Bounty* (1935), opposite Clark Gable, and Quasimodo in the classic 1939 remake of *The HUNCHBACK OF NOTRE DAME.* Laughton was also known for his later work in *Witness for the Prosecution* (1958) and *Advise and Consent* (1962), released shortly before his death.

In 1950, Laughton became a naturalized U.S. citizen. He lived in Los Angeles for the remainder of his life, playing small roles on stage and appearing in the television classic, Dicken's *A Christmas Carol.* He also captured the English stage in a revival of *King Lear* in 1959. He died on December 16, 1962.

References: Charles Higham, *Charles Laughton: An Intimate Biography* (Garden City, N.Y.: Doubleday, 1976); Simon Callow, *Charles Laughton: A Difficult Actor* (London: Methuen, 1988); Kurt Singer, *The Charles Laughton Story* (London: R. Hale, 1954); Elsa Lanchester, *Charles Laughton and I* (New York: Harcourt, Brace, 1938).

See also MOTION PICTURES.

Laurel, Stan (1890–1965) and Oliver Hardy (1892–1957)

Famed comedic duo, composed of an English vaudevillian and an American slapstick artist, known for their comical and jocular routines in films during the interwar period. Born Arthur Stanley Jefferson Jr. on June 16, 1890, in the village of Ulverston, in Lancashire, England, Laurel was the second of five children of theatrical veteran parents. Starting in juvenile theater, Laurel worked his way to Glascow, Scotland, where in 1910 he joined Fred Karno's Troupe, a vaudevillian performance group of which Charlie CHAPLIN was a member. Three years later, Laurel saw the United States for the first time; when Chaplin left the group, Laurel decided to as well. He joined an amateur group led by Alice and Baldwin Cooke and toured America. He left the Cookes for the Australia actress Mae Dahlberg, and the two toured as Stan and Mae Laurel. In 1917 Laurel made a silent short, *Nuts,* and soon after signed a contract with Universal Studio; for the studio he made a few two-reel films. In 1919, while in California, Laurel made a film called *The Lucky Dog,* which also starred a them little-known actor, Oliver Hardy.

Born in Harlem, Georgia, on January 18, 1892, Norvell Hardy was graced with his mother's maiden and married names, Emily Norvell Hardy. His father, a laborer, was killed when Hardy was just 10 months old. To honor the father's memory, he was renamed Oliver Norvell Hardy. Hardy attended a military school and then Young

Harris College. Back with his family in Milledgeville, Georgia, where his mother managed a hotel, Hardy worked as a film projectionist and fell in love with the moving picture. He moved around, through Jacksonville, Florida, and later New Jersey, playing bit parts in short film comedies (his debut was in 1913's *Outwitting Dad*), before going to California in 1919, where he landed a role in *The Lucky Dog.*

After the film Laurel was cast for the next several years in other movies, while Hardy struggled to find work (he starred in the original [1925] version of *The Wizard of Oz,* in which he played the Tin Woodsman). In 1926, however, movie producer Hal Roach teamed them up in *Forty-Five Minutes From Hollywood* (starring Theda Bara), the first of 108 films that the men would undertake together. (Hardy starred in two films, in 1949 and 1950, without Laurel). Their most famous work was in *Babes in Toyland* (also known as *March of the Wooden Soldiers,* 1934). Their last full-length film was *The Bullfighters* (1945). Hardy died in North Hollywood, California, on August 7, 1957. In 1960, Laurel was awarded a special Academy Award for "his creative pioneering in the field of cinema comedy." He died in Santa Monica, California, on February 23, 1965.

See also MOTION PICTURES, SILENT; MOTION PICTURES, TALKING.

References: John McCabe, *Babe: The Life of Oliver Hardy* (New York: Carol Publishing Group, 1990); William K. Everson, *The Films of Laurel & Hardy* (New York: Citadel, 1968); Jack Scagnetti, *The Laurel and Hardy Scrapbook* (Middle Village, N.Y.: Jonathan David Publishers, 1976).

Lausanne, Treaty of

Pact, 1923, between Turkey on the one side and Greece, Britain, France, Italy, Japan, and Romania on the other to restore a state of peace. Following the signing of the post–World War I Treaty of SÈVRES on August 10, 1920, Turkish nationalist leader Mustafa KEMAL (Ataturk) refused to honor that pact, in which the frontiers of Turkey had been restricted. The Allies, desiring to avoid a conflict with Turkey, convened a conference in Lausanne, Switzerland, on July 24, 1923. The Sèvres agreement was scrapped and a new plan was conceived. In article one, the contracting powers held that "from the coming into force of the present Treaty, the state of peace will be definitely re-established between the British Empire, France, Italy, Japan, Greece, Roumania and the Serb-Croat-Slovene State of the one part, and Turkey of the other part, as well as between their respective nationals. Official relations will be resumed on both sides and, in the respective territories, diplomatic and consular representatives will receive, without prejudice to such agreements as may be concluded in the future, treatment in accordance with the general principles of international law." The treaty also restored to Turkey eastern Thrace, the Dardanelles Straits, and Smyrna, all of which had been stripped in the Sèvres agreement.

See also IZMIR.

References: Fred L. Israel, ed., *Major Peace Treaties of Modern History: 1648–1967* (New York: Chelsea House Publishers in association with McGraw-Hill, 1967–1980), 4: 2305–68; "The Lausanne Agreement: Statement of Nicholas Murray Butler. Radio Address of William E. Borah. Text of the Final Act of the Lausanne Conference, July 9, 1932, and texts of further documents relation to the settlement reached at Lausanne, June 16–July 9, 1932" (Worcester, Mass.: Carnegie Endowment for International Peace, Division of Intercourse and Education, 1932); Edmund Jan Osmańczyk, *The Encyclopedia of the United Nations and International Agreements* (Philadelphia: Taylor & Francis, 1985), 456.

Law, Andrew Bonar (1858–1923)

British politician and prime minister. The only person ever born outside of the United Kingdom to attain the office of prime minister, Law was born in the village of Rexton, on the Richibucto River in New Brunswick, Canada, on September 16, 1858. The fourth son of Scottish parents, Presbyterian minister James Law and Eliza Anne (Kidston) Law, Law was two years old when his mother died during childbirth. He was soon under the care of his aunt, Janet Kidston, who came from Scotland. When his father remarried, Kidston returned to Scotland with seven-year-old Law in tow, the only sibling ever to return to Scotland. After a short time in the common schools of Glasgow, he dropped out at age 16 to become a bank clerk.

He worked for an iron merchant in Glasgow, and then used some money he received from a cousin's will to run for politics. In 1900 he was elected to the British House of Commons as a Conservative from the Blackfriar and Hutchesontown area of Glasgow. Although his election came in the wake of the national debate on the British army's role in the Boer War in South Africa, Law never made a serious comment on the debate. He did, however, speak on the possibility of a duty on corn, which won him praise and led to his appointment on August 8, 1902, to the post of parliamentary secretary to the Board of Trade by Prime Minister Arthur James Balfour. At the Board of Trade Law made a name for himself as a rising star in the Conservative Party. In 1905, however, Law lost his seat in the general election, although four months later he was returned to Parliament as a member from Dulwich. In 1910 he again lost this seat, but was returned a second time when another seat, this one representing the village of Bootle, opened up. He was then named privy counsellor. In 1911, Law was elected head of the Conservative Party, in essence making him the next man in line for the prime ministership if the Conservatives attained a majority in Parliament.

When Prime Minister Herbert Asquith introduced the Irish Home Rule bill in Parliament in 1912, Law offered the opposition reply, denouncing the legislation in the strongest terms. Two years later, when the bill received royal assent from King GEORGE V, Law resigned from the House of Commons in protest and went to Belfast, where he called for continued Union rule over Ireland.

World War I strained political relations in Great Britain to the breaking point, and by 1915, Asquith decided to include a well-known Conservative in his cabinet. He named Law secretary for the colonies. On December 5, 1916, however, when Asquith refused War Minister David LLOYD GEORGE's plan for a War Committee, both the prime minister and Lloyd George resigned. In the House of Commons, Law was invited to form a government; he refused because Asquith did not consent to serve with him. The Parliament then turned to Lloyd George, who formed a government five days later with Law as chancellor of the exchequer.

Responsible for forming the national budget during the war, Law raised money through extensive war loan campaigns. Stunned by the war deaths of his two eldest sons, James and Charles, Law continued to serve with distinction. On January 10, 1919, he was named lord privy seal and Conservative leader in the House of Commons. In 1919 he was the British representative at the VERSAILLES peace conference. He resigned both positions because of ill health on March 17, 1921, and moved to France. It seemed as if his career was over.

When he returned to England later that year, Law gave enthusiastic support to the new Irish Home Rule bill, which separated Northern Ireland from the rest of that country. Law's speech on December 15, 1921, helped carry the day, and the bill was overwhelmingly enacted. Frustration with Lloyd George's handling of the government led to the Carlton Club Meeting, where Conservative members of Parliament decided that they would end their support of Lloyd George's government. Lloyd George ultimately resigned, and the king asked Law to form a government. Four days later, Law did so. During his short reign as prime minister, Law handled negotiations over the American debt settlement, in which England accepted terms to repay the United States for munitions sold to England during World War I. Law developed throat cancer and resigned his post, after barely seven months, on May 20. He died on October 31, 1923.

See also BALDWIN, STANLEY; ELECTIONS, BRITISH.

References: Finton Codd, "Andrew Bonar Law" in Dermot Englefield, Janet Seaton, and Isobel White, *Facts about the British Prime Ministers: A Compilation of Biographical and Historical Information* (New York: H. W. Wilson Co., 1995), 246–52; "Mr. Bonar Law Dead. Life Given to Service. The

King's Tribute. Work for the Empire," *The Times* (London), October 31, 1923, p. 15; "Memoir, A Beloved Leader. Statesmanship and Character," *The Times* (London), October 31, 1923, p. 16; "Mr. Bonar Law," *The Times* (London), October 31, 1923, p. 15.

Lawrence, D. H. (1885–1930)

English writer known for his provocative novels of the 1920s. Born David Herbert Lawrence on September 11, 1885, in Eastwood, England, he was the fourth child in a coal-mining family. On a scholarship he attended Nottingham University College in 1906, after which he took up a teaching position at the Davidson Road School in Croydon in 1908. Desiring to make a living as a writer, he published his first novel, *The White Peacock*, in 1911. Over the years Lawrence and his family resided in England, Germany, and Italy.

Although *Sons and Lovers* (1913) and *The Rainbow* (1915) are considered his greatest novels, Lawrence's sexually provocative interwar books garnered much attention and incited much controversy. They include *Women in Love* (1920), *The Lost Girl* (1920), *The Plumed Serpent* (1926), *Lady Chatterley's Lover* (1928), and *The Virgin and the Gipsy* (1930). At least two of his novels (*The Rainbow* and *Lady Chatterley's Lover*) were banned in the United States and in Great Britain for years. Also writing short stories, novellas, poetry, plays, and essays, Lawrence examined the problems of modern society that dehumanize culture and explored the role of sex in human interactions. His *Fantasia of the Unconscious* (1922) looked at the psychological realm.

Lawrence's lyrical and detailed writing style—ahead of its time in many ways—greatly influenced many 20th-century fiction writers. On March 2, 1930, he died after a lifetime of poor health and long-neglected tuberculosis.

References: Fiona Becket, *D. H. Lawrence: The Thinker as a Poet* (New York: St. Martin's, 1997); Jack Stewart, *The Vital Art of D. H. Lawrence: Vision and Expression* (Carbondale: Southern Illinois University Press, 1999).

Lawrence, Ernest Orlando (1901–1958)

American physicist and Nobel laureate. Born in Canton, South Dakota, on August 8, 1901, Lawrence received his bachelor's degree from the University of South Dakota in 1922, his master's from the University of Minnesota in 1923, and his doctorate from Yale University in 1925. Working as a physics professor at Yale University (1925–28) and the University of California at Berkeley (1928–58), Lawrence invented and developed the cyclotron, which "permitted nuclear particle acceleration to very high velocities. The particles were used to bombard atoms, leading to many new isotopes and elements." For this landmark invention, Lawrence was awarded the 1939 Nobel Prize in physics. Because of the outbreak of World War II, however, he could not go to Europe to receive his prize; he was later presented with the Nobel in Berkeley on February 29, 1940.

During the war Lawrence worked on the Manhattan Project to build an atomic bomb; he called on the U.S. government to demonstrate the technology in a neutral test before actually using it in warfare. He died in Palo Alto, California, on August 27, 1958.

References: Bernard S. Schlessinger, "Lawrence, Ernest Orlando" in Bernard S. and June H. Schlessinger, eds., *The Who's Who of Nobel Prize Winners* (Phoenix, Ariz.: Oryx, 1986), 164.

League of Nations

World conference of countries, established 1920, to diplomatically debate and settle questions and problems between nations before the outbreak of war. The subject of a "coalition" or "alliance" of nations has been of general interest since the early years of the 18th century. After World War I, leaders from the United States (President Woodrow WILSON), as well as England, France, and Italy, assembled at VERSAILLES to formulate a peace treaty with Germany and its defeated allies. Wilson brought to the conference his program for a just peace, the so-called Fourteen Points. But the English and French delegates, David LLOYD GEORGE and Georges Clemenceau, had earlier decided to use Versailles to punish Germany so that the country would never rise again militarily to threaten Europe.

To establish peaceful order for the future, the founders of the League sought to include as many of the world's nations as possible. The Versailles document, one of the longest treaties at the time, encompasses the divvying up of major portions of Europe and the "re-bordering" of many of the nations that had fought on the side of Germany, most notably Austria and Hungary. Such treaties as the pact of TRIANON came out of the Versailles Conference.

In 1919, Wilson returned to the United States, but because of Senate opposition to the Versailles Treaty, which Wilson was unable to resolve, the United States never ratified the agreement and never become a League member. Nevertheless, the organization went into effect on January 10, 1920, composed of five bodies: the Council, the Assembly, the Secretariat, the INTERNATIONAL LABOUR ORGANIZATION, and the PERMANENT COURT OF INTERNATIONAL JUSTICE (later the World Court), located at the Hague, the Netherlands. A secretary-general sat as the organization's leader. The League, which was found to be the toothless tiger many had feared, was rendered useless throughout the 1930s by Japanese aggression in China and German aggression in Europe. After World War II,

An early meeting of the League of Nations in Geneva, Switzerland *(CORBIS/Bettmann)*

the League was replaced by the United Nations, which was allowed more of a peacekeeping role and allowance for military action.

See also JOHNSON, Hiram Warren; LEAGUE OF NATIONS CONTROVERSY; LODGE, Henry Cabot.

References: William Ladd, *Dissertation on the Subject of Congress of Nations. For the Adjustment of International Disputes Without Recourse to Arms. By a Friend of Peace* (New York: Ezra Collier, 1837); Stephen Pierce Duggan, *The League of Nations: The Principle and the Practice* (Boston: Atlantic Monthly Press, 1919); Janet M. Manson, "League of Nations" in Bruce W. Jentleson and Thomas G. Paterson, senior eds., *Encyclopedia of U.S. Foreign Relations* (New York: Oxford University Press, 1997), 3: 51–54; "League of Nations and Japan" in Dorothy Perkins, *Encyclopedia of Japan: Japanese History and Culture, from Abacus to Zori* (New York: Facts On

File, 1991), 195–96; "League of Nations Holds First Meeting," New York *Herald* (European Edition), January 17, 1920, p. 1.

League of Nations Controversy

U.S. political conflict, 1919–20, between the forces who supported American participation in the League of Nations as drafted at the VERSAILLES Conference in 1919 and those who wished for the United States to remain aloof or join the organization only with certain conditions. After U.S. President Woodrow WILSON returned to the United States, he submitted the League covenant to the U.S. Senate, which has the power to pass or decline treaties. Many senators refused to consider the treaty, however, and became known as the IRRECONCILABLES. When a leader in this group, Senator Henry Cabot LODGE of Massachusetts, pro-

LEAGUE OF NATIONS MEMBERSHIP FROM INCEPTION

NATION, YEAR OF JOINING

Afghanistan, 1934	Japan, 1920[2]
Albania, 1920	Iraq, 1932
Argentina, 1920	Irish Free State, 1923
Australia, 1920	Italy, 1920
Austria, 1920	Latvia, 1921
Belgium, 1920	Liberia, 1920
Bolivia, 1920	Lithuania, 1921
Brazil, 1920	Luxembourg, 1920
Bulgaria, 1920	Mexico, 1931
Canada, 1920	Netherlands, 1920
Chile, 1920	New Zealand, 1920
China, 1920	Nicaragua, 1920
Colombia, 1920	Norway, 1920
Costa Rica, 1920	Panama, 1920
Cuba, 1920	Paraguay, 1920
Czechoslovakia, 1920	Persia, 1920
Denmark, 1920	Peru, 1920
Dominican Republic, 1923	Poland, 1920
Ecuador, 1920	Portugal, 1920
El Salvador, 1920	Romania, 1920
Estonia, 1921	Siam, 1920
Ethiopia (Abyssinia), 1923	Spain, 1920
Finland, 1920	Sweden, 1920
France, 1920	Switzerland, 1920
Germany, 1926[1]	Turkey, 1932
Greece, 1920	U.S.S.R., 1934
Guatemala, 1920	Union of South Africa, 1920
Haiti, 1920	
Honduras, 1920	United Kingdom, 1920
Hungary, 1922	Uruguay, 1920
India, 1920	Venezuela, 1920
	Kingdom of Serbs, Croats, and Slovenes, 1920

[1]Germany announced its withdrawal from the League on October 21, 1933.

[2]Japan announced its withdrawal from the League on March 27, 1933.

States into the League of Nations over the next several months, Wilson remained huddled in the White House, many of his private affairs being attended to (secretly) by the First Lady, Edith Bolling Galt Wilson.

In the Senate, amendments were attached to the covenant, and there were several votes on its Wilsonian form and its amended form. Both went down to defeat, with friends of the president voting against the latter and backers of Lodge holding against the former. Senator Porter J. McCumber, Republican of North Dakota (later coauthor of the FORDNEY-MCCUMBER ACT of 1922), was the lone Republican to vote for the so-called "Underwood resolution," the Treaty submitted without any added reservations. Part of a group called the "mild reservationists"—almost all Democrats who desired to see the treaty pass with or without reservations—McCumber implored his fellow Republicans to give the treaty a chance in unamended form: "Mr. President, I am not the molder of my brother's convictions nor the keeper of his conscience, but speaking for myself as just one American citizen, I could not cast my vote against any reasonable agreement to secure future world peace without a conviction that would follow me to the grave, that I had committed an unpardonable offense against all future generations."

Some Democrats, among them James Alexander Reed of Missouri, attacked the League. Other pro-League Democrats abandoned their president and party to vote for the so-called "Lodge Reservations." In all, 15 Democrats "defect[ed] from Wilsonianism." Although history has not labeled these Democrats as Irreconcilables, they nonetheless aided in the effort to kill the treaty.

In the end the treaty was defeated, and the United States never joined the League of Nations. It was perhaps Wilson's worst legislative defeat.

References: Harold Tiffany Butler, "Partisan Positions on Isolationism vs. Internationalism, 1918–1933," (Ph.D. dissertation, Syracuse University, 1963), 39, 55, 76; Ashurst comment in Thomas A. Bailey, *Woodrow Wilson and the Great Betrayal* (New York: Macmillan, 1945), 271; Lee Meriwether, *Jim Reed: "Senatorial Immortal"* (Webster Groves, Mo.: International Mark Twain Society, 1948), 61–62; John Chalmers Vinson, *Referendum for Isolation: Defeat of Article Ten of the League of Nations Covenant* (Athens: University of Georgia Press, 1971); a history of the League fight can be found in George A. Finch, "The Treaty of Peace with Germany in the United States Senate," *The American Journal of International Law* 14 (1920): 155–206.

posed changes in the treaty, Wilson refused to budge and instead went out on a national tour to inform American citizens about the plan.

The tour hit Wilson hard; after a speech at Pueblo, Colorado, on September 25, he collapsed and was taken back to Washington a sick, and, in some ways, defeated man. As the Senate debated the inclusion of the United

League to Enforce Peace

American organization, established 1915, which attempted during the 1920s to raise public awareness of the LEAGUE OF NATIONS in the United States. The year after the start of World War I, a group of pacifists established the league to fight for peace and keep the United States out of the war.

The founders of the organization were peace advocates Hamilton Holt, editor of *The Independent*; Abbott Lawrence Lowell, the president of Harvard University; and Theodore Marburg. On June 17, 1915, these men and others met in Philadelphia and instituted the organizational structure of the group, with former President William Howard Taft as the league's first president. In 1916, President Woodrow WILSON told the group that he supported their aims and planned to keep America out of the war. After the United States entered the war, however, the group called for the establishment of a League of Nations. Taft broke with the group in 1920, when he called for the defeat of Wilson's Fourteen Points and campaigned for Republican Warren G. HARDING an enemy of the VERSAILLES Treaty which had set up the League of Nations, for president. The League to Enforce Peace further split when some members backed Republican changes to the treaty, while others denounced the alterations. The intraparty fight destroyed the group, leaving it moribund after the 1920 election. In 1923 it was formally disbanded.

References: Ruhl J. Bartlett, *The League to Enforce Peace* (Chapel Hill: University of North Carolina Press, 1944); John H. Latané, ed., *Development of the League of Nations Idea: Documents and Correspondence of Theodore Marburg* (New York: Macmillan, 1932); Theodore Marburg and Horace Edgar Flack, eds., *Taft Papers on the League of Nations* (New York: Macmillan, 1920); Carol A. Jackson, "League to Enforce Peace" in Bruce W. Jentleson and Thomas G. Paterson, senior eds., *Encyclopedia of U.S. Foreign Relations* (New York: Oxford University Press, 1997), 3: 54–55.

Lebensborn

Gestapo organization of NAZI Germany, literally meaning "source of life" or "fount of life," which "encourage[d] the propagation of large 'racially pure' German families as well as to take care of illegitimate children who were [of] 'pure Aryan blood.'" Established in December 1935 as an office in the SS Race and Settlement Main Office, the Lebensborn program called on the statute of September 13, 1936, that directed every SS officer to produce four children, so that the Aryan race could quickly propagate. The program records were destroyed during World War II, however, so its actual success cannot be ascertained. Historians Christian Zentner and Friedemann Bedüftig believe that approximately eleven thousand children were raised in so-called Lebensborn homes.

References: Edmund Jan Osmañczyk, *The Encyclopedia of the United Nations and International Agreements* (Philadelphia: Taylor & Francis, 1985), 468; Catrine Clay and Michael Leapman, *Master Race: The Lebensborn Experiment in Nazi Germany* (London: Hodder & Stoughton, 1995); "Lebensborn" in Christian Zentner and Friedemann Bedüftig, eds., *Encyclopedia of the Third Reich* (New York: Macmillan, 1991), 1: 534.

Lebensraum

Government policy of Nazi Germany, literally meaning "living space," which was used to justify Nazi expansion into neighboring countries. Although the idea of an expanded German empire was promulgated in the 1870s, it took shape during the era of Nazi rule (1933–45). As early as 1920, the German Workers' Party, the infant genesis of the NAZI PARTY, called for "land and territory (colonies) for the nourishment of our people and for settling our excess population." These plans were also laid out in Adolf HITLER's 1924–26 work, *Mein Kampf*, but until Hitler attained power in 1933 these plans seemed unreal.

Hitler eyed the agricultural Ukraine as well as the German-speaking areas of the Sudetenland and Austria for takeover. By 1938 these two latter areas had been conquered; in 1941, Hitler initiated Operation Barbarossa to capture the third region. But during this military operation the German army became bogged down in Russia, leading to the ultimate defeat of the Third Reich in 1945.

See also ANSCHLUSS.

References: Kamenetsky, Ihor, *Secret Nazi Plans for Eastern Europe: A Study of Lebensraum Policies* (New Haven, Conn.: College and University Press, 1961); "Living Space" in Christian Zentner and Friedemann Bedüftig, eds., *Encyclopedia of the Third Reich* 2 vols. (New York: Macmillan, 1991), 1: 554.

Lenin, Vladimir Ilyich (1870–1924)

Russian Communist leader, originator of the Russian Revolution of 1917, which established Communist rule. Born into a middle-class family in Simbirsk on April 10, 1870, as Vladimir Ilyich Ulyanov, Lenin became a revolutionary when his older brother was hanged in 1887 for plotting to kill the czar. Most of Lenin's early life is bathed in mystery, as are many of his activities. He spent much of his life in exile from his native Russia. An intense reader, he was a dedicated socialist and an early student of Karl Marx and the *Communist Manifesto*. For his socialist propaganda work, he was arrested in 1895 and exiled to Siberia in 1897, where he wrote *The Development of Capitalism in Russia* in 1899. Even before World War I had heightened problems in czarist Russia, Lenin had published several revolutionary works: *What Next? Burning Questions of Our Movement* (1902), *Two Tactics of the Social-Democratic Party in the Democratic Revolution* (1905), and *The Dispersal of the Duma and the Tasks of the Proletariat* (1906). He also founded several revolutionary periodicals, including *Pravda*.

When the war broke out in August 1914, Lenin was in Germany. Using money passed to him by the German government—which wished to see its military enemy to the east, Russia, neutralized—Lenin joined his friend Leon TROTSKY, Menshevik ("minority") revolutionary (Lenin was a member of the Bolshevik ("majority") faction of the Social Democratic Party), to destabilize the government of Czar Nicholas II. Lenin denounced the war as imperialistic and called on all socialists to rise against their governments. When Russia lost horribly in the battles fought against Germany on the eastern front, the czar abdicated and was replaced by another member of the Menshevik wing, Alexandr Kerensky. When the Kerensky government sent more troops into battle to be senselessly slaughtered, Lenin and his fellow socialists staged a coup in November 1917, dislodged Kerensky (who fled into exile), executed the czar and his family (who had been under house arrest), and established a "dictatorship of the proletariat." Lenin and the men around him—Trotsky, Joseph STALIN, Nikolai BUKHARIN, Grigorii Zinoviev, and Lev Kamenev—established workers' councils ("soviets") and instituted a campaign of "food and bread" for the masses. Lenin sued for peace from the Germans, signing the humiliating Treaty of Brest-Litovsk, and handing over both land in western Russia and a large sum of gold.

As head of the Council of People's Commissars, Lenin battled with a rapidly deteriorating economy. From 1918 through 1921, Lenin defended the Soviet government against several counterrevolutionary armies. In 1921, Lenin introduced the NEW ECONOMIC POLICY, which sought to reconstruct the nation's shattered economy through a number of socialistic reforms. By this time, however, Lenin's health was going downhill. An assassination attempt in 1918 had left him impaired, and a series of strokes starting in 1922 led to his death. In his final days he hinted that Stalin, then Lenin's friend and comrade, was a dangerous radical who should not be allowed to take over, but that advice was not taken.

Lenin died on January 21, 1924. Five days after his death, the Second Congress of the Soviets renamed St. Petersburg as Leningrad. Today Lenin is considered the formulator of official communist ideology. Leninism is on an equivalent par with other powerful leftist ideologies—Stalinism, Marxism, and Trotskyism.

References: Elyse Topalian, *V. I. Lenin* (New York: Franklin Watts, 1983); Robert D. Warth, *Lenin* (New York: Twayne Publishers, 1973); Adam Bruno Ulam, *The Bolsheviks: The Intellectual and Political History of the Triumph of Communism in Russia* (New York: Collier Books, 1968); Alexander Rabinowitch, *The Bolsheviks Come to Power: The Revolution of 1917 in Petrograd* (New York: W. W. Norton, 1976); Theodore H. Von Laue, *Why Lenin? Why Stalin? A Reappraisal of the Russian Revolution* (Philadelphia: J. B. Lippincott, 1964); "Lenin Dies of Cerebral Hemorrhage: Moscow Throngs Overcome with Grief; Trotsky Departs Ill, Radek in Disfavor," *New York Times*, January 23, 1924, p. 1.

Leopold, Nathan Freudenthal, Jr. (1905–1971), and Richard Loeb (1906–1936)

American murderers, convicted and sentenced to life in prison for their roles in the murder of 14-year-old Bobby Franks in 1924. Their case became a cause célèbre in the attempt of their attorney, Clarence DARROW, to spare them from the death penalty. Both boys were the products of rich homes and had received elite educations. They were bored youths, however, who desired to commit the perfect murder and get away with it. On May 22, 1924, they kidnapped Franks, heir to the Sears Roebuck fortune and a cousin of both boys. One of the two sat in the back of an automobile, stuffed a rag into Franks's mouth, and bludgeoned him with a chisel. They then drove the near-dead boy out near a railway, poured acid over Franks's face, and left. Using an alias, they sent ransom notes demanding $10,000 to Franks's frantic parents. Two birdwatchers stumbled across the dead body, however; among the items found at the scene were a pair of eyeglasses that police eventually traced to Leopold. The boys were brought in and, in separate rooms, confessed and blamed the other for committing the act.

The case seemed to be an easy peg for the death penalty. Leopold's father hired Darrow, then considered one of the finest attorneys in the nation for defense. Darrow spent 33 days in July and August 1924 trying to get the boys acquitted. When that failed, he appealed in a lengthy speech to Judge John Caverly that the boys should be spared a death sentence. Caverly agreed and sentenced both to life imprisonment for the murder and 99 years for kidnapping.

The two were sent to the Northern Illinois Penitentiary near Joliet, where they served their sentences in anonymity. On January 28, 1936, Loeb was murdered in prison. Leopold served his sentence quietly, working in the prison and earning several degrees. In 1958, he was released by the governor of Illinois after 34 years in prison. Leopold moved to Puerto Rico, where he spent his remaining years working as a hospital orderly. He died in San Juan on August 29, 1971. Leopold told his life story in *Life Plus 99 Years* (1958).

References: Randall Eugene Majors, "Clarence Darrow in Defense of Leopold and Loeb: A Case Study in Forensic Argumentation" (Ph.D. dissertation, Indiana University, 1978); Meyer Levin, "Compulsion" (New York: Simon & Schuster, 1956).

Leticia dispute

Land question, 1932–34, over the territory of Leticia Trapezium in the Amazon basin claimed by both Peru and Colombia, which led to threats of war. Under the Treaty of Solomon-Lozano, signed in Lima, Peru, on March 24,

1922, Peru gave the area to Colombia as Colombia's only access to the Amazon River. Soon after both nations had ratified the treaty (Colombia in 1925, Peru in 1927), however, conflict broke out. On September 1, 1932, Peruvian troops under Col. Luis Sánchez Cerro seized the area. Brazilian mediation failed, and Colombia asked the LEAGUE OF NATIONS to intervene. In 1931 Sánchez Cerro was elected president of Peru, further intensifying the conflict. The League of Nations named a commission, called the Administrative Committee for Leticia Trapezium, to investigate the problem from June 1933 until June 1934. Cerro's death on April 30, 1934, allowed both nations to peacefully end the situation. His successor, O. R. Benevides, restored the Treaty of Solomon-Lozano and a new agreement was signed in Rio de Janiero on May 21, 1934.

References: Edmund Jan Osmańczyk, *The Encyclopedia of the United Nations and International Agreements* (Philadelphia: Taylor & Francis, 1985), 470; Daniel M. Masterson, *Militarism and Politics in Latin American: Peru from Sanchez Cerro to Sendero Luminoso* (New York: Greenwood, 1991); Barry William Loveday, *Sanchez Cerro and Peruvian Politics, 1930–1933* (Glasgow: University of Glasgow Institute of Latin-American Studies, 1973).

Lewis, Sinclair (1885–1951)

American novelist, and Nobel laureate, known for several interwar novels, and "for his great and living art of painting life, with a talent for creating types, with wit and humor." Born Harry Sinclair Lewis in Sauk Centre, Minnesota, on February 7, 1885, the third of three sons of town doctor Emmet J. Lewis and Emma (Kermott) Lewis, he went from an early age by his middle name. Educated in public schools and later at Yale University (1907), Lewis became a journalist and served on newspapers in several cities before becoming a writer. Lewis's reputation as a novelist was established with the publication of *Main Street: The Story of Carol Kennicott* (1920), a story of smalltown America. His other works during the period include *Babbitt* (1922), *Arrowsmith* (1925), and *Elmer Gantry* (1927), a portrait of a minister. His later novels, which include *Cass Timberlane* (1945) and *Kingsblood Royal* (1947), were not as successful. With his Nobel victory in 1930, Lewis became the first American to win the Literature Prize. In his acceptance speech, known as "The American Fear of Literature," Lewis spoke out against the failure of the United States to recognize radical authors, such as Ernest HEMINGWAY and Mike Gold, after diplomat Henry Van Dyke declared that it was an insult for a leftwinger such as Lewis to represent America's first literature Nobel. Lewis died in Rome, Italy, on January 10, 1951.

References: John Smith, "Lewis, Harry Sinclair" in Bernard S. and June H. Schlessinger, eds., *The Who's Who of Nobel Prize Winners* (Phoenix, Ariz.: Oryx, 1986), 57–58; Jon Pahl, "Sinclair Lewis" in Charles H. Lippy, ed., *Twentieth-Century Shapers of American Popular Religion* (New York: Greenwood, 1989), 241–47; "The American Fear of Literature" in Louis Filler, *A Dictionary of American Conservatism* (Secaucus, N.J.: Citadel, 1988), 33; Thomas Watson MacCallum and Stephen Taylor, eds., *The Nobel Prize-Winners and the Nobel Foundation, 1901–1937* (Zurich: Central European Times Publishing, 1938), 313–15.

Lindbergh, Charles Augustus, Jr. (1902–1974)

American aviator whose solo flight across the Atlantic Ocean in 1927 captivated the world. Born in Detroit, Michigan, on February 4, 1902, he was the son of Charles Augustus Lindbergh Sr., a Republican congressman from the Sixth District of Minnesota (1907–17). Lindbergh attended the University of Wisconsin. As a young man he was interested in airplanes and landed a job as an airmail pilot. He then heard about Harry Guggenheim's offer of a sum of money to anyone who could cross the Atlantic solo in a plane. Several had attempted the feat and failed. Lindbergh had his own plane built, which he christened the *Spirit of St. Louis,* and he began his attempt from Floyd Bennett Field on Long Island in New York on May 20, 1927. Thirty-three-and-a-half hours later, he landed at Le Bourget Field in Paris, becoming the first person to make a solo flight across the Atlantic Ocean. In 1927, *Time* magazine named Lindbergh as its first Man of the Year.

After marrying the writer Anne Spencer Morrow, the daughter of the U.S. ambassador to Mexico, Lindbergh went on a survey mission across Europe and South America. When he returned, he was hired as an adviser to Trancontinental Air Transport and also worked for Pan-American Airways. The 1932 kidnapping and murder of his baby son destroyed him. The couple moved to England.

In 1938, Lindbergh made a tour of the military machine of Nazi Germany, which tainted his name as an American hero. On May 5, 1939, Lindbergh was named to the so-called Kilner-Lindbergh Board, established by General H. H. Arnold, to recommend a redraft of military characteristics of all U.S. military aircraft, including the B-29. The board was composed of General W. C. Kilner, Lindbergh, Col. Carl Spaatz and others. During the first years of World War II, Lindbergh was one of the leaders of the America First movement, an organization committed to keeping the United States out of the war in Europe. When the Japanese attacked Pearl Harbor, however, he volunteered for service and flew 50 missions over the Far East. In 1954, President Dwight D. Eisenhower made him a reserve brigadier general.

In his final years, Lindbergh became an environmentalist, opposing the construction of the Supersonic Trans-

A Parisian crowd mobs the *Spirit of St. Louis* as Charles Lindbergh lands the plane on May 31, 1927, after his historic transoceanic flight. *(CORBIS/Bettmann)*

port because of noise concerns and building a small home on Maui, Hawaii, overlooking the ocean. He died there on August 26, 1974.

References: Wayne S. Cole, "Lindbergh, Charles Augustus" in Bruce W. Jentleson and Thomas G. Paterson, senior eds., *Encyclopedia of U.S. Foreign Relations* (New York: Oxford University Press, 1997), 3: 73; "Lindbergh Arrives on Record-Breaking Flight; 50,000 Roar Welcome at Field as Lone American Lands After Ocean Dash of 33hr. 30min," New York *Herald* (European Edition), May 22, 1927, p. 1; "Lindbergh Does It! To Paris in 33 1/2 Hours; Flies 1,000 Miles Through Snow and Sleet; Cheering French Carry Him Off Field," *New York Times*, May 22, 1927, p. 1; "Lindbergh at Paris in 33 1/2 Hours; Slept on Way: Ran Through Storm," *Brooklyn Daily Eagle*, May 22, 1927, p. 1; "America First" in

Louis Filler, *A Dictionary of American Conservatism* (Secaucus, N.J.: Citadel, 1988), 31.

Litvinov, Maxim Maximovich (1876–1951)
Russian Communist leader, politician, and diplomat. Litvinov was born in Bialystok, Russia (now Poland), on July 17, 1876. He served in the czarist army but joined the Social Democratic Worker's Party in 1898. He was arrested in 1901 but escaped to Switzerland to join other anti-czarist revolutionaries abroad. Two years later, he returned to Russia and began organizing against the government. In 1907 he and Maxim Gorki founded in St. Petersburg a radical newspaper called *New Life*. Avoiding a second arrest, he fled to France and then England; Litvinov was in London when the Bolshevik revolution took place in 1917; he was then named as the Soviet ambas-

sador to Great Britain. The British government arrested him, however, and sent him back to Russia in exchange for Bruce Lockhart, a British agent who had been captured by the Soviets.

Back in Russia, Litvinov became a close adviser to Vladimir LENIN, serving as vice commissar of foreign affairs (1918–29) under Grigori Chicherin, then as Chicherin's successor until 1940. In 1928 Litvinov signed for the Soviet Union the KELLOGG-BRIAND PACT, which outlawed war. Litvinov also represented the U.S.S.R. at the GENEVA DISARMAMENT CONFERENCE (1932–34) and at both of the LONDON NAVAL CONFERENCES (1930 and 1935–36). He also signed the LITVINOV PROTOCOL, which outlawed war between the Soviet Union and its neighbors.

For much of the 1930s Litvinov called for a united stand of the West and East against the growing Axis threat; he was forced into retirement by STALIN's growing cooperation with Hitler. He resigned just after the SOVIET-GERMAN NONAGGRESSION PACT was signed on August 23, 1939, and was replaced by the more isolationist Vyacheslav Molotov. After Nazi Germany attacked the Soviet Union on June 22, 1941, Litvinov came out of retirement to rally a concerted Soviet response. Stalin then named Litvinov as Soviet ambassador to the United States (1941–43) and as deputy commissar for foreign affairs (1943–46).

After World War II, Litvinov again fell out of favor with Stalin because of his advocacy of a closer relationship with the West in general and the United States in particular. He died in Moscow on December 31, 1951.

References: Zinovy Sheinis (Vic Schneierson, trans.), *Maxsim Litvinov* (Moscow: Progress Publishers, 1990); Hugh D. Phillips, *Between the Revolution and the West: A Political Biography of Maxim M. Litvinov* (Boulder, Colo.: Westview Press, 1992); Hugh D. Phillips, *Maxim M. Litvinov and Soviet-American Relations, 1918–1946* (Washington, D.C.: Kennan Institute for Advanced Russian Studies, 1996); Donald G. Bishop, *The Roosevelt-Litvinov Agreement: The American View* (Syracuse, N.Y.: Syracuse University Press, 1965).

Litvinov Protocol

Pact, signed February 9, 1929, between Estonia, Latvia, Poland, Romania, and Maxim Maximovich LITVINOV of the Soviet Union, outlawing war as an instrument of state policy. Modeled on the Kellogg-Briand Pact, it is also known as the Moscow Protocol. In the agreement, the signatories and the Soviet Union, "animated by the desire to contribute to the maintenance of the peace existing between their countries and to this end to put forthwith into force between the people of these countries, the treaty of renunciation of war as an instrument of national policy [Kellogg-Briand], signed at Paris, on August 27, 1928, have decided to realize these intentions through the effects of the present protocol." The pact's provisions were also

extended to Turkey on February 28, 1929, to Persia (later Iran) on April 4, 1929, and to Lithuania on April 5, 1929.

References: Arthur Upham Pope, *Maxim Litvinoff* (New York: L. B. Fischer, 1943); Edmund Jan Osmańczyk, *The Encyclopedia of the United Nations and International Agreements* (Philadelphia: Taylor & Francis, 1985), 477.

Lloyd George, David (1863–1945)

British politician and diplomat, prime minister (1916–22). Born in Manchester, England, on January 17, 1863, Lloyd George was the eldest son of four children of teacher and farmer William George and Elizabeth (Lloyd) George. His ancestors were Welsh farmers. When Lloyd George was only 17 months old, his father died, after which his uncle Richard Lloyd raised the boy. His only formal education appears to have occurred when he attended a village school in Llanystumdwy, in Caernarvonshire, Wales. When he was 14, however, Lloyd George passed the preliminary examination of the Wales Law Society and began work at a solicitors firm in Portmadoc.

In 1884, Lloyd George took his law examinations in London and was admitted to the English bar. The following year, he opened a practice in the village of Criccieth, joined two years later by his younger brother William. In 1889 he started his political career with his election as alderman of the Caernarvonshire County Council. In 1890 he was elected to Parliament from the Caernarvon district of Boroughs. His term was marked by his support of temperance measures, the introduction of an old age pensions law, and his denunciation of British participation in the Boer War in South Africa, a stand that nearly got him killed at a 1901 rally. Four years later, Prime Minister Henry Campbell-Bannerman named Lloyd George president of the English Board of Trade, and at the same time he became a privy counsellor. In 1908, when Campbell-Bannerman resigned, incoming prime minister Herbert ASQUITH named Lloyd George chancellor of the exchequer, the British equivalent of the U.S. secretary of the treasury.

In 1909, Lloyd George's budget, known as "the people's budget," sent the Parliament into a frenzy of disagreement until it ultimately was defeated in the House of Lords. During World War I, Lloyd George's "war budgets" doubled the income tax to pay for exploding military expenditures. In Asquith's coalition government, Lloyd George was named minister of munitions, but his time in this post lasted a year. On June 5, 1916, War Minister Lord Kitchener was drowned when his ship was torpedoed by a German ship; a week later, Lloyd George was named as his successor. Joining with the Conservatives, led by Andrew Bonar LAW, Lloyd George criticized the English war effort; he was asked to resign, but on December 5, 1916, Asquith handed in his resignation.

The Conservatives asked Lloyd George to form a new government. As prime minister, Lloyd George oversaw a tumultuous era in Britain. Under his administration the Balfour Declaration, calling for a homeland for Jews in Palestine, was drawn up under the direction of Foreign Minister Arthur James Balfour; the VERSAILLES Conference was held in Paris; the Representation of the People Act, which gave British women over the age of 30 the right to vote, was enacted; the IRISH FREE STATE was established; and Lloyd George interceded in the Chanak crisis to head off war in Turkey. On October 19, 1922, when the Conservatives demanded an end to the coalition government, Lloyd George resigned.

Remaining as a member of Parliament, he nonetheless was out of power. In 1926, during the GENERAL STRIKE of British miners, Liberal Party head Asquith resigned and was succeeded by Lloyd George. Lloyd George wrote *Britain's Industrial Future* (1928) and the four-volume *War Memoirs* (1933–36). In 1935 he called for an economic program to end the depression, but it was not enacted. In 1940 his criticism of Prime Minister Neville CHAMBER-LAIN's handling of World War II ultimately led to Chamberlain's resignation and the beginning of Winston Churchill's rule. Lloyd George's last speech in the House of Commons, on May 7, 1941, concerned granting aid to Greece at the height of the war.

Before his death, he was made earl of Dwyfor and viscount Gwynedd of Dwyfor. He died two months later at Ty Newydd, Llanystumdwy, Wales, on March 26, 1945.

See also ELECTIONS, BRITISH.

References: Thomas Jones, "Lloyd George, David" in Sir Leslie Stephen and Sir Sidney Lee et al., eds., *The Dictionary of National Biography* (Oxford: Oxford University Press, 22 volumes and eight supplements, 1917–1993), 515–29; Stephen E. Fritz, "Lloyd George, David" in Warren F. Kuehl, ed., *Biographical Dictionary of Internationalists* (Westport, Conn.: Greenwood, 1983), 439–41; Finton Codd, "David Lloyd George" in Dermot Englefield, Janet Seaton, and Isobel White, *Facts about the British Prime Ministers: A Compilation of Biographical and Historical Information* (New York: H. W. Wilson Co., 1995), 237–45.

Locarno Pact

Covenant, 1925, constituted by several European heads of state and foreign ministers to assure the integrity of territorial boundaries of European states after World War I. Officially called the Treaty of Mutual Guarantee between Germany, Belgium, France, Great Britain, and Italy, its provisions were negotiated among the leaders of those countries, Czechoslovakia, and Poland. France called the meeting, held in the southern Swiss village of Locarno, on Lake Maggiore, October 5–16, 1925. The treaty itself was signed in London on December 1, 1925, by German chancellor Hans Luther, German president Gustav STRESE-MANN, Belgian foreign minister Émile Vandervelde, French prime minister Aristide BRIAND, British foreign minister Austen CHAMBERLAIN, and Italian premier Benito MUSSOLINI.

In the treaty's final language, the borders of the several European states were defined to avoid war. For their work on this pact, Chamberlain was awarded the 1925 Nobel Peace Prize, and Stresemann and Briand shared the 1926 Nobel Peace Prize.

References: George J. Lerski, *Historical Dictionary of Poland, 966–1945* (Westport, Conn.: Greenwood, 1996), 311; Michael Dockrill and Brian McKercher, eds., *Diplomacy and World Power: Studies in British Foreign Policy, 189–1950* (Cambridge: Cambridge University Press, 1996); Jon Jacobson, *Locarno Diplomacy: Germany and the West, 1925–1929* (Princeton, N.J.: Princeton University Press, 1972); Friedrich Joseph Berber, ed., *Locarno: A Collection of Documents* (London: W. Hodge & Company, 1936); Edmund Jan Osmańczyk, *The Encyclopedia of the United Nations and International Agreements* (Philadelphia: Taylor & Francis, 1985), 477–78; John Ashley Soames Grenville, *The Major International Treaties, 1914–1973: A History and Guide with Texts* (New York: Stein & Day, 1975), 95–96.

Lodge, Henry Cabot (1850–1924)

American politician. Lodge was born in Boston, Massachusetts, on May 12, 1850; he attended Harvard College (now Harvard University), where he received an undergraduate degree (1871), a law degree (1874), and a doctorate (1876). He was an editor of the influential magazine *The North American Review* (1873–76), and also served as a lecturer in American history at Harvard (1876–79).

In 1880, Lodge was elected to the Massachusetts House of Representatives, serving until 1881, and within five years he was elected to the U.S. House of Representatives (1886–93). He was then elected to the U.S. Senate (1893–1924). In his more than three decades in the Senate, Lodge became one of the most powerful of American politicians, eventually rising to become the chair of the Senate Foreign Relations Committee.

Leader of the anti-Wilsonian faction in the Senate, Lodge opposed the VERSAILLES Treaty the president had negotiated after World War I. Biographer Janet Manson calls these differences between Wilson and Lodge "mutual personal and political enmity." Even before the treaty had been drawn, Lodge displayed his opposition as one of the IRRECONCILABLES. In a speech delivered in the Senate on December 21, 1918, Lodge asked, "Is it not our first duty and our highest duty to bring peace to the world at this moment and not encumber it by trying to provide against wars which never may be fought and against difficulties which lie far ahead in a dim and unknown future?" His belief that the United States should stay clear of foreign entanglements, particular those regarding Europe, dictated his fierce opposition to the LEAGUE OF NATIONS. In the end, the League was defeated. Wilson left office, a broken man, never to forgive Lodge. Lodge worked better with Wilson's successor, Warren G. HARDING, and was rewarded with a position on the U.S. delegation to the Washington Conference on the Limitation of Armaments in 1922. Lodge died on November 9, 1924. His work on the LEAGUE OF NATIONS CONTROVERSY, *The Senate and the League of Nations,* appeared posthumously in 1925. His grandson, Henry Cabot Lodge, Jr., served as a U.S. Senator from Massachusetts, as well as on the Republican presidential ticket with Richard Nixon in 1960.

References: Janet M. Manson, "Lodge, Henry Cabot, Sr." in Bruce W. Jentleson and Thomas G. Paterson, senior eds., *Encyclopedia of U.S. Foreign Relations* (New York: Oxford University Press, 1997), 3: 79–80; William C. Widenor, "Lodge, Henry Cabot" in Warren F. Kuehl, ed., *Biographical Dictionary of Internationalists* (Westport, Conn.: Greenwood, 1983), 442–43; John A. Garraty, *Henry Cabot Lodge: A Biography* (New York: Alfred A. Knopf, 1953); Henry Cabot Lodge, *The Senate and the League of Nations* (New York: Charles Scribner's Sons, 1925); "Senator Lodge Dies from Stroke That Followed Surgery; End Comes Late Sunday in Cambridge, Mass., Hospital," *Washington Post,* November 10, 1924, p. 1.

Loewi, Otto (1873–1961)

German-American pharmacologist and Nobel laureate. Born in Frankfurt am Main, Germany, on June 3, 1873, he received his M.D. at the University of Strasbourg (then in Germany, now in France), and then worked as a researcher at the City Hospital in Frankfurt (1897–98), as an assistant to Professor Hans Horst Meyer at the University of Marburg, as a professor of pharmacology at the University of Vienna (1909–38), and at New York University (1940–61). Researching several functions of the human body, including nerve impulses, the kidneys, how insulin works to combat diabetes, and cocaine's effect on adrenaline, Loewi was the corecipient (with Henry Hallett DALE) of the 1936 Nobel Prize in medicine and physiology.

He also devised Loewi's test for the detection of pancreatic cancer. He died on December 25, 1961.

References: Rashelle Karp, "Loewi, Otto" in Bernard S. and June H. Schlessinger, eds., *The Who's Who of Nobel Prize Winners* (Phoenix, Ariz.: Oryx, 1986), 90; Thomas Watson MacCallum and Stephen Taylor, eds., *The Nobel Prize-Winners and the Nobel Foundation, 1901–1937* (Zurich: Central European Times Publishing, 1938), 241–42.

London Economic Conference

Meeting, 1933, at which many of the world's nations met to try to stabilize the world economy and end the GREAT DEPRESSION. Also known as the World Monetary and Economic Conference, the parley opened in London on June 12 and lasted until July 27, with 66 nations in attendance; U.S. Secretary of State Cordell HULL presided. The conferees discussed ways to stabilize world currencies, but neglected to consider the impact of war debt and REPARATIONS on the world's fragile economies. On July 3, U.S. President Franklin D. ROOSEVELT claimed to the conferees that no progress was being made and that he was unhappy with the course of action being taken. This bombshell only served to deflate the morale of the conferees. The conference lasted for three additional weeks, but no solution could be found to the pressing problems Roosevelt had illustrated; a total failure, the meeting broke up on July 27. No further economic conferences were held until after World War II.

See also PITTMAN, KEY.

References: Kendall W. Stiles, "London Economic Conference" in Bruce W. Jentleson and Thomas G. Paterson, senior eds., *Encyclopedia of U.S. Foreign Relations* (New York: Oxford University Press, 1997), 3: 81; Herbert Feis, *1933: Characters in Crisis* (Boston: Little, Brown, 1966); Dean Elizabeth Traynor, *International Monetary and Financial Conferences in the Interwar Period* (Washington, D.C.: Catholic University of America Press, 1949).

London Naval Conference Treaties

Pacts, agreed to at the first London Naval Conference in 1930 between the United States, Great Britain, and Japan, and at the second conference in 1936 between the United States, Great Britain, Japan, and Italy. The first conference assembled on January 21, 1930, and closed on April 22 of that same year. The main goal of this gathering, as historian J. Garry Clifford writes, was to "extend . . . the moratorium on battleship construction arranged at the WASHINGTON NAVAL CONFERENCE of 1921–1922, and provide . . . for the limitation of less ship categories—cruisers, destroyers, and submarines." An agreement between U.S. President Herbert HOOVER and British prime minister Ramsay MACDONALD was to preserve the equilibrium between American heavy cruisers and British light cruisers. The treaty that came out of the 1930 meeting established a 10:10:7 ratio in cruiser tonnage for United States, Britain, and Japan. Despite the vigorous opposition by such senators as Hiram Warren JOHNSON and Kenneth McKellar, the treaty was approved by the U.S. Senate by a vote of 58–9 on July 21, 1930. However, the Japanese, who had promised to curtail battleship construction, set to work after the conference to beef up their fleet; with the invasion of China and the MUKDEN INCIDENT of 1931, the possibility of an extension of the 1930 arrangement at a proposed conference in Geneva in 1932 quickly died.

By 1934 the factors that had led to such optimism relating to the 1930 London treaty were in serious decline. Writes historian Meredith Berg, "Important signs pointed towards the early collapse of naval limitation. The rise of militarism in Japan intensified the demand of the Japanese government for complete naval equality with Britain and the United States. In Britain the Admiralty was dissatisfied with the light cruiser allotment given to the Royal Navy, just as naval elements in the United States were unhappy with the heavy cruiser restrictions imposed by the London Treaty. Finally, France and Italy continued their dispute over the principle of parity between themselves." Under the auspices of the British government, a second conference opened in the Locarno Room in London's Foreign Office on December 9, 1935. Through the four months of negotiations until the signing of the second treaty on March 25, 1936, the impasse over the division of naval armaments expectedly arose. Finally, Italy refused to sign the treaty because Britain and France had leveled sanctions against it for its aggression in the ETHIOPIAN WAR. In the end, however, the signatories agreed to the 1930 treaty restriction of 35,000-ton, 16-inch gun caliber for each ship, as well as the new limitation that further naval construction would be announced to the other signatories, and that annual naval reports would be furnished to them.

References: Garry J. Clifford, "London Naval Conferences of 1930 and 1935–36" in Bruce W. Jentleson and Thomas G. Paterson, senior eds., *Encyclopedia of U.S. Foreign Relations* (New York: Oxford University Press, 1977), 3: 81; Raymond G. O'Connor, *Perilous Equilibrium: The United States and the London Naval Conference of 1930* (Lawrence: University Press of Kansas, 1962); Harold Tiffany Butler, "Partisan Positions on Isolationism vs. Internationalism, 1918–1933," (Ph.D. dissertation, Syracuse University, 1963), 130; Meredith William Berg, "Admiral William H. Standley and the Second London Naval Treaty, 1934–36," *The Historian* 33, 2 (February 1971): 215–36; Stephen E. Pelz, *Race to Pearl Harbor: The Failure of the Second London Naval Conference and the Onset of World War II* (Cambridge: Harvard University Press, 1974).

Long, Huey Pierce (1893–1935)

American politician, nicknamed "the king fish." In a blistering 1932 exposé, journalist John K. Fineran called Long "a tinpot Napoleon." Born on a farm in the town of Winnfield, Louisiana, on August 30, 1893, Long attended the University of Oklahoma in 1912; he later studied the law at Tulane University in New Orleans. Admitted to the state bar in 1915, he gave up a law career for a position as State Railroad Commissioner. In 1928 he assembled a coalition that elected him governor, and he rose to become the most powerful state chief executive in U.S.

Huey Long *(CORBIS/Bettmann)*

history. Under his command, the state legislature and the courts did his bidding; in 1929 an attempt at impeaching him failed. During the first years of the GREAT DEPRESSION, he used state funds to build schools, highways, and other internal improvements, and he doled out funds to the populace to alleviate their economic situation.

In 1930, Long was elected to the U.S. Senate but, fearing that his opponents in Louisiana would capture the governor's seat, did not go to Washington until January 1932, when his close friend and associate, Oscar K. Allen, had been elected as governor. Long is best known, particularly during his tenure in the Senate, for his optimistic but naïve radical "Share the Wealth" plan. In it, the Louisianan claimed that he would have the government give each American family $5,000 a year, allow no American to have an annual income more than $1 million, and confiscate all estates in excess of $5 million (which he later revised to $3 million). The plan never was put into action, although at the time it was very popular and "Share the Wealth" clubs sprung up throughout the country. On August 15, 1935, Long announced that if Herbert HOOVER received the Republican presidential nomination again, as seemed likely, Long himself would run on a liberal or Progressive ticket in the 1936 election.

On September 8, 1935, as Long was touring the State House in Baton Rouge, a young physician, Carl Weiss, who blamed Long for destroying his father-in-law's business, shot Long several times, with Long's bodyguards returning fire and killing Weiss. Some historians speculate that the bodyguards accidentally shot Long. He was rushed to a hospital, where he died two days later. In 1946, writer Robert Penn WARREN used Long as the inspiration for the character Willie Stark in his Pulitzer Prize–winning novel *All The King's Men*.

References: John Kingston Fineran, *The Career of a Tinpot Napoleon: A Political Biography of Huey P. Long* (New Orleans: Printed by J. K.. Fineran, 1932); Hugh Davis Graham, ed., *Huey Long* (Englewood Cliffs, N.J.: Prentice-Hall, 1970); "Long Will Run If Roosevelt's Foe Is Hoover," *Washington Post*, August 16, 1935, p. 2; Glen Jeansonne, *Huey at 100: Centennial Essays on Huey P. Long* (Ruston, La.: McGinty Publications, 1995); "The Assassination of Huey P. Long of Louisiana" in Murray Clark Havens, Carl Leiden, and Karl M. Schmitt, *The Politics of Assassination* (Englewood Cliffs, N.J.: Prentice-Hall, 1970), 74–84.

Long March

Journey across China, 1934–35, by the Red Army under Chinese Communist Party leader MAO Tse-tung, to escape capture and certain death at the hands of the Nationalist government of CHIANG Kai-shek. Officially called the Chang Zheng ("Long March"), the evacuation began when Mao decided to retreat from a potential civil war with Chiang's Nationalist forces. On October 16, 1934, the 90,000 strong Red Army started what would turn out to be a six-thousand-mile forced march. Led by Generals Lin Piao and Teng Hsiao-p'ing (Deng Xiaoping) the army was forced to leave behind twenty thousand wounded men. Several weeks later, this contingent, led by Fang Chih Min, were captured by Chiang's troops and beheaded en masse.

On October 25, 1935, after a year of marching, seven thousand survivors of the initial ninety thousand who had started the march ended up in north Shaanxi Province. Mao's forces had been decimated, but they regained their strength two years later to help Chiang's troops attempt to stave off the Japanese invasion of China. In 1970 China named the rocket that carried the first two Chinese satellites into orbit the *Long March,* and it continues to use the name for its modern launch vehicles.

References: Jean Fritz, *China's Long March: 6,000 Miles of Danger* (New York: Putnam, 1988); Benjamin Yang, *From Revolution to Politics: Chinese Communists on the Long March* (Boulder, Colo.: Westview, 1990); *China: From the Long March to Tiananmen Square* (New York: Henry Holt, 1990).

Look Homeward Angel, A Story of the Buried Life
See WOLFE, Thomas Clayton.

Lost Generation

Designation, applied to the expatriate American writers of the 1920s residing particularly in Paris, including Ernest HEMINGWAY, F. Scott FITZGERALD, Henry MILLER, John DOS PASSOS, and Ezra POUND, whose works expressed their sense of spiritual alienation. The term derives from a remark attributed to Gertrude STEIN and used as an inscription in Hemingway's *The Sun Also Rises* (1926).

Reference: Linda Patterson Miller, ed., *Letters from the Lost Generation: Gerald and Sara Murphy and Friends* (New Brunswick, N.J.: Rutgers University Press, 1991).

Luce, Clare Boothe (1903–1987)

American editor and playwright, known for her witty and satirical plays in the 1930s. Born in New York City to an ex-chorus girl and an itinerant musician, Clare Boothe was educated at private schools. During the 1930s she edited *Vogue* and *Vanity Fair* magazines and married magazine publisher and magnate Henry LUCE in 1935. She also wrote three popular and critically acclaimed plays: *The Women* (1936), *Kiss the Boys Goodbye* (1938), and *Margin for Error* (1939).

During the early part of World War II, Luce was an on-location war correspondent for *Life* magazine, although she considered this merely time off from her true vocation as a playwright. These observations resulted in Luce's only book, *Europe in the Spring* (1940), an anecdotal account of her four-month visit to Europe. Through this work she intended to convince Americans about the dangers of isolationism. Luce set her sights on politics in the 1940s and 1950s, serving in the U.S. House of Representatives for Connecticut (1943–47) and as the U.S. ambassador to Italy (1953–56), at the time being only the second woman to serve as an ambassador. In 1983 she was awarded the Presidential Medal of Freedom. She died in October 1987 in Washington, D.C.

References: Ted Yanak and Pam Cornelison, *The Great American History Fact-Finder* (Boston: Houghton Mifflin, 1993), 253; Wilfred Sheed, *Clare Boothe Luce* (New York: E. P. Dutton, 1982).

Luce, Henry Robinson (1898–1967)

American editor, publisher, and founder of such magazines as *Time, Life,* and *Fortune.* The son of American Presbyterian missionary parents, Luce was born on April 3, 1898, in Tengchow, China, but in 1914 moved to the United States to attend the prestigious Hotchkiss School in Connecticut, where he befriended Briton Hadden. The two men later changed the world of American journalism. Together they attended Yale University, where they coedited the college newspaper; during World War I they also served together in the army. They returned to Yale after the war and graduated in 1920.

For two years Luce and Hadden dreamed of starting the first weekly national news magazine. By 1922 they had raised $86,000, and through a series of conferences with writers and printers, they printed the first issue of *Time* on March 3, 1923, with a drawing of former House Speaker Joseph G. Cannon on the cover. The magazine was denoted by its departments—national news, world news, and so on—all of which became the periodical's standard. The freshness of the reporting in *Time* gave rise to a competitor, *Newsweek,* in 1933, but Luce complimented his publication with the addition of *Fortune,* a business magazine, in 1930. Although *Fortune* appeared at the height of the GREAT DEPRESSION, with a $1-a-copy price, it was able to survive. He also published *Architectural Forum* in 1932 and *Life,* a pictorial publication, in 1936. Luce extended the *Time* empire in 1935 to filmed news reels with *The March of Time.*

Luce was constantly criticized because his publications seemed to mirror his ideological bent: anticommunist and Republican. He remained the quintessential journalist, always reinventing, always catering to the moods of the American public. In 1964 he turned over the duties of running Time-Life, the parent company of his publishing empire, and retired to his home in Phoenix, Arizona, where he died on February 28, 1967. His second wife was Clare Boothe LUCE, who served in Congress (1943–47) and as the U.S. ambassador to Italy (1953–57).

References: Robert Edwin Herzstein, *Henry R. Luce: A Political Portrait of the Man Who Created the American Century* (New York: Charles Scribner's Sons, 1994); Robert T. Elson, *Time Inc.: The Intimate History of a Publishing Enterprise, 1923–1941* (New York: Atheneum, 1968); Donna Tully Cummings, "Luce, Henry Robinson" in Bruce W. Jentleson and Thomas G. Paterson, senior eds., *Encyclopedia of U.S. Foreign Relations* (New York: Oxford University Press, 1997), 3: 85–86.

Ludlow Amendment

Proposed modification of the U.S. Constitution, requiring that three-quarters of the American people must approve a resolution of war before the nation could enter into hostilities. Proposed by Rep. Louis L. Ludlow, Democrat of Indiana, in December 1937, the resolution called on American citizens to give their approval of a declaration of war after Congress had formally voted on such a proclamation. After the infamous PANAY INCIDENT, in which an American ship was bombed in China by Japanese planes, Ludlow garnered enough votes on his

petition to get it out of committee and to the House floor. President Franklin D. ROOSEVELT opposed the measure as an infringement on a president's right to conduct the nation's foreign relations. On January 10, 1938, however, the House voted to return the resolution to committee, and thus it was never officially voted on.

References: Wayne S. Cole, "Ludlow Amendment" in Bruce W. Jentleson and Thomas G. Paterson, senior eds., *Encyclopedia of U.S. Foreign Relations* (New York: Oxford University Press, 1997), 3: 86; Ernest C. Bolt, *Ballots Before Bullets: The War Referendum Approach to Peace in America, 1914–1941* (Charlottesville: University Press of Virginia, 1977).

Lugosi, Bela   *See* DRACULA.

Lytton Commission

Important conference of advisers, 1931–32, appointed by the LEAGUE OF NATIONS to investigate the SINO-JAPANESE WAR and advise the League on a plan of action. On September 18, 1931, Japanese troops invaded the northern China area known as Manchuria and implemented a series of systematic and brutal crackdowns that resulted in the slaughter of countless tens of thousands of men, women, and children, almost all civilians. The League asked Victor Alexander George Robert Bulwer-Lytton to head a commission to examine this MANCHURIAN CRISIS and recommend action. The group was officially called the Commission of Enquiry into the Sino-Japanese Dispute.

On November 4, 1932 the Lytton Commission released its final report to the League, and after debate it was adopted on February 4, 1933. The Commission completely rejected Japan's assertion that the Manchurian incident that justified its occupation was in fact an independence movement, and declared that the creation of the puppet state of Manchukuo was a fraud. The members recommended that Manchuria be governed by the Chinese government with the assistance of international advisers; that Japanese economic interests, which had been threatened by a Chinese boycott, be recognized; and that Japan withdraw immediately. Japan denounced the report and threatened to withdraw from the League, the first time such a threat had been issued in the League's short life. Rather than submitting to some of the report's recommendations, Japan poured more troops into the region and between January and March 1933 advanced on areas south of the Great Wall and the city of Jehol (now Chengde).

The failure of the Lytton Commission was not in its work, but in the organization it was working for. The Japanese response to the report revealed the League's fatal weakness and the volatile state of affairs in Asia as Japan consolidated her holdings. The world plunged closer to a world war that would occur in a few short years.

References: Biography of Lytton in Philip W. Goetz, ed. in chief, *The New Encyclopædia Britannica* (Chicago: Encyclopædia Britannica, Inc., 1995), 7: 596, as well as C. M. Woodhouse, "Bulwer-Lytton, Victor Alexander George Robert" in Sir Leslie Stephen and Sir Sidney Lee et al., eds., *The Dictionary of National Biography* (Oxford: Oxford University Press, 1917–1993), 5: 118–20; Westel W. Willougby, *The Sino-Japanese Controversy and the League of Nations* (Westport, Conn.: Greenwood, 1968); Edward F. Witsell, *The Lytton Report* (Washington, D.C.: War Department, 1932); Edmund Jan Osmañczyk, *The Encyclopedia of the United Nations and International Agreements* (Philadelphia: Taylor & Francis, 1985), 485.

MacDonald, James Ramsay (1866–1937)
British politician, prime minister (1924, 1929–35). Esteemed leader of the British Labour Party, MacDonald was born in a two-room house in the seaside village of Lossiemouth, Morayshire, Scotland, on October 12, 1866. He attended a village school in Lossiemouth, but never received a formal secondary education except for some scientific classes he sought later in London. After serving as an assistant to a priest who had established a Boys' and Young Men's Guild, MacDonald moved to London, where he worked as a clerical assistant.

From an early age, MacDonald was involved in politics; he joined the local Social Democratic Federation even while he lived in Lossiemouth. In 1888 he became the private secretary to Thomas Lough, who won election to Parliament. MacDonald craved the political scene, and after aligning himself with several socialist-leaning groups and joining the Labour Party in 1894, he ran for a seat in Parliament in 1895, representing Southampton, but came in dead last; a similar result happened when he ran in 1900. The following year, however, he was elected to the London County Council, serving until 1904. Two years later, he ran for a seat in Parliament on the Labour ticket, representing Leicester, and was elected. That same year, he was elected as the head of the Independent Labour Party (ILP). When the ILP members in Parliament reformed as the Parliamentary Labour Party, they elected MacDonald as their chair in 1911.

During World War I, MacDonald was a bitter critic of British government policy toward the war; he exhibited his criticism in an article in the August 13, 1914, edition of the *Labour Leader,* the official party publication. Censured loudly for attempting to visit Russia after the overthrow of the czar in 1917 (he was prevented from leaving after a union blocked the ship) and for his overall stand on the war, MacDonald was defeated for reelection in 1918. Out of politics for the first time since 1900, he vis-

ited Berlin and Soviet Georgia. An attempt to return to Parliament was scuttled in 1921, but he was successful in 1922, representing Aberavon. The elections of 1923 left Labour as the second strongest party in Parliament; however, with Liberal support and on MacDonald's urging, the House of Commons called for a vote of no confidence on the government of Prime Minister Stanley BALDWIN. Baldwin promptly resigned, and MacDonald was asked to form a government. He quickly accepted the prime ministership on January 22, 1924, as well as the portfolios of foreign minister and First Lord of the Treasury. Among his earliest moves was to work with French prime minister Édouard HERRIOT to accept the YOUNG PLAN, the report on German REPARATIONS, to secure financial indemnification from Germany. MacDonald lost his position in the next general election on October 29, 1924, when the Labour Party took a stunning blow. Four days before the election, a letter was circulated from Soviet revolutionary Gregorii Zinoviev (called the Zinoviev Letter) to British communists, which intimated that MacDonald and the Labourites were "cozy" with the Ccommunist government in Moscow and that the prime minister could not be trusted. Labour lost 40 seats, MacDonald's government fell, and Stanley Baldwin was reinstated.

In 1929, however, the political fortunes of his party having changed, MacDonald oversaw a large Labour victory in the general election and for the second time became prime minister. Traveling to the United States (the first prime minister to do so), MacDonald negotiated with U.S. President Herbert HOOVER to initiate the LONDON NAVAL CONFERENCE. He also oversaw the India Round Table Conference, where dominion status for India was discussed. Yet the Depression that swept over the world soon after he assumed office had a severe impact on his second administration. Within two years MacDonald was forced to call for harsh austerity measures to alleviate growing unemployment. His allies in Parliament opposed such a course, and with their resignation on August 24, 1931, MacDonald was forced to form a coalition government with Baldwin and Herbert Samuel of the Liberal Party, with MacDonald heading the National government. This unique situation in British history led candidates from this coalition to run in the general election that year as National nominees: the National ticket won an astounding 554 seats in the House of Commons against 56 for the opposition, marking an enormous public acceptance of the unusual arrangement. MacDonald was installed as prime minister for a record fourth time.

MacDonald attended the GENEVA DISARMAMENT CONFERENCE in 1932, as well as the World Monetary and Economic Conference (also called the LONDON ECONOMIC CONFERENCE) in 1933, but the Depression wracked his administration. He released a white paper calling for the rearmament of the British armed forces in 1935, but rapidly declining health ruined his chances to institute the program. On June 7, 1935, he shocked the nation by resigning as prime minister and assuming the office of Lord President of the Council in Baldwin's cabinet, who had again succeeded him. Defeated that year for his seat in Parliament, MacDonald left the government when Baldwin was thrown out of office in May 1937.

On November 9, 1937, after sailing on the liner *Reina del Pacifico* to South America to regain his health, MacDonald suffered heart failure and died.

See also ELECTIONS, BRITISH; HENDERSON, ARTHUR.

References: Bamber Gascoigne, *Encyclopedia of Britain* (New York: Macmillan, 1993), 396; Elton, "MacDonald, James Ramsay" in Sir Leslie Stephen and Sir Sidney Lee et al., eds., *The Dictionary of National Biography* (Oxford: Oxford University Press, 1917–1993), 4: 562–70; David C. Lukowitz, "MacDonald, James Ramsay" in Warren F. Kuehl, ed., *Biographical Dictionary of Internationalists* (Westport, Conn.: Greenwood, 1983), 458–60; Helen Holden, "Ramsay MacDonald" in Dermot Englefield, Janet Seaton, and Isobel White, *Facts about the British Prime Ministers: A Compilation of Biographical and Historical Information* (New York: H. W. Wilson Co., 1995), 262–69; "Death of Ramsay MacDonald. Heart Failure at Sea. A Voyage for Health," *The Times* (London), November 10, 1937, p. 14; "Obituary: Mr. MacDonald's Career. Four Times Prime Minister. Labour and National Leader," *The Times* (London), November 10, 1937, p. 19.

MacLeod, John James Rickard (1876–1935)

Scottish physiologist and Nobel laureate. Born in New Clunie, Perthshire, Scotland, on September 6, 1876, he was educated at the universities of Aberdeen, Leipzig, and Cambridge, afterward traveling to the United States to become a professor of physiology at Western Reserve University in Cleveland, Ohio (1903–18). While there, he studied diabetes, the condition by which human insulin

(which regulates sugar levels in the blood) is retarded or lacking. When MacLeod began his researches, diabetes was little understood. MacLeod then became a professor of physiology at the University of Toronto (1918–28), where he collaborated on his diabetes research with Frederick Grant BANTING. The two men discovered the properties of insulin, for which they were the corecipients of the 1923 Nobel Prize in physiology and medicine. Five years later, MacLeod was named as a professor of physiology at the University of Aberdeen in his native Scotland (1928–35). He died in Aberdeen on March 16, 1935. His published works included *Insulin and Its Use in the Treatment of Diabetes* (1925), *Carbohydrate Metabolism and Insulin* (1926), and *The Fuel of Life* (1928).

References: Carol Somers, "MacLeod, John James Rickard" in Bernard S. and June H. Schlessinger, eds., *The Who's Who of Nobel Prize Winners* (Phoenix, Ariz.: Oryx, 1986), 85; Thomas Watson MacCallum, and Stephen Taylor, eds., *The Nobel Prize-Winners and the Nobel Foundation, 1901–1937* (Zurich: Central European Times Publishing, 1938), 208–209.

Maginot, André (1877–1932)

French politician, the Maginot Line was named in his honor. Born in Paris on February 17, 1877, he served as a deputy in the French legislature representing the area of Bar-le-Duc. In 1913 he was named an undersecretary of war, but he volunteered for service the following year in World War I as a private. After being wounded, Maginot was promoted to sergeant; upon recovery he was named as the minister of colonies in the cabinet of French prime minister Alexander Ribot. He served in subsequent cabinets as the minister of pensions.

In 1922, Prime Minister Raymond POINCARÉ named Maginot as the minister of war (1922–24, 1929–32), where Maginot was instrumental in enacting a law that established the Ministry of Air to oversee the French air force. A firm advocate of military preparedness, he served as the minister of colonies in André Tardieu's cabinet, but he was moved back to war in November 1929, where he served until his death. During his second tenure in this position, Maginot formulated a plan to defend the Franco-German frontier with a series of fortresses that would halt for a time a potential German invasion of France while the nation readied for war. Construction began on Maginot's plan of a series of pillboxes and casements that ran from Switzerland to Luxembourg on France's eastern border. The plan was grand, magnificent, and, where it was constructed, impenetrable. Unfortunately, money ran out before the line was continued across the border with Belgium; here was the Achilles' heel. When Nazi Germany decided to invade France in summer 1940, the Germans did not dare to cross the Maginot Line where it was manned; instead, the Germans took advantage of the lack of a fortification at the Belgian border and crossed there, taking Paris quickly and destroying the philosophy that had created the line in the first place. Maginot was spared the horror his plan had sought to avoid: he had died in Paris on January 7, 1932. Today, the phrase "Maginot Line" connotes a policy doomed to failure.

References: Anthony Kemp, *The Maginot Line: Myth and Reality* (New York: Stein & Day, 1982); J. E. Kaufmann, and H. W. Kaufmann, *The Maginot Line: None Shall Pass* (Westport, Conn.: Praeger, 1997); Robert Boyce, eds., *French Foreign and Defense Policy, 1918–1940: The Decline and Fall of a Great Power* (London: Routledge, 1998).

Maginot Line   *See* MAGINOT, ANDRÉ.

Mallory and Irvine Expedition

Noted voyage, 1924, in which English explorers George Leigh Mallory and Andrew Irvine were lost while attempting to become the first party to conquer Mount Everest. Originally called Peak XV, the peak was renamed Everest in 1856 to honor Sir George Everest, the British surveyor of India from 1830 to 1843. The mountain was not mapped until 1907, when an official Indian surveyor created a blueprint from the Nepalese side. In 1920 a route up the mountain from Tibet was opened, making the mountain accessible to climbers.

In 1921, British explorers led by Colonel C. K. Howard-Bury, an Irishman, made an attempt on Everest, but the first to make a full-fledged effort at the top were Mallory and Irvine. Mallory, who had been on the earlier Howard-Bury expedition, is known for his answer to "Why climb mountains?" He replied, "Because it's there." Mallory himself had tried in 1922 and earlier in 1924, while George Ingle Finch and Geoffrey Bruce reached 27,000 feet in 1922—but none could attain Everest's full 29,000 feet. In 1921, Mallory had written his wife, Ruth, "I'll tell you about Everest. . . . It has the most steep ridges and appalling precipices that I have ever seen, and that all the talk of an east snow slope is a myth." On the Mallory and Irvine's 1924 expedition, a witness reported seeing them "going strong for the top" but both were men on heavy oxygen. They were never seen again, however, and their bodies have never been found. In 1930 a summit team found their camp with a working torch, perhaps left behind by Mallory and leading to their fate. Historians surmise that the team did not make the summit, but their disappearance ranks among the more interesting mysteries of the 20th century.

On May 14, 1995, Mallory's grandson, George Mallory, reached the summit of Everest, nearly 71 years after his grandfather's attempt. In 1999, 75 years after George Leigh Mallory vanished, his body was discovered on Ever-est's northridge, about 27,000 feet up on the Tibetan side of the mountain. Irvine's body has never been found, but evidence suggests that both men were descending the peak when they died.

References: Tom Holzel, *The Mystery of Mallory and Irvine* (London: Cape, 1986); David Allan Robertson, *George Mallory* (London: Faber, 1969); Charles Howard-Bury, *Everest Reconnaissance: The First Expedition of 1921* (London: Hodder & Stoughton, 1991).

Manchukuo   *See* MANCHURIAN CRISIS.

Manchurian Crisis

Emergency situation, 1931–32, in which Japanese troops invaded and occupied Manchuria, setting off a global crisis that eventually led to the beginning of World War II in Asia. As "the northeast part of China, roughly identical with the three provinces [of] Liaoning, Kirin, and Heilungkiang," with an area of 1,950,000 square kilometers, Manchuria was ripe for Japanese expansion. Tensions between China and Japan had been mounting since an earlier boycott of Japanese goods by China led to the battle of Shanghai, in which Japanese aircraft carriers attacked positions inside of China (the first time this type of ship was used in war), setting off the SINO-JAPANESE WAR. The LEAGUE OF NATIONS condemned the conflict but was powerless to stop it.

Japanese troops rushed into Manchuria and renamed it Manchukuo, making it a Japanese colony. They decided that the city of Changchun, renamed as Hsinking, the capital of Kirin Province, would be the capital of this puppet state. On September 15, 1932, Pu Yi, China's last emperor, was crowned by the Japanese as Emperor Kang of Manchukuo. No nation in the world recognized the leader or the state.

On February 24, 1933, after the League of Nations had condemned Japan's actions, the Japanese ambassador to the League, Yosuke Matsuoka, led a walkout of the Japanese delegation; they did not return, effectively ending any chance the League had of resolving the crisis. The invasion of Manchuria revealed the League's utter helplessness and weakness, and would be the beginning of the League's undoing. Japan did not end its occupation of Manchuria until the end of World War II.

See also LYTTON COMMISSION.

References: Edmund Jan Osmańczyk, *The Encyclopedia of the United Nations and International Agreements* (Philadelphia: Taylor & Francis, 1985), 494; "Manchurian Incident (1931)" in Hugh D. Phillips, "Manchurian Crisis" in Bruce W. Jentleson and Thomas G. Paterson, senior eds., *Encyclopedia of U.S. Foreign Relations* (New York: Oxford University Press,

1997), 3: 97–99; Sara Rector Smith, *The Manchurian Crisis, 1931–1932: A Tragedy in International Relations* (New York: Columbia University Press, 1948); "Japan Sets Drastic Terms; Chinese to Reject Peace Plan," *New York World-Telegram,* February 18, 1932, p. 1.

Mandate system

Plan, instituted by the LEAGUE OF NATIONS after World War I, to allow certain conquered territories of Germany and the Ottoman Empire to be administered by victorious Allied nations. Under section 22 of the League covenant, a system of three trusteeships, or mandates, were established: A, B, and C mandates. These were specified by levels of development that would allow a mandate to become independent: A nations, all Arab countries, were in an advanced stage of development and would only be controlled by Britain or France for a short time; B nations, those in Africa, were not considered as advanced, but independence in a number of years was a possibility; and C countries, those for which independence was doubtful and which needed strong support indefinitely.

From 1920 to 1922 all of the mandates and their separate administrators were approved by the League of Nations with the exception of Iraq; after the installation by Great Britain of King Faisal, the League allowed that pseudonation to be ruled on its own. This system held even during World War II. After the war, however, the mandate system met the same fate as the League—the successor organization, the United Nations, assumed control over all of the B and C mandates (except South-West Africa) under the trusteeship system, which gradually offered a chance for independence.

References: Edmund Jan Osmańczyk, *The Encyclopedia of the United Nations and International Agreements* (Philadelphia: Taylor & Francis, 1985), 494–95; Rayford Whittingham Logan, *The Senate and the Versailles Mandate System* (Westport, Conn.: Greenwood, 1975); Aaron Morris Margalith, *The International Mandates* (Baltimore: Johns Hopkins University Press, 1930); Quincy Wright, *Mandates under the League of Nations* (New York: Greenwood Press, 1968); Robert LaRoy Bradford, "The Origin and Concession of the League of Nations' Class 'C' Mandate for South-West Africa and Fulfillment of the Sacred Trust, 1919–1939" (Master's Thesis, Yale University, 1965); Harold K. Jacobson, "Mandates and Trusteeships" in Bruce W. Jentleson and Thomas G. Paterson, senior eds., *Encyclopedia of U.S. Foreign Relations* (New York: Oxford University Press, 1997), 3: 99–103.

Mann, Thomas (1875–1955)

German American novelist and Nobel laureate. The son of Johann Heinrich Mann and Julia (da Silva-Bruhns) Mann, Mann was born in Lübeck, Germany, on June 6, 1875. In 1901 he began a series of works that encompassed daily life in his native land. *Buddenbrooks* (1901) was an examination of four generations of a German family. His 1912 novella, *Der Tod in Venedig* (*Death in Venice*), which explored the probability of decadence in artistic life, was made into an opera by English composer Benjamin Britten in 1970. Perhaps Mann's greatest work, the symbolic *Der Zauberberg* (*The Magic Mountain*, 1924), concerns the life story of a disenchanted German soldier who served in World War I. For this body of work, Mann was awarded the 1929 Nobel Prize in literature. Mann's work considered changing European values and inner conflicts, artistic creativity in a bourgeois society, and the connection between genius and disease. He also wrote short fiction and political essays. His later work included *Joseph and his Brothers* (1933–43), the masterpiece *Doctor Faustus* (1947), and *Confessions of Felix Kroll* (1954).

Mann, who opposed the rise of the NAZI PARTY in Germany, was in Switzerland in January 1933 when Adolf HITLER rose to power; Mann decided not to return home. In 1938, he settled in the United States. In 1936 the German government stripped Mann of his citizenship, and he became a naturalized American citizen in 1944. During World War II he urged listeners during radio broadcasts to fight the Nazis at all costs. After the war he settled in Zurich, where he died on August 12, 1955.

References: Tyler Wasson, ed., *Nobel Prize Winners: An H. W. Wilson Biographical Dictionary* (New York: H. W. Wilson Co.,

THE MANDATE SYSTEM AND THE MANDATORIES		
TERRITORY	MANDATE CODE	MANDATORY
Cameroons	B	France and Great Britain
Iraq	A	France
Lebanon	A	France
Marianas, Caroline, and Marshall Islands	C	Japan
Nauru	C	Australia
New Guinea	C	Australia
Palestine	A	Great Britain
Rwanda-Urundi	B	Belgium
South-West Africa	C	South Africa
Syria	A	France
Tanganyika	B	Great Britain
Togoland	B	France and Great Britain
Transjordan	A	Great Britain
Western Samoa	C	New Zealand

1987), 662–65; Edra, Bogle, "Mann, Paul Thomas" in Bernard S. and June H. Schlessinger, eds., *The Who's Who of Nobel Prize Winners* (Phoenix, Ariz.: Oryx, 1986), 57; Thomas Watson MacCallum and Stephen Taylor, eds., *The Nobel Prize-Winners and the Nobel Foundation, 1901–1937* (Zurich: Central European Times Publishing, 1938), 310–12.

Mao Tse-tung (1893–1976)

Chinese leader and revolutionary, initiator of communist rule in mainland China, 1949. Born on December 29, 1893, into a well-to-do family in the village of Shao-shan, in Hunan Province, he rebelled against his strict father. He was schooled in the nationalist fervor of the area and eventually moved to Chang-sha in 1911. While in the Hunan First Normal school, he joined the May Fourth Movement in 1919 and worked as a local school principal in Hunan.

By 1920, when he married Yang K'ai-hui (daughter of one of his teachers in Chang-sha, she was executed in 1930), Mao was a confirmed communist and follower of the Soviet revolution in Russia. In July 1921 he was one of the founders of the Chinese Communist Party in Shanghai, and began to formulate a policy to oppose the Nationalist government of CHIANG KAI-SHEK. Mao's 1927 work, *Report on the Peasant Movement in Hunan*, concluded that the people of the land in China would help in a communist revolution.

For most of the 1920s, Chiang and the Communists cooperated loosely to oppose the Japanese. In 1927, however, Chiang secretly decided to liquidate the Commu-

Mao Tse-tung *(CORBIS)*

nists and began a series of precise military strikes. In response, on August 1, 1927, Mao began a peasant rebellion, called the Autumn Harvest Uprising, at Chingkang-shan. There, he assembled a force of some fifteen thousand men, including Korean Communists who had attempted to oust Japan from their own homeland. With the establishment of this first division, Mao forged a new kind of military structure, a People's Army founded on what he called "the three duties": to fight to the death against the enemy, to arm the peasants, and to raise money to support the army. Mao marched the force to Canton, to liberate Kwantung Province, but they were defeated by Chiang's Nationalists. Mao was taken prisoner and sentenced to death, but before the sentence could be carried out, he escaped. At this time Mao started a guerrilla army that he intended to use to topple China's republican government and install a communist regime.

In 1934, after several skirmishes with Chiang's forces, Mao, facing disaster, led his troops (some ninety thousand) on the six thousand-mile infamous LONG MARCH toward what he considered their Salvation: the northwestern mountains of Shoanxi Province. When he arrived in western China in 1935, his army was decimated; slowly, he rebuilt it. In response to the 1937 Japanese invasion of China Mao and Chiang formed a united front against the aggressors. After World War II, however, the two sides picked up their campaign against one another, locked in a death struggle. This time Mao's overwhelming forces slowly defeated the Nationalists, eventually driving them to the island of Formosa (Taiwan). In 1949 the Communists were victorious, and Mao, in Red Square in Peking (now Beijing), proclaimed the People's Republic of China.

Over the next thirty years, Mao established himself as the leading theoretician of Chinese communism. He adapted Marxism to Chinese conditions by focusing on the peasantry (rather than the proletariat) as the revolutionaries. In 1957 he launched the Great Leap Forward, an unsuccessful attempt to decentralize the economy through a system of nationwide communes; scholars estimate that some 30–40 million Chinese perished as a result. The Cultural Revolution (1966–69) represented Mao's attempt to reenergize the nation with the Communist Party's revolutionary principles. Mao's revolutionary Red Guards, many of them youths, attacked so-called bourgeois elements in society; the movement resulted in widespread disorder and violence.

By the end of his life, Mao was considered a respected world leader who had done much to change the face of China. In 1972, he renewed ties to the United States during President Richard Nixon's historic visit to the mainland—the first president to do so. Mao's final years were spent in near seclusion; he died on September 9, 1976.

References: Jeffrey G. Barlow, "Mao Zedong" in Anne Commire, ed., *Historic World Leaders* (Detroit: Gale Research,

1994), 1: 384–89; Zhang Shu Guang, "Mao Zedong" in Bruce W. Jentleson and Thomas G. Paterson, senior eds., *Encyclopedia of U.S. Foreign Relations* (New York: Oxford University Press, 3: 107–109; "Mao Tse-Tung is Dead at 82; Peking Leadership Succession Is Uncertain," *International Herald-Tribune*, September 10, 1976, p. 1.

March First Movement

Social movement, particularly during March–April 1919, in which the people of Korea, under the yoke of Japanese colonialism, sought to gain independence. From 1910, Korea had been a colony of Japan. By early 1919 the combination of colonial oppression, Korean student protests at universities across the peninsula, the effects of the "Koreanization" movement to educate and enlighten the people about national pride and heritage, and calls by U.S. President Woodrow WILSON for the right of self-determination for colonial powers made the area a powder keg liable to explode.

Several inspired Korean dissidents, including Kwon Tong-jun, O Se-Chang, and Choe Rin, planned a peaceful protest timed during the funeral of the former Emperor Kojong, who had died of a stroke on January 22, 1919. They believed in the concept of *Ajiashugi* ("Asianism"), a pride in their national culture. These events gave rise to the drafting of the so-called Korean Declaration of Independence. On March 1, 1919, the 33 signers of this document appeared before a crowd of supporters in Pagoda Park in Seoul, the capital, and read from the declaration. They waited for the Japanese police to arrest them, but instead the Japanese panicked at the sight of the large crowd and fired into the throng, killing an untold number of protesters.

This event, called the March First Movement, gave rise to the Korean independence movement. For several weeks, demonstrations broke out throughout Korea demanding independence from Tokyo. The Japanese crackdown led to more than fifty thousand arrests, six thousand deaths, and the torture and execution of many of the 33 signatories of the declaration. The movement had sprung from the hope that Wilson would fight for the theory of colonial independence. Little did the two million marchers who participated that March day realize that their fate had already been sealed: Wilson had agreed in advance with the Japanese delegation to VERSAILLES that Korea would remain under Japanese occupation and domination.

The Japanese crackdown also led to external pressures: on April 8, 1919, the Korean Provisional Government was established in the Chinese city of Shanghai. Syngman Rhee, a Korean nationalist, was named president, Yi Tong Whi as defense minister, and Kim Kyu Sik as foreign minister. The following month, Korean nationalist Kim Wong Bom, alias Kim Yak San, organized the *Uiyoldan* ("Practice Justice Bravely Society"), a secret ter-

rorist cell which carried out some three hundred terrorist acts against Japanese targets until 1924, including the bombing of Governor-General Baron Makoko Saito's office in Seoul on September 4, 1919, the attempted assassinations of General Gi-ichi Tanaka on March 28, 1922, and of Emperor Yoshihito on January 4, 1924, and the bombing of Takushoku University in Tokyo of December 28, 1926. On September 3, 1923, anti-Korean riots took place in Tokyo, resulting in the deaths of some eight hundred Korean students in Japan and the expulsion of more than a hundred thousand Koreans from that nation. Other Koreans, on both the right and left of the political spectrum, formed the Korean Independence Army as part of the Chinese army effort to fight Japanese troops in China. In the 1930s, Japanese destruction of Korean culture continued unabated. In 1937 the Japanese ordered that the Korean language be extinguished, to be replaced by Japanese, and that Japanese names be substituted for Korean ones. During World War II thousands of Koreans were taken by Japan and used as slave labor.

In the end the March First Movement failed to dislodge the Japanese from the Korean Peninsula; nonetheless, it is among Asia's first independence movements, setting precedence for the nationalist movements following World War II.

References: Robert T. Oliver, *A History of the Korean People in Modern Times: 1800 to the Present* (Newark: University of Delaware Press, 1993), 133–42; Frank Prentis Baldwin, Jr., "The March First Movement: Korean Challenge and Japanese Response" (Ph.D. dissertation, Columbia University, 1969); Carl Crow, *Japan's Dream of World Empire: The Tanaka Memorial* (London: Allen & Unwin, 1943).

March on Rome   *See* CIANO, GALEAZZO; FASCISM; MUSSOLINI, BENITO.

Martin du Gard, Roger (1881–1958)

French writer and Nobel laureate. Born in Neuilly-sur-Seine, France, on March 22, 1881, he received his baccalaureate from the École des Chartes. Starting in 1908, he began writing a series of works dealing with the leitmotif of human suffering, including *Devener* (1908) and *Jean Barois* (1913). The body of work that won him the Nobel Prize in literature in 1937 was part of a device in French literature called a *roman fleuve,* in which a central character is involved in several novels, in this case Jacques Thibault in Martindu Gard's *Les Thibault* (1922–1940). Of this work, Per Hallström, the Permanent Secretary of the Swedish Academy, said, "It represents modern French life by means of a whole gallery of characters and an analysis of the intellectual currents and the problems that occupied France during the ten years preceding the First World

War, a gallery as full and an analysis as complete as the subject of the novel permitted."

Martin du Gard spent the remainder of his life writing such works as *Vieille France* (1933) and *Note sur André Gide* (Recollections of André Gide, 1951). He died in Belleme, France, on August 22, 1958.

References: Sharon Charette, "Martin du Gard, Roger" in Bernard S. and June H. Schlessinger, eds., *The Who's Who of Nobel Prize Winners* (Phoenix, Ariz.: Oryx, 1986), 59–60; Thomas Watson MacCallum and Stephen Taylor, eds., *The Nobel Prize-Winners and the Nobel Foundation, 1901–1937* (Zurich: Central European Times Publishing, 1938), 326.

Marx Brothers

American comedy team, famed for their zany Broadway acts and films during the interwar period. Best known for their comedic movies of the 1920s and 1930s, the brothers— Groucho (real name Julius, 1890–1977), Chico (Leonard, 1886?–1961), Harpo (born Adolph, later Arthur, 1893–1964), Gummo (Milton, 1894?–1977), and Zeppo (Herbert, 1901–1979)—got their start in vaudeville. Illinois comic Art Fisher gave the brothers their nicknames in 1914. Gummo left the act in 1918 and was replaced by the youngest Marx, Zeppo. For more than 70 years, the brothers performed on Broadway, over the radio, in films, and later on television.

In 1924 their Broadway show *I'll Say She Is* opened and became a roaring success. The brothers followed up with *The Cocoanuts*, which ran for a record 275 performances (a popular film version was produced in 1929). Next was the 1928 stage play *Animal Crackers* (film 1930). The brothers moved to California in 1931 and signed a film contract with MGM in 1934. Many film historians consider as classics the Marx brothers' *Monkey Business* (1931), *Duck Soup* (1933), and *A Night at the Opera* (1935). An accomplished writer, Groucho published numerous essays and articles in such publications as *Collier's*, the *Hollywood Reporter*, the *New Yorker*, the *New York Times*, *Redbook*, the *Saturday Evening Post*, the *Saturday Review*, and *Variety*.

Although Zeppo quit the team in 1934 and the group announced an official breakup in 1941, several of the brothers continued doing film and radio work through World War II. After the war Groucho starred in the long-running television game show *You Bet Your Life*. He, Harpo, and Chico continued to make regular television appearances throughout their lives. On January 16, 1977, the Marx Brothers were inducted into the Motion Picture Hall of Fame.

References: Allen Eyles, *The Marx Brothers: Their World of Comedy* (Cranbury, N.J.: A. S. Barnes & Co., 1968); Ted Yanak and Pam Cornelison, *The Great American History Fact-Finder* (Boston: Houghton Mifflin, 1993), 263.

Masaryk, Tomás Garrigue (1850–1937)

Czechoslovak politician and philosopher, first president of Czechoslovakia (1918–35). Born simply Tomás Masaryk in the village of Hodonín, Moravia (later Czechoslovakia), on March 7, 1850, he married American Charlotte Garrigue in 1878 and took her maiden name as his middle name. After acquiring his doctorate in Vienna, Masaryk moved to Leipzig, where he met Charlotte Garrigue. Two months later, Masaryk followed her back to the United States and the two were married.

In 1882, Masaryk became a professor of philosophy at Charles University in Prague. He became one of a number of Czech nationalists who called for independence for his homeland. In 1885 he wrote *The Foundations of Concrete Logic*, a document on philosophy, but he set his sights on political theory. In 1891 he was elected to the Imperial Diet as a member of the nationalist Young Czech Party. Two years later he resigned over differences in his party, however, and wrote during this period *Ceská Otázka* (The Czech question, 1895), *Nase Nynejsj Krise* (Our present crisis, 1895), and *Parackého Idea Naroda Ceského* (Palacky's idea of the Czech nation, 1898), all of which expressed a nationalist point of view. In 1900 he founded the Progressive Party and toured the United States, Russia, and Great Britain to espouse his cause. During World War I he lived in the United States and was a constant advocate of his nation's independence.

After the war and the breakup of the Austro-Hungarian Empire in 1918, Masaryk, who had founded the Czechoslovak National Council in Paris in 1916, returned to Prague and proclaimed on October 28, 1918, the Czechoslovak Republic. Two months later, the 68-year-old Masaryk was named as the first president of the republic. His dream of a free Czechoslovakia had become a reality. He was called *stary pán* ("the old man") by his friends and admirers. During his presidency, Masaryk spent much time trying to consolidate power and heal fractures among the electorate. A strong supporter of the LEAGUE OF NATIONS, he called on his people to support peace in Europe. Reelected as president in 1927 and 1934, he became the object of a cult of personality, even though old age was approaching. In 1935 he suffered a stroke that ended his career; the Czech people presented him with a castle in the village of Lány, near Prague, where on September 14, 1937, he died. His other writings include *Jan Hus* (1896; English translation, 1908) and *Svêtová Revoluce* (The making of a state, 1925).

References: Stanley B. Winters and Robert B. Pynsent, eds., *T.G. Masaryk (1850–1937)* (London: School of Slavonic and East European Studies, University of London, 1989); Simon Rosengard Green, "Thomas Garrigue Masaryk: Educator of a Nation" (Ph.D. dissertation, University of California at Berkeley, 1976); Thomas Whigham, "Thomas G. Masaryk" in Anne Commire, ed., *Historic World Leaders* (Detroit: Gale Research, 1994), 3: 895–98.

Matteotti, Giacomo (1885–1924)

Italian socialist leader, outspoken critic of Mussolini's Fascist regime. Born in the village of Fratta Polesine, Italy, on May 22, 1885, he was an early exponent of Italian socialism. In 1910, after studying the law at the University of Bologna, he published a work on criminal law. A pacifist, he decried the outbreak of World War I and spoke out publicly against Italian participation in the conflict. In 1919, his place among fellow Socialists assured, he was elected to the Italian Parliament.

When the Italian Socialist Party broke into two factions, one tied to Moscow and the other more moderate, Matteotti founded the PSU, a middle-of-the-road faction. He directed his anger at Benito MUSSOLINI, the fascist dictator who rose to become prime minister of Italy after his March on Rome in 1922. During one Mussolini speech in Parliament, Matteotti rose to yell, "Long Live Parliament!" To counter the Socialists, Mussolini enacted the Acerbo Law of 1923, which made it easier for Fascists to be elected to Parliament. In April 1924, amid widespread corruption, the Fascists won a majority in Parliament. Matteotti declared the election a fraud and asked for it to be declared null and void. Aware of his doom, Matteotti said to a colleague afterward, "Now you can prepare my funeral oration." Historians believe that Mussolini moved to silence Matteotti. On June 10, 1924, Matteotti disappeared and was apparently killed by six Fascists. He was 39 years old.

The murder caused a worldwide scandal and seemed to shake Mussolini's regime. The Socialists demanded that Mussolini be removed from the prime ministership. However, when King Victor Emmannuel III did not act Mussolini moved against the Socialists in 1925, arresting them and ending all parliamentary controls over his leadership. During World War II some Italian partisans who fought for the Allies formed so-called Matteotti brigades. After the war seven suspects in Matteotti's murder (three of whom could not be found, and were tried in absentia) were tried; three were found guilty and sentenced to 30 years imprisonment and four were acquitted.

References: Neil Heyman, "Giacomo Matteotti" in Anne Commire, ed., *Historic World Leaders* (Detroit: Gale Research, 1994), 3: 903–906; Adrian Lyttelton, *The Seizure of Power: Fascism in Italy, 1919–1929* (New York: Charles Scribner's Sons, 1973); Spencer DiScala, "Matteotti Crisis" in Frank J. Coppa, ed. in chief, *Dictionary of Modern Italian History* (Westport, Conn.: Greenwood, 1985), 262.

Mayer, Louis B. (1885–1957)

Russian-American MOTION PICTURE producer. Born as Eliezer or Lazar Mayer in Minsk, Russia, on July 4, 1885, he migrated with his parents as a child to Canada and was educated in the schools of St. John, New Brunswick. Until 1906 he worked as a partner in his father's scrap metal dealership, later opening a similar business in Boston. About 1907, he began his motion picture career, operating a cinema in Haverhill, Massachusetts. In 1912 he became an American citizen, and in 1915 was the exclusive New England distributor for D. W. Griffith's *Birth of a Nation*. In 1916, Mayer moved into the area of film production, teaming up for a time with the Alco Company (later Metro). Leaving Alco in 1917 to establish his own company, Mayer opened Louis B. Mayer Pictures in Los Angeles, California, in 1918. In 1919 he produced one picture, *Virtuous Wives*.

In 1924 he merged his firm with Metro Pictures Corp. and later with Goldwyn Pictures to form Metro-Goldwyn-Mayer (MGM). As vice president in charge of production, Mayer ruled the studio with a firm and sometimes dictatorial hand until he was ousted in a power struggle in 1951. During the late 1920s and throughout the 1930s, he built MGM into one of the most important movie studios. Billing the company as having "more stars than there are in the heavens," he produced such films as *Ben Hur* (1926), *Grand Hotel* (1932), *Dinner at Eight* (1933), and *The Good Earth* (1937), discovering such stars as Greta GARBO, Rudolph VALENTINO, and Clark GABLE. Mayer died in California on October 29, 1957.

See also GOLDWYN, Samuel; HAYS OFFICE; HOLLYWOOD.

References: Ephraim Katz, *The Film Encyclopedia* (New York: HarperPerennial, 1994), 792; Bosley Crowther, *Hollywood Rajah* (New York: Holt, 1960).

McKay, Claude   *See* HARLEM RENAISSANCE.

McCumber, Porter J.   *See* FORDNEY-MCCUMBER ACT; LEAGUE OF NATIONS CONTROVERSY.

McDaniel, Hattie   *See* GONE WITH THE WIND.

Meighen, Arthur (1874–1960)

Canadian politician, prime minister (1920–22, 1926), opposition leader in the House of Commons and Canadian Senate. Born on a farm in Anderson, Perth County, Ontario, on June 16, 1874, he was the son of Irish immigrants to Canada. Meighen graduated from the University of Toronto, spent some time as a schoolteacher, then studied the law. After earning his license, he opened a small practice in Portage la Prairie, Manitoba. In 1908, Meighen ran for a seat in the House and Commons and won. In his 24 years there, he was known as a skilled orator. In 1913, Prime Minister Robert L. Borden named Meighen as his solicitor general. Meighen helped draft the 1917 Conscription Bill, was instrumental in the formation of the Canadian National Railways in 1919, and worked to end the Winnipeg General Strike that same year.

In 1920, Borden retired and Meighen was named as his successor. His main accomplishment as prime minister was the argument against the renewal of the Anglo-Japanese alliance between the British Commonwealth and Japan. In 1921, Meighen was saddled by a depressing economic situation, and the rise of the Progressive Party spelled doom for his Conservatives. In the November elections the Conservatives were beaten by the Liberals, led by Mackenzie KING, who was elected prime minister. Meighen served as the opposition leader in Parliament until 1926, when the Conservatives again came to power and Meighen picked up another short term as prime minister, 29 June–25 September 1926. In 1932, Prime Minister Richard BENNETT named him to the Senate, where he served until 1942. Meighen retired to Toronto, where he died on August 5, 1960.

References: Roger Graham, "Meighen, Arthur" in *The Canadian Encyclopedia* (Edmonton: Hurtig Publishers, 1988), 3: 1332–33; "Rt. Honourable Arthur Meighen" in *Canada, the Founders and the Guardians: Fathers of Confederation, Governors General, Prime Ministers – A Collection of Biographical Sketches and Portraits* (Ottawa: The Queen's Printer, 1968), 136; Elisabeth Ann Matthews, "Meighen and the West, 1921–1926; the National Policy revisited" (Master's thesis, Carleton University [Ottawa], 1966); Roger Graham, *Arthur Meighen: A Biography* (Toronto: Clarke, Irwin, 1960); "Arthur Meighen of Canada Dead; Prime Minister in 1920 and Again in 1926 Was 86—An Outstanding Orator," *New York Times*, August 6, 1960, p. 19.

Mein Kampf

Two-volume work, published 1924–26, by Nazi German politician Adolf HITLER. In 1924, Hitler tried to overthrow the WEIMAR REPUBLIC in the BEER HALL PUTSCH. Sentenced to Landsberg am Lech prison for five years (he ultimately served only eight months), Hitler composed, with the aid of his secretary, Rudolf Hess, his memoirs, which were eventually published as *Mein Kampf* (My struggle). Describing his upbringing and the shaping of the political philosophy that would eventually plunge the world into a horrific war, Hitler blended half-truths and distortions to meld his vision of a future Germany, returned to greatness after its numbing defeat in World War I.

In the preface, Hitler wrote, "German-Austria must return to the great German mother country, and not because of any economic considerations. No, and again no: even if such a union were unimportant from an economic point of view; yes, even if it were harmful, it must nevertheless take place. One blood demands one Reich. Never will the German nation possess the moral right to engage in colonial politics until, at least, it embraces its own sons within a single state. Only when the Reich borders include the very last German, but can no longer guarantee his daily bread, will the moral right to acquire foreign soil arise from the distress of our own people. Their sword will become our plow, and from the tears of war the daily bread of future generations will grow."

Since its publication, *Mein Kampf* has become one of the most incendiary works in the world's history. Although countless numbers of people have read it, its impact cannot be estimated.

References: R. H. Barry, trans., *Hitler's "Mein Kampf": An Analysis* (London: Faber, 1970); Hans Staudinger, *The Inner Nazi: A Critical Analysis of "Mein Kampf"* (Baton Rouge: Louisiana State University Press, 1981); Adolf Hitler, *Germany's Foreign Policy as Stated in "Mein Kampf"* (London: Friends of Europe, 1936?).

Mencken, H. L. (1880–1956)

American journalist and critic, noted for his numerous interwar publications as well as his work on the influential magazines *The Smart Set* and *American Mercury*. Born Henry Louis Mencken in Baltimore, Maryland, on September 12, 1880, he attended Baltimore Polytechnic Institute before becoming a newspaper writer. In 1906 he became the editor of the Baltimore *Evening Herald*, then joined the Baltimore *Sun*, with which he was associated for the remainder of his life. In 1908, Mencken became the literary critic for *The Smart Set*, of which he served as the part owner and joint editor (1914–23) with writer George Jean Nathan. In 1924, a year after dissolving *The Smart Set*, Mencken and Nathan founded *American Mercury*, which became until 1950 the leading literary criticism magazine in the United States. Among the magazine's early writers were Charles BEARD, the American Fascist Lawrence Dennis, the Spanish-American poet and philosopher George Santayana, and the English journalist and writer G. K. Chesterton. Mencken also became one of the best-known U.S. writers and dramatists of his era, through such works as *The American Language* (1919), *Notes on Democracy* (1926), *Selected Prejudices* (1927), and *Treatise on the Gods* (1937). He continued to write until just shortly before his death in Baltimore on January 29, 1956.

References: William H. Nolte, "H. L. Mencken" in Gregory S. Jay, ed., *Modern American Critics, 1920–1955* (Detroit: Gale Research Co., 1988), 149–62; Douglas C. Stenerson, "Mencken, Henry Louis" in Allen Johnson and Dumas Malone et al., eds., *Dictionary of American Biography* (New York: Charles Scribner's Sons, 1930–95), 6: 443–47; "Mencken, H. L." in William H. Taft, *Encyclopedia of Twentieth-Century Journalists* (New York: Garland, 1986), 231; "H. L. Mencken, 75, Dies in Baltimore," *New York Times*, January 30, 1956, pp. 1, 20.

Merz   *See* DADA.

Metaxas, Ioannis   (1871–1941)

Greek general and politician. Born in Ithaca, Greece, on April 12, 1871, Metaxas received his military education in Greece and Germany, and was assistant chief of staff to the Greek army (1913–17) during the First Balkan War. He served as the chief military assistant to King Constantine during World War I. He was exiled from Greece when his nation entered the war on the side of the Allies and he remained, as did his benefactor Constantine, sympathetic to the Germans. Imprisoned by the French for his pro-German attitude from 1917 to 1920, he returned to Greece in 1923 and seemed at first to support the regime of King George II, who took the throne when a pro-Allied republic was established under the leadership of Prime Minister Eleutherios Venizelos.

When George II was restored to the Greek throne in 1935, Metaxas served in several cabinet positions, including war minister, foreign minister, and in 1936 as prime minister. In August of that year, claiming that civil unrest forced his hand, he declared himself head of a new government and established a fascist state with pro-Nazi sympathies. When Italy attempted to infringe on Greek independence in October 1940, however, Metaxas turned against the Axis powers and declared war on Germany and Italy. Metaxas died on January 29, 1941, but his country continued the fight, building a line of defense in eastern Macedonia (the Metaxas Line). The line held off the German onslaught until April 1941, when the Greek government collapsed.

References: Panayiotis J. Vatikiotis, *Popular Autocracy in Greece, 1936–41: A Political Biography of General Ioannis Metaxas* (London: Frank Cass, 1998); Jon V. Kofas, *Authoritarianism in Greece: The Metaxas Regime* (Boulder, Colo.: East European Monographs, 1983).

Meyerhof, Otto   (1884–1951)

German biochemist and Nobel laureate. Born in Hannover, Germany, on April 14, 1884, he received his M.D. from the University of Heidelberg in 1909. He then worked as a researcher there (1909–11) and a biology professor at the University of Kiel, (1912–24) also in Germany.

During this period Meyerhof conducted studies on how muscles metabolize lactic acid, and what relationship that process had with the use of oxygen by these same muscles. For this work, Meyerhof shared the 1922 Nobel Prize in medicine and physiology with Archibald V. HILL. In 1924, Meyerhof joined the Kaiser Wilhelm Institute of Biologie in Berlin, and in 1929 became director of the physiology department of the Kaiser Wilhelm Institute for Medical Research in Heidelberg. In 1938, he left his native Germany to do research work at the Centre Nationale in Paris, rising to become director before becoming a professor of biology at the University of Pennsylvania (1940–51). Meyerhof died in Philadelphia on October 6, 1951.

References: Barbara I. McNutt, "Meyerhof, Otto" in Bernard S. and June H. Schlessinger, eds., *The Who's Who of Nobel Prize Winners* (Phoenix, Ariz.: Oryx, 1986), 84; Thomas Watson MacCallum and Stephen Taylor, eds., *The Nobel Prize-Winners and the Nobel Foundation, 1901–1937* (Zurich: Central European Times Publishing, 1938), 206.

Meyer v. Nebraska   (1923)

Landmark U.S. Supreme Court decision, which held that "a state law forbidding, under penalty, the teaching in any private, denominational, parochial or public school, of any modern language, other than English, to any child who has not attained and successfully passed the eighth grade, invades the liberty guaranteed by the Fourteenth Amendment and exceeds the power of the State." Under a law passed by the state of Nebraska, approved April 9, 1919, "No person, individually or as a teacher, shall, in any private, denominational or public school, teach any subject to any person in any language other than the English language." Plaintiff Meyer, a teacher in the Zion Parochial School, was tried and convicted in the District Court for Hamilton County on May 25, 1920, of breaking that law. The Nebraska state Supreme Court upheld the conviction, and Meyer appealed to the U.S. Supreme Court. Arguments were heard before the Court on February 23, 1923.

A little less than five months later, on June 4, 1923, Justice James McReynolds spoke for a unanimous Court (Justices Oliver Wendell HOLMES and George Sutherland wrote separate but concurring opinions) in striking down the Nebraska law as a violation of the Fourteenth Amendment. McReynolds explained, . . . "As the statute undertakes to interfere only with teaching which involves a modern language, leaving complete freedom as to other matters, there seems no adequate foundation for the suggestion that the purpose was to protect the child's health by limiting his mental activities. It is well known that proficiency in a foreign language seldom comes to one not instructed at an early age, and experience shows that this is not injurious to the health, morals or understanding of the ordinary child. The judgment of the court below must be reversed, and the cause remanded for further proceedings not inconsistent with this opinion."

References: Paul L. Murphy, "Meyer v. Nebraska" in Kermit L. Hall, ed. in chief, *The Oxford Companion to the Supreme Court of the United States* (New York: Oxford University Press, 1992), 543–44; *Meyer v. Nebraska*, 262 US 390 (1919).

Mies van der Rohe, Ludwig (1886–1969)

German architect, noted for his minimalist design philosophies as director of the BAUHAUS. Born on March 27, 1886, in Aachen, Germany, Mies worked in the family stone-carving business before joining the Berlin design firm of Peter Behrens at age 19 in 1908. Under Behrens's influence, Mies developed a unique design approach that was sympathetic with the Dutch group DE STIJL. In 1923 he worked on the progressive design magazine *G*. Known for his "less is more" aesthetic, Mies made major contributions to the architectural philosophies of the late 1920s and 1930s, first as artistic director of the Werkbund-sponsored Weissenhof project and then as director of the Bauhaus school in WEIMAR GERMANY.

Mies moved to the United States in 1937 and became the director of architecture at the Illinois Institute of Technology in 1938. Throughout his life, he strove to create "skin and bone architecture," contemplative spaces based on structural and material integrity. Some of his most well-known designs include the Barcelona Pavilion in Spain, Chicago's Crown Hall, Berlin's New National Gallery, the Czech Republic's Tugendhat House, and Stuttgart's Weissenhof Apartments. He received the American Institute of Architects Gold Medal in 1960. Mies died in Chicago in 1969.

References: Dennis Sharp, *The Illustrated Encyclopedia of Architects and Architecture* (New York: Whitney Library of Design, 1991); Franz Schulze, *Mies van der Rohe: A Critical Biography* (Chicago: University of Chicago Press, 1995).

Migratory Bird Protection Act   *See Missouri v. Holland.*

Miller, Glenn   *See* SWING.

Miller, Henry (1891–1980)

American writer, known for his controversial novels of the 1930s and beyond. Born in New York on December 28, 1891, to American parents of German ancestry, Miller spent his early years in Brooklyn. He enrolled in City College of New York in 1909, but dropped out after two months. After a series of jobs, Miller wrote his first book, *Clipped Wings,* in 1922 and was determined to make a living as a writer. In the late 1920s and 1930s, Miller toured Europe and eventually settled in Paris, where he met the writer Anaïs Nin. This was a period of great productivity, as he created *Tropic of Cancer* (1934), *Aller Retour New York* (1935), *Black Spring* (1936), and *Tropic of Capricorn* (1939) during these years. Because of their explicit sexual description, however, both of the *Tropic* titles were banned in the United States until 1961. Often autobiographical, his novels explored self-realization, philosophy, literature, and society.

At the outbreak of World War II, Miller's source of regular income—his Paris publisher, the Obelisk Press—ceased operations, and he returned to New York. His later works include *The Colossus of Maroussi* (1941), *Air-Conditioned Nightmare* (1945), and *The Rosy Crucifixion* trilogy, which contained *Sexus* (1949), *Plexus* (1953), and *Nexus* (1959). Also a travel writer and essayist, Miller painted and exhibited watercolors throughout his lifetime. In 1957 he was elected a member of the National Institute of Arts and Sciences. His autobiography *My Life and Times* was published in 1971.

Reference: Henry Miller, *My Life and Times* (New York: Playboy Press, 1971).

Millikan, Robert Andrews (1868–1953)

American physicist and Nobel laureate. Born in Morrison, Illinois, on March 22, 1868, he received his bachelor's (1891) and master's (1893) degree from Oberlin College in Ohio, and his doctorate from Columbia University (1895). Millikan worked as a professor of physics at the University of Chicago (1896–1921) and as a professor and administrator at the Norman Bridge Laboratory of Physics at the California Institute of Technology (1921–46). At these two institutions, Millikan explored the photoelectric effect dealing with the properties of electricity and atoms. For this work he was awarded the 1923 Nobel Prize in physics.

He wrote *The Electron* (1917), *Evolution in Science and Religion (1927)*, and *Science and the New Civilization (1930)*, among other works. Millikan died in Pasadena, California, on December 19, 1953.

References: I. Helen Gross, "Millikan, Robert Andrews" in Bernard S. and June H. Schlessinger, eds., *The Who's Who of Nobel Prize Winners* (Phoenix, Ariz.: Oryx Press, 1986), 157; Thomas Watson MacCallum, and Stephen Taylor, eds., *The Nobel Prize-Winners and the Nobel Foundation, 1901–1937* (Zurich: Central European Times Publishing, 1938), 78–79.

Milne, A. A. (1882–1956)

English poet and playwright, author of *Winnie the Pooh* (1926) and other delightful children's tales during the interwar period. Born Alan Alexander Milne in London on January 18, 1882, he was educated at Trinity College, Cambridge University, where he was the editor of *Granta*. After leaving college, in 1906 he became the assistant editor of the British humor magazine *Punch,* serving until 1914. Milne's articles from *Punch* were collected and published in 1929 as *Those Were the Days*.

Although he wrote several works in the years surrounding World War I, he reached a higher level of fame with his first children's book. *When We Were Very Young*

A. A. Milne poses with his son Christopher Robin in 1926, just before publication of the first book featuring the boy and his stuffed toys' adventures. *(CORBIS/Bettmann)*

(1924). Two years later, he published *Winnie the Pooh,* an enchanting fable about a little boy, Christopher Robin (Milne's son's name), who dreams about his life in a magical world with a small talking bear, and a host of other characters, including Tigger, Eeyore, Kanga, and Piglet. Milne continued the theme in such works as *The House at Pooh Corner* (1928).

Milne also composed several comedies, which were showcased on the London and New York stages, including *The Romantic Age* (1920), *The Ivory Door* (1927), *Toad of Toad Hall* (1930), and *Miss Elizabeth Bennet* (1936). Yet it was his creation of Winnie the Pooh, the indomitable little bear loved by so many millions of children, for whom Milne is remembered. He died on January 13, 1956.

References: Ann Thwaite, *A. A. Milne: His Life* (London: Faber, 1990); Thomas Burnett Swann, *A. A. Milne* (New York: Twayne, 1971); Tori Haring-Smith, *A. A. Milne: A Critical Bibliography* (New York: Garland, 1982).

Minot, George Richards (1885–1950)

American physician and Nobel laureate. Born in Boston, Massachusetts, on December 2, 1885, Minot received his bachelor's and two master's degrees from Harvard University. Working at a series of hospitals, including Johns Hopkins University Hospital in Baltimore, Minot worked collectively with William P. MURPHY and George H. WHIPPLE to discover the effects of anemia on the liver, and its relation to causing cancer, arthritis, and dietary diseases. For their work, the three were corecipients of the 1934 Nobel Prize in medicine and physiology. Professor I. Holmgren, a member of the Staff of Professors of the Royal Caroline Institute, commented to the prize winners: "You have spread a new light over the process of regeneration of the blood, you have discovered a function of the liver, before you unknown to science, you have invented and elaborated a new method for the treatment of anaemia, especially pernicious anaemia, that dreadful disease, which hitherto has killed practically everyone who was afflicted by it. This new method, the liver treatment, has saved already thousands of lives, and will in the future save innumerable human beings from death."

Minot continued to work until his death on February 25, 1950.

References: Rashelle Karp, "Minot, George Richards" in Bernard S. and June H. Schlessinger, eds., *The Who's Who of Nobel Prize Winners* (Phoenix, Ariz.: Oryx, 1986), 88–89; Thomas Watson MacCallum and Stephen Taylor, eds., *The Nobel Prize–Winners and the Nobel Foundation, 1901–1937* (Zurich: Central European Times Publishing, 1938), 234–35.

Miró, Joan   *See* SURREALISM.

Missouri ex rel. Gaines v. Canada (1938)

Landmark U.S. Supreme Court decision, in which the Court struck down state laws that proscribed "separate but equal" school facilities for black Americans at law schools. Petitioner Lloyd Gaines, a black man, was denied admission to the School of Law at the State University of Missouri because of his race. When the school offered to send him to Lincoln University, a separate state law school for blacks, Gaines refused. He sued the state of Missouri and the admissions officer, Canada, for violating his equal protection rights per the Fourteenth Amendment to the U.S. Constitution. Gaines requested a writ of mandamus to compel the school to admit him. Canada answered the suit by noting that the state universities of four adjacent states (Kansas, Nebraska, Iowa, and Illinois) allowed "nonresident negroes" to attend. The trial court denied Gaines's writ, a circuit court denied the issuance of a peremptory writ, and the Supreme Court of Missouri affirmed these findings. The U.S. Supreme Court granted the right to hear the case, and the justices heard arguments on November 9, 1938, in what was officially called *Missouri ex rel. Gaines v. Canada, Registrar of the University of Missouri et al.*

Less than five weeks later, on December 12, 1938, the Court struck down the university's refusal to admit Gaines and reversed the judgment of the state Supreme Court. In the 8–1 opinion (Justice James McReynolds dissented), Chief Justice Charles Evans HUGHES argued that "it is manifest that this discrimination . . . would constitute a denial of equal protection." Hughes wrote, "The equal protection of the laws is 'a protection of equal laws.' Manifestly, the obligation of the State to give the protection of equal laws can be performed only where its law operates, that is, within its own jurisdiction. It is there that the equality of legal right must be maintained. That obligation is imposed by the Constitution upon the States severally as governmental entities—each responsible for its own laws establishing the rights and duties of persons within its borders." Unfortunately, Gaines never enjoyed his judicial victory: mysteriously, he disappeared shortly after the case was filed. Still, the triumph cracked the wall of legalized segregation in education in the United States for the first time.

Reference: Kenneth L. Karst, "Missouri ex rel. Gaines v. Canada" in Leonard W. Levy, ed. in chief, *Encyclopedia of the American Constitution* (New York: Macmillan, 1986–92), 3: 1269; *Missouri ex rel. Gaines v. Canada*, 305 US 337 (1938).

Missouri v. Holland (1920)

Landmark U.S. Supreme Court decision, in which the Court upheld the right of the federal government to intrude on the "protection of [a state's] quasi-sovereign right to regulate the taking of game." The Migratory Bird Treaty Act, signed July 3, 1918, provided "for the protection, by closed seasons and in other ways, of migratory birds in the United States and Canada," and bound "each power to take and propose to their [respective] lawmaking bodies the necessary measures for carrying it out." The state of Missouri filed suit in court to enjoin game warden Ray P. Holland from carrying out provisions of the act, claiming that the federal government was intruding on matters deemed to be under state jurisdiction, such as wild birds within state borders. The U.S. district court for the Western District of Missouri ruled against the state, after which the U.S. Supreme Court offered to hear the facts in the case. Arguments were heard before the court on March 2, 1920.

Less than seven weeks later, Justice Oliver Wendell HOLMES held for a 7–2 court (Justices Willis Van Devanter and Mahlon Pitney dissented) in holding that the federal government did have a right to regulate the protection of wild birds in a state. Holmes explained: "As most of the laws of the United States are carried out within the States and as many of them deal with matters which in the silence of such laws the State might regulate, such general grounds are not enough to support Missouri's claim. . . . Here a national interest of very nearly the first magnitude

is involved. It can be protected only by national action in concert with that of another power. The subject-matter is only transitorily within the State and has not permanent habitat therein. But for the treaty and the statute there soon might be no birds for any powers to deal with. We see nothing in the Constitution that compels the government to sit by while a food supply is cut off and the protectors of our forests and our crops are destroyed. It is not sufficient to rely upon the States. The reliance is vain, and were it otherwise, the question is whether the United States is forbidden to act. We are of the opinion that the treaty and statute must be upheld. Decree affirmed."

U.S. historian Henry Steele Commager has written that "the opinion of the Court in this case is one of the most far-reaching assertions of national power in our constitutional history."

References: Henry Steele Commager, ed., *Documents of American History* (New York: Appleton-Century-Crofts, 1949), 343; Mark Grossman, *The ABC-Clio Companion to the Environmental Movement* (Santa Barbara, Calif.: ABC-Clio, 1994), 202–203; Charles A. Lofgren, "Missouri v. Holland" in Leonard W. Levy, ed. in chief, *Encyclopedia of the American Constitution* (New York: Macmillan, 1986–92), 3: 1267–68; Charles A. Lofgren, "Missouri v. Holland in Historical Perspective," Supreme Court Review, 1975 (1975), 77–122; *Missouri v. Holland*, 252 US 416 (1920).

Mitchell, Margaret (1900–1949)

American writer, noted for her 1936 work, GONE WITH THE WIND, which became one of the most famed books of the interwar period. Born in Atlanta, Georgia, she graduated from the Washington Seminary there, and spent her entire life save one year (when she was at Smith College) in Atlanta. She worked as a writer for the Atlanta *Journal*, and in 1925 married John R. Marsh.

In 1936, Mitchell published what would become her only published book, *Gone with the Wind*, a thousand-page romantic glance at the South before, during, and after the U.S. Civil War. Mitchell created a panoply of characters, including the brusque but gentlemanly Rhett Butler and the womanly but scorned Scarlett O'Hara. Mitchell detailed their interlocked lives as the war swept away their traditional way of life. For this work, Mitchell was awarded the 1937 Pulitzer Prize for Fiction. The book was made into a film in 1939 starring Clark GABLE and Vivian Leigh.

Mitchell never wrote another work. She died in Atlanta on August 16, 1949, when she was hit and killed by a drunk driver. She was only 48.

References: Elizabeth I. Hanson, *Margaret Mitchell* (Boston: Twayne Publishers, 1990); Finis Farr, *Margaret Mitchell of Atlanta: The Author of Gone with the Wind* (New York: Morrow, 1965); Anne Edwards, *The Road to Tara: The Life of Margaret Mitchell* (New Haven, Conn.: Ticknor & Fields, 1983).

Mitchell, William (1879–1936)

U.S. Army officer, court-martialed for his criticism of U.S. military policy regarding the use of aviation. Born in Nice, France, on December 29, 1879, he grew up in Wisconsin, the son of U.S. Senator John Lendrum Mitchell. After attending Racine College in Wisconsin and graduating from George Washington University in Washington, D.C., in 1899, Mitchell enlisted in the U.S. Army as a private and rose through the ranks, graduating from the Army Staff College in 1909 and attaining the rank of brigadier general. During World War I, he served as chief of the U.S. Air Service (the forerunner of the Air Force), and after the war was named as director of the U.S. Army's military aviation program.

For many years, Mitchell witnessed the potential, both military and civilian, that airplanes could have. Yet, he saw that the military and their strict adherence to old weaponry was a detriment to the establishment and buildup of a comprehensive aviation policy. He began to speak out publicly on the army's failure to exploit this new technology. Mitchell saw that naval power, which the major military powers looked to for defense, would be easily destroyed in the hands of a country that controlled the skies. In 1921 he demonstrated his belief in air power, when he was given six Martin bombers and allowed to bomb, from the air, the German battleship *Ostfriesland*, which had been surrendered after World War I. On July 21, 1921, Mitchell and the six planes scored a direct hit on the ship and sank it, proving Mitchell's assertion of the superiority of air power over sea power. The military was not impressed, however, and continued to deny him a forum.

Mitchell continued to speak out, until he said that his superiors were guilty of "incompetency, criminal negligence, and almost treasonal administration of national defense." He was then court-martialed; General Douglas MacArthur, a friend of Mitchell, served on the board, composed mostly of men who favored land and sea warfare. Mitchell's court-martial lasted from October to November 1925. His defense was led by Congressman Frank R. Reid of Illinois, a staunch air power supporter. Reid used the trial to charge the military with a failure to use air power. Although he and Mitchell made fools of the military and their beliefs were vindicated, the board found against Mitchell, all but MacArthur voting for his conviction. He was stripped of his rank, command, and salary (half of which was later restored by President Calvin COOLIDGE, who upheld the guilty verdict), but even in civilian life Mitchell continued to speak out on behalf of aviation.

He died in New York City on February 19, 1936, before he could see the impact aviation would have during World War II. In the end, he was proven right—air power, not sea power, proved the decisive factor in the Allies' winning the war. In 1941 the U.S. Congress enacted a resolution that restored Mitchell's rank to brigadier general. The 1955 Otto Preminger film, *The Court-Martial of Billy Mitchell,* highlighted his case. In 1964 the Civil Air Patrol, an auxiliary of the U.S. Air Force, established the General Billy Mitchell Award, given to a cadet in the Civil Air Patrol program.

References: Roger Burlingame, *General Billy Mitchell: Champion of Air Defense* (New York: McGraw-Hill, 1952); Emile H. Ganvreu and Lester Cohen, *Billy Mitchell: Founder of Our Air Force and Prophet without Honor* (New York: Dutton, 1942); "Gen. Mitchell, Chief of A. E. F. Air Force, Dies," *New York Herald-Tribune,* February 20, 1936, p. 14; "Funeral of Gen. Mitchell Will Be in Milwaukee; Veterans Pay Honor to Former Air Chief at Station Here," *New York Herald-Tribune,* February 21, 1936, p. 12.

Mondrian, Piet (1872–1944)

Dutch painter, credited with developing a geometric, nonobjective style called neoplasticism. Influenced by cubism, his work is characterized by vertical and horizontal lines at 90-degree angles in wide swathes of primary colors or blacks and grays. Cofounder of DE STIJL movement and the group's magazine, he published a book about his theories in 1920 titled *Neo-Plasticisme.* His theories influenced the *Bauhaus.*

Montagu-Chelmsford Reforms   *See* GOVERNMENT OF INDIA ACTS.

Moody, Helen Newington Wills   *See* TENNIS.

Moral Re-Armament

Nondenominational religious movement, founded by American evangelist Frank Nathan Daniel Buchman. In 1922, Buchman, a lecturer in personal evangelism at the Hartford Seminary Foundation in Hartford, Connecticut, resigned his position to launch a social and religious movement based on the direction of God and moral perfection. He originally offered his thoughts at Princeton University; however, when he discussed sexual matters openly, he was asked to leave the college. He moved to Oxford University in England; where his group took the name "the Oxford Group." Over the next 16 years, the Oxford Group held conferences around the world on various religious subjects, at which thousands of people gathered. In 1938, to broaden the movement's appeal, Buchman and his followers changed the name of the group to "Moral Re-Armament," in an attempt to awaken the world to a religious revitalization that he believed would head off any threat of war. The move failed, however, and although the group continued to attract members during and after World War II, the deaths of Buchman in 1961 and his successor, Peter Howard, in 1965 left the movement in decline. It still exists in a limited form today. Buchman authored *Rising Tide* (1937), *Moral Re-Armament* (1938), *The Fight to Serve* (1943), *Remaking the World* (1948), and *The World Rebuilt* (1951).

References: D. G. Bloesch, "Moral Re-Armament" in Walter A. Elwell, ed., *Evangelical Dictionary of Theology* (Grand Rapids, Mich.: Baker Book House, 1987), 733–34; Walter Houston Clark, *The Oxford Group: Its History and Significance* (New York: Bookman Associates, 1951); Tom Driberg, *The Mystery of Moral Re-Armament* (New York: Alfred A. Knopf, 1965).

Morgan, Thomas Hunt (1866–1945)

American geneticist and Nobel laureate. Born in Lexington, Kentucky, on September 25, 1866, he received his bachelor of science degree from the State College of Kentucky in 1888, and his master's and doctoral degrees from Johns Hopkins University in 1890. He served as a professor at Bryn Mawr College (1891–1903), at Columbia University (1904–28), and at the California Institute of Technology (1928–45). During these years Morgan investigated, utilizing the fruit fly (*Drosophilia melanogaster*), the operation of chromosomes in heredity, becoming the first scientist to determine the role genetics played in the formation of all life. For this work, he was awarded the 1933 Nobel Prize in medicine and physiology.

His works include *Regeneration* (1901), *Heredity and Sex* (1913), *Evolution and Genetics* (1925), *The Theory of the Gene* (1926), and *Embryology and Genetics* (1933). Morgan died in Pasadena, California, on December 4, 1945.

References: Rashelle Karp, "Morgan, Thomas Hunt" in Bernard S. and June H. Schlessinger, eds., *The Who's Who of Nobel Prize Winners* (Phoenix, Ariz.: Oryx, 1986), 88; Thomas Watson MacCallum and Stephen Taylor, eds., *The Nobel Prize-Winners and the Nobel Foundation, 1901–1937* (Zurich: Central European Times Publishing, 1938), 228–31.

Morgenthau, Henry (1891–1967)

American politician and diplomat, noted as one of the most important financial figures of the NEW DEAL program of President Franklin D. ROOSEVELT. The son of American diplomat Henry Morgenthau Sr., who served as the U.S. ambassador to Turkey, Morgenthau Jr. was born in New York City on May 11, 1891. He studied architecture at Cornell University for three semesters before dropping out and retiring to a farm in Dutchess County, New York, in 1913. The farm was near that of the Roosevelt family estate

at Hyde Park, New York, and Morgenthau and Roosevelt became friends. When Roosevelt was elected governor of New York in 1928, he named Morgenthau as the chair of the State Agricultural Advisory Committee. Roosevelt depended on Morgenthau for advice on conservation matters, and he teamed his close adviser Harry HOPKINS with Morgenthau to work on several state environmental projects, including those dealing with reforestation. In 1932, Roosevelt, now president, named Morgenthau as the head of the Farm Credit Bureau. In this capacity, Morgenthau was loaning some $1 million a day in loan credits to financially-strapped farmers by the end of 1933, helping to avert a collapse in the national farm economy. When Roosevelt disagreed with Morgenthau over a financial policy, he moved his friend to the post of assistant secretary of the Treasury in November 1933.

In December 1933, Secretary of the Treasury William H. Woodin announced his retirement, and the next month Morgenthau was became the 52nd secretary of the treasury. He served from 1934 until 1945, the second longest tenure in that position in U.S. history (Albert Gallatin, who served from 1801 to 1814, is the record holder). During Morgenthau's tenure, he stabilized the economy by shoring up the value of the dollar, working within the strictures of Roosevelt's New Deal policies. During the 1930s he used stabilization fund payments to purchase foreign currencies, gold, and U.S. dollars so that, by the end of the decade, the dollar had become the strongest currency in the world, making recovery from the GREAT DEPRESSION much easier. During World War II he sold war bonds and was a leader in several meetings with other world economic leaders, helping to establish the International Monetary Fund and the World Bank after the war.

Roosevelt's death in April 1945 left Morgenthau as an outsider in the new government of Harry S. Truman. When he suggested to Truman that a defeated Germany be urged to move toward a more agrarian economy to stave off any future attempt to militarize, the idea was dismissed. Increasingly ineffectual, Morgenthau resigned in July 1945 and returned to his New York farm.

In his final decades, Morgenthau was involved in numerous philanthropic pursuits. He died in Poughkeepsie, New York, on February 6, 1967.

References: Otis L. Graham Jr., and Meghan Robinson Wander, eds., *Franklin D. Roosevelt: His Life and Times: An Encyclopedic View* (Boston: G. K. Hall, 1985), 265–66; Philip Abbott, "Morgenthau, Henry, Jr." in Bruce W. Jentleson and Thomas G. Paterson, senior eds., *Encyclopedia of U.S. Foreign Relations* (New York: Oxford University Press, 1997), 3: 168–69.

Morro Castle Disaster

Tragic accident, September 8, 1934, on board the passenger ship *Morro Castle*, in which 134 people were killed.

Part of the Ward Line of passenger ships, the liner was named after two Spanish fortifications in Cuba that had been captured by the United States during the Spanish-American War. Its maiden voyage was in August 1930. On September 5, 1934, despite the ship's state of decay and deterioration, it sailed in the midst of a hurricane between Havana and New York City. Piloted by Captain Robert R. Wilmott, who was ill at the time, the ship carried 455 passengers and crew. Wilmott retreated to his cabin and by 7 P.M. on September 7 was found dead. First mate William F. Warms took control. The following day, about 2 A.M., a fire broke out on deck. Chief engineer Eben Abbott and some of the crew slipped off the boat and fled in a lifeboat, leaving the passengers to fend for themselves. Off the coast of Sea Girt, New Jersey, the fire was soon out of control; some of the passengers jumped ship into the Atlantic Ocean. Warms did not send an SOS, instead hoping to fight the fire with what remained of the crew. Flames could be seen from the shore, however, and rescue vessels tried to help fight the impending disaster. Despite efforts of the U.S. Coast Guard, nearby fishers, and the Merchant Marines to rescue passengers from the ocean and the burning ship, 134 people died. The *Morro Castle's* anchor snapped, and the ship slipped toward Asbury Park, where it beached itself while it smoldered.

A federal investigation led to the indictments and convictions of Warms and Abbott, but these were overturned by a higher court. No one went to prison; the Ward Line merely paid a fine. The line leased another ship, the *Mohawk*, to take the *Morro Castle's* place. On January 25, 1935, however, that ship sank off of Manasquan Inlet in New Jersey, leaving 45 dead. A third ship, the *Havana*, ran aground on a Florida reef and was never used again.

References: Dan Perkes, "Holocaust on the High Seas" in *Eyewitness to Disaster* (New York: Gallery Books, 1985), 38–47; Michael Prideaux, comp., *World Disasters* (London: Phoebus Publishing Co., 1976), 12–16; "186 Dead, 39 Missing as Liner Morro Castle Burns; 333 Survivors Tell of Heroic Rescues Off Jersey," *New York Herald-Tribune*, September 9, 1934, p. 1.

Mosley, Sir Oswald Ernald (1896–1980)

British politician, supporter of Adolf Hitler, founder of the British Union of Fascists. Born in London on November 16, 1896, he served in the House of Commons from 1918 to 1931, during which he moved from the Conservative, to the Independent, to the Labour Party; in 1929 he served in a ministry in the Labour government. In 1931, however, Mosley deserted the Labour Party to establish a British Socialist Party, but because of his politics he was defeated for reelection to Parliament. In 1932 he founded the British Union of Fascists (BUF), an anti-Semitic organization that sympathized with Adolf HITLER's platform. Through the union's official publication *Action*, speeches by Mosley and his colleagues, and the wearing of uniforms with prominent swastikas, the BUF became known as the Blackshirts. Mosley conducted a campaign against Jews in England, which led to his arrest after the outbreak of the war in 1939. In 1943 he was released because he was ill, only to continue his activities. In 1948 the BUF was modified into the Union Movement, an amalgamation of anti-Semitic and other fringe groups in England. Mosley remained the head of the Union Movement until his death in Orsay, Paris, France, on December 3, 1980.

References: Christian Zentner and Friedemann Bedüftig, eds., *Encyclopedia of the Third Reich* (New York: Macmillan, 1991), 2: 603–604; "Mosley Memorandum 1930" in Christopher Haigh, ed., *The Cambridge Historical Encyclopedia of Great Britain and Ireland* (Cambridge: Cambridge University Press, 1985), 296; John D. Brewer, *Mosley's Men: The British Union of Fascists in the West Midlands* (Aldershot, Hampshire, England: Gower Publishing Co., 1984); Robert Benewick, *Political Violence and Public Order: A Study of British Fascism* (London: Allen Lane, 1969); "Story of Olympia 'Battle' in Fascist Slander Suit; Men Alleged to Have Been Struck Down," *The Daily Telegraph* (London), February 7, 1936, p. 6; "Sir Oswald Mosley, British Fascist Who Urged Peace with Nazis, Dies," *The New York Times*, December 4, 1980, p. D23.

motion pictures, silent

Major entertainment method in the 1920s, until the late 1920s, when the advent of "talking" pictures brought sound to the screen. The genre of silent motion pictures began with the first flickering images in the early 1890s, when Thomas Edison invented moving pictures and the Lumière brothers, Louis and Auguste, established the camera and the theater as a part of everyday life.

The 1920s was the golden era of filmmaking in the United States, particularly in HOLLYWOOD, where new and innovative directors and actors were coming on the scene. The image of Italian-born Rudolph VALENTINO first shook the scene with his performance as Julio Desnoyers in the anti-war drama *The Four Horsemen of the Apocalypse* (1921). His role as Sheik Ahmed Ben Hassan in *The Sheik* (1921) made him a national heartthrob. Valentino followed up that role in *Blood and Sand* (1922), *The Eagle* (1925), *Cobra* (1925), and *The Son of the Sheik* (1926). Charlie CHAPLIN's the "Little Tramp," opened the era up with *The Kid* (1920). Chaplin's works during and after the silent era, which included *A Woman of Paris* (1923), *The Gold Rush* (1924), and *The Circus* (1928), are some of the masterpieces of silent film. Besides Chaplin, the most gifted comic of the silent era was Buster KEATON. Appearing in such side-splitting comedies as *The Three Ages* (1923), *Our Hospitality* (1923), *Sherlock, Jr.* (1924), *The*

Navigator (1924), the classic Civil War story *The General* (1927), *College* (1927), *Steamboat Bill, Jr.* (1928), and *The Cameraman* (1928), Keaton is the period's most prolific comedian on film.

The 1920s was also the era of tremendous cinematic productions in Hollywood, such as director Fred Niblo's *Ben-Hur: A Tale of the Christ* (1926), starring Ramon Novarro and Francis X. Bushman, and Cecil B. DEMILLE's lavish *The Ten Commandments* (1926), starring Theodore Roberts and Charles De Roche. Perhaps one of the greatest directors of the period was Austrian Erich von STRO-HEIM, whose first work, *Blind Husbands* (1919), was a moderate success; his second film, *Foolish Wives* (1922), was the first movie to have a budget of more than $1 million. Stroheim followed up his success with *Greed* (1923), based on the book *McTeague* by Frank Norris. Stroheim then directed *The Merry Widow* (1925) for MGM. In 1921 director Henry David presented Richard Barthelmess's performance in *Tol'able David* (1921), a story of youth. German director Friedrich Wilhelm MURNAU directed the first film with a speaking portion, *Sunrise* (1927). In 1927, Clara BOW became the "It" girl with that magical allure. Frank Borzage's *Seventh Heaven* (1927) won three Academy Awards, including Best Picture, at the 1928 awards ceremonies.

In 1927, Warner Brothers released *The JAZZ SINGER*, starring Al JOLSON. Laced with speaking sections, the film was a big hit. Studios flocked to film with sound, and in 1928, *The Lights of New York*, the first film with no silent scenes, appeared, marking the end of the silent era. With the advent of sound, many of Hollywood's European stars—Vilma Banky, Emil JANNINGS, Erich Von Stroheim, Alla Nazimova, and Valentino—were adversely affected, as they could not hide their accents.

The 1920s was also a landmark decade in European filmmaking. During the economic hardships of WEIMAR Germany, people paid to see the era's great impressionist films with lumps of coal, choosing to escape life's pressures for an hour or so rather than stay warm. Swedes Mauritz Stiller and Victor Sjostrom and the Dane Carl Dreyer used film to show new forms of art. Among the brilliant artists who emerged from this dismal time after World War I were the Germans Fritz LANG, F. W. Murnau, Georg Wilhelm, G. W. PABST, and Ernst Lubitsch, the Frenchman Abel GANCE, whose 1927 epic *Napoléon* set the medium for realism, and the Englishman Alfred HITCHCOCK, whose shadowy 1927 melodrama *The Lodger* became perhaps the silent era's most famous dark drama. Lang directed *Dr. Mabuse der Spieler* (Dr. Mabuse, the gambler, 1922), the classic utopian nightmare *Metropolis* (1926), and *Spione* (Spies, 1928). Murnau is famed for his horror picture *Nosferatu eine Symphonie des Grauens* (Nosferatu, a symphony of horror, 1922). Pabst's contributions include *Die Freudlose Gasse* (Joyless street, 1925), *Die Liebe der Jeanne Ney* (The Love of Jeanne Ney, 1927),

and his most famous, *Die Büchse der Pandora* (Pandora's box, 1928), starring the mesmerizing Louise BROOKS. The Russian directors Sergei Mikhailovitch EISENSTEIN (*Bronenosets Potemkin* {THE BATTLESHIP POTEMKIN, 1927), and Vselvolod Illarionovich Pudovkin (*Konyets Sankt-Peterburga* {"The End of St. Petersburg," 1927), also exhibited original filming devices that became standards for movie makers in the years to come.

See also ACADEMY AWARDS; ALL QUIET ON THE WESTERN FRONT.

References: Roy Kinnard, *Horror in Silent Films: A Filmography, 1896–1929* (Jefferson, N. C.: McFarland, 1996); Pauline Kael, "*Vampyr* (1932)," Michael Sragow, "*Sabotage* (1936)," Terrence Rafferty, "*L'Atalante* (1934)," John Powers, "*Zéro de Conduite* (1933)," Peter Rainer, "*Bizarre, Bizarre* (1937)," Pauline Kael, "*Á Nous la Liberté* (1931)," Pauline Kael, "*Pépé Le Moko* (1937)," Pauline Kael, "*The Baker's Wife* (1938)," Morris Dickstein, "*Metropolis* (1927)" and "*M* (1931)," Pauline Kael, "*Nosferatu* (1922)," Jay Carr, "*Pandora's Box* (1928)," Pauline Kael, "*The Blue Angel* (1929)," Pauline Kael, "*The Cabinet of Dr. Caligari* (1919)," Kathy Schulz Huffhines, "*Alexander Nevsky* (1938)," Andrew Sarris, "*Potemkin* (1925)," and Pauline Kael, "*Earth* (1930)" and "*Mother* (1926)" in Kathy Schulz Huffhines, ed., *Foreign Affairs: The National Society of Film Critics' Video Guide to Foreign Films* (San Francisco: Mercury House, 1991), 6, 10, 21–25, 26–28, 29–30, 32, 33, 34–39, 93–98; Roger Manvell and Heinrich Fraenkel, *The German Cinema* (New York: Praeger Publishers, 1971); Eric Rhode, *A History of the Cinema from Its Origins to 1970* (London: Penguin Books, 1984), 161–262.

motion pictures, talking

The effort to create sound in the filming of motion pictures began in the infant days of silent pictures. American Thomas Edison, whose first flickering images were the earliest movies, experimented but failed to establish a complete technique to film with sound. In the 1920s the Bell Telephone Laboratories investigated the superphonograph system, which led to the Vitaphone system, which allowed a disc of the sounds to be synchronized with film. The art of sound actually being placed on the film was still years away.

The Vitaphone system was first used during a showing of *Don Juan*, starring actor John BARRYMORE, which debuted in New York City on August 6, 1926. Soon after, many other films began to use sounds in their dialogues. Many pictures claim to be the first to use talking dialogue; some historians credit the mostly silent *The JAZZ SINGER* (1929) as being the first, while others assert that 1927's *Sunrise*, in which people on a street can be heard to holler a sound at a car, is the first to use the synchronized human voice in film. Universal's first "talkie" was supposed to

The first "talkie," *The Jazz Singer,* featured Al Jolson performing "Mammy" in vaudeville-style blackface—a veritable collision of old-fashioned entertainment and new. (*CORBIS/Bettmann*)

have been *Melody of Love* (1928), but instead it was *Broadway* (1929). *The Lights of New York,* directed by Brian Foy and starring Helene Costello and Cullen Landis, was the first to have speaking parts all the way through.

HOLLYWOOD used motion pictures to entertain, particularly as the GREAT DEPRESSION became more a part of American life. New faces were used in productions, as were storylines regarding real people. The advent of talking pictures closed the door on many actors futures; for instance, Clara BOW was laughed at for her thick Brooklyn accent and European actors such as Marlene DIETRICH and Rudolf VALENTINO could not hide their accents. But sound also opened the door for many other actors. Film historian Eric Rhode explains, "Sound allowed [the movie studios] to employ talented people whose gifts had been previously unusable, and who had built reputations in the theater or on radio: comedians like Mae West, W. C. Fields and the Marx BROTHERS; singers and dancers like Ruby Keeler, Joan Blondell, Eddie Cantor and Fred ASTAIRE; straight actors like Bette DAVIS, Katharine Hepburn, James CAGNEY and Spencer Tracy; directors and choreographers

like Rouben Mamoulian, James Whale and Busby BERKELEY. Many of the films that seem to define aspects of the thirties had been popular novels or plays of the previous decade."

The first ACADEMY AWARDS in 1928 had all been handed out to silent films. In 1929 they were overtaken by the so-called talkies. The leading film that broke ground like no other in this new medium was Lewis Milestone's epic antiwar drama *All Quiet on the Western Front,* based on the book by Erich Maria Remarque. British actor George ARLISS won Best Actor in *Disraeli,* and in 1931, *Cimarron* became the first Western (Clint Eastwood's *Unforgiven* was the second in 1993) to win the Best Picture. In 1936 Oscars were first presented in the Supporting Actor and Actress categories. The honors went to Walter Brennan for *Come and Get It* and to Gale Sondergaard for *Anthony Adverse.*

The use of film noir, with a blackened look to the scenery, came into vogue in the early 1930s, although it didn't become popular until the 1940s and 1950s. Fritz LANG's haunting 1931 *M,* starring the Hungarian actor Peter

Lorre, was the first crime picture made with sound; in it, Lorre portrays a demented and deranged child murderer who is methodically and systematically hunted down (the story was based on the true case of serial murderer Peter Kürten, who himself was beheaded for his crimes). Charlie CHAPLIN, known for his silent comedies, refused to add speaking to his first movies in the 1930s, including *City Lights* (1931) and *Modern Times* (1936). Many of these early films with speaking parts also included music, and the MUSICAL became a major form of entertainment. Berkeley's work led the way, with dance numbers in such productions as *Footlight Parade* (1933), *Forty-Second Street* (1933), and *Gold Diggers of 1933* (1933). The crime drama also became popular. Such films as *Little Caesar* (1930), directed by Mervyn Le Roy and starring Edward G. Robinson and Douglas FAIRBANKS, and *Scarface* (1932), directed by Howard Hawks and starring Paul Muni, were two of the major films of the period. The main actor in the crime genre was James CAGNEY, however. Starring in *The Public Enemy* (1931) and *Angels with Dirty Faces* (1938), Cagney exemplified the tough guy image of the early PROHIBITION era.

Horror films also were in vogue. FRANKENSTEIN (1931), featuring Boris KARLOFF's magnetic performance as the Monster, to DRACULA (1931), featuring Bela Lugosi, and KING KONG (1933), these films were extremely popular. The MARX BROTHERS became the decades' leading comedians with their numerous pictures, including *The Cocoanuts* (1929), *Horse Feathers* (1932), and *A Night at the Opera* (1935). Marlene DIETRICH, who first appeared in *The Blue Angel* (1930), continued her success with *Morocco* (1930) and *The Devil is a Woman* (1935).

The decade ended with opportunities to use color in films. *Gone With the Wind* and *The Wizard of OZ* (both 1939) both used color for the first time and were widely popular. Within a decade Hollywood had gone from talking to color.

See also ACADEMY AWARDS.

References: Eric Rhode, *A History of the Cinema from Its Origins to 1970* (London: Penguin Books, 1984), 268; Roy Liebman, *From Silents to Sound: A Biographical Encyclopedia of Performers Who Made the Transition to Talking Pictures* (Jefferson, N. C.: McFarland & Co., 1998); Andrew Bergman, *We're in the Money: Depression America and Its Films* (New York: New York University Press, 1971); Margaret Farrand Thorp, *America at the Movies* (New Haven, Conn.: Yale University Press, 1939).

Mukden Incident

Event, September 18, 1931, in which the murder of a Japanese captain in the Chinese city of Mukden was used as a pretext by the Japanese to invade China and establish a puppet government in Manchuria. Mukden (also called Shenyang, or, earlier, Fungtienfu), was the capital of the Manchurian province of Liaoning before the invasion and takeover by Japan. It was the original home of the Manchu dynasty, who made it their capital in 1631; all of the tombs of the Manchu emperors are located at Mukden. Throughout the mid to late 19th century, the Russians, Chinese, and Japanese built railroads to the city, making it a major center of commerce and trade.

After the defeat of the Japanese in the Russo-Japanese War of 1905, Japan was the area's leading military power, and for many years Japan had sought to control China as part of its sphere of influence, with Mukden as the center. Following the incident, the Japanese army seized the city of Kirin three days later, and began establishing the puppet state of Manchukuo. The LEAGUE OF NATIONS sent the LYTTON COMMISSION, headed by Victor Alexander Bulwer-Lytton, to investigate the Japanese invasion of Manchuria, and called for a full Japanese withdrawal. Japan dismissed the Lytton report as a provocation and withdrew from the League instead. That action was the start of a long and protracted war, referred to as the MANCHURIAN CRISIS. After the Chinese capitulation in Mukden was complete, the Japanese started to build factories and other industrial centers in the city, making it an important nucleus of their ability to fight World War II. On August 20, 1945, however, after the United States had dropped two atomic bombs on Japan, the U.S.S.R., which had declared war on Japan, marched into Mukden and stripped all of the factories bare, taking the parts back to the Soviet Union. When Chinese nationalist troops entered the city in early 1946, they found a decimated and devastated locale.

Starting in the late 1970s, stories began to leak that a Japanese military unit, called Unit 731, used both Chinese and American prisoners captured at Mukden for biological warfare experiments. Recently these declassified files have shown that horrible experiments did indeed occur.

References: Takehiko Yoshihashi, *Conspiracy at Mukden: The Rise of the Japanese Military* (New Haven: Yale University, Conn. Press, 1963); League of Nations, "Commission of Enquiry of the League of Nations into the Sino-Japanese Dispute [The Lytton Report]" (London: *The Economist*, 1932); Ching-chun Liang, *The Sinister Face of the Mukden Incident* (New York: St. John's University Press, 1969).

Muni, Paul   *See* BUCK, PEARL S.

Munich Crisis-Munich Pact

Emergency situation, August–September 1938, in which British prime minister Neville CHAMBERLAIN used APPEASEMENT to attempt to avoid war in Europe. Adolf HITLER's demands to annex the Sudetenland, the German-speaking areas of Czechoslovakia, led to the worst crisis on the

European continent since World War I. On September 22, Chamberlain met Hitler in the German city of Godesberg; finding the German leader's demands unreasonable, Chamberlain postponed all action on a treaty to confer with the Allies. He then met Hitler a week later in Munich, where Chamberlain agreed to allow German armies to take the Sudetenland in exchange for a promise that no further territorial possessions would be demanded. Hitler agreed, and the two men signed an understanding, known as the Munich Pact, on September 30. The document reads: "We, the German Führer and Chancellor and the British Prime Minister, ... regard the agreement signed last night and the ANGLO-GERMAN NAVAL AGREEMENT as symbolic of the desire of our two peoples never to go to war with one another again."

Chamberlain returned home to jubilant crowds, who thought he had helped to avert a second calamitous war in Europe. But time would tell that Chamberlain's appeasement of Hitler had only emboldened the German dictator; this would lead to the occupation of Czechoslovakia in March 1939 and the outbreak of war in September.

Refer also to Appendix 1 for text of the Munich Agreement, September 30, 1938.

References: Edmund Jan Osmańczyk, *The Encyclopedia of the United Nations and International Agreements* (Philadelphia: Taylor & Francis, 1985), 529; "Czechs Accept Munich Decision with Resignation; 'Peace Heroes' Get Triumphal Welcome on Return as Europe Relaxes, Forecasts General Settlement," New York *Herald-Tribune* (European Edition), October 1, 1938, p. 1.

Murnau, Friedrich Wilhelm (1889–1931)

German motion picture director, noted director of the silent film era. Born in Bielefeld, Germany, on December 28, 1889, he studied art and literature at the University of Heidelberg before going to Berlin to work under the direction of Max Reinhardt. Murnau served as a fighter pilot during World War I, spending some time in Switzerland when his plane accidentally landed there. After the war he returned to Germany to direct motion pictures. He directed a total of 22 films; the first was 1919's *Der Knabe in Blau* (The blue boy), the last was 1931's *Tabu*. Those he made before 1921 have been lost forever. He directed what many film historians consider two of the best silent films ever made: *Nosferatu, a Symphony of Horror* (1922) and *Sunrise: A Story of Two Humans* (1927). He had just finished filming *Tabu*, a story set in the South Seas of the Pacific, when he was killed in a car crash in Santa Barbara, California, on March 11, 1931.

References: Ephraim Katz, *The Film Encyclopedia* (New York: HarperPerennial, 1994), 840–41; Lotte H. Eisner, *Murnau* (Berkeley: University of California Press, 1973).

Murphy, William Parry (1892–1987)

American researcher and Nobel laureate. Born in Stoughton, Wisconsin, on February 6, 1892, he received his bachelor's degree from the University of Oregon (1914) and his master's and doctorate degrees from Harvard University (1920). After serving in the U.S. Army (1917–18), Murphy worked at the Rhode Island Hospital as a physician (1920–22). In 1922 he joined the staff of the Peter Bent Brigham Hospital in Boston (now Brigham and Women's Hospital), where he worked until his retirement. His work with George Richards MINOT on the liver disease anemia and how to treat it earned him, Minot, and George Hoyt WHIPPLE of the University of Rochester in New York the 1934 Nobel Prize in medicine and physiology.

Murphy died at his home in Brookline, Massachusetts, on October 9, 1987.

References: Rashelle Karp, "Murphy, William Parry" in Bernard S. and June H. Schlessinger, eds., *The Who's Who of Nobel Prize Winners* (Phoenix, Ariz.: Oryx, 1986), 89; Thomas Watson MacCallum and Stephen Taylor, eds., *The Nobel Prize–Winners and the Nobel Foundation, 1901–1937* (Zurich: Central European Times Publishing, 1938), 236–37.

musicals

Form of stage entertainment using song, wildly popular during the interwar period. Also known as comic opera, operetta, or musical comedy, the musical as it is known in the American tradition originated in the mid-1800s with French and Viennese operettas. In the late 1800s continental operettas were well received in England, embodied by the satiric shows of William Gilbert and Arthur Sullivan, including *H.M.S. Pinafore* (1878) and *The Mikado* (1885). But audiences across the Atlantic preferred the looser, less formal format of the Music Hall. Such variety and minstrel shows combining song, dance, magic, and comedy sketches eventually gave way to vaudeville revues in the United States beginning in the 1880s.

During the early 20th century, such imports as the Hungarian composer Franz Lehár's opera *The Merry Widow* (1905) had enormous influence on the early Broadway musical, but the American composer George M. Cohan gave the U.S. musical comedy its distinctive sound and style. Among Cohan's hits were "Give My Regards to Broadway" and "Yankee Doodle Dandy" (both from 1904's *Little Johnny Jones*) and "You're a Grand Old Flag" (from 1906's *George Washington Jr.*). In 1907 theatrical producer Florenz Ziegfeld, whom many consider the father of Broadway, introduced his elaborate stage revue, the *Follies,* which ran for an unprecedented 24 years. But the American musical gained worldwide influence after World War I, with the Broadway debuts of such composers as Jerome KERN, Cole PORTER, Richard RODGERS, Moss HART, Ira and George GERSHWIN, the multitalented British playwright Noel Coward, and others. Their productions introduced realistic characters and situations to the musical stage. During this period Kern and Oscar HAMMERSTEIN wrote the innovative *Show Boat* (1927), which became the most enduring hit of the 1920s.

European cabaret musical theater burst onto the scene in the 1920s and early 1930s, especially in Paris and Berlin. These cabarets were filled with intellectual punch, satire, and a decadent blend of comedy sketches and torch songs. The classic German film *The Blue Angel* (1930) with Marlene DIETRICH captures pre-Nazi cabaret performance in Germany. The cabaret trend spread to the United States with PROHIBITION, when entrepreneurs across the country opened illegal cabaret-style nightclubs or speakeasies featuring elaborate floor shows or female solo singers. When Prohibition ended in 1933, although the GREAT DEPRESSION was at its worst, large nightclubs with lavish floor shows became quite popular; the material and performance style were very much in the European musical cabaret tradition.

Americans seemed to find escape during the depression era in such lighthearted Broadway musicals as Gershwin's *Of Thee I Sing* (1931), the first musical to win the Pulitzer Prize; Rodgers and Hart's *On Your Toes* (1936); and Porter's *Anything Goes* (1934). The musical was also successfully transferred to the medium of film by director-choreographer Busby BERKELEY in such hits as *Forty-Second Street* (1933) and *Footlight Parade* (1933). Berkeley introduced elaborately choreographed dance numbers that opened the door for Agnes de Mille's balletic choreography in Rodgers and Hammerstein's smash production *Oklahoma* (1943). *Oklahoma* was the first fully integrated musical play, using song and dance to develop the characters and the plot. German composer Kurt Weill's *Lady in the Dark* (1941) opened the way for the more realistic musicals that would come to the fore in the post-World War II period.

See also BERLIN, Irving.

References: David Ewen, *American Musical Theatre* (New York: Holt, Rinehart, & Winston, 1970); Stanley Green, *Encyclopedia of the Musical* (London: Cassell & Company, 1976); Alan Jay Lerner, *The Musical Theatre: A Celebration* (New York: McGraw Hill, 1986); Gerald Mast, *Can't Help Singing: The American Musical on Stage and Screen* (Woodstock, N.Y.: Overlook, 1987).

Muslim Brotherhood   *See* AL-BANNA, HASAN.

Mussolini, Benito (1983–1945)

Italian dictator (1922–45). Born in the village of Predappio in 1883, Mussolini became a political agitator for the Italian Socialist Party by 1904. He was expelled from the party in 1914, however, for supporting World War I. He served in the war until wounded, thereafter editing his radical paper *Popolo d'Italia.* Mussolini founded a paramilitary organization in 1919, which eventually folded into the Fascist Party. His followers took their name from the Italian word *fascio,* from the Latin *fasces,* meaning "group" or "bundle," the emblem of authority of a Roman magistrate.

By 1921, Mussolini was elected to the Italian Parliament. The following year, he directed the Fascist march on Rome to seize power. When the Facta cabinet resigned, King Victor Emmanuel III asked Mussolini to form a new government. He quickly changed electoral law to ensure a Fascist majority, and within a few years, Mussolini had earned the name "Il Duce" (leader), as he had turned Italy into a totalitarian state. By 1925 the country was a full-blown dictatorship; Mussolini suppressed all opposition. When Socialist Giacomo MATTEOTTI challenged Mussolini's power, fascist thugs kidnapped and murdered Matteotti. This scandal almost brought down Mussolini's government, but the dictator survived because the opposition did not act quickly enough.

Mussolini wanted a diplomatic solution to national questions of instability when he negotiated and signed with the Vatican the LATERAN TREATY of 1929, which preserved the right of the Holy See to exist within the boundaries of Italy, ending a 59-year dispute. On December 5, 1934, to avenge the Battle of Adowa, in which Ethiopian troops had defeated Italians in 1896, Mussolini forced a series of border clashes that led to the Italian invasion of Ethiopia on October 2, 1935, and the ETHIOPIAN WAR. Although his action was condemned by the LEAGUE OF NATIONS, the League was powerless to act against the conflict, and by May 1936, Italy had conquered and annexed Ethiopia to Italy. That same year, Mussolini courted further hostility and instability on the European continent when he sent troops to aid General Francisco FRANCO in his civil war against the Spanish government. On July 14, 1938, Mussolini seemed to announce his alignment with Nazi leader Adolf HITLER, when he released the *Manifesto della Razza,* which stated that "Jews do not belong to the Italian Race."

When Germany invaded Poland on September 1, 1939, Italy remained neutral only because of Mussolini's military disorganization; he entered the war on the side of Germany in June 1940. After a series of military defeats including the loss of the African colonies, Mussolini's government was dismissed by the king and Mussolini was arrested. Hitler sent German paratroopers to rescue Mussolini, however, and brought him back to Germany to organize a pro-Fascist puppet regime in northern Italy. In the last days of the war, when the Nazi government was collapsing under Allied and Soviet bombardment, Mussolini attempted to escape to Switzerland. He was seized near Lake Como by Italian Communists; on trial, he was found guilty of crimes against Italy and was executed on April 28, 1945.

References: Richard Collier, *Duce! A Biography of Benito Mussolini* (New York: Viking, 1971); Bernard V. Burke, "Mussolini, Benito" in Bruce W. Jentleson and Thomas G. Paterson, senior eds., *Encyclopedia of U.S. Foreign Relations,* 4 vols. (New York: Oxford University Press, 1997), 3: 184; "Fascist Chief Dictator of Italy; Called by King to Form Cabinet," New York *Herald-Tribune* (European edition), October 30, 1922, p. 1.

Nanking

Chinese city, located on the Yangtze River, site of the infamous Rape of Nanking by invading Japanese troops in 1937. The capital of the Ming Dynasty from 1368 to 1421, the city had previously been invaded by Chinese rebels during the T'aiping Insurrection (1853–64). In 1912 Chinese nationalist Sun Yat-Sen made Nanking the capital of the Chinese Republic; it was also the site of the Nationalist Chinese government (1928–29, 1945–49).

On December 13, 1937, after several months of fighting, the Japanese army took over Nanking and instituted a mass slaughter of the city's residents. Some historians estimate that as many as 300,000 people died; tens of thousands of women were raped, and others were beheaded. In one mass execution, 57,000 people were shot. In 1938, H. J. Timperley, a correspondent for the *Manchester Guardian* newspaper, wrote, "As a consequence of the Sino-Japanese hostilities which began in the summer of 1937, some eighteen million people were forced to flee from their homes in and around Shanghai, Soochow and Wusih, in August, September, October, and during the course of November and December from Hangchow, Chinkiang, Wuhu and Nanking. Camps were established by Chinese and foreigners in the Shanghai International Settlement and French Concession which fed and housed, at their height, some 450,000 destitute Chinese refugees."

Reporter Michael Browning, in observing the 50th anniversary of the event in 1987, wrote, "[It was] an orgy of murder, rape, looting and incendiarism that shocked the world and gave a horrible foretaste of what World War II would be like: a total war, in which innocent civilians and whole urban populations would become legitimate military targets." The siege ended in January 1938, when the Japanese withdrew but retained control of the area. On September 9, 1945, China took back Nanking from the Japanese, and on May 5, 1946, the Nationalists under Chiang Kai-Shek returned the civilian government there for the first time in nearly a decade.

In 1985 the Nanking Memorial Hall was opened to memorialize the countless thousands who died during the reign of terror.

References: Iris Chang, *The Rape of Nanking: The Forgotten Holocaust of World War II* (New York: Basic Books, 1997); H. J. Timperley, comp. and ed., *What War Means: The Japanese Terror in China—A Documentary Record* (London: Victor Gollancz, 1938), 13; Michael Browning, "China's Quiet Anger Builds Over 1937 Rape of Nanking," *Miami Herald,* December 20, 1987, p. 1B.

Nansen, Fridtjof (1861–1930)

Norwegian explorer, peace activist, and Nobel laureate. Born in Fröen, Norway, on October 10, 1861, he studied zoology at the University of Christiana (now Oslo), and in 1882 made a voyage to the Arctic to study animal life there. When he returned, he was hired by the Museum of Natural History at Bergen. In 1897 he became a professor of zoology and oceanography at Oslo University, and in 1901 he was appointed as director of an international laboratory that investigated deep-sea research. In fact, Nansen was on his way to becoming a noted explorer.

He turned to writing in 1893 and became a peace activist. He joined the Interparliamentary Union, which had been founded in 1889, and spent the remainder of his life in the quest for peace. In 1905 he urged the independence of Norway from Sweden, and, after that was accomplished, served as Norway's first minister to Great Britain until 1908. He continued his polar explorations during World War I, and after the war asked the United States to relax its blockade of the Baltic to allow for food shipments. In 1919 he was in Paris to urge the creation of a LEAGUE OF NATIONS; afterward, he was named as president of the Norwegian Union for the League of Nations, serving as Norway's representative to that body.

In 1920 the League asked Nansen to head up a commission to arrange for the repatriation of prisoners of war, some of whom had been held for several years. Using his political power, he helped to repatriate more than 450,000 prisoners in the years that followed his appointment, and brought badly needed food and other matériel into Soviet Russia, which was then suffering from famine. Because of this work, in June 1921 Nansen was asked to head up the League's High Commission for Refugees. He agreed and invented the "Nansen Passport," which was used by countless refugees to find protection and asylum around the world after the war. In 1925 the League asked him to help Armenian refugees who had suffered from a massacre by Turkish forces; Nansen's plan, to move these fifty thousand refugees to an Armenian homeland, was shelved, but they were rescued and sent to Lebanon and Syria. Nansen also called on the League from 1921 on to recognize Germany and seat her as a member.

For his extraordinary work to accomplish peace all over the world, Nansen was awarded the 1922 Nobel Peace Prize. He died in Oslo on December 11, 1938. Mount Fridtjof Nansen, located in Antarctica at the head of the Ross Ice Shelf, was named in his honor.

References: Solveig Olsen, "Nansen, Fridtjof" in Bernard S. and June H. Schlessinger, eds., *The Who's Who of Nobel Prize Winners* (Phoenix, Ariz.: Oryx, 1986), 132; Thomas Watson MacCallum, and Stephen Taylor, eds., *The Nobel Prize-Winners and the Nobel Foundation, 1901–1937* (Zurich: Central European Times Publishing, 1938), 362–63.

Narutowicz, Gabriel (1865–1922)

Polish diplomat and president (1922) of the Second Polish Republic. A scientist, Narutowicz was born into a noble Polish family in Lithuania in 1865, later studying in St. Petersburg and Zurich. In 1906 he was named chair of the Hydro-Engineering Department at the University of Switzerland and operated his own construction business in Zurich. During World War I he worked for humanitarian assistance programs in Zurich for Polish exiles and for Poles trapped in Poland. After the war he returned to Warsaw, where he worked on ways to harness the Vistula River. In 1920 he was named minister of public works, where he served for two years; he was also the chair of the Polish Reconstruction Council to rebuild the nation's infrastructure. In November 1922, he was invited to run for president of Poland as head of the Polish Peasant Party. Elected from a field of five candidates, he was denounced by the political right because most of his support came from the leftist and minority parties. On the day Narutowicz was inaugurated, then chief of state Joseph Pilsudski turned over the reins of power. To the

new Polish president, Pilsudski said, "I served in the army but never stood at attention before anybody. Today I'm standing before you." Two days later, on December 16, 1922, Narutowicz was shot and killed by Polish painter Eligiusz Niewiadomski.

References: George J. Lerski, *Historical Dictionary of Poland, 966–1945* (Westport, Conn.: Greenwood, 1996), 374; "Polish President Murdered. Only a Week in Office," *The Times* (London), December 18, 1922, p. 12; "The Murder of the Polish President," *The Times* (London), December 18, 1922, p. 13; "Army Calms Poles; Plotters Arrested. Many Haller Veterans Are Seized, Following Murder of President Narutowicz," *New York Times*, December 18, 1922, p. 1.

National Association for the Advancement of Colored People (NAACP)

U.S. civil rights organization that worked to improve the social, economic, and legal conditions of African Americans in the interwar period. Founded on February 12, 1909 (the hundredth anniversary of Abraham Lincoln's birthday) in New York City by a group of social and legal activists, including journalist Ida Wells-Barnett and educator W. E. B. DUBOIS, the organization advanced "the call" to renew the struggle for civil and political liberty among black Americans. Early on the group focused on ending discrimination and racial violence, such as lynchings, through legal action. In 1919 they published *Thirty Years of Lynching in the United States, 1899–1918,* to open the public's eyes to the issue and to establish anti-lynching laws. Throughout the 1920s NAACP efforts to increase public exposure and to mobilize public pressure helped to bring an end to excessive violence against black Americans.

Lynching declined in the 1930s, and the NAACP shifted its focus to improving the poor economic conditions for black Americans brought about by the GREAT DEPRESSION. The group lobbied against racial discrimination in NEW DEAL programs, which ultimately led U.S. President Franklin D. ROOSEVELT to create the Fair Employment Practices Committee. The NAACP also successfully blocked the nomination to the U.S. Supreme Court of John Parker, who openly favored discrimination. In the educational realm, NAACP lawyers Charles Houston and Thurgood Marshall in 1935 won the legal battle for a black student to be admitted to the University of Maryland. In 1939, when the Daughters of the American Revolution banned noted African American soprano Marian Anderson from singing in Constitution Hall, the NAACP (in cooperation with First Lady Eleanor ROOSEVELT) moved Anderson's concert to the Lincoln Memorial, where more than 75,000 people attended.

After World War II and throughout the 1950s and 1960s, the NAACP continued through many legal battles to fight discrimination and to end segregation in the armed services, in public schools, in businesses, and in real estate practices. Through grassroots tactics (such as sit-in demonstrations and voter registration drives) as well as through the courts, the NAACP protested injustice and won major battles, ensuring constitutional guarantees to liberty and justice for black Americans. By the early 1970s the nonviolent social revolution of the NAACP and other civil rights advocacy groups had transformed American society. The organization continues in its commitments today.

Reference: Douglas Brinkley, *History of the United States* (New York: Viking, 1998).

National Labor Relations Act

U.S. legislation enacted by Congress, also known as the Wagner Labor Relations Act, on July 5, 1935. Sponsored by Senator Robert F. Wagner of New York, the law affirmed workers' rights to organize and participate in (or refrain from) collective bargaining (that is, through a union). As one of the most important NEW DEAL reforms, the law also forbade employers from interfering with union organizers seeking to enlist workers in their factories and created the NATIONAL LABOR RELATIONS BOARD. The Wagner Act was amended by the Labor Management Relations Act (also called the Taft-Hartley Act) of 1947, and by the Labor Management Reporting and Disclosure (or Landrum-Griffin Act) of 1959.

National Labor Relations Board

U.S. government committee, established by the National Labor Relations Act (NLRA) of 1935. The U.S. Congress enacted the NLRA to have a government entity to negotiate relations between business and labor. The board was charged with supervising factory elections to determine whether workers wanted union representation. The board also could investigate employers and mediate disputes between labor and management. The creation of the board permanently changed employer-worker relations. In five cases decided in 1937 the U.S. Supreme Court upheld the rulings of the board: these were *NATIONAL LABOR RELATIONS BOARD V. JONES & LAUGHLIN STEEL CORPORATION*, *National Labor Relations Board v. Freuhauf Trailer Company*, *National Labor Relations Board v. Friedman-Harry Marks Clothing Company*, *Associated Press Co. v. National Labor Relations Board*, and *Washington, Virginia & Maryland Coach Co. v. National Labor Relations Board*. The modern regulations of the NLRB can be found at volume 29 of the Code of Federal Regulations. Refer also to the entry on an important Wagner Act case: *NATIONAL LABOR RELATIONS BOARD V. JONES & LAUGHLIN STEEL CORPORATION*.

References: Paul L. Murphy, "Taft-Hartley Labor Relations Act" in Leonard W. Levy, ed. in chief, *Encyclopedia of the*

American Constitution (New York: Macmillan, 1986–92), 4: 1855.

National Labor Relations Board v. Jones & Laughlin Steel Corporation

Landmark U.S. Supreme Court decision, which held that the act that had established the National Labor Relations Board in 1935 was indeed constitutional, and that the government had a right to end what it considered to be unfair labor practices. Under the NATIONAL LABOR RELATIONS ACT, Congress had established the "right of employees to self-organization and to bargain collectively through representatives of their own choosing." The Jones & Laughlin Steel Corporation of Pittsburgh, Pennsylvania, was sued by Beaver Valley Lodge No. 200, which was affiliated with the Amalgamated Association of Iron, Steel and Tin Workers of America, for firing 10 workers who had attempted to organize the workers at the company into a union. The NATIONAL LABOR RELATIONS BOARD then ordered the company to cease and desist from coercing the workers. The company refused to comply, and the board asked a Circuit Court of Appeals to order the company to stop; that court ruled that such as order was "out of the range of federal power." The union then sued to the U.S. Supreme Court, which granted a hearing of arguments on February 10 and 11, 1937. On April 12 of that same year, the court handed down its decision.

Holding for a unanimous court, Chief Justice Charles Evans HUGHES found that the NLRA was constitutional, and that the board had the right to order a company to stop harassing workers who were organizing a labor union. After discussing the act itself, and explaining how the court found it and the board to be constitutional, the chief justice simply wrote, "Our conclusion is that the order of the Board was within its competency and that the act is valid as here applied. The judgment of the Circuit Court of Appeals is reversed and the cause is remanded for further proceedings in conformity with this opinion. It is so ordered." The decision was a major one; it marked the first time that a major piece of NEW DEAL legislation had been found to pass constitutional muster by the Court. That same day, in several other cases, the Court also found the NLRB to be constitutional.

References: Richard C. Cortner, *The Jones & Laughlin Case* (New York: Alfred A. Knopf, 1970); Paul R. Benson, Jr. *The Supreme Court and the Commerce Clause, 1937–1970* (New York: Dunellan, 1970); text of decision at 301 U.S. 1.

National Recovery Administration (NRA)

U.S. administration agency, established as part of President Franklin D. ROOSEVELT'S NEW DEAL of government programs that sought to stimulate industrial recovery and foster greater employment during the GREAT DEPRESSION. On June 16, 1933, Congress enacted the National Industrial Recovery Act, which established the NRA to fight the depression by shortening the hours of labor to lessen unemployment, increase wages for workers, and eliminate price cutting and unfair business practices. Much of the power to do these specific things were enclosed in Section 3 of Title I of the act, which was soon challenged by several U.S. companies. In signing the legislation, Roosevelt said, "The law I have just signed was passed to put people back to work, to let them buy more of the products of farms and factories and start our business at a living rate again. This task is in two stages; first, to get many hundreds of thousands of the unemployed back on the payroll by snowfall and, second, to plan for a better future for the longer pull. While we shall not neglect the second, the first stage is an emergency job. It has the right of way . . . The second part of the Act gives employment through a vast program of public works. Our studies show that we should be able to hire many men at once and to step up to about a million new jobs by October 1st and a much greater number later. We must put at the head of our list those works which are fully ready to start now. Our first purpose is to create employment as fast as we can, but we should not pour money into unproved projects."

Soon after the act was signed into law, Roosevelt named Brigadier General High S. Johnson as head of the agency. Under Johnson, the NRA established more than five hundred industrial fair practice codes, to encourage "fair competition," the abolition of child labor, and increased wages. Johnson resigned on September 24, 1934, and he was replaced by what Roosevelt called the National Industrial Recovery Board.

A May 27, 1935, U.S. Supreme Court decision invalidated many of these codes, however. In *A.L.A. SCHECHTER POULTRY CORPORATION V. UNITED STATES,* the Court held that the act that had created the NRA violated the Constitution through the use of compulsory fair practice labor codes. Chief Justice Charles Evans HUGHES commented in the case that "the attempted delegation of legislative power and the attempted regulation of intrastate transactions which affect interstate commerce only indirectly . . . we hold the code provisions . . . to be invalid." Thus, with its internal "backbone" struck down, the NRA was in effect a toothless horse; on January 1, 1936, it ceased to exist as a government entity.

References: David Gordon, "National Industrial Recovery Act" in Leonard W. Levy, ed. in chief, *Encyclopedia of the American Constitution* (New York: Macmillan, 1986–92), 3: 1293–94; Vincent Murray Brown, "Contemporary Appraisal: The National Industrial Recovery Program," (Ph.D. dissertation, Georgetown University, 1954).

National Socialism   *See* NAZI PARTY.

Nazi Party

Political party led by German dictator Adolf HITLER, founder of National Socialism, or Nazism. Embittered after his service in World War I, Hitler blamed Germany's defeat in that war on the Jews and the marxists. He then joined with other nationalists (among them Josef GOEBBELS, Hermann Goering, and Heinrich HIMMLER) and formed the National Socialist German Workers' Party in 1920. In 1923, Hitler attempted to overthrow Bavaria's WEIMAR government in an action known as the BEER HALL PUTSCH, and to thereby establish a dictatorship. President of the republic Friedrich EBERT put down the revolt and Hitler was imprisoned for nine months, during which he wrote his treatise MEIN KAMPF. The work—filled with ANTI-SEMITISM and disdain for morality—outlined Hitler's strategy for ultimate world domination. Soon it became the Nazi Party's bible. Among the party's principles were the superiority of an Aryan "master race," led by an infallible Führer; the establishment of a pan-Germanic Third Reich; and the extermination of those whom Hitler considered to be Germany's enemies—the Jews and the Communists.

The Nazi movement grew slowly until 1929, when the difficulties of economic depression in Germany brought mass support for Hitler's ideas. With his keen understanding of mass psychology and through his powerful oration of hate and nationalism, anti-Semitism, and anticommunism, Hitler's Nazi Party soon won the support of the workers, the bankers, and the industrialists alike. With Hitler's rise to power as the chancellor in 1933, the Nazi Party crushed all opposition in the Reichstag and enacted anti-Semitism into law. As the party enforced its policies, millions of Jews, Poles, Russians, and others were interned in concentration camps and later killed. The terror of the Nazi rule ended in defeat during World War II.

References: James D. Forman, *Nazism* (New York: F. Watts, 1978); Charles Freeman, *The Rise of the Nazis* (Austin, Tex.: Raintree Steck-Vaughn, 1998).

Nehru, Jawaharlal   (1889–1964)

Indian nationalist leader, general secretary and president of the Indian National Congress (1927–29), president of the Indian Congress (1937). Born in Allahabad, India, on November 14, 1889, the son of Indian nationalist leader Motilal Nehru, he was named Jawaharlal ("red jewel"). His father and mother were Brahmins, the highest caste in India; as such, Nehru and his two sisters were taught by English tutors in what was then British-ruled India. In 1905, Nehru was enrolled in the prestigious English school Harrow; he later attended Trinity College at Cambridge University, and then studied the law in London, after which he was admitted to the English bar. By this time, however Nehru was an Indian nationalist who desired independence for his homeland.

Supporters greet Jawaharlal Nehru with flowers on his arrival in London, 1935. *(CORBIS/Hultch Deutsch Collection)*

In 1912 he returned to India, where at first he practiced law. During a 1916 session of the Congress Party in Lucknow, which Nehru attended, he met and became friends with Mohandas K. GANDHI. A devout Hindu, Gandhi believed that violent resistance to British rule was wrong and felt that *swaraj* ("freedom") must be attained by peaceful means only. Following the JALIANWALLA BAGH MASSACRE in Amritsar in April 1919, in which several hundred Indians were shot by British troops, Nehru and his father joined Gandhi's movement to end British rule. Because of his caste, however, Nehru had never really "seen" the poverty of India. Joining the movement, he traveled the country and saw the plight of his fellow Indians. He wrote of a visit to a settlement on the banks of the Jumna River in his hometown of Allahabad, "That visit was a revelation to me. . . . Looking at them and their misery and overflowing gratitude, I was filled with shame and sorrow, shame at my own easy-going and comfortable way of life and our petty politics of the city which ignored this vast multitude of seminaked sons and daughters of India, sorrow at the degradation and overwhelming poverty of India. A new picture of India seemed to rise before me: naked, starving, crushed and utterly miserable. And their faith in us, casual

visitors from the distant city, embarrassed me and filled me with a new responsibility that frightened me." In December 1921, Nehru was arrested for calling for strikes against the British government; he served three months in prison.

In 1925 Nehru traveled to Europe with his wife, who had become ill with tuberculosis. At this time, he saw India not just as a free and independent nation, but as one nation among all others. He visited Moscow and sympathized with the Bolshevik revolution there, which he felt would make a good model for freedom in his own land. On returning to Indian in 1927, he indoctrinated this radicalism in his speeches, a revolutionary rhetoric that was dismissed by Gandhi and other party leaders. Nehru and Gandhi remained friends, however, even during these periods of disagreement. In 1929, Gandhi endorsed Nehru to lead the Indian National Congress. Both Gandhi and Nehru were jailed repeatedly during the 1930s for practicing civil disobedience against the British authorities.

Nehru continued to study socialism and apply his teachings to India. When World War II broke out, he was jailed for speaking against Britain's war declaration against Germany. In 1942 he presided over a meeting of the All-India Congress that declared that the British should pull out of India immediately. Gandhi and Nehru were both arrested, and Nehru was not released until June 1945. In 1946 the British viceroy of India asked Nehru to form a government under a home-rule doctrine. Finally, in July 1947, the British Parliament enacted the Indian Independence Act and, on August 15, 1947, India passed from a colony to a free nation. The 57-year-old Nehru was named as the nation's first prime minister. Serving for 17 years, Nehru battled such issues as the partition of northern India into the Islamic state of Pakistan, and border skirmishes with China that exploded into a short conflict in 1962. He died on May 27, 1964. Nehru's daughter, Indira Gandhi, and one of his grandsons, Rajiv, later served as prime minister.

References: Frank Moraes, *Jawaharlal Nehru: A Biography* (New York: Macmillan, 1956); Bal Nanda, *The Nehrus: Motilal and Jawaharlal* (New York: John Day, 1963); Michael Edwardes, *Nehru: A Pictorial Biography* (New York: Viking, 1962); Jawaharlal Nehru, *Toward Freedom: The Autobiography of Jawaharlal Nehru* (New York: John Day, 1941); "Nehru Dead at 74; Led India 17 Years," *New York Times,* May 27, 1964, pp. 1, 15.

Nernst, Walther Hermann   (1864–1941)

German chemist and Nobel laureate. Born in Briesen, Germany, on June 25, 1864, Nernst was educated in Switzerland, Austria, and Germany. In 1890 he was named professor of physical chemistry at Göttingen. Fourteen years later, he was named to the same chair at the University of Berlin, where he served until 1933. In 1925, he was appointed at that school's Institute for Physics.

During his life, Nernst worked on thermochemistry and the "theory of galvanic cells," for which he was awarded the 1920 Nobel Prize in chemistry.

Nernst died in Berlin on November 18, 1941. His works, which were famed in the late 19th century and in the first half of the 20th, include *Theoretical Chemistry from the Standpoint of Avogadro's Rule and Thermodynamics* (1891), and *Die theoretischen und experimentellen Grundlagen des neuen Wärmesatzes* (1918), which was released in English as *The New Heat Theorem* (1926).

References: Lisa Kammerlocher, "Nernst, Walther Hermann" in Bernard S. and June H. Schlessinger, eds., *The Who's Who of Nobel Prize Winners* (Phoenix, Ariz.: Oryx, 1986), 8–9; Thomas Watson MacCallum and Stephen Taylor, eds., *The Nobel Prize–Winners and the Nobel Foundation, 1901–1937* (Zurich: Central European Times Publishing, 1938), 141–42.

Neuilly, Treaty of

Pact, 1919, between the victorious Allied Powers (the United States, England, France, Japan, and Italy) and Bulgaria, ending that nation's participation with Germany during World War I. Signed on November 27, 1919, in the French village of Neuilly-sur-Seine, the agreement fixed the borders of Bulgaria with its neighbors, namely the Serb-Croat-Slovene State (which in 1929 became Yugoslavia), with Greece, with Romania, and to the Black Sea.

Historian John Ashley Soames Grenville writes of this pact, "By the armistice terms [of Neuilly], Bulgaria had to withdraw its troops to the pre-war frontier. The territorial terms required Bulgaria to return the southern Dobruja to Romania regardless of ethnic considerations; and to cede to Yugoslavia most of the four small regions occupied by Serbia in 1918. To the Allies, Bulgaria had to cede nearly the whole of western Thrace, thus losing Bulgaria's Aegean littoral [coast]; the Allies transferred this territory to Greece by treaty on August 10, 1920, and at the same time a treaty was signed with Turkey [for references to this particular pact, see SÈVRES, TREATY of]. REPARATIONS were required and the Bulgarian army was limited to 33,000 professionals."

References: Edmund Jan Osmańczyk, *The Encyclopedia of the United Nations and International Agreements* (Philadelphia: Taylor & Francis, 1985), 542; John Ashley Soames Grenville, *The Major International Treaties, 1914–1973: A History and Guide with Texts* (New York: Stein & Day, 1975), 47.

Neutrality Acts of 1935, 1936, and 1937

Series of three sets of U.S. congressional legislation designed to keep America out of Europe between 1935 and the outbreak of World War II.

The first legislation, enacted August 31, 1935, was passed after Italy invaded Ethiopia. By 1935, Republican Senator Gerald Nye of North Dakota was investigating the national munitions industry. Nervous about the routes the Nye Committee was taking, President Franklin ROOSEVELT asked Nye on March 19, 1935, to draft neutrality legislation. Nye's bill, which went through hearings in the Senate Foreign Relations Committee, headed by Democratic Senator Key PITTMAN of Nevada, contained what historian Justus Doenecke called "a mandatory arms embargo, but gave the president the power to define 'implements of war' and to say when the embargo should go into effect." On August 31, 1935, Roosevelt signed the measure, but it was in effect a toothless tiger because of the provisions that allowed the president to skate around the enactment's meaning. It led to the passage of the NEUTRALITY ACT OF 1936.

Enacted February 29, 1936, the second neutrality act extended the first by an additional 14 months past the original period established. Introduced by Senator Elbert D. Thomas, Democrat of Utah, it extended a ban on loans to belligerents, made it mandatory for the president to embargo arms to those belligerent nations, and added travel restrictions on U.S. citizens. It is the least known of the three neutrality acts. The third neutrality act, passed during the Spanish civil war, was enacted May 1, 1937. It "prohibit[ed] . . . the export of arms, ammunition, and implements of war to belligerent countries" and reinforced the second act.

The impetus for the passage of these neutrality acts was the general isolationism of the United States at this time, based on a widespread feeling that the country should stay out of European affairs and regret that the country had fought in World War I.

References: Manfred Jonas, "Neutrality Acts of the 1930s" in Bruce W. Jentleson and Thomas G. Peterson, senior eds., *Encyclopedia of U.S. Foreign Relations* (New York: Oxford University Press, 1997) 3: 231–33; United States Congress, Senate Committee on Foreign Relations, "Neutrality: Act of 1937. Hearings before the Committee on Foreign Relations, U.S. Senate, Seventy-fifth Congress, first session, Relative to Proposed Legislation on Neutrality, February 13, 1937" (Washington, D.C.: U.S. Government Printing Office, 1937); text of act at 50 Stat. 121 et seq.

New Deal

National U.S. economic policy, 1935–45, enunciated by President Franklin D. ROOSEVELT to combat the effects of the GREAT DEPRESSION. The name of this expansive program came from a line in Roosevelt's acceptance speech before the Democratic National convention. Appearing before the convention's delegates (the first time a nominated candidate showed up at a nominating convention), Roosevelt said, "I pledge you—I pledge myself—to a new deal for the American people. This is more than a political campaign; it is a call to arms."

After taking office in March 1933, Roosevelt set to work establishing a series of programs through congressional action or presidential initiative. His first hundred days in office were marked by a series of enactments, including government control over industrial and agricultural planning, labor relations, employment, banking, and other relief measures. Many of these domestic achievements were achieved through the creation of such ALPHABET AGENCIES as the Agricultural Adjustment Administration (AAA), the CIVILIAN CONSERVATION CORPS, the Civil Works Administration, the NATIONAL RECOVERY ADMINISTRATION (NRA), and the Public Works Administration, which created a substantial federal works program. In 1936 the new relief program called the WORKS PROGRESS ADMINISTRATION was created, which created hundreds of thousands of jobs for the unemployed. The last major achievement of Roosevelt's New deal administration was the passage of the 1938 FAIR LABOR STANDARDS ACT.

Although these measures were popular and created broad support for Roosevelt, for many years conditions did not improve. Although the GNP increased from $56 billion in 1933 to $72 billion in 1935, by 1936 there were still more than seven million unemployed. In addition, from 1935 to 1937 the U.S. Supreme Court struck down several New Deal acts as unconstitutional, including the AAA and the NRA. Historians believe that although Roosevelt's New Deal program alleviated the worst conditions of the depression, it was not until the country built up its industrial base to fight World War II that the depression itself ended.

References: Arthur Meier Schlesinger, *The Coming of the New Deal* (Boston: Houghton Mifflin, 1959); Joseph P. Lash, *Dealers and Dreamers: A New Look at the New Deal* (Garden City, N.Y.: Doubleday, 1988); Otis L. Graham, Jr., and Meghan Robinson Wander, eds., *Franklin D. Roosevelt: His Life and Times: An Encyclopedic View* (Boston: G. K. Hall, 1985), 285–88.

New Economic Policy

National Soviet economic plan, enacted in 1921 after the imposition of so-called "War Communism." For four years after the Bolsheviks took power in Russia, civil war and famine served to bring an already precarious economic situation almost to the point of collapse. To placate the farm-

---

SUPREME COURT DECISIONS THAT UPHELD OR STRUCK DOWN NEW DEAL LEGISLATION, 1935–1937

CASE	VOTE	BASIS FOR DECISION
Panama Refining Co. v. Ryan	8-1	Invalidated Section 9(c) of the National Industrial Recovery Act
Schechter Poultry Corporation v. U.S.	9-0	Invalidated the National Industrial Recovery Act's "unfair trade" provisions
Louisville Joint Stock Land Bank v. Redford	9-0	Struck down the Frazier- Lemke Act of 1934
Humphrey's Executor v. U.S.	9-0	Held that the President did not have the power to remove an officer not working in the Executive Branch
United States v. Butler et al	6-3	Struck down the Agricultural Adjustment Act of 1993
Ashwander v. T.V.A.	8-1	Upheld the Tennessee Valley Authority Act of 1933
Carter v. Carter Coal Co.	6-3	Struck down the Guffey-Snyder Bituminous Coal Stabilization Act of 1935
Wright v. Vinton Branch of Mountain Trust	9-0	Upheld the new Frazier-Lemke Mortgage Act of 1935
National Labor Relations Act Cases[1]	5-4	Upheld the National Labor Relations Act of 1935
Social Security Cases		
Helvering v. Davis	7-2	Upheld the Social Security
Carmichael v. Southern Coal & Coke Co.	5-4	Act of 1935

[1] These were *National Labor Relations Board v. Jones & Laughlin Steel Corporation* (301 U.S. 1), *National Labor Relations Board v. Freuhauf Trailer Company* (301 U.S. 49), *National Labor Relations Board v. Friedman-Harry Marks Clothing Company* (301 U.S. 58), *Associated Press Co. v. National Labor Relations Board* (301 U.S. 103), and *Washington, Virginia & Maryland Coach Co. v. National Labor Relations Board* (301 U.S. 142).

Sources: James Stuart Olson, *Historical Dictionary of the New Deal: From Inauguration to Preparation for War* (Westport, Conn.: Greenwood, 1985); Otis L. Graham, Jr. and Meghan Robinson Wander, eds., *Franklin D. Roosevelt: His Life and Times: An Encyclopedic View* (Boston: G. K. Hall, 1985), 410.

ers and peasants, who were on the point of backing another revolution, Lenin instituted a plan called the New Economic Policy. In this scheme, farmers were taxed only on the surplus of what they produced, at a graduated rate; thus, the more a farmer grew, the more he would pay, but this also would allow the farmer to sell his surplus for a profit. This injection of capitalism served to save the Soviet Union from another possible revolution in the early 1920s.

By 1926 the Soviet Union had regained most of its pre–World War I levels of industry, and two years later the government instituted the first FIVE-YEAR PLAN.

References: Paul R. Gregory and Robert C. Stuart, *Soviet Economic Structure and Performance* (HarperCollins Publishers, 1990), 58–76; Lionel Kochan and Richard Abraham, *The Making of Modern Russia* (New York: Penguin Books, 1983), 339.

New Woman/Women

U.S. concept, referring to the educated and self-supporting (often unmarried) American women of the 1920s. This second generation of "new women," many of whom were raised by women with similar ideas and ideals in the 1880s and educated in the 1890s, helped revolutionize U.S. women's notions of themselves. Seeing broadened opportunities after World War I, these women had careers, for the first time stepping into the public's eye in large numbers, leaving the traditional domestic role of homemaker and mother behind. They were leaders of social, political, and educational reform movements; they were journalists, nurses, and writers. Settlement house advocate Jane ADDAMS, poet Gertrude STEIN, and anthropologist and novelist Zora Neale HURSTON exemplify such women.

References: Carroll Smith-Rosenberg, "The New Woman," in *The Reader's Companion to U.S. Women's History,* ed. Wilma Mankiller, Gwendolyn Mink, Marysa Navarro, Barbara Smith, and Gloria Steinem (Boston: Houghton Mifflin, 1998), 430.

Nicaragua, U.S. Occupation of

Period of occupation of Nicaragua by the U.S. Marines as the "protector" of American interests in that country during internal political strife. The roots of the conflict between the Liberal and Conservative Party factions goes back to the early 1800s, and led to numerous flare-ups in the years leading up to the 20th century. In 1912, to defend American interests, both economic and political, in Nicaragua, President William Howard Taft ordered U.S. Marines there. As many as 2,700 Marines were involved and they remained until 1925.

When the Marines departed, they had established a nonpartisan government, as well as a constabulary, to pave the way for normal internal relations between the two warring factions. However, soon after the troops departed, the Conservatives seized power, and, in 1926, the Liberals started a civil war to fight them. To again bring stability there, in January 1927 President Calvin Coolidge ordered Marines to again occupy Nicaragua, and by the following month there were 5,400 Marines in that country. The United States provided economic and military aid to the Conservatives, but did not openly take part in the hostilities. In May 1927 the Liberals settled, after Coolidge threatened that the Americans would side in the field with the Conservatives if there was not a settlement. Starting in July 1927, Augusto Sandino, a Liberal rebel leader, led a band of armed guerrillas (known as Sandinistas) to oppose the American occupation. He rallied his forces with speeches about the unacceptable domination of his country by external forces. On July 16, 1927, he and his band attacked the Marine garrison at Ocotal. The United States used air power for the first time in Central America, and Sandino suffered heavy losses (about 300 of his 400 men), while one American marine was killed. Sandino took to the hills but used hit-and-run attacks to fight over the next few years. In 1931, the Nicaraguan National Guard, trained by the American troops, replaced the Marines, and, after the United States supervised the 1932 elections, which led to inauguration of Liberal President Juan Sacasa, the Marines departed in January 1933. Sandino met with Sacasa and agreed to end the insurrection. However, Anastasio Somoza, Sacasa's nephew and appointed head of the Nicaraguan National Guard, saw Sandino as a continuing threat and ordered his troops to kill the rebel. In February 1934, Sandino was hunted down and murdered. In 1978, when leftist troops fought against the government of Somoza's son, Anastasio Somoza Debayle, they adopted the name "Sandinistas."

References: John A. Booth, *The End and the Beginning: The Nicaraguan Revolution* (Boulder, Colo.: Westview, 1982), 31; William S. Brooks, "Bombing Liberals in Nicaraguan War," *New York Times,* May 29, 1927, 10; "800 Marines Board Ships for Nicaragua," *New York Times,* May 12, 1927, 29; Neill Macaulay, *The Sandino Affair* (Durham, N.C.: Duke University Press, 1985), 33; Bernard C. Nalty, *The United States Marines in Nicaragua* (Washington: Government Printing Office, 1962), 14; Bernard Diederich, *Somoza: The Legacy of U.S. Involvement in Central America* (New York: E. P. Dutton, 1981).

Nicolle, Charles-Jean-Henri (1866–1936)

French bacteriologist and Nobel laureate. The son of Eugène Nicolle, he was born in Rouen, France, on September 21, 1886, and received his M.D. degree from the Rouen School of Medicine, where he worked from 1895 to 1903. In 1903 he became the director of the Pasteur Institute, a post he hold until his death in 1936. During this period Nicolle worked on the properties of typhus, and how a serum derived from patients who suffered from it could be used as a treatment for those who did not. He also applied this idea to measles and undulant fever. For this groundbreaking work, Nicolle was awarded the 1928 Nobel Prize in medicine and physiology. "When the Great War broke out and many Russian and Serbian prisoners were interned in German and Austrian prison camps, typhus, which until then had hardly attracted the attention of European doctors at all, was not long in making an appearance," explained Professor F. Henschen, a member of the Staff of Professors of the Royal Caroline Institute, in presenting the Nobel to Nicolle. "In spite of the precautions ordinarily taken against epidemics, it was quickly transmitted from one man to another, from home to home, regardless of age and in defiance of all the laws of epidemiology. The armies were threatened with a veritable catastrophe. The epidemic broke out in the same way amongst the civilian population in regions of the eastern front devastated by war. The Balkan Peninsula was affected badly, but the disease spared no part along the whole front, from Finland to Mesopotamia. The value of Nicolle's discovery was once again made apparent. The Great War provided the opportunity for a clinico-experimental application of Nicolle's work on a large scale."

Nicolle died on February 28, 1936.

References: Rashelle Karp, "Nicolle, Charles Jules Henri" in Bernard S. and June H. Schlessinger, eds., *The Who's Who of Nobel Prize Winners* (Phoenix, Ariz.: Oryx, 1986), 86; Thomas Watson MacCallum and Stephen Taylor, eds., *The Nobel Prize-Winners and the Nobel Foundation, 1901–1937* (Zurich: Central European Times Publishing, 1938), 215–16.

Night of Long Knives   *See* ROEHM, ERNST.

Nine-Power Treaty

Pact, February 6, 1922, signed at the WASHINGTON NAVAL CONFERENCE, which served to preserve certain interests in China while removing Japanese troops from SHANTUNG. Signed alongside the FOUR POWER TREATY at the Washington Conference for the Limitation of Armaments, the treaty, officially entitled "Treaty Between the United of States of America, Belgium, the British Empire, China, France, Italy, Japan, the Netherlands, and Portugal. Signed at Washington February 6, 1922," pledged: "(1) To respect the sovereignty, the independence, and the territorial and administrative integrity of China; (2) To provide the fullest and most unembarrassed opportunity to China to develop and maintain for herself an effective and stable government; (3) To use their influence for the purpose of effectually establishing and maintaining the principle of equal opportunity for the commerce and industry of all nations throughout the territory of China; (4) To refrain from tak-

ing advantage of conditions in China in order to seek special rights or privileges which would abridge the rights of subjects or citizens of friendly States, (5) and from countenancing action inimical to the security of such States."

As part of the agreement, Japan agreed to remove its troops from the Chinese province of Shantung. Soon after passage of the pact, these troops were removed.

References: Emily O. Goldman, "Washington Conference on the Limitation of Armaments" in Bruce W. Jentleson and Thomas G. Paterson, senior eds., *Encyclopedia of U.S. Foreign Relations* (New York: Oxford University Press, 1997), 4: 311, "Powers Adopt Treaties to Cut Navies and Restrict Use of Submarines and Gas; Shantung Accord Hailed; 'Absolutely Ends' the Naval Race, Asserts Hughes," *The World* (New York), February 2, 1922, p. 1; "President to Close Conference After Signing of Treaties Today; Pacts to be Hurried to Senate," *Washington Post,* February 6, 1922, p. 1.

Nineteenth Amendment

Amendment to the Constitution of the United States, adopted in 1920, that guaranteed American women the right to vote. Although an amendment was first introduced in the U.S. Congress in 1878, it took decades of struggle, agitation, and protest among supporters of woman suffrage before final victory was attained. Beginning in the mid-19th century, suffragists lectured, wrote, marched, lobbied, practiced civil disobedience, and even staged hunger strikes to achieve what many Americans considered a radical change of the Constitution.

Suffragists pursued various strategies: some sought to pass suffrage acts in each state (by 1912 nine western states had adopted woman suffrage legislation); others challenged male-only voting laws in the courts. Political reformers Alice Paul and Lucy Burns founded the Congressional Union in 1913, which later became the National Woman's Party, to organize would-be women voters in large numbers. By 1916 suffrage organizations were united behind the goal of creating and pushing forward a constitutional amendment. U.S. president Woodrow WILSON announced his support in 1918 for such an amendment, and the political balance shifted in favor of the idea. When Tennessee became the 36th state to ratify the amendment on August 18, 1920, the amendment had achieved the agreement of three-fourths of the states. Secretary of State Bainbridge Colby certified the ratification on August 26, 1920, changing the face of the American electorate forever.

Reference: Ellen Carol DuBois, "Suffrage Movement," in *The Reader's Companion to U.S. Women's History,* ed. Wilma Mankiller, Gwendolyn Mink, Marysa Navarro, Barbara Smith, and Gloria Steinem (Boston: Houghton Mifflin, 1998), 577–81.

Nobel Prize

The Nobel Foundation, established in 1900 under the terms of Swedish inventor Alfred Bernhard Nobel's 1895 will, grants annual prizes "to those who, during the preceding year, have conferred the greatest benefit to mankind" in the fields of physics, chemistry, physiology or medicine, literature, peace, and economics. The prize-awarding institutions are the Royal Swedish Academy of Sciences, the Nobel Assembly at the Karolinska Institute, the Swedish Academy, the Norwegian Nobel Committee, and the Bank of Sweden.

The lists that follow name the Nobel laureates in the various categories during the interwar period, along with the nations they represented when the prize was awarded. See under the laureates' names for details of their achievements.

PHYSICS

1919 Johannes Stark, Germany
1920 Charles E. Guillaume, France
1921 Albert Einstein, United States
1922 Francis W. Aston, Great Britain
      Niels Bohr, Denmark
1923 Robert A. Millikan, United States
1924 Karl M.G. Siegbahn, Sweden
1925 James Franck, Germany
      Gustav Hertz, Germany
1926 Jean B. Perrin, France
1927 Arthur H. Compton, United States
      Charles T. R. Wilson, Great Britain
1928 Owen W. Richardson, Great Britain
1929 Louis-Victor de Broglie, France
1930 Chandrasekhara V. Raman, India
1931 No Prize
1932 Werner Heisenberg, Germany
1933 Paul A.M. Dirac, Great Britain
      Erwin Schrödinger, Austria
1934 No Prize
1935 Sir James Chadwick, Great Britain
1936 Carl D. Anderson, United States
      Victor F. Hess, Austria
1937 Clinton J. Davisson, United States
      George P. Thomson, Great Britain
1938 Enrico Fermi, United States
1939 Ernest O. Lawrence, United States

CHEMISTRY

1919 No Prize
1920 Walther H. Nernst, Germany
1921 Frederick Soddy, Great Britain
1922 No Prize
1923 Fritz Pregl, Austria
1924 No Prize
1925 Richard A. Zsigmondy, Germany
1926 Theodor Suedberg, Sweden
1927 Heinrich O. Wieland, Germany
1928 Adolf O. R. Windaus, Germany
1929 Arthur Harden, Great Britain
      Hans von Euler-Chelpin, Sweden
1930 Hans Fischer, Germany
1931 Friedrich Bergius, Germany
      Carl Bosch, Germany
1932 Irving Langmuir, United States
1933 No Prize
1934 Harold C. Urey, United States
1935 Frédéric Joliot-Curie, France
      Irène Joliot-Curie, France
1936 Peter J.W. Debye, Netherlands
1937 Walter N. Haworth, Great Britain
      Paul Karrer, Switzerland
1938 Richard Kuhn, Germany
1939 Adolf F.J. Butenandt, Germany
      Leopold Ruzicka, Switzerland

MEDICINE AND PHYSIOLOGY

1919 Jules Bordet, Belgium
1920 August Krogh, Denmark
1921 No Prize
1922 Archibald V. Hill, Great Britain
      Otto F. Meyerhof, Germany
1923 Frederick G. Banting, Canada
      John J.R. Macleod, Scotland
1924 Willem Einthoven, Netherlands
1925 No Prize
1926 Johannes A. G. Fibiger, Denmark
1927 Julius Wagner von Jauregg, Austria
1928 Charles J.H. Nicolle, France
1929 Christiaan Eijkman, Netherlands
      Frederick G. Hopkins, Great Britain
1930 Karl Landsteiner, United States
1931 Otto H. Warburg, Germany
1932 Edgar D. Adrian, Great Britain
      Charles S. Sherrington, Great Britain
1933 Thomas H. Morgan, United States
1934 George R. Minot, United States
      William P. Murphy, United States
      George H. Whipple, United States
1935 Hans Spemann, Germany
1936 Henry H. Dale, Great Britain
      Otto Loewi, United States
1937 Albert von Nagyrapolt Szent-Györgyi, United States
1938 Corneille J. F. Heymans, Belgium
1939 Gerhard Domagk, Germany

LITERATURE

1919	Carl F. G. Spitteler, Switzerland
1920	Knut Hamsun, Norway
1921	Anatole France, France
1922	Jacinto Benevente, Spain
1923	William Butler Yeats, Ireland
1924	Wladyslaw S. Reymont, Poland
1925	George Bernard Shaw, Great Britain
1926	Grazia Deledda, Italy
1927	Henri-Louis Bergson, France
1928	Sigrid Undset, Norway
1929	Thomas Mann, Germany
1930	Sinclair Lewis, United States
1931	Erik A. Karlfeldt, Sweden
1932	John Galsworthy, Great Britain
1933	Ivan A. Bunin, France
1934	Luigi Pirandello, Italy
1935	No Prize
1936	Eugene O'Neill, United States
1937	Roger Martin du Gard, France
1938	Pearl S. Buck, United States
1939	Frans E. Sillanpää, Finland

Peace

1919	Woodrow Wilson, United States
1920	Léon-Victor Auguste Bourgeois, France
1921	Karl H. Branting, Sweden
	Christian Lange, Norway
1922	Fridtjof Nansen, Norway
1923	No Prize
1924	No Prize
1925	Joseph Austen Chamberlain, Great Britain
	Charles G. Dawes, United States
1926	Aristide Briand, France
	Gustav Stresemann, Germany

1927	Ferdinand-Édouard Buisson, France
	Ludwig Quidde, Germany
1928	No Prize
1929	Frank B. Kellogg, United States
1930	Nathan Söderblom, Sweden
1931	Jane Addams, United States
	Nicholas Murray Butler, United States
1932	No Prize
1933	Sir Norman Angell, Great Britain
1934	Arthur Henderson, Great Britain
1935	Carl von Ossietsky, Germany
1936	Carlos de Saavedra Lamas, Argentina
1937	Robert Cecil, Great Britain
1938	Nansen, Fridtjof
1939	No Prize

Nye, Gerald Prentice   *See* Neutrality Acts of 1935, 1936, and 1937.

Nyon Agreement

Understanding, 1937, which attempted to end attacks by Spanish submarines against merchant vessels not belonging to either side during the SPANISH CIVIL WAR. Signed in the village of Nyon, France, by the so-called Nine Powers (Bulgaria, Egypt, France, Great Britain, Greece, Romania, Turkey, the USSR, and Yugoslavia), the pact held that "any submarine which attacks such a ship shall be counterattacked and, if possible, destroyed." A supplemental agreement was signed in Geneva on September 17, 1937.

References: Text of "The Nyon Agreement" in Dietrich Schindler and Jiøi Toman, eds., *The Laws of Armed Conflicts: A Collection of Conventions, Resolutions and Other Documents* (Geneva: Sijthoff & Noordhoff, 1981), 799–802; Edmund Jan Osmañczyk, *The Encyclopedia of the United Nations and International Agreements* (Philadelphia: Taylor & Francis, 1985), 576.

O

Obregón, Alvaro (1880–1928)

Mexican general, politician, and president (1920–24, 1928). Once a planter in Sonora, Obregón rose through the military ranks to become a powerful general in the Mexican revolution (1910–17). During Mexico's civil war he aided President Venustiano Carranza as minister of war. When Carranza did not enforce a reform constitution in 1917, however, Obregón led a revolt against him. Carranza fled Mexico and was later murdered. After a provisional administration of Adolfo de la Huerta, Obregón was elected president in 1920.

Obregón's administration worked to enact agrarian, labor, and educational reforms; he also thwarted a revolt led by de la Huerta in 1923–24. The United States delayed in recognizing Obregón's regime until 1923, primarily because of proclamations by radicals who urged the nationalization of oil deposits. Obregón was also involved in a long battle with the church. Upon his reelection in 1928, he was assassinated by Roman Catholic Jose de Leon Toral, presumably because of his anticlerical opinions.

See also BUCARELI AGREEMENTS.

Reference: "Alvaro Obregón" in *Columbia Encyclopedia*, 5th ed. (New York: Columbia University Press, 1993).

Odets, Clifford (1906–1963)

American playwright, known for his social protest plays of the 1930s. Born in Philadelphia, Pennsylvania, Odets took to the stage in minor roles throughout the 1920s. He founded Group Theatre in New York and wrote a series of acclaimed plays, including *Waiting for Lefty* (1935); *Awake and Sing* (1935), considered his finest work; and *Golden Boy* (1937). He then moved to Hollywood, where he wrote screenplays and directed a few films, including *The General Died at Dawn* (1936) and *None but the Lonely Heart* (1944), for which actress Ethel BARRYMORE won an Oscar. Odets's later plays include *Clash by Night* (1942) and *The Country Girl* (1950).

Despite his early promise, Odets did not achieve similar professional successes later in life. Lacking further creative inspiration, he referred to himself as a "playwright *manqué*." His later plays were poorly received. Furthermore, during the late 1940s and early 1950s, he was labeled a Communist by the House Committee on Un-American Activities and blacklisted in Hollywood, which in effect ended his career.

Reference: Roberta Smith, "Clifford Odets: Anguish of Many Colors in Paintings," *New York Times,* April 26, 1996.

O'Keeffe, Georgia (1887–1986)

American painter, known for her geometric cityscapes of the 1920s and her mystical landscapes and flowers of the 1930s. Born Georgia Totto O'Keeffe on November 15, 1887, she was raised on a dairy farm in Sun Prairie, Wisconsin. Women's education was a family tradition, and by age 16, O'Keeffe had enjoyed five years of private art lessons. She then attended the Art Institute of Chicago (1905) and the Art Student League in New York City (1907). Discouraged with her work, however, O'Keeffe did not return to the League, and for a time she abandoned painting altogether. During this time she worked as a commercial artist in Chicago and later as an art instructor, teaching in Texas, South Carolina, and Virginia schools.

O'Keeffe's first solo exhibition was in 1917 at Alfred Stieglitz's 291 Gallery in New York. Stieglitz was her most avid supporter, arranging annual shows and selling her paintings; the two were married in 1924. During the 1920s O'Keeffe painted New York cityscapes in an abstract geometric style. By 1928, however, she sought other subject matter. She made the first of many trips to New Mexico in 1929, where she returned each summer for inspiration until Stieglitz's death in 1946. In that year she moved permanently to her New Mexico home at Ghost Ranch. Among other guests to visit the ranch over the years were the writer D. H. LAWRENCE and the photographer Ansel Adams.

O'Keeffe's work from the 1930s and beyond is characterized by sculptural and organic forms painted in strong, clear colors. The subject matter is often such southwestern motifs as bleached bones, rolling hills, clouds, and desert blooms. In 1962 she was elected to the American Academy of Arts and Letters. Despite failing eyesight in her final years, O'Keeffe continued to paint. She died on March 6, 1986, in Santa Fe, New Mexico.

References: Jeffrey Hogrefe, *O'Keeffe: The Life of an American Legend* (New York: Bantam, 1994); Laurie Lisle, *Portrait of an Artist* (New York: Washington Square Press, 1986); Charles C. Eldredge, *Georgia O'Keeffe* (New York: Harry N. Abrams, 1991).

Olympic Games

International sporting event, which after an eight-year hiatus because of World War I, resumed in 1920 in Antwerp. Since their inauguration in classical Greece, the Olympic Games had always been a way of putting aside military conflicts and bringing communities together for a festive time of competitive sport. The modern games are no different; in fact, starting with the 1920 games, the world looked toward these global sporting events to calm and soothe the intense animosity many nations held for each other after the war. By 1936, however, the games were unfortunately used for political purposes, and by 1940 they were again canceled, not to be restarted again until 1948. How, and why the games degenerated into such a spectacle is just part of the story of how the world slid back into a warlike posture in the 1930s.

1920, *Antwerp Summer Games.* The first since 1912 in Stockholm, the Antwerp Summer Games opened on April 20 and lasted until September 12. In all, 2,607 athletes (2,543 men and 64 women) from 29 nations competed. The losing powers of World War I—Germany, Austria, Bulgaria, Hungary, and Turkey (the former Ottoman Empire)—were not allowed to participate. Without those nations, the games were poorly attended and did not make much money. Little is known about the Olympic history of the Antwerp games. The American team sailed to Europe on the *Princess Matoika*, which had just returned from Europe with dead soldiers from the war and still smelled of formaldehyde. Although the American team finished with 96 team medals (41 gold, 27 silver, and 28 bronze), the Finnish team was the darling of the games. This Olympiad marked the debut of Paavo Nurmi, the

"Finnish Phantom," whose daring running exploits in the next few games wowed the world. Nurmi was leading the 5,000 meter race, when Joseph Guillemot of France, a World War I veteran who had been gassed, passed Nurmi and won the gold; Nurmi came in a close second. Nurmi then beat Guillemot in the 3,000 meter the following day and won a second gold the day after. In all, Finland tied the United States with eight gold medals in track and field. In tennis, Suzanne Lenglen of France won two medals in tennis; in swimming, American Aileen Riggin won a gold in the springboard at age 14. The games were noted for their simplicity, but after the horrors of the war just two years earlier, such an event brought the nations of wartorn Europe a little closer together.

1924, *Chamonix Winter Games.* With Paris set to hold the annual Olympics in 1924, skiing and other winter sporting events enthusiasts demanded that such sports be added to the roster of events held at the games, slated to start in July. Instead, the French Olympic Committee established a small winter sports festival, which opened in the French Alpine resort of Chamonix on January 25, 1924, and lasted until February 4. Sixteen nations, including Norway, Finland, and Austria, sent 294 athletes (281 men and 13 women) to participate in several sports, including the four-man bobsled (won by the United States team in 3:20:5), and ice hockey (which had been played at the 1920 games as a lone sport and at Chamonix was won by the Canadians over the Americans). Austria, Finland, and Norway took most of the skating and skiing awards (Norway's Thorlief Haug won three golds), while Canada won the ice hockey tourney and Switzerland won at the bobsled. Yet the entire games were overtaken by the performance of Sonja Henie, an eleven-year-old Norwegian skater who became the darling of the games (she was bested by Finland's Clas Thunberg but took two golds and one silver). Henie became the Norwegian skating champion in 1925. The overall success of the Chamonix games led the International Olympic Committee to sanction winter events as official Olympic games; in 1928 they opened the next winter games in St. Moritz, Switzerland.

Paris Summer Games. The 1924 summer games were held in Paris, the second time an Olympiad was held in that city (the first was 1900). These games opened on May 4 in Colombes Stadium and closed on July 27. Forty-four nations were represented; there were nearly 3,000 male athletes and only 136 female. Finland, which had won or seriously competed for many of the track and field medals in the 1920 games, gave notice that it would be repeating that performance in 1924. While Paavo Nurmi was a strong competitor, he was bested in the 10,000 meter by fellow Finn Ville Ritola, who cut twelve full seconds off the world record; Ritola also scored gold in the 3,000 meter steeplechase. Ritola and Nurmi faced each other in the 5,000 meter, with Nurmi taking the gold over Ritola and fellow Finn (but racing for Sweden) Edvin Wide coming in third. Nurmi beat Ritola again in the 9,000 meters a few days later, but did not run in the marathon, which was bested by Finnish runner Albin Stenroos. Finn runner Jonni Myrrä, who won the javelin at Antwerp, repeated the performance in Paris. Scottish athlete Eric Henry Liddell won gold in the 400 meters; his life was later memorialized in the 1981 film *Chariots of Fire*. British runner Harold Abrahams bested such favored Americans as Jackson Scholz, Loren Murchison, and Charley Paddock in the 100 meter sprint and the 200 meter, while fellow Brit Douglas Lowe beat Swiss Paul Martin in the 800 meters. American William De Hart Hubbard became the first African American to win a gold when he won the long jump. In the end, the United States finished with 12 track and field gold medals to Finland's eight. One of the lesser stars of the 1924 games, who showed great promise, was American swimmer Johnny Weissmuller, who took home gold in the 100 meter freestyle, the 400 meter freestyle, and the 4 x 200 meter freestyle relay.

1928, *St. Moritz Winter Games*. The second winter games saw the return of Norwegian skater Sonja Henie, now 15 years old. Twenty-five nations competed in these second winter games, with 468 men and 27 women participating from February 11–19 at St. Moritz, Switzerland, and participating in such events as the Skeleton or Cresta Run (utilizing a heavy sled, a sport only held when the Winter Olympics are held in St. Moritz, which has been 1928 and 1948 only). Henie won the gold in women's figure skating, which would become the first of three such medals over the next two Olympics. American William "Billy" Fiske led the U.S. bobsled team at age 16 to gold, becoming the youngest gold medal winner in Olympic history. Finn Clas Thunberg won medals in the 500 meter and 1500 meter speedskating events. Canada won the gold in ice hockey (beating Sweden, which took the silver), and Johan Gröttumsbråten of Norway took the 18 kilometer cross-country skiing race. Norway took 15 medals in total, with the United States in second with six and Sweden in third with five.

Amsterdam Summer Games. These were the first games during which women were allowed to compete in track and field events. Although the Soviet Union and China were excluded from participating, the Germans were allowed for the first time since 1912, and came in second in medals with 16 (behind the 22 of the United States). In all, 46 nations, represented by 2,724 male athletes and 290 female athletes, competed from May 17 to August 12. The stars of the games were Nurmi of Finland and Weissmuller of the United States. Nurmi came for this third games and picked up his 10th, 11th, and 12th gold medals, including one in which he bested Ritola in the 10,000 meters for the second straight time. Weissmuller

won two golds by winning the 100 meter freestyle and the 4 x 200 meter freestyle relay. Canadian sprinter Percy Williams, an unknown, won two gold in the 100 meter and 200 meter sprints. British runner David Cecil won gold in the 400 meter hurdles, while South African Sid Atkinson was best in the 110 meter hurdles. In these games, the United States beat Finland's five gold medals in track and field with eight of their own.

1932, *Lake Placid Winter Games*. The first Olympics held in the United States came to the New York resort of Lake Placid, held February 4–15, and involving 17 nations, presented 272 male athletes and 32 female athletes. These games saw the debut of the two-man bobsled, and three so-called "demonstration sports," including women's speedskating. In male speedskating, Americans Irving Jaffee and John Shea took all four golds in the 500 meter and 1,500 meter competitions, the first time athletes from the Scandinavian nations—Sweden and Norway—had not captured all of these medals in the winter games. In women's figure skating, Henie continued her performance first started at the 1924 games and took gold against Austria's Fritzi Burger in women's figure skating. The three-man Norwegian team of Birger Ruud, Hans Beck, and Kaare Wahlberg took all three medals in the ski jump (90 meter hill) competition. Canada beat the United States in ice hockey, with Germany coming in third. In total, the United States came in first with 12 medals, with Norway in second with 10, and Sweden with three.

Los Angeles Summer Games. The first summer games in the United States were held in the midst of the GREAT DEPRESSION, and the number of attendees was the lowest in Olympic history: only 1,281 men and 127 women, representing 37 nations, appeared from July 30 to August 14. The star, however, for the first time, was a woman: American Mildred "Babe" Didrickson, who won gold in the javelin and 80 meter hurdles, and silver in the high jump, making her one of the most famous women athletes in the world. Duncan McNaughton of Canada won the high jump, and American Edward Gordon took gold in the pole vault. American Thomas "Eddie" Tolan came in first in both the 100-meter and 200-meter dash, while Juan Carlos Zabala of Argentina took gold in the marathon. In the women's categories, Stanislawa Walasiewicz of Poland took the gold in the 100-meter dash, and American Jean Shiley won the high jump, while the American team took the 4 x 100 meter relay. The United States came in first with 104 medals, with Italy in second with 36, and France in third with 19.

1936, *Garmisch-Partenkirchen Winter Games*. For the second time in Olympic history, both the winter and summer games in one year were held in the same country, this time Germany. The winter games were held in the resort village of Garmisch-Partenkirchen, February 6–16, with 28 nations attending represented by 675 male athletes and 80 females athletes. The events of men's and women's alpine skiing made its first appearance. Canada lost the gold in ice hockey for the first time when the British team, led by Edgar Brenchley and two Canadians, Alex Archer and James Foster, who actually lived in England, beat them in the semifinals, and survived a 0–0 tie with the United States in the finals. The German team, which came in fifth, was led by Rudi Ball, a Jew who had fled Nazi Germany but returned to his homeland to lead his beloved hockey squad. Figure skater Henie repeated her gold-winning performance in the 1936 games. Norwegian Ivar Ballangrund took gold in men's speedskating in the 500-meter, 5,000-meter, and 10,000-meter competitions, and silver in the 1,500-meter race. Along with three others (one gold, one silver, and one bronze) that he had won in 1928 and 1932, Ballangrund finished with seven medals, four of them gold. Norway came in first with 15 total medals, with Sweden in second with seven, and Germany in third with six. (The United States was tied in fifth with five.) The Garmisch games would be the last winter games until the St. Moritz games in 1948.

Berlin Summer Games. The games held in Berlin marked the last Olympics for twelve years. Germany was allowed to host the games after having had them taken away in 1916, during World War I, but this Olympiad came in the midst of a massive military buildup by the new leaders of Germany, namely Adolf HITLER and the Nazi Party; this undoubtedly clouded the festivities. There were strong international calls to boycott the games; but they went on, and the Germans made it the showcase of their propaganda theme. An alternative People's Olympics, to be held in Barcelona, Spain, was canceled when the SPANISH CIVIL WAR broke out. Forty-nine nations, represented by 3,738 male athletes and 328 females, competed from August 1 to August 16. Perhaps the greatest story of the games came from American runner Jesse Owens, the grandson of slaves, who took four golds in the 100 meter, 200 meter, the 4 x 100 meter relay, and the long jump and demolished the theory of Aryan superiority as Hitler looked on and Owens bested German athletes. Hitler snubbed Owens (as did U.S. President Franklin D. ROOSEVELT, who refused to congratulate Owens and did not invite him to the White House). The United States beat Canada to win the gold in basketball; British rower Jack Beresford became the greatest Olympic oarsman of all time when he won a gold in the Double Sculls race in Berlin, completing the last of five medals in five Olympics, including three gold. Kee-Chung Sohn of Korea, then occupied by Japan, competed for his occupiers and won a gold in the Marathon. American Helen Stephens won the women's 100 meter dash, while the American team captured the women's 4 x 100 meter relay. Germany led the field with 89 medals, with the United States in second with 56, and Hungary in third with 16. Sports writer

Shirley Povich wrote, "Germany claimed to have won the 1936 Olympics, and in a manner of speaking it did. It won the most medals, succeeding in such sports as fencing, canoeing, yachting and weightlifting. But in the most featured sports of track and field and swimming, the Americans dominated." German filmmaker Leni Riefenstahl, who documented the entire Berlin games on film, released a four-hour documentary in 1938 entitled *Olympia*. The 1940 games set for Tokyo (and later moved to Helsinki, but called off nonetheless), as well as the 1944 games scheduled for London, were canceled because of World War II; the games eventually resumed in London in 1948.

References: David Wallechinsky, *The Complete Book of the Olympics* (New York: Penguin Books, 1984); William Oscar Johnson, *The Olympics: A History of the Games* (New York: Oxmoor House, 1992); Shane J. Maddock, "Olympic Games" in Bruce W. Jentleson and Thomas G. Paterson, senior eds., *Encyclopedia of U.S. Foreign Relations* (New York: Oxford University Press, 1997), 3: 322–23; Richard Mandell, *The Nazi Olympics* (Urbana: University of Illinois Press, 1987); "Hitler Opens 11th Olympic Games, With 5,000 Athletes;

U.S. athletes Jesse Owens and Ralph Metcalfe run their gold-medal-winning—and politically significant—400-meter relay in the 1936 Berlin Olympics. *(CORBIS/Bettmann)*

110,000 Attend Stadium Rites, Teams' Parade," *New York Herald-Tribune* (European Edition), August 1, 1936, p. 1; Shirley Povich, "Berlin, 1936: At the Olympics, Achievements of the Brave in a Year of Cowardice," *Washington Post,* July 6, 1996, p. D1.

O'Neill, Eugene (1888–1953)

American writer, considered one of the greatest writers of the early 20th century, whose prose was exemplified in such interwar works as *The Emperor Jones* (1920), *Desire under the Elms* (1924), and *Mourning Becomes Electra* (1931), a body of work for which he was awarded the Pulitzer Prize in 1920 and 1922 and the Nobel Prize in literature in 1936. Born in New York City on October 16, 1888, he was the son of actor James O'Neill. O'Neill went to private schools, and in 1906 entered Princeton University; he was forced out after a year because of failing grades. He spent the next five years as a sailor on trips to Europe and South America, and worked for a time as a laborer in Argentina. When O'Neill finally returned to the United States, he spent much of his time at a bar in New York City, where he picked up stories he later used in many of his works.

Working part-time as an actor in his father's troupe, O'Neill became a reporter for the *New London* (Connecticut) *Times.* He then entered Harvard University to study the art of play writing with George Pierce Baker. In 1916, O'Neill's first play, *Bound East for Cardiff,* was performed in Massachusetts. He then moved to the Greenwich Village section of New York City, where he continued to write. Because of his ill health, he was not drafted to fight in World War I.

O'Neill's first major play, *Beyond the Horizon,* which was produced in 1920, won the Pulitzer Prize for drama. His *Anna Christie* (1922) and *Strange Interlude* (1927) also received Pulitzers. One of his lesser known but equally important works is *All God's Chillun Got Wings,* a two-act play written in 1923 and produced for the stage the following year. This work complemented *The Emperor Jones* (1921), which reflected O'Neill's attraction and fascination with African-American life and race in American society, particularly during the 1920s. The story of Jim Harris, an intelligent black man, who marries a white girl, Ella Downey, *All God's Chillun Got Wings* tackled this touchy and incendiary subject with frankness and clarity. At first their marriage and life in France seem to go well, but their return to the United States shows the cracks in their lives and exposes them to pressures based on their respective races. O'Neill's tragic melodrama is considered progressive for its time. His *Desire Under the Elms* (1924) studied how a father, son, and stepmother bitterly contend for possession of a New England farm, in a struggle between Puritanism and desire that ends in the sacrificial murder of an infant. *In Mourning Becomes Electra* (1931), O'Neill borrowed from Aeschylus's trilogy *Oresteia* to place his more modern story during the American Civil War. Other plays produced during this period include *Dynamo* (1928), *Ah, Wilderness!* (1932), *Days without End* (1933) and *The Iceman Cometh* (1939).

O'Neill was awarded the 1936 Nobel Prize "for dramatic works of vital energy, sincerity and intensity of feeling, stamped with an original conception of tragedy." In becoming the second American to win this coveted award (Sinclair LEWIS was the first in 1930), O'Neill joined a select group of writers in American history. He continued to write after winning the Nobel Prize, and began a nine-part play entitled *A Tale of Possessors Self-Dispossessed,* of which he produced several parts. O'Neill died in Boston, Massachusetts, on November 27, 1953. One of his final plays, *Long Day's Journey into Night,* was produced in 1956 and made into a movie in 1962. For this work, O'Neill was posthumously awarded his fifth Pulitzer Prize.

References: Charles Bruce, "O'Neill, Eugene Gladstone" in Bernard S. and June H. Schlessinger, eds., *The Who's Who of Nobel Prize Winners* (Phoenix, Ariz.: Oryx, 1986), 59; Thomas Watson MacCallum, and Stephen Taylor, eds., *The Nobel Prize–Winners and the Nobel Foundation, 1901–1937* (Zurich: Central European Times Publishing, 1938), 324–25.

Ossietzky, Carl von (1889–1938)

German peace advocate, writer, and Nobel laureate. Born in Hamburg, Germany, on October 3, 1889, the son of a minor government official, he attended a school of the well-to-do. Service in the German army during World War I confirmed in him an intense hatred of war and bred a pacifist stance.

In the 1920s, Ossietsky spoke against war; in 1918 he had founded the *Nie Wieder Krieg* (Never again war) movement. By 1927 he found his voice in literature, working as the editor-in-chief of the *Die Weltbühne,* the official paper of the leftist intellectuals in WEIMAR Germany. Ossietsky used the journal to criticize the left and right with equal fervor, lending support to Foreign Minister Gustav STRESEMANN's attempt to reconcile with France. In 1932 Ossietsky was arrested and tried by the military authorities for bringing notice to the world that Germany was secretly rearming, which had been outlawed by the VERSAILLES Treaty. He served seven months of an 18-month sentence, being freed in a general amnesty. A month later, however, Adolf HITLER became the chancellor of Germany, and Ossietsky set about to call attention to what he saw the greatest danger to the German state. On February 28, 1933, just a month after Hitler came to power, Ossietsky and other enemies of Hitler's new regime were rounded up. Within a year, reports began to surface that Ossietsky was being tortured inside concentration camps. For being "a symbol of the struggle for peace," he was secretly nominated for the Nobel Peace Prize.

In October 1935 the Red Cross was allowed to visit him; the representative later wrote that he found Ossietsky as "a trembling deadly pale something, a creature that appeared to be without feeling, an eye swollen, teeth apparently smashed . . . it dragged a broken, badly healed leg . . . a human being that had reached the uttermost limits of what can be borne." On November 23, 1936, Ossietsky was awarded the Nobel, which had originally gone without being issued, "recognizing his valuable contribution to the cause of peace." Nazi Germany was indignant at the slight; the government protested to the Norwegian government, and Hitler ordered that no citizen of the Reich could accept a Nobel. Ossietsky never received the award, and the money that came with the prize was embezzled.

German Reichsmarshal Hermann Göring offered freedom for Ossietzky if he renounced the Nobel, but the peace advocate refused. Within 17 months of his award, on May 4, 1938, Ossietzky died in a Reich hospital in Berlin at the age of 48. Relatives who survived the war believe that Nazi doctors injected him with tuberculosis.

References: Bernard S. Schlessinger, "Ossietzky, Carl von" in Bernard S. and June H. Schlessinger, eds., *The Who's Who of Nobel Prize Winners* (Phoenix, Ariz.: Oryx, 1986), 136; Istvan Deak, "Ossietzky, Carl von" in Harold Josephson, ed. in chief, *Biographical Dictionary of Modern Peace Leaders* (Westport, Conn.: Greenwood, 1985), 714–15; Thomas Watson MacCallum and Stephen Taylor, eds., *The Nobel Prize-Winners and the Nobel Foundation, 1901–1937* (Zurich: Central European Times Publishing, 1938), 384; Robert S. Wistrich, *Who's Who in Nazi Germany* (London: Routledge, 1995), 186; Irwin Abrams, *The Nobel Peace Prize and the Laureates: An Illustrated Biographical History, 1901–1987* (Boston: G. K. Hall & Co., 1988), 126; Stephen Kinzler, "Exoneration Still Eludes an Anti-Nazi Crusader" *New York Times*, January 13, 1996. p. A2.

Ottawa Economic Conference

Conference, 1932, during which Richard Bedford BENNETT, prime minister of Canada, arranged preferential trade agreements with Britain and other Commonwealth countries. Also called the Imperial Economic Conference, this meeting was hosted in Ottawa by Conservative Party leader Bennett, who was also Canada's minister of finance and secretary of state for external affairs. Economic problems stemming from the GREAT DEPRESSION had dominated Bennett's tenure as prime minister; unemployment had reached one-third of Canada's population. The gross national product fell 43 percent from 1929 to 1933. The drought-stricken western provinces were particularly hard hit as grain prices toppled 83 percent from 1928 to 1932. In addition, exports had dropped by about $600 million (Canadian dollars), a disaster for a country so dependent on foreign markets. The government's priority thus shifted from nation building to the pursuit of social well-being for Canadians.

At the conference Bennett vigorously promoted a system of empire trade preferences. He had hoped to penetrate the lucrative British market for raw materials while retaining a measure of protection for Canadian manufacturers. Despite his efforts, however, the Canadian economy did not recover. In 1935 the prime minister announced a more radical reform package similar to U.S. President Franklin D. ROOSEVELT'S NEW DEAL: unemployment insurance, a reduced workweek, make-work programs such as environmental restoration, a minimum wage, industrial codes, and permanent economic planning. A series of measures aimed at controlling competition was passed, but eventually most of this legislation was disallowed by the British Privy Council as being outside the constitutional powers of the federal government to enact.

References: Robert Bothwell, Ian Drummond, and John English, *Canada, 1900–1945* (Toronto: University of Toronto Press, 1987); M. C. Urquhart, *Canadian Economic Growth, 1870–1980* (Kingston, Ont.: Institute for Economic Research, Queen's University, 1988).

Oxford Group Movement   *See* MORAL RE-ARMAMENT.

P

Pabst, Georg Wilhelm (1885–1967)

Austrian film director, noted for his films during the silent film era which are distinguished by their innovative realistic techniques and their social criticism of German decadence and nationalism. Born in the village of Raudnitz, Austria, he was raised in Vienna, where he trained to become an engineer. He became interested in the arts, however, and studied for two years at the Vienna Academy of Decorative Arts, afterward going to Switzerland, where he acted on the stage. Sometime after 1906 he came to the United States, where he remained until the beginning of World War I.

In France during the early part of the war, he was prevented from returning to Vienna; instead, he staged plays in Paris. Turning down an offer to work as a theater director, he later went to Berlin, where he worked as an actor and screenwriter for the German director Carol Froelich. By 1923, however, Pabst was moving away from expressionism and toward pessimism, an area of the human psyche he explored in many of his films. Starting with *The Street of Sorrow,* (1925), a dark commentary on life in postwar WEIMAR Germany (which starred a Pabst discovery, Swedish actress Greta GARBO), Pabst used the camera to paint a dark portrait of existence. He continued this ideal in *Secrets of a Soul* (1926) and *The Love of Jeanne Ney* (1926), which explored Freudian ideas. In 1929 he brought the beautiful and sensuous American actress Louise BROOKS to Germany to star in *Pandora's Box* (1929), based on Alban Berg's opera *Lulu*. That same year, he cast Brooks in *Diary of a Lost Girl* (1929). In these and other films, he exhibited camera techniques that were later used by Alfred HITCHCOCK; many of these techniques are today erroneously considered "Hitchcockian." Pabst's other films include *The White Hell of Piz Palu* (1929), *Westfront 1918* (1930), and *The Threepenny Opera* (1931).

In 1939, Pabst fled Germany in the midst of the Nazi invasion of Poland. Pabst's first postwar film, *The Trial,* highlighted the problem of anti-Semitism. After a career of groundbreaking techniques and classic films, Pabst died in Vienna on May 29, 1967.

References: Lee Atwell, *G. W. Pabst* (Boston: Twayne Publishers, 1977); Eric Renschler, ed., *The Films of G. W. Pabst: An Extraterritorial Cinema* (New Brunswick, N.J.: Rutgers University Press, 1990); G. W. Pabst, Maker of Films Abroad; Early Viennese Producer and Director Dies at 82," *New York Times,* May 31, 1967, p. 43.

pacifism

Social movement based on the premise of opposition to war, which gained renewed vigor in the West during the interwar period. The trauma of World War I revived the advancement of pacifism and international cooperation, as evidenced by the LEAGUE OF NATIONS and by Mohandas GANDHI's practice of nonviolent resistance in India. In addition to those who supported pacifism on religious grounds, such as the Quakers, after the war a "moral and utilitarian condemnation of war and preparation for it permeated Western civilization." The 1929 novel ALL QUIET ON THE WESTERN FRONT became a primary text for peace advocates.

Local peace societies sprouted up throughout the United States, and women in particular played a central role in these movements against militarism. For example, the social reformer Jane ADDAMS, who had spoken out against America's involvement in the war, founded in 1919 the Women's International League for Peace and Freedom. For her continued antiwar efforts, she earned the Nobel Prize for Peace in 1931. The journalist Dorothy Day worked for a number of antiwar newspapers in New York City before launching in 1933 the *Catholic Worker.* Originally a newspaper, the *Worker* grew into a broad-based pacifist and social justice movement. Peace advocates such as the politician Jeannette Rankin and the reformer Carrie Chapman Catt worked tirelessly in the name of peace. The Women's Peace Union campaigned steadily throughout the interwar period for a constitutional amendment that would declare war illegal.

References: Dennis E. Showalter, "Pacifism," in *The Reader's Companion to Military History,* ed. Robert Cowley and Geoffrey Parker (Boston: Houghton Mifflin, 1996), 351–52; Peter Brock and Nigel Young, *Pacifism in the Twentieth Century* (Syracuse, N.Y.: Syracuse University Press, 1999); Richard J. Evans, *Comrades and Sisters: Feminism, Socialism, and Pacifism in Europe, 1870–1945* (New York: St. Martin's, 1987).

painting

During the interwar period, painters experimented with and embraced a variety of innovative styles. Modern European styles of painting representing DADA, expressionism, and SURREALISM had first been exhibited in 1913 at the famous Armory show in New York. These radical new styles continued to develop in the interwar period. Dada—embraced by such artists as Jean Arp, Marcel Duchamp, and Man Ray—rejected traditional aesthetic standards, aiming instead to create anti-art and non-art, often employing a sense of the absurd. German Dadaist Kurt Schwitters created Merz, an art form made from refuse and other "found" objects. By the mid-1920s, however, Dada had petered out and was replaced by surrealism.

Beginning in France in the early 1920s, surrealism explored the unconscious, often using images from dreams. Such artists as André Breton, Salvador Dalí, Max Ernst, René Magritte, Joan Miro, and Yves Tanguy used spontaneous techniques and featured unexpected juxtapositions of objects in their surrealist works. Like much art of the 1920s, surrealism was a reaction to the kind of "rationalism" that had led to the trauma of World War I. The modernism of the early 1920s also included the artistic movements known as pure abstraction and cubism. Typified by the geometric work of the Dutch artist Piet Mondrian, leader of the harmony-loving DE STIJL artists, pure abstraction was embraced by Wassily Kandinsky, Kasimir Malevich, and Theo van Doesburg. Although cubism had been invented in Paris in 1908, some of the genre's most sophisticated works were produced in the 1920s by such artists as Georges Braque, Marc Chagall, Juan Gris, Fernand Léger, and Pablo PICASSO. Such American artists as Lyonel Feininger and Charles Demuth tried their hands during the 1920s at what became known as American cubism. Feininger developed a complex cubist-influenced style using colors and lines to produce multidimensional images.

After World War I the anger and despair of German artists over the war's atrocities led to the founding of a new expressionistic movement called the New Objectivity, exemplified by such artists as George Grosz and Otto Dix, whose paintings and drawings bluntly portrayed the violence of war as well as the decadent aspects of life in the postwar WEIMAR Republic. Other prominent European artists working in the style included Oskar Kokoschka, Georges Rouault, and Chaim Soutine, whose rough style of thick layers of paint revealed the dark and grotesque side of humanity.

In the United States postwar American realism was taking root. George Bellows painted scenes that captured the rough side of city life. Illustrator John Held, known for his colorful magazine-cover depictions of flappers for *Life* and the *New Yorker,* painted some of the most well-known images of the 1920s, mixing humor and innocent sexuality. Watercolorist John Marin used geometry and color in innovative ways in his landscapes and cityscapes. During the HARLEM RENAISSANCE, African-American painters created art that affirmed their identity and introduced black themes into American modernism. Taking their inspiration from Harlem's thriving political and cultural milieu, such artists as Aaron Douglas and Jacob Lawrence are part of this rich artistic legacy. Henry Tanner was a member of a small cadre of black American artists in the freer atmosphere of Paris; his paintings featured religious themes. Watercolorist Georgia O'KEEFFE emerged in the mid-1920s as an inspirational painter of distinctive and innovative American tradition. Her art was more abstract, often representing enlarged plants and flowers, and was infused with a kind of surrealism she called "magical realism."

During the GREAT DEPRESSION artists of the American Scene movement, also known as regionalists, responded to the country's cry for renewal by instilling a sense of nationalism in their works. With government support through the Federal Arts Project, part of the WORKS PROGRESS ADMINISTRATION, such painters as Thomas Hart Benton and Grant Wood created vivid renderings of rural Midwestern scenes. Benton is known for his quirky and vibrant panels and murals of rural American life. Wood is famous for his *American Gothic* (1930), a stylized portrait of a farming couple in Iowa. Other regionalists, such as the anti-urban painters Richard Coe, Lamar Dodd, and John McCrady, painted hard-working laborers on southern farms. Their depictions of African-American subjects, captured either in the joyous act of spiritual song or as victims in brutal attacks and violent lynchings, were critically acclaimed.

Another great painter of the American scene was Edward Hopper, who gave visual form to the loneliness, vacuity, and boredom of big-city life. His work was strongly realist, and his precise images of American desolate landscapes and cityscapes and isolated individuals reflected the social mood of the times. Hopper painted with a disturbing truth, expressing the world as a chilling and alienating place. This was something new in art, an expression of the sense of hopelessness that characterized the depression era. Ben Shahn achieved fame in the 1930s with his gouache paintings on the 1920s trials of SACCO AND VANZETTI. His images of the depression are also admired.

The Mexican painters Diego Rivera and Frida Kahlo are also regarded as great artists of the interwar period. Kahlo was largely an autobiographical painter, and most of her works reflect her own sufferings. Her tumultuous marriage to Rivera also greatly influenced her work. Diego's immense frescoes were homages to the masses, showing workers, farmers, and historical figures in dense scenes. His earliest great works include the murals in Mexico City's National Palace, *Workers of the Revolution* (1929). Rivera's work sparked a renaissance in Mexican mural painting.

References: Ian Chilvers, *A Dictionary of Twentieth-Century Art* (New York: Oxford University Press, 1998); Matthew Biagell, *The American Scene: American Paintings of the 1930s* (New York: Praeger, 1974); Alfred Barr, *What Is Modern Painting?* (New York: Museum of Modern Art; distributed by Simon and Schuster, 1953); Milton Brown, *American Painting from the Armory Show to the Depression* (Princeton, N.J.: Princeton University Press, 1955); Paul Wood, ed., *The Challenge of the Avant-Garde* (New Haven, Conn.: Yale University Press, 1999).

Palmer, Alexander Mitchell   *See* PALMER RAIDS.

Palmer Raids

Series of attacks in the United States, 1919–1920, on suspected socialists, anarchists, and communists, under the authority of Attorney General Alexander Mitchell Palmer. During World War I many newspapers attacked persons who spoke out against U.S. participation in the war; after the war ended, these newspapers and a portion of the public called out for the removal from society of these persons. Palmer, a Quaker, ordered federal agents, without search warrants or writs of arrest, to enter and search the homes of suspected left-wingers and to detain those found with incendiary material, without writs of habeas corpus. Many of these invididuals were deported from the United States.

References: Stanley Coben, *A. Mitchell Palmer: Politician* (New York: Columbia University Press, 1963); Dennis J. Mahoney, "Palmer Raids" in Leonard W. Levy, ed. in chief, *Encyclopedia of the American Constitution* (New York: Macmillan, 1986–92), 3: 1361–62.

Panay Incident

Military action, December 12, 1937, in which Japanese aircraft, operating illegally inside China territory, attacked three American ships, including the gunboat at the U.S.S. *Panay*, as well as three ships belonging to the Standard Oil Company: the steamers *Meiping*, *Meian*, and *Meihsia*. The SINO-JAPANESE WAR, while condemned by many nations, had not had an effect on the foreign policies of these nations. On December 12, 1937, however, when Japanese planes either mistakenly or purposefully attacked these ships, causing American diplomats to be evacuated from Nanking to Shanghai, the outlook of the United States changed. The following day, President Franklin D. ROOSEVELT expressed "deep shock" to the Japanese ambassador to the United States and added that he wanted an expression of regret and compensation for those killed and injured. Secretary of State Cordell HULL believed that the attack was deliberate and asked Roosevelt to impose sanctions on Japan. Congress was hesitant to pick a fight with Japan that might escalate into a war. The attitude forced Roosevelt to accept from the Japanese a statement of apology and a fine of $2,214,007.36. It was a portent of things to come, however: four years later, almost to the day, Japanese planes attacked U.S. ships at the Pearl Harbor naval station in Hawaii:

References: Hugh D. Phillips, "Panay Episode" in Bruce W. Jentleson and Thomas G. Paterson, senior eds., *Encyclopedia of U.S. Foreign Relations* (New York: Oxford University Press, 1997), 3: 358; Hamilton D. Perry, *The Panay Incident: Prelude to Pearl Harbor* (New York: Macmillan, 1969); Manny T. Koginos, *The Panay Incident: Prelude to War* (Lafayette, Ind.: Purdue University Studies, 1967).

Pandora's Box   *See* BROOKS, LOUISE.

Parker, Dorothy   (1893–1967)

American writer, a founder and member of the ALGONQUIN ROUND TABLE, a literary luncheon group that was popular in the 1920s. Born in West End, New Jersey, on August 22, 1893, she was educated in the public schools of Morristown, New Jersey, and the Blessed Sacrament Convent in New York City. She first worked for *Vogue* (1916) and then landed a job as the drama critic of *Vanity Fair* magazine (1917–20). In 1919 she formed with two other writers on that magazine, Robert Benchley and Robert Sherwood, the ALGONQUIN ROUND TABLE, which met in a hotel in New York City to discuss literature and other matters.

Known for her acerbic wit, Parker was fired in 1920 from *Vanity Fair* for her bitter reviewing style, and she began to work as a freelance writer. Her pieces were collected in *A Month of Saturdays* (1971). Her other works issued during this period included verse, short stories, and other literary forms in *Enough Rope* (1926), *Sunset Gun* (1928), *Laments for the Living* (1930), *Death and*

Taxes (1931), and *After Such Pleasures* (1933). In 1933, she began to write for motion pictures, and her writing earned her an Academy Award nomination for *A Star is Born* (1937). She reported on the SPANISH CIVIL WAR from a left-wing perspective. After the end of World War II, her politics got her blacklisted in cold war America, and she did little work, writing only a few plays. When she died on June 7, 1967, the *New York Times* said, "[She was a] sardonic humorist who purveyed her wit in conversation, short stories, verse and criticism."

References: Marion Meade, *Dorothy Parker: What Fresh Hell Is This?* (New York: Villard Books, 1988); Arthur F. Kinney, *Dorothy Parker* (Boston: Twayne Publishers, 1978); Alden Whitman, "Dorothy Parker, 73, Literary Wit, Dies," *New York Times,* June 8, 1967, p. 1.

Peel Commission

Council, 1937, which recommended the final partition of the British mandate of Palestine between the Jews and the Arabs. The issue of Palestine had been a touchy one since Foreign Minister Arthur James Balfour in 1917 announced that it would become British policy for Palestine to be a homeland for the Jews. The immigration situation in what is today Israel exploded onto the international scene just before World War II. Between 1920, when Jewish immigration to what was then known as Palestine stepped up, and 1937, when the Peel Commission report was released, the Jewish population increased from 50,000 to approximately 400,000. In 1929, Britain had assembled the Shaw Commission to investigate a series of attacks on Jews by Arabs; the commission found that the attacks were justified. This report did little to ease the situation; it was an additional eight years before another commission was assembled to study the problem. Officially known as the Palestine Royal Commission, the council acquired its name from its chair, Lord Peel. Other members included Horace Rumbold, Laurie Hammond, Morris Carter, and Harold Morris.

The Peel Commission investigated the Jewish-Arab situation in Palestine from October 1936 until January 1937, and released its final report on July 8, 1937. The commission recommended that Palestine be partitioned into two states, one Jewish and one Arab, with the Arab state joined to the artificial state of Transjordan (today known as Jordan). The Zionists in Palestine, who had long demanded from the British the establishment of some entity to achieve security for the Jews there, adopted the commission report on August 2, 1937. The Arabs, who had taken the Balfour Declaration as a hope and not a blueprint and who desired to see the Jews all driven from Palestine, denounced the report. The LEAGUE OF NATIONS, in an effort to calm the situation, sent a team headed by John Woodhead in 1938 to further investigate; he

reported that no firm plan for partition could be reached. Further Jewish emigration to Palestine, and numerous attacks on both sides, led to the creation of the Jewish state of Israel in 1948.

References: Aaron S. Klieman, ed., *The Rise of Israel: Zionist Evidence Before the Peel Commission, 1936–1937* (New York: Garland, 1987); "Policy for Palestine: Partition Recommended by Royal Commission," *The Times* (London), July 8, 1937, p. 10; John M. Machover, *Jewish State or Ghetto: Dangers of Palestine Partition: Royal Commission's Proposals Examined* (London: R. Anscombe, 1937).

Perkins, Frances (1882–1965)

American politician, the first female cabinet officer. Born in Boston, Massachusetts, on April 10, 1882, she graduated from Mount Holyoke College and was awarded a master's degree from Columbia University in New York in 1910. She served first as the executive secretary of the Consumers' League of New York for two years, then until 1917 holding the same position with the New York Committee on Safety. In 1917, she worked as the executive director of the New York Council of Organization for War Service. In 1919 she was named as a commissioner on the New York State Industrial Commission, where she served until 1921, and again in that position from 1929 to 1933.

Perkins served under New York governor Franklin D. ROOSEVELT; when he was elected president, he sought to name her to a cabinet position, the first woman to hold such a post. He named her secretary of labor in 1933, and she served until June 1945, one of the longest tenures of a cabinet secretary in U.S. history. As labor secretary, Perkins dealt with issues involving unemployment, unions, strikes, and wages, and in many ways became Roosevelt's personal labor adviser while his NEW DEAL economic program was being implemented.

In 1946, Perkins published *The Roosevelt I Knew,* a biographical account of her friendship with the president. That same year, she was named by President Harry S Truman a member of the U.S. Civil Service Commission, where she served until 1953. Perkins died on May 14, 1965.

References: George Whitney Martin, *Madam Secretary: Frances Perkins* (Boston: Houghton Mifflin, 1976); Winifred D. Wandersee, "Perkins, Frances" in Richard S. Kirkendall, ed., *The Harry S Truman Encyclopedia* (Boston: G. K. Hall & Co., 1989), 275; "Frances Perkins, the First Woman in Cabinet, Is Dead," *New York Times,* May 15, 1965, pp. 1, 31.

Permanent Court of International Justice

Intergovernmental body, part of the Treaty of VERSAILLES, known as the official law-interpreting institution of the LEAGUE OF NATIONS. In article 14 of the Versailles Treaty, the leaders who had signed the treaty established a council to draft a blueprint for the establishment of a world court. The charter of the court was adopted by 44 members of the League of Nations on December 13, 1920, 10 judges were chosen for terms of nine years (in 1930 the number of judges was increased to 15), and the court began its work on December 15, 1922. As per its mandate, it was "competent to hear and determine any dispute of an international character which the parties thereto submit to it. The Court may also give an advisory opinion upon any dispute or question referred to it by the Council or by the Assembly."

Because the United States was not a signatory to the Treaty of Versailles, however, it did not join the Court. President Franklin D. ROOSEVELT's 1932 platform called on the Senate to ratify at least this part of the treaty. Once in office, it took Roosevelt three years to gain the necessary support for such a move. Democratic Senator Claude Augustus Swanson of Virginia introduced the resolution in Congress for the United States to join the Court, but on January 29, 1935, the Senate vote was seven votes shy of the two-thirds required. Leading the opposition to the Court were Senators Hiram JOHNSON and William BORAH, members of the "IRRECONCILABLES" who had helped to defeat passage of the treaty in 1919. Although the United States never officially joined the court, a U.S. citizen was allowed to sit as a representative.

On January 1, 1946, the Permanent Court was superseded by the International Court of Justice, located (as was its predecessor) at the Hague in the Netherlands.

References: Christopher C. Joyner, "Permanent Court of International Justice" in Bruce W. Jentleson and Thomas G. Paterson, senior eds., *Encyclopedia of U.S. Foreign Relations,* 4 vols. (New York: Oxford University Press, 1997), 3: 383; "Root's Plan for International Court as Washington Receives It in Outline; Its Functions Intertwine with League," *New York Times,* August 28, 1920, p. 1; Gilbert N. Kahn, "Presidential Passivity on a Nonsalient Issue: President Franklin D. Roosevelt and the 1935 World Court Fight," *Diplomatic History* 4, no. 2 (Spring 1980): 137–59.

Perrin, Jean-Baptiste (1870–1942)

French physicist and Nobel laureate. Born in Lille, France, on September 30, 1870, Perrin attended the École Normale Supérieure in Paris, where he studied physics and earned a doctorate in 1897; in 1910 he became a professor of physical chemistry at the University of Paris. In 1925 he was admitted as a member of the Académie de Sciences and the Institut de France.

During this time Perrin worked on "the discontinuous structure of matter," and for this and his discovery of sedimentation equilibrium, he was awarded in 1926 the Nobel Prize in physics. His labors were published in such works as *The Atoms* (1913) and *The Physical Elements* (1930). Perrin died in New York City on April 17, 1942. His son, François-Henri Perrin, became head of the French atomic research program after World War II.

References: Alison Staton, "Perrin, Jean Baptiste" in Bernard S. and June H. Schlessinger, eds., *The Who's Who of Nobel Prize Winners* (Phoenix, Ariz.: Oryx, 1986), 158–59; Thomas Watson MacCallum and Stephen Taylor, eds., *The Nobel Prize–Winners and the Nobel Foundation, 1901–1937* (Zurich: Central European Times Publishing, 1938), 86.

Picasso, Pablo (1881–1973)

Spanish painter and artist, whose espousal of the technique of cubism became a basis for one of the most important art movements in the 20th century. Born Pablo Ruiz y Picasso in Malaga, Spain, on October 25, 1881, he was the son of a Basque art teacher, who taught his son the love of painting. To supplement this education, Picasso attended the School of Fine Arts in Barcelona, where he studied all the great masters. Influenced by the French impressionist painters, including Paul Cézanne, he settled in Barcelona in 1900 and two years later began what is called his "blue period": a course of time during which his paintings examined the seedier side of life. In 1904 he moved to Paris and began his "rose period": these paintings contemplate a more positive outlook on life. His *Boy Leading a Horse* (1906) reflects that change in Picasso's persona as well.

Influenced by African sculpture, in 1907 Picasso embarked on cubism, a distorted view of life in abstract paintings and drawings using geometric formations. In 1915 he embraced naturalism, and in the 1920s surrealism. His 1925 work *Three Dancers* exhibits this surrealism. Biographer Ronald Alley called this era "a new period of emotional violence and expressionist distortion, in which the human figure was torn apart and reinvented with an unprecedented freedom to produce highly charged images of a metamorphic and dreamlike character which nevertheless always retained a strong formal design." A champion of the Loyalists during the SPANISH CIVIL WAR, Picasso expressed his outrage at the failure of the West to come to the Spanish government's aid when he painted his well-known work *Guernica,* which highlighted the death of a Spanish city when German planes bombed it.

Picasso was a member of the Spanish Communist Party, and in his later years was twice awarded the Lenin Peace Prize by the Soviet Union. He spent his last years calling for world peace. Picasso died in Mougins, in Alpes-Maritimes, France, on April 4, 1973.

References: Ernest Lloyd Raboff, *Pablo Picasso* (Garden City, N.Y.: Doubleday, 1968); John W. Selfridge, *Pablo Picasso* (New York: Chelsea House, 1994); Ronald Alley, "Picasso, Pablo" in Alan Bullock and R. B. Woodings, eds., "20th Century Culture: A Biographical Companion" (New York: Harper & Row, 1983), 598.

Pierce v. Society of Sisters

Landmark U.S. Court case, in which the court held in 1925 that a government law "requiring all children between the ages of eight and sixteen years to attend the public schools unconstitutionally interferes with the liberty of parents and guardians to direct the upbringing and education of children under their control." In 1922 Oregon voters passed the Compulsory Education Act, which required "that every parent, guardian, or other person having control of charge or custody of a child between eight and sixteen years send him 'to a public school for the period of time a public school shall be held during the current year' in the district where the child resides," and that failure do so would result in a misdemeanor. The Society of the Sisters of the Holy Names of Jesus and Mary, a private institution established in 1880 with the power to care for and educate orphans and other youth, felt the immediate wrath of the new statute. The society ran secular (and not public) schools outside the parameters of the Oregon law, and therefore faced fines and jail because of these policies; parents responded by pulling their children out of the Society's school. In turn, the Society's profits declined. They then sued Oregon's governor, Walter M. Pierce, as well as other state officials, to have the law struck down as too vague and constricting to the Society's attempt to provide a religious education. Hill Military Academy of Oregon, which offered a military-style form of education and suffered the same fate under the new law, joined the Society in their lawsuit. A local court held that the law challenged the two groups' rights under the Fourteenth Amendment to the U.S. Constitution, that it served to deprive them of their property without the due process of the law, and that parents' rights to send their children to the educational facility of their choice was being infringed by the enactment. The U.S. Supreme Court granted the right to hear the case, and arguments were held on March 16 and 17, 1925.

On June 1, Justice James McReynolds held for a unanimous Court in striking down the Oregon law as a violation of the Fourteenth Amendment as well as the rights of parents to freely contract with noncompulsory parties for the education of their children. In 1965, the Court upheld the principle established in *Pierce* in the landmark ruling *Griswold v. Connecticut.*

References: Gerald Gunther, *Constitutional Law* (Mineola, N.Y.: Foundation Press, 1985), 455; Henry Steele Commager, ed., *Documents of American History* (New York: Appleton-Century-Crofts, 1949), 377–78; Text of decision at 268 U.S. 510 (1925).

Pilsudski, Józef Klemens (1867–1935)

Polish general and statesman, who served as provisional president, first marshal, and premier of post–World War I Poland. Born in Zulou, near Wilno, Poland, on December 5, 1867, he was of Lithuanian parentage who strained under the Russian domination of their adopted Polish homeland. Pilsudski studied medicine at the University of Kharkiv (now Kharkov) in Russia; in 1886, after returning to Wilno and joining a revolutionary group known as the Young Poles, however, he was arrested by the Russian police and accused of plotting to assassinate Czar Alexander III. Found guilty, he was deported to eastern Siberia for five years, returning to Poland in 1892. That year, Pilsudski joined the Polish Socialist Party, and two years later founded and became the first editor of the Polish nationalist journal *The Worker,* where he remained for six years until arrested again in a sweep of radicals. This time he escaped and fled to London; he returned two years later to organize an underground Socialist Party and an army to fight the Russians. Over the next decade Pilsudski became one of the most influential Polish radicals.

At the outbreak of World War I, Pilsudski offered to recruit ten thousand men to send to Austria to fight Russia, an overture that was accepted. By 1916, dissatisfied with German and Austrian interference in Polish affairs, he resigned as head of the Polish army. The Central Powers, seeing a need for his power in Poland, offered him and his nation independence in exchange for help in defeating the Allies on the Western Front. Pilsudski refused; he was imprisoned, to be released only when Germany and her allies were defeated in November 1918. This experience was described in depth in his 1931 work, *My First War Experience.*

Pilsudski returned to Poland, declared an independent Polish state free from Russia, and in 1919 was elected the provisional president of a free Poland. His task, from the beginning, seemed impossible: unite the nation, evacuate German and Austrian soldiers, and assert Polish territorial claims. These claims led Pilsudski to launch a war in 1919–20 against Lithuania, which led to the almost-disastrous RUSSO-POLISH WAR later that year. Pushing deep into Lithuanian territory, Pilsudski's armies brought down on themselves the wrath of the newly-instituted Soviet Red Army, which attacked deep into Poland and seemed, for a time, to be on the verge of capturing Warsaw. A last-minute move by Pilsudski led to the great victory known as "Miracle on the Vistula." This resulted in the Treaty of Riga on March 18, 1921, which ended the war and established the Polish-Soviet frontier, a border which held until 1939. The pact confirmed from Soviet Russia to Poland the rights to Galicia, an area that played a tremendous role during the Eastern Front portion of World War I. The area was then divided into four zones: Krakov and Lvov in the section west of the San River and Stanislavov and Tarnopol in the east.

In December 1922, Pilsudski resigned from the government and retired to his home in Sulejowek. In May 1926 the government of Wincentry Witos, battered by a devastated economy, veered toward collapse as the *Sejm,* the Polish Parliament, lost most of its authority in a power struggle. Pilsudski came out of retirement and, overthrowing the Witos government by force (the battle lasted two days), installed a new cabinet under Kazimierz Bartel, with Pilsudski serving as minister of war. Later that year, Bartel stepped aside as Pilsudski became the premier, then holding virtual dictatorial powers. He served until 1928, and again for a short time in 1930. He controlled the posts of commander in chief of the Polish army and minister of war.

Pilsudski died in Warsaw on May 12, 1935.

References: Stanley S. Sokol, *The Polish Biographical Dictionary* (Waucaonda, Ill.: Bolchazy-Carducci Publishers, 1992), 309–10; William Fiddian Reddaway, *Marshal Pilsudski* (London: Routledge, 1939); Waclaw Jedrzejewicz, *Pilsudski, a Life for Poland* (New York: Hippocrene Books, 1982); Grace Humphrey, *Pilsudski: A Builder of Poland* (New York: Scott & More, 1936); Christopher Blackburn, "Józef Pilsudski" in Anne Commire, ed., *Historic World Leaders* (Detroit: Gale Research, 1994), 3: 1087–91.

Pirandello, Luigi (1867–1936)

Italian author and Nobel laureate. Born in Girgenti (now Agrigento), on the island of Sicily, on June 28, 1867, he received a doctorate of philosophy from the University of Bonn in Germany in 1891. He served as a professor of aesthetics and stylistics at the Real Instituto Superiore di Majistrero Femminile in Rome (1898–1921) and worked at the Teatro d'Arte di Roma (1925–28). Pirandello's first love was his literary work. Examining the lives of ordinary Italians, he composed a series of works that brought him international acclaim. His novels include *The Late Mattia Pascal* (1904), *The Old and the Young* (1913), *Shoot!* (1916), and *One, None, and a Hundred Thousand* (1926). His plays, many written during the interwar period, include *Six Characters in Search of An Author* (1921), *Henry IV* (1922), *To Clothe the Naked* (1923), and *The Life I Gave You* (1924). Biographer Ara D. Jared explains, "Pirandello's influence as a modern dramatist who not confined to the Italian theater. He was recognized as a major international figure in the theater of the twentieth century for his innovative techniques of philosophical and psychological drama, and he produced notable works as dramatist, novelist, short story writer, poet, and critic."

Perhaps Pirandello's greatest work was *Novelle per un anno* (1922–37), a series of 15 volumes of novellas. For this work, as well as the entire body of his literary achievements, he was awarded the 1934 Nobel Prize in literature.

Pirandello died in Rome on December 10, 1937.

References: Gaspare Guidice, *Pirandello: A Biography* (New York: Oxford University Press, 1975); Olga Ragusa, *Luigi*

Luigi Pirandello *(CORBIS/Hulton: Deutsch Collection)*

Pirandello (New York: Columbia University Press, 1968); Ara D. Jared, "Pirandello, Luigi" in Bernard S. and June H. Schlessinger, eds., *The Who's Who of Nobel Prize Winners* (Phoenix, Ariz.: Oryx, 1986), 59; Thomas Watson MacCallum and Stephen Taylor, eds., *The Nobel Prize–Winners and the Nobel Foundation, 1901–1937* (Zurich: Central European Times Publishing, 1938), 322–23.

Pittman, Key (1872–1940)

American politician, leading American spokesman on foreign matters during the 1930s. Born into a wealthy family in Vicksburg, Mississippi, on September 19, 1872, he was educated by private tutors, then studied law at Southwestern Presbyterian University in Clarksville, Tennessee, but he did not receive his degree. After leaving college, he traveled West, earning his fortune in the mines of Alaska and Nevada. He found more of a challenge in defending miners than in prospecting, however, and in 1901 settled in Tonopah, Nevada, rising to prominence as one of that state's finest attorneys. In 1910 he ran for the U.S. Senate against Republican George Nixon; Nixon won in a statewide race. Two years later, however, Nixon died, and Pittman was elected to the seat, which he held until he died in 1940.

In 1916, Pittman became a member of the Senate Foreign Relations Committee, and although his principle interests in the Senate were mining issues and how they affected the American West, by the late 1920s he had become a leading authority on foreign affairs issues. In 1933 he was named as chair of the Senate Committee on Foreign Affairs, and became one of President Franklin ROOSEVELT's allies. Writes historian Wayne Cole, "Serving in this responsible capacity in the critical years preceding the American entry into World War II, Senator Pittman was in the middle of the struggle between the 'isolationists' and the 'internationalists' for control of American foreign policy." He was a key member in the drafting of the NEUTRALITY ACT of 1935; he was also named as one of the American representatives to the LONDON MONETARY AND ECONOMIC CONFERENCE held in July 1933.

He died on November 10, 1940, in Reno, Nevada.

References: Jeannette P. Nichols, "Pittman, Key" in Allen Johnson and Dumas Malone et al., eds., *Dictionary of American Biography* (New York: Charles Scribner's Sons, 1930–95), 530–32; Key Pittman to Keefer Wilson Pittman, February 6, 1939, Folder "Key Pittman Genealogy—Correspondence," container 1, Key Pittman Papers, Library of Congress; Wayne S. Cole, "Senator Key Pittman and American Neutrality Policies, 1933–1940," *Mississippi Valley Historical Review* 46, 4 (March 1960): 644–62; "Senator Pittman Dies Unexpectedly; Foreign Relations Committee Head Stricken in Nevada—George Slated for Post," *New York Times*, November 11, 1940, p. 1.

Pius XI (1857–1939)

Roman Catholic leader and pope (1922–39). Born Ambrogio Damiano Achille Ratti in Desio, Italy, on May 30, 1857, he was the son of a silk factory manager. For his education, the young Ambrogio Ratti attended the gymnasium at San Pietro Martire, the lyceum in the city of Monza, and the College of St. Charles in Milan. At this time he felt the calling to enter the priesthood, and he began his religious training at the Grand Seminary in Milan. Further instruction came at the Lombard College in Rome as well as the Gregorian University; he was ordained a priest on December 20, 1879. Three years later he began to teach at Milanese seminary, where he remained until 1888. He was then made a librarian at the Ambrosian Library in Milan, where, after being named to the college of doctors, he was part of the archive's staff for the next 20 years, serving as head librarian from 1907 to 1910. In 1910, Pope Pius X called him to Rome, where he was asked to rearrange the collections of the Vatican Library; after four years of this work, he was named Prefect in 1914.

In April 1918, Pope BENEDICT XV sent Ratti, now a Monsignor, to Poland as the official apostolic visitor (later the apostolic nuncio) to that nation to handle the negotia-

tions over the Polish-Russian border. On October 28, 1919, at the Cathedral of Warsaw, Ratti was consecrated Archbishop of Lepanto. His work on the border issue led the Interallied Commission to name him as the high ecclesiastical commissioner to oversee the plebiscite held in the area of Upper Silesia. The Polish government awarded Ratti the Order of the White Eagle, and he received an honorary doctorate from the University of Warsaw. His final work in Poland came during the RUSSO-POLISH WAR of 1920–21, when he remained in Warsaw during the Russian occupation of that city. For this work he was named a cardinal and appointed to the See of Milan on June 13, 1921.

Seven months later, on January 22, 1922, Pope Benedict XV died; on February 6, Ratti was chosen as his successor. He was seated as Pope Pius XI, taking the name of the man who had originally brought him to Rome. He chose as his motto "To seek the peace of Christ in the reign of Christ," and selected, as one of his secretaries, Eugenio Pacelli, later Pope Pius XII. As head of the Catholic Church from 1922 until 1939, Pius saw the world come out of one world war and begin preparations for another. He signed the LATERAN TREATIES with Italy's fascist leader Benito MUSSOLINI on February 11, 1929, in which Italy recognized the power of the pope to rule over Vatican City and compensated the Vatican for lands confiscated by Italy in 1870. As enemy of communism, he issued the encyclical *Divine Redemption* to condemn the repressive and murderous regime of the Soviet Union's Joseph STALIN.

Almost all of Pius's reign came in the interwar years between the end of World War I and the start of the next war. In the 1930s, he became concerned with the growing Nazi threat and its repressive policies. As war crept ever closer, Pius lashed out angrily at growing hatred, including that against Jews, bigotry he labeled as "anti-Christian." Pius warned against the peril of anti-Semitism. In the months before his death, he mourned for the world's children, particularly those in the dictatorships of Germany and Russia. In one of his last encyclicals, *Mit brennender Sorge,* released on March 14, 1937, Pius railed against the recent German trials of church officials "with burning sorrow and growing surprise."

He died on February 10, 1939, wracked by uncertainty whether he had done enough to stop the horrendous war that was sweeping the globe.

References: Philip Hughes, *Pope Pius the Eleventh* (New York: Sheed & Ward, 1937), 5–20; Philip Hughes, *The Popes' New Order: A Systematic Summary of the Social Encyclicals and Addresses, From Leo XIII to Pius XII* (New York: Macmillan, 1944); John Norman Davidson Kelly, *The Oxford Dictionary of Popes* (Oxford: Oxford University Press, 1986), 316–18; Matthew Bunson, *The Pope Encyclopedia: An A to Z of the Holy See* (New York: Crown Trade Paperbacks, 1995), 287–88;

Hubert Jedin, "Pope Benedict XV, Pius XI, and Pius XII: Biography and Activity within the Church" in Gabriel Adriányi-Quinton Aldea Vaquero et al., *The Church in the Modern Age* (New York: Crossroad, 1989), 23–29, 47–77; James F. Minifie, "Pope Rests in State at Vatican; To Be Borne to St. Peter's Today; New York Ceremonies Arranged," *New York Herald-Tribune,* February 11, 1939, p. 1; "Pius XI to Be Entombed in Chapel of the Popes," *New York Herald-Tribune,* February 11, 1939, p. 2.

Pius XII (1876–1958)

Roman Catholic leader and pope (1939–58). Born Eugenio Maria Guiseppe Giovanni Pacelli in Rome on March 2, 1876, he was the second of four children of attorney Filippo Pacelli and Virginia (Graziosi) Pacelli. Desiring to become a priest at an early age, he attended the Gregorian University at Rome, where he studied philosophy. After being ordained in the priesthood in 1899, he entered the Vatican Secretariat of State, the diplomatic corps of the Holy See, rising within a few years to nuncio of Munich and archbishop of Sardes. After World War I, Pacelli became the first apostolic nuncio to the new German republic, where he served until 1929. Called to Rome, he was named a cardinal by Pope PIUS XI. He advanced to secretary of state, and the office of *camerlengo* (a cardinal who administers papal affairs when there is no pope) on February 10, 1939, upon the death of Pius XI. On March 2, 1939, he was elected Pope and took the name of his predecessor becoming the 12th man to use the designation Pius.

Just seven months after his ascension to the papacy, Pius was forced to face the onslaught of World War II. Although he pledged the Church's neutrality in the conflict and offered some support for Jews trying to escape the Nazi slaughter, many of his subordinates quietly worked for the Axis powers, particularly against Communist nations and, at the end of the war, to aid Nazi war criminals to escape prosecution. Many historians criticize Pius for the church's stand during the war and in its aftermath.

From the time of the war until his death in 1958, Pius attempted some minor reforms of church doctrine. All in all, Pius's reign is considered conservative in scope and nature; he served 19 years, seven months and seven days, the second longest tenure in the 20th century (he was surpassed in 1998 by Pope John Paul II). Pius died at the papal residence of Castel Gandolfo on October 11, 1958.

References: Richard J. Wolff, "Pius XII" in Frank J. Coppa, ed. in chief, *Dictionary of Modern Italian History* (Westport, Conn.: Greenwood, 1985), 335–36; R. Lieber, "Pius XII, Pope" in *New Catholic Encyclopedia* (New York: McGraw-Hill, 1967–89), II: 414–18; John Norman Davidson Kelly, *The Oxford Dictionary of Popes* (Oxford: Oxford University Press, 1986), 318–20; Matthew Bunson, *The Pope Encyclopedia: An A to Z of the Holy See* (New York: Crown Trade Paperbacks, 1995), 89–91; Hubert Jedin, "Pope Benedict XV, Pius XI, and Pius XII: Biography and Activity within the Church" in Gabriel Adriányi-Quinton Aldea Vaquero et al., *The Church in the Modern Age* (New York: Crossroad, 1989), 29–34, 77–96; "Pius XII: Quick Choice of New Pope. Cardinal Pacelli Succeeds. An Enthusiastic Multitude," *The Times* (London), March 3, 1939, p. 14.

Poincaré, Raymond (1860–1934)

French politician, president (1913–20), prime minister (1912–13, 1922–24, 1926–29). A conservative and a nationalist, Poincaré rose to become a leader of the progressive Republicans, holding several cabinet positions from 1893 to 1903. He was then elected a senator (1903–12), after which he served as prime minister (the first of several terms) and as president. As prime minister, Poincaré influenced legislation and strengthened the French military. His tenure spanned the entire World War I period, and Poincaré sustained patriotism through his stirring oratory and by fighting defeatism in the government and populace at large. He disagreed with Great Britain over the REPARATIONS issue for Germany after World War I, which had been established in the Treaty of VERSAILLES in 1919. Poincaré sent the French troops into the Ruhr region in northwestern Germany to force the defeated country to begin making payments. In the 1924 election Poincaré was defeated by the Radicals and Socialists, but he was again elected prime minister in 1926. During his final term he stabilized the franc, laying the foundation for a period of new prosperity in France.

References: Raymond Poincaré, *The Memoirs of Raymond Poincaré* (Garden City, N.Y.: Doubleday; four volumes, 1926–31); John F. V. Keiger, *Raymond Poincaré* (Cambridge: Cambridge University Press, 1997).

Porter, Cole (1891–1964)

American composer and lyricist. Born to parents Kate Cole and Sam Porter on June 9, 1891, in Peru, Indiana, Porter learned to play the piano and violin as a young child. By age 10 he had composed his first piano piece, dedicated to his mother. In 1905 he attended Worcester Academy, where he studied the dynamic relationship between words and music. Porter then attended Yale University, where he wrote football fight songs and developed a half-dozen full-scale MUSICALS for school clubs and fraternities. A zany, witty surreality and high energy marked his early productions.

After college Porter briefly attended Harvard Law School, at the urging of his grandfather. His heart was not in it, however, and after one year he switched to the school of arts and sciences to pursue music. Soon Porter left school altogether and moved to New York in 1914.

His first Broadway show, *See America First* (1916), was a flop, but he continued to compose songs for other musicals. "Let's Do It" was his first big hit, in 1928. Porter's clever lyrics and tropical rhythms proved wildly popular in such interwar hits as "You Do Something to Me" (which appeared in 1929's *Fifty Million Frenchmen*), "Night and Day" (in 1932's *Gay Divorce*), "I Get a Kick out of You" and "You're the Top" (both in 1934's *Anything Goes*), and "Begin the Beguine" (in 1935's *Jubilee*). His "I've Got You under My Skin" (1936) and "In the Still of the Night" (1937) were written for Hollywood films.

A horse-riding accident in 1937 crushed both of Porter's legs and left him in constant pain. His health and energy quashed, Porter continued to create light-hearted musical scores. Among his memorable show tunes written after World War II are "Wunderbar" (in 1948's *Kiss Me, Kate,* a remake of Shakespeare's *Taming of the Shrew*), "I Love Paris" (in 1953's *Can-Can*), and "All of You" (in 1955's *Silk Stockings*).

Reference: William McBrien, *Cole Porter: A Biography* (New York: Alfred A. Knopf, 1998).

Pound, Ezra (1885–1972)

American poet, editor, and critic. Born Ezra Weston Loomis Pound on October 30, 1885, in Hailey, Idaho, Pound was the son of Homer Loomis Pound and Isabel Weston Pound. He grew up in Philadelphia, Pennsylvania, and at age 13 embarked on a life-changing three-month tour of Europe with his great-aunt, traveling through London, Brussels, Cologne, Paris, the Alps, Venice, Granada, and Tangiers. He studied at the University of Pennsylvania (1901–03, 1906) and at Hamilton College (1903–05), but after a brief stint teaching romance languages at Wabash College in Crawfordsville, Indiana, Pound returned to Europe, where he spent the remainder of his life. Over the years he lived in London (1909–19), Paris (1920–24), and Italy (1925–45, 1958–72).

In London, Pound became a regular contributor to the weekly *New Age* and an editor with the magazines *Poetry* and *The Little Review.* An acclaimed poet himself, Pound led the Imagists and influenced and encouraged other writers during the interwar period, including T. S. ELIOT, James JOYCE, William Butler YEATS, and later Robert Frost, Ernest HEMINGWAY, and D. H. LAWRENCE. Pound's major poetical works include *Lustra* (1916), *Homage to Sextus Propertius* (1918), *Hugh Selwyn Mauberley* (1920), and *Cantos* (1925–60), a sweeping epic that reconstructs the history of Western civilization.

Pound moved to Italy in 1925, where he developed economic theories and became obsessed with monetary reform, publishing his controversial *What Is Money For* in 1939. During World War II he broadcast these theories for the Italian Fascist regime; after the war he was indicted for treason and confined to a mental hospital until 1958. He then returned to Italy, where he died in Venice on November 1, 1972.

References: Noel Stock, *The Life of Ezra Pound: An Expanded Edition* (San Francisco: North Point, 1982); Donald Gallup, *Ezra Pound: A Bibliography* (Charlottesville: University Press of Virginia, 1983); and John Tytell, *Ezra Pound: The Solitary Volcano* (London: Bloomsbury, 1987).

Pregl, Fritz (1859–1930)

Austrian chemist and Nobel laureate. Born in Laibach, Austria, on September 3, 1859, he was educated at the University of Graz (Austria), from which he earned an M.D. degree in 1894. He served as a professor of chemistry at the University of Graz (1893–1907) as a forensic chemist at the Medico-Chemical Institute in Graz (1907–10), as a professor of chemistry at the University of Innsbruck (1910–13), and again at the University of Graz from 1913 until his death. During these periods, Pregl became unhappy with the way chemistry was studied; he set out to discover a new way to analyze chemical reactions. His plan, called micro-analysis, was considered a landmark in his day. Writes one biographer, Philip Hight, "[The plan came about as] a result of his dissatisfaction with the lengthy, complicated, and inexact analytical methods for organic chemistry of his time. The use of very small quantities for analysis made possible the progress in a great many areas of biochemistry." For this discovery, Pregl was awarded the 1923 Nobel Prize in chemistry.

Pregl died in Graz, Austria, on December 13, 1930.

References: Phillip Hight, "Pregl, Fritz" in Bernard S. and June H. Schlessinger, eds., *The Who's Who of Nobel Prize Winners* (Phoenix, Ariz.: Oryx, 1986), 9; Thomas Watson MacCallum and Stephen Taylor, eds., *The Nobel Prize–Winners and the Nobel Foundation, 1901–1937* (Zurich: Central European Times Publishing, 1938), 145.

Prohibition

National American program, 1919–33, which prohibited "the manufacture, sale, or transportation" of intoxicating liquors in the United States. It was called "the defeat of Gambrinus," after the mythical Flemish king who is credited with inventing beer: a reform movement that had sprouted up among other reform movements such as women's rights and rights for freed slaves. Prior to 1919, there was what was called "local option"—the ability of localities to ban, through the ballot, drinking in that state or district. The passage of the Eighteenth Amendment, which established prohibition, in 1919 marked the government's first major attempt to regulate personal behavior. The Volstead Act attempted to enforce prohibition, but it failed miserably. Hundreds of federal agents spread out across the nation to crack down on illegal liquor. But bootlegging, the springing up of speakeasies, where liquor was sold, as well as the birth of "bathtub gin" made in people's private homes was widespread.

Prohibition was a complete failure, and by the late 1920s it was evident that either the law would have to go or more law enforcement would be needed. The Wickersham Commission, headed by former attorney general George W. Wickersham, released a meaningless report in 1931 that held that laws needed to be strengthened. It was too late. Democrat Franklin D. ROOSEVELT ran for president on the platform that among other reforms, if elected he would push to have the Eighteenth Amendment repealed. Upon Roosevelt's election, Congress drafted a new amendment, the twenty-first, and just nine months later, Prohibition was ended. It has been called "the noble experiment."

See also WICKERSHAM REPORT.

References: "Nation Dry Today, But Law Will Be Inoperative in Case of 2 3/4 Per Cent Beer until Court Decides" *Washington Post,* July 1, 1920, p. 1; "Roosevelt Proclaims Prohibition Repeal Today; Special Utah Wire to Give Signal; Drys Seeks 11th Hour Injunction," New York *Herald* (European Edition), December 6, 1933, p. 1; "Prohibition Era Ended! Loop Crowds Hail Repeal; Utah Records Final Vote; U.S. Proclama-tion Follows," *Chicago Herald and Examiner,* December 6, 1933, p. 1; "Repeal Ratified; City Celebrates," *Daily News* (New York), December 6, 1933, p. 1.

Public Works Administration   *See* NEW DEAL.

Pulitzer Prizes

Since 1917, as specified in a provision in the 1904 will of the American journalist Joseph Pulitzer, Pulitzer Prizes have been awarded annually as an incentive toward excellence in journalism, letters, and drama. The newspaper publisher specified that four awards in journalism, four in letters and drama, one in education, and four traveling scholarships be granted. Pulitzer entrusted his mandate to an advisory board then composed primarily of newspaper publishers. He also included a provision that allowed for changes to be made as necessary in the awards system. Since the inception of the prizes, the categories have been expanded and redefined as American journalism has evolved. In 1922, for example, the awards for poetry and cartoons were created.

The table below lists Pulitzer Prize winners in the major categories during the interwar period.

	PUBLIC SERVICE	REPORTING	EDITORIAL WRITING	NOVEL	DRAMA
		PULITZER PRIZES: MAJOR CATEGORIES 1920–1940			
1920	no award	John J. Leary Jr., *New York World*	Harvey E. Newbranch, *Evening World Herald* (Omaha)	no award	Eugene O'Neill, *Beyond the Horizon*
1921	*Boston Post*	Louis Seibold, *New York World*	no award	Edith Wharton, *The Age of Innocence*	Zona Gale, *Miss Lulu Bett*
1922	*New York World*	Kirke L. Simpson, Associated Press	Frank M. O'Brien, *New York Herald*	Booth Tarkington, *Alice Adams*	Eugene O'Neill, *Anna Christie*
1923	*Memphis Commercial Appeal*	Alva Johnston, *New York Times*	William Allen White, Emporia (Kan.) *Gazette*	Willa Cather, *One of Ours*	Owen Davis, *Icebound*
1924	*New York World*	Magner White, *San Diego Sun*	no author, *Boston Herald*	Margaret Wilson, *The Able McLaughlins*	Hatcher Hughes, *Hell-Bent fer Heaven*
1925	no award	James W. Mulroy and Alvin H. Goldstein, *Chicago Daily News*	no author, *Charleston* (S.C.) *News and Courier*	Edna Ferber, *So Big*	Sidney Howard, *They Knew What They Wanted*
1926	*Columbus* (Ga.) *Enquirer Sun*	William Burke Miller, *Louisville Courier-Journal*	Edward M. Kingsbury, *New York Times*	Sinclair Lewis, *Arrowsmith*	George Kelly, *Craig's Wife*

	PUBLIC SERVICE	REPORTING	EDITORIAL WRITING	NOVEL	DRAMA
1927	Canton (Oh.) Daily News	John T. Rogers, St. Louis Post-Dispatch	F. Lauriston Bullard, Boston Herald	Louis Bromfield, Early Autumn	Paul Green, In Abraham's Bosom
1928	Indianapolis Times	no award	Gorver Cleveland Hall, Montgomery (Ala.) Advertiser	Thornton Wilder, The Bridge of San Luis Rey	Eugene O'Neill, Strange Interlude
1929	New York Evening World	Paul Y. Anderson, St. Louis Post-Dispatch	Louis Isaac Jaffe, Norfolk Virginian-Pilot	Julia Peterkin, Scarlet Sister	Elmer L. Rice, Street Scene
1930	no award	Russell D. Owen, New York Times	no award	Oliver La Farge, Laughing Boy	Marc Connelly, The Green Pastures
1931	Atlanta Constitution	A.B. Macdonald, Kansas City (Mo.) Star	Charles S. Ryckman, Fremont (Neb.) Tribune	Margaret Ayer Barnes, Years of Grace	Susan Glaspell, Alison's House
1932	Indianapolis News	W.C. Richards et al., Detroit Free Press	no award	Pearl S. Buck, The Good Earth	George S. Kaufman, Morrie Riskind and Ira Gershwin, Of Thee I Sing
1933	New York World-Telegram	Francis S. Jamieson, Associated Press	no author, Kansas City (Mo.) Star	T. S. Stribling, The Store	Maxwell Anderson, Both Your Houses
1934	Medford (Ore.) Mail Tribune	Royce Brier, San Francisco Chronicle	E. P. Chase, Atlantic (Ia.) News-Telegraph	Caroline Miller, Lamb in his Bosom	Sidney Kingsley, Men in White
1935	Sacramento Bee	William H. Taylor, New York Herald-Tribune	no award	Josephine Winslow Johnson, Now in November	Zoë Akins, The Old Maid
1936	Cedar Rapids (Ia.) Gazette	Lauren D. Lyman, New York Times	Felix Morley, Washington Post; George B. Parker, Scripps-Howard Newspapers	Harold L. Davis, Honey in the Horn	Robert E. Sherwood, Idiot's Delight
1937	St. Louis Post-Dispatch	five individual awards	John W. Owens, Baltimore Sun	Margaret Mitchell, Gone With the Wind	Moss Hart and George S. Kauffman, You Can't Take It With You
1938	Bismarck (N.D.) Tribune	Raymond Sprigle, Pittsburgh Post-Gazette	William Wesley Waymack, Register and Tribune (Des Moines)	John Phillips Marquand, The Late George Apley	Thornton Wilder, Our Town
1939	Miami Daily News	Thomas Lunsford Stokes, Scripps-Howard	Ronald G. Callvert, The Oregonian (Portland, Ore.)	Marjorie Kinnan Rawlings, The Yearling	Robert E. Sherwood, Abe Lincoln in Illinois
1940	Waterbury (Conn.) Republican & American	S. Burton Heath, New York World-Telegram	Bart Howard, St. Louis Post-Dispatch	John Steinbeck, The Grapes of Wrath	William Saroyan, The Time of Your Life

Source: http//www.pulitzer.org

"quarantine" speech

Remarks, delivered in Chicago, Illinois, by U.S. President Franklin D. ROOSEVELT, on October 5, 1937, in which he called for the "quarantine" of war-making nations in Europe and Asia. The president said: "The peace-loving nations must make a concerted effort in opposition to those violations of treaties and those ignorings of humane instincts which today are creating a state of international anarchy and instability from which there is no escape through mere isolation or neutrality." He continued: "Those who cherish their freedom and recognize and respect the equal right of their neighbors to be free and live in peace, must work together for the triumph of law and moral principles in order that peace, justice, and confidence may prevail in the world. There must be a return to a belief in the pledged word, in the value of a signed treaty. These must be recognition of the fact that national morality is as vital as private morality."

In the *New York Herald Tribune*, Ernest K. Lindley wrote: "Washington officials interpreted the President's speech as notice to League of Nations powers that this country was ready to join them in a denunciation of international lawbreakers, but it was not believed that the United States would take the lead in applying any punitive measures. Officials doubted that Mr. Roosevelt's phrase 'quarantine' meant economic sanctions, a measure which would require action by Congress."

International reaction to the speech was swift. The Japanese claimed that they had the "right" to intervene anywhere and live anywhere they wanted to. In London the British Foreign Office "evinced surprise" at the "anti-isolationist" tone of the remarks. In Berlin and Rome spokespeople for both governments claimed that they were among the "peace-loving" nations of the world.

References: Dorothy Borg, *The United States and the Far Eastern Crisis of 1933–1938: From the Manchurian Incident* *through the Initial Stage of the Undeclared Sino-Japanese War* (Cambridge: Harvard University Press, 1964); "President Calls for 'Quarantine' of Aggressors in Chicago Speech; Asserts Neutrality is 'No Escape'," *New York Herald-Tribune*, October 6, 1937, p. 1.

Quidde, Ludwig (1858–1941)

German peace advocate and Nobel laureate. Born in Bremen, Germany, on March 23, 1858, he studied at the Universities of Strassburg and Göttingen, thereafter becoming a professor at the University of Munich, as well as a member of the Bavarian Landtag and on the board of aldermen. From 1892, Quidde was a leader in the German peace movement; in 1894 he published *Caligula: A Study of Imperial Insanity,* a biography of the Roman emperor but a thinly disguised attack on Kaiser Wilhelm II. Tried on charges of treason, Quidde defended himself and was acquitted. When the prosecutor asked who Quidde had in mind when he wrote the book, Quidde replied, "Caligula, of course. Whom do *you* have in mind?"

Quidde joined the Council of the International Peace Council in Bern, Switzerland, as well as the World Peace Congress in Glasgow, Scotland, in 1901. He rose to oversee the meeting of the congress in Munich in 1907, and became president of the German Peace Society in 1914. When World War I broke out, he went to the Hague to meet with English and French peace activists in an attempt to quickly end the war; when he failed, he returned to Germany but by then was branded a traitor and jailed for treason, although the charges were later dropped. After the war, he rose to become vice president of the International Peace Council.

For "his long and arduous service in the course of peace," Quidde was the corecipient (with Ferdinand BUISSON) of the 1927 Nobel Peace Prize. Fredrik Stang, a professor of jurisprudence at the University of Oslo and chairman of the Nobel Committee, said in presenting the Nobel to Quidde, "Two qualities stand out in Quidde's writing and in his work as a whole: moderation and courage. Although he has never had a chance to publish major works outside his professional field of history, all of his work bears the stamp of the historian and the scholar."

When Hitler came to power in Germany in 1933, Quidde went into exile in Geneva, where he lived until his death on March 5, 1941. His final work, *German Pacifism during the World War,* was never completed.

References: Sheila K. Arestad, "Quidde, Ludwig" in Bernard S. and June H. Schlessinger, eds., *The Who's Who of Nobel Prize Winners* (Phoenix, Ariz.: Oryx, 1986), 134; Thomas Watson MacCallum and Stephen Taylor, eds., *The Nobel Prize–Winners and the Nobel Foundation, 1901–1937* (Zurich: Central European Times Publishing, 1938), 373–74.

R

radio

Entertainment medium, popularized on a mass scale during the 1920s and 1930s in the household, where regular music and amusement programs held the attention of millions. Radio started in 1895 with its invention by Guglielmo Marconi; within a few years, it was used mainly for the promoting of small broadcasts on which violin was played. In 1912, David Sarnoff, a telegraph operator, used the radio to keep the world updated on the facts of the *Titanic* disaster. Seven years later, Sarnoff founded the Radio Corporation of America (RCA) to make the radio available to the masses. In 1920 the presidential election returns were delivered to the American people via radio for the first time. In 1921 the Jack Dempsey–Georges Carpentier fight was the first sports event broadcast.

In 1924 Americans spent $358 million on radio sets and parts. Radio music programs such as the Grand Ole Opry from Nashville were popular in these early years. Radio announcers became famous; Norman Brokenshire, Phillips Carlin, Milton Cross, Niles T. Granlund (who identified himself as NTG), Ted Husing, Graham McNamee, and Jimmy Wallington became household names. In 1929 the *Amos 'n' Andy Show*, featuring two white players imitating black comedians, debuted and became enormously popular, as did the family shows *The Goldbergs* and *The Aldrich Family*.

The 1930s saw the introduction of news programs, including those featuring Lowell Thomas and Father Charles COUGHLIN. The most popular shows of the period included *Jack Armstrong, the All-American Boy,* which ran almost 20 years (the last program aired on June 28, 1951); *Ma Perkins*, a serial that featured the "homespun philosophies" of the title character, ran for 7,065 episodes, from 1933–60; *The Lone Ranger* ran from 1933–55; and *One Man's Family* was also quite popular (1932–60). "Talk radio" was also an important segment of radio entertainment; one such program was *The Mary Margaret McBride Show,* hosted by McBride, which lasted from 1934 to 1954. The explosion and destruction of the HINDENBURG was broadcast live on WLS radio in Chicago by announcer Herb Morrison. In England the British Broadcasting Corporation (BBC) became one of the largest radio concerns in the 1920s and 1930s.

In the late 1930s and early 1940s, the advent of television, which did not become popular in a mass scale until the 1950s, marked the beginning of the end of radio as the standard entertainment tool.

References: Lawrence Wilson Lichty, comp., *American Broadcasting: A Source Book on the History of Radio and Television* (New York: Hastings House, 1975); Asa Briggs, *The Birth of Broadcasting* (London: Oxford University Press, 1961); Henry Petroski, "Radio Days," *Civilization* 4, 1 (March 1997): 64–67; Melvin Patrick Ely, *The Adventures of Amos 'n' Andy: A Social History of an American Phenomenon* (New York: Free Press, 1991).

Rainey, Ma (1886–1939)

African-American jazz singer and entertainer, famed for her interwar blues renditions such as "C. C. Rider" and "Black Bottom," which earned her the nickname "Mother of the Blues." Born Gertrude Malissa Nix Pridgett in Columbus, Georgia, on April 26, 1886, she was the second of five children of Thomas Pridgett and Ella (Allen) Pridgett. Little is known of her life before she married singer William "Pa" Rainey sometime between 1900 and 1904, except that she was a singer at the Springer Opera House in Columbus. The duo became known as "Ma and Pa Rainey, Assassinators of the Blues." They toured the southern United States with the Rabbit Foot Minstrels for the next two decades as part of the Negro T.O.B.A. (Theater Owners and Bookers Association).

During one such tour Rainey met and befriended another young blues singer, Bessie SMITH. Although the two singers never professionally worked together, the experience of seeing Rainey perform profoundly affected Smith. In 1923, Rainey signed a record contract with Paramount Records, and began her career at age 37, belting out impressive renditions. In her six years with Paramount, she recorded some of the finest jazz and blues pieces in history. Some of her recordings from this time include "Jelly Bean Blues" and "Gone Daddy Blues." Biographer Hollie West writes, "Ma Rainey was not the first to record the blues (Mamie Smith preceded her by two years), but it was Rainey, along with Bessie Smith, who introduced the earthy sounds of the South, the raw blues of field workers, to the general record-buying public. . . . Rainey usually sang in a moaning, poignant style, but she could also perform with lusty vigor." Rainey performed with many of the leading musicians of the time, including Tampa Red and Blind Blake, Tommy DORSEY, Coleman Hawkins, and Louis ARMSTRONG.

In 1928 Rainey cut her last record. She returned to touring professionally to earn a living; only after the death of her mother and sister in 1935 did she retire to her home in Columbus. In her last years, Rainev ran and owned two theaters in Rome, Georgia, where she died on December 22, 1939.

Of her larger impact on the jazz world, biographer Marshall Stearns intones, "On her records, and in person, she sang only for Negro audiences. Not until after her death, when a growing popular interest in jazz and its origins led to a discovery of many of the earlier 'race recordings' did 'Ma' Rainey win recognition among students of jazz as one of its important figures . . . the greatest of the blues singers."

References: Sandra R. Lieb, "Rainey, Ma" in Darlene Clark Hine, ed., Black Women in America: An Historical Encyclopedia, 2 vols. (Brooklyn, N.Y.: Carlson Publishing, 1993), 2: 958–60; Sandra R. Lieb, Mother of the Blues: A Study of Ma Rainey (Amherst: University of Massachusetts Press, 1981); Hollie I. West, "Rainey, 'Ma'" in Rayford W. Logan and Michael R. Winston, eds., Dictionary of American Negro Biography (New York: W. W. Norton & Company, 1982), 511; Marshall W. Stearns, "Rainey, Gertrude Malissa Nix Pridgett" in Allen Johnson and Dumas Malone et al., eds., Dictionary of American Biography (New York: Charles Scribner's Sons, 1930–95), 2: 547–48.

Raman, Chandrasekhara Venkata   (1888–1970)

Indian physicist, educator, and Nobel laureate. Born in the village of Turuvanaikkaval in Madras, India, on November 7, 1888, he received both his bachelor's (1902) and master's (1907) degrees from Presidency College in India. He served as a researcher in the Finance Department of the Indian government in New Delhi (1907–17), as a profes-

sor of physics at Calcutta University (1917–33), and at the Indian Institute of Science in Bangalore, India (1933–48). During these years, Raman worked on the scattering of light and developed the so-called "Raman Effect," which biographer Bernard Schlessinger says "became a powerful tool for the studies of molecular structure and chemical analysis." For this discovery, Raman was awarded the 1930 Nobel Prize in physics.

Raman continued to work on various areas of physics, including the effect of x rays on infrared vibrations in light-irradiated crystals. He headed the Raman Institute of Research in Bangalore from 1948 until his death on November 21, 1970.

References: Bernard S. Schlessinger, "Raman, Chandrasekhara Venkata, Sir" in Bernard S. and June H Schlessinger, eds., The Who's Who of Nobel Prize Winners (Phoenix, Ariz.: Oryx, 1986), 160–61; "Raman, Sir (Chandrasekhara) Venkata" in Charles Moritz, ed., Current Biography 1948 (New York: H. W. Wilson, 1948), 510–12; Thomas Watson MacCallum and Stephen Taylor, eds., The Nobel Prize-Winners and the Nobel Foundation, 1901–1937 (Zurich: Central European Times Publishing, 1938), 95–96.

Rankin, Jeannette   See PACIFISM.

Rapallo, Treaty of

Pact, signed April 16, 1920, in which the Soviet Union and Germany settled their differences from World War I. Representatives of the two nations met at Rapallo, Italy, and hammered out an agreement that came into force on January 31, 1923. In article 2, Germany renounced claims against the Soviet Union for actions that occurred during revolutionary times; in article 3, the nations pledged to establish diplomatic relations as soon as possible. On November 5, 1922, the treaty was expanded to include the Ukraine, Belorussia, and other Soviet republics. The treaty was annulled by the Soviet Union on June 22, 1941, with the German invasion of that nation.

References: Carole Fink, Axel Frohn, and Jürgen Heideking, eds., Genoa, Rapallo, and European Reconstruction in 1922 (Cambridge: Cambridge University Press, 1991); Edmund Jan Osmańczyk, The Encyclopedia of the United Nations and International Agreements (Philadelphia: Taylor & Francis, 1985), 655.

Ray, Man   See DADA; SURREALISM.

Red Scare

Period of extreme anticommunism in the United States, 1919–20, in which the U.S. government used all of its political and judicial resources to harass and deport those suspected of sympathy with the Communist Party in Russia. During World War I a number of Russians in the United States who sympathized with the aims of the Bolshevik regime in Russia were arrested and tried for trying to stop American participation in the war. A series of Supreme Court cases followed, in which the rights of these dissenters to speak was curtailed. In 1919 the Communist Party of America was founded with the expressed intent of bringing down the American government.

Beginning in fall 1919, Attorney General A. Mitchell Palmer began a series of raids and arrests on Communist hideouts, when it was proven that those suspected were aliens without citizenship, they were deported. On December 22, 1919, the U.S. *Buford* sailed with 249 deportees, including anarchists Alexander Berkman and Emma Goldman. On January 2, 1920, Palmer conducted still more raids, when more than 2,700 Communists in 33 cities were taken into custody. The raids ended that May, but the "scare" over communism in America continued. It reached its height with the trial, and subsequent execution, of anarchists Nicola SACCO and Bartolomeo VANZETTI for the murder of two guards in a robbery. Although Socialist and Communist Party candidates ran in the 1920, 1924, 1928, and 1932 elections, their parties gradually were left alone as they presented less and less of a threat. The recognition by the United States of the Soviet Union in 1933 ended the scares until the rise of the cold war, when similar distrust and panic swept the country in the late 1940s and 1950s.

See also ABRAMS V. UNITED STATES; PALMER RAIDS.

References: Robert K. Murray, *Red Scare: A Study in National Hysteria, 1919–1920* (Minneapolis: University of Minnesota Press, 1955); Ellen W. Schrecker, "Anticommunism" in Eric Foner and John A. Garraty, eds., *The Reader's Companion to American History* (Boston: Houghton Mifflin, 1991), 38.

reparations

System of settlement or repayment due to injured parties (in this case, countries) implemented after World War I in the Treaty of VERSAILLES, signed on June 28, 1919, by the Allies and Germany. According to international law, reparations are legally due for injuries sustained by war. They represent an economic way for the victors to recover costs accrued as a result of the war and to hinder the defeated country's postwar military activity. Reparations also may control the enemy's postwar political behavior.

In Germany's case, the treaty imposed the burden of reparations and also placed limits on the German armed forces. Britain and France, growing poorer and already indebted to the United States, had hoped to transfer much of the cost of the war to Germany. U.S. president Woodrow WILSON's peace program called the Fourteen Points, presented in 1918, had established the legal basis for repara-

tions, calling for "restoration" of invaded territories, which many interpreted to mean "compensation." An initial $33 billion settlement was set in 1921, and Germany found itself unable to make payments. Germany's inability to live up to the settlement led to the French occupation of the Ruhr Valley, in northwestern Germany, from 1923 through 1925.

The reparations terms were eased somewhat in 1924 with the DAWES PLAN, but problems returned with the onset of the GREAT DEPRESSION. In 1929 the YOUNG PLAN revised the terms yet again, but by the early 1930s the entire reparations structure had collapsed. Historians suggest that the Allies' failure to resolve this reparations issue undermined stability in Europe and contributed to the rise of the Nazi regime and ultimately to World War II.

References: Gideon Rose, "Reparations," in *The Reader's Companion to Military History*, ed. Robert Cowley and Geoffrey Parker (Boston: Houghton Mifflin, 1996), 385–86; Philip Mason Burnett, *Reparation at the Paris Peace Conference from the Standpoint of the American Delegation* (New York: Octagon Books, 1940; reprint 1965); Alan Sharp, *The Versailles Settlement: Peacemaking in Paris, 1919* (New York: St. Martin's, 1991).

Reymont, Wladyslaw Stanislaw (1867–1925)

Polish novelist and Nobel laureate. Born in the village of Kobiele Weilkie, near Piotrkow, Poland, on May 7, 1867, he was the son of Josef Rejment and Antonia (Kupcynska) Rejment. As an infant, he and his parents moved to a settlement seven miles from Lvov called Tuszyn. This upbringing in the countryside did not allow for much formal education. To earn a living, he joined an actor's troupe and for a time labored as a railway clerk. Before he was 30 years old, he wrote his first story, *The Comedians* (1896; English translation, 1920). Both this work and his second publication, *Ferments* (1897), were based on his real-life experiences as an actor and clerk. Yet his two most famous works were based on agriculture and life in the rural Polish countryside: *The Promised Land* (1898; English translation, 1927) and the four-volume *The Peasants* (1902–9; English translation, 1924–25). When the first volume of the latter work was released to English-speaking audiences outside of Poland, their impact was immediate: Reymont, who had changed the spelling of his last name, was awarded the 1924 Nobel Prize in literature and secured worldwide fame for his realistic examination of farmlife in late 19th-century Poland. Reymont's last works—*Vampire* (1911) and *The Year 1794* (1914–19)—while important and successful to a degree, were not as popular as his earlier works.

Reymont died on December 5, 1925.

References: Jerzy K. Krzyzanowski, *Wladyslaw Stanislaw Reymont* (New York: Twayne, 1972); Schlessinger, June H.,

"Reymont, Wladyslaw Stanislaw" in Bernard S. and June H. Schlessinger, eds., *The Who's Who of Nobel Prize Winners* (Phoenix, Ariz.: Oryx, 1986), 55; Stanley S. Sokol, *The Polish Biographical Dictionary* (Waucaonda, Ill.: Bolchazy-Carducci Publishers, 1992), 333–34; Thomas Watson MacCallum and Stephen Taylor, eds., *The Nobel Prize-Winners and the Nobel Foundation, 1901–1937* (Zurich: Central European Times Publishing, 1938), 300–301.

Rhee, Syngman (1875–1965)

Korean independence leader and politician, president of provisional government in exile (1919–41). He was born in Korea's Hwanghae province on April 26, 1875; noted historian on Korea Robert T. Oliver writes that "Rhee descended through seventeen generations from Prince Yi Yang-yong, grandson of the founder of the Choson or Yi dynasty." When family fortunes declined, Rhee's grandfather, Yi Hwang, moved from their ancestral estate in Seoul, in the Haeju District, to the Ongjin Peninsula. Driven to help his country achieve independence from Japan, Rhee helped found the Independence Club in 1896. Arrested and tortured by authorities of the Yi dynasty, he spent seven years in prison before being released in 1904.

As early as 1905, Rhee was in the United States, meeting with U.S. President Theodore Roosevelt and pleading for American aid in establishing Korean independence. Because of his pressure, the United States and other nations removed their diplomatic missions from Seoul. Rhee enrolled at George Washington University in Washington, D.C., and spent two years at Harvard. In 1907 he became the first Korean national to earn a doctorate.

In 1910, Rhee returned to his homeland to begin a revolution, starting with students who were constantly staging demonstrations against first the Yi court and then the Japanese, who took over Korea in 1904 following the Russo-Japanese War. Although he was forced to flee to Hawaii to avoid arrest, he was the force behind fresh protest in Korea. He watched from exile the machinations of his fellow revolutionaries to assemble the MARCH FIRST MOVEMENT of 1919, which resulted in a brutal crackdown by Japanese authorities. Dismayed at the lack of progress in gaining liberty for his people, Rhee founded in 1919 the provisional Korean government, of which he served as president. Although he asked for American recognition of his government-in-exile, it was not granted until the Japanese were defeated at the end of World War II.

Rhee returned to Korea in 1945 to find his country freed from the Japanese but occupied in the south by the United States and in the north by the Soviet Union. Forming the National Society for the Rapid Realization of Korean Independence, he ran as president of the south in United Nations–sponsored elections in 1948 and was elected as the first Korean-born president of the Republic of Korea. Rhee was opposed in the Communist north by another Korean revolutionary, Kim Il-Sung, who like Rhee was part of student demonstrations. Kim was chosen as the head of North Korea.

From 1948 until he left office in 1960, Rhee urged the United States to march to the North Korean capital, Pyongyang, and liberate northern Korea. In 1950 he was forced to flee when North Korean troops invaded the south, but he led his fragile government through the Korean War (1950–53), gradually growing more authoritarian in his attitude. After the war, although he led in a massive rebuilding of his shattered nation, corruption in his government soured many on his presidency. In April 1960 a coup led by students forced Rhee from office; he went into exile again in Hawaii, where he died on July 19, 1965.

References: Jeffrey D. Bass, "Rhee, Syngman" in Bruce W. Jentleson and Thomas G. Paterson, senior eds., *Encyclopedia of U.S. Foreign Relations* (New York: Oxford University Press, 1997), 4: 9–10; Robert Tarbell Oliver, *A History of the Korean People in Modern Times: 1800 to the Present* (Newark: University of Delaware Press, 1993), 332; Robert Tarbell Oliver, *Syngman Rhee: The Man Behind the Myth* (New York: Dodd, Mead, 1955); Quee-Young Kim, "The Fall of Syngman Rhee" (Berkeley, Calif.: Institute of East Asian Studies, University of California, Berkeley, Center for Korean Studies, 1983).

Rhineland Crisis

Crucial period, starting March 7, 1936, in which Germany, which was beginning to rebuild its demilitarized armed forces, renounced the VERSAILLES Treaty of 1919, as well as the LOCARNO PACT of 1925, and occupied the Rhineland in western Germany. The Rhineland, located along the western edge of the Rhine River, includes the province of Prussia, the Rhenish Palatinate, western Baden, and the area called Rhenish and southern Hesse; its historical capital is the city of Cologne. In total, the area is about nine thousand square miles. Germany had used this area as a staging point for many of its military maneuvers during World War I, and in the Treaty of Versailles the Allies had sought to demilitarize the region.

German troops began to move into the Rhineland on March 7, 1936, and the Allies refused to pressure Hitler to withdraw. The German leader constructed the so-called Siegfried Line to defend the territory, which the Allies were forced to breach during World War II. The area, under a reunified Germany, is now part of two west German states, North Rhine-Westphalia and Rhineland-Palatinate.

References: Ernst Fraenkel, *Military Occupation and the Rule of Law: Occupation Government in Rhineland, 1918–1923* (London: Oxford University Press, 1944); James Thomas Emmerson, *The Rhineland Crisis, 7 March 1936: A Study in Multilateral Diplomacy* (London: Temple Smith for the London School of Economics and Political Science, 1977);

Edmund Jan Osmańczyk, *The Encyclopedia of the United Nations and International Agreements* (Philadelphia: Taylor & Francis, 1985), 665.

Ribbentrop, Joachim von (1893–1946)

German signatory of the Anti-Comintern Pact in 1936, also known as the ROME-BERLIN-TOKYO AXIS AGREEMENT. Born on April 30, 1893, in the village of Wesel to a middle-class family as Joachim Ribbentrop (he added the more aristocratic "von" later), he attended schools in Kassel and Metz. Entering business, he was sent on a commercial trip to Canada and returned to Germany just as World War I was starting. He then served for a short time on the eastern front against Russia, but was moved to the German military mission in Turkey. After the war, he worked as a wine salesman.

In 1932 von Ribbentrop joined the National Socialist (NAZI) PARTY, and was named a *Standartenfuehrer* (colonel) in the infamous Nazi protection unit (Schutzstaffeln) known as the SS. Considered by his enemies to be arrogant and conceited about his own potential (he was called "Von Ribbensnob"), von Ribbentrop was close to Adolf HITLER, who appreciated his ideas on foreign policy. In 1933, when Hitler assumed the chancellorship of Germany, he made Ribbentrop his chief adviser on foreign affairs. In 1934 von Ribbentrop was made German ambassador-at-large, in which capacity he signed the ANGLO-GERMAN NAVAL TREATY on June 18, 1935. This work led to his appointment as German ambassador to Great Britain, which failed (he offered the king a Nazi salute). On February 4, 1938, Hitler named von Ribbentrop as the minister of foreign affairs. He was instrumental in the signing of the Ribbentrop-Molotov Agreement with the Soviet Union on August 23, 1939, which opened the doors to the German invasion of Poland and the commencement of World War II.

As Nazi Germany collapsed, von Ribbentrop disappeared, but was arrested by the British and put on trial at Nuremberg with the rest of the Nazi hierarchy. Charged with conspiracy to commit crimes alleged in other counts, committing crimes against peace, committing war crimes, and committing crimes against humanity, he was found guilty on all charges. On October 16, von Ribbentrop became the first of the Nuremberg defendants to be executed.

After he was taken down from the scaffold and his corpse photographed, von Ribbentrop was taken to Dachau concentration camp, where he and other Nuremberg defendants were cremated, their ashes dumped in the Isar River near Munich. In 1953 his memoirs, *Zwischen London und Moskau* (Between London and Moscow) were published; they were later translated as *The Ribbentrop Memoirs*.

References: Louis L. Snyder, *Encyclopedia of the Third Reich* (New York: McGraw-Hill Book Co., 1976), 295–96; James Taylor and Warren Shaw, *The Third Reich Almanac* (New York: World Almanac, 1987), 274; Louis L. Snyder, *Encyclopedia of the Third Reich* (New York: McGraw-Hill Book Co., 1976), 295–96; Joachim von Ribbentrop, (Oliver Watson, trans.), *The Ribbentrop Memoirs* (London: Weidenfeld & Nicolson, 1954); Paul Schwartz, *This Man Ribbentrop: His Life and Times* (New York: Julian Messner, 1943); Christian Zentner, and Friedemann Bedürftig, eds., *Encyclopedia of the Third Reich* (New York: Macmillan, 1991), 2: 803–804; Ann and John Tusa, *The Nuremberg Trial* (New York: Atheneum, 1986).

Richardson, Owen Willans (1879–1959)

British physicist and Nobel laureate. Born in Dewsbury, Yorkshire, England, on April 26, 1879, he received his bachelor's degree from Cambridge University in 1900 and a doctor of science degree from the University of London in 1904. He worked at the Cavendish Laboratory in England (1900–1906), as a professor of physics at Princeton University (1906–14), and at the University of London (1914–44). During these years, he worked on "the thermionic phenomenon," which he called the Richardson Effect, which "quantified the theory of electron emission from hot bodies and enabled the development of devices like radio tubes and television tubes." For this discovery, Richardson was awarded the 1928 Nobel Prize in physics.

He died in Hampshire, England, on February 15, 1959.

References: Frank Kellerman, "Richardson, Owen Williams, Sir" in Bernard S. and June H. Schlessinger, eds., *The Who's Who of Nobel Prize Winners* (Phoenix, Ariz.: Oryx, 1986), 160; Thomas Watson MacCallum and Stephen Taylor, eds., *The Nobel Prize-Winners and the Nobel Foundation, 1901–1937* (Zurich: Central European Times Publishing, 1938), 90–92.

Riga, Treaty of   *See* PILSUDSKI, JÓZEF KLEMENS.

Rivera, Diego   *See* PAINTING.

Robeson, Paul (1898–1976)

African-American actor, singer, and civil rights activist, noted for his strong interwar stage and film performances. Born in Princeton, New Jersey, on April 9, 1898, he was the son of a former slave. Robeson was educated at Rutgers University in New Jersey, from which he graduated in 1919. Four years later he was awarded a law degree from the Columbia University law school in New York. He ini-

Paul Robeson in the 1933 film *The Emperor Jones* *(CORBIS/Bettmann)*

tially entered a New York law office to practice law, but sensing that his race would limit him in the profession, Robeson turned to the stage. There he starred in several theatrical productions of writer Eugene O'NEILL, including the plays *The Emperor Jones* (1925) and *All God's Chillun Got Wings* (1923). Although many critics were impressed with his bass singing and his unique interpretation of spirituals, his acting landed him his first and only silent film role, 1925's *Body and Soul,* in which he played both the Reverend and the Reverend's brother.

With the advent of sound, Robeson showcased his enormous singing talent in such films as *The Emperor Jones* (1933), *Sanders of the River* (also called *Bosambo,* a British production, 1935), and Jerome KERR's *Show Boat* (1936), in which he played Joe.

In the 1930s Robeson made various trips to Europe, and espoused several left-wing causes. Upon his return to the United States after a trip to the Soviet Union, he spoke out against racism, joined the National Association for the Advancement of Colored People (NAACP), picketed the White House, refused to sing before segregated audiences, and expressed sympathy for the Communist Party. In the 1940s and 1950s his popularity waned, and the U.S. State Department seized his passport. (It was returned after a 1958 Supreme Court ruling.) Robeson then left the United States and lived for a time in the Soviet Union. His last American film was *Tales of Manhat-*

tan (1942), and on stage he played Othello (1943–44). He later appeared in a singing role in the 1954 German documentary *Song of the Rivers.* In all, he appeared in 13 pictures.

Robeson died on January 23, 1976. The marker on his stone reads: "The Artist Must Elect to Fight for Freedom or Slavery. I Have Made My Choice. I Had No Alternative." His autobiography, first published in 1958, is entitled *Here I Stand.*

References: Rob Nagel, "Robeson, Paul" in Barbara Carlisle Bigelow, ed., *Contemporary Black Biography* (Detroit: Gale Research, 1992), 2: 204–208; Ephraim Katz, *The Film Encyclopedia* (New York: HarperPerennial, 1994), 1161; Paul Robeson, *Here I Stand* (Boston: Beacon, 1988).

Robinson, Joseph Taylor   (1872–1937)

American politician, considered a key player in President Franklin ROOSEVELT's controversial COURT PACKING CONTROVERSY before his untimely death in the midst of the debate on the matter. Born in the small village of Lonoke, Arkansas, on August 26, 1872, Robinson studied law at the University of Arkansas and was admitted to the state bar in 1895. Elected to the state legislature in 1894, he served one term before entering the private practice of law. In 1902, Robinson was elected to the U.S. House of Representatives, where he served five full terms (1903–13). In 1912, he was elected governor of Arkansas, and he took office that following January. Upon the death of Senator Jeff Davis, the state legislature named him to fill the vacant seat, and Robinson immediately returned to Washington, where he served from 1913 to 1937.

A loyal Democrat, Robinson supported the Woodrow WILSON plan of U.S. participation in the LEAGUE OF NATIONS as well as the Federal Reserve Bill. In 1923, he became minority leader in the Senate; 10 years later, when the Democrats recaptured control of that body, he was elevated to majority leader. In 1928, he was nominated for vice president by the Democrats to run with Governor Al SMITH of New York. The election that year was run on the economic performance of the Republicans, who had been in power for eight years, and on Smith's religion. Even though the two men toured widely, Smith and Robinson were defeated. Robinson thus became one of only two men from Arkansas to be named to a national ticket (Bill Clinton is the other). Returning to his Senate duties as majority leader, Robinson led the fight for passage of Roosevelt's NEW DEAL economic program, even though he was not completely in sympathy with the plan.

In 1937, Roosevelt put Robinson in charge of getting the president's "Supreme Court Reorganization Plan" passed in the Senate. Robinson saw immediately the difficulty and danger in supporting such a strategy, but as a faithful Democrat he gave his all for the president. As support for the plan waned even among Democrats, Robinson worked night and day for it; some historians have speculated that Roosevelt had offered Robinson a coveted Supreme Court seat if the plan were approved.

On July 14, 1937, however, Robinson was found dead in his Washington home of a massive heart attack. Shortly thereafter, the court packing bill was shelved once and for all.

References: Nevin Neal, "A Biography of Joseph T. Robinson," (Ph.D. dissertation, University of Oklahoma, 1958); Robert Sobel and John Raimo, *Biographical Dictionary of the Governors of the United States* (Westport, Conn.: Meckler Books, 1978), 1: 84; Beryl Pettus, "The Senatorial Career of Joseph Taylor Robinson," Master's thesis, University of Illinois, 1952; Joseph Alsop, Jr., and Turner Catledge, "Joe Robinson, The New Deal's Old Reliable," *The Saturday Evening Post* 209, no. 15 (September 26, 1936): 5–7, 66–74; "Senator Robinson Dies Suddenly; Senate Faces Fight on Leadership and Fate of Court Bill Is Doubtful," *New York Times,* July 15, 1937, p. 1.

Rockne, Knute Kenneth (1888–1931)

Norwegian-American coach, famed head of the Notre Dame Fighting Irish football team, killed in a tragic plane crash. Born in the village of Voss, Norway, on March 4, 1888, as Knute Rokne, he was brought to the United States by his parents when he was five. He grew up in Chicago, Illinois. After graduating from high school, he worked for a time as a brakeman and mail clerk to earn enough for a college education. In 1914 he graduated from Notre Dame University in Indiana with a bachelor of science degree.

Rockne became known as one of the finest college football players the school had ever seen; the teams that he played on were undefeated for the entire period. After college graduation, he worked as a professor of chemistry at Notre Dame, but Rockne wanted to coach. Working first under assistant coach Jesse Harper, Rockne honed his skills as a manager. In 1918 he was named head coach of the Fighting Irish, where over the next 13 years he compiled a record of 105 wins, 12 losses, and five ties, a winning percentage of 0.897; in his last two seasons, 1929–30, his teams were 19–0. Notre Dame won only one national championship, with Rockne at the helm, in 1924. Four of his players—Don Miller, Elmer Layden, Jim Crowley, and Harry Stuhldreher—became nationally known as "The Four Horsemen." College football historians John McCallum and Charles H. Pearson write, "Between 1920 and 1930, football came into its own and Knute Rockne was its prophet . . . the 'Swede'—as Notre Damers called this Norwegian—was more than just a technical expert. He was a master psychologist, an unerring student of human nature. He knew which player needed praise and which needed a verbal lashing to produce superior effort. He handled each man individually and differently. But he even made practice a delight. Rock's wit was so bouncy and so sharp that there never was a dull moment" on the Notre Dame field. His on-field innovations—including the forward pass and the single-wing formation—were used for many years afterwards.

On March 31, 1931, Rockne and eight others were flying from Kansas City to Los Angeles when their plane crashed in Bazaar, Kansas, killing all aboard. Rockne was just 43 years old. Soon after his death, *The Autobiography of Knute K. Rockne,* edited by his widow, Bonnie Skiles Rockne, appeared. In 1940, his life was memorialized in the film *Knute Rockne, All American,* starring Pat O'Brien.

See also FOOTBALL, COLLEGIATE.

References: Jerry Brondfield, *Rockne: The Coach, the Man, the Legend* (New York: Random House, 1976); John Dennis McCallum and Charles H. Pearson, *College Football U.S.A., 1869–1972* (New York: McGraw-Hill, 1972), 162–63; John Dennis McCallum and Paul Castner, *We Remember Rockne* (Huntington, Ind.: Our Sunday Visitor, Inc., 1975).

Rodgers, Richard (1902–1979)

American composer, whose interwar productions were some of the most popular on Broadway. Born in New York City on June 28, 1902, he studied at Columbia University and at the Institute for Musical Art in New York City. Starting at Columbia, Rodgers wrote a series of shows that revealed his talent for composing songs. During his collaboration with the American lyricist Moss Hart, which lasted from 1919 until 1937, the duo composed the scores for such interwar MUSICALS as *The Garrick Gaieties* (1925), *The Girl Friend* (1926), *A Connecticut Yankee* (1927), *Evergreen* (1930), *Jumbo* (1935), *Babes in Arms* (1937), *I'd Rather Be Right* (1937), and *The Boys from Syracuse* (1938). From *On Your Toes* (1937) came the dance number "Slaughter on Tenth Avenue," choreographed by George Balanchine. From these numerous plays, many of which became favorites of the American stage, such songs as "Thou Swell," "With a Song in My Heart," "Bewitched, Bothered, and Bewildered" and "My Funny Valentine" were featured. The partnership ended with Hart's death in 1943. During Rodgers's association with lyricist Oscar HAMMERSTEIN, the two men wrote the scores for such musicals as *Oklahoma* (1943), *Carousel* (1945), *Allegro* (1947), *South Pacific* (1948), *The King and I* (1951), *Me and Juliet* (1953), *Pipe Dream* (1955), *Flower Drum Song* (1958), and *The Sound of Music* (1959). Rodgers received the U.S. Navy's Distinguished Public Service Award in 1953 for his score for the popular television series *Victory at Sea.* He died in New York City on December 30, 1979.

References: Richard Rodgers, *Musical Stages: An Autobiography* (New York: Random House, 1975); William Hyland, *Richard Rodgers* (New Haven, Conn.: Yale University Press, 1998); Samuel Marx, *Rodgers & Hart: Bewitched, Bothered, and Bedeviled: An Anecdotal Account* (New York: Putnam, 1976); Milton Kaye, "Richard Rodgers: A Comparative Melody Analysis of His Songs with Hart and Hammerstein Lyrics" (Master's thesis, New York University, 1969).

Roehm, Ernst (1887–1934)

German Nazi politician, leader of the Sturmabteilung (SA), murdered by Adolf HITLER in the so-called Night of Long Knives, or "The Great Blood Purge." Born in Munich on November 28, 1887, he served in World War I, where he was wounded three times (including having part of his nose shot off). By the early 1920s he had moved into the realm of radical politics, siding with infant German Workers' Party, the predecessor of the NAZI PARTY. Roehm had assembled a private army, which in October 1921 became the SA, a group of toughs noted for their distinctive brown shirts. Roehm made this army available to Hitler for use in his failed attempt to take over the Bavarian government (known as the BEER HALL PUTSCH). When the putsch failed, Roehm was briefly imprisoned.

Roehm wanted the SA to become Germany's leading paramilitary group, to oversee the German army, the *Wehrmacht*. In 1930 he went to Bolivia to study the army there, but returned when Hitler took power in 1933 to receive a place in Hitler's cabinet. But Hitler made the SA a subordinate of the Nazi Party, angering Roehm. Hermann Göring and Heinrich HIMMLER, head of the SS, convinced Hitler that Roehm was a threat to his rule. On June 30, 1934, rumors were spread that elements of the SA were planning a coup against Hitler. The chancellor called Roehm to meet to discuss the situation, instead, Hitler had Roehm arrested. He was taken to Stadelheim prison outside of Munich, where he was shot without a trial. Other elements of the SA were decimated that same day, called the Night of Long Knives. Of this, Hitler later told the Reichstag, "If anyone reproaches me and asks why I did not resort to the regular courts of justice, then all I can say is this: In this hour I was responsible for the fate of the German people, and thereby I became the supreme judge of the German people."

References: "Röhm, Ernst" in Robert S. Wistrich, *Who's Who in Nazi Germany* (London: Routledge, 1995), 205–207; Elisheva Shaul, "Homosexuality in the Third Reich" in Israel Gutman, ed. in chief, *Encyclopedia of the Holocaust* (New York: Macmillan, 1990), 2: 688; Roger Manvell, *The Hundred Days to Hitler* (London: Dent, 1974).

Roerich Pact

Agreement signed by 21 nations, 1935, which sought to preserve cultural property. Officially called the Treaty on the Protection of Artistic and Scientific Institutions and Historic Monuments, it was first proposed, and later drawn up, by Professor Nicholas Roerich, a Russian-born artist who desired to see cultural property protected by international law. Using the Red Cross as an example of his aims, Roerich explained that he desired that a flag—which he called the Banner of Peace—would fly over all places considered protected under his law. The so-called Roerich Movement to initiate such worldwide legislation gained momentum when three conferences—in Bruges, Belgium; Montevideo, Uruguay; and Washington, D.C.—were held to discuss the proposed legislation. After a meeting of the Pan American Union in Washington, D.C., in April 1935, the Roerich Pact was signed by 21 nations, including the United States, before President Franklin D. ROOSEVELT. The pact calls for "historic monuments, museums, scientific, artistic, educational and cultural institutions" to be "considered as neutral and as such respected and protected by belligerents." The pact also expands "the same respect and protection" to "the personnel of the institutions named." The agreement certified that "the neutrality of, and protection and respect to, the monuments and institutions mentioned . . . shall be recognized in the entire expanse of territories subject to the sovereignty of each of the Signatory and Acceding States, without any discrimination as to the State allegiance of said monuments and institutions."

Reference: Text of Roerich Pact in Dietrich Schindler and Jiøí Toman, eds., *The Laws of Armed Conflicts: A Collection of Conventions, Resolutions and Other Documents* (Geneva: Sijthoff & Noordhoff, 1981), 653–55.

Rogers, Will (1879–1935)

American comedian and social commentator, star of the stage and screen particularly during the interwar era. Born in the small town of Oologah, Indian Territory (now Oklahoma), on November 4, 1879, Rogers was christened William Penn Adair Rogers. His parents, Clem and Mary Rogers, were part Cherokee Indian. Rogers started on the entertainment circuit as a youth, using the rope and lasso tricks he had learned on his father's ranch. He played in vaudeville shows, Wild West shows, and other venues. He made his debut in 1917 with the Ziegfeld Follies. He starred in several motion pictures, including *A Connecticut Yankee* (1931), *State Fair* (1933), and *David Havum* (1934).

Known for his wit, Rogers started a newspaper column that was syndicated weekly in 1922 and daily four years later. With his homespun humor, he soon became one of the most popular political commentators in the United

States. He declined to run for governor of Oklahoma, but did assist Franklin D. ROOSEVELT's election in 1932.

Rogers was also an avid adventurer; on his round-the-world aviating adventure with Wiley Post, both men perished on August 15, 1935, as their plane crashed upon takeoff. He is the author of *Cowboy Philosopher on Prohibition* (1919) and *Will Rogers's Political Follies* (1929). On his gravestone is the passage, "If You Live Life Right, Death Is a Joke as Far as Fear Is Concerned."

References: Will Rogers (Donald Day, ed.), *The Autobiography of Will Rogers* (Chicago: People's Book Club, 1949); Will Rogers (Steven K. Gragert, ed.), *"How to Be Funny" & Other Writings of Will Rogers* (Stillwater: Oklahoma State University Press, 1983); Will Rogers (Steven K. Gragert, ed.), *Radio Broadcasts of Will Rogers* (Stillwater: Oklahoma State University Press, 1983); "Will Rogers and Post Die in Airplane Crash; Pair Forced Down by Faulty Motor; Fall in Take-Off," *New York World-Telegram,* August 16, 1935, p. 1; "Plane Returning Rogers, Post; Air Tragedy Saddens Millions," *Washington Post,* August 17, 1935, p. 1.

Rogers Act

U.S. congressional legislation, May 24, 1924, that established the U.S. Foreign Service. In enacting this law, sponsored by Representative John Jacob Rogers of Massachusetts and written with the help of State Department official Wilbur J. Carr, Congress sought to "reorganize and improv[e] the foreign service," at the same time implementing a system of examinations for advancement for diplomatic officers and constituting a salary method. Historian Ronald Swerczek writes that "the law merged the consular and diplomatic services into a foreign service with a single personnel board to oversee appointments, transfers, and promotions."

References: Ronald E. Swerczek, "Hugh Gibson and Disarmament: The Diplomacy of Gradualism" in Kenneth Paul Jones, ed., *U.S. Diplomats in Europe, 1919–1941* (Santa Barbara, Calif.: ABC-Clio, 1981), 77; United States Congress, House of Representatives, Committee on Foreign Affairs, "Hearings on H.R. 17 and H.R. 6357) (H.R. 6357 Reported Favorably) for the Reorganization and Improvement of the Foreign Service of the United States, and for Other Purposes, January 14–18, 1924," Sixty-eighth Congress, First Session (1924).

Roosevelt, Eleanor (1884–1962)

American social reformer, politician, First Lady (1933–45). Niece of President Theodore Roosevelt, she was born in New York City on October 11, 1884. Her mother died when she was eight, and her father died two years later. She attended the prestigious Allenswood School for Girls in England. She met them young aspiring politician Franklin Roosevelt, a fifth cousin once removed, in 1903, and the two were married in 1905. She was politically active early on, attending her first Democratic convention in 1912. She worked during World War I as a nurse with the American Red Cross, as her husband served as the assistant secretary of the Navy. In 1920, Franklin was nominated for vice president by the Democrats, and Eleanor worked the campaign trail with him. The race was unsuccessful, and afterward Eleanor joined the League of Women Voters to campaign for women's use of suffrage.

While vacationing at Campobello in Canada, Franklin was stricken with polio and Eleanor acted as his political stand-in during his recuperation. During the 1920s she worked for his reentry into political life. In 1928, she pushed him to run for governor and, once he was elected, became an adviser on ways to combat the GREAT DEPRESSION. In 1932 when Franklin was elected president, Eleanor transformed the role of America's First Lady, as the first president's wife to have a public life as well as a career. In 1933 she became the first First Lady to hold a press conference; to get newspapers to hire female reporters, she demanded that only women could attend. She spent her time advocating the rights of minorities; she resigned from the Daughters of the American Revolution when they refused to let African-American singer Marian Anderson perform in their hall, and later set up an outside concert at the Lincoln Memorial for Anderson's performance. She also advocated the improvement of living conditions for the poor and underprivileged, women's equality, and world peace.

After her husband's death in April 1945, she continued her activities, embarking on a career that led many to call her "the First Lady of the World." President Harry S. Truman named her as the U.S. delegate to the General Assembly of the United Nations in 1945, where she served until 1953, and again in 1961 she held the same position. She served as the chair of the United Nations Commission on Human Rights, where she was instrumental in the drafting of the Universal Declaration of Human Rights in 1948. She died on November 7, 1962.

References: Jane Goodsell, *Eleanor Roosevelt* (New York: T. Y. Crowell, 1973); James R. Kearney, *Anna Eleanor Roosevelt: The Evolution of a Reformer* (Boston: Houghton Mifflin, 1968); Tamara K. Hareven, *Eleanor Roosevelt: An American Conscience* (Chicago: Quadrangle Books, 1968).

Roosevelt, Franklin Delano (1882–1945)

American politician, president of the United States (1933–1945). Born in Hyde Park, New York, on January 30, 1882, he studied at Groton School and graduated from Harvard University. He entered Columbia Law School in 1904. Although he was admitted to the state bar in 1907, he never seemed interested in the law, and never practiced it. Rather, he was attracted to the political arena, and in 1910 ran for and won a seat in the New York State Senate as a Democrat, where he showed himself a fighter against the big city Tammany bosses. In 1912, after he campaigned for New Jersey governor Woodrow WILSON for president, Wilson returned the favor when president by naming Roosevelt assistant secretary of the navy (1915–21). Roosevelt dealt with Congress and learned the ins and outs of labor relations in the military, skills that would help him years later. During his seven years with the Navy Department, he earned an outstanding reputation as a hard worker.

In 1920, Roosevelt was nominated by the Democrats to run for vice president on the ticket with Governor James M. COX of Ohio, mainly to balance the conservative Cox with the more liberal Roosevelt. Although Roosevelt

toured nationally and delivered many speeches, his youth and inexperience, showed, and the defeat by Republicans Warren G. HARDING and Calvin COOLIDGE left him unemployed for the first time in a decade. He turned to the private sector, serving as vice president of the Fidelity and Deposit Company in Maryland. Then, in August 1921, while he was visiting his summer home at Campobello Island, New Brunswick, he contracted poliomyelitis and lost the use of his lower limbs. His wife, Eleanor ROOSEVELT, whom Roosevelt had married in 1905, came to his aid and spent the next three years trying to rehabilitate him. With great courage and strength, he came to walk with the aid of crutches and leg braces.

In 1924, Roosevelt appeared at the Democratic National Convention in New York City to nominate his friend Governor Al SMITH for the presidency. The appearance reinvigorated Roosevelt, and four years later, when Smith got the

U.S. president Franklin D. Roosevelt's inimitable rapport with the average voter was a major factor in his four victorious national election campaigns. *(CORBIS/Hulton-Deutsch Collection)*

presidential nomination, he convinced Roosevelt to run for governor in his stead. Although Smith lost in a Republican landslide, Roosevelt was elected governor. A year later, however, the GREAT DEPRESSION struck, and Roosevelt set out with innovative new programs to alleviate and ameliorate the effects of the economic downturn in New York. Reelected overwhelmingly in 1930, he was praised for his handing of the crisis, and his name began to come up as a candidate for the presidency in 1932. By then the depression had deepened, and Roosevelt threw his hat into the ring for the nomination. Opposed by House Speaker John Nance GARNER, Roosevelt early won the nomination outright, but he was forced to give the second spot on the ticket to Garner in exchange for Garner's delegates. Roosevelt appeared at the Democratic National Convention in Chicago to officially accept the nomination, the first candidate to do so. Here he called for a NEW DEAL for the American people—the name stuck to his proposed national program to deal with the depression. His campaign was smooth, and the American people ended 12 years of Republican rule by tossing out President Herbert HOOVER in a landslide. On March 4, 1933, Roosevelt took office as the 32nd president.

As he was sworn in, millions of Americans were in bread lines, unemployment had exploded, and people had little confidence that things would not worsen. Roosevelt declared war on the situation, explaining that he was asking Congress for extraordinary powers to fight the crisis. In a special session that lasted a hundred days, Congress drafted several landmark pieces of legislation to abate the plight of the American people. Roosevelt declared a "bank holiday" and closed all such financial institutions to end the rush on money by frightened Americans. A series of ALPHABET AGENCIES were created to address these needs; farmers were covered under the Agricultural Adjustment Act; the unemployed were helped by the CIVILIAN CONSERVATION CORPS; dams were built and electricity supplied to rural areas in the American South with the help of the Tennessee Valley Authority; industry was shaken up with the passage of the National Industrial Recovery Act. In advancing these ideas, Roosevelt took to the radio in a series of "FIRESIDE CHATS" to discuss with the electorate the pace of reform. His skills learned in the New York State Senate and at the Navy Department were used to cajole and buy influence among weary congressional supporters and opponents.

In 1936, Roosevelt was overwhelmingly elected over his Republican opponent, Governor Alf LANDON of Kansas. This came, however, after the U.S. Supreme Court started a three-year run in striking down as unconstitutional major pieces of the New Deal legislation. Emboldened by his electoral victory, Roosevelt desired to "pack" the court with justices friendly to his thinking; his "Court Packing Plan," sent to the Senate, was bottled up and came under such strict scrutiny by Democrats and Republicans alike that it failed in the end. This episode led to serious losses among congressional Democrats in the 1938 midyear elections.

Later in the decade, Roosevelt attempted to deal with the growing threat of war from Europe and Japan. Numerous diplomatic entreaties did little to solve the situation, and Roosevelt's inattention and fear of being involved in another massive war gave rise to the APPEASEMENT European leaders used to mollify German chancellor Adolf HITLER. The start of the war in Europe in September 1939 did not involve the United States, even though it was closely tied to its ally, Great Britain. The passage of the LEND LEASE ACT in 1940 gave Britain aid that exposed the United States not as a neutral but as a partner. Eventually, U.S. participation in the war was inevitable. The act that led to U.S. entry was the Japanese sneak attack on the naval base at Pearl Harbor, Hawaii, on December 7, 1941, which killed more than two thousand American sailors. Mobilizing his nation to defeat the enemies of Germany and Japan, Roosevelt engaged in the construction of a great military force. Numerous battles in the Pacific led to slow but steady progress against the Japanese; a planned invasion of Europe, which came on June 6, 1944, in Normandy, France, opened the war up to two distinct fronts. Roosevelt's electoral victories in 1940 and 1944 made him the only American president ever to win four terms (this led to the passage in 1947 of the Twenty-second Amendment to the U.S. Constitution, allowing a president only two elected terms).

Roosevelt was in failing health when he ran for his fourth term in 1944, a fact that was hidden from the nation he was leading to victory. He began his fourth them by heading off to Yalta, on the Black Sea, for a meeting with Soviet leader Joseph STALIN and British prime minister Winston Churchill to discuss how Europe would be ruled after the defeat of Germany. Roosevelt, sick with a bad heart, was pressured by Stalin into allowing Eastern Europe to come under Soviet domination. The three men agreed to a meeting in the United States at which a United Nations, a successor to the moribund LEAGUE OF NATIONS, would be drawn up. Roosevelt returned from Yalta, but his doubts grew over the power he had given the Soviets in Eastern Europe. As part of his rest, he vacationed at Warm Springs, Georgia, where on April 12, 1945, he died.

See also COURT PACKING CONTROVERSY. Refer to **Appendix 1** for text of Franklin Delano Roosevelt's first "Fireside Chat" with the American people, March 12, 1933.

References: Ted Morgan, *F.D.R.: A Biography* (New York: Simon & Schuster, 1985); James MacGregor Burns, *Roosevelt: The Soldier of Freedom* (New York: Harcourt Brace Jovanovich, 1970); William Emerson, "Franklin Roosevelt as Commander-in-Chief in World War II," *Military Affairs* 22 (Winter 1958–59): 181–207.

Rosenberg, Alfred (1893–1946)

Estonian-German politician, considered the ideologist of Nazism and the leading advocate in the Nazi regime of the full-scale extermination of European Jews. Born in Reval (now Tallinn), Estonia, on January 12, 1893, the son of a Lithuanian cobbler father and an Estonian mother, Rosenberg studied at a technology school in Riga, then went to France, but left in 1919 for Munich, where the NAZI PARTY was beginning to gain strength in post–World War I Germany. In 1920 he became a German citizen and a major force in the Nazi Party. In 1921 Adolf HITLER, sensing Rosenberg's editorial and writing skills, made him the editor of the official Nazi newspaper, *Völkisher Beobachter.* In addition, he published several anti-Semitic pamphlets, outlining the future Nazi strategy when they attained power in Germany.

When Hitler tried to seize power in 1923 in the unsuccessful BEER HALL PUTSCH, he made Rosenberg the titular head of the party while Hitler was in prison. In 1927, Rosenberg published *The Future Direction of a German Foreign Policy,* which discussed the Nazi ideal of taking over Russia and Poland. In 1930 he published *The Myth of the Twentieth Century: A Valuation of the Spiritual-Intellectual Conflicts of Our Time.* When Hitler was elected chancellor in 1933, Rosenberg was appointed head of the office of foreign politics, to teach potential Nazi Party members the ideology. On October 17, 1941, Hitler named Rosenberg as minister for the eastern occupied territories, where he used all of his energy to ship captured refugees back to Germany as slaves and to exterminate as many Jews as possible.

At the end of World War II, Rosenberg was captured by the Allies, and put on trial at Nuremberg in November 1945. On October 1, 1946, he was found guilty of committing crimes alleged in other counts, of committing crimes against peace, of committing war crimes, and of committing crimes against humanity. Fifteen days later, on October 16, 1946, he was hanged. According to biographer Louis Snyder, "It was reported that he looked at the chaplain but said nothing. In ninety seconds he was dead, in the swiftest execution of the condemned men." Rosenberg's corpse was photographed, then cremated, with his ashes scattered in the Isar River near Munich. His autobiography, *Selected Writings,* was published in 1970.

References: Alfred Rosenberg, *Selected Writings* (London: Jonathan Cape, 1970); Robert Cecil, *The Myth of the Master Race: Alfred Rosenberg and Nazi Ideology* (New York: Dodd, Mead, 1972); Fritz Nova, *Alfred Rosenberg: Nazi Theorist of the Holocaust* (New York: Hippocrene Books, 1986); James Taylor and Warren Shaw, *The Third Reich Almanac* (New York: World Almanac, 1987), 282; Christian Zentner and Friedemann Bedüftig, eds., *Encyclopedia of the Third Reich* (New York: Macmillan, 1991), 2: 812–13; Ann and John Tusa, *The Nuremberg Trial* (New York: Atheneum, 1986); Telford Taylor, *The Anatomy of the Nuremberg Trials: A Personal Memoir* (New York: Alfred A. Knopf, 1992); Louis L. Snyder, *Encyclopedia of the Third Reich* (New York: McGraw-Hill Book Co., 1976), 300.

Ross, Harold Wallace   *See* ALGONQUIN ROUND TABLE.

Rowlatt Acts

Series of enactments by the British Parliament, 1919, which precipitated near civil war in India. Because of disturbances in India, British justice S. A. T. Rowlatt recommended that the British government in India pass a number of laws that included the rights to arrest and imprison persons without trial; to conduct a trial without a jury; and to use torture in interrogation. Edwin Montagu, the former secretary of state for India who later became Lord Irwin, was reportedly repulsed at the thought of such enactments. Indian nationalist Mohandas K. GANDHI led the expressions of Indian outrage at the acts, and his call for protests to have them annulled led to the JALLIANWALA BAGH MASSACRE in April 1919, and to Gandhi's Noncooperation Movement in 1920. Although enacted into law, these acts were never put into use.

References: "Rowlatt Acts" in Surjit Mansingh, *Historical Dictionary of India* (Lanham, Md.: Scarecrow Press, 1996), 358; Ravinder Kumar, *Essays on Gandhian Politics: The Rowlatt Satyagraha of 1919* (Oxford: Clarendon Press, 1971).

Russo-Polish War

Conflict, 1919–20, between the infant Bolshevist regime instituted in Russia and the government of Poland. In 1919, Poland invaded the Ukraine, the breadbasket of Russia, in an attempt to take over the area while the Bolshevik Revolution was being challenged by civil war. The war was short; the Soviets were able to beat the Polish troops, led by Polish president Józef Klemens PILSUDSKI, back so that it seemed for a time that the Soviets would take Warsaw, the Polish capital. However, a military maneuver by Pilsudski led to the great Polish victory known as the "Miracle on the Vistula" and ended the war as a stalemate for both sides. The Treaty of Riga was signed the following year, and a demarcation line, called the CURZON LINE, was instituted, held until the German invasion of Poland in September 1939.

References: Thomas C. Fiddick, *Russia's Retreat from Poland, 1920: From Permanent Revolution to Peaceful Coexistence* (Houndmills, Basingstoke, Hampshire: Macmillan, 1990); Norman Davies, *White Eagle, Red Star: The Polish-Soviet War, 1919–1920* (New York: St. Martin's, 1972); "Bolsheviki Making a Stand at Grodno," *New York Times,* August 28, 1920, p. 1.

Ruth, Babe (1895–1948)

American baseball player, considered one of the finest. His record of 714 home runs was eclipsed only by Hank Aaron in 1974 and his record of 60 home runs in a single season was surpassed by Mark McGwire and Sammy Sosa in 1998. Born George Herman Ruth, the son of a Baltimore tavern owner, on February 6, 1895, Ruth learned from an early age to play baseball when his parents enrolled the rowdy youngster in St. Mary's Industrial School. There, he came under the influence of a coach who taught him the fundamentals of the game. Ruth began his professional career in 1914, when he was chosen by the Baltimore team of the American League as a pitcher; later that season, however, he was sold to the Boston Red Stockings (later the Red Sox), where he made a name for himself as both a pitcher and a hitter.

In the era of the so-called "dead ball," which did not fly very well even when accurately hit, Ruth excelled. In 1919, his last full year with Boston, he hit 29 home runs—at that time a remarkable record. It would not be his last. In 1920 he was sold to the New York Yankees for the then-unheard of sum of $100,000, including a loan to the Red Sox owner of an additional $370,000. Ruth spent the next 15 years with the Yankees, and he blazed a series of records and accomplishments. As an integral member of "Murderers' Row"—a number of Yankee players including Lou Gehrig, Tony Lazzeri, Bob Meusel, and Earle Combs—Ruth helped his team become the predominant sports team of the century. In 1927, Ruth hit an astonishing 60 home runs. In the 1928 World Series alone, he hit an astonishing 0.628 batting average. The $10 million stadium built by Yankee

Babe Ruth (center) flanked by Earle Combs and Bob Meusel, his fellow outfielders for the 1927 Yankees—one of the greatest baseball teams of all time. (CORBIS/Underwood & Underwood)

owner Jacob Ruppert was dubbed "The House That Ruth Built." During the 1920s, aside from his teammate Lou Gehrig, Ruth *was* baseball. In 1934, he signed with the Boston Braves of the National League, but played little during the 1935 season, when he was really too old. He desired a managing position, but none was ever offered, and he retired, beloved by multitudes of fans.

In his 22-year career, Ruth set or tied 76 different records, including 2,056 bases on balls and 1,330 strikeouts, and helped his team win four of the seven World Series in which he played. In 1933 he hit the first home run in All-Star Game history, and he was one of the first players to be elected to the Baseball Hall of Fame. Ruth was a born showman; when he knew he was dying of throat cancer, he appeared before the fans he had once played for in Yankee Stadium and spoke in a choking, husky voice of the love he had for them and the game. When he died on August 16, 1948, at the age of 53, he was memorialized by having his body lie in state at Yankee Stadium. His plaque in the Baseball Hall of Fame reads, "Greatest drawing card in the history of baseball. Holder of many home run and other batting records. Gathered 714 home runs in addition to 15 in World Series."

References: Lee Allen, *Babe Ruth: His Story in Baseball* (New York: Putnam, 1966); Donald Honig, *The New York Yankees: An Illustrated History* (New York: Crown Publishers, 1987), 38–111; "Igoe Tells How Babe Ruth Smashes Out His Homers," *The World* (New York), September 18, 1921, p. 13.

Ruzicka, Leopold Stephen (1887–1976)

Swiss chemist and Nobel laureate. Born in Vukovar, then in Austria-Hungary, now in Yugoslavia, on September 13, 1887, he received his education at the Technische Hochschule in Germany. He served as a professor of chemistry at the Federal Institute of Technology in Zurich (1923–26), at the University of Utrecht in the Netherlands (1926–29), and again at the Federal Institute of Technology in Zurich (1929–57). During these years Ruzicka worked on the synthesis of sex hormones. Writes biographer Connie Dowell, "In 1916, Ruzicka began researching natural odoriferous compounds, which culminated in the discovery that the molecules of muskone and civetone, important to the perfume industry, contain rings of 15 and 17 carbon atoms respectively. Prior to his work, rings with more than eight atoms were thought to be unstable, if they did exist. By 1933/34, Ruzicka was able to offer the first complete proof of the constitution of a sex hormone and accomplish the first artificial production of a sex hormone." This work earned Ruzicka the Nobel Prize in chemistry in 1939, which he shared with German chemist Adolf BUTENANDT. The discovery earned Ruzicka worldwide acclaim and a fortune on a patent. He died in Zurich on September 26, 1976.

References: Connie Dowell, "Ruzicka, Leopold Stephen" in Bernard S. and June H. Schlessinger, eds., *The Who's Who of Nobel Prize Winners* (Phoenix, Ariz.: Oryx, 1986), 15–16; "Dr. Leopold Ruzicka Dies in Switzerland at Age 89; Won Nobel in Chemistry," *New York Times*, September 27, 1976, p. 34.

Saar Basin

Area of controversy, 1919–1935, between Germany and France. The region is composed of approximately 2,569 square kilometers, with the capital of Saarbrücken. With a base economy of coal mines, the Saar was an attractive target for conflict between the two European powers. When Napoleonic France was defeated in 1815, it ceded the Saar to Prussia (later the nucleus of Germany). After Germany's defeat in World War I, sections of the Saar, particularly the Bavarian Palatinate and Rhenish Prussia, were sectioned off and given to France under the VERSAILLES Treaty of 1919, "as compensation for the destruction of the coal-mines in the north of France and as part payment towards the total reparation due from Germany for the damage resulting from the war."

The treaty established the border of the region and constituted "the Government of the Territory of the Saar Basin." It also allowed that after 15 years of occupation, a vote would be taken among the populace whether the region would remain with France or return to German control. Accordingly, a plebiscite was held on January 12, 1935, and the residents voted to rejoin Germany. On March 1, 1935, the provisions of the treaty that had established French control over the area were annulled, and the Saar became part of the German Reich.

On December 18, 1955, the people of the Saar once again voted for union with West Germany, and that same year the region was incorporated into the Federal Republic of Germany.

References: Edmund Jan Osmańczyk, *The Encyclopedia of the United Nations and International Agreements* (Philadelphia: Taylor & Francis, 1985), 687; Laing Gray Cowan, *France and the Saar, 1680–1948* (New York: Columbia University Press, 1950); Frank Marion Russell, *The Saar: Battleground and Pawn* (Stanford, Calif.: Stanford University Press, 1951); Sarah Wambaugh, *The Saar Plebiscite, with a Collection of Official Documents* (Cambridge: Harvard University Press, 1940).

Saavedra Lamas, Carlos (1878–1959)

Argentine jurist, diplomat, and Nobel laureate. Born in Buenos Aires on November 1, 1878, the son of Mariano Saavedra Zavaleta and Luisa Lamas, Saavedra Lamas earned a law degree from the National University in Buenos Aires. He became a professor of international law at the University of Buenos Aires and the University of La Plata. For many years he was known as one of the finest law professors in Argentina, serving as a delegate to the Conference of Jurists in Rio in 1927 and the Seventh Pan American Conference in Montevideo, Uruguay, in 1933. He also served as the chair of the International Labor Congress in 1928. His government work included stints in 1915 as minister of the interior and of justice and public instruction in the cabinet of President Victorino de la Plaza's administration.

In 1932, Saavedra Lamas was named foreign minister in the government of President Augustín Justo; in his six years in this post, he developed the so-called Latin American Anti-War Pact (the *tratado anti-bellico*) to prevent the outbreak of war in his region, and worked for interhemispheric cooperation at the Pan American Conference in Buenos Aires in 1936. That same year, he served as president of the LEAGUE OF NATIONS general assembly. Yet Saavedra Lamas is best known for negotiating an end to the CHACO BOUNDARY WAR (1932–35) between Bolivia and Paraguay. For his labors to end the controversy, he was awarded the 1936 Nobel Prize for Peace.

After leaving the office of foreign minister in 1938, Saavedra Lamas returned to the teaching of law. The author of numerous books on international law and foreign relations, he died in Buenos Aires on May 5, 1959.

References: Reynaldo Ayala, "Saavedra Lamas, Carlos" in Bernard S. and June H. Schlessinger, eds., *The Who's Who of Nobel Prize Winners* (Phoenix, Ariz.: Oryx, 1986), 136–37; Paul E. Masters, Jr., "Saavedra Lamas, Carlos" in Harold Josephson, ed. in chief, *Biographical Dictionary of Modern Peace Leaders* (Westport, Conn.: Greenwood, 1985), 829–31; Thomas Watson MacCallum and Stephen Taylor, eds., *The Nobel Prize–Winners and the Nobel Foundation, 1901–1937* (Zurich: Central European Times Publishing, 1938), 385; Daniel Lewis, "Saavedra Lamas, Carlos" in Barbara A. Tenenbaum, ed. in chief, *Encyclopedia of Latin American History and Culture*, 5 vols. (New York: Charles Scribner's Sons), 5: 3.

Sacco, Nicola (1891–1927), and Bartolomeo Vanzetti (1888–1927)

Italian Americans executed in 1927, amid great controversy, after being charged with a violent burglary that resulted in two deaths. On April 15, 1920, in South Braintree, Massachusetts, a shoe company paymaster and his security guard were robbed and murdered, while carrying more than $15,000 cash in bank deposits. The next month, two men were seized for the crime. Both Italian immigrants and anarchists, Nicola Sacco (29, a factory worker) and Bartolomeo Vanzetti (32, a fish peddler) were charged and convicted on July 14, 1921, after a six-week trial, of the robbery and murder.

Critics charged that the evidence supporting the conviction was slim, however, Vanzetti even had an alibi that he was selling fish at the time. The case made worldwide headlines, as many felt that the court had been prejudiced against Sacco and Vanzetti for their radical views. It was an era of fear, after all, as the anticommunist PALMER RAIDS were occurring in the United States. Socialist lawyer Fred H. Moore was hired by the Sacco-Vanzetti Defense Fund, money that had been raised by leftist organizations throughout the country. From 1921 until 1927, Sacco and Vanzetti's lawyers filed numerous motions for the verdict to be set aside, for a new trial to be held, in both the state and federal courts. The judge who presided over their trial, however, Webster Thayer, thought the men guilty and denied all motions.

On April 9, 1927, after all of the appeals had run out, Thayer sentenced both men to death in the electric chair. National outrage led Massachusetts governor Alvan T. Fuller to appoint a committee of leading thinkers, headed by A. Lawrence Lowell of Harvard University, to review the case again. The Lowell Committee claimed that the trial was just, however, and that clemency was not warranted. On August 23, 1927, first Sacco and then Vanzetti were executed. On July 19, 1977, on the 50th anniversary of their execution, the two men received pardons from Governor Michael S. Dukakis: "There are . . . compelling grounds for believing that the Sacco and Vanzetti legal proceedings were permeated with unfairness . . . Any stigma and disgrace should be forever removed from the names of their families and descendents."

References: Robin D. G. Kelley, "Sacco-Vanzetti Case" in Mari Jo Buhle, Paul Buhle, and Dan Georgakas, eds., *Encyclopedia of the American Left* (New York: Garland, 1990), 667–86; "Sacco and Vanzetti: Myth and Reality" in Julian Symons, *A Pictorial History of Crime* (New York: Crown Publishers, 1966), 128–29; Bernard Ryan, Jr., "Sacco-Vanzetti Trial: 1923" in Edward W. Knappman, ed., *Great American Trials* (Detroit: Visible Ink Press, 1994), 289–93; Herbert B. Ehrman, *The Case That Will Not Die: Commonwealth v. Sacco and Vanzetti* (Boston: Little, Brown & Company, 1964); *The Sacco-Vanzetti Case: Transcript of the Record of the Trial of Nicola Sacco and Bartolomeo Vanzetti in the Courts of Massachusetts and Subsequent Proceedings, 1920–7* (New York: Henry Holt & Company; four volumes, 1928); "Madeiros, Sacco, Vanzetti Died in Chair This Morning," *Boston Daily Globe*, August 23, 1927, p. 1.

Saint-Germain-en-Laye, Treaty of

Pact, signed September 10, 1919, in which the nations victorious in World War I separated Austria from Hungary (formerly the Austro-Hungarian Empire), and established in the western section the state of Czechoslovakia (now separated in the Czech and Slovak Republics). Its text, which was completed by the delegates at the VERSAILLES Peace Conference, was handed to the Austrian delegates on July 20, 1919; after being signed, it was ratified by the Austrian Parliament on October 17, 1919.

The treaty established the nation of Austria as a separate and independent republic and fixed its boundaries for the first time. The Treaty of Brest-Litovsk, which had ended Russian involvement in the war, was voided, as were all further agreements with the Russian and subsequent Soviet governments. The future Austrian army was limited to thirty thousand men; the region of Upper Adige was assigned to Italy, and some areas were given to Romania and the new nation of Yugoslavia. A protocol (addition) was signed in Geneva on October 4, 1922, that prevented Austria from future political alignment with Germany. The protocol was broken when Austria invited German troops to occupy that nation in 1938.

See also ANSCHLUSS.

References: Jacob Viner, *The Customs Union Issue* (New York: Carnegie Endowment for International Peace, 1950); Edmund Jan Osmańczyk, *The Encyclopedia of the United Nations and International Agreements* (Philadelphia: Taylor & Francis, 1985), 689.

Salt March   *See* GANDHI, MOHANDAS KARAMCHAND; NEHRU, JAWAHARLAL; SALT SATYAGRAHA.

Salt Satyagraha

Protest, 1930–31, by members of the Indian National Congress, including Mohandas K. GANDHI. Gandhi, a nationally known figure who had long protested social injustice in India, sought to change social conditions and unjust government laws though the *satyagraha,* or "soul force." From 1906 until 1914, he conducted a number of these protests, which forced the rulers of South Africa to change their laws regarding minorities. In 1930 the first *satyagraha* was instituted against the despised salt taxes imposed by the British government. Through marches and nonviolent protests, Gandhi bought pressure on the government to lessen the tax. Finally, the government jailed Gandhi and sixty thousand of his followers; however, by 1931, the government saw the danger of keeping such a popular figure in prison and released him, at the same time giving in to his demands. Soon after his release, Gandhi took part in the 1931 Indian Round Table Conference, where he demanded that Britain become more sympathetic to the problems of India.

References: Parshotam Mehra, *A Dictionary of Modern Indian History, 1707–1947* (Delhi: Oxford University Press, 1985), 181–85; S. R. Bakshi, "The Dandi March of Gandhi," *The Modern Review* 134, no. 4 (April 1974): 250–58; *Reader's Digest Great Events of the 20th Century: How They Changed Our Lives* (Pleasantville, N.Y.: The Reader's Digest Association, 1977), 163.

Sandino, Augusto César (1893–1934)

Nicaraguan rebel leader, leader of a peasant revolt, assassinated in 1934. Born Augusto Nicolás Calderón Sandino in the village of Niquinohomo, Nicaragua, he was the son of a wealthy coffee plantation owner and a peasant worker. Abandoned by his mother, he spent time with his maternal grandmother before living with his father; he was educated in local schools, but otherwise little is known about his early life. In 1921 he shot the son of a town leader and fled to Honduras to avoid prison. By 1926, however, he returned to his homeland to raise a rebel army to fight the conservative government of president Adolfo Díaz, which had been backed by American troops before their evacuation in 1925. Sandino raised a force of some eight hundred men, and attacked several army garrisons, including that at El Jícaro.

In May 1927, U.S. President Calvin COOLIDGE again sent troops to Nicaragua to quell the violence, but by then Sandino had acquired arms and other matériel. An agreement reached by the Americans and the liberal opposition at Tipitapa on May 3, 1927, was not recognized by

Sandino, and he continued his guerrilla war by hiding in the mountains. He renamed El Jícaro, the site of his first major attack, Ciudad Sandino and issued a manifesto that claimed he was a mystic designed to drive American influence from the country. For nearly six years, Sandino defied all efforts by either the Nicaraguan government or the Americans to drive him out of his mountain retreat.

On January 3, 1933, the last American Marines pulled out, and on February 2, 1933, Sandino signed a peace accord with the newly elected president, Juan Bautista Sacasa, and came out of the mountains. After a while, however, Sandino began to have differences with the Nicaraguan National Guard and their head, Anastasio SOMOZA. He desired to meet with Sacasa to discuss the problem. After dinner with the president on February 21, 1934, Sandino, his brother Socrates, and two aides were taken to the airport in the capital of Managua and shot to death. Somoza's men then raided Sandino's headquarters and executed most of his followers.

Historians debate whether Sandino was a bandit or a patriot. In 1979 rebels opposed to Somoza's son, Anastasio Somoza DeBayle, took up the name of Sandino, calling themselves *Sandinistas* ("followers of Sandino") in their successful revolution to topple the Nicaraguan government.

See also NICARAGUA, AMERICAN OCCUPATION OF.

References: Robert Edgar Conrad, ed. and trans., *Sandino: The Testimony of a Nicaraguan Patriot, 1921–1934* (Princeton, N.J.: Princeton University Press, 1990); Mark Everingham, "Sandino, Augusto César" in Barbara A. Tenenbaum, ed. in chief, *Encyclopedia of Latin American History and Culture* (New York: Charles Scribner's Sons, 1996), 5: 45–47; LeeAnna Y. Keith, "Sandino, Augusto César" in Bruce W. Jentleson and Thomas G. Paterson, senior eds., *Encyclopedia of U.S. Foreign Relations* (New York: Oxford University Press, 1997), 4: 58; Neill Macaulay, *The Sandino Affair* (Chicago: Quadrangle Books, 1967).

Sanger, Margaret (1879–1966)

American birth control advocate and founder of the American Birth Control League (1921). Born Margaret Louise Higgins on September 11, 1879, in Corning, New York, she was the sixth of 11 children born to Michael Hennessey Higgins and Anne (Purcell) Higgins. She attended Claverack College and was trained as a nurse at White Plains (New York) Hospital. She briefly taught on the Lower East Side of New York, where she came in contact with numerous immigrant women with unwanted pregnancies. In some cases these women resorted to illegal or self-inflicted abortions, which left many sterile, injured, or dead. Sympathetic to their plight, Sanger began to dispense birth control advice.

In 1914, Sanger founded *The Woman Rebel*, a magazine on birth control. She was arrested and charged with violating the state's Comstock Law, which prohibited the dissemination of birth control information through the mail. In 1916 Sanger, her sister Ethel Higgins Byrne, and Fania Mindell opened the first birth control clinic, located in the Brownsville section of Brooklyn in New York. The women served 30 days in prison, for at this time providing birth control was illegal, but Sanger's appeals led to federal judges ruling that doctors indeed had the right to dispense birth control advice.

In 1921, Sanger convened the first American birth control conference, held in New York. During the meeting, Sanger and another advocate, Mary Winsor, were arrested for speaking publicly about birth control. That same year, Sanger established the Planned Parenthood Federation of America (PPFA) and, following the New York conference, formed the American Birth Control League in 1922. Sanger believed that the control of births by immigrants, whom she saw as a growing threat to the United States, was important and, to this end, she was a founding member of the American Eugenics Society, which advocated the control of immigrant populations in America and the sterilization of those thought by society to be "unfit." These radical ideas were advanced in her 1922 work, *The Pivot of Civilization*. In her later years, Sanger served as the president of the International Planned Parenthood Federation. She is the author of *What Every Mother Should Know* (1917), *My Fight for Birth Control* (1931), and *Margaret Sanger: An Autobiography* (1938). She died on September 6, 1966.

See also EUGENICS; STOPES, MARIE CARMICHAEL.

References: Ellen Chesler, *Woman of Valor: Margaret Sanger and the Birth Control Movement in America* (New York: Simon & Schuster, 1992); David M. Kennedy, "Birth Control: Its Heroine and Its History in America: The Career of Margaret Sanger," (Ph.D. dissertation, Yale University, 1968); Jay Robert Nash, *Encyclopedia of World Crime*, 6 vols. (Wilmette, Ill.: CrimeBooks, 1990); "Profile: Margaret Sanger" in John H. Rhodehamel, Stephen F. Rohde, and Paul Von Blum, *Foundations of Freedom* (Los Angeles: Constitutional Rights Foundation, 1991), 75.

Saukel, Fritz (1894–1946)

German politician, head of Reich labor during World War II. Born in Hassfurt, in Germany's Lower Franconia area, on October 27, 1894, as Ernst Friedrich Christoph Saukel, he entered the German merchant marines and became an experienced seaman. Captured by the French, he served much of World War I in internment. After the war, he shied away from politics, becoming an apprentice locksmith.

That all changed in 1922, however, when he became a member of the growing NAZI PARTY. A devoted aide to Adolf HITLER, Saukel was rewarded for his loyalty in 1925 by being named as district party leader in the region of Thuringia. After serving in the Thuringian legislature from 1927 to 1933 as the Nazi Party leader, he was named by Hitler the Reich governor of Thuringia. His work in this area, particularly his ability to have foreign guest workers come to Germany to help build its industries in the years before the Germans invaded Poland in September 1939, made him Hitler's logical choice for Reich defense commissioner for labor deployment and allocation. Initially, Saukel treated the workers humanely: "All these people must be fed, housed, and treated in such a way that with the least possible outlay the greatest possible results will be achieved." Yet as costs rose, and the German armies conquered territory rich with civilians, Saukel instigated slave labor on a mass scale. From 1942 until 1945, some five million people were sent through the German factories as slaves, many of them dying under torturous conditions. As many perished, Saukel fervently reported to Hitler that work was going ahead on schedule and that the Reich needed more and more workers to fill his quotas.

With the collapse of Nazi Germany in 1945, Saukel was captured by the Allies and tried at Nuremberg later that year. After being convicted of committing crimes against humanity and other war crimes, Saukel pleaded that he was merely following orders. When films were shown in the courtroom of the labor camps which he oversaw, he pleaded, "I'd choke myself with these hands if I thought that I had the slightest thing to do with those murders. It is a shame! It is a disgrace for us and our children!" But his earlier reports to Hitler surfaced. He was sentenced to death on October 1, 1946. Saukel was the eighth of the 10 Nazi criminals to be hanged. The corpses were trucked to a crematorium (rumored to be that at Dachau), where they were cremated and unceremoniously dumped into the Isar River near Munich.

References: Christian Zentner and Friedemann Bedüftig, eds., *Encyclopedia of the Third Reich* (New York: Macmillan, 1991), 2: 830; James Taylor and Warren Shaw, *The Third Reich Almanac* (New York: World Almanac, 1987), 291; Ann and John Tusa, *The Nuremberg Trial* (New York: Atheneum, 1986); Telford Taylor, *The Anatomy of the Nuremberg Trials: A Personal Memoir* (New York: Alfred A. Knopf, 1992), 610.

Schechter Poultry Corporation v. United States

Landmark U.S. Supreme Court decision, in which the court struck down the NATIONAL RECOVERY ADMINISTRATION, a key component of President Franklin Roosevelt's NEW DEAL economic program, as unconstitutional. The petitioners were convicted in the District Court of the United States for the Eastern District of New York on 18 counts of an indictment charging violations of the so-called "Live Poultry Code" of the National Industrial

Recovery Act (NIRA), which regulated interstate commerce, as well as violations of the minimum wage and maximum hour provisions of the code. The petitioners then sued to the U.S. Supreme Court for relief and the Court heard arguments on May 2 and 3, 1935.

The Court handed down its decision a little more than three weeks later. On May 27, Chief Justice Charles Evans HUGHES held for a unanimous court in striking down the section of the NIRA as an unconstitutional exercise of power of the federal government over interstate commerce. Writing for the court, Hughes said, "We are of the opinion that the attempt through the provisions of the code to fix the hours and wages of employees of defendants in their intrastate business was not a valid exercise of federal power. . . . The other violations for which defendants were convicted related to the making of local sales. Ten counts, for violation of the provision as to 'straight killing,' were for permitting customers to make 'selections of individual chickens taken from particular coops and half coops.' Whether or not this practice is good or bad for the local trade, its effect, if any, upon interstate commerce was only indirect. The same may be said of violations of the code by intrastate transactions consisting of the sale 'of an unfit chicken' and of sales which were not in accord with the ordinances of the city of New York. The requirement of reports as to prices and volumes of defendants' sales was incident to the effort to control their intrastate business."

The *Schechter* decision came down on the same day that the Court struck down other key portions of Roosevelt's New Deal economic program, a date historians call "BLACK MONDAY."

See also COURT PACKING CONTROVERSY.

References: Leonard W. Levy, "Schechter Poultry Corp. v. United States" in Leonard W. Levy, ed. in chief, *Encyclopedia of the American Constitution* (New York: Macmillan, 1986–92), 4: 1622–23; Vincent Murray Brown, "Contemporary Appraisal: The National Industrial Recovery Program," (Ph.D. dissertation, Georgetown University, 1954); Frank Friedel, "The Sick Chicken Case" in John A. Garraty, ed., *Quarrels That Have Shaped the Constitution* (New York: Harper & Row, Publishers, 1987), 233–52; *Schechter Poultry Corp. v. United States* 295 US 495 (1935).

Schenck v. United States

Landmark U.S. Supreme Court decision, holding that speech considered a "clear and present danger" to the United States in wartime could be restricted. Schenck and two other men were accused of printing anti-American leaflets, violating the Espionage Act of June 15, 1917, "by causing and attempting to cause insubordination . . . in the military and naval forces of the United States, and to obstruct the recruiting and enlistment service of the

United States, when the United States was at war with the German Empire." Convicted, the three men appealed to the U.S. Supreme Court, which heard arguments on January 9 and 10, 1919.

On March 3 the Court unanimously held that the Espionage Act was constitutional, and that the government, in time of war, was allowed to ban certain types of speech. Holding for the court, Justice Oliver Wendell HOLMES wrote, "The question in every case is whether the words used are used in such circumstances and are of such a nature as to create a clear and present danger that they will bring about the substantive evils that Congress has a right to prevent. It is a question of proximity and degree. When a nation is at war many things that might be said in time of peace are such a hindrance to its effort that their utterance will not be endured so long as men fight and that no Court could regard them as protected by any constitutional right. It seems to be admitted that if an actual obstruction of the recruiting service were proved, liability for words that produced that effect might be enforced."

Starting with *Schenck*, the Court found in six separate sedition cases between 1919 and 1920 that certain speech was not protected by the U.S. Constitution. These cases are *Frohwerk v. United States*, DEBS V. UNITED STATES, ABRAMS V. UNITED STATES, Schaefer v. United States, and *Pierce v. United States*.

See also PALMER RAIDS; RED SCARE.

References: Martin Shapiro, "Schenck v. United States" in Leonard W. Levy, ed. in chief, *Encyclopedia of the American Constitution* (New York: Macmillan, 1986–92), 4: 1623–24; Elder Witt, ed., *Congressional Quarterly's Guide to the U.S. Supreme Court* (Washington, D.C.: Congressional Quarterly, 1979), 397; *Schenck v. United States,* 249 US 47 (1919).

Schrödinger, Erwin (1887–1961)

Austrian physicist and Nobel laureate. Born in Vienna on August 12, 1887, the son of Rudolf Schrödinger, Erwin attended the University of Vienna, which awarded him a doctorate degree in 1910. A researcher from 1910 until 1914, he then joined the Austrian army and saw action in World War I. He returned to Austria in 1920, settling in the town of Jena as an assistant to the Austrian physicist Max Wien.

From 1920 until 1927, he served at various universities, including the Stuttgart Polytechnic and Breslau University. In 1927 he succeeded Max Planck in his chair at Berlin University. It was during these years that Schrödinger formulated his investigations into atomic theory, which established him as a leading physicist. Biographer Alison Staton writes, "Early in his career, Schrödinger worked on specific heats of solids, thermodynamics, atomic spectra, and physiological studies of color, culminating this period with the development of his wave equations." For this work, Schrödinger was the corecipient (with Paul DIRAC) of the 1933 Nobel Prize in physics.

The rise of the Nazis in Germany and Austria marked the end of Schrödinger's rise in the scientific circles of Europe. He was a rabid anti-Nazi and paid with his professional career when Germany invaded Austria in 1938; Schrödinger fled to Ireland, where he taught until 1956 at the School for Advanced Studies in Dublin. He died in Vienna on January 4, 1961. His publications include *What Is Life?* (1945) and *Space-Time Structure* (1950).

References: Alison Staton, "Schrödinger, Erwin" in Bernard S. and June H. Schlessinger, eds., *The Who's Who of Nobel Prize Winners* (Phoenix, Ariz.: Oryx, 1986), 161–62.

Schuschnigg, Kurt von (1897–1977)

Austrian chancellor (1934–38), who attempted to stave off the German invasion and occupation of his nation known as the ANSCHLUSS. Born in Riva, in South Tyrol (now in Italy), on December 14, 1897, he was the son of an Austro-Hungarian army officer. During World War I, he served in the Austro-Hungarian army but was taken prisoner by the Italians near the end of the war. After being repatriated, he attended the Universities of Freiburg and Vienna, where he studied the law. He opened a law office in 1924. In 1927, he was elected as a deputy to the Austrian National Council as a member of the Christian Social Party. Regarded by his fellow party members as a rising figure, in 1932 he was chosen as the minister of justice in the cabinet of Chancellor Engelbert DOLLFUSS; he was then minister of education (1933–34).

On July 25, 1934, a team of Austrian Nazis, intent on overthrowing the government, besieged the capital and assassinated Dollfuss. On that same day, von Schuschnigg was named as his replacement. In the next four years, he also held the posts of minister of defense, foreign minister, and minister for public security (1937–38). He ruled the Austrian state with a dictatorial hand and was key in the ousting of Prince Ernst Rüdiger von Starhemberg, an Austrian Nazi who had participated in Hitler's BEER HALL PUTSCH in 1923. Serving as vice chancellor under Dollfuss and von Schuschnigg, von Starhemberg had been head of the Austrian fascist militia since 1930.

Von Schuschnigg staved off the German annexation of Austrian as long as he had the support of Italian leader Benito MUSSOLINI; in 1937, however, he lost Mussolini's support and the takeover was but a matter of time. Von Schuschnigg later wrote, "The 12th of February, 1938, the day of my interview with Adolf Hitler at his mountain retreat, Berghof, near Berchtesgaden, will for ever remain one of the darkest and most fateful days in the annals of Austria. It was the beginning of the end, for exactly one month later the German army invaded Austria. Indeed, it

was rather the beginning of the last act, since the meeting at Berchtesgaden was the outcome of a long period of friction between Austria and Germany, the last desperate attempt of a small State to stave off the end of its national existence." Hitler forced von Schuschnigg to accept the quasi leadership of Artur SEYSS-INQUART, the Nazi minister of the interior, who was to be named as the new Austrian minister for internal administration and security—in other words Austria was now a Nazi puppet state. Von Schuschnigg attempted to hold a plebiscite for or against Nazi rule; when German troops massed at the Austrian border, von Schuschnigg called off the vote. Hitler then demanded his resignation, which came on March 11, 1938.

When the German army entered Austria, von Schuschnigg was interned for a time in a Vienna hotel before being arrested and sent to a series of concentration camps. Liberated by the Allies in 1946, he went to the United States, where he served as a professor of government at the University of St. Louis, becoming a naturalized American citizen in 1956. In 1967 he returned to Austria, settling down in the Tyrol area of that country. Von Schuschnigg died at Mutters near Innsbruck on November 18, 1977.

References: Robert S. Wistrich, *Who's Who in Nazi Germany* (London: Routledge, 1995), 230–31; Kurt von Schuschnigg (Franz von Hildebrand, trans.), *Austrian Requiem* (London: Victor Gollancz, 1947), 13; Count Galeazzo Ciano (Malcolm Muggeridge, ed.), *Ciano's Diplomatic Papers, Being a Record of Nearly 200 Conversations Held during the Years 1936–42 with Hitler, Mussolini, Franco, Goering, Ribbentrop, Chamberlain, Eden, Sumner Welles, Schuschnigg, Lord Perth, François-Poncet, and many other World Diplomatic and Political Figures, Together with Important Memoranda, Letters, Telegrams, etc.* (London: Odhams, 1948).

Schutzstaffeln (SS)   See KALTENBRUNNER, ERNST; HIMMLER, HEINRICH; NAZI PARTY; WORLD WAR II.

Scopes, John Thomas   See SCOPES TRIAL.

Scopes trial

Landmark American trial, in which the teaching of Charles Darwin's theory of evolution in the public schools was put on trial. Defendant John Thomas Scopes, a 25-year-old biology teacher, broke a state law prohibiting the teaching of evolution. The law in question, the Butler Act, had been passed by the Tennessee legislature in 1924. In 1925 the AMERICAN CIVIL LIBERTIES UNION (ACLU) advertised in a Tennessee newspaper asking for someone to test the law. Scopes stepped forward, and two local attorneys,

Herbert and Sue Hicks, who were friends of Scopes, agreed to "prosecute" him.

The Scopes trial soon became about the clash of two cultures. The trial opened in the small village of Dayton, the seat of Rhea County, Tennessee, located about 38 miles from Chattanooga. John R. Neal, a law school dean from Knoxville, asked to join the defense. Former Secretary of State William Jennings BRYAN, who eschewed the theory of evolution, joined the prosecution; this move prompted famed attorney Clarence DARROW to volunteer for the defense. The ACLU actually wanted wanted former Solicitor General John W. DAVIS for the defense and former Supreme Court Justice Charles Evans HUGHES for the prosecution. When Darrow and Bryan came forward, the ACLU sent attorneys Arthur Garfield Hays and Dudley Field Malone to support Darrow. Backing Bryan was his son, William Jennings Bryan Jr., a federal prosecutor.

Nearly a thousand people jammed into the Rhea County Courthouse on July 10, 1925, including H. L. MENCKEN, covering the trial for the *Baltimore Sun*. Presiding judge John T. Raulston allowed a prayer to open the trial over Darrow's objections. A jury of 12 men, 11 of whom were avid churchgoers, were selected. Darrow opened the trial by asking to have the indictment against Scopes quashed based on state and federal law, but the judge denied the motion. In his opening statement, Bryan claimed that "if evolution wins, Christianity goes." Darrow remarked that "Scopes isn't on trial; civilization is on trial." Bryan called just seven witnesses, all of them students of Scopes. All reported that Scopes had taught them that man evolved from one-celled organisms. The prosecution rested.

The first defense witness, Maynard Metcalf, a zoologist from the Johns Hopkins University, was disallowed by the judge, who held Metcalf's testimony to be irrelevant. Darrow became upset and was cited for contempt by the judge. By this time, hundreds of people had packed the courtroom, and with the more than hundred-degree heat, the judge ordered the trial to be moved outside. When asked if he had any further evidence, Darrow called Bryan to the stand as a Bible expert. Darrow thoroughly questioned Bryan about his steadfast belief in stories of the Bible.

He tested Bryan on every facet of biblical history. When he was through, he rested and asked for a directed

Clarence Darrow speaks at the 1925 Scopes trial. *(CORBIS/Bettmann)*

verdict. The jury returned after only eight minutes of deliberation with a verdict of guilty, however. Scopes had broken the law, even if it was an unjust law. The judge ordered Scopes to pay a fine of $100. Scopes responded, "I will continue in the future . . . to oppose this law in any way I can. Any other action would be in violation of my idea of academic freedom."

Five days after the trial ended, on July 30, 1925, Bryan died. Although the law remained on the books, it was never again enforced. The trial represented an advance for progressive ideas and the laws of science. A film version of the trial, *Inherit the Wind,* was released in 1960. It was not until the 1968 case of *Epperson v. Arkansas* that the U.S. Supreme Court struck down all state laws that prohibited the teaching of evolution.

References: Michael E. Parrish, "State of Tennessee v. Scopes" in Leonard W. Levy, ed. in chief, *Encyclopedia of the American Constitution* (New York: Macmillan, 1986–92), 4: 1743; Ray Ginger, *Six Days or Forever? Tennessee v. John Thomas Scopes* (New York: Oxford University Press, 1958); Leslie Henri Allen, *Bryan and Darrow at Dayton: The Record and Documents of the "Bible-Evolution Trial"* (New York: Arthur Lee & Co., 1925); "Bryan, On Stand, Charges Darrow Assails Religion; Fighting Bigots, Is Reply," *Washington Post,* July 21, 1925, p. 1; Peter Applebome, "70 Years after Scopes Trial, Creation Debate Lives," *New York Times,* March 10, 1996, p. A1.

Scottsboro Case

American landmark trial in which nine African-American youths were accused in 1931 of raping two white women, which stirred the nation to examine its judicial system. On March 25, 1931, Charlie Weems, Ozie Powell, Clarence Norris, Olin Montgomery, Willie Roberson, Haywood Patterson, Andy and Roy White, and Eugene Williams (ages 13–21) were charged with raping two white women on a train near Paint Rock, Alabama. They were taken to the town of Scottsboro, Alabama, quickly arraigned, and, without adequate counsel, put on trial just 12 days after their arrests. Although the evidence was slim, four days later they were convicted by an all-white jury; all except 13-year-old Wright were sentenced to death.

The case of the nine "Scottsboro Boys" captured the public's outrage. There were protests around the United States. The National Association for the Advancement of Colored People (NAACP) searched for adequate counsel to aid in the youths' appeals. On November 8, 1932, after lawyers representing the left-wing International Labor Defense filed a motion for a new trial, in *Powell v. Alabama* the U.S. Supreme Court held that the youths' constitutional rights to fair and impartial trial had been violated and set aside the convictions. The original trial judge, Alfred E. Hawkins, set new trial dates for all nine during the March 1933 term in Scottsboro. For these new trials, the ILD employed the famed New York attorney Samuel Leibowitz. Leibowitz asked for the arrest warrants to be quashed; when this was denied, he asked for a change of venue. This was granted and the second trial opened in Decatur, Alabama, on March 28, 1933. The second trial also excluded African-Americans from the jury. Despite the fact that one of the women repudiated her rape accusation, the all-white jury convicted all nine a second time, and again they were sentenced to death.

Leibowitz founded the American Scottsboro Committee in 1934, and on his own, he sued the U.S. Supreme Court, which in 1935 in *Norris v. Alabama* again struck down the convictions. But in November 1935 a grand jury again indicted all of the accused. Charges against four of the defendants were dropped, but five were sentenced to long prison terms. The Supreme Court refused to review their convictions a third time, and eventually all were paroled in the 1940s after serving many years in prison.

References: Bernard Ryan, Jr., "The Scottsboro Trials: 1931–37" in Edward W. Knappman, ed., *Great American Trials* (Detroit: Visible Ink Press, 1994), 351–56; James Haskins, *The Scottsboro Boys* (New York: Henry Holt and Co., 1994).

Securities Act of 1933

U.S. congressional legislation, enacted May 27, 1933, which required all new securities (stocks, bonds, and so on) for sale to be registered with the Federal Trade Commission and reliable information about the securities to be provided to investors. Those who failed to do so, or who provided false or misleading information, paid civil and criminal penalties. The law was initiated in reaction to the practice of many companies throughout the "roaring" 1920s of issuing stocks and bonds on the basis of fantastic promises of outrageous profits, without disclosing meaningful information to investors. The stock market kept rising until the wave of this speculative euphoria ended with the STOCK MARKET CRASH of 1929 and the GREAT DEPRESSION that followed. Congress created these securities laws, as well as the SECURITIES EXCHANGE ACT in 1934, in an effort to curb future excesses and to provide full and fair disclosure to investors.

References: Securities Act 15 U.S. 77 (1933); Michael Parish, *Anxious Decades: America in Prosperity and Depression, 1920–1941* (New York: W. W. Norton, 1992).

Securities Exchange Act of 1934

U.S. congressional legislation, enacted June 6, 1934, which for the first time regulated and controlled the buying and selling of securities. Congress explained that it was enacting the legislation "to protect interstate commerce, the national credit, the Federal taxing power, to protect and make more effective the national banking system and Federal Reserve System, and to insure the maintenance of fair and honest markets in such transactions." The act provides for investor access to current financial and other information regarding securities, particularly those that trade publicly. The act prohibits fraudulent and unfair behavior on the part of securities brokers and dealers and governs the conduct of securities exchanges.

References: Ralph F. De Bedts, "The New Deal's SEC: The Formative Years" (New York: Columbia University Press, 1964); "Securities Exchange Act of 1934, as amended to July 1, 1991" (Washington, D.C.: United States Securities and Exchange Commission, 1991); Securities Exchange Act 48 Stat. 881 (1934).

Settlement House Movement   *See* ADDAMS, JANE.

Sèvres, Treaty of
Pact, August 10, 1920, which ended the state of war between the Allies and Turkey. Officially called the Treaty of Peace between the Allied and Associated Powers, it laid down Turkey's new boundaries with Greece and other surrounding nations. Turkey was allowed to keep only Constantinople (later Istanbul) and a portion of Anatolia in Asia Minor, while the Hejaz was made into an independent Arab state; Armenia was sectioned off as a republic; Palestine, Mesopotamia, and Transjordan were made mandates of Great Britain; and Syria was made a mandate of France. The treaty was signed by Ottoman Sultan Mohammed VI but was repudiated by the Turkish National Assembly and its leader, MUSTAFA KEMAL, later known as Ataturk. Kemal sent troops into Armenia and defeated Greece in a war in 1922. After the sultan was overthrown in 1922, the Allies established a new agreement, the Treaty of LAUSANNE, which was signed by Turkey in 1923 on terms more favorable to Ataturk's government.

See also MANDATE SYSTEM.

References: "Treaty between the Principal Allied and Associated Powers and Greece. Signed at Sèvres, August 10, 1920" (London: His Majesty's Stationery Office, 1920); *The Treaties of Peace, 1919–1923* (New York: Carnegie Endowment for International Peace, 1924).

Seyss-Inquart, Artur (1892–1946)
Austrian politician and supporter of the German Nazi regime. Born in the Moravian village of Stannern bei Iglau on July 22, 1892, he practiced law in Vienna starting in 1921. A lover of all things German, he supported Austria's forced ANSCHLUSS with Germany and belonged to a number of Austrian organizations that championed that goal. In 1931 he formed a relationship with the German NAZI PARTY; however, since he was not a formal member, he could not attain high offices given to party members. Instead, he was appointed the *Staatsrat* (state counselor) in 1937 in talks between the Austrian and German governments.

Seyss-Inquart was made Austrian minister for internal administration and security, in essence in charge of all state police. Thus, when German troops were readied at the border to invade Austria, Seyss-Inquart was ready to counter any and all Austrian opposition. After the invasion, he was named Reich governor of Austria and Reich minister without portfolio. He later served for a time under Hans Frank, governor-general of occupied Poland, then as Reich commissioner for the occupied Netherlands, where he viciously rooted out opposition to Nazi rule and deported most of that nation's Jews to concentration camps. When the war ended, Seyss-Inquart was seized by Canadian troops and taken to Nuremberg, where he was tried for war crimes and crimes against humanity.

On October 1, 1946, Seyss-Inquart was found not guilty of conspiring to wage aggressive war but guilty of committing crimes against peace and humanity, and of violating the laws of war. Along with other Nazi leaders, he was sentenced to death on October 15. According to several witnesses, Seyss-Inquart's last words as he mounted the gallows were, "I hope this execution is the last act in the tragedy of World War II." After death his body was cremated, and the ashes dumped in the Isar River near Munich.

References: James Taylor and Warren Shaw, *The Third Reich Almanac* (New York: World Almanac, 1987), 301–302; Christian Zentner and Friedemann Bedüftig, eds., *Encyclopedia of the Third Reich* (New York: Macmillan, 1991), 2: 872–73; Ann and John Tusa, *The Nuremberg Trial* (New York: Atheneum, 1986); Telford Taylor, *The Anatomy of the Nuremberg Trials: A Personal Memoir* (New York: Alfred A. Knopf, 1992).

Shantung
Chinese province, the subject of Japanese encroachment during the interwar period. Shantung is located in eastern China, with an area of 153,000 square kilometers (95,070 square miles). Germany was granted the right to construct a railroad in the area by the Chinese-German Treaty of March 6, 1898. However, by the Treaty of VERSAILLES, Germany abrogated these rights to Japan, "particularly those concerning the territory of Kiaochow, railways, mines and submarine cables," which Germany had received in the 1898 pact. Japan also acquired "all German rights in the Tsingtao-Tsinanfu Railway, including its branch lines together with its subsidiary property of all kinds, stations, shops, fixed and rolling stock, mines, plant and material for the exploitation of the mines."

Shantung was a thorn in Sino-Japanese relations even before the Versailles Treaty had been signed in Paris in 1919. Chinese delegates objected to Japanese control of the area, and Japan declared that it would not sign the document if forced to abandon Shantung immediately. U.S. President Woodrow WILSON conceded to Tokyo, allowing for the stationing of Japanese troops in Shantung for a limited time if Japan signed the treaty and joined the LEAGUE OF NATIONS. Japan accepted. As historian Hugh Phillips writes, "Many of Wilson's critics believed that this arrangement sacrificed Chinese interests to Japanese expansionism." In 1922, after signing the NINE POWER TREATY, Japan kept its pledge and removed all of its troops from Shantung.

References: "Eve of Shantung Decision. Brighter Prospects. Japan's Disclaimer about Siberia," *The Times* (London), January 26, 1922, p. 10; Edmund Jan Osmańczyk, *The Encyclopedia of the United Nations and International Agreements* (Philadelphia: Taylor & Francis, 1985), 753; Westel W. Willoughby, *China at the Conference: A Report* (Baltimore: Johns Hopkins University Press, 1922), 277–83; text of the Treaty of Versailles, sections 156–58; Hugh D. Phillips, "Shandung Question" in Bruce W. Jentleson and Thomas G. Paterson, senior eds., *Encyclopedia of U.S. Foreign Relations* (New York: Oxford University Press, 1997), 3: 79.

Shaw, George Bernard (1856–1950)

Irish playwright, critic, pacifist, and Nobel laureate. Born in Dublin, Ireland, on July 26, 1856, Shaw received only a primary school education. He enjoyed a series of jobs, including as an art, music, and drama critic for a few London papers from 1888 to 1898. Starting in 1893, Shaw began to write a series of works that would make him a leading literary figure of his times. These works include *Widowers' Houses: A Comedy* (1893), *Man and Superman* (1903), *Caesar and Cleopatra: A History* (1905), and *Pygmalion: A Play in Five Acts* (1912). After World War I he published *Heartbreak House* (1921) and *Back to Methuselah: A Metabiological Pentateuch* (1921). For this body of work—"marked by idealism and humanity, its stimulating satire often being infused with a singular poetic beauty"—he was awarded the 1925 Nobel Prize in literature.

In the quarter of a century in which he lived after the bestowal of his Nobel, he only wrote two other works: *The Apple Cart: A Political Extravaganza* (1930) and *The Political Madhouse in America and Nearer Home: A Lecture* (1933). Shaw died in Hertfordshire, England, on November 2, 1950.

References: James Lee and June H. Schlessinger, "Shaw, George Bernard" in Bernard S. and June H. Schlessinger, eds., *The Who's Who of Nobel Prize Winners* (Phoenix, Ariz.: Oryx, 1986), 55–56; Thomas Watson MacCallum and Stephen Taylor, eds., *The Nobel Prize-Winners and the Nobel Foundation,* *1901–1937* (Zurich: Central European Times Publishing, 1938), 302–4.

Sheppard-Towner Maternity and Infancy Protection Act of 1921

U.S. congressional legislation enacted on November 23, 1921, extending federal aid to states for the welfare of poor women and children. Sponsored by Texas senator Morris Sheppard and Iowa state representative Horace Towner, it was the first federally funded social measure in the United States. The law appropriated $480,000 in the first year and $240,000 a year for the next five years in matching grants to the states for prenatal care, child health clinics, and nutrition and hygiene information. Infant and maternal mortality rates had been high in the 1910s and the new Sheppard-Towner programs contributed to a significant drop in those rates. However, many states saw the act as federal intrusion into state matters and refused to accept the funds. Opponents of the act forced the bill's repeal in 1929, but federal funds for maternal and infant care were restored in the SOCIAL SECURITY ACT of 1935.

References: U.S. Statutes at Large, Vol. 42, 224–25; Henry Steele Commager, ed., *Documents of American History* (New York: Appleton-Century-Crofts, 1949), 353–54; J. Stanley Lemons, *The Woman Citizen: Social Feminism in the 1920's* (Urbana: University of Illinois Press, 1973).

Sherrington, Charles Scott (1857–1952)

British neurophysicist and Nobel laureate. Born in London on November 27, 1857, he received his M.B. degree from Cambridge University in 1885. He served as a researcher at the Koch Laboratory in Berlin, as a physician at the St. Thomas Hospital in London, as a professor and administrator at the University of London, and as a professor at the University of Liverpool. In these positions, Sherrington investigated the activity of the neurons of the brain and the spinal cord. His numerous writings, including *The Integrative Action of the Nervous System* (1906), demonstrated his research in this field. For his pioneering work on the human nervous system, Sherrington was co-awarded (with Edgar ADRIAN) the 1932 Nobel Prize in medicine and physiology.

Sherrington was knighted in 1922 and continued to work on the problems of neurons until his retirement from the University of Edinburgh in 1938. He died in Eastbourne, Sussex, England, on March 4, 1952.

References: Rashelle Karp, "Sherrington, Charles Scott, Sir" in Bernard S. and June H. Schlessinger, eds., *The Who's Who of Nobel Prize Winners* (Phoenix, Ariz.: Oryx, 1986), 88; Tyler Wasson, ed., *Nobel Prize Winners: An H. W. Wilson Biographical Dictionary* (New York: H. W. Wilson Co., 1987),

962–62; Judith P. Swazey, "Sherrington, Charles Scott" in Charles Coulston Gillespie, ed. in chief, *Dictionary of Scientific Biography* (New York: Charles Scribner's Sons, 1980–90), 12: 395–403; Thomas Watson MacCallum and Stephen Taylor, eds., *The Nobel Prize–Winners and the Nobel Foundation, 1901–1037* (Zurich: Central European Times Publishing, 1938), 227.

Sherwood, Robert Emmet   *See* ALGONQUIN ROUND TABLE.

Showa Era   *See* HIROHITO.

Siegbahn, Karl Manne Georg (1886–1978)
Swedish physicist and Nobel laureate. Born in Örebro, Sweden, on December 3, 1886, he received his master's degree and doctorate from the University of Lund, where he served as a professor of physics (1911–23). Then he worked at the University of Uppsala (1923–27), and as a professor and administrator at the Swedish Royal Academy of Sciences (1937–64). During these years, Siegbahn worked on the properties of X-ray spectroscopy, demonstrating techniques for the measurement of X-ray wavelengths. For this discovery, he was awarded the 1924 Nobel Prize in physics.

Siegbahn spent the remainder of his professional life studying nuclear physics. He died in Stockholm, Sweden, on September 26, 1978.

References: Carol Somers, "Siegbahn, Karl Manne Georg" in Bernard S. and June H. Schlessinger, eds., *The Who's Who of Nobel Prize Winners* (Phoenix, Ariz.: Oryx, 1986), 158; Thomas Watson MacCallum and Stephen Taylor, eds., *The Nobel Prize–Winners and the Nobel Foundation, 1901–1937* (Zurich: Central European Times Publishing, 1938), 80–82.

Sillanpää, Frans Eemil (1888–1964)
Finnish writer and Nobel laureate "for his deep comprehension and exquisite art in painting the nature of his country and the life of its peasants in their mutual relations." Born in the village of Hämeen Kyro, Finland, on September 16, 1888, Sillanpää received limited formal education. He began to write books on his native Finland starting in 1916 with *Life and Sun*. Other works include *Children of Man in Life's Procession* (1917), *Meek Heritage* (1919), *Beloved Fatherland* (1919), and *Hiltu and Ragnar* (1923). For these works, Sillanpää was awarded the 1939 Nobel Prize in literature.

After winning the Nobel, he wrote only two novels: *August* (1944) and *The Loveliness and Wretchedness of Human Life* (1945). His memoirs were published as *The Boy Lived His Life* (1953). He died in Helsinki, Finland, on June 3, 1964.

References: June H. Schlessinger, "Sillanpää, Frans Eemil" in Bernard S. and June H. Schlessinger, eds., *The Who's Who of Nobel Prize Winners* (Phoenix, Ariz.: Oryx, 1986), 60; Stanley J. Kunitz and Howard Haycraft, eds., *Twentieth Century Authors: A Biographical Dictionary of Modern Literature* (New York: H. W. Wilson Co., 1942), 1286–88.

Sino-Japanese War, Second
The second armed conflict of the modern era between the two nations—the first occurred in 1894–95 and ended with the victorious Japanese forcing the Chinese to sign the humiliating Treaty of Shimonoseki. Preceding the second Sino-Japanese War, known by the Chinese as the War of Resistance against Japan, tensions were high between the Chinese and Japanese following the Japanese conquest of Manchuria. On July 7, 1937, Chinese and Japanese troops exchanged shots across the bridge at Luguoqiao, known in English as the Marco Polo Bridge. The Japanese used this incident as a pretext to invade. Within just a few weeks, Japanese troops had quickly taken major Chinese cities in the east, including Nanking, where for six weeks they inflicted mass murders and other brutalities. The forces of CHIANG KAI-SHEK and MAO TSE-TUNG, once enemies, combined to start an ineffective guerrilla war against the Japanese. The actions did not make much headway until 1945, when the United States had defeated Japan in World War II. Japan signed a peace treaty with Taiwan in 1952 and with the People's Republic of China in 1978, effectively ending the war. The number of deaths estimated from the conflict amount to 1.3 million Chinese and more than 571,000 Japanese soldiers.

References: C. Walter Young, *Japan's Special Position in Manchuria* (Baltimore: Johns Hopkins University Press, 1931); Andrew Tolstoy, "Post-Mortem on an 'Incident,'" *Current History* 48, no. 1 (January 1938): 24.

Smith, Al (1873–1944)
American politician, governor of New York (1919–21, 1923–29), presidential nominee of the Democratic Party (1928). Born in New York City on December 30, 1873, he attended a parochial school before joining his father's trucking business. In 1895 he was appointed as a clerk in the office of the New York Commissioner of Jurors, where he served until 1903, the same year that he was elected to the state assembly as a Democrat. He became majority leader in 1911 and floor leader in 1912. In 1913, when the Democrats regained the majority, he was elected speaker of the state assembly.

In 1915, after serving as a member of the state constitutional convention, Smith was elected sheriff of New York County, and he served until 1917, when he was elected president of the New York Board of Aldermen. In 1919 he became governor of New York, eventually serving four terms. He worked for a minimum wage for female workers and for mandatory health insurance for industrial workers, and oversaw the convention that approved the Nineteenth Amendment to the U.S. Constitution, which granted the suffrage to women. In 1924, Smith was a leading figure for the Democratic presidential nomination, but the convention in New York City deadlocked between Smith and former secretary of the treasury William Gibbs McAdoo, and turned instead to former U.S. ambassador to Great Britain John William DAVIS as the presidential candidate.

Smith's victories in 1924 and 1926, in the face of growing Republican victories nationwide, and his close run for the presidency in 1924, made him the foremost politician in his party for the 1928 presidential nomination. However, as the Democratic convention neared, opposition to him sprang up in his own party, based on the fact that he was a Roman Catholic, that he was "wet" (an opponent of PROHIBITION), and that he was a member of Tammany, the corrupt New York City political organization. Nonetheless, at the convention in Houston, he was nominated by former assistant secretary of the navy Franklin ROOSEVELT who called him "the Happy Warrior." Senator Joseph T. ROBINSON of Arkansas was named as his running mate, and both men conducted a campaign on the issues of farm relief and water conservation. The nation was satisfied with eight years of Republican rule, however, and elected Herbert Hoover over Smith by 444 electoral votes to 87.

In 1930, Smith nominated Roosevelt for a second term as governor of New York in the midst of the GREAT DEPRESSION. In 1932 he supported Roosevelt's campaign for president, but things soon changed after Roosevelt was elected. Although Smith as governor had pushed to change the lives of the populace, he saw Roosevelt's attempts at changing the federal government as overreaching and dangerous. Smith joined the American Liberty League and opposed Roosevelt's programs as approaching a Soviet-style government. In the 1936 election, he signed an open letter calling for Roosevelt's defeat; he even campaigned for Republican Alf LANDON.

After Landon's defeat, Smith retreated from politics, his power in New York, which had once been so strong, now broken. He died on October 5, 1944.

References: Frank Graham, *Al Smith, American: An Informal Biography* (New York: G. P. Putnam's Sons, 1945); Richard O'Connor, *The First Hurrah: A Biography of Alfred E. Smith* (New York: Putnam, 1970); Roy V. Peel and Thomas C. Donnelly, *The 1928 Campaign: An Analysis* (New York: R. R. Smith, 1931); Edmund Arthur Moore, *A Catholic Runs for President: The Campaign of 1928* (New York: Ronald Press Co., 1956).

Smith, Bessie (1894 or 1898–1937)

American singer known as the "Empress of the Blues." Born in Chattanooga, Tennessee, into a poor family, she started singing when a child. In her teens, she joined the Rabbit Foot Minstrel Show, run by the legendary Ma RAINEY, who became Smith's mentor. Her first record, *Down Hearted Blues,* released by Columbia Records in 1923, presaged her rise as a blues star. She later recorded with such jazz stars as Louis ARMSTRONG, Benny GOODMAN, and Fletcher Henderson, among others. By 1926, she was one of the highest-paid stars in the world and had earned the epithet "Empress of the Blues." Known for emotional intensity and earthy style, Smith's greatest performances include *Ticket Agent, Ease Your Window Down* (1923), *Jailhouse Blues* (1923), *House Rent Blues* (1924), and *Follow the Deal on Down* (1924). By 1930, however, alcoholism had destroyed Smith's ability to tour and sing. Her last appearance was at the Famous Door Club in New York in 1936. Over her career, Smith had recorded more than 200 songs.

She died on September 26, 1937.

References: William Barlow, "Smith, Bessie" in Darlene Clark Hine, ed., *Black Women in America: An Historical Encyclopedia* (Brooklyn, N.Y.: Carlson Publishing, 1993), 2: 1074–78; Elaine Feinstein, *Bessie Smith* (New York: Viking, 1985); Clifford Richter, eds., *Bessie Smith: Empress of the Blues* (New York: Schirmer Books, 1975).

Smith, Kate (1909–1986)

American singer and radio entertainer, famed for her stirring rendition of Irving BERLIN's "God Bless America." Born Kathryn Elizabeth Smith in Greenville, Virginia, on May 1, 1909, she initially trained to become a nurse, but later followed her heart and became an entertainer. Radio announcer "Ted" Joseph Martin Collins discovered Smith's voice in 1929, and he became her manager and producer. Her theme song became "When the Moon Comes over the Mountain." In 1930 Smith formed a partnership with Collins and developed the radio show, *Kate Smith Sings,* one of the most popular of the era, lasting until 1947. She also conducted a radio news program in 1938. In the 1950s and 1960s she had several variety shows on television. In 1982, shortly before her death, she was awarded the Medal of Freedom by President Ronald Reagan. Smith died on June 17, 1986.

References: Richard K. Hayes, *Kate Smith: A Biography, with a Discography, Filmography, and List of Stage Appearances*

Kate Smith *(CORBIS/Bettmann)*

(Jefferson, N.C.: McFarland, 1995); Michael R. Pitts, *Kate Smith: A Bio-bibliography* (New York: Greenwood, 1988).

Smoot, Reed (1862–1941)

American politician, U.S. senator from Utah (1903–33) who introduced the SMOOT-HAWLEY TARIFF in the Senate. A Mormon, Smoot was born in Salt Lake City, Utah, on January 10, 1862. He attended Deseret University and the Brigham Young Academy in Provo. After entering the business world, Smoot soon became wealthy through the purchase of a series of industrial enterprises. In 1895 he was named to the presidency of the Utah Stake of the Church of Jesus Christ of Latter Day Saints, known better as the Mormons; in 1900 he was elected an apostle of the church. In 1903, Smoot was elected to the U.S. Senate, but his election was immediately contested by Senator Fred Dubois of Idaho on the grounds that, as a Mormon, Smoot sanctioned the practice of polygamy. Smoot denied the charge. Senator Boises Penrose of Pennsylvania joked during the debate, "I don't see why we can't get along just as well with a polygamist who doesn't 'polyg' as we do with a lot of monogamists who don't 'monog.'" The Senate eventually cleared Smoot.

Smoot rose to chair of the Senate Finance Committee, where he became an expert in economic and tax matters

as well as tariff legislation. The onset of the GREAT DEPRESSION in 1929 gave Smoot a chance to enact a law to protect American industries in such hard economic times. Teaming up with Representative Willis Chatman Hawley of Oregon, the men cosponsored the Smoot-Hawley Tariff of 1930, which made foreign items more expensive in the United States. Instead of preserving American industries, however, it forced foreign nations to raise their tariffs against American goods, plunging the world deeper into depression.

Because of Smoot's support for the tariff, and the unpopularity of Republican President Herbert HOOVER in 1932, Smoot was defeated in the next election. He died in St. Petersburg, Florida, on February 9, 1941.

References: Milton R. Merrill, "Reed Smoot: Apostle-Senator," *Utah Historical Quarterly* 28 (1961): 343–50; James B. Allen, "The Great Protectionist: Senator Reed Smoot of Utah," *Utah Historical Quarterly* 45 (1977): 325–45; Jan Shipps, "The Public Image of Senator Reed Smoot," *Utah Historical Quarterly* 45 (1977): 380.

Smoot-Hawley Tariff

Levy, enacted by the U.S. Congress in 1930 on imported goods, which many historians consider to have been a major factor worsening the effects of the GREAT DEPRESSION. Also called the Tariff Act of 1930, it boosted tariff rates on imported goods in an effort to protect those American industries hard hit by the depression. On the day that it was signed into law by President Herbert HOOVER, June 17, 1930, however, the stock markets around the world plummeted further into depression. The act was amended in 1934 by the Reciprocal Trade Agreement Act.

References: Donald R. Kennon and Rebecca M. Rogers, "The United States House of Representatives Committee on Ways and Means: A Bicentennial History, 1789–1989" (House Document 100–244, 1990), 265–70; Joseph Marion Jones, "Tariff Retaliation: Repercussions of the Hawley-Smoot Bill" (Philadelphia: University of Pennsylvania Press, 1934); "Not Smitten with Smoot," *New York Times*, November 16, 1987, B6.

Smuts, Jan Christiaan (1870–1950)

South African military figure and politician, representative of his nation at the Versailles Peace Conference (1919), prime minister (1919–24). Born near Ribeek West, in the Malmesbury District of the Cape Colony of what is now South Africa on May 24, 1870, he was of Dutch and French-Huguenot descent. He attended Victoria College and, when he was 21, won a scholarship to England, where he studied the law at Christ College, Cambridge. After being admitted to the bar in 1894, Smuts returned to his homeland the following year and opened a law practice in Capetown.

At that time the colony of South Africa was ruled by the British but was populated by the Dutch *Boers* (literally Dutch settlers; also called Afrikaners). Smuts, a Boer, believed in reconciliation between the two groups. By 1897, however, Smuts had turned against the British; he gave up his British citizenship and moved to Pretoria in the Transvaal, where in 1898 he was named state's attorney by President Paul Kruger. In 1899 the Boers attacked the Cape Colony and the Natal in what is called the Boer War. Smuts joined with the Boer guerrillas after the British occupation of Pretoria and rose to become the commander in chief of all Boer forces in the Cape Colony.

In 1904, Smuts became a political partner of General Louis Botha, another hero of the Boer War, and together they formed the People's Party. Smuts won self-government from London for the defeated nation-state in 1906. In 1910 Botha and Smuts unified all of the former Dutch republics under one government, forming the Union of South Africa in 1910. Botha served as prime minister, while Smuts served as minister of defense (1910–20), minister of the interior and mines (1910–12), and minister of finance (1912–13). When World War I broke out in August 1914, Smuts assumed command of all South African military forces.

In 1917, Smuts was named as a member of the Imperial War Cabinet under British prime minister David LLOYD GEORGE, and served until the end of 1918. In 1919, he and Botha were the South African representatives to the VERSAILLES Peace Conference. After Botha's death, Smuts led the country. As the leader of the South African Party, he merged with the Unionist Party (dominated by persons of British ancestry), and established a coalition government. In 1922 he was forced to deal with an uprising among the workers in the goldfields of Witwatersrand, and he was compelled to call out troops to diffuse the situation. The situation allowed the Labour Party, which had supported the strike, to align itself with the Nationalist Party, and allowed their candidate, James B. M. Hertzog, to defeat Smuts in the 1924 election. After writing a philosophical work, *Holism and Evolution* (1926), Smuts joined the Hertzog government as the minister of justice (1933–39). With the death of Hertzog, Smuts once again became prime minister, and during World War II he commanded South African forces with the rank of field marshal.

After the war, Smuts represented South Africa at the United Nations Conference in San Francisco, where he was one of the writers of the organization's preamble. He later served as the South African representative at the Paris Peace Conference in 1946, as well as at two sessions of the United Nations General Assembly (1946–47). In the national elections of May 1948, however, his government was defeated, and Smuts retired. He died at Irene, near Pretoria, on September 11, 1950.

See also HERTZOG, JAMES BARRY MUNNIK.

References: Jan Christiaan Smuts, *Jan Christiaan Smuts* (London: Cassell, 1952); Sarah Gertrude Liebson Millin, *General Smuts* (London: Faber & Faber, 1936); Thomas Pakenham, *The Boer War* (London: Weidenfeld & Nicolson, 1997).

Social Security Act

U.S. congressional legislation, August 14, 1935, which established a federal social system of security payments during the GREAT DEPRESSION. Specifically, it was "an act to provide for the general welfare by establishing a system of federal old-age benefits, and by enabling the several States to make more adequate provisions for aged persons, blind persons, dependent and crippled children, maternal and child welfare, public health, and the administration of their unemployment compensation laws; to establish a Social Security Board; and for other purposes." It was also enacted to enable those elderly Americans without savings to support themselves. On June 8, 1934, President Franklin ROOSEVELT announced his intention to provide a program for the nation's social security needs. To study the problem of nation social "insecurity" and to make legislative recommendations to the president and to Congress, Roosevelt created the Committee on Economic Security, headed by Frances PERKINS, secretary of labor; Henry Morganthau, secretary of the treasury; Henry A. Wallace, secretary of agriculture; Homer Stille Cummings, attorney general; and Harry L. HOPKINS, administrator, Federal Emergency Relief Administration. In early January 1935, the group reported to Roosevelt and he presented the report to Congress. Although each chamber passed differing versions of a social security law, they reconciled in conference, enacted the law, and it was signed by Roosevelt on August 14, 1935. Nine days later, on August 23, the Senate confirmed Roosevelt's appointees to the Social Security Board: John G. Winant, chairman; Arthur J. Altmeyer, and Vincent M. Miles. The board was abolished in 1946 and replaced with the Social Security Administration.

Major portions of the act were upheld in 1937 by the U.S. Supreme Court in *Stewart Machine Company v. Davis.*

References: Melvin I. Urofsky, ed., *Documents of American Constitutional and Legal History* (Philadelphia: Temple University Press, 1989), 2: 194–97; Arthur Joseph Altmeyer, *The Formative Years of Social Security* (Madison: University of Wisconsin Press, 1968); Roy Lubove, *The Struggle for Social Security, 1900–1935* (Cambridge: Harvard University Press, 1968).

Soddy, Frederick (1877–1956)

British chemist and Nobel laureate. Born in Eastbourne, Sussex, England, on September 2, 1877, he was awarded bachelor's (1898) and master's (1910) degrees from Oxford University. He served as a researcher at McGill University (1900–1902) in Montreal, Canada, and at the

University of London (1903–1904). He then became a professor of chemistry at the University of Glascow (1904–14), eventually moving to Aberdeen University in Scotland and finally to Oxford University (1919–36).

During his years of research and teaching, Soddy worked on the theory of radioactive isotopes with Ernest Rutherford (who was awarded the 1908 Nobel Prize in chemistry), helping to "clarify the relations of elements in the periodic table." For his work on radioactivity, Soddy was awarded the 1921 Nobel Prize in chemistry.

After retiring in 1936, Soddy spent his final years in England. He died in Brighton on September 22, 1956.

References: Frank Kellerman, "Soddy, Frederick" in Bernard S. and June H. Schlessinger, eds., *The Who's Who of Nobel Prize Winners* (Phoenix, Ariz.: Oryx, 1986), 9; George B. Kauffman, ed., *Frederick Soddy (1877–1956): Early Pioneer in Radiochemistry* (Dordrecht and Boston: D. Reidel Publishing Co., 1986); Linda Merricks, *The World Made New: Frederick Soddy, Science, Politics, and Environment* (New York: Oxford University Press, 1996); Thomas Watson MacCallum and Stephen Taylor, eds., *The Nobel Prize-Winners and the Nobel Foundation, 1901–1937* (Zurich: Central European Times Publishing, 1938), 143.

Söderblom, Nathan (1866–1931)

Swedish theologian, peace advocate, and Nobel laureate. Born Lars Olof Jonathan Söderblom in Trönö, Sweden, on January 15, 1866, he received his bachelor's degree from Uppsala University in 1886 and a doctor of theology degree from the Sorbonne in 1901. A member of the Swedish church, Söderblom was promoted to archbishop in 1901, then served as a professor of theology at the University of Uppsala (1901–12) and at the University of Leipzig (1912–14).

An outspoken pacifist, Söderblom spent most of his life using religion to bring peace to the world, leading to his establishment of the Universal Christian Congress on Life and Work in 1925. For his lifetime of labor for peace, he was awarded the 1930 Nobel Peace Prize. In his comments on the occasion of Söderblom's award, Johan Ludwig Mowinckel, a member of the Nobel Committee, said, "Archbishop Nathan Söderblom's great achievement is that he has thrown the power of the spirit into the fight for peace. A holder of high ecclesiastical office, he understands the enormous importance of the church in this fight, the powerful influence which it can bring to bear." Söderblom died in Uppsala on June 12, 1931.

References: Leslie Sandlin, "Söderblom, Nathan" in Bernard S. and June H. Schlessinger, eds., *The Who's Who of Nobel Prize Winners* (Phoenix, Ariz.: Oryx, 1986), 134–35; Thomas Watson MacCallum and Stephen Taylor, eds., *The Nobel Prize-Winners and the Nobel Foundation, 1910–1937* (Zurich: Central European Times Publishing, 1938), 376.

Soil Conservation Service

U.S. governmental agency, established under the Soil Conservation Act of 1935, to advance research into soil conservation, particularly during the DUST BOWL and the GREAT DEPRESSION. Prior to its creation, there was a Soil Conservation Service in the Department of the Interior, which operated on a nonpermanent basis. This act, which made it a permanent government entity, created a service under the leadership of Hugh Hammond Bennett, a renowned soil specialist. The act created soil conservation districts around the United States, and, through the CIVILIAN CONSERVATION CORPS and the WORKS PROGRESS ADMINISTRATION, provided work for people in an effort to preserve the nation's soil resources. Historian James S. Stuart writes, "With CCC and WPA labor, the soil conservation districts began providing a variety of programs to farmers, including research on wind and water erosion; model projects; land-use planning for general areas as well as for farms and ranches; financial and technical advice to farmers; loans or gifts of seed, supplies, and conservation equipment; removal of steep slopes from cultivation; use of grasses and think-growing crops; implementations of strip cropping, terracing, and crop rotation; and widespread wind and water control projects." The Soil Conservation Service turned out to be one of the most successful of the NEW DEAL programs.

References: Denton Harper Simms, *The Soil Conservation Service* (New York: Praeger, 1970); Robert Lee Geiger, *A Chronological History of the Soil Conservation Service and Related Events: Our Soil, Our Strength* (Washington, D.C.: U.S. Government Printing Office, 1955); James Stuart Olson, *Historical Dictionary of the New Deal: From Inauguration to Preparation for War* (Westport, Conn.: Greenwood, 1985), 466–67.

Soviet-German Nonaggression Pact

Agreement, signed August 23, 1939, by German foreign minister Joachim von RIBBENTROP and his partner Soviet foreign minister Vyacheslav Mikhailovich Molotov, in which Moscow gave its permission for Berlin to attack and annex parts of Poland in exchange for the eastern half of Poland and a guarantee that Germany would never attack the Soviet Union. Also known as the Nazi-Soviet Pact, the Pact of Steel, the Russo-German Nonaggression Pact, or the Ribbentrop-Molotov Agreement, the move, according to the *Herald-Tribune,* "dropped a diplomatic bombshell into the current European crisis."

On August 23, Molotov and Ribbentrop met in Moscow to initial the pact that in essence sold out Eastern Europe to the Germans and western Poland to the Soviets, and pushed the continent even further on the road toward World War II. When Germany swept across Poland on September 1, Britain became the first nation to declare war on the Reich. World War II had begun.

See also ANSCHLUSS.

Refer to Appendix 1 for text of the Soviet-German Nonaggression Pact, August 23, 1939.

References: Vladimir Petrov, "Soviet-German Nonaggression Pact" in Thomas Parrish and Samuel Lyman Atwood Marshall, eds., *The Simon and Schuster Encyclopedia of World War II* (New York: Simon & Schuster, 1978), 585; "Soviet-German Non-Aggression Pact Announced in Brief Berlin Broadcast; Ribbentrop Flies to Moscow Tomorrow," New York *Herald-Tribune* (European Edition), August 22, 1939, p. 1; "The Russo-German Nonaggression Pact, 1939" in Louis L. Snyder, eds., *Documents of German History* (New Brunswick, N.J.: Rutgers University Press, 1958), 447; text of agreement in German Library of Information, *Documents on the Events Preceding the Outbreak of the War. Compiled and Published by the German Foreign Office* (New York: German Library of Information, 1940), 370–71.

Spa Conference

Meeting, held July 5–16, 1920, at the Belgian resort of Spa, "to consider . . . the delay of Germany in the implementation of military restrictions ensuring from the provisions of the Treaty of VERSAILLES and Germany's failure to deliver coal within reparation payments." Two earlier meetings on this issue were held at HYTHE and BOULOGNE. After these two conferences, Germany announced that it could not afford further REPARATIONS payments. At the Spa Conference the wartime Allies agreed that if payments were not started again by January 1, 1921, occupation zones by various nations would be extended; furthermore, reparations were to be divided as follows: 52.5 percent for France, 22 percent for Britain, 10 percent for Italy, 8 percent for Belgium, 5 percent for Yugoslavia, with the remaining percentages going to Romania, Japan, and Greece.

Reference: Edmund Jan Osmańczyk, *The Encyclopedia of the United Nations and International Agreements* (Philadelphia: Taylor & Francis, 1985), 771.

Spanish Civil War

Armed hostilities, 1936–39, in which the forces of Francisco FRANCO took over the Spanish government. The Spanish government had been a monarchy, first under the regency of Maria Christina, then under ALFONSO XIII, who ruled as a constitutional monarch from 1902 until 1931 under a series of Conservative and Liberal governments. The crisis over the uprising by Rif tribesmen under the command of ABD EL-KRIM and the collapse of the Spanish army at Anual in 1921 led to a coup d'état by General Miguel Primo de Rivera y Orbaneja in 1923; Alfonso's consent for him to rule under a military directorate served to push the nation closer to civil war between the rightists and the leftists. After defeating Abd el-Krim in 1925, Primo de Rivera ruled for an additional five years, until he was succeeded by a shared government ruled by General Dámaso Berenguer y Fusté and Admiral Juan Bautista Aznar, who called for national elections for Parliament. This plebiscite, held on April 12, 1931, did not give any one party a majority, but the vote against the monarchist parties was large, particularly in the cities, and on April 14, Alfonso went into exile to avoid civil war.

On that same day, a provisional government led by Niceto Alcalá Zamora, holding both the presidency and prime ministership, came to power, but it led to the Spanish Left instituting such unpopular reforms as the separation of church and state and state-run education. A rightist revolt at the ballot box brought a more conservative government to power in 1933. These measures were further extended, however, and the far right (called the Falangists) launched a violent campaign against the government. In October 1936 Franco was declared chief of the Spanish State, and several Spanish cities, including Burgos, Cadiz, Seville, and Zaragoza, came out in favor of Franco. The regimes in Nazi Germany and Fascist Italy sent troops to aid Franco in establishing his insurgent government, while Soviet Russia sent matériel to the beleaguered Republican government in Madrid. In the United States, among other nations, calls from leftists came to raise troops to save the Madrid government. The Abraham Lincoln Brigade, in which some 2,800 Americans took up guns and went to fight, came from the United States. Other nations, like France, sent upwards of ten thousand troops. Germany dispatched five thousand troops to aid Franco.

By the end of 1936, Franco's troops held half of Spain, and with the help of Germany and Italy they soon extended this reach. During the conflict the term *fifth column* was coined, to delineate those supporters of the Republican cause who worked behind the lines to commit sabotage and spy on the enemy. Photographers Hans Namuth and Georg Reisner, who were set to cover the 1936 Berlin OLYMPICS, instead went to Spain to cover the war; some of their photographs of the people and the conflict have become famous. The battle at Guernica, in which German planes strafed a Spanish village, was later captured in Pablo PICASSO's painting of the same name. Strategic victories by the Nationalists led to Moscow's aid becoming less and less effective. A series of military victories in early 1939, including the capture of Barcelona and Valencia, brought about the collapse of the government. Historian Eric Hobsbawn explains, "unlike the Nationalists, who enjoyed a single military and political direction, the Republicans remains politically divided, and—in spite of the communists' contribution—did not acquire a single military will and strategic command, or not until it was too late. The best it could do was from time to time throw back potentially fatal offensives by the other side, thus prolonging a war which might have been effectively ended in November 1936 by the capture of Madrid." On March 27, 1939, Madrid capitulated to Franco's forces, and the Fascist government swept into power. On that same day the new regime joined, through a prearranged treaty, the ROME-BERLIN-TOKYO AXIS AGREEMENT (also called the Anti-Comintern Pact of 1936).

See also NYON AGREEMENT.

References: Gabriel Jackson, *The Spanish Republic and the Civil War, 1931–1939* (Princeton, N.J.: Princeton University Press, 1965); Robert Rosenstone, *Crusade of the Left: The Lincoln Battalion in the Spanish Civil War* (New York: Pegasus, 1969); Edmund Jan Osmańczyk, *The Encyclopedia of the United Nations and International Agreements* (Philadelphia: Taylor & Francis, 1985), 772; "Spanish Rebels Drive to 10 Miles from Madrid; Halt Called as Leader Prepare for Concerted Attack on Capital," New York *Herald-Tribune* (European Edition), August 2, 1936, p. 1; Eric Hobsbawn, *Age of Extremes: The Short Twentieth Century, 1914–1991* (London: Abacus, 1996), 160–61; "Franco Occupies Madrid without Shot; Defenders Join 'Arriba Espana' Ovation; All Fronts Crumble as Long Siege Ends," New York *Herald-Tribune* (European edition), March 29, 1939, p. 1.

Fascist troops confront government soldiers at Torrejou, Spain, during the Spanish Civil War. *(CORBIS/Bettmann)*

Spemann, Hans (1869–1941)

German embryologist and Nobel laureate. Born in Stuttgart, Germany, on June 27, 1869, he received his doctorate at the University of Würzburg in 1895. He served as a researcher at the University of Würzburg (1894–1908), at the University of Rostock (1908–13), as the director of the Kaiser Wilhelm Institute of Biology (1914–18), and as a professor of zoology at the University of Freiburg-im-Breisgau (1919–35). During these tenures, Spemann demonstrated that when transferring one embryo section into another whole embryo, certain chemicals in the original embryo might or might not induce further development of the second embryo. For this work, Spemann was awarded the 1935 Nobel Prize in medicine and physiology. He died in Freiburg-im-Breisgau on September 12, 1941.

References: Rashelle Karp, "Spemann, Hans" in Bernard S. and June H. Schlessinger, eds., *The Who's Who of Nobel Prize Winners* (Phoenix, Ariz.: Oryx, 1986), 89; Thomas Watson MacCallum and Stephen Taylor, eds., *The Nobel Prize-Winners and the Nobel Foundation, 1901–1937* (Zurich: Central European Times Publishing, 1938), 238.

Spitteler, Carl Friedrich Georg (1845–1924)

Swiss writer and Nobel laureate. Born on April 24, 1845, in Liesthal, Switzerland, he received a theology degree from the University of Basel. He served as a private tutor in Saint Petersburg, Russia, in the Neuveville schools in Berne, Switzerland, and as a reporter for two Swiss newspapers in the late 1880s and early 1890s. Starting in 1898, however, he began to publish several works under the pseudonym Carl Felix Tandem, including *Laughing Truths* (1898) and *Bell Songs* (1906). His most famous work, however, was *Olympian Spring* (1900–05), a series of exchanges in which a solitary individual seems to remain hopeful in a world of pessimism. For this work, Spitteler was awarded the 1919 Nobel Prize in literature.

He wrote epics, poems, prose, and a novel. He died in Lucerne, Switzerland, on December 28, 1924.

References: Cheryl Chan and June H. Schlessinger, "Spitteler, Carl Friedrich Georg" in Bernard S. and June H. Schlessinger, eds., *The Who's Who of Nobel Prize Winners* (Phoenix, Ariz.: Oryx, 1986), 53; Thomas Watson MacCallum and Stephen Taylor, eds., *The Nobel Prize-Winners and the Nobel Foundation, 1901–1937* (Zurich: Central European Times Publishing, 1938), 289–90.

Sports   *See* BASEBALL, MAJOR LEAGUE; BASEBALL, NEGRO LEAGUE; BOXING; HORSE RACING; OLYMPIC GAMES; TENNIS.

St. Valentine's Day Massacre

Gangster rubout, masterminded by mob boss Al CAPONE, occurring on St. Valentine's Day, February 14, 1929. During PROHIBITION, gangs nationwide battled for control of the illegal business in bootleg liquor. In Chicago the two crime gangs were led by Capone and George "Bugs" Moran. On February 14, 1929, Moran's men were in a warehouse at 2122 Clark Street when a number of men dressed as police raided the warehouse. They were not police but in fact gangsters belonging to Capone's gang. The imposters waited for Moran, who never showed up. Seven members of Moran's gang were lined up against a brick wall and executed. When the police arrived on the scene, it was a blood bath.

The police suspected Capone in the carnage, but he had a firm alibi: he was vacationing in Florida. The killers were never found. Moran's hold on the Chicago liquor business dried up, and Capone took over the entire city. The massacre ranks as the most famous mob rubout in American history.

References: Ruth Dudley Edwards, *The Saint Valentine's Day Murders* (New York: St. Martin's, 1984); "Calls Chicago Police Killers of Gangmen; Federal Dry Chief Expects Slayers Named Today," *Wisconsin News* (Milwaukee), February 15, 1929, p. 1.

Stalin, Joseph (1879–1953)

Soviet leader, who ruled the Soviet Union from 1922 to 1953 with an iron hand, and converted his nation from an agricultural country to an industrial and military giant in the years before and during World War II. Born Josief Vissarionovich Dzhugashvili in the village of Gori, in the area of Georgia in the Caucasus Mountains region, on December 21, 1879, he was the son of poor serfs (his father was a shoemaker and his mother cleaned clothes). Although the young Georgian was educated in the Orthodox Theological Seminary in Tiflis (now Tbilisi, in the independent republic of Georgia), he was expelled for radicalism. When he was 19 he joined the local social-democratic movement, which adhered to the teachings of Karl Marx. He then worked as a clerk in an observatory, but he remained a radical, and in 1901 he became the editor of a Georgian marxist newspaper. A year later he was arrested by the czarist police and spent two years in prisons in the Caucasus, then was exiled to Siberia. During this period he assumed the name "Stalin" ("steel"). After the split in the Social Democratic movement into Bolsheviks ("majority") and Mensheviks ("minority"), Stalin identified with the Bolshevik wing headed by Vladimir LENIN.

Joseph Stalin *(CORBIS/Bettmann)*

After being exiled to Siberia, Stalin escaped and attended Social Democratic conventions in several nations, including Finland. He returned to Georgia, where he became the head of a band of roving criminals, robbing to augment Bolshevik funds. Arrested, he escaped twice before settling underground in St. Petersburg. In 1912, Lenin elected him to the Bolshevik Central Committee. Stalin founded the party newspaper, *Pravda,* and served as its first editor for a short period. In 1916, there was an attempt to draft him into the czarist army to fight in World War I, but a childhood injury to his left arm had made him unfit. With the czar's abdication in March 1917, he returned as editor of *Pravda,* and, shortly before the October Revolution, was named by Lenin to the Politburo, the Bolshevik party congress.

The first Soviet government saw Stalin included as commissar of nationalities, a post he held until 1923. In 1919 he was also named as commissar of workers' and peasants' inspection, a position designed to end corruption in state-run industries. An assassination attempt on Lenin in 1918 made Stalin a closer adviser of the Soviet leader, and in 1922 he was named secretary general of the Soviet Communist Party. Although it seemed that Lenin's inner circle of Leon TROTSKY, Nikolai BUKHARIN, Grigorii Zinoviev, Lev Kamenev, and Stalin worked together, Stalin was secretly scheming to take over upon Lenin's death. When Lenin succumbed on January 21, 1924, Stalin served as the ruler of the USSR because of his post as Communist Party leader. The other leaders desired power-sharing, but Stalin turned on them: all four were expelled from the Politburo and the party in 1927.

On June 9, 1930, *Time* Magazine said of him, "Stalin acts without warning. At his sudden fiat, Trotsky . . . was bundled out of Moscow on a few hours notice, exiled to Turkestan for a year, then banished. . . . In decisions of state Stalin is equally abrupt. One day he orders wholesale 'liquidation' (extermination) of the *kulak* or 'rich peasant' class, and the grim campaign begins. . . . A week, six months or two years later the Dictator may change his mind. As in the case of the anti-Religion campaign, he may modify or relax his whole program, reserving if not the Right then the Power to redouble persecution of the pious at his pleasure." By 1934, Stalin had eliminated all of his political opposition, and he instituted a national system of purges and arrests, which terrorized the people and crushed all dissent. This period is called the Great Terror: untold millions of people who were considered dangerous were arrested and exiled into labor and prison camps without charge or trial, and, in many cases, executed. Desiring to show his might, Stalin conducted show trials of his leading political enemies from 1936 to 1938, in which thousands of people were put to death for imaginary crimes. The Communist Party hierarchy was purged time and time again.

By 1939, Stalin had created a most terrorized society.

He represented a cult of personality, in which *he* became the state, and the state became him: songs were sung in his honor; cities were named for him; children sung his praises. But Stalin's purges had also decimated the Soviet military; and when the Nazi army attacked the Soviet Union in 1941, the Russians were thrown back. While most leaders would have been overthrown under such an onslaught, Stalin brought forward the love of country and the rise to its defense in urging and inspiring the people to fight the Nazis at all costs. Gradually, the Red Army, using resources both from Russia and from the Allies, pushed the Nazis back, until ultimate victory was won in May 1945. Afterward, however, Stalin desired to undertake a barrier against further aggression from Europe by setting up puppet governments in the Eastern European nations from eastern Germany to the Soviet border, establishing an "iron curtain" behind which he created little satellites of his country.

After the war Stalin continued to lead, but he was seen less and less frequently, owing to ill health attributed to heart disease. By the early 1950s, he was in a state of isolation. On March 5, 1953, the Kremlin announced his death—an era ended. The following day, the Communist Party Central Committee named Georgi Malenkov as Stalin's successor. Stalin's impact is immeasurable—from his cult of personality to his purges and destruction of Soviet society, to the heroic victories of the Red Army in helping the Allies to win World War II, to his imposition of state socialism in the Eastern European nations.

References: Robert D. Warth, *Joseph Stalin* (New York: Twayne Publishers, 1969); James L. Heizer, "The Cult of Stalin, 1929–1939" (Master's thesis, University of Kentucky, 1977); *Time* magazine, June 9, 1930, 8; Wolfgang Leonhard (Richard D. Bosley, trans.), *Betrayal: The Hitler-Stalin Pact of 1939* (New York: St. Martin's, 1989); Nikita Sergeevich Khrushchev, *The Anatomy of Terror: Khruschev's Revelations about Stalin's Regime* (Washington: Public Affairs Press, 1956).

Stamboliski, Alexander Stoimenov (1879–1923)

Bulgarian politician and prime minister (1919–23). Born in Slavovitsa, Bulgaria, on March 1, 1879, he completed his secondary education at the State Vinicultural Institute in Pleven in 1898 and later studied agronomy at the University of Halle (1901–02). He became leader of the Bulgarian Agrarian Union in 1900.

Stamboliski opposed Bulgaria's entry into World War I on the side of the Germans, and, as an opponent of King Ferdinand of Bulgaria, he was imprisoned for life. However, he was released after the war. He immediately led a soldiers' mutiny, overthrew the government of King Boris III in what has been called "the Peasant Revolution," and proclaimed the Republic of Radomir. In 1920 he established the Agrarian Union as the government entity. He enacted laws to provide more land for the peasants in June 1921—a move that turned the bourgeoisie against him.

In 1923, Stamboliski's Agrarian Party won elections to the national parliament. On June 9, 1923, however, a military coup overthrew his government; when he attempted to raise a resistance, he was arrested. History differs on his exact fate, but newspapers at the time reported that some of the villagers betrayed him, and he was executed on the spot. Biographer John Bell called him "the most original and dynamic of the peasant leaders who inspired Eastern Europe's 'Green Rising' in the era between the two world wars."

References: John D. Bell, "Stamboliski, Alexander Stoimenov" in Harold Josephson, ed. in chief, *Biographical Dictionary of Modern Peace Leaders* (Westport, Conn.: Greenwood, 1985), 895–98; John D. Bell, *Peasants in Power: Alexander Stamboliski and the Bulgarian Agrarian National Union, 1899–1923* (Princeton, N.J.: Princeton University Press, 1977); Jay Robert Nash, *Encyclopedia of World Crime* (Wilmette, Ill.: CrimeBooks, 1990), 3: 2837; "Stambulisky [sic] Killed. Betrayal by Villagers. Capture Followed by Rescue. Shot in Fight," *The Times* (London), August 16, 1923, p. 12; "The Peasant Premier. M. Stambulisky's Career. Friend of Allies," *The Times* (London), August 16, 1923, p. 11.

Stark, Johannes (1874–1957)

German physicist and Nobel laureate, discovered the Doppler Effect. Born in Schickenhof, Bavaria, on April 15, 1874, he received his doctorate from the University of Munich (1897). Stark served as a professor of physics at the University of Munich (1897–1900), at the University of Göttingen (1900–06), as a professor at the Technische

Hochschule in Aachen (1909–17), and a professor of physics at the University of Greifswald (1917–20). During this period he conducted research into atomic theory and the splitting of spectral lines. He discovered the Doppler Effect, or the Stark Effect, a disclosure that earned him the 1919 Nobel Prize in physics.

Stark continued to work on electrical conduction in gases and atomic theory until his retirement in 1922. He died in Traunstein, Bavaria, on June 21, 1957.

References: Bullit Lowry, "Stark, Johannes" in Bernard S. and June H. Schlessinger, eds., *The Who's Who of Nobel Prize Winners* (Phoenix, Ariz.: Oryx, 1986), 155; Thomas Watson MacCallum and Stephen Taylor, eds., *The Nobel Prize-Winners and the Nobel Foundation, 1901–1937* (Zurich: Central European Times Publishing, 1938), 71.

Statute of Westminster

British parliamentary legislation, enacted 1931, which proclaimed the equality of the Commonwealth nations, such as Australia, New Zealand, and Canada, on the same political and social footing as Great Britain, and ended the British Parliament's right to enact legislation dealing with these countries. As part of the program enacted by the IMPERIAL CONFERENCE held in London in 1930, the conferees drafted the statute, which reads, in part, "It is hereby declared and enacted that the Parliament of a Dominion has full power to make laws having exra-territorial operation. . . . No act of Parliament of the United Kingdom passed after the commencement of this Act shall extend, or be deemed to extend, to a Dominion as part of the law of that Dominion, unless it is expressly declared in that Act that that Dominion requested, and consented to, the enactment itself."

The action also ended the application of England on the Commonwealth nations the Colonial Laws Validity Act of 1865, which made invalid all laws passed by Commonwealth nations that conflicted with laws enacted by the British Parliament. In response, South Africa enacted the Status of the Union Act in 1934, declaring that nation to be a "sovereign independent state." In Australia the act became law in 1942, although the Parliament there claimed that it was retroactive back to 1939.

References: Text of statute at British Statutes, 22 George V, chapter 4; "Statute of Westminster" in Graeme Aplin, Stephen Glynn Foster, and Michael McKernan, eds., *Australians: A Historical Dictionary* (New South Wales: Fairfax, Syme & Weldon Associates, 1987), 379.

Stein, Gertrude (1874–1946)

American writer, leader of a cultural salon of writers and artists in Paris during the 1920s. Born February 3, 1874, into upper-middle-class surroundings in Allegheny, Pennsylvania, Stein was the fifth child of Daniel and Amelia Stein. She was three years old when the family moved to Vienna and then to Paris before returning to the United States in late 1878. A trilingual child, Stein was an avid reader. In 1893 she entered Radcliffe College in Cambridge, Massachusetts, where she studied psychology and philosophy under Harvard scholar William James. After briefly studying medicine at Johns Hopkins University and for a time in Europe, Stein abandoned that course to travel through Italy, Germany, and England before earnestly pursuing a writing career.

Back in the United States in 1903, she wrote her first novel *Q.E.D.* (published posthumously as *Things as They Are*), which explores the jealousies and desires among three young women. Later that year, Stein moved to Paris, where she largely remained for the rest of her life. During the 1920s her home became a beacon for such artists as Pablo PICASSO and Henri Matisse and such writers as Ernest HEMINGWAY, Sherwood Anderson, and F. Scott FITZGERALD—members of the LOST GENERATION.

This interaction motivated much of Stein's own experimental writing, which typically used language imaginatively and explored the sounds and rhythms of words. Her works include the short stories of *Three Lives* (1909), the "cubist" prose-poem *Tender Buttons* (1914), the narrative *The Making of Americans* (1925), the critical essays in *How to Write* (1931), her life story in *The Autobiography of Alice B. Toklas* (1933), and the opera *Four Saints in Three Acts* (1934, music by Virgil Thomson).

References: John Malcolm Brinnin, *The Third Rose: Gertrude Stein and Her World* (Reading, Mass.: Addison-Wesley, 1987); Howard Greenfeld, *Gertrude Stein: A Biography* (New York: Crown, 1973).

Steinbeck, John (1902–1968)

American writer, novelist, and Nobel laureate, whose interwar work reflected American life during the GREAT DEPRESSION. Steinbeck was born on February 27, 1902, in Salinas, California, which he used as a backdrop for many of his works, starting with *Cup of Gold* (1929), *Pastures of Heaven* (1932), *To a God Unknown* (1933), *Tortilla Flat* (1935), and *In Dubious Battle* (1936). His *Of Mice and Men* (1937) earned him instant international recognition for the story of two drifters caught in the depression-era dream of having a piece of land of their own. Steinbeck's last interwar work, *The Grapes of Wrath* (1939), which was made into a major motion picture and won Steinbeck the Pulitzer Prize for fiction in 1940, is the story of the Joad family and their trek to California during the DUST BOWL to seek a better life. For this body of work, Steinbeck was awarded the 1962 Nobel Prize in literature. He died in New York City on December 20, 1968.

References: Kiernan, Thomas, "The Intricate Music: A Biography of John Steinbeck" (Boston: Little, Brown, 1979); Robert Bartlett Harmon, "The Collectible John Steinbeck: A Practical Guide" (Jefferson, N.C.: McFarland, 1986); Tetsumaro, Hayashi, "John Steinbeck: A Concise Bibliography, 1930–65" (Metuchen, N.J.: Scarecrow Press, 1967).

Stimson Doctrine

Statement of principles, enunciated January 7, 1932, by U.S. Secretary of State Henry Lewis Stimson, which called for the "nonrecognition" of all Japanese-acquired territories in China. In December 1931 the LEAGUE OF NATIONS established the LYTTON COMMISSION under the leadership of Victor Alexander George Robert Bulwer-Lytton, second Earl of Lytton, to investigate Japanese aggression in China. However, this action only delayed dealing with what became in 1932 a major international crisis as Japanese troops advanced rapidly. Stimson, having discussed a plan of action with President Herbert HOOVER as early as November 9, 1931, when after long deliberations the United States secretly changed its policy of opposing an embargo by the major powers against Japan to noninterference of such a move, decided to send notes to the governments in Tokyo and Peking that the United States would refuse to recognize any territorial conquests of Japan in China, based, according to historian Lester Brune, "on Japan's violation of the NINE-POWER TREATY and the KELLOGG-BRIAND Peace Pact."

In the identical notes sent to both governments, Stimson wrote,

> With the recent military operations about Chinchow, the last remaining administrative authority of the Government of the Chinese Republic in South Manchuria, as it existed prior to September 18th, 1931, has been destroyed. The American Government continues confident that the work of the neutral commission recently authorized by the Council of the League of Nations will facilitate an ultimate solution of the difficulties now existing between China and Japan. But in view of the present situation and of its own rights and obligations therein, the American Government deems it to be its duty to notify both the Imperial Japanese Government and the Government of the Chinese Republic that it cannot admit the legality of any situation de facto nor does it intend to recognize any treaty or agreement entered in to between those Governments, or agents thereof, which may impair the treaty rights of the United States or its citizens in China, including those which relate to the sovereignty, the independence, or the territorial and administrative integrity of the Republic of China, or to the international policy relative to China, commonly known as the open door policy; and that it does not intend to recognize any situation, treaty or agreement which may be brought about by meancontrary to the covenants and obligations of the Pact of Paris of August 27, 1928 [Kellogg-Briand], to which Treaty both China and Japan, as well as the United States, are parties.

The Stimson notes had little aftereffect; if the United States was hoping for the world to join and not recognize the Japanese conquest of China, it failed. Historian Brune writes of the consequence of the doctrine, "The Hoover-Stimson policy was moralistic in tone but had no constructive results beyond putting the United States on record."

References: Gary B. Ostrower, "Stimson, Henry Lewis" in Warren F. Kuehl, ed., *Biographical Dictionary of Internationalists* (Westport, Conn.: Greenwood, 1983), 693–96; Thomas P. Brockway, *Basic Documents in United States Foreign Policy* (Princeton, N.J.: D. Van Nostrand Company, 1968), 87–88; Lester H. Brune, *Chronological History of United States Foreign Relations, 1776 to January 20, 1981* (New York: Garland, 1985), 2: 687.

Stock Market Crash

Plummet in the U.S. stock market on October 29, 1929, also known as Black Tuesday, caused by overspeculation in the market during the 1920s. On this day thousands of investors tried to sell off their stock and more than 16 million shares of stock were traded. With few buyers, stock prices dropped far below what investors had originally paid for them. Accordingly, investors lost billions of dollars within a matter of hours. Banks and businesses that had invested in the market were forced to shut down. This crash put an end to the excesses of the JAZZ AGE and the Roaring Twenties—what had been a decade-long rise in stock values.

The crash shocked the world, and the U.S. government seemed frozen by the crisis. U.S. President Herbert HOOVER refused to intervene, believing the fundamentals of the American economy to be sound. Although the market recovered somewhat throughout November and December of 1929, the crash was in effect the opening event of the 1930s, the preamble to the GREAT DEPRESSION. Historians cite loose regulation of the banking system as well as a sharp rise in consumer credit-based spending as contributing factors to this market precariousness.

References: Douglas Brinkley, *History of the United States* (New York: Viking, 1998), 399–400; Dixon Wecter, *The Age of the Great Depression, 1929–1941* (New York: Macmillan, 1948).

Stopes, Marie Carmichael (1880–1958)

British birth control advocate, founder, 1921, of the world's first birth control clinic. Born in Edinburgh, Scotland, in 1880, she was educated at the Universities of London and Munich, and studied paleobotany, serving as a lecturer in the science at University College in London and at the University of Manchester. In 1918, she changed direction, however, and started to advocate the distribution of birth control information and devices. That year, she published *Married Love,* which claimed that women enjoyed sex as much as men did. Although she barely mentioned birth control in the book, she was asked for advice on the subject, and published that same year *Wise Parenthood,* which was a guide for the use of contraceptive devices such as the sponge. With her second husband, Humphrey Vernon Roe, she founded, on March 17, 1921, the first birth control clinic in the British Empire, the Mothers' Clinic for Constructive Birth Control. Conservatives demanded its closing, and she was sued in the famed Sutherland libel case in 1923, which she lost. Her clinic remained open, however, and expanded to the Population Services Family Planning Programme, now called Marie Stopes International.

Stopes died in 1958. Her other writings include *Contraception* (1923) and *Wartime Harvest* (1944).

References: Ruth E. Hall, *Passionate Crusader: The Life of Marie Stopes* (New York: Harcourt Brace Jovanovich, 1977); Keith Briant, *Passionate Paradox: The Life of Marie Stopes* (New York: Norton, 1962).

Straits Treaty

Pact, approved July 24, 1923, in which the nations comprising the High Contracting Parties agreed "to recognise and declare the principle of freedom of transit and of navigation by sea and by air in the Strait of the Dardanelles, the Sea of Marmora and the Bosphorus." Signed by representatives of the British Empire, France, Italy, Japan, Bulgaria, Greece, Romania, the Soviet Union, the Serb-Croat-Slovene State (later called Yugoslavia), and Turkey, it was initialed in the Swiss city of Lausanne at the same time that the Treaty of LAUSANNE was being signed.

In time of peace, the treaty called for the "complete freedom of navigation and passage by day and by night under any flag and with any kind of cargo, without any formalities, or tax, or charge whatever (subject, however, to international sanitary provisions) unless for services directly rendered, such as pilotage, light, towage or other similar charges, and without prejudice to the rights exercised in this respect by the services and undertakings now operating under concessions granted by the Turkish Government." During wartime the treaty specified what actions could or could not be taken if Turkey was at peace or was a belligerent. It also allowed for the passing of "Merchant Vessels, including Hospital Ships, Yachts and Fishing Vessels and non-Military Aircraft" during wartime without incident.

Reference: Fred L. Israel, ed., *Major Peace Treaties of Modern History: 1648–1967* (New York: Chelsea House Publishers in association with McGraw-Hill, 1967–1980), 4: 2305–68.

Streicher, Julius (1885–1946)

German journalist and propagandist, editor and official propaganda voice of the NAZI PARTY. Born in Fleinshausen, Germany, on February 12, 1885, he worked as a schoolteacher, but after World War I he converted to National Socialism. In 1923, Streicher was a major participant in the BEER-HALL PUTSCH, the attempted Nazi revolt against the WEIMAR government established in Germany after the end of the war. That same year, he founded *Der Stürmer* (The storm), an obscene, anti-Semitic Nuremberg newspaper that the Nazis distributed throughout Germany. Soon, Streicher became the official mouthpiece of the Nazi Party. When Hitler came to power as German chancellor in 1933, he named Streicher the Nazi Party district leader of Franconia (northern Bavaria).

In the next several years, Streicher was most responsible for the passage of the Nuremberg Laws, a series of enactments meant to strip Jews of their rights in German life. He also became the director of the Central Committee for Deflecting Jewish-Atrocity and Boycott-Mongering, a group designed to distribute the official German government line on the atrocities being committed against Jews and other undesirables. Streicher was at the forefront for the entire Nazi period.

Captured by the Allies at the end of World War II (where he was disguised as a fleeing refugee artist, a *Kunstmaler*), Streicher was tried at Nuremberg, where he was found guilty of crimes against humanity for his vicious anti-Semitic activities. On October 16, 1946, he was hanged and, with the other Nazis executed on that same day, was cremated; his remains were dumped into the Isar River near Munich.

References: Christian Zentner and Friedemann Bedüftig, eds., *Encyclopedia of the Third Reich* (New York: Macmillan, 1991), 2: 921–22; James Taylor and Warren Shaw, *The Third Reich Almanac* (New York: World Almanac, 1987); Ann and John Tusa, *The Nuremberg Trial* (New York: Atheneum, 1986); Telford Taylor, *The Anatomy of the Nuremberg Trials: A Personal Memoir* (New York: Alfred A. Knopf, 1992).

Stresemann, Gustav (1878–1929)
German politician, chancellor (1923), and foreign minister (1923–29). Born in Berlin on May 10, 1878, he was educated at the universities of Berlin and Leipzig. Elected in 1917 to the German Reichstag as a member of the National Liberal Party, he became the party leader that same year. Six years later, in 1923, he was elected, as part of the "Grand Coalition," to the post of chancellor of the WEIMAR REPUBLIC and served under President Friedrich EBERT. Soon after, he was named foreign minister; in this office he made more progress in the name of Germany toward peace with the rest of Europe than any German leader this century save Chancellor Helmut Kohl.

As foreign minister, he helped stabilize the German mark during the financial panic of 1923, initiated the peace talks which resulted in the LOCARNO PACT of 1925, and oversaw Germany's admittance into the LEAGUE OF NATIONS in 1926. For his work on Locarno, he was awarded, with Aristide BRIAND, the 1926 Nobel Prize for Peace. Stresemann was the only one of the four laureates to pick his award up in person. Writes biographer Irwin Abrams, "Stresemann . . . recognized the opportunity to interpret 'The Way of the New Germany' to a foreign audience. His address was delivered in the Aula of the University [of Oslo] in June 1927 and broadcast throughout Scandinavia . . . Stresemann declared that the Germany he represented was trying to achieve a synthesis of the best of the old and the new."

Stresemann, perhaps one of Weimar Germany's best chances for post–World War I peace, died suddenly on October 3, 1929. His contributions to peace and economic stability in Europe, however, were swept away with the onslaught of the Nazi Party's rise to power just four years after his death.

References: Solveig Olsen, "Stresemann, Gustav" in Bernard S. and June H. Schlessinger, eds., *The Who's Who of Nobel Prize Winners* (Phoenix, Ariz.: Oryx, 1986), 133–34; Kenneth Paul Jones, "Stresemann, Gustav" in Warren F. Kuehl, ed., *Biographical Dictionary of Internationalists* (Westport, Conn.: Greenwood, 1983), 702–703; Thomas Watson MacCallum, and Stephen Taylor, eds., *The Nobel Prize-Winners and the Nobel Foundation, 1901–1937* (Zurich: Central European Times Publishing, 1938), 369–70; Henry A. Turner, *Stresemann and the Politics of the Weimar Republic* (Princeton, N.J.: Princeton University Press, 1963); Irwin Abrams, *The Nobel Peace Prize and the Laureates: An Illustrated Biographical History, 1901–1987* (Boston: G. K. Hall & Co., 1988), 104–105; Niles Holt, "Gustav Stresemann" in Anne Commire, ed., *Historic World Leaders* (Detroit: Gale Research, 1994), 3: 1231.

Stroheim, Erich von (1885–1957)
German actor and director, known for numerous interwar silent film masterpieces. Born Erich Oswald Stroheim on September 22, 1885, in Vienna, Austria, he graduated from the Imperial and Royal Military Academy in Wiener Neustadt, Austria. He seemed for a time to be headed for a career in the Austrian cavalry. In 1909, however, he emigrated to the United States and earned a living doing odd jobs. In 1914 he moved to Hollywood, California, and the following year got a bit part in the D. W. GRIFFITH motion picture *The Birth of a Nation*. Seeing his talent in acting as well as directing, movie studios allowed him to direct *Blind Husbands* (1918), which was moderately successful. However, it was with his next film, *Foolish Wives,* that he went ridiculously over budget and wound up spending over $1 million, the first picture to do so. He wrote and directed the film version of Frank Norris's *McTeague* as *Greed* (1923), which is now considered a classic by film historians. Von Stroheim directed *The Merry Widow* (1925), but it was his work on *The Wedding March* that proved to be his undoing. Wildly over budget and with reels and reels of film being shot, he was fired from the production. He never again directed an American film. For his obstinate desire for perfection, he was called "the man you love to hate."

Von Stroheim moved to France in 1937, acting as the Prussian officer in Jean Renoir's *The Grand Illusion* (1938). During World War II, he returned to the United States, and worked in several films. His last appearance was *Sunset Boulevard* (1949) opposite Gloria Swanson. Von Stroheim died in Maurepas, near Montfort-d'Amaury, France, on May 12, 1957.

References: Peter Noble, *Hollywood Scapegoat: The Biography of Erich von Stroheim* (New York: Arno, 1972); Richard Koszarski, *The Man You Loved to Hate: Erich Von Stroheim and Hollywood* (Oxford: Oxford University Press, 1983); Herman G. Weinberg, comp., *The Complete Greed of Erich von Stroheim: A Reconstruction of the Film in 348 Still Photos Following the Original Screenplay Plus 52 Production Stills* (New York: E. P. Dutton, 1972).

Sudetenland   See HITLER, ADOLF; MUNICH CRISIS; APPEASEMENT.

Sunday, William Ashley (1862–1935)
American preacher and evangelist, known for his flamboyant revivals in the 1920s. Born in Ames, Iowa, on November 19, 1863, he was orphaned at an early age and later attended Northwestern University. He played professional baseball for the Chicago White Stockings (later White Sox), as well as the Pittsburgh and Philadelphia clubs from 1883 to 1890. It was during this period, when with his teammates he would roam city bars, that he heard while walking along the sidewalk hymns against alcohol sung by members of the Pacific Garden Mission band. He declared

that he would never drink again. In 1890 he left baseball forever, and the following year joined the Young Men's Christian Association in Chicago, where he served as assistant secretary.

In 1896, Sunday began as an evangelist, and seven years later was ordained as a Presbyterian minister by the Chicago Presbytery. Over the next several years, he hit the road with sermons on the "proper" way of living. He spoke out against liquor, socialism, immigrants, and during World War I denounced draft dodgers, asking God to "strike down in his tracks" any man who would shirk his duty. His conversations, held at huge rallies, attracted tens of thousands of supporters.

After the war, however, Sunday was in decline. He continued to preach, but he was not as successful as he had once been. For the remaining 15 years of his life, he preached in the tents of the Midwestern towns where he had begun.

References: John Pahl, "Billy Sunday" in Charles H. Lippy, ed., *Twentieth-Century Shapers of American Popular Religion* (New York: Greenwood, 1989), 410–17; Lyle W. Dorsett, *Billy Sunday and the Redemption of Urban America* (Grand Rapids, Mich.: W. B. Eerdmans Publishing Co., 1991); William Thomas Ellis, *"Billy" Sunday, The Man and His Message, with His Own Words Which Have Won Thousands for Christ* (Philadelphia: John C. Winston Company, 1914).

surrealism

Major art and literary movement of the 1920s and 1930s, established circa 1924, by the French poet André Breton. Breton rallied against DADA, an art movement that had sprung up in Europe during World War I. He declared that Dada had only been "a state of mind," and thus needed to be superceded by a new movement that was

Surrealist poets Paul Éluard, André Breton, and Robert Desnos *(CORBIS/Stefano Bianchetti)*

more realistic. To these ends, Breton published a proclamation in Paris that year called the *Manifeste du surréalisme*, which called for a new order in the arts. "We must burst the bonds of reason," he wrote. Every artist must attempt to become "the modest recording device of his dreams." He thus defined the new name of the movement, surrealism, as "the principles, ideals or practice of producing fantastic or incongruous imagery or effects in art, literature, film or theater by means of unnatural juxtapositions and combinations." Surrealism took all forms: from the literary works of Louis Aragon, Paul Éluard, Philippe Soupault, and René Crevel, to the art of René Magritte, Yves Tanguy, Salvador Dalí, Albert Giacometti, and Joan Miró, to the photographs and films of Jean COCTEAU and Man Ray.

Dalí's dream-inspired images, such as his melting clocks, and Miró's paintings from the subconscious came to symbolize the movement. Because Breton called for "free, revolutionary, independent art," the movement moved to the left of the political spectrum, and allied itself in the late 1920s with the Communist Party. However, because they did not follow strict communist dogma, many were booted out of the party, including Breton, who was forced out in 1936. Although the movement continued in different directions (Dali worked with filmmaker Luis Buñuel to produce the 1929 film *The Andalusian Dog*), surrealism rapidly moved into other world centers, including London, New York, and Copenhagen. The last large exhibition of surrealist art was shown at the Galerie des Beaux-Arts in Paris in January 1938. The movement ended with the start of World War II.

References: Wallace Fowlie, *Age of Surrealism* (New York: Swallow, 1950); Robert Short, *Dada & Surrealism* (New York: Mayflower Books, 1980); J. H. Matthews, *The Imagery of Surrealism* (Syracuse, N.Y.: Syracuse University Press, 1977); *Reader's Digest Great Events of the 20th Century: How They Changed Our Lives* (Pleasantville, N.Y.: Reader's Digest Association, 1977), 186–91.

Svedberg, Theodor (1884–1971)

Swedish chemist and Nobel laureate. Born in the village of Flerang, in Valbo, Sweden, on August 30, 1884, he graduated with a bachelor of science degree (1905) and a doctorate (1907) from the University of Uppsala. He then served as a professor of chemistry there (1912–49). During these years Svedberg instituted a series of researches into colloidal chemistry: specifically, he invented the ultracentrifuge to separate the colloids from solutions and to study them more closely. For this work, Svedberg was awarded the 1926 Nobel Prize in chemistry.

With Arne Tiselius (who later won the 1948 Nobel Prize in chemistry), Svedberg invented the use of electrophoresis, an electronic sorter that led to the discovery of DNA fingerprinting. Svedberg spent his final working years as director of the Gustaf Werner Institute of Nuclear Chemistry in Uppsala, retiring in 1967. He died in Orebro, Sweden, on February 25, 1971.

References: Cheryl N. Broome, "Svedberg, Theodor" in Bernard S. and June H. Schlessinger, eds., *The Who's Who of Nobel Prize Winners* (Phoenix, Ariz.: Oryx, 1986), 10; Thomas Watson MacCallum and Stephen Taylor, eds., *The Nobel Prize-Winners and the Nobel Foundation, 1901–1937* (Zurich: Central European Times Publishing, 1938), 148.

swing

Style of JAZZ music that swept the United States during the 1930s and beyond. Clarinetist and bandleader Benny Goodman, who came to be known as "the King of Swing," helped develop this innovative twist on traditional New Orleans–style improvisational jazz. Swing compositions, characterized by the big-band sound played by large groups of musicians, were carefully arranged and featured improvisation only during solos. Goodman recruited such musical talents as drummer Gene Krupa and vibraphonist Lionel Hampton in his trio; he also was one of the earliest bandleaders to bring together black and white musicians in his performing groups.

Bandleaders Count Basie, Duke ELLINGTON, and Fletcher Henderson also helped introduce this popular music to audiences across the country. The singing voices of Ella Fitzgerald, Frank Sinatra, and Sarah Vaughan typified the swing sound. *Life* magazine captured the swing era in several issues, as its cover featured photographs of dancers taken in New York's Savoy Ballroom and Cotton Club. In the 1940s "be-bop" jazz developed as a revolt against swing's carefully arranged formulas, led by musicians Charlie Parker and Dizzy Gillespie.

Reference: Stanley Dance, *The World of Swing* (New York: Charles Scribner's Sons, 1974).

Szent-Györgyi, Albert von Nagyrapolt (1893–1986)

Hungarian-American biochemist and Nobel laureate. Born in Budapest, Hungary, on September 16, 1893, he received his M.D. degree from the University of Budapest (1917) and his doctorate from Cambridge University (1927). After serving in the Hungarian army during World War I, he worked as a researcher at various universities until 1931, when he became the administrator of the University of Szeged in Hungary. During this period, Szent-Györgyi worked on the combustion processes of certain vitamins, including vitamin C, and the catalysis of fumaric acid. For this work, he was awarded the 1937 Nobel Prize in medicine and physiology.

Szent-Györgyi spent the remainder of his life as a researcher. Today, his name is remembered for his studies of adenosine triphosphate and his numerous investigations into human cancers. He is memorialized with the Albert Szent-Györgyi Medical University, located in Dumter, Hungary.

References: Marlene Latuch, "Szent-Györgyi, Albert von Nagyrapolt" in Bernard S. and June H. Schlessinger, eds., *The Who's Who of Nobel Prize Winners* (Phoenix, Ariz.: Oryx, 1986), 90–91; Thomas Watson MacCallum and Stephen Taylor, eds., *The Nobel Prize–Winners and the Nobel Foundation, 1901–1937* (Zurich: Central European Times Publishing, 1938), 243–44.

T

Tacna-Arica Controversy

Territorial dispute over the area between the Peruvian town of Tacna and the Chilean port of Arica. The dispute, which occurred from 1922 to 1926, centered on events that transpired a half-century earlier. In 1879 Chile and Peru went to war over this territory, in what has been called the War of the Pacific. The conflict lasted until 1883 and ended in the Treaty of Ancón, signed that same year, which allowed for Chilean ownership of the entire area for 10 years, after which a plebiscite would be held to determine its final status. In 1893, Chile refused to hold the election, however, and for the next 30 years the possibility of war between the two nations became ever closer. In July 1922, U.S. President Warren G. HARDING offered to use his nation as a mediating influence to settle the dispute peacefully. Famed World War I General John "Black Jack" Pershing was chosen to chair the Tacna-Arica Boundary Commission. The Pershing commission found that conditions were not proper for a new plebiscite and disbanded. In 1928 negotiations were resumed by the two nations, but again they went nowhere. In 1929, President Herbert HOOVER again offered the United States as a mediator, suggesting that Tacna be given fully to Peru and Arica to Chile. This was accepted, and on August 28, 1929, the two nations signed the Tacna-Arica Agreement in Washington, D.C. It allowed Tacna as well as a portion of Arica Bay to remain with Peru; at the same time, Chile kept control of Arica, and paid Peru $6 million for its complete right to the port.

References: Important documents and letters dealing with the controversy can be found in *Papers Relating to the Foreign Relations of the United States: 1921* (Washington, D.C.: U.S. Government Printing Office, 1936), 1: 237–57; further information can be found in Edmund Jan Osmańczyk, *The Encyclopedia of the United Nations and International Agreements* (Philadelphia: Taylor & Francis, 1985), 792; William F. Sater, "Tacna-Arica Dispute" in Barbara A. Tenenbaum, ed. in chief, *Encyclopedia of Latin American History and Culture* (New York: Charles Scribner's Sons, 1996), 5: 194; William Jefferson Dennis, *Tacna and Arica: An Account of the Chile-Peru Boundary Dispute and of the Arbitrations by the United States* (Hamden, Conn.: Archon Books, 1967); William Jefferson Dennis, *Documentary History of the Tacna-Arica Dispute* (Port Washington, N.Y.: Kennikat, 1971).

Taisho *See* HIROHITO.

Takahashi, Korekiyo (1854–1936)

Japanese diplomat and financier, prime minister (1921–22), member of several cabinets as finance minister (1913–36). Born in Edo (now Tokyo) on July 7, 1854, he was the son of an artist with the surname Kawamura but was adopted by the samurai of the Sendai domain (now Miyagi Prefecture). Under their tutelage, he studied English in Japan for a year and then was sent to the United States. Upon his return, he became the houseboy of Japanese politician Mori Arinori.

For several years, Takahashi served in several bureaucratic posts, including an office in the Department of Agriculture and Commerce. Later, he held posts at the Bank of Japan (in 1911) and the Yokohama Specie Bank, where he became an expert in Japanese financial matters. In 1913 he was named finance minister in the cabinet of Prime Minister Yamamoto Gonnohyoei, serving until 1914, and again held the post from 1918 to 1921 in the cabinet of Takashi Hara, who was assassinated on November 4, 1921. Takahashi, who had worked to increase Japan's naval capabilities during his tenure at finance, was quickly installed as Hara's successor. His term lasted a brief seven months because of divisions within his own party. Japanese biographer Michio Umegaki writes of the period, "His tenure as prime minister was brief and undistinguished, but his contributions as a financial expert were widely praised."

In 1927, Takahashi was elected to the lower house of the Japanese Diet (parliament), but that same year was named minister of agriculture and commerce. He later served as finance minister in three separate cabinets (1927–29, 1931–32, 1934–36). In his final term he increasingly spoke out against increased military appropriations as unnecessary. On February 26, 1936, in a widespread coup some 1,400 soldiers of the right-wing Kodo, or Imperial Way, faction of the Japanese army attacked five major politicians, assassinating former prime minister Makoko Saito (who at the time was lord keeper of the privy seal), Premier Keisuke Okada, General Jotaro Watanabe, the military inspector general, Admiral Soruku Suzuki, grand chamberlain, and Takahashi, who was 71. Takahashi's death cleared the way for the increase in the influence of the military on Japan's foreign and domestic policy, culminating during World War II.

References: "Takahashi Korekiyo" in Gen Itasaka, gen. ed., *Kodansha Encyclopedia of Japan* (Tokyo: Kodansha, 1983), 7: 312; Michio Umegaki, *Takahashi Korekiyo* in Ainslee T. Embree, ed. in chief, *Encyclopedia of Asian History* (New York: Charles Scribner's Sons, 1988), 4: 56; "Takahashi Installed; New Japanese Premier Keeps Finance Portfolio Also" *Washington Post*, November 14, 1921, p. 1; "Martial Law Invoked, Warships Ring Tokyo; New Cabinet Resigns," *Washington Post*, February 27, 1936, p. 1; "Tokyo Rebels Reject Peace; Marines Land to Guard City; Censorship Is Evoked Again," *Washington Post*, February 28, 1936, p. 1.

Tarzan   *See* EDGAR RICE BURROUGHS.

Taylor, Deems (1885–1966)

American composer, noted for his scores for *The King's Henchman* (1927) and *Peter Ibbetson* (1931), as well as his work as music writer for the *New York World* (1921–32). Born Joseph Deems Taylor in New York City on December 22, 1885, Taylor graduated from New York University in 1906 after studying to be an architect. While there, he found an interest in writing operas, and in 1909 he composed a comedy, *The Echo*, which found its way onto Broadway. Over the next several years, he composed the musical poem *The Siren Song* (1912), and two cantatas, *The Chambered Nautilus* and *The Highwayman* (both 1914), which increased his reputation as a serious composer.

In 1916, Taylor was hired as the assistant Sunday editor of the *New York Tribune*, eventually moving to become the paper's war correspondent when the United States entered World War I. Taylor was sent to cover the conflict in France. After he returned, he left the *Tribune*, but continued to do newspaper work for such papers as the *New York World*. In 1925 he resigned his newspaper duties to concentrate full time on composing. That year, Walter Damrosch of the New York Symphony hired Taylor to compose a symphony for the poem *Jurgen*, based on the book by James Branch Cabell. Taylor's work on that composition led his commission the following year from the Metropolitan Opera Company to compose the music for *The King's Henchman*. Writer Edna St. Vincent Millay wrote the libretto. When the play opened in New York on February 17, 1927, critics called it the greatest American opera ever staged. A second commission followed, and Taylor composed the music for *Peter Ibbetson*, based on the book by George du Maurier, with the words supplied by Constance Collier. For this opera, Taylor was hailed as perhaps the greatest composer ever.

Starting in 1931, Taylor also served as the voice of the Metropolitan over radio; he had narrated the airing of *The King's Henchman* over the Columbia network in 1927, and his popularity and smooth speaking voice served to call for his return. In 1936 he started a stint as the voice of the New York Philharmonic Orchestra, which lasted until 1943. His other work during this period that earned him high acclaim include the orchestral pieces *The Portrait of a Lady* (1919), *A Kiss in Xanadu* (1923), *Lucrece* (1932), and *Circus Day* (1934). He also worked as the editor of the magazine *Musical America* (1927–29), and as the music editor of the *New York American* newspaper (1931–32), and wrote several books, including *Of Men and Music* (1937). He died in New York on July 3, 1966.

Reference: Stanley Green, *The World of Musical Comedy: The Story of the American Musical Stage as Told Through the Careers of its Foremost Composers and Lyricists* (South Brunswick, N.J.: A.S. Barnes, 1968).

Teapot Dome scandal

U.S. political scandal, in which the secretary of the interior illegally leased federal oil reserves to cronies for bribes. President William Howard Taft established the federal oil reserves at Teapot Dome, Wyoming, and Elk Hills, California, in case of a fuel emergency. In 1921, President Warren G. HARDING's secretary of the interior, former New Mexico senator Albert Bacon FALL, took bribes totaling $260,000 from two men—Harry F. Sinclair of the Mammoth Oil Company and Edward F. Doheny of the Pan-American Oil Company—so that he might sign leases without bidding for the men to profit from.

In 1923 a Senate committee heard about allegations that Fall had been bribed in exchange for the leases, but before it could hold hearings, Fall resigned and returned to New Mexico. Nevertheless, Senator Thomas J. Walsh of Montana opened hearings, which lasted until 1924. Walsh's committee uncovered the bribes, and Fall was indicted and found guilty (after eight trials). He served one year in prison, emerging broken both in spirit and health. Teapot Dome was thereafter known as the code name for many Harding administration scandals, including ones that forced the resignation of Attorney General Harry DAUGHERTY and payoffs found in the Veterans Administration.

References: Thomas G. Alexander, "Teapot Dome Revisited: Reed Smoot and Conservation in the 1920s," *Utah Historical Quarterly* 45 (1977): 352–68; Burl Noggle, *Teapot Dome: Oil and Politics in the 1920s* (Baton Rouge: Louisiana State University Press, 1962).

technocracy

American social movement, popular for a short time in the United States during the GREAT DEPRESSION, which predicted the collapse of capitalism, fostered by New York engineer Howard Scott. Influenced by the ideas of noted economist and writer Thorstein Veblen, Scott predicted the end of capitalism and the transfer of the control of society from politicians and businesspeople to technicians. He illustrated his ideas in a speech delivered at the Hotel Pierre in New York City on January 13, 1933. From 1935 to 1942, Scott published *Technocracy: For the New America, The Official Magazine of Technocracy*. After the depression, he continued to write on the subject, but he was largely ignored.

Reference: William E. Akin, *Technocracy and the American Dream: The Technocrat Movement, 1900–1941* (Berkeley: University of California Press, 1977).

tennis

The sport of tennis remained a formal event during the 1920s and 1930s. The leading female players of the period undoubtedly were the American player Helen Newington Wills Moody and the French singles and doubles player Suzanne Lenglen, who between them won *fourteen* championships at Wimbledon from 1919 to 1939. Wills Moody won the U.S. singles championship continuously from 1923–25, 1927–29, and 1931, as well as the French Open four times, and the Wightman Cup singles 18 times before retiring in 1938. The French Open ladies' singles tournament is known as the *Coupe Suzanne Lenglen*. In 1996, the main court at the Open was renamed the Court Suzanne Lenglen.

On the men's side, William ("Big Bill") Tilden was perhaps the finest player. From 1920 until 1925, he won 66 straight matches, winning the U.S. Open six times, the

WIMBLEDON SINGLES CHAMPIONS, 1919–1939		
	MEN'S	WOMEN'S
1919	Gerald Patterson	Suzanne Lenglen
1920	Bill Tilden	Suzanne Lenglen
1921	Bill Tilden	Suzanne Lenglen
1922	Gerald Patterson	Suzanne Lenglen
1923	William Johnston	Suzanne Lenglen
1924	Jean Borotra	Kathleen McKane
1925	René Lacoste	Suzanne Lenglen
1926	Jean Borotra	Kathleen McKane Godfree
1927	Henri Cochet	Helen Wills
1928	René Lacoste	Helen Wills
1929	Henri Cochet	Helen Wills
1930	Bill Tilden	Helen Wills Moody
1931	Sidney Wood	Cilly Aussem
1932	Ellsworth Vines	Helen Wills Moody
1933	Jack Crawford	Helen Wills Moody
1934	Fred Perry	Dorothy Round
1935	Fred Perry	Helen Wills Moody
1936	Fred Perry	Helen Jacobs
1937	Don Budge	Dorothy Round
1938	Don Budge	Helen Wills Moody
1939	Bobby Riggs	Alice Marble

All-England Championship at Wimbledon twice (a third win came in 1930), and was ranked first in the world in 1919. During the interwar years, only one man won all four major tennis championships—the United States National Championships, which in 1968 became the U.S. Open, Wimbledon, the Australian Open, and the French Open—Don Budge, in 1938. Two others won three of the four: Jack Crawford (1933), and Fred Perry (1934).

Thomas, Norman Mattoon   *See* AMERICAN CIVIL LIBERTIES UNION.

Thomson, George Paget (1892–1975)

British physicist and Nobel laureate. Born in Cambridge, England, on May 3, 1892, he received his baccalaureate from Cambridge University in 1914. Working at Cambridge University, the University of Aberdeen, and the Imperial College of Science in England, Thomson worked on electron diffraction by crystals and moved to the area of fission and the development of an atomic weapon, unknown at this time. For this work, he shared the 1937 Nobel Prize in physics with Clinton Joseph DAVISSON, who was honored for the same research. Professor H. Pleijel, the chair of the Nobel Committee for Physics of the Royal Swedish Academy of Sciences, explained Thomson's experiments: "For his experiments Thomson made use of exceedingly thin films of celluloid, gold, platinum, or aluminum. He made the electron beam fall perpendicularly upon the film and examined the diffraction figures produced on a fluorescent screen placed behind the film, or else had them reproduced on a photographic plate."

Thomson was knighted in 1943. He continued his work until he retired in 1962; he died in Cambridge on September 10, 1975.

References: Thomas McGinty, "Thomson, George Paget, Sir" in Bernard S. and June H. Schlessinger, eds., *The Who's Who of Nobel Prize Winners* (Phoenix, Ariz.: Oryx, 1986), 163; Thomas Watson MacCallum and Stephen Taylor, eds., *The Nobel Prize–Winners and the Nobel Foundation, 1901–1937* (Zurich: Central European Times Publishing, 1938), 106–107.

Transportation Act of 1920   *See* ESCH-CUMMINS (TRANSPORTATION) ACT.

Travers, P. L.   (1899–1996)

Australian-British author, noted for her creation of the character of Mary Poppins, the nonsensical housekeeper who, through several books and a film, delighted millions. Born Helen Lyndon Goff in North Queensland, Australia, on August 9, 1906, she was the daughter of an Irish father and a mother of Scottish and Irish descent, and as such was brought up with stories of the British Isles. As a youth, she wrote mystery novels and for a time acted on the stage. She left Australia for England in 1924 with little money and began to contribute poems to a British literary magazine. In 1934, while watching two small children, she concocted the story of a stately British woman who was a nanny, and Travers's most famous character, Mary Poppins, was born. That year, the story of the mystical governess who cares for the Banks children at 17 Cherry Tree Lane was released under the pseudonym P. L. Travers (she had adopted the name Pamela Lyndon Travers as her stage name in Australia, but for her works only used the initials). She wrote in 1978, "Nothing I had written before 'Mary Poppins' had anything to do with children, and I have always assumed, when I thought about it at all, that she had come out of the same wall of nothingness as the poetry, myth, and legend that had absorbed me all my writing life." She followed up that popular work with *Mary Poppins Comes Back* (1935), *Mary Poppins Opens the Door* (1943), among other works. In 1964, Walt DISNEY approached Travers to turn the book into a movie; although Travers collaborated on the screenplay, she was dissatisfied with the final product and disassociated herself from it. The film was translated into more than 20 languages and sold millions of copies, exhibiting a sense of a childhood she wished to recapture. Travers died in London on April 23, 1996.

References: Margalit Fox, "P. L. Travers, Creator of the Magical and Beloved Nanny Mary Poppins, Is Dead at 96," *New York Times*, April 25, 1996, p. C19.

Trianon, Treaty of

Settlement, signed in 1920 after World War I, between the victorious Allies and Hungary, which reduced the borders of that nation to just 28 percent of its prewar size. At the end of the war, harsh terms were imposed by the Allies on all of Germany's military partners, and Hungary was not spared. The imposition for a time of a Bolshevik government led by Béla KÚN scared the Allies into carving up Hungary among its neighbors. The powers at VERSAILLES met and drafted the so-called Hungarian Peace Treaty, and forced the Hungarian delegation to sign it at the palaces named the Grand Trianon and Petit Trianon on July 26, 1920, as part of the overall Versailles peace agreement. The pact transferred Hungary's non-Magyar territories to the so-called "successor states": Austria, Czechoslovakia, Romania, and Yugoslavia. The U.S. Senate, when it refused to ratify the treaty, cited in the arguments of many senators the fact that Hungary was so decapitated. In 1933, in a work published in London, historian Roland E. L. Vaughan Williams wrote, "No one will to-day seriously deny that the Treaty of Trianon violated the principle of self-determination. Three and a half million Hungarians were left outside Treaty Hungary, forming in several instances solid 'blocks' immediately adjoining the new frontier."

References: "Hungary Peace Treaty, 1920" in Edmund Jan Osmańczyk, *The Encyclopedia of the United Nations and International Agreements* (Philadelphia: Taylor & Francis, 1985), 362–63; Carlile Aylmer Macartney, *Hungary and Her Successors: The Treaty of Trianon and Its Consequences, 1919–1937* (London: Oxford University Press, 1965); *The Hungarian Question in the British Parliament: Speeches, Questions and Answers Thereto in the House of Lords and the House of Commons from 1919 to 1930* (London: Grant Williams, 1933), v–vii.

Tripartite Treaty   *See* CIANO, GALEAZZO; MUSSOLINI, BENITO.

Triple Crown   *See* HORSE RACING.

Trotsky, Leon   (1879–1940)

Russian Communist revolutionary, who lost a massive struggle for the power of the party and the nation with

Joseph STALIN. Born Lev Davidovich Bronstein in the village of Yanoivka, near Elisavetgrad (later Kirovograd), on the steppes of the Ukraine, on October 25, 1879, he was the son of Jewish farmers. From his earliest years, Bronstein leaned to the left politically and was an early reader of Karl Marx. In his teens he became identified with the Russian revolutionary movement that sought to overthrow the established order led by the monarchy of the Romanov dynasty. Arrested in 1898 for subversive activities, he was exiled to Siberia, but escaped four years later and reached London with the use of a passport that listed him as Leon Trotsky. In London he took the name as his own and became an established figure in the Russian underground with such men as Nikolai Lenin and Georgi Plekhanov. For a time he wrote for *Iskra* ("Spark"), a revolutionary publication.

In 1905, Trotsky returned to Russia but was again arrested by the czarist authorities and exiled a second time to Siberia. He escaped, on this occasion going to Vienna, where he became the editor of *Pravda*. When World War I broke out, he went to Zurich, then to Germany, where he was arrested for speaking out against the war and sentenced to prison. After his release in 1915, Trotsky made his way to France, where he edited a socialist daily in which he continued to denounce the war. Even in France, however, he was made unwelcome, and he left, making his way through Cuba to New York City in January 1917, where he settled down as the editor of the socialist sheet *New World*. He sailed for Russia two months later, when the Russian Revolution broke out, and even though he was detained for a month in Halifax, Canada, he made his way back to Russia by May. In Petrograd (later Leningrad), he established *Forward*, a propaganda sheet designed to aid the Bolsheviks in their quest for power. Although he was arrested by the provisional government of Aleksandr Kerensky for fomenting revolu-

Leon Trotsky and his wife in 1932, during his exile from the USSR *(CORBIS/Bettmann)*

tion Trotsky was quickly released, and participated in the October 1917 revolution, in which the Bolsheviks seized power.

In the new Soviet government, which was formed with Lenin as its leader, Trotsky became a chief adviser and was given the post of People's Commissar of Foreign Affairs. One of his first responsibilities was to serve as the chief Soviet delegate to the peace conference at Brest-Litovsk, where the Soviets negotiated an end to World War I with Germany. Once the treaty was signed, Lenin made him commissar of war, in which post he reorganized the Red Army and conducted war on the so-called "white" troops who sought to overthrow the infant Bolshevik government. After the Whites were defeated, Trotsky transformed the Red army units into labor units designed to rehabilitate and stimulate the ruined Russian economy. Although at times Trotsky and Lenin disagreed about the direction of Soviet policies, the men worked closely together. Lenin groomed Trotsky as his successor, particularly after an assassination attempt on Lenin's life in August 1918 that left him incapacitated. Trotsky was in the Caucasus on vacation when Lenin died, and his failure to return during Lenin's funeral allowed one of Trotsky's rivals for power, Stalin, to take over the party hierarchy and remove Trotsky as commissar of war. Trotsky was subjugated to a series of lower echelon posts. In 1927 he was suspected of attempting to overthrow Stalin; that November he was expelled from the Communist Party. Early the next year, he was exiled to Alma Alta, Kazakhstan, where he wrote a series of books and articles that harshly criticized the Stalin government. Stalin ordered Trotsky to leave Russia forever, and in early 1929 he did so, never to return.

Starting in 1929, Trotsky lived for a time outside Istanbul, Turkey, then in 1933 moved to France, where he continued to denounce Stalin. The Soviet leader put pressure on the French, and in 1935 Trotsky was ordered to leave. Refused entry to Great Britain, he settled in Norway for a time, but a series of purge trials in the Soviet Union targeted him as the alleged underground leader of a supposed massive movement to overthrow the Soviet government; the Norwegians refused to extend his residency permit. At the invitation of communist painter Diego García, Trotsky moved in 1937 to a villa outside of Mexico City. He continued his unending attacks on Stalin; and in doing so, he signed his own death warrant. Stalin ordered Soviet hit squads to get Trotsky. On August 20, 1940, an assassin mortally wounded Trotsky.

References: Robert Wistrich, *Trotsky: Fate of a Revolutionary* (New York: Stein & Day, 1979); Christopher Phelps, "Leon Trotsky" in Anne Commire, ed., *Historic World Leaders* (Detroit: Gale Research, 1994), 3: 1268–72; Philip Pomper, *Lenin, Trotsky, and Stalin: The Intelligentsia and Power* (New York: Columbia University Press, 1990); Robert Payne, *The Life and Death of Trotsky* (New York: McGraw-Hill, 1977).

Tutankhamen, discovery of   *See* CARTER, Howard.

Tydings-McDuffie Act

U.S. congressional legislation, also called the Philippine Independence Act, enacted March 24, 1934, to offer the Philippine Islands independence from the United States. The history of U.S. attempts to offer the Philippines independence stretches across two decades. In 1916, Congressman William Atkinson Jones introduced a bill in the U.S. Congress that would have granted the islands independence by 1921. The House did not consider it, though, and it died in committee. In 1933, the HARES-HAWES-CUTTING ACT passed over President Herbert HOOVER's veto, but the Philippine legislature voted it down because of objections over trade and immigration. New legislation that addressed these two areas was demanded; a year later, Senator Millard Tydings in the Senate and Rep. John McDuffie in the House introduced a new act, which called for a period of commonwealth status under American leadership to last for 10 years, and full independence to be granted in 1946. The new law did not address the concerns of the Philippine legislation, however, and codified the original limits on immigration and trade. The political situation in the Philippines had changed in the year since the Hares-Hawes-Cutting Act had been defeated. The leading advocate for the law was Manuel Luis Quezon Molina but he was outvoted in the legislature; in 1934, however, Quezon's National Consolidation Party won an overwhelming victory at the polls for seats in the new legislature. On November 15, 1935, the Commonwealth of the Philippine Islands was born with Quezon elected as president.

References: Teodoro A. Agoncillo and Oscar M. Alfonso, *History of the Filipino People* (Quezon City: Malaya Books, 1967); Norman G. Owen, ed., *Compadre Colonialism: Studies on the Philippines under American Rule* (Ann Arbor, Mich.: Center for South and Southeast Asian Studies, 1971); Sol H. Gweckoh, *The Autobiography of Manuel L. Quezon* (Manila: Art Printing and Publishing Co., 1940); Aruna Gopinath, *Manuel L. Quezon: The Tutelary Democrat* (Quezon City: New Day Publishers, 1987).

Undset, Sigrid (1882–1949)

Norwegian writer and Nobel laureate. Born in the village of Kalundborg, Denmark, on May 20, 1882, she began in 1909 to publish a series of works that reflected the life of the Scandinavian people; these include *Gunnar's Daughter* (1909), *Spring* (1914), and *Kristin Lavansdatter,* her major work, which appeared in three volumes (1920–22). For this entire body of work, she was awarded the 1928 Nobel Prize in literature. Per Hallström, the chair of the Nobel Committee of the Swedish Academy, commented on Undset: "In her first novels or novellas, all of them remarkable works, Sigrid Undset painted the present-day world of young women in the environs of Christiania. It was a restless generation, prompt to make the gravest decisions as soon as its aspirations for happiness were at stake, ready to take the ultimate logical and sentimental consequences of its impulsive nature, and impassioned for truth. . . . The women of this generation were strangely isolated in this disconcerting world. Far from finding support in a firmly established social rule, they had, in full consciousness, renounced the heritage of the past. Hostile to all established social order, which they considered a useless yoke, they counted only on themselves to create a new society, consistent with a conviction, doubtless sincere at bottom, but easily misled."

The outset of World War II forced Undset to flee her homeland and go to the United States, where she worked to support the Norwegian resistance. After the war, she returned to Norway a heroine and received the Cross of St. Olav for her wartime labors. She died in Lillehammer, Norway, on June 10, 1949.

References: June H. Schlessinger, "Undset, Sigrid" in Bernard S. and June H. Schlessinger, eds., *The Who's Who of Nobel Prize Winners* (Phoenix, Ariz.: Oryx, 1986), 57; Thomas Watson MacCallum and Stephen Taylor, eds., *The Nobel Prize–Winners and the Nobel Foundation, 1901–1937* (Zurich: Central European Times Publishing, 1938), 308–309; "Faces of a Nation," *The European* Magazine, December 5–11, 1996, 6.

United States v. Carolene Products Company

1938 U.S. Supreme Court decision in which the Court upheld a federal ban on the interstate shipment of filled milk (milk in which butterfat has been replaced with coconut oil). Historian Aviam Soifer admits, "Today, the decision seems unremarkable; at the time, however, not only was the result of Carolene Products controversial but the theory of variable judicial scrutiny suggested by its footnote four was new and perhaps daring." In writing the majority opinion, Justice Harlan Fiske Stone expanded on the power of the judiciary to examine issues relating directly to the Constitution. He wrote, "There may be narrower scope for operation of the presumption of constitutionality when legislation appears on its face to be within a specific prohibition of the Constitution, such as those of the first ten Amendments, which are deemed equally specific when held to be embraced within the Fourteenth."

References: Aviam Soifer, "*Carolene Products Company, United States v.*" in Leonard W. Levy, ed. in chief, *Encyclopedia of the American Constitution* (New York: Macmillan, 1986–92), 1: 213–15; Lewis F. Powell, Jr., "Carolene Products Revisited," *Columbia Law Review* 82 (1982); Geoffrey P. Miller "The True Story of Carolene Products," *The Supreme Court Review* 1987 (1987), 397–420; *United States v. Carolene Products Company* 304 U.S. 144 (1938).

Urey, Harold Clayton (1893–1981)

American chemist and Nobel laureate. Born in Walkerton, Indiana, on April 29, 1893, he was educated at the universities of Montana and California before he entered the Bohr Institute in Copenhagen, Denmark. He then returned to the United States, where he taught for a time at the University of Montana, at Johns Hopkins University, and at Columbia University. During this period he worked on the fundamentals of heavy hydrogen, which he called "deuterium," a component of hydrogen and nuclear bombs. For this groundbreaking advance in the study of radioactivity, which was eventually used in the construction of the first atomic bombs, Urey was awarded the 1934 Nobel Prize in chemistry.

He worked on the Manhattan Project to build an atomic bomb during World War II. After the war, he researched chemical reactions that might have caused the formation of the earth and the moon. Urey retired in 1970; he died in La Jolla, California, on January 5, 1981.

References: Dorothy Riemenschneider, "Urey, Harold Clayton" in Bernard S. and June H. Schlessinger, eds., *The Who's Who of Nobel Prize Winners* (Phoenix, Ariz.: Oryx, 1986), 12–13; Thomas Watson MacCallum and Stephen Taylor, eds., *The Nobel Prize–Winners and the Nobel Foundation, 1901–1937* (Zurich: Central European Times Publishing, 1938), 162–63.

Valentino, Rudolph (1895–1926)

Italian-American actor, the consummate matinee idol of the 1920s. Born Rodolfo Alfonzo Rafaelo Pierre Filibert Guglielmi di Valentine D'Antonguolla in Italy in 1895, he migrated to the United States in 1913 and worked a series of odd jobs. In 1918 he headed west to try to break into motion pictures. Valentino was cast in 1919 in *The Delicious Little Devil*, followed by a series of roles that defined his Casanova image. Rex Ingram's 1921 feature *The Four Horsemen of the Apocalypse* propelled Valentino into stardom. That same year he filmed *The Conquering Power*, *Camille*, and *The Sheik*, the latter role earning him superstardom. He also drew large crowds to *Blood and Sand* (1922) and as *Monsieur Beaucaire* (1924). He played opposite Vilma Banky in *The Eagle* (1925), playing a Russian nobleman. His popular role as Ahmed Ben Hassan in *The Sheik* demanded a sequel, the first ever done; in 1926 he filmed *The Son of the Sheik*. A few months later, however, he was rushed to the hospital in New York with a perforated ulcer. On August 23, 1926, he died suddenly at age 31. Film historians consider the few films Valentino made classics.

References: Alexander Walker, *Rudolph Valentino* (New York: Stein & Day, 1976); Robert Oberfirst, *Rudolph Valentino: The Man behind the Myth* (New York: Citadel, 1962); "Valentino Is Dead! Sheik Dies Nonchalantly Asking for More Sunlight" *Wisconsin News* (Milwaukee), August 23, 1926, p. 1.

Versailles, Treaty of

Pact, signed in 1919 by the leaders of the Allied Powers (U.S. President Woodrow WILSON, French premier Georges Clemenceau, British prime minister David LLOYD GEORGE, and Italian premier Vittorio Orlando), which ended World War I in Europe. Among the peace terms, the treaty placed limits on German armed forces and imposed REPARATIONS on Germany and Austria. The key portion of the treaty called for the creation of the LEAGUE OF NATIONS, which the U.S. Senate opposed; the United States therefore refused to ratify the pact. The treaty also restored Alsace and Lorraine to France, gave Prussian Poland to Poland, made Danzig a free city, called for plebiscites in territories newly freed from the Central Powers, and called for the demilitarization of the Rhineland. The Committee of Responsibilities, a council composed of fifteen international law experts, also met at the Versailles Peace Conference to prepare the section of the treaty that dealt with war crimes and who should be charged. In 1935, Adolf Hitler broke most terms of the treaty.

See ANSCHLUSS; IRRECONCILABLES.

References: "World Peace Pact Signed at Versailles," New York *Herald* (European Edition), June 29, 1919, p. 1; George A. Finch, "The Treaty of Peace with Germany in the United States Senate," *The American Journal of International Law* 14 (1920): 155–206.

Versailles Peace Conference   *See* VERSAILLES, TREATY OF.

Volstead Act   *See* PROHIBITION.

W

Wagner, Robert Ferdinand   *See* NATIONAL LABOR RELATIONS BOARD.

Wagner-Connery Labor Relations Act   *See* NATIONAL LABOR RELATIONS ACT.

Wagner von Jauregg, Julius   (1857–1940)
Austrian neurologist and Nobel laureate. Born in Wels, Austria, on March 7, 1857, he received his doctorate from the University of Vienna in 1880. He spent his entire career as a researcher and professor of medicine at the University of Vienna (1881–1928), where he conducted experiments to find the cure to certain dementia-related diseases by inoculating the patients with malaria, a treatment which he discovered worked. He also introduced the earliest form of shock therapy and worked on diseases of the thyroid gland and treatment of the mentally ill. For his work, he was awarded the 1927 Nobel Prize in medicine and physiology.

Wagner von Jauregg retired in 1928. He died in Vienna on September 27, 1940.

References: Rashelle Karp, "Wagner von Jauregg, Julius" in Bernard S. and June H. Schlessinger, eds., *The Who's Who of Nobel Prize Winners* (Phoenix, Ariz.: Oryx, 1986), 86; Thomas Watson MacCallum and Stephen Taylor, eds., *The Nobel Prize–Winners and the Nobel Foundation, 1901–1937* (Zurich: Central European Times Publishing, 1938), 213–14.

Wallace, Henry Cantwell   *See* AGRICULTURAL ADJUSTMENT ACTS; AMERICAN FARM BUREAU FEDERATION.

Warburg, Otto Heinrich   (1883–1970)
German biochemist and Nobel laureate. Born in Freiburg, Germany, on October 8, 1883, he received a doctorate in chemistry at the University of Berlin (1906) and a doctorate in medicine at the University of Heidelberg (1911). Working at the Kaiser-Wilhelm Institute (later the Max Planck Institute) in Berlin, Warburg investigated respiratory enzymes, work that earned him the 1931 Nobel Prize in medicine and physiology. Writes biographer Joel Schlessinger, "In a career spanning 65 years and over 500 papers, Otto Warburg distinguished himself as probably the greatest biochemist of this century."

Warburg spent the remainder of his career working on photosynthesis and the metabolism. He died in Berlin on August 1, 1970.

References: Joel J. Schlessinger, "Warburg, Otto Heinrich" in Bernard S. and June H. Schlessinger, eds., *The Who's Who of Nobel Prize Winners* (Phoenix, Ariz.: Oryx, 1986), 87; Thomas Watson MacCallum and Stephen Taylor, eds., *The Nobel Prize–Winners and the Nobel Foundation, 1901–1937* (Zurich: Central European Times Publishing, 1938), 224–25.

War Communism   *See* NEW ECONOMIC POLICY.

Warren, Robert Penn   (1905–1989)
American novelist, poet, and critic. Born in Guthrie, Kentucky, Warren became the youngest member of the group of southern poets called the FUGITIVES when he was a student at Vanderbilt University in 1921. His first poems were published in *The Fugitive*, a magazine published from 1922 to 1925 by the group. The poets advocated the rural southern agrarian tradition and based their work on classical aesthetic ideals. Many of Warren's literary pieces also dealt with the troubling social issues that plagued the U.S. South, where he made his home. After college Warren obtained his master's degree at the University of California. Next he studied at Oxford University as a Rhodes

scholar, returning to the United States in 1930. Over the years he taught at Vanderbilt, Louisiana State University, the University of Minnesota, and Yale University.

He and writer Cleanth BROOKS edited the *Southern Review,* a journal of literary criticism and political thought, from 1935 to 1942. The two also collaborated on widely read college textbooks, including *Understanding Poetry* (1938). After World War II, Warren wrote his first novel, *All the King's Men* (1946), a character study of a powerful Southern governor, for which he earned a Pulitzer Prize in 1947. He also won Pulitzers for *Promises: Poems 1954–1956* (1957) and for *Now and Then: Poems 1976–1978* (1979). Warren was appointed as the first U.S. poet laureate in 1986.

References: William Bedford Clark, *The American Vision of Robert Penn Warren* (Lexington: University Press of Kentucky, 1992); Joseph Blotner, *Robert Penn Warren: A Biography* (New York: Random House, 1997).

Washington Naval Conference

Meeting, 1921–22, in which several matters dealing with naval armaments from World War I were cleared up between the United States and other Allied nations. Meeting in Washington, D.C., this was the first major arms limitation conference. Historian Akira Iriye writes, "In Washington, [the representatives of the attending nations] readily agreed on a formula for multilateral naval disarmament. According to it, the United States and Britain would scuttle some of the existing warships and refrain from the construction of some others, so that the total capital-ship tonnage of each ('capital ships referred to warships displacing more than 10,000 tons of water and equipped with eight-inch guns) would not exceed 535,000 tons. As the existing tonnages were far greater, the naval agreement would result in America's destroying 30 of its 48 ships [those in existence or under construction]. Britain would reduce its navy from 45 to 20 warships. Japan, on its part, would be limited to 315,000 tons and would destroy 17 of its 27 warships. This was the famous 5-5-3 ration, giving Japan the equivalent of 60 percent of each of the navies of the United States and Britain."

See also FOUR-POWER TREATY; NINE-POWER TREATY.

References: Akira Iriye, *The Cambridge History of American Foreign Relations: III: The Globalizing of America, 1913–1945* (Cambridge: Cambridge University Press, 1993), 76–77; "President to Close Conference After Signing of Treaties Today; Pacts to Be Hurried to Senate" *Washington Post,* February 6, 1922, p. 1.

Weimar Germany

Name commonly applied to Germany in the post–World War I period, from 1919 to 1933, with particular significance in the realms of politics and the arts.

Weimar Republic In 1919 the Bavarian city of Weimar was the scene of the national assembly that established the government known as the Weimar Republic, the first representative government in German history. German politician Friedrich ebert was elected as the republic's first president. Ebert suppressed the Kapp Putsch in 1920, during which Wolfgang kapp led a monarchist revolt against the government. Ebert also staved off Adolf hitler's first attempt in 1923 to establish a dictatorship, known as the beer hall putsch. Hitler was imprisoned for nine months for his crimes, during which he wrote the influential treatise mein kampf.

The government was hamstrung throughout its existence by unstable parliamentary alliances and ceaselessly rising inflation. By 1929 the republic was ruled by a coalition cabinet of the Social Democrats and the People's Party, with Hermann Müller as chancellor and Paul von HINDENBURG as president. Müller resigned in 1930 because of party disagreements over how to deal with the republic's rising unemployment and worsening economic crisis. Heinrich Brüning, leader of the Catholic Center Party, was appointed chancellor. In the 1930 Reichstag elections, while unemployment was about three million, the NAZI PARTY made sweeping gains and the Communist Party enjoyed smaller gains. At this point a coalition government was no longer possible, and Germany ceased to be a parliamentary regime. The republic thereafter became a presidential regime ruling through the chancellor.

With unemployment continuing to rise at alarming rates, Hindenburg was reelected as president in 1932, although Hitler had gained 37 percent of the vote. Because of his failure to deal with Germany's growing economic problems, Brüning was forced to resign; Hindenburg replaced him with moderate Franz von Papen. Shortly after his appointment, Papen met with Hitler, who convinced Papen that the Nazis might support the new government in exchange for Papen's dissolving the current Reichstag and holding new elections. Papen agreed and dissolved the parliament. Presidential rule was thereafter imposed, which gave the chancellor direct control, and in the new elections Hitler made startling gains. The Nazis, along with the Communists, now held a blocking majority in the Reichstag and Hitler broke his earlier agreement to support Papen.

The new Reichstag met in September, and the Communists moved for a vote of no-confidence in the government; the vote was counted at 512–42 against the government. The elections showed some losses for Hitler, but gains by the Communists kept the Reichstag deadlocked. By this time Germany was already a presidential dictatorship; Papen had lost any support he once held in the cabinet and resigned. In December, Hitler demanded the chancellorship, which Hindenburg granted him in January 1933. Massive intimidation by the Nazis in the 1933 elections ensured that only Nazis and Nationalists were able to campaign. Nazi opponents were beaten up; some were killed. Despite these tactics, however, the Nazis won only 43.9 percent of the vote. With the Nationalists, however, they now held a majority.

An act giving dictatorial powers to Hitler's government was put to the Reichstag; the Nationalists, the Peoples Party, and the Catholics provided the necessary two-thirds majority. Hitler then essentially outlawed opposition parties and the right to free speech. Upon Hindenburg's death in 1934, Hitler consolidated the offices of the Reichspresident and the chancellor in the all-powerful position of the Führer. The Weimar Republic had officially ended.

The Arts The Weimar region has a rich cultural and literary tradition. In the eighteenth and nineteenth centuries it was frequented by such figures as the poets Johann Goethe and Friedrich von Schiller, the composer Franz Liszt, and the philosopher Friedrich Nietzsche. This tradition of extraordinary artistic and literary output continued well into the 20th century, before the Nazi regime condemned the creative element as "decadent" in the late 1920s and early 1930s. For example, the cutting-edge

BAUHAUS school of art and architecture, headed by Walter GROPIUS, was founded in Weimar in 1919. With such faculty as the innovative artists Paul Klee, Wassily Kandinsky, and Marcel Breuer and later headed by architect Ludwig MIES VAN DER ROHE, the controversial school moved to Dessau in 1925, then to Berlin in 1932, before being closed by the Nazis in 1933.

The politically conscious playwright Bertoldt Brecht, known for his revolutionary "epic theater," also wrote in Weimar, producing such works as *Mann ist Mann* (1926, A man is a man). During the Nazi period he went into exile in Denmark and later settled in the United States. The composer Kurt Weill, best known for the satirical operas *The Threepenny Opera* (1928) and *The Rise and Fall of the City of Mahagonny* (1930)—both with librettos by Brecht—left Weimar for the United States in 1935.

References: Michael Brenner, *The Renaissance of Jewish Culture in Weimar Germany* (New Haven, Conn.: Yale University Press, 1996). Walter Horace Bruford, *Culture and Society in Classical Weimar, 1775–1806* (London: Cambridge University Press,

German jazz band during the Weimar period: "decadence" in action *(CORBIS/Bettmann)*

1962). Siegfried Kracauer, *The Salaried Masses: Duty and Distraction in Weimar Germany,* trans. Quintin Hoare (New York: Verso, 1998); Ben Lieberman, *From Recovery to Catastrophe: Municipal Stabilization and Political Crisis in Weimar Germany* (New York: Berghahn Books, 1998). Anthony Phelan, *The Weimar Dilemma: Intellectuals in the Weimar Republic* (Manchester: Manchester University Press, 1985); Thomas J. Saunders, *Hollywood in Berlin: American Cinema and Weimar Germany* (Berkeley: University of California Press, 1994); Donald Jenks Ziegler, *Prelude to Democracy: A Study of Proportional Representation and the Heritage of Weimar Germany, 1871–1920* (Lincoln: University of Nebraska Press, 1958).

Wheeler, Burton Kendall   *See* COURT-PACKING CONTROVERSY.

Whipple, George Hoyt (1878–1976)

American pathologist and Nobel laureate. Born on August 28, 1878, in Ashland, New Jersey, he received a bachelor's degree from Yale University (1900) and his M.D. degree from Johns Hopkins University (1905). Whipple worked at Johns Hopkins University, the University of California, and the University of Rochester, where he investigated liver therapy to cure anemia. He also did research into bile, intestinal obstructions, and iron metabolism. For this combined work, he was the corecipient (with George R. MINOT and William P. MURPHY) of the 1934 Nobel Prize in medicine and physiology.

Whipple retired as the administrator of the University of Rochester School of Medicine in 1955. He died in Rochester on February 1, 1976.

References: Rashelle Karp, "Whipple, George Hoyt" in Bernard S. and June H. Schlessinger, eds., *The Who's Who of Nobel Prize Winners* (Phoenix, Ariz.: Oryx, 1986), 89; Thomas Watson MacCallum and Stephen Taylor, eds., *The Nobel Prize–Winners and the Nobel Foundation, 1901–1937* (Zurich: Central European Times Publishing, 1938), 232–33.

Wickersham Report

Landmark American document, produced 1930–31, by the National Commission on Law Observance and Enforcement, which examined the impact of PROHIBITION on the populace of the United States. During the 1928 presidential campaign, Herbert HOOVER, the Republican nominee, promised that if elected he would convene a commission to investigate whether Prohibition was working or was allowing the nation to become consumed by crime and lawlessness. After his inauguration, Hoover appointed former attorney general George W. Wickersham to head up this commission, whose mission was expanded to include an investigation into the national criminal justice system.

The first two volumes of this five-volume report deal with Prohibition. The first volume, *Proposal to Improve Enforcement of Criminals in the United States,* was issued on January 13, 1930. The second, *Report on the Enforcement of the Prohibition Laws of the United States,* was released on January 7, 1931. In the end, however, all of the commission's recommendations (one of which was to call for more agents to enforce prohibition laws) were for naught; two years later, in December 1933, the Twenty-first Amendment to the Constitution ended the era of Prohibition in the United States.

References: David Gordon, "Wickersham, George" in Leonard W. Levy, ed. in chief, *Encyclopedia of the American Constitution* (New York: Macmillan, 1986–92), 4: 2062; *Enforcement of the Prohibition Laws: Official Records of the National Commission on Law Observance and Enforcement, Pertaining to Its Investigation of the Facts as to the Enforcement, the Benefits, and the Abuses Under the Prohibition Laws, Both Before and Since the Adoption of the Eighteenth Amendment to the Constitution* (Washington, D.C.: Government Printing Office; five volumes, 1931).

Wieland, Heinrich Otto (1877–1957)

German chemist and Nobel laureate. Born in the village of Pforzheim, Germany, on June 4, 1877, he graduated from the University of Munich with a doctorate in 1901. While working at that institution as a professor of chemistry (1901–17), as well as during his later work at the Technische Hochschule in Berlin (1917–21), and at the University of Freiburg (1921–25), Wieland researched the composition and physical nature of bile acids, which are necessary for human digestion. For his contributions to the study of the reactions of bile acids, he was awarded the 1927 Nobel Prize in chemistry.

In his last two decades of work, Wieland worked as a professor of chemistry at the University of Munich (1925–50). He died in Pforzheim, Germany, on June 4, 1937. One of his numerous publications was the work *On the Mechanism of Oxidation* (1932).

References: Ralph Johnson, "Wieland, Heinrich Otto" in Bernard S. and June H. Schlessinger, eds., *The Who's Who of Nobel Prize Winners* (Phoenix, Ariz.: Oryx, 1986), 10; Thomas Watson MacCallum and Stephen Taylor, eds., *The Nobel Prize–Winners and the Nobel Foundation, 1901–1937* (Zurich: Central European Times Publishing, 1938), 149.

Wilson, Charles Thomson Rees (1869–1959)

Scottish physicist and Nobel laureate. Born in Glencorse, Midlothian, Scotland, on February 14, 1869, he received his bachelor of science degree from Owens College in England (1887), and his bachelor's degree from Cambridge University (1892). Working as a researcher at the Cavendish Laboratory in England (1892–96), and at Cambridge University (1896–1934), Wilson researched the expansion method of rendering visible the tracks of electrically charged particles, utilizing his discovery, today called the Wilson Cloud Chamber. For this important invention, he was co-awarded, with American physicist Arthur Holly COMPTON, the 1927 Nobel Prize for physics.

Wilson retired in 1934. He died in Carlops, Peeblesshire, Scotland, on November 15, 1959.

References: Frank Kellerman, "Wilson, Charles Thomson Rees" in Bernard S. and June H. Schlessinger, eds., *The Who's Who of Nobel Prize Winners* (Phoenix, Ariz.: Oryx, 1986), 159; Thomas Watson MacCallum and Stephen Taylor, eds., *The Nobel Prize–Winners and the Nobel Foundation, 1901–1937* (Zurich: Central European Times Publishing, 1938), 89.

Wilson, Woodrow (1856–1924)

U.S. statesman and president (1913–21), awarded the 1919 Nobel Peace Prize "for his sincere attempts at peace negotiations" that he advanced at the VERSAILLES peace conference in France that same year. Born in Staunton, Virginia, on December 28, 1856, Wilson graduated from Princeton University in 1879, studied law at the University of Virginia, and was admitted to the Virginia bar in 1881. He opened a law office in Atlanta, but soon decided he preferred to teach. He entered the Johns Hopkins Graduate School, where he earned a doctorate in history in 1885. He taught history at Bryn Mawr College (1885–88) and at Wesleyan University (1888–90), then served as a professor of jurisprudence and political economics at Princeton (1890–1902), where he became an expert in governmental relations. In 1902 he was named as the first nonclerical president of Princeton, where he remained until 1910. In that year, he ran for and won the governorship of New Jersey as a reformist politician.

In 1912, conservative Democrats pushed the candidacy of Wilson for president to stop that of William Jennings Bryan, who had lost in 1896, 1900, and 1908. Wilson received the nomination and won when the Republicans split their vote between William Howard Taft and Theodore Roosevelt. His first term (1913–17) as president was noted for such reforms as the Federal Reserve Act (1913) and the Clayton Anti-trust Act (1914). Following the sinking of the *Lusitania,* he strove to keep the United States out of war, and ran for reelection in 1916 on that platform. He was reelected in a close race, but soon after starting his second term he was forced to ask Congress to declare war against Germany because of the use of unrestricted submarine warfare. After the war he laid out his framework for peace that came to be known as the Fourteen Points. Wilson's plan of a LEAGUE OF NATIONS, an international deliberative body to prevent war, became a

Woodrow Wilson *(CORBIS/Bettmann)*

major part of the final treaty. For this accomplishment, Wilson was awarded the 1919 Nobel Peace Prize. He thus became the third American to be awarded the Peace Prize (after Theodore Roosevelt in 1906 and Secretary of State Elihu Root in 1912).

However, there were American voices opposed to the treaty. The obstacles facing its passage in the Senate were obvious and, to many observers, too difficult to overcome unless the president gave in a little to his opposition. Instead, he dug in his heels and decided that the treaty would be passed his way or no way. On March 11, 1920, Senator Henry Ashurst of Arizona, a loyal Democrat, simply said, "As a friend of the President, as one who has loyally followed him, I solemnly declare to him this morning: If you want to kill your own child because the Senate straightens out its crooked limbs, you must take the responsibility and accept the verdict of history." Instead of listening to this advice, however, Wilson took to a presidential train and, against the advice of his doctors, set out on a nationwide train tour to speak to the American people and convince them of the righteousness of an unadulterated treaty. In a tour that started on September 4 in Columbus, Ohio, and ran west for more than eight thousand miles, Wilson spoke at more than three dozen stops and delivered more than thirty speeches.

On September 25, after delivering an address at Pueblo, Colorado, Wilson suffered a mild stroke. With the blinds of the *Mayflower* drawn, he was rushed back to the nation's capital. A few days later, unbeknownst to the Congress or the American people, Wilson suffered a debilitating stroke from which he never recovered. According to historians, for weeks the president could not sit up in bed or even write his own name on important pieces of legislation. For the rest of his tenure, which ended on March 4, 1921, the president's duties were assumed by his wife, Edith Bolling Galt Wilson, who forged his name on documents and kept all but his doctor and secretary away from the family bedroom. Even Vice President Thomas Marshall was kept out of the loop. From the White House, letters apparently from the president to supporters of the treaty urged them to hold on for ratification of an unaltered pact; even after the treaty went down to defeat there was no give-and-take from the White House. With the election of Warren HARDING to the presidency in 1920 and Wilson's departure in March 1921, the treaty was never ratified by the U.S. Senate.

Wilson spent his final two years as an invalid in his Washington, D.C., home, where he died on February 3, 1924.

References: Daniel Bergen, "Wilson, Thomas Woodrow" in Bernard S. and June H. Schlessinger, eds., *The Who's Who of Nobel Prize Winners* (Phoenix, Ariz.: Oryx, 1986), 131; Thomas Watson MacCallum and Stephen Taylor, eds., *The Nobel Prize–Winners and the Nobel Foundation, 1901–1937* (Zurich: Central European Times Publishing, 1938), 356–57; Kendrick A. Clements, "Wilson, Thomas Woodrow" in Bruce W. Jentleson and Thomas G. Paterson, senior eds., *Encyclopedia of U.S. Foreign Relations* (New York: Oxford University Press, 1997), 4: 324–30.

Windaus, Adolf Otto Reinhold (1876–1959)

German chemist and Nobel laureate. Born in Berlin, Germany, on December 25, 1876, he received his medical license from the University of Berlin in 1897. He served as a researcher at the University of Berlin (1900–01), as a professor of chemistry at the University of Innsbruck, Austria (1906–15), and as a professor of chemistry at the University of Göttingen (1915–44). It was during this period that Windaus investigated sterols and their reactions. As biographer Bernard S. Schlessinger writes, "Windaus, in accordance with his view that sterols were parents to other groups of natural substances, converted cholesterol to cholanic acid, proving the relationship of sterols to bile acids. He also showed that histidine, a protein component, was an imidazole alanine, and discovered histamine." For these discoveries, Windaus was awarded the 1928 Nobel Prize in chemistry. Professor H. G. Söderbaum, Secretary of the Royal Swedish Academy of Sciences, remarked, "As

a result of patient and skillful work, Windaus succeeded in producing several of the digitalis glucosides and their components in the pure state. In this way it was shown that these vegetable cardiac poisons are directly related on the one hand to cholesterol and the bile acids, and on the other hand to the animal cardiac poison bufotoxin, which Wieland studied with great success."

After winning the Nobel, Windaus later went on to study vitamins and their reactions in the human body, and the reaction of the body to chemotherapy. He died in Göttingen on June 9, 1959.

References: Bernard S. Schlessinger, "Windaus, Adolf Otto Reinhold" in Bernard S. and June H. Schlessinger, eds., *The Who's Who of Nobel Prize Winners* (Phoenix, Ariz.: Oryx, 1986), 10–11; Thomas Watson MacCallum and Stephen Taylor, eds., *The Nobel Prize–Winners and the Nobel Foundation, 1901–1937* (Zurich: Central European Times Publishing, 1938), 150.

Wolfe, Thomas Clayton (1900–1938)

American novelist, noted for such interwar works as *Look Homeward, Angel,* (1929) and *Of Time and the River* (1935). Born October 3, 1900, in Asheville, North Carolina, he graduated from the University of North Carolina in 1920. He wanted to become a playwright, and while in college he put on an exhibition of his show *The Return of Buck Gwinn,* with Wolfe himself in the starring role. He studied for a time at Harvard. When his plays did not succeed he earned a master of arts degree in 1922 and took a position as a professor of English at Washington Square College at New York University, working there until 1930.

In 1929, Wolfe published his first novel, *Look Homeward, Angel,* a sprawling examination of Wolfe's life as a youth and in college through the autobiographical but fictional Gant family, using allegory to describe the violence of the family, particularly the mother figure, Eliza Gant. The work received much praise and made Wolfe into one of the leading literary figures of the mid-20th century. His following works included *Of Time and the River* (1935), a book of short stories entitled *From Death to Morning* (1935), and the memoir *The Story of a Novel* (1936). Wolfe was hospitalized in Seattle throughout July and August 1938; later he was removed to Johns Hopkins University Hospital in Baltimore, where he underwent two operations. On September 15, he died at age 37. Several works were posthumously edited and published, including *The Web and the Rock* (1939), *You Can't Go Home Again* (1940), *The Hills Beyond* (1941), and *Letters to His mother* (1943).

References: Thomas Wolfe, (Leslie Field, ed.), *The Autobiography of an American Novelist* (Cambridge: Harvard University Press, 1983); Neal F. Austin, *A Biography of Thomas Wolfe* (Austin, Tex.: R. Beacham, 1968); David Herbert Donald,

Look Homeward: A Life of Thomas Wolfe (Boston: Little, Brown, 1987).

Wood, Grant   *See* PAINTING.

Woolf, Virginia (1880–1941)

English novelist, critic, and leader in the interwar literary movement of modernism. Born Adeline Virginia Stephen into an upper-class Victorian family, she married writer Leonard Woolf in 1912. Together the two launched the literary press Hogarth and became central figures in London's BLOOMSBURY GROUP.

Woolf celebrated a European literary tradition and the high cultural aesthetic values of a Victorian upbringing. In the 1920s she began to experiment with a new method of revealing her characters' thoughts by their effects on their surroundings; *Jacob's Room* (1922) and *Mrs. Dalloway* (1925) brilliantly exhibit this innovative stream-of-consciousness technique. Always poetic, symbolic, and visual, her interwar novels include *Night and Day* (1919), *Monday or Tuesday* (1921), *The Waves* (1931), and *The Years* (1937). Her best-known work, *To the Lighthouse* (1927), portrays the fragility of human relationships and the collapse of social values. *Orlando* (1928) examines the meanings of masculinity and femininity and presents a feminist historical overview of English history.

One of the most influential writers of the 20th century, Woolf also wrote criticism (*The Common Reader,* 1925), essays, letters, and diaries. Her timeless *A Room of One's Own* (1929) examines this necessary material precondition for a woman's creativity. Despite these literary achievements, Woolf suffered from chronic depression; she died on March 28, 1941, it is believed by drowning herself.

References: Linda Anderson, *Women and Autobiography in the Twentieth Century: Remembered Futures* (New York: Prentice Hall/Harvester Wheatsheaf, 1997); Quentin Bell, *Virginia Woolf: A Biography* (London: Hogarth Press, 1990).

Works Progress Administration (WPA)

U.S. federal relief agency, established in 1935 under President Franklin Delano ROOSEVELT'S NEW DEAL as an innovative attempt to provide emergency aid and public jobs rather than "handouts" to the unemployed. Headed by Harry Hopkins, the WPA employed more than 8.5 million people—men and women, young and old, skilled and unskilled—during its eight years in existence. The name was changed in 1939 to Works Projects Administration. The WPA undertook massive building and improvement projects, constructing thousands of buildings, bridges, and public roads. Other innovative WPA relief programs included the Federal Writers' Project (FWP), the Federal Arts Project (FAP), the Federal Theatre Project (FTP), and the National Youth Administration, which found work for students.

The FWP was initiated to use the skills of unemployed white-collar workers, mainly editors, researchers, historians, and writers, such as Saul Bellow, John Cheever, and Ralph Ellison. The FWP began work on November 1, 1935, with 2,381 employees located in 48 states and the District of Columbia. In 1936 the project reached its height of employment with 6,686 employees, about 40 percent of them women. Because of the WPA's strict equal-opportunity rules, women were hired in unheard-of numbers through the WPA's various programs; by 1938, 372,000 women had WPA jobs. More than 25 percent of these women were professionals: teachers, artists, photographers, librarians, nurses, musicians, and administrators.

Under the Federal Arts Project (FAP), such artists as Willem de Kooning, Jackson Pollock, and Thomas Hart Benton were commissioned to create public murals, sculptures, and mosaics. The Federal Theatre Project (FTP), headed by Hallie Flanagan, put on some 1,500 productions starring such actors as Burt Lancaster and Burgess Meredith.

References: Michael E. Parrish, *Anxious Decades: America in Prosperity and Depression, 1920–1941* (New York: W. W. Norton, 1992); Blanche Weisen Cook, "New Deal," in *The Reader's Companion to U.S. Women's History,* ed. Wilma Mankiller, Gwendolyn Mink, Marysa Navarro, Barbara Smith, and Gloria Steinem (Boston: Houghton Mifflin, 1998), 426–28; Douglas Brinkley, *History of the United States* (New York: Viking, 1998).

World Court   *See* PERMANENT COURT OF INTERNATIONAL JUSTICE.

World Monetary and Economic Conference   *See* LONDON MONETARY AND ECONOMIC CONFERENCE.

Wright, Richard   *See* HARLEM RENAISSANCE.

Yeats, William Butler (1865–1939)

Irish poet, playwright, and Nobel laureate. Born in Dublin on June 13, 1865, Yeats was the son of an artist. As a young man he studied painting but soon developed a strong interest in Gaelic literary traditions and Irish folklore. By the 1890s he had formed his own lyrical style of verse and had written several poetic plays, folk stories, critical essays, and collections of poetry, including *The Celtic Twilight* (1893), *Secret Rose* (1897), and *The Wanderings of Oisin* (1899). During this time Yeats assumed leadership of Irish literary revival, establishing the Irish Literary Theatre, which later became the Abbey Theatre. Here his plays *The Countess Cathleen* (1899), *Cathleen in Houlihan* (1902), *The Hour Glass* (1904), *The Land of Heart's Desire* (1904), and *Deirdre* (1907) were staged. For this body of work, Yeats was awarded in 1923 the Nobel Prize in literature.

Later works included *The Wild Swans at Coole* (1919), *The Player Queen* (1919), *The Cat and the Moon* (1924), *The Resurrection* (1927), *The Tower* (1928), *The Winding Stair* (1929), *Wheels and Butterflies* (1934), *The Words upon the Window Pane* (1934), and *Dramatis Personae* (1936). His prose work *A Vision* (1925), an occult view of history written with his wife Georgie Hyde-Lees, explores Yeats's personal mythology and theories of art and poetry.

One of the greatest poets of the 20th century, Yeats also intensely believed in the cause of Irish national identity; to this end, he was elected a senator of the IRISH FREE STATE (1922–28). His final poems, completed days before his death on January 28, 1939, deal with heroic resolution in the face of death.

References: Keith Alldritt, *Yeats: The Man and the Milieu* (New York: Clarkson Potter, 1997); Douglas N. Archibald, *Yeats* (Syracuse, N.Y.: Syracuse University Press, 1986).

Yokohama Earthquake

Massive quake which struck the major Japanese cities of Yokohama and Tokyo, September 1, 1923, killing an estimated 143,000 people. Yokohama, the capital of Kanagawa Prefecture, located on Tokyo Bay approximately twenty miles (32 kilometers) from Tokyo, developed primarily as a major trading city and port after the establishment of the open door policy of the Japanese leadership with the Harris Treaty of 1858. The city was virtually destroyed by the 1923 quake, as it was again by Allied bombing in 1945 in World War II. The September quake is considered one of the largest in history. U.S. President Calvin COOLIDGE telegraphed Emperor Yoshihito, "At the moment when the news of the great disaster has befallen the people of Japan is being received I am moved to offer you in my own name and in that of the American people the most heartfelt sympathy and to express to your Majesty my sincere desire to be of any possible assistance in alleviating the terrible suffering to your people." It is estimated that 143,000 people lost their lives in the quake, with more than 600,000 homes destroyed.

References: "The Great Kanto Earthquake" in Kaari Ward, ed., *Great Disasters: Dramatic True Stories of Nature's Awesome Powers* (Pleasantville, N.Y.: Reader's Digest Association, 1989), 192–95; "Tokyo and Yokohama in Ruins; Fire aAfter Earthquake; Great Loss of Life Feared," *Washington Post,* September 2, 1923, p. 1; "More Than 200,000 in Japan Killed by Quake, Typhoon, Tidal Wave and Fire," *Washington Post,* September 3, 1923, p. 1; Coolidge to Emperor Yoshihito, September 1, 1923 (telegram 894. 48B/52a) in *Papers Relating to the Foreign Relations of the United States: 1923* (Washington, D.C.: U.S. Government Printing Office; two volumes, 1938), 465.

Yoshihito   *See* HIROHITO

Young, Owen D. (1874–1962)

American lawyer and business executive, whose work on the DAWES PLAN for German REPARATIONS to the Allies after World War I, as well as his own YOUNG PLAN for a revision of those reparations payments, made him internationally known. Born in Van Hornesville, New York, on October 27, 1874, Young was the second son (the first died as an infant) of farmer Smith Young and Ida (Brandow) Young. He studied at St. Lawrence University, earning a bachelor's degree, and Boston University Law School, which awarded him a law degree in 1894. He opened a practice in Boston, and for a time taught law at the Boston University Law School. In 1913, Young was hired as the general counsel for the General Electric Company, and moved to New York to take up his duties. He eventually moved up to become vice president, then chair of the board, serving in that latter post from 1922–39 and 1942–44.

Young was hired in 1919 by the U.S. government to coordinate all American radio patents into a single company that would control that infant industry. Young established the Radio Corporation of America (RCA), changing communications forever. RCA led that sector of commerce in radio and television for the next several decades. In 1923, Young was requested to sit as a member of the Expert Commission on German Finances and Reparations (headed by Charles Gates DAWES), which sought to devise an equitable scheme for the payment of German reparations without bankrupting that nation's economy. The Dawes Plan earned Dawes a share of the 1925 Nobel Peace Prize, but by the end of the decade it was unraveling. Young was asked by the European powers to revise Dawes's blueprint. His own formula, known as the Young Plan, is considered by many to be one of the finest pieces of economic diplomacy.

Young served as chair of the board of the General Electric from 1922 to 1939, and chair of the board of RCA until 1929. He died on July 11, 1962.

References: Ida M. Tarbell, *Owen D. Young: A New Type of Industrial Leader* (New York: Macmillan, 1932), 9–11; John M. Carroll, "Young, Owen D." in Warren F. Kuehl, ed., *Biographical Dictionary of Internationalists* (Westport, Conn.: Greenwood, 1983), 809–10; John M. Carroll, "Owen D. Young: The Diplomacy of an Enlightened Businessman" in Kenneth Paul Jones, ed., *U.S. Diplomats in Europe, 1919–1941* (Santa Barbara, Calif.: ABC-Clio, 1981), 43–60; "Owen D. Young, 87, Industrialist, Dies," *New York Times*, July 12, 1962, p. 1.

Young Plan

Formula, devised in 1929, by American business executive Owen D. YOUNG to get Germany to pay REPARATIONS after World War I. Eight years after Germany was faced with reparations charges in the Treaty of VERSAILLES, signed in 1919, the nation was caught in an economic downturn and announced that it was unable to pay. On September 16, 1928, representatives of several nations, including Germany, France, Great Britain, Japan, and Italy, met in Geneva, Switzerland, to lay out a blueprint for German payments. The conference agreed that a "Committee of Financial Experts," headed by Young, would advise on proper German payments. In their report, known to history as the Young Plan, the committee members came up with a scheme in which Germany would pay about 1,700 million Reichsmarks per year from 1929 until 1988. On August 31, 1929, the conference agreed to the plan in what was called "The Protocol Concerning Approval in Principle of Report of Experts on Reparations." In Article 8, the German government declared that "it is firmly determined to make every possible effort to avoid a declaration of postponement and not to have recourse thereto until it has come to conclusion in good faith that Germany's exchange and economic life may be seriously endangered by the transfer in part or in full of the postponable portion of the annuities. It remains understood that Germany alone has authority to decide whether occasion has arisen for declaring a postponement" as provided for in the Young Plan. The onset of the GREAT DEPRESSION, however, and the rise of Adolf HITLER (who decried any reparations and suspended their payment) made the reparations issue, a major question of the 1920s, moot.

References: Ida M. Tarbell, *Owen D. Young: A New Type of Industrial Leader* (New York: Macmillan, 1932), 183–91; John M. Carroll, "Young, Owen D." in Warren F. Kuehl, ed., *Biographical Dictionary of Internationalists* (Westport, Conn.: Greenwood, 1983), 809–10; John Ashley Soames Grenville, *The Major International Treaties, 1914–1973: A History and Guide with Texts* (New York: Stein & Day, 1975), 101.

Z

Zaghlul Pasha Ibn Ibrahim, Ahmad Saad
(1857–1927)
Egyptian politician, prime minister (1924). Born in Gharbiya Province, Egypt, about 1860, he was educated at the University of al-Azhar. Although in 1882 he was arrested for his participation in the rebellion of Arabi Pasha, also known as Ahmed Arabi, Zaghlul was released and within two years became an attorney. By 1892 he became a judge in the Court of Appeal, and by 1906 he was appointed as minister of public instruction. Four years later, he was named minister of justice.

Egypt at this time labored under British rule, and the nationalist Zaghlul sought independence. It was not until after the end of World War I, however, that British authorities saw him as a real threat. In early 1919 he was deported to the island of Malta, and on March 10, 1919, nationalist riots broke out in Cairo. He returned a national hero in 1921. Massive anti-British revolts followed, which caused

the British to again deport him, until he was allowed to return in 1923. By 1924 Zaghlul was elected prime minister. He died in 1927.

References: Yaacov Shimoni, ed., *Biographical Dictionary of the Middle East* (New York: Facts On File, 1991); Joan Wucher King, *Historical Dictionary of Egypt* (Metuchen, N.J.: Scarecrow, 1984), 645–48; Israel Gershoni and James P. Jankowski, *Egypt, Islam and the Arabs: The Search for Egyptian Nationhood, 1900–1930* (New York: Oxford University Press, 1986), 185–89; Ralph M. Coury, "The Politics of the Funereal: The Tomb of Saad Zaghlul," *Journal of the American Research Center in Egypt* 29 (1992): 191–200.

zeppelins and dirigibles
Major mode of transportation, particularly during the interwar period, until the destruction of the German zep-

MAJOR DIRIGIBLE ACCIDENTS, 1919–37				
DATE	NAME OF SHIP	PLACE	CAUSE	FATALITIES
July 15, 1919	British *NS-11*	North Sea	Lightning	12
July 21, 1919	*Wingfoot Express*	Chicago	Burned	10
January 12, 1921	British *R-34*	Howden, England	Storm	0
August 25, 1921	British *ZR-2*	Hull, England	Structural	44
February 21, 1922	Italian *Roma*	Hampton Roads, Va.	Rudder failure	34
December 31, 1923	French *Dixmude*	Sicilian Coast	Unknown	52
September 3, 1925	*Shenandoah*	Caldwell, Ohio	Line squall	14
May 17, 1928	*Italia*	North Pole	Incompetency	9
October 5, 1930	British *R-101*	Beauvais, France	Unknown	46
April 4, 1933	*Akron*	Barnegat, N.J.	Storm	73
April 4, 1933	*J-3*	Beach Haven, N.J.	Storm	2
April 4, 1933	French *E-9*	St-Nazaire, France	Engine Trouble	0
May 6, 1937	*Hindenburg*	Lakehurst, N.J.	Explosion	36

pelin HINDENBURG in 1937. After World War I the United States and several European countries desired to build airships as a new form of transportation. The Germans led the way with the *Graf Zeppelin,* which, in service from 1928 to 1937, flew some one million miles (1.6 million km); it also flew around the world with only three stops. Its sister ship, the *Hindenburg,* was 804 feet (245 meters) in length and was considered the finer of the two ships, but after only 10 flights it crashed and burned at Lakehurst, New Jersey, on May 6, 1937, killing 36 people. In the 1920s the U.S. Navy established a program of constructing three airships—one by Germany, one by Great Britain, and one by the United States. These ships were the German *Los Angeles,* the British *ZR-2,* and the American-built *Shenandoah.* The 'Los Angeles was nearly crushed on a mooring mast, and the *Shenandoah* crashed in Ohio on September 3, 1925, 1925, leaving fourteen dead. In England, the *R-101* was thought to be that nation's leading ship. However, on October 5, 1930, it crashed and burned on its maiden voyage, killing 46. One of the victims of the *R-101* crash was Christopher Birdwood Thomson, first baron Thomson of Cardigan, secretary of state for air in the first British Labour government.

In 1933 the U.S. Congress formed the Joint Committee to Investigate Dirigible Disasters. Senator William Henry King of Utah served as the chair. After two months of hearings, the committee issued its final report on June 14, 1933. The committee recommended "that the Navy continue in the maintenance, development, and operation of airships," and that "it is recommended that the naval air station at Lakehurst, N.J., be the center of training and a center of experiment; that a most experienced airship commander be assigned to its command and that there be placed at his disposal experts in airship operation, aerology, radio, and other fields of instruction and research, and that free balloons and nonrigid airships be provided for training." Less than four years later, the *Hindenburg* exploded over Lakehurst, ending the era of the dirigibles.

References: Jay Robert Nash, *Darkest Hours: A Narrative Encyclopedia of Worldwide Disasters from Ancient Times to the Present* (New York: Wallaby Books, 1977), 11–12, 149–50; 238–43, 456, 457–58, 478, 515; "R-34 Across; Short of Fuel; May Need a Tow," *St. Louis Post-Dispatch,* July 5, 1919, p. 1;

"The Wreck of R.38. Causes of the Disaster. Survivors' Stories. Official Inquiry To-morrow," *The Times* (London), August 26, 1921, p. 10; "Change in Course Led Akron to Doom; Aerologist Says Ship Could Have Escaped Storm by Continuing to West," *New York Times,* April 14, 1933, p. 5; "Records from RG 128: Records of the Joint Committee to Investigate Dirigible Disasters, 1933," National Archives, Washington, D.C.; "Dirigible Disasters: Report of the Joint Committee to Investigate Dirigible Disasters, Pursuant to H. Con. Res. 15, A Concurrent Resolution to Investigate the Causes of Dirigible Disasters," Senate Document 75, Seventy-third Congress, First Session (1934), 15–16; "33 Reported Killed as Hindenburg Explodes and Crashes to Earth in Flames at Lakehurst," New York *Herald-Tribune* (European Edition), May 7, 1937, p. 1.

Zinoviev Letter   *See* ELECTIONS, BRITISH.

Zsigmondy, Richard Adolf (1865–1929)

Austrian chemist and Nobel laureate. Born in Vienna, Austria, on April 1, 1865, he graduated from the University of Munich in 1890. While working as a researcher at the University of Berlin and at the Technische Hochschule in Graz, Austria, Zsigmondy began researches into the colors produced by the presence of metallic oxides on glass, which gave rise to his lifelong studies into colloid chemistry. With H. F. W.. Siedentopf, Zsigmondy invented the ultramicroscope, which he used to study the action of colloidal particles. For this entire body of work, Zsigmondy was awarded the 1925 Nobel Prize in chemistry, "for his demonstration of the heterogeneous nature of colloid solutions and for the methods he used, which have since become fundamental in modern colloid chemistry."

Zsigmondy worked at the University of Göttingen until his death on September 24, 1929.

References: Phillip Hight, "Zsigmondy, Richard Adolf" in Bernard S. and June H. Schlessinger, eds., *The Who's Who of Nobel Prize Winners* (Phoenix, Ariz.: Oryx, 1986), 9–10; Thomas Watson MacCallum and Stephen Taylor, eds., *The Nobel Prize–Winners and the Nobel Foundation, 1901–1937* (Zurich: Central European Times Publishing, 1938), 146–47.

LIST OF DOCUMENTS

League of Nations Covenant

The High Contracting Parties,
    In order to promote international co-operation and
    to achieve international peace and security
    by the acceptance of obligations not to resort to war,
    by the prescription of open, just and honourable
    relations between nations,
    by the firm establishment of the understandings of
    international law as the actual rule of conduct among
    Governments,
    and by the maintenance of justice and a scrupulous
    respect for all treaty obligations in the dealings of
    organised peoples with one another,
    Agree to this Covenant of the League of Nations.

ARTICLE 1

1.   The original Members of the League of Nations shall be those of the Signatories which are named in the Annex to this Covenant and also such of those other States named in Annex as shall accede without reservation to this Covenant. Such accession shall be effected by a Declaration deposited with the Secretariat within two months of the coming into force of the Covenant. Notice thereof shall be sent to all other members of the League.

2.   Any full self-governing State, Dominion or Colony not named in the Annex may become a Member of the League if its admission is agreed to by two-thirds of the Assembly, provided that it shall give effective guarantees of its sincere intention to observe its international obligations, and shall accept such regulations as may be prescribed by the League in regard to its military, naval and air forces and armaments.

3.   Any Member of the League may, after two years' notice of its intention to do so, withdraw from the League, provided that all its international obligations and all its obligations under this Covenant shall have been fulfilled at the time of its withdrawal.

ARTICLE 2

The action of the League under this Covenant shall be effected through the instrumentality of an Assembly and of a Council, with a permanent Secretariat.

ARTICLE 3

1.   The Assembly shall consist of Representatives of the Members of the League.

2.   The Assembly shall meet at stated intervals and from time to time as occasion may require at the Seat of the League or at such other place as may be decided upon.

3.   The Assembly may deal at its meetings with any matter within the sphere of action of the League or affecting the peace of the world.

4.   At meetings of the Assembly, each Member of the League shall have one vote, and may have not more than three Representatives.

ARTICLE 4

1.   The Council shall consist of Representatives of the Principal Allied and Associated Powers[1], together with Representatives of four other Members of the League. These four Members of the League shall be selected by the Assembly from time in its discretion. Until the appointment of the Representatives of the four Members of the League first selected by the Assembly, Representatives of Belgium, Brazil, Spain and Greece shall be Members of the Council.

2.   With the approval of the majority of the Assembly, the Council may name additional Members of the League, whose Representatives shall always be Members of the Council[2]; the Council with like approval may increase the number of Members of the League to be selected by the Assembly for representation on the Council[3].

2 bis.[4] The Assembly shall fix by a two-thirds majority the rules dealing with the election of the non-permanent Members of the Council, and particularly such regulations as relate to their term of office and the conditions of reeligibility.

3.   The Council shall meet from time to time as occasion may require, and at least once a year, at the Seat of the League, or at such other place as may be decided upon.

4.   The Council may deal at its meetings with any matter within the sphere of action of the League or affecting the peace of the world.

5.   Any Member of the League not represented on the Council shall be invited to send a Representative to sit as a member at any meeting of the Council during consideration of matters specially affecting the interests of that Member of the League.

6.   At meetings of the Council, each Member of the League represented on the Council shall have one vote, and may have not more than one Representative.

ARTICLE 5

1.   Except where otherwise expressly provided in this Covenant or by the terms of the present Treaty, decisions at any meeting of the Assembly or of the Council shall require the agreement of all the Members of the League represented at the meeting.

2.   All matters of procedure at meetings of the Assembly or of the Council, including the appointment of Committees to investigate particular matters, shall be regulated by the Assembly or by the Council and may be

decided by a majority of the Members of the League represented at the meeting.

3.   The first meeting of the Assembly and the first meeting of the Council shall be summoned by the President of the United States of America.

ARTICLE 6

1.   The permanent Secretariat shall be established at the Seat of the League. The Secretariat shall comprise a Secretary-General and such secretaries and staff as may be required.

2.   The first Secretary-General shall be the person named in the Annex; thereafter the Secretary-General shall be appointed by the Council with the approval of the majority of the Assembly.

3.   The secretaries and staff of the Secretariat shall be appointed by the Secretary-General with the approval of the Council.

4.   The Secretary-General shall act in that capacity at all meetings of the Assembly and of the Council.

5.   The expenses of the League shall be borne by the Members of the League in the proportion decided by the Assembly.

ARTICLE 7

1.   The Seat of the League is established at Geneva.

2.   The Council may at any time decide that the Seat of the League shall be established elsewhere.

3.   All positions under or in connection with the League, including the Secretariat, shall be open equally to men and women.

4.   Representatives of the Members of the League and officials of the League when engaged on the business of the League shall enjoy diplomatic privileges and immunities.

5.   The buildings and other property occupied by the League or its officials or by Representatives attending its meetings shall be inviolable.

ARTICLE 8

1.   The Members of the League recognise that the maintenance of peace requires the reduction of national armaments to the lowest point consistent with national safety and the enforcement by common action of international obligations.

2.   The Council, taking account of the geographical situation and circumstances of each State, shall formulate plans for such reduction for the consideration and action of the several Governments.

3.   Such plans shall be subject to reconsideration and revision at least every ten years.

4.   After these plans shall have been adopted by the several Governments, the limits or armaments therein fixed shall not be exceeded without the concurrence of the Council.

5.   The Members of the League agree that the manufacture by private enterprise of munitions and implements of war is open to grave objections. The Council shall advise how the evil effects attendant upon such manufacture can be prevented, due regard being had to the necessities of those Members of the League which are not able to manufacture the munitions and implements of war necessary for their safety.

6.   The Members of the League undertake to interchange full and frank information as to the scale of their armaments, their military, naval and air programmes and the condition of such of their industries as are adaptable to warlike purposes.

ARTICLE 9

A permanent Commission shall be constituted to advise the Council on the execution of the provisions of Articles 1 and 8 and on military, naval and air questions generally.

ARTICLE 10

The Members of the League undertake to respect and preserve as against external aggression the territorial integrity and existing political independence of all Members of the League. In case of any such aggression or in case of any threat or danger of such aggression the Council shall advise upon the means by which this obligation shall be fulfilled.

ARTICLE 11

1.   Any war or threat of war, whether immediately affecting any Members of the League or not, is hereby declared a matter of concern to the whole League, and the League shall take any action that may be deemed wise and effectual to safeguard the peace of nations. In case any such emergency should arise the Secretary-General shall on the request of any Member of the League forthwith summon a meeting of the Council.

2.   It is also declared to be the friendly right of each member of the League to bring to the attention of the Assembly or of the Council any circumstance whatever affecting international relations which threatens to disturb international peace or the good understanding between nations upon which peace depends.

ARTICLE 12[6]

1.   The Members of the League agree that if there should arise between them any dispute likely to lead to a rupture they will submit the matter either to arbitration or

judicial settlement or to enquiry by the Council, and they agree in no case to resort to war until three months after the award by the arbitrators or the judicial decision or the report by the Council.

2.   In any case under this Article the award of the arbitrators or the judicial decision shall be made within a reasonable time, and the report of the Council shall be made within six months after the submission of the dispute.

ARTICLE 13[6]

1.   The Members of the League agree that whenever any dispute shall arise between them which they recognise to be suitable for submission to arbitration *or judicial settlement,* and which cannot be satisfactorily settled by diplomacy, they will submit the whole subject-matter to arbitration *or judicial settlement.*

2.   Disputes as to the interpretation of a treaty, as to any question of international law, as to the existence of any fact which, if established, would constitute a breach of any international obligation, or as to the extent and nature of the reparation to be made for any such breach, are declared to be among those which are generally suitable for submission to arbitration *or judicial settlement.*

3.   *For the consideration of any such dispute, the court to which the case is referred shall be the Permanent Court of International Justice, established in accordance with Article 14, or any tribunal agreed on by the parties to the dispute or stipulated in any convention existing between them.*

4.   The Members of the League agree that they will carry out in good faith any award *or decision* that may be rendered, and that they will not resort to war against a Member of the League which complies therewith. In the event of any failure to carry out such an award *or decision,* the Council shall propose what steps should be taken to give effect thereto.

ARTICLE 14

The Council shall formulate and submit to the Members of the League for adoption plans for the establishment of a Permanent Court of International Justice. The Court shall be competent to hear and determine any dispute of an international character which the parties thereto submit to it. The Court many also give an advisory opinion upon any dispute or question referred to it by the Council or by the Assembly.

ARTICLE 15

1.[7]   If there should arise between Members of the League any dispute likely to lead to a rupture, which is not submitted to arbitration *or judicial settlement* in accordance with Article 13, the Members of the League agree that they will submit the matter to the Council. Any party

to the dispute may effect such submission by giving notice of the existence of the dispute to the Secretary-General, who will make all necessary arrangements for a full investigation and consideration thereof.

2.   For this purpose the parties to the dispute will communicate to the Secretary-General, a promptly as possible, statements of their case with all the relevant facts and papers, and the Council may forthwith direct the publication thereof.

3.   The Council shall endeavour to effect a settlement of the dispute, and if such efforts are successful, a statement shall be made public giving such facts and explanations regarding the dispute and the terms of settlement thereof as the Council may deem appropriate.

4.   If the dispute is not thus settled, the Council either unanimously or by a majority vote shall make and publish a report containing a statement of the facts of the dispute and the recommendations which are deemed just and proper in regard thereto.

5.   Any Member of the League represented on the Council may make public a statement of the facts of the dispute and of its conclusions regarding the same.

6.   If a report by the Council is unanimously agreed to by the members thereof other than the Representatives of one or more of the parties to the dispute, the Members of the League agree that they will not go to war with any party to the dispute which complies with the recommendations of the report.

7.   If the Council fails to reach a report which is unanimously agreed to by the members thereof, other than the Representatives of one or more of the parties to the dispute, the Members of the League reserve to themselves the right to take such action as they shall consider necessary for the maintenance of right and justice.

8.   If the dispute between the parties is claimed by one of them, and is found by the Council, to arise out of a matter which by international law is solely within the domestic jurisdiction of that party, the Council shall so report, and shall make no recommendation as to its settlement.

9.   The Council may in any case under this Article refer the dispute to the Assembly. The dispute shall be so referred at the request of either party to the dispute provided that such request be made within fourteen days after the submission of the dispute to the Council.

10.   In any case referred to the Assembly, all the provisions of this Article and of Article 12 relating to the action and powers of the Council shall apply to the action and powers of the Assembly, provided that a report made by the Assembly, if concurred in by the Representatives of this Members of the League represented on the Council and of a majority of the other Members of the League, exclusive in each case of the Representatives of the parties to the dispute, shall have the same force as a report by the Council concurred in by all the members thereof other than the Representatives of one or more of the parties to the dispute.

ARTICLE 16

1. Should any Member of the League resort to war in disregard of its covenants under Articles 12, 13 or 15, it shall *ipso facto* be deemed to have committed an act of war against all other Members of the League, which hereby undertake immediately to subject it to the severance of all trade or financial relations, the prohibition of all intercourse between their nationals and the nationals of the covenant-breaking State, and the prevention of all financial, commercial or personal intercourse between the nationals of the covenant-breaking State and the nationals of any other State, whether a Member of the League or not.

2. It shall be the duty of the Council in such case to recommend to the several Governments concerned what effective military, naval or air force the Members of the League shall severally contribute to the armed forces to be used to protect the covenants of the League.

3. The Members of the League agree, further, that they will mutually support one another in the financial and economic measures which are taken under this Article, in order to minimise the loss and inconvenience resulting from the above measures, and that they will mutually support one another in resisting any special measures aimed at one of their number by the covenant-breaking State, and that they will take the necessary steps to afford passage through their territory to the forces of any of the Members of the League which are co-operating to protect the covenants of the League.

4. Any Member of the League which has violated any covenant of the League may be declared to be no longer a Member of the League by a vote of the Council concurred in by the Representatives of all the other Members of the League represented thereon.

ARTICLE 17

1. In the event of a dispute between a Member of the League and a State which is not a Member of the League, or between States not Members of the League, the State or States not Members of the League shall be invited to accept the obligations of membership in the League for the purposes of such dispute, upon conditions as the Council may deem just. If such invitation is accepted, the provisions of Articles 12 to 16 inclusive shall be applied with such modifications as may be deemed necessary by the Council.

2. Upon such invitation being given the Council shall immediately institute an enquiry into the circumstances of the dispute and recommend such action as may seem best and most effectual in the circumstances.

3. If a State so invited shall refuse to accept the obligations of membership in the League for the purposes of such dispute, and shall resort to war against a Member of the League, the provisions of Article 16 shall be applicable as against the State taking such action.

4. If both parties to the dispute when so invited refuse to accept the obligations of membership in the League for the purposes of such dispute, the Council may take such measures and make such recommendations as will prevent hostilities and will result in the settlement of the dispute.

ARTICLE 18

Every treaty or international engagement entered into hereafter by any Member of the League shall be forthwith registered with the Secretariat and shall as soon as possible be published by it. No such treaty or international engagement shall be binding until so registered.

ARTICLE 19

The Assembly may from time to time advise the reconsideration by Members of the League of treaties which have become inapplicable and the consideration of international conditions whose continuance might endanger the peace of the world.

ARTICLE 20

1. The Members of the League severally agree that this Covenant is accepted as abrogating all obligations or understandings inter se which are inconsistent with the terms thereof, and solemnly undertake that they will not hereafter enter into any engagements inconsistent with the terms thereof.

2. In case any Member of the League shall, before becoming a Member of the League, have undertaken any obligations inconsistent with the terms of this Covenant, it shall be the duty of such Member to take immediate steps to procure its release from such obligations.

ARTICLE 21

Nothing in this Covenant shall be deemed to affect the validity of international engagements, such as treaties of arbitration or regional understandings like the Monroe doctrine, for securing the maintenance of peace.

ARTICLE 22

1. To those colonies and territories which as a consequence of the late war have ceased to be under the sovereignty of the States which formerly governed them and which are inhabited by peoples not yet able to stand by themselves under the strenuous conditions of the modern world, there should be applied a principle that the well-being and development of such peoples form a sacred trust of civilisation and that securities for the performance of this trust should be embodied in this Covenant.

2.   The best method of giving practical effect to this principle is that the tutelage of such peoples should be entrusted to advanced nations who by reasons of their resources, their experience or their geographical position can best undertake this responsibility, and who are willing to accept it, and that this tutelage should be exercised by them as Mandatories on behalf of the League.

3.   The character of the mandate must differ according to the stage of the development of the people, the geographical situation of the territory, its economic conditions and other similar circumstances.

4.   Certain communities formerly belonging to the Turkish Empire have reached a stage of development where their existence as independent nations can be provisionally recognised subject to the rendering of administrative advice and assistance by a Mandatory until such time as they are able to stand alone. The wishes of these communities must be a principal consideration in the selection of the Mandatory.

5.   Other peoples, especially those of Central Africa, are at such a stage that the Mandatory must be responsible for the administration of the territory under conditions which will guarantee freedom of conscience and religion, subject only to the maintenance of public order and morals, the prohibition of abuses such as the slave trade, the arms traffic and the liquor traffic, and the prevention of the establishment of fortifications or military and naval bases and of military training of the natives for other than police purposes and the defence of territory, and will also secure equal opportunities for the trade and commerce of other Members of the League.

6.   There are territories, such as South-West Africa and certain of the South Pacific Islands, which, owing to the sparseness of their population, of their small size, or their remoteness from the centres of civilisation, or their geographical contiguity to the territory of the Mandatory, and other circumstances, can be best administered under the laws of the Mandatory as integral portions of its territory, subject to the safeguards above mentioned in the interests of the indigenous population.

7.   In every case of mandate, the Mandatory shall render to the Council and annual report in reference to the territory committed to its charge.

8.   The degree of authority, control or administration to be exercised by the Mandatory shall, if not previously agreed upon by the Members of the League, be explicitly defined in each case by the Council.

9.   A permanent Commission shall be constituted to receive and examine the annual reports of the Mandatories and to advise the Council on all matters relating to the observance of the mandates.

ARTICLE 23

Subject to and in accordance with the provisions of international conventions existing or hereafter to be agreed upon, the Members of the League:

(a)   will endeavour to secure and maintain fair and humane conditions of labour for men, women and children, both in their own countries and in all countries to which their commercial and industrial relations extend, and for that purpose will establish and maintain the necessary international organisations;

(b)   undertake to secure just treatment of the native inhabitants of territories under their control;

(c)   will entrust the League with the general supervision over the execution of agreements with regard to the traffic in women and children, and the traffic in opium and other dangerous drugs;

(d)   will entrust the League with the general supervision of the trade in arms and ammunition with the countries in which the control of this traffic is necessary in the common interest;

(e)   will make provision to secure and maintain freedom of communications and of transit and equitable treatment for the commerce of all Members of the League. In this connection, the special necessities of the regions devastated during the war of 1914–1918 shall be borne in mind;

(f)   will endeavour to take steps in matters of international concern for the prevention and control of disease.

ARTICLE 24

1.   There shall be placed under the direction of the League all international bureaux already established by general treaties if the parties to such treaties consent. All such international bureaux and all commissions for the regulation of matters of international interest hereafter constituted shall be placed under the direction of the League.

2.   In all matters of international interest which are regulated by general conventions but which are not placed under the control of international bureaux or commissions, the Secretariat of the League shall, subject to the consent of the Council and if desired by the parties, collect and distribute all relevant information and shall render any assistance which many be necessary or desirable.

3.   The Council may include as part of the expenses of the Secretariat the expenses of any bureau or commission which is placed under the direction of the League.

ARTICLE 25

The Members of the League agree to encourage and promote the establishment and co-operation of duly authorised voluntary national Red Cross organisations having as purposes the improvement of health, the prevention of disease and the mitigation of suffering throughout the world.

ARTICLE 26

1. Amendments to this Covenant will take effect when ratified by the Members of the League whose Representatives compose the Council and by a majority of the Members of the League whose Representatives compose the Assembly.

2. No such amendments shall bind any Member of the League which signifies its dissent therefrom, but in that case it shall cease to be a Member of the League.

FOOTNOTES

[1]The Principal Allied and Associated Powers were defined as including the United States, the British Empire, France, Italy, and Japan.

[2]In virtue of this paragraph of the Covenant, Germany was nominated as a permanent Member of the Council on September 8, 1926.

[3]The number of Members of the Council selected by the Assembly was eventually increased to six instead of four by virtue of a resolution adopted at the third ordinary meeting of the Assembly, held September 25, 1922. A further increase, from six to nine, came on a motion adopted by the Assembly on September 8, 1926.

[4]This Amendment, not included in the original Covenant but added here in its proper and lawful position, came into force on July 29, 1926, in accordance with Article 26 of the Covenant.

[5]This amendment, not included in the original Covenant but added here in its proper and lawful position, came into force on August 13, 1934, in accordance with Article 26 of the Covenant.

[6]The additions printed in italics relating to those Articles came into force on September 26, 1924, in accordance with Article 26 of the Covenant.

[7]The italicized Amendment to the first paragraph of this Article came into force on September 26, 1924, in accordance with Article 26 of the Covenant.

Source: League of Nations: Ten Years of World Co-Operation (Geneva: Secretariat of the League of Nations, 1930), 417–30.

Extracts from the Weimar Constitution, August 11, 1919

The Weimar Constitution, a remarkable document, emerged from a time of turmoil and anarchy. In less than a year, the Imperial German Government headed by Kaiser Wilhelm II had been overthrown, and a Spartacist (communist) revolt had been put down. On January 19, 1919, a National Constituent Assembly of 423 members was elected, with a majority of seats, 165, being held by Socialists. Centrists (with 91 seats) and Democrats (75) came in second and third, and between these groups power was shared. The Assembly convened in the German city of Weimar on February 6, 1919; five days later, Friedrich Ebert was elected president of the Republic. Those assembled then turned to a draft constitution written by Dr. Hugo Preuss, a professor of constitutional law who was named minister of the interior. The constitution, excerpts of which appear here, was enacted on July 31, 1919, and went into effect on August 11. Historian Louis L. Snyder writes of it, "[It embodied] the best features of the British Bill of Rights, the French Declaration of the Rights of Man, and the first Ten Amendments of the American Constitution."

PREAMBLE

The German people, united in all their racial elements, and inspired by the will to renew and strengthen their Reich in liberty and justice, to preserve peace at home and abroad and to foster social progress, have established the following Constitution:

CHAPTER 1: STRUCTURE AND FUNCTIONS OF THE REICH

Section 1: REICH AND STATES

Article 1.   The German Reich is a Republic. Political authority emanates from the people.

Article 2.   The territory of the Reich consists of territories of the German member states . . .

Article 3.   The Reich colors are black, red, and gold. The merchant flag is black, white, and red, with the Reich colors in the upper inside corner.

Article 4.   The generally accepted rules of international law are to be considered as binding integral parts of the German Reich.

Article 5.   Political authority is exercised in national affairs by the national government in accordance with the Constitution of the Reich, and in state affairs by the state governments in accordance with state constitutions . . .

Article 12.   Insofar as the Reich does not exercise its jurisdiction, such jurisdiction remains with the states . . . with the exception of cases in which the Reich possesses exclusive jurisdiction.

Article 17.   Every state must have a republican constitution. The representatives of the people must be elected by universal, equal, direct, and secret suffrage of all German citizens, both men and women, in accordance with the principles of proportional representation.

Section II: THE REICHSTAG

Article 20.   The Reichstag is composed of delegates of the German people.

Article 21.   The delegates are representatives of the whole people. They are subject only to their own conscience and are not bound by any instructions.

Article 22.   The delegates are elected by universal, equal, direct, and secret suffrage by men and women over twenty years of age, according to the principle of proportional representation. Election day must be a Sunday or a public holiday.

Article 23.   The Reichstag is elected for four years. New elections must take place at the latest on the sixtieth day after this term has run its course . . .

Article 32.   For decisions of the Reichstag a simple majority vote is necessary, unless the Constitution prescribes another proportion of votes . . .

Article 33.   The Reichstag and its committees may require the presence of the Reich Chancellor and every Reich Minister . . .

Section III: THE REICH PRESIDENT AND THE REICH CABINET

Article 41.   The Reich President is elected by the whole German people. Every German who has completed his thirty-fifth year is eligible for election . . .

Article 42.   On assuming office, the Reich President shall take the following oath before the Reichstag:

> I swear to devote my energies to the well-being of the German people, to further their interests, to guard them from injury, to maintain the Constitution and the laws of the Reich, to fulfill my duties conscientiously, and to administer justice for all.

It is possible to add a religious affirmation.

Article 43.   The term of office of the Reich President is seven years. Re-election is permissible.

Before the expiration of his term, the Reich President, upon motion of the Reichstag, may be recalled by a popular vote. The decision of the Reichstag shall be by a two-thirds majority. Through such decision the Reich President is denied any further exercise of his office. The rejection of the recall motion by the popular referendum counts as a new election and results in the dissolution of the Reichstag.

Article 48.   If any state does not fulfill the duties imposed upon it by the Constitution of the laws of the Reich, the Reich President may enforce such duties with the aid of the armed forces.

In the event that the public order and security are seriously disturbed or endangered, the Reich President may take measures necessary for their restoration, intervening, if necessary, with the aid of the armed forces. For this purpose he may temporarily abrogate, wholly or in part, the fundamental principles laid down in Articles 114, 115, 117, 118, 123, 124, and 153.

The Reich President must, without delay, inform the Reichstag of all measures taken under Paragraph 1 or Paragraph 2 of this Article. These measures may be rescinded on demand of the Reichstag.

Article 50.   All orders and decrees of the Reich President, including those relating to the armed forces, must, in order to be valid, be countersigned by the Reich Chancellor or by the appropriate Reich Minister. Responsibility is assumed through the countersignature . . .

Article 52.   The Reich Cabinet consists of the Reich Chancellor and the Reich Ministers.

Article 53.   The Reich Chancellor and, on his recommendation, the Reich Ministers, are appointed and dismissed by the Reich President.

Article 54.   The Reich Chancellor and the Reich Ministers require for the exercise of their office the confidence of the Reichstag. Any one of them must resign if the Reichstag by formal resolution withdraws its confidence.

Article 55.   The Reich Chancellor presides over the government of the Reich and conducts its affairs according to the rules of procedure laid down by the government of the Reich and approved by the Reich President.

Article 56.   The Reich Chancellor determines the political program of the Reich and assumes responsibility to the Reichstag. Within this general policy each Reich Minister conducts independently the office entrusted to him and is held individually responsible to the Reichstag.

Section IV: THE REICHSRAT

Article 60.   A Reichsrat is formed to give the German states representation in the law-making and administration of the Reich.

Article 61.   Each state has at least one vote in the Reichsrat. In the case of the larger states one vote shall be assigned for every million inhabitants1 . . . No single state shall have more than two-fifths of the total number of votes . . .

Article 63.   The states shall be represented in the Reichsrat by members of their governments . . .

Section V: REICH LEGISLATION

Article 68.   Bills are introduced by the Reich cabinet, with the concurrence of the Reichsrat, or by members of the Reichstag. Reich laws shall be enacted by the Reichstag . . .

Article 73.   A law of the Reichstag must be submitted to popular referendum before its proclamation, if the Reich President, within one month of its passage, so decides . . .

Article 74.   The Reichsrat may protest against laws passed by the Reichstag. In case of such protest, the law is returned to the Reichstag, which may override the objection by a two-thirds majority. The Reich President must either promulgate the law within three months or call for a referendum . . .

Article 76.   The Constitution may be amended by law, but acts . . . amending the Constitution can only take effect if two-thirds of the legal number of members are present and at least two-thirds of those present consent . . .

CHAPTER II: FUNDAMENTAL RIGHTS AND DUTIES OF THE GERMANS

Section I: THE INDIVIDUAL

Article 109.   All Germans are equal before the law. Men and women have the same fundamental civil rights and duties. Public legal privileges or disadvantages or birth or of rank are abolished. Titles of nobility . . . may be bestowed no longer . . . Orders and decorations shall not be conferred by the state. No German shall accept titles or orders from a foreign government.

Article 110.   Citizenship of the Reich and the states is acquired in accordance with the provisions of a Reich law . . .

Article 111.   All Germans shall enjoy liberty of travel and residence throughout the whole Reich . . .

Article 112.   Every German is permitted to emigrate to a foreign country . . .

Article 114.   Personal liberty is inviolable. Curtailment or deprivation of personal liberty by a public authority is permissible only by authority of law.

Persons who have been deprived of their liberty must be informed at the latest on the following day by whose authority and for what reasons they have been held. They shall receive the opportunity without delay of submitting objections to their deprivation of liberty.

Article 115.   The house of every German is his sanctuary and is inviolable. Exceptions are permitted only by authority of law . . .

Article 117.   The secrecy of letters and all postal, telegraph, and telephone communications is inviolable. Exceptions are inadmissible except by national law.

Article 118.   Every German has the right, within the limits of general laws, to express his opinion freely by word, in writing, in print, in picture form, or in any other way . . . Censorship is forbidden.

Section II: THE GENERAL WELFARE

Article 123.   All Germans have the right to assembly peacefully and unarmed without giving notice and without special permission . . .

Article 124.   All Germans have the right to form associations and societies for purposes not contrary to the criminal law . . .

Article 126.   Every German has the right to petition . . .

Section III: RELIGION AND RELIGIOUS SOCIETIES

Article 135.   All inhabitants of the Reich enjoy full religious freedom and freedom of conscience. The free exercise of religion is guaranteed by the Constitution and is under public protection . . .

Article 137.   There is no state church . . .

Section IV: EDUCATION AND THE SCHOOLS

Article 142.   Art, science, and the teaching thereof are free . . .

Article 143.   The education of the young is to be provided for by means of public institutions . . .

Article 144.   The entire school system is under the supervision of the state . . .

Article 145.   Attendance at school is compulsory . . .

Section V: ECONOMIC LIFE

Article 151.   The regulation of economic life must be compatible with the principles of justice, with the aim of attaining humane conditions of existence for all. Within these limits the economic liberty of the individual is assured . . .

Article 152.   Freedom of contract prevails . . . in accordance with the laws . . .

Article 153.   The right of private property is guaranteed by the Constitution . . . Expropriation of property may take place . . . by due process of law . . .

Article 159.   Freedom of association for the preservation and promotion of labor and economic conditions is guaranteed to everyone and to all vocations. All agreements and measures attempting to restrict or restrain this freedom are unlawful . . .

Article 161.   The Reich shall organize a comprehensive system of [social] insurance . . .

Article 165.   Workers and employees are called upon to co-operate, on an equal footing, with employers in the regulation of wages and on the conditions of labor, as well as in the general development of the productive forces . . .

CONCLUDING PROVISIONS

Article 181.   . . . The German people have passed and adopted this Constitution through their National Assembly. It comes into force with the date of its proclamation. Schwarzburg, August 11, 1919.

The Reich President
EBERT
The Reich Cabinet
BAUER
ERZBERGER   HERMANN MÜLLER   DR. DAVID
NOSKE   SCHMIDT
SCHLICKE   GIESBERTS   DR. BAYER
DR. BELL

FOOTNOTES

[1]Changed by the law of March 24, 1921 to read "every 700,000 inhabitants."

Source:"Extracts from the Constitution of the German Republic, August 11, 1919" in Louis L. Snyder, ed., *Documents of German History* (New Brunswick, N.J.: Rutgers University Press, 1958), 386–92.

Treaty of Peace between the United States and Germany, August 25, 1921

Following the defeat of the League of Nations Covenant in the United States Senate, the members of that body proceeded to initiate the Treaty of Peace with Germany, which effectively ended the state of war between the United States and Germany that had existed since 1917. The treaty was enacted as a resolution in the House and Senate, but was vetoed by President Woodrow Wilson on May 27, 1919, and an official state of peace did not come until the following treaty was signed on August 25, 1921: The United States of America and Germany:

Considering that the United States, acting in conjunction with its co-belligerents, entered into an Armistice with Germany on November 11, 1918, in order that a Treaty of Peace might be concluded;

Considering that the Treaty of Versailles was signed on June 28, 1919, and came into force according to the terms of its Article 440, but has not been ratified by the United States;

Considering that the Congress of the United States passed a Joint Resolution, approved by the President July 2, 1921, which reads in part as follows:

Resolved by the Senate and House of Representatives of the United States of America in Congress Assembled:

That the state of war declared to exist between the Imperial German Government and the United States of America by the joint resolution of Congress approved April 6, 1917, is hereby declared at an end.

Section 2.   That in making this declaration, and as a part of it, there are expressly reserved to the United States of America and its nationals any and all rights, privileges, indemnities, reparations or advantages, together with the right to enforce the same, to which it or they have become entitled under the terms of the Armistice signed November 11, 1918, or any extensions or modifications thereof; or which were acquired by or are in the possession of the United States of America by reason of its participation in the war or to which its nationals have thereby become rightfully entitled; or which, under the Treaty of Versailles, have been stipulated for its or their benefit; or to which it is entitled as one of the Principal Allied and Associated powers; or to which it is entitled by virtue of any Act or Acts of Congress; or otherwise.

. . . Being desirous of restoring the friendly relations existing between the two Nations prior to the outbreak of war:

Have for that purpose appointed their plenipotentiaries:

The President of the United States of America: Ellis Loring Dressel, Commissioner of the United States of America to Germany, and

The President of the German Empire, Dr. Friedrich Rosen, Minister for Foreign Affairs,

Who, having communicated their full powers, found to be in good and due form have agreed as follows:

Art. 1.   Germany undertakes to accord to the United States, and the United States shall have and enjoy, all the rights, privileges, indemnities, reparations or advantages specified in the aforesaid Joint Resolution of the Congress of the United States of July 2, 1921, including all the rights and advantages stipulated for the benefit of the United States in the Treaty of Versailles which the United States shall fully enjoy notwithstanding the fact that such Treaty has not been ratified by the United States.

Art. 2.   With a view to defining more particularly the obligations of Germany under the foregoing Article with respect to certain provisions in the Treaty of Versailles, it is understood and agreed between the High Contracting Parties:

(1)   That the rights and advantages stipulated in that Treaty for the benefit of the United States, which it is intended the United States shall have and enjoy, are those defined in Section 1 of Part IV, and Parts V, VI, VIII, IX, X, XI, XII, XIV, and XV.

The United States, in availing itself of the rights and advantages stipulated in the provisions of that Treaty mentioned in this paragraph, will do so in a manner consistent with the rights accorded to Germany under such provisions.

(2)   That the United States shall not be bound by the provisions of Part I of that Treaty, nor by any provisions of that Treaty, including those mentioned in Paragraph (1) of this Article, which relate to the Covenant of the League of Nations, or by Council of by the Assembly thereof, unless the United States shall expressly give assent to such action.

(3)   That the United States assumes no obligations under or with respect to the provisions of Part II, Part III, Sections 2 to 8 inclusive of Part IV, and Part XIII of that Treaty.

(4)   That while the United States is privileged to participate the Reparation Commission, according to the terms of Part VIII of that Treaty, and in any other Commission established under the Treaty or under any agreement supplemental thereto, the United States is not bound to participate in any such commission unless it shall elect to do so.

(5)   That the periods of time to which reference is made in Article 440 of the Treaty of Versailles shall run,

with respect to any act or election on the part of the United States, from the date of the coming into force of the present Treaty.

Art. 3   The present Treaty shall be ratified in accordance with the constitutional forms of the High Contracting Parties and shall take effect immediately on the exchange of ratifications, which shall take place as soon as possible at Berlin.

In witness whereof, the respective plenipotentiaries have signed this Treaty and have hereunto affixed their seals.

Done in duplicate in Berlin this twenty-fifth day of August, 1921.

————(signed, Ellis Loring Dressel)

————(signed, Friedrich Rosen)

Source: U.S. Statutes at Large, Vol. XXXXII, p. 1939.

The Final Mandates for Mesopotamia and Palestine, Presented for Approval Before the Council of the League of Nations, 1921

FINAL DRAFT OF MANDATE FOR MESOPOTAMIA FOR THE APPROVAL OF THE LEAGUE OF NATIONS:

THE COUNCIL OF THE LEAGUE OF NATIONS.

Whereas by Article 132 of the Treaty of Peace signed at Sèvres on the tenth day of August, 1920, Turkey renounced in favour of the Principal Allied Powers all rights and title over Mesopotamia, and whereas by Article 94 of the said treaty the High Contracting Parties agreed that Mesopotamia should, in accordance with the fourth paragraph of Article 22 of Part I (Covenant of the League of Nations), be provisionally recognised as an independent State, subject to the rendering of administrative advice and assistance by a Mandatory until such time as it is able to stand alone, and that the determination of the frontiers of Mesopotamia, other than those laid down in the said treaty, and the selection of the Mandatory would be made by the Principal Allied Powers; and

Whereas the Principal Allied Powers have selected His Britannic Majesty as Mandatory for Mesopotamia; and

Whereas the terms of the Mandate in respect to Mesopotamia have been formulated in the following terms and submitted to the Council of the League for approval; and

Whereas His Britannic Majesty has accepted the Mandate in respect of the said territories and undertaken to exercise it on behalf of the League of Nations in conformity with the following provisions:

Hereby approves the terms of the said Mandate as follows:

ARTICLE 1

The Mandatory will frame within the shortest possible time, not exceeding three years from the date of the coming into force of this Mandate, an Organic Law for Mesopotamia, which shall be submitted to the Council of the League of Nations for approval, and shall, as soon as possible, be published by it. This Organic Law shall be framed in consultation with the native authorities, and shall take account of the rights, interests and wishes of all the populations inhabiting the mandated territory. It shall contain provisions designed to facilitate the progressive development of Mesopotamia as an independent State. Pending the coming into effect of the Organic Law, the administration of Mesopotamia shall be conducted in accordance with the spirit of this Mandate.

ARTICLE 2

The Mandatory may maintain armed forces in the territories under his Mandate for the defence of these territories. Until the entry into force of the Organic Law and the re-establishment of public security, he may organise and employ local forces necessary for the maintenance of order and for the defence of these territories. Such local forces may only be recruited from the inhabitants of the territories under the Mandate.

The said local forces shall thereafter be responsible to the local authorities, subject always to the control to be exercised over these forces by the Mandatory. The Mesopotamian Government shall not employ them for other than the above-mentioned purposes, except with the consent of the Mandatory.

Nothing in this article shall preclude the Mesopotamian Government from contributing to the cost of the maintenance of any forces maintained by the Mandatory in Mesopotamia.

The Mandatory shall be entitled at all times to use the roads, railways, and ports of Mesopotamia for the movement of armed forces and the carriage of fuel and supplies.

ARTICLE 3

The Mandatory shall be entrusted with the control of the foreign relations of Mesopotamia, and the right to issue exequaturs to consuls appointed by foreign Powers. It shall also be entitled to afford diplomatic and consular protection to citizens of Mesopotamia when outside its territorial limits.

ARTICLE 4

The Mandatory shall be responsible for seeing that no Mesopotamian territory shall be ceded or leased to or in any way placed under the control of the Government of any foreign Power.

ARTICLE 5

The immunities and privileges of foreigners, including the benefits of consular jurisdiction and protection as formerly enjoyed by Capitulation or usage in the Ottoman Empire, and definitely abrogated in Mesopotamia.

ARTICLE 6

The Mandatory shall be responsible for seeing that the judicial system established in Mesopotamia shall safeguard (a) the interests of foreigners; (b) the law, and (to the extent deemed expedient) the jurisdiction now existing in Mesopotamia with regard to question arising out of the religious beliefs of certain communities (such as the laws of Wakf and personal status). In particular the Mandatory agrees that the control and administration of Wakf shall be exercised in accordance with religious law and the dispositions of the founders.

ARTICLE 7

Pending the making of special extradition agreements with foreign Powers relating to Mesopotamia, the extradition treaties in force between foreign Powers and the Mandatory shall apply to Mesopotamia.

ARTICLE 8

The Mandatory will ensure to all complete freedom of conscience and the free exercise of all forms of worship, subject only to the maintenance of public order and morals. No discrimination of any kind shall be made between the inhabitants of Mesopotamia on the ground of race, religion or language. Instruction in and through the medium of the native languages of Mesopotamia shall be promoted by the Mandatory.

The right of each community to maintain its own schools for the education of its own members in its own language (while conforming to such educational requirements of a general nature as the Administration may impose) shall not be denied or impaired.

ARTICLE 9

Nothing in this Mandate shall be construed as conferring upon the Mandatory authority to interfere with the fabric or the management of the sacred shrines, the immunities of which are guaranteed.

ARTICLE 10

The Mandatory shall be responsible for exercising supervision over missionary enterprise in Mesopotamia as may be required for the maintenance of public order and good government. Subject to such supervision, no measures shall be taken in Mesopotamia to obstruct or interfere with such enterprise or to discriminate against any missionary on the ground of his religion or nationality.

ARTICLE 11

The Mandatory must see that there is no discrimination in Mesopotamia against the nationals of any State member of the League of Nations (including companies incorporated under the laws of such State) as compared with the nationals of the Mandatory or of any foreign State in matters concerning taxation, commerce or navigation, the exercise of industries or professions, or in the treatment of merchant vessels or civil aircraft. Similarly, there shall be no discrimination in Mesopotamia against goods originating in or destined for any of the said States, and there shall be freedom of transit under equitable conditions across the mandated area.

Subject as aforesaid the Mesopotamian Government may on the advice of the Mandatory impose such taxes and customs duties as it may consider necessary and take such steps as it may think best to promote the development of the natural resources of the country and to safeguard the interests of the population.

Nothing in this article shall prevent the Mesopotamian Government on the advice of the Mandatory, from concluding a special customs arrangement with any State, the territory of which in 1914 was wholly included in Asiatic Turkey or Arabia.

ARTICLE 12

The Mandatory will adhere on behalf of Mesopotamia to any general international conventions already existing or that may be concluded hereafter with the approval of the League of Nations respecting the slave traffic, the traffic in arms and ammunition, and the traffic in drugs, or relating to commercial equality, freedom of transit and navigation, laws of aerial navigation, railways and postal, telegraphic and wireless communication, or artistic, literary or industrial property.

ARTICLE 13

The Mandatory will secure the co-operation of the Mesopotamian Government, so far as social, religious and other conditions may permit, in the execution of any common policy adopted by the League of Nations for preventing and combating disease, including diseases of plants and animals.

ARTICLE 14

The Mandatory will secure the enactment within twelve months from the coming into force of this Mandate, and will ensure the execution of a Law of Antiquities, based on the contents of Article 421 of Part XIII of the Treaty of Peace with Turkey. This law shall replace the former Ottoman Law of Antiquities, and shall ensure equality of treatment in the matter of archaeological research to the nationals of all States, members of the League of Nations.

ARTICLE 15

Upon the coming into force of the Organic Law an arrangement shall be made between the Mandatory and the Mesopotamian Government for settling the terms on which the latter will take over Public Works and other services of a permanent character, the benefit of which will pass to the Mesopotamian Government. Such arrangement shall be communicated to the Council of the League of Nations.

ARTICLE 16

Nothing in this Mandate shall prevent the Mandatory from establishing a system of local autonomy for predominantly Kurdish areas in Mesopotamia as he may consider suitable.

ARTICLE 17

The Mandatory shall make to the Council of the League of Nations an annual report as to the measures taken during the year to carry out the provisions of the Mandate. Copies of all laws and regulations promulgated or issued during the year shall be communicated with the report.

ARTICLE 18

The consent of the Council of League of Nations is required for any modification of the terms of the present Mandate, provided that in the case of the modification proposed by the Mandatory such consent may be given by a majority of the Council.

ARTICLE 19

If any dispute whatever should arise between the members of the League of Nations relating to the interpretation or the application of these provisions which cannot be settled by negotiation, this dispute shall be submitted to the Permanent Court of International Justice provided for by Article 14 of the Covenant of the League of Nations.

ARTICLE 20

In the event of the termination of the Mandate conferred upon the Mandatory by this Declaration, the Council of the League of Nations shall make such arrangements as may be deemed necessary for securing under the guarantee of the League that the Mesopotamian Government will fully honour the financial obligations legally incurred by the Mandatory during the period of the Mandate, including the rights of public servants to pensions or gratuities.

The present copy shall be deposited in the archives of the League of Nations. Certified copies shall be forwarded by the Secretary-General of the League of Nations to all Powers Signatories of the Treaty of Peace with Turkey. Made at——the——day of——

Final Draft of the Mandate for Palestine for the Approval of the League of Nations

Whereas by Article 132 of the Treaty of Peace signed at Sèvres on the tenth day of August, 1920, Turkey renounced in favour of the Principal Allied Powers all rights and title over Palestine; and

Whereas by Article 95 of the said treaty the High Contracting Parties agreed to entrust, by application of the provisions of Article 22, the Administration of Palestine, within such boundaries as might be determined by the Principal Allied Powers, to a Mandatory to be selected by the said Powers; and

Whereas by the same article the High Contracting Parties further agreed that the Mandatory should be responsible for putting into effect the declaration originally made on November 2, 1917, by the Government of His Britannic Majesty, and adopted by the other Allied Powers, in favour of the establishment in Palestine of a national home for the Jewish people, it being clearly understood that nothing should be done which might prejudice the civil and religious rights of existing non-Jewish communities in Palestine, or the rights and political status enjoyed by Jews in any other country; and

Whereas recognition has thereby been given to the historical connection of the Jewish people with Palestine and to the grounds for reconstituting their National Home in that country; and

Whereas the Principal Allied Powers have selected His Britannic Majesty as the Mandatory for Palestine; and

Whereas the terms of the Mandate in respect of Palestine have been formulated in the following terms and submitted to the Council of the League for approval; and

Whereas His Britannic Majesty has accepted the Mandate in respect of Palestine and undertaken to exercise it on behalf of the League of Nations in conformity with the following provisions:

Hereby approves the terms of the said Mandate as follows:

ARTICLE 1

His Britannic Majesty shall have the right to exercise as Mandatory all the powers inherent in the Government of a Sovereign State, save as they may be limited by the terms of the present Mandate.

ARTICLE 2

The Mandatory shall be responsible for placing the country under such political, administrative and economic conditions as will secure the establishment of the Jewish national home, as laid down in the preamble, and the development of self-governing institutions, and also for safeguarding the civil and religious rights of all the inhabitants of Palestine, irrespective of race and religion.

ARTICLE 3

The Mandatory shall encourage the widest measure of self-government for localities consistent with the prevailing conditions.

ARTICLE 4

An appropriate Jewish agency shall be recognised as a public body for the purpose of advising and co-operating with the Administration of Palestine in such economic, social and other matters as may effect the establishment of the Jewish national home and the interests of the Jewish population in Palestine, and, subject always to the control of the Administration, to assist and take part in the development of the country.

The Zionist organisation, so long as its organisation and constitution are in the opinion of the Mandatory appropriate, shall be recognised as such agency. It shall take steps in consultation with His Britannic Majesty's Government to secure the co-operation of all Jews who are willing to assist in the establishment of the Jewish national home.

ARTICLE 5

The Mandatory shall be responsible for seeing that no Palestine territory shall be ceded or leased to, or in any way placed under the control of the Government of any foreign Power.

ARTICLE 6

The Administration of Palestine, while ensuring that the rights and positions of other sections of the popula-

tion are not prejudiced, shall facilitate Jewish immigration under suitable conditions and shall encourage in co-operation with the Jewish agency referred to in Article 4 close settlement by Jews on the land, including State lands and waste lands not required for public purposes.

ARTICLE 7

The Administration of Palestine will be responsible for enacting a nationality law. There shall be included in this law provisions framed so as to facilitate the acquisition of Palestinian citizenship by Jews who take up their permanent residence in Palestine.

ARTICLE 8

The immunities and privileges of foreigners, including the benefits of consular jurisdiction and protection as formerly enjoyed by Capitulation or usage in the Ottoman Empire, are definitely abrogated in Palestine.

ARTICLE 9

The Mandatory shall be responsible for seeing that the judicial system established in Mesopotamia shall safeguard (a) the interests of foreigners; (b) the law, and (to the extent deemed expedient) the jurisdiction now existing in Palestine with regard to question arising out of the religious beliefs of certain communities (such as the laws of Wakf and personal status). In particular the Mandatory agrees that the control and administration of Wakfs shall be exercised in accordance with religious law and the dispositions of the founders.

ARTICLE 10

Pending the making of special extradition agreements with foreign Powers relating to Palestine, the extradition treaties in force between foreign Powers and the Mandatory shall apply to Palestine.

ARTICLE 11

The Administration of Palestine shall take all necessary measures to safeguard the interests of the community in connection with the development of the country and, subject to Article 311 of the Treaty of Peace with Turkey, shall have full power to provide for public ownership or control of any of the natural resources of the country or of the public works, services and utilities established or to be established therein. It shall introduce a land system appropriate to the needs of the country, having regard, among other things, to the desirability of promoting the close settlement and intensive cultivation of the land.

The Administration may arrange with the Jewish agency mentioned in Article 4 to construct or operate, upon fair and equitable terms, any public works, services and utilities, and to develop any of the natural resources of the country, in so far as these matters are not directly undertaken by the Administration. Any such arrangements shall provide that no profits distributed by such agency, directly or indirectly, shall exceed a reasonable rate of interest on the capital, and any further profits shall be utilised by it for the benefit of the country in a manner approved by the Administration.

ARTICLE 12

The Mandatory shall be entrusted with the control of the foreign relations of Palestine, and the right to issue exequaturs to consuls appointed by foreign Powers. It shall also be entitled to afford diplomatic and consular protection to citizens of Palestine when outside its territorial limits.

ARTICLE 13

All responsibility in connection with the Holy Places and religious buildings or sites in Palestine, including that of preserving existing rights, of securing free access to the Holy Places, religious buildings and sites and the free exercise of worship, while ensuring the requirements of pubic order and decorum, is assumed by the Mandatory, who will be responsible solely to the League of Nations in all matters connected therewith: provided that nothing in this article shall prevent the Mandatory from entering into such arrangement as he may deem reasonable with the Administration for the purpose of carrying the provisions of this article into effect; and provided also that nothing in this Mandate shall be construed as conferring upon the Mandatory authority to interfere with the fabric or the management of purely Moslem sacred shrines, the immunities of which are guaranteed.

ARTICLE 14

In accordance with Article 95 of the Treaty of Peace with Turkey, the Mandatory undertakes to appoint as soon as possible a special Commission to study and regulate all questions and claims relating to the different religious communities. In the composition of this Commission the religious interests concerned will be taken into account. The Chairman of the Commission will be appointed by the Council of the League of Nations. It will be the duty of this Commission to ensure that certain Holy Places, religious buildings or sites regarded with special veneration by the adherents of one particular religion, are entrusted to the permanent control of suitable bodies representing the adherents of the religion concerned. The selection of the Holy Places, religious buildings or sites to be

entrusted, shall be made by the Commission, subject to the approval of the Mandatory.

In all case dealt with under this article, however, the right and duty of the Mandatory to maintain order and decorum in the place concerned shall not be affected, and the buildings and sites will be subject to the provisions of such laws relating to public monuments as may be enacted in Palestine with the approval of the Mandatory.

The rights of control conferred under this article will be guaranteed by the League of Nations.

ARTICLE 15

The Mandatory will see that complete freedom of conscience and the free exercise of all forms of worship, subject only to the maintenance of public order and morals, is ensured to all. No discrimination of any kind shall be made between the inhabitants of Palestine on the ground of race, religion or language. No person shall be excluded from Palestine on the sole ground of his religious belief.

The right of each community to maintain its own schools for the education of its own members in its own language (while conforming to such educational requirements of a general nature as the Administration may impose) shall not be denied or impaired.

ARTICLE 16

The Mandatory shall be responsible for exercising such supervision over religious or eleemosynary [charitable] bodies of all faiths in Palestine as may be required for the maintenance of public order and good government. Subject to such supervision, no measures shall be taken in Palestine to obstruct or interfere with the enterprise of such bodies or to discriminate against any representative or member of them on the ground of his religion or nationality.

ARTICLE 17

The Administration of Palestine may organise on a voluntary basis the forces necessary for the preservation of peace and order, and also for the defence of the country, subject, however, to the supervision of the Mandatory, but shall not use them for purposes other than those above specified save with the consent of the Mandatory. Except for such purposes, no military, naval or air forces shall be raised or maintained by the Administration of Palestine.

Nothing in this article shall preclude the Administration of Palestine from contributing to the cost of the maintenance of forces maintained by the Mandatory.

The Mandatory shall be entitled at all time to use the roads, railways and ports of Palestine for the movement of armed forces and the carriage of fuel and supplies.

ARTICLE 18

The Mandatory must see that there is no discrimination in Palestine against the nationals of any of the States members of the League of Nations (including companies incorporated under their laws) as compared with those of the Mandatory or of any foreign State in matter concerning taxation, commerce or navigation, the exercise of industries or professions, or in the treatment of merchant vessels or civil aircraft. Similarly, there shall be no discrimination in Palestine against goods originating in or destined for any of the said States, and there shall be freedom of transit under equitable conditions across the mandated area.

Subject as aforesaid and to the other provisions of this Mandate, the Administration of Palestine may on the advice of the Mandatory impose such taxes and customs duties as it may consider necessary, and take such steps as it may think best to promote the development of the natural resources of the country and to safeguard the interests of the population.

Nothing in this article shall prevent the Government of Palestine, on the advice of the Mandatory, from concluding a special customs agreement with any State, the territory of which in 1914 was wholly included in Asiatic Turkey or Arabia.

ARTICLE 19

The Mandatory will adhere on behalf of the Administration to any general international conventions already existing or that may be concluded hereafter with the approval of the League of Nations respecting the slave traffic, the traffic in arms and ammunition, or the traffic in drugs, or relating to commercial equality, freedom of transit and navigation, aerial navigation and postal, telegraphic and wireless communication or literary, artistic or industrial property.

ARTICLE 20

The Mandatory will co-operate on behalf of the Administration of Palestine, so far religious, social and other conditions may permit, in the execution of any common policy adopted by the League of Nations for preventing and combating disease, including diseases of plants and animals.

ARTICLE 21

The Mandatory will secure, within twelve months from the coming into force of this Mandate, the enactment, and will ensure the execution of a Law of Antiquities based on the provisions of Article 421 of Part XIII of the Treaty of Peace with Turkey. This law shall replace the former Ottoman Law of Antiquities, and shall ensure equality of treatment in the matter of archaeological research to the nationals of all States, members of the League of Nations.

ARTICLE 22

English, Arabic and Hebrew shall be the official languages of Palestine. Any statement or inscriptions in Arabic on stamps or money in Palestine shall be repeated in Hebrew and any statements or inscriptions in Hebrew shall be repeated in Arabic.

ARTICLE 23

The Administration of Palestine shall recognise the holy days of the respective communities in Palestine as legal days of rest of the members of such communities.

ARTICLE 24

The Mandatory shall make to the Council of the League of Nations an annual report as to the measures taken during the year to carry out the provisions of the Mandate. Copies of all laws and regulations promulgated or issued during the year shall be communicated with the report.

ARTICLE 25

In the territories lying between the Jordan [River] and the eastern boundary of Palestine to be ultimately determined, the Mandatory shall be entitled to postpone or withhold application of such provisions of this Mandate as he may consider inapplicable to the existing local conditions, and to make such provision for the administration of the territories as he may consider suitable to those conditions, provided no action shall be taken which is inconsistent with the provisions of Articles 15, 16, and 18.

ARTICLE 26

If any dispute whatever should arise between the members of the League of Nations relating to the interpretation or the application of these provisions which cannot be settled by negotiation, this dispute shall be submitted to the Permanent Court of International Justice provided for by Article 14 of the Covenant of the League of Nations.

ARTICLE 27

The consent of the Council of the League of Nations is required for any modification of the terms of the present Mandate, provided that in the case of any modification proposed by the Mandatory, such consent may be given by a majority of the Council.

ARTICLE 28

In the event of the termination of the Mandate conferred upon the Mandatory by this Declaration, the Council of the League of Nations shall make such arrangements as may be deemed necessary for safeguarding in perpetuity, under guarantee of the League, the rights secured by Articles 13 and 14, and for securing, under the guarantee of the League, that the Government of Palestine will fully honour the financial obligations, legitimately incurred by the Administration of Palestine during the period of the Mandate, including the rights of public servants to pensions or gratuities.

The present copy shall be deposited in the archives of the League of Nations and certified copies shall be forwarded by the Secretary-General of the League of Nations to all Powers Signatories of the Treaty of Peace with Turkey. Made at——the——day of——

Source: Mandates. Final Drafts of the Mandates for Mesopotamia and Palestine for the Approval of the Council of League of Nations. Presented to Parliament by Command of His Majesty, August, 1921 (London: His Majesty's Stationery Office, 1921), 2–13.

Excerpts from the Limitation Treaty Signed at Washington, February 6, 1922

Treaty between the United States, the British Empire, France, Italy and Japan agreeing to a limitation of naval armament. Signed at Washington, February 6, 1922; ratification advised by the Senate, March 29, 1922; ratified by the President, June 9, 1923; ratifications deposited with the Government of the United States, August 17, 1923; proclaimed, August 21, 1923.

BY THE PRESIDENT OF THE UNITED STATES OF
AMERICA
A PROCLAMATION

Whereas a Treaty between the United States of America, the British Empire, France, Italy and Japan, agreeing to a limitation of naval armament, was concluded and signed by their respective plenipotentiaries at Washington on February 6, 1922, the original of which Treaty, in the English and French languages, is word for word as follows:

The United States of American, the British Empire, France, Italy and Japan;

Desiring to contribute to the maintenance of the general peace, and to reduce the burdens of competition in armament;

Have resolved, with a view to accomplishing these purposes, to conclude a treaty to limit their respective naval armament, and to that end have appointed as their Plenipotentiaries . . .

Who, having communicated to each other their respective full powers, found to be in good and due form, have agreed as follows:

CHAPTER 1

ART. I. The Contracting Powers agree to limit their respective naval armaments as provided in the present Treaty.

ART. II. The Contracting Powers may retain respectively the capital ships which are specified in Chapter II, Part 1. On the coming into force of the present Treaty, but subject to the following provisions of this Article, all other capital ships, built or building, of the United States, the British Empire and Japan shall be disposed of as prescribed in Chapter II, Part 2.

In addition to the capital ships specified in Chapter II, Part 1, the United States may complete and retain two ships of the *West Virginia* class now under construction. On the completion of these two ships the *North Dakota* and *Delaware* shall be disposed of as prescribed in Chapter II, Part 2.

The British Empire may, in accordance with the replacement table in Chapter II, Part 3, construct two new capital ships not exceeding 35,000 tons (36,560 metric tons) standard displacement each. On the completion of the said two ships the *Thunderer, King George V, Ajax* and *Centurion* shall be disposed of as prescribed in Chapter II, Part 2.

ART. III. Subject to the provisions of Article II, the Contracting Powers shall abandon their respective capital ship building programs, and no new capital ships shall be constructed or acquired by any of the Contracting Powers except replacement tonnage which be may constructed or acquired as specified in Chapter II, Part 3.

Ships which are replaced in accordance with Chapter II, Part 3, shall be disposed of as prescribed in Part 2 of that Chapter.

ART. IV. The total capital ship replacement tonnage of each of the Contracting Powers shall not exceed in standard displacement, for the United States 525,000 tons (533,400 metric tons); for the British Empire 525,000 tons (533,400 metric tons); for France 175,000 tons (177,800 metric tons); for Italy 175,000 tons (177,800 metric tons); for Japan 315,000 tons (320,040 metric tons).

ART. V. No capital ship exceeding 35,000 tons (35,560 metric tons) standard displacement shall be acquired by, or constructed by, for, or within the jurisdiction of, any of the Contracting Powers.

ART. VI. No capital ship of any of the Contracting Powers shall carry a gun with a calibre in excess of 16 inches (406 millimetres).

ART. VII. The total tonnage for aircraft carriers of each of the Contracting Powers shall not exceed in standard displacement, for the United States 135,000 tons (137,160 metric tons); for the British Empire 135,000 tons (137,160 metric tons); for France 60,000 tons (60,960 metric tons); for Italy 60,000 tons (60,090 metric tons); for Japan 81,000 tons (82,296 metric tons).

ART. VIII. The replacement of aircraft carriers shall be effected only as prescribed in Chapter II, Part 3, provided, however, that all aircraft carrier tonnage in existence or building on November 12, 1921, shall be considered experimental, and may be replaced, within the total tonnage limit prescribed in Article VII, without regard to its age.

ART. IX. No aircraft carrier exceeding 27,000 (27,432 metric tons) standard displacement shall be acquired by, or constructed by, for or within the jurisdiction of, any of the Contracting Powers.

However, any of the Contracting Powers may, provided that its total tonnage allowance of aircraft carriers in not thereby exceeded, build not more than two aircraft carriers, each of a tonnage of not more than 33,000 tons (33,528 metric tons) standard displacement, and in order to effect economy any of the Contracting Powers may use for this purpose any two of their ships, whether constructed or in course of construction, which would otherwise be scrapped under the provisions of Article II. The armament of any aircraft carriers exceeding 27,000 tons (27,432 metric tons) standard displacement shall be in accordance with the requirements of Article X, except that the total number of guns to be carried in case any of such guns be of a calibre exceeding 6 inches (152 millimetres) except anti-aircraft guns not exceeding 5 inches (127 millimetres), shall not exceed eight.

ART. X. No aircraft carrier of any of the Contracting Powers shall carry a gun with a calibre in excess of 8 inches (203 millimetres). Without prejudice to the provisions of Article IX, if the armament carried includes guns exceeding 6 inches (152 millimetres) in calibre the total number of guns carried, except anti-aircraft guns and guns not exceeding 5 inches (127 millimetres), shall not exceed ten. If alternately the armament contains no guns exceeding 6 inches (152 millimetres) in calibre, the number of guns is not limited. In either case the number of anti-aircraft guns and of guns not exceeding 5 inches (127 millimetres) in not limited.

ART. XI. No vessel of war exceeding 10,000 tons (10,160 metric tons) standard displacement, other than a capital ship or aircraft carrier, shall be acquired by, or constructed by, for, or within the jurisdiction of, any of the Contracting Powers. Vessels not specifically built as fighting ships nor taken in time of peace under government control for fighting purposes, which are employed on fleet duties or as troop transports or in some other way for the purpose of assisting in the prosecution of hostilities otherwise than as fighting ships, shall not be within the limitations of this Article.

ART. XII. No vessel of war of any of the Contracting Powers, hereafter laid down, other than a capital ship, shall carry a gun with a calibre in excess of 8 inches (203 millimetres).

ART. XIII. Except as provided in Article IX, no ship designated in the present Treaty to be scrapped may be reconverted into a vessel of war.

ART. XIV. No preparation shall be made in merchant ships in time of peace for the installation of warlike armaments for the purpose of converting such ships into vessels of war, other than the necessary stiffening of decks for the mounting of guns not exceeding 6 inch (152 millimetres) calibre.

ART. XV. No vessel of war constructed within the jurisdiction of any of the Contracting Powers for a non-Contracting Power shall exceed the limitations as to displacement and armament prescribed by the Treaty for vessels of a similar type which may be constructed by or for any of the Contracting Powers; provided, however, that the displacement for aircraft carriers constructed for a non-Contracting Power shall in no case exceed 27,000 tons (27,432 metric tons) standard displacement.

ART. XVI. If the construction of any vessel of war for a non-Contracting Power is undertaken within the jurisdiction of any of the Contracting Powers, such Power shall promptly inform the other Contracting Powers of the date of the signing of the contract and the date on which the keel of the ship is laid; and shall also communicate to them the particulars relating to the ship prescribed in Chapter II, Part 3, Section I(b), (4) and (5).

ART. XVII. In the event of a Contracting Power being engaged in a war, such Power shall not use as a vessel of war any vessel of war which may be under construction within its jurisdiction for any other Power, or which may have been constructed within its jurisdiction for another Power and not delivered.

ART. XVIII. Each of the Contracting Powers undertakes not to dispose by gift, sale or any mode of transfer of any vessel of war in such a manner that such a vessel may become a vessel of war in the Navy of any foreign Power.

ART. XIX. The United States, the British Empire and Japan agree that the status quo at the time of the signing of the present Treaty, with regard to fortifications and naval bases, shall be maintained in their respective territories and possessions specified hereunder:

(1) The insular possessions which the United States now holds or may hereafter acquire in the Pacific Ocean, except (a) those adjacent to the coast of the United States, Alaska and the Panama Canal Zone, not including the Aleutian Island, and (b) the Hawaiian Islands;

(2) Hongkong and the insular possession which the British Empire now holds or may hereafter acquire in the Pacific Ocean, east of the meridian of 110° east of longitude, except (a) those adjacent to the coast of Canada, (b) the Commonwealth of Australia and its Territories, and (c) New Zealand;

(3) The following insular territories and possessions of Japan in the Pacific Ocean, to wit: the Kurile Islands, the Bonin Islands, Amami-Oshima, the Loochoo Islands, Formosa and the Pescadores, and any insular territories or possessions in the Pacific Ocean which Japan may hereafter acquire.

The maintenance of the status quo under the foregoing provisions implies that new fortifications or naval bases shall be established in the territories and possessions specified; that no measures shall be taken to increase the existing naval facilities for the repair and maintenance of naval forces, and that no increase shall be made in the coast defences of the territories and possessions above specified. This restriction, however, does not preclude such repair and replacement of worn-out weapons and equipment as is customary in naval and military establishments in time of peace.

ART. XX. The rules for determining tonnage displacement prescribed in Chapter II, Part 4, shall apply to the ships of each of the Contracting Powers.

PART 2: RULES FOR SCRAPPING VESSELS OF WAR

The following rules shall be observed for the scrapping of vessels of war which are to be disposed of in accordance with Articles II and III.

I. A vessel to be scrapped must be placed in such condition that it cannot be put to combatant use.

II. This result must be finally effected in any way of the following ways:

(a) Permanent sinking of the vessel;

(b) Breaking the vessel up. This shall always involve the destruction or removal of all machinery, boilers and armour, and all deck, side and bottom plating;

(c) Converting the vessel to target use exclusively. In such case all the provisions are paragraph III of this Part, except subparagraph (6), in so far as may be necessary to enable the ship to be used as a mobile target, and except subparagraph (7), must be previously complied with. Not more than one capital ship may be retained for this purpose at one time by any of the Contracting Powers.

(d) Of the capital ships which would otherwise be scrapped under the present Treaty in or after the year 1931, France and Italy may each retain two sea-going vessels for training purposes exclusively, that is, as gunnery or torpedo schools. The two vessels retained by France shall be of the *Jean Bart* class, and of those retained by Italy one shall be the *Dante Alighieri*, the other of the *Giulio Cesare* class. On retaining these ships for the purpose above stated, France and italy respectively undertake to remove and destroy their conning-towers, and not to use the said ships as vessels of war.

III. (a) Subject to the special exceptions contained in Article IX, when a vessel is due for scrapping, the first stage of scrapping, which consists in rendering a ship incapable of further warlike service, shall be immediately undertaken.

(b) A vessel shall be considered incapable of further warlike service when there shall have been removed and landed, or else destroyed in the ship:

(1) All guns and essential portions of guns, fire-control tops and revolving parts of all barbettes and turrets;

(2) All machinery for working hydraulic or electric mountings;

(3) All fire-control instruments and range-finders;

(4) All ammunition, explosives and mines;

(5) All torpedoes, war-heads and torpedo tubes;

(6) All wireless telegraphy installations;

(7) The conning tower and all side armour, or alternatively all main propelling machinery; and

(8) All landing and flying-off platforms and all other aviation accessories.

IV. The periods in which scrapping of vessels is to be effected are as follows:

(a) In the case of vessels to be scrapped under the first paragraph of Article II, the work of rendering the vessels incapable of further warlike service, in accordance with paragraph III of this Part, shall be completed within six months from the coming into force of the present Treaty, and the scrapping shall be finally effected within eighteen months from such coming into force . . .

In faith whereof the above named Plenipotentiaries have signed the present Treaty.

Done at the City of Washington the sixth day of February, One Thousand Nine Hundred and Twenty-Two.

Charles Evans Hughes [seal]
Henry Cabot Lodge [seal]
Oscar W. Underwood [seal]
Elihu Root [seal]
Arthur James Balfour [seal]
Lee of Fareham [seal]
A.C. Geddes [seal]
R.L. Borden [seal]
G.F. Pearce [seal]
John W. Salmond [seal]
Arthur James Balfour [seal]
V.S. Srinivasa Sastri [seal]
A. Sarraut [seal]
Jusserand [seal]
Carlo Schanzer [seal]
V. Rolandi Ricci [seal]
Luigi Albertini [seal]
T. Kato [seal]
K. Shidehara [seal]
M. Hanihara [seal]

Sources: Conference on the Limitation of Armament: Address of the President of the United States, Submitting the Treaties and Resolutions Approved and Adopted by the Conference on the Limitation of Armament, Together with the report of the American Delegation of the Proceedings of the Conference on the Limitation of Armament, Submitted to the President, February 9, 1922, Senate Document No. 125, 67th Congress, 2nd Session (1922); *Armament Conference Treaties: Treaties and Resolutions, Approved and Adopted by the Conference on the Limitation of Armament, Submitted by the President of the United States for Advice and Consent to their Ratification,* Senate Document No. 124, 67th Congress, 2nd Session (1922); Text of Naval Limitation Treaty at U.S. Statutes at Large, Vol. XXXXIII, 1655–84.

Text of the Locarno Treaty, December 1, 1925

From October 5 to 16, 1925, delegates from Belgium, Czechoslovakia, France, Germany, Great Britain, Italy, and Poland met at the instigation of France so that the borders of the European states could be defined by treaty to avoid future conflict. The negotiations were held in the Swiss village of Locarno, but the treaty itself was signed in London on December 1, 1925. Herewith is the entire text of that document:

The President of the German Reich, His Majesty the King of the Belgians, the President of the French Republic, and His Majesty the King of the United Kingdom of Great Britain and Ireland and of the British Dominions beyond the Seas, Emperor of India, his Majesty the King of Italy;

Anxious to satisfy the desire for security and protection which animates the peoples upon whom fell the scourge of war [from] 1914–18;

Taking note of the abrogation of the treaties for the neutralisation of Belgium, and conscious of necessity of ensuring peace in the area which has so frequently been the scene of European conflicts;

Animated also with the deepest desire of giving to all the signatory Powers concerned supplementary guarantees within the framework of the Covenant of the League of Nations and the treaties in force between them;

Have determined to conclude a treaty with these objects, and have appointed as plenipotentiaries: Who, having communicated their full powers, found in good and due form, have agreed as follows:

ART. 1. The high contracting parties collectively and severally guarantee, in the manner provided in the following articles, the maintenance of the territorial status quo resulting from the frontiers between Germany and Belgium and between Germany and France and the inviolability of the said frontiers as fixed by or in pursuance of the Treaty of Peace signed at Versailles on the 28th June, 1919, and also the observance of the stipulations of articles 42 and 43 of the said treaty concerning the demilitarized zone.

ART. 2. Germany and Belgium, and also Germany and France, mutually undertake that they will in no case attack or invade each other or resort to war against each other. This stipulation shall not, however, apply in the case of

(1) The exercise of the right of legitimate defence, that is to say, resistance to a violation of the undertaking contained in the previous paragraph or to a flagrant breach of articles 42 or 43 of the said Treaty of Versailles, if such breach constitutes an unprovoked act of aggression and by reason of the assembly of armed forces in the demilitarized zone immediate action is necessary.

(2) Action in pursuance of article 16 of the Covenant of the League of Nations.

(3) Action as the result of a decision taken by the Assembly or by the Council of the League of Nations or in pursuance of article 15, paragraph 7, of the Covenant of the League of Nations, provided that in this last event the action is directed against a state which was the first to attack.

ART. 3. In view of the undertakings entered into by article 2 of the present treaty, Germany and Belgium and Germany and France undertake to settle by peaceful means and in the manner laid down herein all questions of every kind which may arise between them and which it may not be possible to settle by the normal methods of diplomacy:

Any question with regard to which the parties are in conflict as to their respective rights shall be submitted to judicial decision, and the parties undertake to comply with such decision.

All other questions shall be submitted to a conciliation commission. If the proposals of this commission are not accepted by the two parties, the question shall be brought before the Council of the League of Nations, which will deal with it in accordance with article 15 of the Covenant of the League. The detailed arrangements for effecting such peaceful settlement are the subject of special agreements signed this day.

ART 4. (1) If one of the high contracting parties alleges that a violation of article 2 of the present treaty of a breach of articles 42 or 43 of the Treaty of Versailles has been or is being committed, it shall bring the question at once before the Council of the League of Nations.

(2) As soon as the Council of the League of Nations is satisfied that such violation or breach has been committed, it will notify its finding without delay to the Powers signatory of the present treaty, who severally agree that in such case they will each of them come immediately to the assistance of the Power against whom the act complained of is directed.

(3) In case of a flagrant violation of article 2 of the present treaty or of a flagrant breach of articles 42 or 43 of the Treaty of Versailles by one of the high contracting parties, each of the other contracting parties hereby undertakes immediately to come to the help of the party against whom such a violation or breach has been directed as soon as the said Power has been able to satisfy itself that this violation constitutes an unprovoked act of aggression and that by reason either of the Assembly of armed forces in the demilitarized zone immediate action is necessary. Nevertheless, the Council of the League of Nations, which will be seized of the question in accordance with the first paragraph of this article, will issue its findings, and the high contracting parties undertake to act in accordance with the recommendations of the Council provided that they are concurred in by all the members others than the representatives of the parties which have engaged in hostilities.

ART. 5. The provisions of article 3 of the present treaty are placed under the guarantee of the high contracting parties as provided by the following stipulations:

If one of the Powers referred to in article 3 refuses to submit a dispute to a peaceful settlement or to comply with an arbitral or judicial decision and commits a violation of article 2 of the present treaty or a breach of article 42 or 43 of the Treaty of Versailles, the provisions of article 4 shall apply.

Where one of the Powers referred to in article 3 without committing a violation of article 2 of the present treaty or a breach of article 42 or 43 of the Treaty of Versailles, refuses to submit a dispute to peaceful settlement or to comply with an arbitral or judicial decision, the other party shall bring the matter before the Council of the League of Nations, and the Council shall propose what steps shall be taken; the high contracting parties shall comply with these proposals.

ART. 6. The provisions of the present treaty do not affect the rights and obligations of the high contracting parties under the Treaty of Versailles or under arrangements supplementary thereto, including the agreements signed in London on the 30th August, 1924.

ART. 7. The present treaty, which is designed to ensure the maintenance of peace, and is in conformity with the Covenant of the League of Nations, shall not be interpreted as restricting the duty of the League to take whatever action may be deemed wise and effectual to safeguard the peace of the world.

ART. 8. The present treaty shall be registered at the League of Nations in accordance with the Covenant of the League.

It shall remain in force until the Council, acting on a request of one or other of the high contracting parties notified to the other signatory Powers three month in advance, and voting at least a two-thirds' majority, decides that the League of Nations ensures sufficient protection to the high contracting parties; the treaty shall cease to have effect on the expiration of a period of one year from such decision.

ART. 9. The present treaty shall impose no obligation upon any of the British dominions, or upon India, unless the Government of such dominion, or of India, signifies its acceptance thereof.

ART. 10. The present treaty shall be ratified and the ratifications shall be deposited at Geneva in the archives of the League of Nations as soon as possible.

It shall enter into force as soon as all the ratifications have been deposited and Germany has become a member of the League of Nations.

The present treaty, done in a single copy, will be deposited in the archives of the League of Nations, and the Secretary-General will be requested to transmit certified copies to each of the high contracting parties.

In faith whereof the above-mentioned plenipotentiaries have signed the present treaty.
Done at Locarno, the 16th October, 1925.

[Hans] LUTHER
[Gustav] STRESEMANN
EMILE VANDERVELDE
A. BRIAND
AUSTEN CHAMBERLAIN
BENITO MUSSOLINI
Sources: Edmund Jan Osmańczyk, *The Encyclopedia of the United Nations and International Agreements* (Philadelphia: Taylor & Francis, 1985), 477–78; Louis L. Snyder, ed., *Documents of German History* (New Brunswick, N.J.: Rutgers University Press, 1958), 398–401.

The Kellogg-Briand Pact, Proclaimed July 24, 1929

On August 27, 1928, members of several nations met in Paris to sign the treaty known as the Kellogg-Briand Pact. This agreement, mediated between U.S. Secretary of State Frank Kellogg and French foreign minister Aristide Briand, sought to abolish war "as an instrument of national policy." And although such nations as Germany and Japan signed the covenant, within a decade both would be involved in starting World War II; in fact, in 1931 Japan was already moving into Manchuria in China. Although Kellogg negotiated the pact and lent his name to it, by the time it was ratified, by July 24, 1929, he had been replaced as U.S. Secretary of State by Henry L. Stimson. The following is the official text of the agreement, with confirmatory language added when all nations being signatories ratified it:

Treaty between the United States and other Powers providing for the renunciation of war as an instrument of national policy. Signed at Paris, August 27, 1928; ratification advised by the Senate, January 16, 1929; ratified by the President, January 17, 1929; instruments of ratification deposited at Washington by the United States of America, Australia, Dominion of Canada, Czechoslovakia, Germany, Great Britain, India, the Irish Free State, Italy, New Zealand, and the Union of South Africa, March 2, 1929; by Poland, March 26, 1929; by Belgium, March 27, 1929; by France, April 22, 1929; by Japan, July 24, 1929; proclaimed, July 24, 1929.

BY THE PRESIDENT OF THE UNITED STATES OF AMERICA. A PROCLAMATION.

WHEREAS a Treaty between the President of the United States of America, the President of the German Reich, His Majesty the King of the Belgians, the President of the French Republic, His Majesty the King of Great Britain, Ireland and the British Dominions beyond the Seas, the Emperor of India, His Majesty the King of Italy, His Majesty the Emperor of Japan, the President of the Republic of Poland, and the President of the Czechoslovak Republic, providing for the renunciation of war as an instrument of national policy, was concluded and signed by their respective Plenipotentiaries at Paris on the twenty-seventh day of August, one thousand nine hundred and twenty-eight, the original of which Treaty, being in the English and the French languages, is word for word as follows:

THE PRESIDENT OF THE GERMAN REICH, THE PRESIDENT OF THE UNITED STATES OF AMERICA, HIS MAJESTY THE KING OF THE BELGIANS, THE PRESIDENT OF THE FRENCH REPUBLIC, HIS MAJESTY THE KING OF GREAT BRITAIN, IRELAND AND THE BRITISH DOMINIONS BEYOND THE SEAS, THE EMPEROR OF INDIA, HIS MAJESTY THE KING OF ITALY, HIS MAJESTY THE EMPEROR OF JAPAN, THE PRESIDENT OF THE REPUBLIC OF POLAND, AND THE PRESIDENT OF THE CZECHOSLOVAK REPUBLIC,

Deeply sensible of their solemn duty to promote the welfare of mankind;

Persuaded that the time has come when a frank renunciation of war as an instrument of national policy should be made to the end that the peaceful and friendly relations now existing between their peoples may be perpetuated;

Convinced that all the changes in their relations with one another should be sought only by pacific means and by the result of a peaceful and orderly process, and that any signatory Power which shall hereafter seek to promote its national interests by resorting to war should be denied the benefits furnished by this Treaty;

Hopeful that, encouraged by their example, all the other nations of the world will join in this humane endeavor and, by adhering to the present Treaty as soon as it come into force, bring their peoples within the scope of its beneficent provisions, thus uniting the civilized nations of the world in a common renunciation of war as an instrument of their national policy;

Have decided to conclude a Treaty and for that purpose have appointed their respective

Plenipotentiaries:
THE PRESIDENT OF THE GERMAN REICH:
Dr. Gustav STRESEMANN, Minister of Foreign Affairs;
THE PRESIDENT OF THE UNITED STATES OF AMERICA:
The Honorable Frank B. KELLOGG, Secretary of State;
HIS MAJESTY THE KING OF THE BELGIANS:
Mr. Paul HYMANS, Minister for Foreign Affairs, Minister of State;
THE PRESIDENT OF THE FRENCH REPUBLIC:
Mr. Aristide BRIAND, Minister for Foreign Affairs;
HIS MAJESTY THE KING OF GREAT BRITAIN, IRELAND AND THE BRITISH DOMINIONS BEYOND THE SEAS, [AND] THE EMPEROR OF INDIA:
For GREAT BRITAIN and NORTHERN IRELAND and all parts of the British Empire which are not separate Members of the League of Nations:
The Right Honourable Lord Cushendun, Chancellor of the Duchy of Lancaster, Acting Secretary of State for Foreign Affairs;
For the DOMINION OF CANADA:
The Right Honourable William Lyon MACKENZIE KING, Prime Minister and Minister for External Affairs;
For the COMMONWEALTH OF AUSTRALIA:
The Honourable Alexander John MCLACHLAN, Member of the Executive Federal Council;
For the DOMINION OF NEW ZEALAND:
The Honourable Sir Christopher James PARR, High Commissioner for New Zealand in Great Britain;
For the UNION OF SOUTH AFRICA:
The Honourable Jacobus Stephanus SMUTS, High Commissioner for the Union of South Africa in Great Britain;
For the IRISH FREE STATE:
Mr. William Thomas COSGRAVE, President of the Executive Council;
For INDIA:

The Right Honourable Lord Cushendun, Chancellor of the Duchy of Lancaster, Acting Secretary of State for Foreign Affairs;

HIS MAJESTY THE KING OF ITALY:

Count Gaetano MANZONI, his Ambassador Extraordinary and Plenipotentiary at Paris;

HIS MAJESTY THE EMPEROR OF JAPAN:

Count UCHIDA, Privy Councillor;

THE PRESIDENT OF THE REPUBLIC OF POLAND:

Mr. A. ZALESKI, Minister for Foreign Affairs;

THE PRESIDENT OF THE CZECHOSLOVAK REPUBLIC:

Dr. Eduard BENEŠ, Minister for Foreign Affairs;

who, having communicated to one another their full powers found in good and due form have agreed upon the following articles:

ARTICLE I

The High Contracting Parties solemnly declare in the names of their respective peoples that they condemn recourse to war for the solution of international controversies, and renounce it, as an instrument of national policy in their relations with one another.

ARTICLE II

The High Contracting Parties agree that the settlement or solution of all disputes or conflicts or whatever nature or of whatever origin they may be, which may arise among them, shall never be sought except by pacific means.

ARTICLE III

The present Treaty shall be ratified by the High Contracting Parties named in the Preamble in accordance with their respective constitutional requirements, and shall take effect as between them as soon as all their several instruments of ratification shall have been deposited at Washington.

This Treaty shall, when it has come into effect as prescribed in the preceding paragraph, remain open as long as may be necessary for adherence by all the other Powers of the world. Every instrument evidencing the adherence of a Power shall be deposited at Washington and the Treaty shall immediately upon such deposit become effect as between the Power thus adhering and the other Powers parties hereto.

It shall be the duty of the Government of the United States to furnish each Government named in the Preamble and every Government subsequently adhering to this Treaty with a certified copy of the Treaty and of every instrument of ratification or adherence. It shall also be the duty of the Government of the United States telegraphically to notify such Governments immediately upon the deposit with it of each instrument of ratification or adherence.

IN FAITH WHEREOF the respective Plenipotentiaries have signed this Treaty in the French and English languages both texts having equal force, and hereunto affix their seals.

DONE at Paris, the twenty seventh day of August in the year one thousand nine hundred and twenty eight.

[SEAL OF STRESEMANN]
[SEAL OF KELLOGG]
[SEAL OF HYMANS]
[SEAL OF BRIAND]
[SEAL OF CUSHENDUN]
[SEAL OF MACKENZIE KING]
[SEAL OF MCLACHLAN]
[SEAL OF PARR]
[SEAL OF SMUTS]
[SEAL OF COSGRAVE]
[SEAL OF CUSHENDUN]
[SEAL OF MANZONI]
[SEAL OF UCHIDA]
[SEAL OF ZALESKI]
[SEAL OF BENEŠ

Certified to be a true copy of the signed original deposited with the Government of the United States of America.

FRANK B. KELLOGG
Secretary of State of the United States of America

AND WHEREAS it is stipulated in the said Treaty that it shall take effect as between the High Contracting Parties as soon as all the several instruments of ratification shall have been deposited at Washington;

AND WHEREAS the said Treaty has been duly ratified on the parts of all the High Contracting Parties and their several instruments of ratification have been deposited with the Government of the United States of America, the last of July 24, 1929;

NOW, THEREFORE, be it known that I, Herbert Hoover, President of the United States of America, have caused the said Treaty to be made public, to the end that the same and every article and clause thereof may be observed and fulfilled with good faith by the United States and the citizens thereof.

IN TESTIMONY WHEREOF, I have hereunto set my hand and caused the seal of the United States to be fixed.

DONE at the city of Washington this twenty fourth day of July in the year of our Lord one thousand nine hundred and twenty nine, and of the Independence of the United States of America the one hundred and fifty-fourth.

HERBERT HOOVER
[Signature of the President]
HENRY L. STIMSON
[signature of the Secretary of State]
Source: U.S. Statutes at Large, 46:2:2343–44.

Excerpts from the London Naval Treaty, Signed April 22, 1930

ARTICLE 1

The High Contracting Parties agree not to exercise their rights to lay down the keels of capital ship replacement tonnage during the years 1931–1936 inclusive as provided in Chapter II, Part 3 of the Treaty for the Limitation of Naval Armament signed between them at Washington of the 6th February, 1922, and referred to in the present Treaty as the Washington Treaty . . .

ARTICLE 2

1.   The United States, the United Kingdom of Great Britain and Northern Ireland, and Japan shall dispose of the following capital ships as provided in this Article:

United States:
   "Florida"
   "Utah"
   "Arkansas" or "Wyoming"
United Kingdom:
   "Benbow"
   "Iron Duke"
   "Marlborough"
   "Emperor of India"
   "Tiger"
Japan:
   "Hiyei"

ARTICLE 3

1.   For the purposes of the Washington Treaty, the definition of an aircraft carrier given in Chapter II, Part 4 of said Treaty is hereby replaced by the following definition:

The expression "aircraft carrier" includes any surface vessel of war, whatever its displacement, designed for the specific and exclusive purpose of carrying aircraft and so constructed that aircraft can be launched therefrom and landed thereon.

2.   The fitting of a landing-on or flying-off platform or deck on a capital ship, cruiser of destroyer, provided such vessel was not designed for adapted exclusively as an aircraft carrier, shall not cause any vessel so fitted to be charged against or classified in the category of aircraft carriers.

3.   No capital ship in existence on the 1st April, 1930, shall be fitted with a landing-on platform or deck.

ARTICLE 4

1.   No aircraft carrier of more than 10,000 tons (10,160 metric tons) or less standard displacement mounting a gun above 6.1-inch (155 mm.) calibre shall be acquired by or constructed by or for any of the High Contracting Parties . . .

ARTICLE 6

1.   The rules for determining standard displacement prescribed in Chapter II, Part 4 of the Washington Treaty shall apply to all surface vessels of war of each of the High Contracting Parties.

2.   The standard displacement of a submarine is the surface displacement of the vessel complete (exclusive of the water in [a] non-water-tight structure) fully manned, engined, and equipped ready for sea, including all armament and ammunition, equipment, outfit, provisions for crew, miscellaneous stores, and implements of every description that are intended to be carried in war, but without fuel, lubricating oil, fresh water or ballast water of any kind on board . . .

ARTICLE 7

1.   No submarine the standard displacement of which exceeds 2,000 tons (2,032 metric tons) of with a gun above 5.1-inch (130 mm.) calibre shall be acquired by or constructed by or for any of the High Contracting Parties.

2.   Each of the High Contracting Parties may, however, retain, build or acquire a maximum of three submarines of a standard displacement not exceeding 2,800 tons (2,845 metric tons); these submarines may carry guns not above 6.1-inch (155 mm.) calibre. Within this number, France may retain one unit, already launched, of 2,880 tons (2,926 metric tons), with guns the calibre of which is 8 inches (203 mm.) . . .

ARTICLE 8

Subject to any special agreements which may submit them to limitation, the following vessels are exempt from limitation:

(a)   naval surface combatant vessels of 600 tons (610 metric tons) standard displacement and under;

(b)   naval surface combatant vessels exceeding 600 tons (610 metric tons), but not exceeding 2,000 tons (2,032 metric tons) standard displacement, provided they have none of the following characteristics:

(1)   mount a gun above 6.1-inch (155 mm.) calibre;

(2)   mount more than four guns above 3-inch (76 mm.) calibre;

(3)   are designed or fitted to launch torpedoes;

(4) are designed for a speed greater than twenty knots . . .

ARTICLE 12

3. Japan may . . . replace the minelayers "Aso" and "Tokiwa" by two new minelayers before the 31st December 1936. The standard displacement of each of the new vessels shall not exceed 5,000 tons (5,080 metric tons); their speed shall not exceed twenty knots, and their characteristics shall conform to the provisions of paragraph (b) of Article 8 . . .

4. The "Asama," "Yakumo," "Izumo," "Iwate" and "Kasuga" shall be disposed of . . .

ARTICLE 21

If, during the term of the present Treaty, the requirements of the national security of any High Contracting Party in respect of vessels of war . . . are in the opinion of that Party materially affected by new construction of any Power . . . , that High Contracting Party will notify the other parties . . . as to the increase required to be made in its own tonnages within one or more of the categories of such vessels of war, specifying particularly the proposed increases and the reasons therefor, and shall be entitled to make such increase. Thereupon the other Parties . . . of this Treaty shall be entitled to make a proportionate increase in the category or categories specified; and the said other Parties shall promptly advise with each other through diplomatic channels as to the situation thus presented . . ."

Sources: London Naval Treaty of 1930, Publications of the United States Department of State, Conference Series No. 2 (Washington, D.C.: U.S. Government Printing Office, 1930); *London Naval Conference: Speeches and Press Statements by Members of the American Delegation, January 20–April 29, 1930,* Publications of the United States Department of State, Conference Series No. 3 (Washington, D.C.: U.S. Government Printing Office, 1930).

Franklin Delano Roosevelt's First "Fireside Chat" with the American People, March 12, 1933

On March 12, 1933, U.S. President Franklin Delano Roosevelt took to the air to address the American people by radio on the bank crisis which was slowly strangling the American economy. In the process, he invented a new form of dialogue: the "fireside chat," a name that evoked images of comfortable familiarity in its listeners. The address, which occurred at 10 P.M. Washington time and lasted less than 14 minutes, is presented verbatim here.

I want to talk for a few minutes with the people of the United States about banking—with the comparatively few who understand the mechanics of banking but more particularly with the overwhelming majority who use banks for the making of deposits and the drawing of checks. I want to tell you what has been done in the last few days, why it was done, and what the next steps are going to be. I recognize that the many proclamations from State Capitols and from Washington, the legislation, the Treasury regulations, etc., couched for the most part in banking and legal terms should be explained for the benefit of the average citizen. I owe this in particular because of the fortitude and good temper with which everybody has accepted the inconvenience and hardships of the banking holiday. I know that when you understand what we in Washington have been about I shall continue to have your cooperation as fully as I have had your sympathy and help during the past week.

First of all let me state the simple fact that when you deposit money in a bank the bank does not put the money into a safe deposit vault. It invests your money in many different forms of credit-bonds, commercial paper, mortgages and many other kinds of loans. In other words, the bank puts your money to work to keep the wheels of industry and of agriculture turning around. A comparatively small part of the money you put into the bank is kept in currency—an amount which in normal times is wholly sufficient to cover the cash needs of the average citizen. In other words the total amount of all the currency in the country is only a small fraction of the total deposits in all of the banks.

What, then, happened during the last few days of February and the first few days of March? Because of undermined confidence on the part of the public, there was a general rush by a large portion of our population to turn bank deposits into currency or gold.—A rush so great that the soundest banks could not get enough currency to meet the demand. The reason for this was that on the spur of the moment it was, of course, impossible to sell perfectly sound assets of a bank and convert them into cash except at panic prices far below their real value.

By the afternoon of March 3 scarcely a bank in the country was open to do business. Proclamations temporarily closing them in whole or in part had been issued by the Governors in almost all the states.

It was then that I issued the proclamation providing for the nation-wide bank holiday, and this was the first step in the Government's reconstruction of our financial and economic fabric.

The second step was the legislation promptly and patriotically passed by the Congress confirming my proclamation and broadening my powers so that it became possible in view of the requirement of time to entend [sic] the holiday and lift the ban of that holiday gradually. This law also gave authority to develop a program of rehabilitation of our banking facilities. I want to tell our citizens in every part of the Nation that the national Congress—Republicans and Democrats alike—showed by this action a devotion to public welfare and a realization of the emergency and the necessity for speed that it is difficult to match in our history.

The third stage has been the series of regulations permitting the banks to continue their functions to take care of the distribution of food and household necessities and the payment of payrolls.

This bank holiday while resulting in many cases in great inconvenience is affording us the opportunity to supply the currency necessary to meet the situation. No sound bank is a dollar worse off than it was when it closed its doors last Monday. Neither is any bank which may turn out not to be in a position for immediate opening. The new law allows the twelve Federal Reserve banks to issue additional currency on good assets and thus the banks which reopen will be able to meet every legitimate call. The new currency is being sent out by the Bureau of Engraving and Printing in large volume to every part of the country. It is sound currency because it is backed by actual, good assets.

As a result we start tomorrow, Monday, with the opening of banks in the twelve Federal Reserve bank cities—those banks which on first examination by the Treasury have already been found to be all right. This will be followed on Tuesday by the resumption of all their functions by banks already found to be sound in cities where there are recognized clearing houses. That means about 250 cities of the United States.

On Wednesday and succeeding days banks in smaller places all through the country will resume business, subject, of course, to the Government's physical ability to complete its survey. It is necessary that the reopening of banks be extended over a period in order to permit the banks to make applications for necessary loans, to obtain currency needed to meet their requirements and to enable the Government to make common sense checkups. Let me make it clear to you that if your bank does not open the first day you are by no means justified in believing that it will not open. A bank that opens on one of the subsequent days is in exactly the same status as the bank that opens tomorrow.

I know that many people are worrying about State banks not members of the Federal Reserve System. These banks can and will receive assistance from members banks and from the Reconstruction Finance Corporation. These state banks are following the same course as the national banks except that they get their licenses to resume business from the state authorities, and these authorities have been asked by the Secretary of the Treasury to permit their good banks to open up on the same schedule as the national banks. I am confident that the state banking departments will be as careful as the National Government in the policy relating to the opening of banks and will follow the same broad policy. It is possible that when the banks resume a very few people who have not recovered from their fear may again begin withdrawals. Let me make it clear that the banks will take care of all needs—and it is my belief that hoarding during the past week has become an exceedingly unfashionable pastime. It needs no prophet to tell you that when the people find that they can get their money—that they can get it when they want it for all legitimate purposes—the phantom of fear will soon be laid. People will again be glad to have their money where it will be safely taken care of and where they can use it conveniently at any time. I can assure you that it is safer to keep your money in a reopened bank than under the mattress.

The success of our whole great national program depends, of course, upon the cooperation of the public—on its intelligent support and use of a reliable system.

Remember that the essential accomplishment of the new legislation is that it makes it possible for banks more readily to convert their assets into cash than was the case before. More liberal provision has been made for banks to borrow on these assets at the Reserve Banks and more liberal provision has also been made for issuing currency on the security of those good assets. This currency is not fiat currency. It is issued only on adequate security—and every good bank has an abundance of such security.

One more point before I close. There will be, of course, some banks unable to reopen without being reorganized. The new law allows the Government to assist in making these reorganizations quickly and effectively and even allows the Government to subscribe to at least a part of new capital which may be required.

I hope you can see from this elemental recital of what your government is doing that there is nothing complex, or radical in the process.

We had a bad banking situation. Some of our bankers had shown themselves either incompetent or dishonest in their handling of the people's funds. They had used the money entrusted to them in speculations and unwise loans. This was of course not true in the vast majority of our banks but it was true in enough of them to shock the people for a time into a sense of insecurity and to put them into a frame of mind where they did not differentiate, but seemed to assume that the acts of a comparative few had tainted them all. It was the Government's job to straighten out this situation and do it as quickly as possible—and the job is being performed.

I do not promise you that every bank will be reopened or that individual losses will not be suffered, but there will be no losses that possibly could be avoided; and there would have been more and greater losses had we continued to drift. I can even promise you salvation for some at least of the sorely pressed banks. We shall be engaged not merely in reopening sound banks but in the creation of sound banks through reorganization. It has been wonderful to me to catch the note of confidence from all over the country. I can never be sufficiently grateful to the people for the loyal support they have given me in their acceptance of the judgment that has dictated our course, even though all of our processes may not have seemed clear to them.

After all there is an element in the readjustment of our financial system more important than currency, more important than gold, and that is the confidence of the people. Confidence and courage are the essentials of success in carrying out our plan. You people must have faith; you must not be stampeded by rumors or guesses. Let us unite in banishing fear. We have provided the machinery to restore our financial system; it is up to you to support and make it work.

It is your problem no less than it is mine. Together we cannot fail.

Source: 1933 volume of Public Papers and Addresses of FDR, note before first F.C., March 12, 1933.

The Munich Agreement, September 30, 1938

On September 30, 1938, after meeting with Adolf Hitler and Benito Mussolini in Munich, British Prime Minister Neville Chamberlain, in order to stave off the threat of war in Europe, agreed to "appease" the German leader and let him occupy so-called German Sudeten sections of Czechoslovakia. Upon arriving home in London, Chamberlain called the agreement reached at the Munich conference a way to guarantee "peace in our time." In fact, the act emboldened Hitler to launch his assault against Poland 11 months later to start World War II. The following is the text of the agreement reached in Munich:

AGREEMENT BETWEEN GERMANY, GREAT BRITAIN, FRANCE, AND ITALY, CONCLUDED IN MUNICH ON SEPTEMBER 29, 1938.

The conversation which the chiefs of the Governments of Germany, Italy, France and Great Britain began on Thursday noon [September 29] have found their conclusion in the late evening.

The agreements, which were reached, and which are laid down in the following documents, have been immediately transmitted to the Czechoslovak Government.

Germany, the United Kingdom, France and Italy, taking into consideration the settlement already agreed upon in principle concerning the cession of the Sudeten German districts, have agreed on the following conditions and procedures and the measures to be taken, and declare themselves individually held responsible by this agreement for guaranteeing the steps necessary for its fulfillment:

1. The evacuation begins on October 1.

2. The United Kingdom of Great Britain, France and Italy agree that the evacuation of the region shall be completed by October 10, without destruction of any of the existing installations, and that the Czechoslovak Government bear the responsibility for seeing that the evacuation is carried out without damaging the aforesaid installations.

3. The conditions governing the evacuation will be laid down in detail by an international commission composed of representatives of Germany, the United Kingdom, France, Italy, and Czechoslovakia.

STAGES OF OCCUPATION

4. The occupation by stages of the predominantly Sudeten German territories by German troops will begin on October 1. The four territories marked on the attached map will be occupied by German troops in the following order:—The territory marked No. 1 on October 1 and 2, the territory marked No. 2 on October 2 and 3, the territory marked No. 3 on October 3, 4 and 5, the territory marked No. 4 on October 6 and 7.

The remaining territories of predominantly German character will be ascertained by the aforesaid international commission forthwith and be occupied by German troops by October 10.

5. The international commission referred to in paragraph 3 will determine the territories in which a plebiscite is to be held. These territories will be occupied by international bodies until the plebiscite has been completed. The same commission will fix the conditions in which the plebiscite is to be held, taking as a basis the conditions of the Saar plebiscite.

The commission will also fix the date at the end of November on which the plebiscite will be held.

6. The final determination of the frontiers will be carried out by the international commission. The commission will also recommend to the four Powers—Germany, the United Kingdom, France, and Italy—in certain exceptional circumstances minor modifications in the strictly ethnographical determination of the zones which are to be transferred without plebiscite.

7. There will be a right of opinion into and out of the transferred territories, the option to be exercised within six months of the date of this agreement. A German-Czechoslovak commission shall determine the details of the options and consider ways of facilitating the transfer of populations and certain questions of principle arising out of the said transfer.

RELEASE OF PRISONERS

8. The Czechoslovak Government will within the period of four weeks from the date of this agreement release from the military and police forces any Sudeten Germans who may wish to be released, and the Czechoslovak Government will within the same period

release German Sudeten prisoners who are serving terms of imprisonment for political offences.

ADOLF HITLER
NEVILLE CHAMBERLAIN
ÉDOUARD DALADIER
BENITO MUSSOLINI

ANNEXE TO THE AGREEMENT

His Majesty's Government in the United Kingdom and the French Government have entered into the above agreement on the basis that they stand by the offer contained in Paragraph 6 of the Anglo-French proposals of September 19 in relation to an international guarantee of the new boundaries of the Czechoslovak State against unprovoked aggression.

When the question of the Polish and Hungarian minorities in Czechoslovakia has been settled Germany and Italy for their part will give a guarantee to Czechoslovakia.

The heads of the Governments of the four Powers declare that the problems of the Polish and Hungarian minorities in Czechoslovakia, if not settled within three months by agreement between the respective Governments, shall form the subject of a further meeting of the heads of Governments of the four Powers here present.

SUPPLEMENTARY DECLARATION

All questions which may arise out of the transfer of the territories shall be considered as coming within the terms of reference of the international commission."

Source: "Text of Munich Agreement. Eight Clauses," *The Times* (London), October 1, 1938, p. 11; full text in *Further Documents Respecting Czechoslovakia. Including the Agreement Concluded at Munich on September 29, 1938. Presented by the Secretary of State for Foreign Affairs to Parliament by Command of His Majesty,* Miscellaneous Report No. 8 (1938) (London: His Majesty's Stationery Office, 1938), 2–6.

The Soviet-German Nonaggression Pact, August 23, 1939

On August 23, 1939, German Foreign Minister Joachim von Ribbentrop and Soviet Foreign Minister Vyacheslav Mikhailovich Molotov signed the so-called Soviet-German Nonaggression Pact, an agreement which allowed Germany to overrun Poland in exchange for Soviet nonaction; the treaty opened the door for the Nazis to initiate the blitzkrieg on the Polish nation which started World War II. The following is the exact text of the treaty signed in Moscow:

Guided by the desire to strengthen the cause of peace between Germany and the Union of Socialist Soviet Republics, and basing themselves on the fundamental stipulations of the Neutrality Agreement concluded between Germany and the Union of Socialist Soviet Republics in April, 1926, the German Government and the Government of the Union of Socialist Soviet Republics have come to the following agreement:

ARTICLE 1. The two contracting parties undertake to refrain from any act of force, any aggressive act, and any attacks against each other undertaken either singly or in conjunction with other powers.

ARTICLE 2. If one of the two contracting parties should become the object of war-like action on the part of a third Power, the contracting party will in no way support the third Power.

ARTICLE 3. The Governments of the two contracting parties will in [the] future remain in consultation with one another in order to inform each other about questions which touch their common interests.

ARTICLE 4. Neither of the two contracting parties will join any group of Powers which is directed, mediately or immediately, against the other party.

ARTICLE 5. In case disputes or conflicts on questions of any kind should arise between the two contracting parties, the two partners will solve these disputes or conflicts exclusively by [the] friendly exchange of views or if necessary by arbitration commissions.

ARTICLE 6. The present agreement is concluded for the duration of ten years with the stipulation that unless one of the contracting parties denounces it one year before its expiration, it will automatically be prolonged by five years.

ARTICLE 7. The present agreement shall be ratified in the shortest possible time. The instruments of ratification are to be exchanged in Berlin. The treaty comes into force immediately [after] it has been signed.

Done in two original documents in the German and Russian languages, respectively.

Moscow, August 23, 1939.

For the German Government
RIBBENTROP

As plenipotentiary of the Government of the Union of Socialist Soviet Republics

MOLOTOV

Source: Text of agreement in German Library of Information, *Documents on the Events Preceding the Outbreak of the War. Compiled and Published by the German Foreign Office* (New York: German Library of Information, 1940), 370–71.

BIBLIOGRAPHY

BOOKS AND ARTICLES

Accinelli, Robert D. "The Hoover Administration and the World Court," *Peace and Change* 4, no. 3 (1977): 28–36.

———. "The Roosevelt Administration and the World Court Defeat, 1935," *Historian* 40, no. 3 (1978): 463–78.

———. "Militant Internationalists: The League of Nations Association, the Peace Movement, and U.S. Foreign Policy, 1934–38," *Diplomatic History,* 4, no. 1 (1980): 19–38.

Adams, R. J. Q. *British Politics and Foreign Policy in the Age of Appeasement, 1935–39.* London: Macmillan, 1992.

Adler, Selig. *The Uncertain Giant, 1921–1941: American Foreign Policy between the Wars.* New York: Macmillan, 1965.

Agoncillo, Teodoro A., and Oscar M. Alfonso. *History of the Filipino People.* Quezon City: Malaya Books, 1967.

Aiken, Conrad. *Conrad Aiken.* Edited by Louis Untermeyer. New York: Simon & Schuster, 1927.

Aleiss, Angela. "The Vanishing American: Hollywood's Compromise to Indian Reform," *Journal of American Studies* (Great Britain), 25, no. 3 (1991): 467–72.

Allen, Frederick Lewis. *Only Yesterday: An Informal History of the Nineteen Twenties.* New York: Perennial, 1964.

Allen, James B. "The Great Protectionist, Sen. Reed Smoot of Utah," *Utah Historical Quarterly* 45, no. 4 (1977): 325–45.

Alsop, Joseph, Jr. *The 168 Days.* Garden City, New York: Doubleday & Co., 1937.

Alsop, Joseph, Jr., and Turner Catledge. "Joe Robinson, The New Deal's Old Reliable," *The Saturday Evening Post,* September 26, 1936, pp. 5–7, 66–74.

Altmeyer, Arthur Joseph. *The Formative Years of Social Security.* Madison: University of Wisconsin Press, 1968.

Amouzegar, P. "The Influence of Kemalism on Reza Shah's Reforms," *Journal of the Regional Cultural Institute* 7 (1974): 31–38.

Andrade, Ernest O., Jr. "The United States Navy and the Washington Conference," *Historian* 31, no. 3 (1969): 345–63.

Anger, Kenneth. *Hollywood Babylon.* San Francisco: Straight Arrow Books, 1975.

Aplin, Graeme, Stephen Glynn Foster, and Michael McKernan, eds. *Australians: A Historical Dictionary.* New South Wales: Fairfax, Syme & Weldon, 1987.

Asquith, Michael. *Famine Quaker Work in Russia, 1921–23.* London: Oxford University Press, 1943.

Aubert, Louis. *The Reconstruction of Europe: Its Economic and Political Conditions, Their Relative Importance.* New Haven, Conn.: Yale University Press, 1925.

Auld, George P. *The Dawes Plan and the New Economics.* London: Allen & Unwin, 1927.

Avrich, Paul. *Kronstadt 1921.* Princeton, N.J.: Princeton University Press, 1970.

Awalt, Francis G. "Recollections of the Banking Crisis of 1933," *Business History Review* 43 (Autumn 1969): 347–71.

Baer, George W. "Sanctions and Security: The League of Nations and the Italian-Ethiopian War, 1935–1936," *International Organization* 27, no. 2 (1973): 165–80.

———. *A Question of Trust: The Origins of U.S.–Soviet Diplomatic Relations: The Memoirs of Loy W. Henderson*. Stanford, Calif.: Hoover Institution Press, 1986.

Bailey, Thomas A. *Woodrow Wilson and the Great Betrayal*. New York: Macmillan, 1945.

Baker, Roscoe. *The American Legion and American Foreign Policy*. New York: Bookman Associates, 1954.

Bakshi, S. R. "The Dandi March of Gandhi," *The Modern Review* 134, no. 4 (April 1974): 249–58.

Ball, Stuart. *Baldwin and the Conservative Party: The Crisis of 1929–1931*. New Haven, Conn.: Yale University Press, 1988.

Barros, James. *Betrayal from Within: Joseph Avenol, Secretary-General of the League of Nations, 1933–1940*. New Haven, Conn.: Yale University Press, 1969.

———. *Office without Power: Secretary-General Sir Eric Drummond, 1919–1933*. London: Clarendon Press, 1979.

Barry, R. H., trans. *Hitler's "Mein Kampf": An Analysis*. London: Faber, 1970.

Beebe, William. *Half Mile Down, by William Beebe, director of the department of tropical research of the New York Zoological Society, with 123 illustrations and 8 colored plates. Published under the auspices of the New York Zoological Society*. New York: Harcourt, Brace & Company, 1934.

———. *The Book of Naturalists, An Anthology of the Best Natural History*. New York: Alfred A. Knopf, 1944.

Beede, Benjamin R. *The War of 1898 and U.S. Interventions, 1898–1934: An Encyclopedia*. New York: Garland, 1994.

Belknap, Michael, ed. *American Political Trials*. Westport, Conn.: Greenwood, 1981.

Bell, John D. *Peasants in Power: Alexander Stamboliski and the Bulgarian Agrarian National Union, 1899–1923*. Princeton, N.J.: Princeton University Press, 1977.

Ben-Ami, Shlomo. *The Origins of the Second Republic in Spain*. New York: Oxford University Press, 1978.

Benston, George J. *The Separation of Commercial and Investment Banking: The Glass-Steagall Act Revisited and Reconsidered*. Houndmills, Basingstoke, Hampshire: Macmillan in association with Dept. of Banking and Finance, City University Business School, London, 1990.

Bergamini, David. *Japan's Imperial Conspiracy*. New York: Pocket Books, 1972.

Berger, Samuel R. *Dollar Harvest: The Story of the Farm Bureau*. Lexington, Mass.: Heath Lexington Books, 1971.

Bergman, Karl. *The History of Reparations*. London: E. Benn, 1927.

Bernard, Philippe, and Henri Dubief. *The Decline of the Third Republic*. Cambridge: Cambridge University Press, 1985.

Bernard, William Spencer, ed. *Americanization Studies: The Acculturation of Immigrant Groups into American Society*. Montclair, N.J.: Patterson Smith, 1971.

Bernstein, Irving. *The Lean Years: A History of the American Worker, 1920–1933*. Boston: Houghton Mifflin, 1960.

Berra, Tim M. *William Beebe: An Annotated Bibliography*. Hamden, Conn.: Archon Books, 1977.

Biel, Steven. "Frederick Lewis Allen's Only Yesterday and the Idea of the Decade," *Journal of American Studies* (Great Britain) 25, no. 2 (1991): 259–66.

Birdsall, Paul. "The Second Decade of Peace Conference History," *Journal of Modern History* 11, no. 3 (1939): 362–78.

Birn, Donald S. *The League of Nations Union, 1918–1945*. Oxford: Clarendon Press, 1981.

Bisceglia, Louis. "The Politics of a Peace Prize," *Journal of Contemporary History* 7 (July–October 1972): 263–73.

Bishop, Donald G. *The Roosevelt-Litvinov Agreements: The American View*. Syracuse, N.Y.: Syracuse University Press, 1965.

Black, Jeremy. *European Warfare, 1660–1815*. New Haven: Yale University Press, 1994.

Bloom, Murray Teigh. "Is It Judge Crater's Body?" *Harper's,* November 1959, pp. 41–47.

Blum, Daniel C. *Great Stars of the American Stage.* New York: Greenberg, 1952.

Boorman, Howard L., ed. *Biographical Dictionary of Republican China.* 5 vols. New York: Columbia University Press, 1967.

Boothe, Leon E. "A Fettered Envoy: Lord Grey's Mission to the United States, 1919–1920," *Review of Politics* 33, no. 1 (1971): 78–94.

Bordman, Gerald Martin. *Jerome Kern: His Life and Music.* New York: Oxford University Press, 1980.

Borg, Dorothy. *The United States and the Far Eastern Crisis of 1933–1938: From the Manchurian Incident through the Initial Stage of the Undeclared Sino-Japanese War.* Cambridge: Harvard University Press, 1964.

Bosanyi, Gyorgy. *The Life of a Communist Revolutionary, Bela Kun.* Boulder, Colo.: Social Science Monographs, 1993.

Bowers, Robert E. "American Diplomacy, the 1933 Wheat Conference, and Recognition of the Soviet Union," *Agricultural History* 11, no. 1 (1966): 39–52.

———. Hull, Russian Subversion in Cuba, and Recognition of the USSR," *Journal of American History* 53, no. 3 (1966): 542–54.

Bowers, William L. *The Country Life Movement in America, 1900–1920.* Port Washington, N.Y.: Kennikat, 1974.

Boyle, Peter E. *American-Soviet Relations: From the Russian Revolution to the Fall of Communism.* London: Routledge, 1993.

Brandes, Joseph. *Herbert Hoover and Economic Diplomacy: Department of Commerce Policy, 1921–1928.* Pittsburgh: University of Pittsburgh Press, 1962.

Brazil, John R. "Murder Trials, Murder, and Twenties America," *American Quarterly* 33 (1981): 163–84.

Briley, Ronald F. "Smith W. Brookhart and Russia," *Annals of Iowa* 42, no. 7 (1975): 541–56.

Brosman, Catharine Savage, ed. *Dictionary of Twentieth Century Culture: French Culture, 1900–1975.* Detroit: Gale Research, 1975.

Browne, Frank C. *They Called Him Billy: A Biography of the Rt. Hon. W. M. Hughes.* Sydney, New South Wales: P. Huston, 1946.

Brownlow, Kevin, and John Kobal. *Hollywood: The Pioneers.* New York: Alfred A. Knopf, 1979.

Bryn-Jones, David. *Frank B. Kellogg: A Biography.* New York: G. P. Putnam's Sons, 1937.

Buckley, Thomas. *The United States and the Washington Conference, 1921–1922.* Knoxville: University of Tennessee Press, 1970.

Buell, Raymond L. *The Washington Conference.* New York: Appleton-Century Co., 1922.

Buhite, Russell D. *Nelson T. Johnson and American Policy Toward China, 1925–1941.* East Lansing: Michigan State University Press, 1968.

Buhle, Mari Jo, Paul Buhle, and Dan Georgakas, eds. *Encyclopedia of the American Left.* New York: Garland, 1990.

Burleigh, Michael, and Wolfgang Wipperman. *The Racial State: Germany 1933–1945.* New York: Cambridge University Press, 1991.

Burns, James MacGregor. *Roosevelt: The Lion and the Fox.* New York: Harcourt, Brace, 1956.

Burns, Richard Dean, and W. Adams Dixon. "Foreign Policy and the 'Democratic Myth': The Debate on the Ludlow Amendment," *Mid-America* 47, no. 4 (1965): 288–306.

Butler, Nicholas Murray. *Across the Busy Years: Recollections and Reflections.* New York: Charles Scribner's Sons; two volumes, 1939.

Byrne, Gary C. *The Great American Convention: A Political History of Presidential Elections.* Palo Alto, Calif.: Pacific Books, 1976.

Campbell, Christiana McFadyen. *The Farm Bureau and the New Deal: A Study in the Making of National Farm Policy, 1933–1940.* Urbana: University of Illinois Press, 1962.

Campbell, James E. *The Presidential Pulse of Congressional Elections.* Lexington: University Press of Kentucky, 1993.

Campbell, John, and Philip Sherrard. *Modern Greece.* London: Ernest Benn, 1968.

Canada, The Founders and the Guardians: Fathers of Confederation, Governors General, Prime Ministers—A

Collection of Biographical Sketches and Portraits. Ottawa: The Queen's Printer, 1968.

Cannistraro, Philip V., Edward D. Wynot, Sr., and Theodore P. Kovaleff, eds. *Poland and the Coming of the Second World War: The Diplomatic Papers of A. J. Drexel Biddle, Jr., United States Ambassador to Poland, 1937–1939.* Columbus: Ohio State University Press, 1976.

Carlisle, Rodney. "The Foreign Policy Views of an Isolationist Press Lord: W. R. Hearst and the International Crisis, 1936–41," *Journal of Contemporary History* 9, no. 3 (1974), 217–27.

Carlton, David. "Disarmament with Guarantees: Lord Cecil, 1922–1927," *Disarmament and Arms Control* 3, no. 2 (1965): 143–64.

———. "Great Britain and the Coolidge Naval Disarmament Conference of 1927," *Political Science Quarterly* 83, no. 4 (1968): 573–98.

———. *MacDonald vs. Henderson: The Foreign Policy of the Second Labour Government.* London: Macmillan, 1970; reprint, New York: Humanities Press, 1970.

Carr, Edward Hallett. *The Twenty Years' Crisis, 1919–1939.* London: Macmillan, 1951.

Carr, Raymond. *Spain: 1808–1975.* Oxford: Oxford University Press, 1982.

Carroll, John M. "Henry Cabot Lodge's Contributions to the Shaping of Republican European Diplomacy, 1920–1924," *Capitol Studies* 3, no. 1 (1975): 153–65.

Carroll, Thomas F. "Freedom of Speech and of the Press in War Time: The Espionage Act," *Michigan Law Review* 17 (June 1919): 621–65.

Carruth, Gordon. *What Happened When.* New York: Signet, 1989.

Cebula, James E. *James M. Cox: Journalist and Politician.* New York: Garland, 1985.

Chadwick, O. *Britain and the Vatican during the Second World War.* Cambridge: Cambridge University Press, 1987.

Chase, Harold W., and Craig R. Ducat. *Constitutional Interpretation: Cases–Essays–Materials.* St. Paul, Minn.: West Publishing Co., 1979.

Chatfield, Charles. *For Peace and Justice: Pacifism in America, 1914–1941.* Knoxville: University of Tennessee Press, 1971.

Clayton, Anthony. *The British Empire as a Superpower, 1919–1939.* Athens: University of Georgia Press, 1986.

Clepper, Henry, ed. *Leaders of American Conservation.* New York: Ronald Press Co., 1971.

Clissold, Stephen, ed. *A Short History of Yugoslavia.* Cambridge: Cambridge University Press, 1966.

Coben, Stanley. *A. Mitchell Palmer: Politician.* New York: Columbia University Press, 1963; reprint, New York: Da Capo Press, 1971.

———. "Ordinary White Protestants: The KKK of the 1920s," *Journal of Social History* 28, no. 1 (Fall 1994): 155–65.

Cockett, Richard. *Twilight of Truth: Chamberlain, Appeasement, and the Manipulation of the Press.* London: Weidenfeld & Nicolson, 1989.

Cole, Wayne S. "Senator Key Pittman and American Neutrality Policies, 1933–1940," *Mississippi Valley Historical Review* 46, no. 4 (March 1960): 644–62.

———. *Senator Gerald P. Nye and American Foreign Relations* Minneapolis: University of Minnesota Press, 1962.

———. *Roosevelt and the Isolationists, 1932–45.* Lincoln: University of Nebraska Press, 1983.

Coletta, Paolo E. "Bryan Briefs Lansing," *Pacific Historical Review* 27, no. 4 (1958): 383–96.

Collins, Bud, and Zander Hollander, eds. *Bud Collins' Modern Encyclopedia of Tennis.* Garden City, N.Y.: Doubleday & Co., 1980.

Colton, Joel G. *Leon Blum: Humanist in Politics.* New York: Knopf, 1966.

Commager, Henry Steele, ed. *Documents of American History.* New York: Appleton-Century-Crofts, 1949.

Commire, Anne, ed. *Historic World Leaders.* Detroit: Gale Research; five volumes, 1994.

Congressional Quarterly. *Congressional Quarterly's Guide to Congress.* Washington, D.C.: Congressional Quarterly, 1991.

———. *Congress A to Z.* Washington, D.C.: Congressional Quarterly, 1993.

———. *Congressional Quarterly's Guide to U.S. Elections.* Washington, D.C.: Congressional Quarterly, 1994.

Conquest, Robert. *The Harvest of Sorrow: Soviet Collectivization and the Terror-Famine.* New York: Oxford University Press, 1986.

Cook, Fred J. *Mob Inc.* New York: Watts, 1977.

Coolidge, Calvin. *The Autobiography of Calvin Coolidge.* Rutland, Vt.: Academy Books, 1984.

Cornebise, Alfred E. *The Weimar in Crisis: Cuno's Germany and the Ruhr Occupation.* Washington: University Press of America, 1977.

Costigiola, Frank C. *The Other Side of Isolationism: The Establishment of the First World Bank, 1929–1930, Journal of American History* 59, no. 3 (1972): 602–20.

Costin, Lela B. *Two Sisters for Social Justice: A Biography of Grace and Edith Abbott.* Urbana: University of Illinois Press, 1983.

Coury, Ralph M. "The Politics of the Funereal: The Tomb of Saad Zaghlul," *Journal of the American Research Center in Egypt* (New York) 29 (1992): 191–200.

Cox, James M. *Journey through My Years.* New York: Simon & Schuster, 1946.

Craig, Gordon. *Europe since 1815.* New York: Holt, Rinehart & Winston, 1971.

Craig, Gordon A., and Felix Gilbert, eds. *The Diplomats, 1919–1939.* Princeton, N.J.: Princeton University Press, 1994.

Cramer, Clarence H. *Newton D. Baker: A Biography.* Cleveland: World Publishing Co., 1961.

Crew, Spencer R. *Field to Factory: Afro-American Migration, 1915–1940.* Washington, D.C.: Smithsonian Institution Press, 1987.

Dallek, Robert. "Beyond Tradition: The Diplomatic Careers of William E. Dodd and George S. Messersmith, 1933–1938," *South Atlantic Quarterly* 66, no. 2 (1967), 233–44.

———. *Democrat and Diplomat: The Life of William E. Dodd.* New York: Oxford University Press, 1968.

Danelski, David J., and Joseph S. Tulchin, eds. *The Autobiographical Notes of Charles Evans Hughes.* Cambridge: Harvard University Press, 1973.

Darling, H. Maurice. "Who Kept the United States Out of the League of Nations?" *Canadian Historical Review* 10 (1929): 196–211.

Davidson, John W. "Brand Whitlock and the Diplomacy of Belgian Relief," *Prologue* 2, no. 3 (1970): 145–60.

Davis, Calvin D. *The United States and the Second Hague Peace Conference.* Durham, N.C.: Duke University Press, 1975.

Dawes, Charles Gates. *A Journal of Reparations.* New York: Macmillan, 1939.

———. *Journal as Ambassador to Great Britain.* Westport, Conn.: Greenwood, 1970.

Dawidowicz, Lucy S. *The War against the Jews, 1933–1945.* New York: Bantam, 1975.

DeBenedetti, Charles. "James T. Shotwell and the Science of International Politics," *Political Science Quarterly* 89, no. 2 (1974): 379–95.

———. "The $100,000 American Peace Award of 1924," *Pennsylvania Magazine of History* 98, no. 2 (1974), 224–49.

———. "The First Détente: America and Locarno," *South Atlantic Quarterly* 75, no. 4 (1976): 407–23.

Debicki, Roman. *Foreign Policy of Poland, 1919–39: From the Rebirth of the Polish Republic to World War II.* New York: Praeger, 1962.

DeConde, Alexander, ed. *Isolation and Security: Ideas and Interests in Twentieth-Century American Foreign Policy.* Durham, North Carolina: Duke University Press, 1957.

De Jonge, Alex. *Weimar Chronicles.* New York: Paddington, 1978.

De Kock, W. J., ed. in chief. *Dictionary of South African Biography.* 3 vols. Pretoria: Nasionale Boekhandel BPK, 1968–77.

Dennis, William Jefferson. *Tacna and Arica: An Account of the Chile-Peru Boundary Dispute and of the Arbitrations by the United States.* Hamden, Conn.: Archon Books, 1967.

———. *Documentary History of the Tacna-Arica Dispute.* Port Washington, N.Y.: Kennikat, 1971.

Detzer, Dorothy. *Appointment on the Hill.* New York: Holt, 1948.

DeWitt, Howard A. "Hiram Johnson and Early New Deal Diplomacy, 1933–1934," *California Historical Quarterly* 53, no. 4 (1974): 377–86.

———. "The 'New' Harding and American Foreign Policy: Warren G. Harding, Hiram W. Johnson, and Pragmatic Diplomacy," *Ohio History* 86, no. 2 (1977): 96–114.

Diefendorf, Elizabeth, ed. *The New York Public Library's Books of the Century.* New York: Oxford University Press, 1996.

DiMento, Joseph F. "Mining the Archives of 'Pennsylvania Coal': Heaps of Constitutional Mischief," *Journal of Legal History* (Great Britain) 11, no. 3 (1991): 396–436.

Diner, Steven. "Scholarship in the Quest for Social Welfare: A Fifty-Year History of the Social Service Review," *Social Service Review* 51, no. 1 (March 1977): 1–66.

Dingman, Roger. *Power in the Pacific: The Origins of Naval Arms Limitation, 1914–1922.* Chicago: University of Chicago Press, 1976.

Divine, Robert A. "Franklin D. Roosevelt and Collective Security, 1933," *Mississippi Valley Historical Review* 48, no. 1 (1961): 42–59.

Documents on Germany: Foreign Policy 1918–1945. Washington, D.C.: United States Government Printing Office, 1949.

Doleschal, Eugene, Anne Newton, and William Hickey. *A Guide to the Literature on Organized Crime: An Annotated Bibliography Covering the Years 1967–81.* Hackensack, N.J.: National Council on Crime and Delinquency, 1981.

Dollar, Charles M. "The South and the Fordney-McCumber Tariff of 1922: A Study in Regional Politics," *Journal of Southern History* 39, no. 1 (1973): 45–67.

Donnelly, J. B. "Prentiss Gilbert's Mission to the League of Nations Council, October 1931," *Diplomatic History* 4, no. 2 (1978): 373–87.

Douglas, James. *Parliaments across Frontiers: A Short History of the Interparliamentary Union.* London: Her Majesty's Stationery Office, 1976.

Doyle, Billy H. *The Ultimate Directory of Silent Screen Performers: A Necrology of Births and Deaths and Essays on 50 Lost Players.* Lanham, Md.: Scarecrow, 1995.

Drennan, James. *B.U.F.: Oswald Mosley and British Fascism.* London: J. Murray, 1934.

Dubay, Robert W. "The Geneva Naval Conference of 1927: A Study in Battleship Diplomacy," *Southern Quarterly* 8, no. 2 (1970): 177–99.

Dunning, John. *Tune in Yesterday: The Ultimate Encyclopedia of Old-Time Radio, 1926–1976.* Englewood Cliffs, N.J.: Prentice-Hall, 1976.

Eisner, Lotte H. *Haunted Screen.* Los Angeles: University of California Press, 1969.

Ellis, Edward Robb. *A Nation's Torment: The Great American Depression, 1929–1939.* New York: Kodansha International, 1995.

Ellis, Lewis Ethan. *Frank B. Kellogg and American Foreign Relations, 1925–1929.* New Brunswick, N.J.: Rutgers University Press, 1961.

———. *Republican Foreign Policy, 1921–1933.* New Brunswick, N.J.: Rutgers University Press, 1968.

Elson, Robert T. *Time Inc.: The Intimate History of a Publishing Enterprise, 1923–1941.* New York: Atheneum, 1968.

Elwell, Walter A., ed. *Evangelical Dictionary of Theology.* Grand Rapids, Mich.: Baker Book House, 1987.

Englefield, Dermot, Janet Seaton, and Isobel White. *Facts about the British Prime Ministers: A Compilation of Biographical and Historical Information.* New York: H. W. Wilson Co., 1995.

Englemann, Bernt. *In Hitler's Germany: Everyday Life in the Third Reich.* Translated by Krishna Winston. New York: Schocken Books, 1986.

Enssle, Manfred J. "Stresemann's Diplomacy Fifty Years after Locarno: Some Recent Perspectives," *Historical Journal* 20, no. 4 (1977): 937–48.

Esposito, John L., ed. in chief. *The Oxford Encyclopedia of the Modern Islamic World.* 5 vols. New York: Oxford University Press, 1995.

Ewing, Cortez Arthur Milton. *Congressional Elections, 1896–1944: The Sectional Basis of Political Democracy in the House of Representatives.* Norman: University of Oklahoma Press, 1947.

Eyck, Erich. *Geschichte der Weimarer Republik* (A history of the Weimar Republic). 2 vols. Zurich: Eugen Rensch,

1954–62; English edition: Cambridge: Harvard University Press, 1962–63.

Farnsworth, Beatrice. *William C. Bullitt and the Soviet Union.* Bloomington: Indiana University Press, 1967.

Farrell, John C. *Beloved Lady: A History of Jane Addams' Ideas on Reform and Peace.* Baltimore: Johns Hopkins University Press, 1967.

Fausold, Martin L., and George T. Mazuzan, eds. *The Hoover Presidency: A Reappraisal.* Albany: State University Press of New York, 1974.

Feigl, Erich. *A Myth of Terror—Armenian Extremism: Its Causes and Its Historical Context.* Freilassing-Salzburg, Austria: Edition Zeitgeschichte, 1986.

Feis, Herbert. *The Road to Pearl Harbor.* Princeton, N.J.: Princeton University Press, 1950.

Ferrell, Robert H. *Peace in Their Time: The Origins of the Kellogg-Briand Pact.* New Haven, Conn.: Yale University Press, 1952.

———. *Woodrow Wilson and World War I, 1917–1921.* Bloomington: Indiana University Press, 1985.

———. *The Strange Deaths of President Harding.* Columbia: University of Missouri Press, 1996.

Filler, Louis. *A Dictionary of American Conservatism.* Secaucus, N.J.: Citadel, 1988.

Firda, Richard Arthur. *All Quiet on the Western Front: Literary Analysis and Cultural Context.* New York: Twayne, 1993.

Fishel, Leslie H., Jr., and Benjamin Quarles, eds. *The Black American: A Brief Documentary History.* Glenview, Ill.: Scott, Foresman & Company, 1970.

Fisher, Harold H. *The Famine in Soviet Rusia, 1919–1923: The Operations of the American Relief Administration.* New York: Macmillan, 1927.

Fleming, Denna Frank. *The United States and the World Court.* New York: Doubleday, Doran & Company, Inc., 1945.

Ford, Franklin L. *Political Murder: From Tyrannicide to Terrorism.* Cambridge: Harvard University Press, 1985.

Fosdick, Raymond B. *Letters on the League of Nations: From the Files of Raymond B. Fosdick.* Princeton, N.J.: Princeton University Press, 1966.

Fowler, Doreen, and Ann J. Abadie, eds. *Faulkner and Popular Culture.* Jackson: University Press of Mississippi, 1990.

Fox, John P. *Germany and the Far Eastern Crisis: A Study in Diplomacy and Ideology.* Oxford, England: Oxford University Press, 1985.

Fox, Stephen R. *Blood and Power: Organized Crime in Twentieth-Century America.* New York: William Morrow, 1989.

Fred, Singleton. *A Short History of the Yugoslav Peoples.* Cambridge: Cambridge University Press, 1985.

Freedland, Michael. *Jerome Kern.* New York: Stein & Day, 1981.

Freund, Ernst. "The Debs Case and Freedom of Speech," *The New Republic,* May 3, 1919, p. 13.

Friedman, Leon. *The Law of War: A Documentary History.* 2 vols. New York: Random House, 1972.

Gardner, Warner W. "Court Packing: The Drafting Recalled," *Journal of Supreme Court History* 1990 (1990): 99–103.

Garraty, John A. *Henry Cabot Lodge: A Biography.* New York: Alfred A. Knopf, 1953.

Gelernter, David. *1939: The Lost World of the Fair.* New York: Free Press, 1995.

Gelfand, Lawrence E. *The Inquiry: American Preparations for Peace, 1917–1919.* New Haven, Conn.: Yale University Press, 1963.

Genizi, Haim. "James G. McDonald: High Commissioner for Refugees, 1933–1935," *Wiener Library Bulletin* (Great Britain) 30, no. 43 (1977): 40–52.

Getzler, Israel. *Kronstadt 1917–1921.* Cambridge: Cambridge University Press, 1983.

Gibbs, Norman. "The Naval Conferences of the Interwar Years: A Study in Anglo-American Relations," *Naval War College Review* 30, no. 1 (1977): 50–63.

Girard, Jolyon P. "Congress and Presidential Military Policy: The Occupation of Germany, 1919–1923," *Mid-America* 56, no. 4 (1974): 211–20.

———. "American Diplomacy and the Ruhr Crisis of 1920," *Military Affairs* 39, no. 2 (1975), 59–61.

Gitelman, H. M. "Welfare Capitalism Reconsidered," *Labor History* 33, no. 1 (1992): 5–31.

Glad, Betty. *Charles Evans Hughes and the Illusions of Innocence: A Study in American Diplomacy* Urbana: University of Illinois Press, 1966.

Goldstein, Erik, and John Maurer, eds. *The Washington Conference, 1921–22: Naval Rivalry, East Asian Stability and the Road to Pearl Harbor* Essex, England: Frank Cass, 1994.

Gómez Robledo, Antonio. *The Bucareli Agreements and International Law.* Translated by Salmón de la Selva. Mexico City: National University of Mexico Press, 1940.

Gompers, Samuel, and William English Walling. *Out of Their Own Mouths: A Revolution and an Indictment of Sovietism.* New York: E. P. Dutton, 1921.

Gopinath, Aruna. *Manuel L. Quezon: The Tutelary Democrat.* Quezon City: New Day Publishers, 1987.

Gordon, Gilbert Andrew Hugh. *British Seapower and Procurement between the Wars: A Reappraisal of Rearmament.* Annapolis, Md.: Naval Institute Press, 1988.

Gorodetsky, Gabriel. *The Other "Zinoviev Letters": New Light on the Mismanagement of the Affair.* Tel Aviv: The Russian and East European Research Center of Tel Aviv University, 1976.

Gottlieb, Moshe. "The Berlin Riots of 1935 and Their Repercussions in America," *American Jewish Historical Quarterly* 59, no. 3 (1970): 302–31.

Gould, Stephen Jay. "Carrie Buck's Daughter," *Natural History* 93, 14–18.

Graebner, Norman A., ed. *An Uncertain Tradition: American Secretaries of State in the Twentieth Century.* New York: McGraw-Hill, 1961.

Graham, Otis L., Jr., and Meghan Robinson Wander, eds. *Franklin D. Roosevelt: His Life and Times: An Encyclopedic View.* Boston: G. K. Hall, 1985.

Graham, Roger. *Arthur Meighen: A Biography.* Toronto: Clarke, Irwin, 1960.

Graham, Stephen. *Alexander of Yugoslavia: The Story of the King Who Was Murdered at Marseilles.* New Haven, Conn.: Yale University Press, 1939.

Gray, Peter. *Weimar Culture.* New York: Harper & Row, 1968.

Greenbaum, Fred. "Hiram Johnson and the New Deal," *Pacific Historian* 18, no. 3 (1974): 20–35.

Gregory, Paul R., and Robert C. Stuart. *Soviet Economic Structure and Performance.* HarperCollins, 1990.

Griffin, Walter R. "Louis Ludlow and the War Referendum Crusade, 1935–1941," *Indiana Magazine of History* 64, no. 4 (1968): 267–88.

Grossman, Mark. *The ABC-Clio Companion to the Civil Rights Movement.* Santa Barbara, Calif.: ABC-Clio, 1993.

———. *The ABC-Clio Companion to the Environmental Movement.* Santa Barbara, Calif.: ABC-Clio, 1994.

Groueff, Stephanie. *Crown of Thorns: The Reign of King Boris III of Bulgaria, 1918–1943.* Lanham, Md.: Madison Books, 1987.

Gulick, Charles. *Austria from Hapsburg to Hitler.* Berkeley: University of California Press, 1948.

Gutman, Israel, ed. in chief. *Encyclopedia of the Holocaust.* 4 vols. New York: Macmillan, 1990.

Gweckoh, Sol H. *The Autobiography of Manuel L. Quezon.* Manila: Art Printing and Publishing Co., 1940.

Hall, Christopher David. *Britain, America and Arms Control, 1921–37.* New York: St. Martin's, 1987.

Hankey, Maurice P. *The Supreme Control at the Paris Peace Conference 1919: A Commentary.* London: Allen & Unwin, 1963.

Hanssen, Helmer Julius. *Voyages of a Modern Viking.* London: G. Routledge & Sons, 1936.

Hardman, Frederick. *The Spanish Campaign in Morocco.* Edinburgh and London: William Blackwood & Sons, 1860.

Harrigan, W. M. "Nazi Germany and the Holy See," *Catholic Historical Review* 47 (1961–62): 164–98.

Hartmann, Edward George. *The Movement to Americanize the Immigrant.* New York: Columbia University Press, 1948.

Havel, James T. *U.S. Presidential Candidates and the Elections: A Biographical and Historical Guide.* 2 vols. New York: Macmillan, 1996.

Hawley, Ellis W. "Herbert Hoover, the Commerce Secretariat, and the Vision of an 'Associative State,'" *Journal of American History* 61 (June 1974): 116–40.

Heinrichs, Waldo H., Jr. *American Ambassador: Joseph C. Grew and the Development of the United States Diplomatic Tradition*. Boston: Little, Brown, 1966.

Heller, Hermann. *Parliament or Dictatorship?: Essays on Fascism in Europe, 1928–1933*. London: Berg, 1992.

Hendrick, Burton J. "Governor Hughes" *McClure's Magazine* 30, no. 5 (March 1908): 520–36.

Herman, Sondra L. *Eleven against War: Studies in American Internationalist Thought, 1898–1921*. Stanford: Calif.: Hoover Institution Press, 1969.

Hickey, D. J., and J. E. Doherty. *A Dictionary of Irish History since 1800*. Dublin: Gill & Macmillan, 1980.

Higham, Robin, ed. *A Guide to the Sources of United States Military History*. Hamden, Conn.: Shoe String, 1975.

Hilberg, Raul. *The Destruction of the European Jews*. New York: Holmes & Meier Publishers, 1985.

Hine, Darlene Clark, ed. *Black Women in America: An Historical Encyclopedia*. 2 vols. Brooklyn, N.Y.: Carlson Publishing, 1993.

Hitchens, Keith. *Rumania: 1866–1947*. Oxford: Clarendon, 1994.

Hitler, Adolf, *Germany's Foreign Policy as Stated in "Mein Kampf."* London: Friends of Europe, 1936?.

Hofstadter, Richard, *The Progressive Historians: Turner, Beard, Parrington*. New York: Knopf, 1968.

———. *Great Issues in American History*. New York: Vintage Books, 1982.

Holli, Melvin G., and Peter d'Alroy Jones, eds. *Biographical Dictionary of American Mayors, 1820–1980: Big City Mayors*. Westport, Conn.: Greenwood, 1981.

Holmes, James Derek. *The Papacy in the Modern World, 1914–1978*. New York: Crossroad, 1981.

Hopkins, George W. "The Politics of Food: United States and Soviet Hungary, March–August, 1919," *Mid-America* 55, no. 4 (1973), 245–70.

Howorth, Muriel. *Pioneer Research on the Atom: Rutherford and Soddy in a Glorious Chapter of Science—The Life of Frederick Soddy*. London: New World Publications, 1958.

Hudson, M. E., and Mary Clark. *Crown of a Thousand Years: A Millennium of British History Presented as a Pageant of Kings and Queens*. New York: Crown Publishers, 1978.

Hudson, Manley O. *The World Court 1921–1938*. Boston: World Peace Foundation, 1938.

International Bibliography of Biography, 1970 to 1987. 10 vols. London: K. G. Saur, 1988.

Jablon, Howard. "The State Department and Collective Security," *Historian* 33, no. 2 (1971), 248–63.

———. "Cordell Hull, His 'Associates,' and Relations With Japan, 1933–1936," *Mid-America* 56, no. 3 (1974), 160–74.

Jablonsky, David. *The Nazi Party in Dissolution: Hitler and the Verbotzeit, 1923–1925*. London: Frank Cass, 1989.

Jackson, George, ed. in chief. *Dictionary of the Russian Revolution*. Westport, Conn.: Greenwood, 1989.

Jacobson, Jon. *Locarno Diplomacy: Germany and the West, 1925–1929*. Princeton, N.J.: Princeton University Press, 1972.

Jessup, Philip C. "The Saavedra Lamas Anti-War Draft Treaty," *American Journal of International Law* 27 (January 1933): 109–14.

Johnpoll, Bernard K. *Pacifist's Progress: Norman Thomas and the Decline of American Socialism*. Chicago: Quadrangle, 1970.

Johnson, Allen, and Dumas Malone et al., eds. *Dictionary of American Biography*. 10 vols., 10 supps. New York: Charles Scribner's Sons, 1930–95.

Johnson, James Weldon. *Along This Way*. New York: Viking, 1967.

Jones, Richard S. *A History of the American Legion*. Indianapolis: Bobbs-Merrill Co., 1947.

Josephson, Harold. *James T. Shotwell and the Rise of Internationalism in America*. Rutherford, N.J.: Fairleigh Dickinson University Press, 1975.

———. "The Dynamics of Repression: New York during the Red Scare," *Mid-America: An Historical Review* 59, no. 3 (October 1977): 131–46.

———. "Outlawing War: Internationalism and the Pact of Paris," *Diplomatic History* 3, no. 4 (1979), 377–90.

———. ed. in chief, *Biographical Dictionary of Modern Peace Leaders*. Westport, Conn.: Greenwood, 1985.

Joyce, James Avery. *Broken Star: The Story of the League of Nations (1919–1939)*. Swansea, Wales: Christopher Davies, 1978.

Joyner, Conrad. *Holman versus Hughes: Extension of Australian Commonwealth Powers*. Gainesville: University of Florida Press, 1961.

Kaes, Anton, ed. *Weimar Republic Sourcebook*. Berkeley: University of California Press, 1994.

Kahn, Gilbert N. "Presidential Passivity on a Nonsalient Issue: President Franklin D. Roosevelt and the 1935 World Court Fight," *Diplomatic History* 4, no. 2 (1980): 137–60.

Kajima, Morinosuke. *Teikoku gaiko no kihon seisaku* (The emergence of Japan as a world power, 1895–1925). Rutland, Vt.: C. E. Tuttle, 1968.

Katz, Ephraim. *The Film Encyclopedia*. New York: HarperPerennial, 1994.

Keith, Arthur Berriedale. *The Sovereignty of the British Dominions*. London: Macmillan, 1929.

Kellogg, Frank B. "The War Prevention Policy of the United States," *American Journal of International Law* 22 (1928): 253–61.

Kenez, Peter. *The Birth of the Propaganda State: Soviet Methods of Mass Mobilization, 1917–1929*. New York: Cambridge University Press, 1985.

Kennan, George F. "Russia and the Versailles Conference," *American Scholar,* 30, no. 1 (1960/1961), 13–42.

Kennon, Donald R., and Rebecca M. Rogers. *The United States House of Representatives Committee on Ways and Means: A Bicentennial History, 1789–1989*. House Document 100–244, 1990.

King, Joan Wucher. *Historical Dictionary of Egypt*. Metuchen, N.J.: Scarecrow, 1984.

Kitchen, Martin. *The Coming of Austrian Fascism*. London: Croom Helm, 1980.

Klehr, Harvey, John Earl Haynes, and Fridrikh Igorevich Firsov. *The Secret World of American Communism*. New Haven, Conn.: Yale University Press, 1995.

Kneeshaw, Stephen J. "The Kellogg-Briand Pact and American Recognition of the Soviet Union," *Mid-America* 56, no. 1 (1974): 16–31.

Knott, Richard C. *A Heritage of Wings: An Illustrated History of Naval Aviation*. Annapolis, Md.: Naval Institute Press, 1997.

Kohn, George C. *Dictionary of Wars*. New York: Facts On File, 1986.

Kracauer, Siegfried. *Caligari to Hitler*. Princeton, N.J.: Princeton University Press, 1966.

Kreuger, Miles. *Show Boat: The Story of a Classic American Musical*. New York: Oxford University Press, 1977.

Krzyzanowski, Jerzy K. *Wladyslaw Stanislaw Reymont*. New York: Twayne, 1972.

Kuehl, Warren F., ed. *Biographical Dictionary of Internationalists*. Westport, Conn.: Greenwood, 1983.

Kunitz, Stanley J., and Howard Haycraft, eds. *Twentieth Century Authors: A Biographical Dictionary of Modern Literature*. New York: H. W. Wilson Co., 1942.

Kusmer, Kenneth L., gen. ed. *Black Communities and Urban Development in America, 1720–1990*. New York: Garland; four volumes, 1990.

Kutulas, Judy. "Becoming 'More Liberal': The League of American Writers, the Communist Party, and the Literary People's Front," *Journal of American Culture* 13, no. 1 (1990), 71–80.

La Follette, Belle C., and Fola La Follette. *Robert M. La Follette, June 4, 1855–June 18, 1925*. New York: Macmillan; two volumes, 1953.

Lamb, Richard. *The Drift to War, 1922–1939*. New York: St. Martin's, 1989.

Langer, William L., and S. Everett Gleason. *Challenge to Isolation*. 2 vols. New York: Harper & Brothers, 1952.

Lansing, Robert. *The Big Four and Others of the Peace Conference*. Boston: Houghton Mifflin, 1921.

———. *The Peace Negotiations, a Personal Narrative*. Boston: Houghton Mifflin, 1921.

Lapp, John Augustus. *The First Chapter of the New Deal*. Chicago, J. A. Prescott & Son, 1933.

Latham, John Grieg. *Australia and the British Commonwealth*. London: Macmillan, 1929.

Laybourn, Keith. *A History of British Trade Unionism, c. 1770–1990*. Stroud, Gloucestershire, England: A. Sutton, 1992.

———. *The General Strike of 1926.* Manchester, England: Manchester University Press, 1993.

———. *The General Strike Day by Day.* Stroud, Gloucestershire, England: A. Sutton, 1996.

The League of Nations in Retrospect: Proceedings of the Symposium Organized by the United Nations Library and the Graduate Institute of International Studies, Geneva, 6–9 November 1980 [with both English and French text]. Berlin: Walter de Gruyter, 1983.

Lederer, Ivo J. *Yugoslavia at the Paris Peace Conference: A Study in Frontier Making.* New Haven, Conn.: Yale University Press, 1963.

Leibman, Roy. *Silent Film Performers: An Annotated Bibliography of Published, Unpublished and Archival Sources for Over 350 Actors and Actresses.* Jefferson, N.C.: McFarland & Co., 1996.

Leff, Leonard J. *The Dame in the Kimono: Hollywood, Censorship, and the Production Code from the 1920s to the 1960s.* New York: Grove Weidenfeld, 1990.

Leffler, Melvyn P. *The Elusive Quest: America's Pursuit of European Stability and French Security, 1919–1933.* Chapel Hill: University of North Carolina Press, 1979.

Lentz, Harry M. III *Assassinations and Executions: An Encyclopedia of Political Violence, 1865–1986.* Jefferson, N.C.: McFarland & Co., 1988.

Lerski, George J. *Historical Dictionary of Poland, 966–1945.* Westport, Conn.: Greenwood, 1996.

Leuchtenberg, William E. *Franklin D. Roosevelt and the New Deal, 1932–1940.* New York: Harper & Row, 1963.

Levine, Erwin L. *Theodore Francis Green: The Washington Years, 1937–1960.* Providence, R.I.: Brown University Press, 1971.

———. *Theodore Francis Green: The Rhode Island Years, 1906–1936.* Providence, R.I.: Brown University Press, 1963.

Levy, Leonard W., ed. in chief. *Encyclopedia of the American Constitution.* 4 vols; 1 supp. New York: Macmillan Publishing Company; 1986–92.

Lewis, Bernard. *The Emergence of Modern Turkey.* London: Oxford University Press, 1968.

Lewis, Beth Irwin. *George Grosz: Art and Politics in the Weimar Republic.* Princeton, N.J.: Princeton University Press, 1991.

Lewis, Chester, Stephen Fay, and Hugo Young. *The Zinoviev Letter.* London: Heinemann, 1967.

Lewis, David Stephen. *Illusions of Grandeur: Mosley, Fascism, and British Society, 1931–81.* Manchester; Wolfeboro, N.H.: Manchester University Press, 1987.

Libby, James K. "Liberal Journals and the Moscow Trials of 1936–38," *Journalism Quarterly* 52, no. 1 (1975): 85–92.

Libby, Justin H. "The Irreconcilable Conflict: Key Pittman and Japan during the Interwar Years," *Nevada Historical Society Quarterly* 18, no. 3 (1975), 128–39.

Linn, James Weber. *Jane Addams: A Biography.* New York and London: Appleton-Century Co., 1935.

Lippy, Charles H., ed. *Twentieth-Century Shapers of American Popular Religion.* New York: Greenwood, 1989.

Little, Douglas. "AntiBolshevism and American Foreign Policy, 1919–1939: The Diplomacy of Self-Delusion," *American Quarterly* 35 (1983): 376–90.

Lodge, Henry Cabot. *The Senate and the League of Nations.* New York: Charles Scribner's Sons, 1925.

Logan, Rayford W., and Michael R. Winston, eds. *Dictionary of American Negro Biography.* New York: W. W. Norton & Company, 1982.

Lora, Ronald. *Conservative Minds in America.* Chicago: Rand McNally, 1971.

Lorentz, John Henry. *Historical Dictionary of Iran.* Lanham, Md.: Scarecrow, 1995.

Lower, Richard C. "Hiram Johnson: The Making of an Irreconcilable," *Pacific Historical Review* 41, no. 4 (1972), 505–26.

Lowitt, Richard. *Bronson M. Cutting: Progressive Politician.* Albuquerque: University of New Mexico Press, 1992.

Macartney, Carlile A. *October Fifteenth: A History of Modern Hungary.* 2 vols. Edinburgh: University of Edinburgh Press, 1956.

MacArthur, Brian. *The Penguin Book of 20th Century Speeches.* New York: Penguin, 1992.

MacCallum, Thomas Watson, and Stephen Taylor, eds. *The Nobel Prize-Winners and the Nobel Foundation, 1901–1937.* Zurich: Central European Times Publishing, 1938.

MacCarthy, Esther. "Catholic Women and the War: The National Council of Catholic Women, 1919–1946," *Peace and Change* 5, no. 1 (1978): 23–32.

Maddox, Robert J. *William E. Borah and American Foreign Policy.* Baton Rouge: Louisiana State University Press, 1969.

Magill, Frank. ed. *Great Lives from History. American Women Series.* 5 vols. Pasadena, Calif.: Salem, 1985.

———, ed. *Great Lives from History: American Series.* 5 vols. Pasadena, Calif.: Salem, 1987.

Maltin, Leonard, ed. *Movie and Video Guide, 1996 Edition.* New York: Plume, 1995.

Mansoor, Menahem. *Political and Diplomatic History of the Arab World, 1900–1967: A Chronological Study.* 16 vols. Englewood, Colo.: Information Handling Services, 1972–77.

Manvell, Roger, and Heinrich Frankell. *German Cinema.* New York: Praeger, 1971.

Marburg, Theodore (John H. Latane, ed.), *Development of the League of Nations Idea: Documents and Correspondence of Theodore Marburg.* 2 vols. New York: Macmillan, 1932.

Marcus, Harold G. *Haile Selassie I: The Formative Years, 1892–1936.* Los Angeles: University of California Press, 1987.

Margulies, Herbert F. "The Senate and the World Court," *Capitol Studies* 4, no. 2 (1976), 37–52.

Marquand, David. *Ramsay MacDonald.* London: Cape, 1976.

Marrin, Albert. *Nicholas Murray Butler.* Boston: Twayne, 1976.

———. *Sir Norman Angell.* Boston: Twayne, 1979.

Martin, Jeffrey Brown. *Ben Hecht: Hollywood Screenwriter.* Ann Arbor, Mich.: UMI Research Press, 1985.

Mason, Alpheus Thomas. *The Supreme Court from Taft to Warren.* Baton Rouge: Louisiana State University Press, 1958.

Mayer, Arno J. *Politics and Diplomacy of Peacemaking: Containment and Counterrevolution at Versailles, 1918–1919.* New York: Harcourt, 1967.

McCallum, John, and Charles H. Pearson. *College Football U.S.A.: 1869–1972.* New York: McGraw-Hill Book Company, 1972.

McClymer, John F. "Gender and the 'American Way of Life': Women in the Americanization Movement," *Journal of American Ethnic History* 10, no. 3 (1991): 3–20.

McCoy, Donald R. *Landon of Kansas.* Lincoln: University of Nebraska Press, 1966.

———. *Calvin Coolidge: The Quiet President.* New York: Macmillan, 1967.

McKenna, Marian Cecilia. *Borah.* Ann Arbor: University of Michigan Press, 1961.

Mehra, Parshotam. *A Dictionary of Modern Indian History, 1707–1947.* Delhi: Oxford University Press, 1985.

Meigs, Cornelia. *Jane Addams, Pioneer for Social Justice: A Biography.* Boston: Little, Brown, 1970.

Melencio, José P. *Arguments against Philippine Independence and Their Answers.* Washington, D.C.: Philippine Press Bureau, 1919.

Melton, J. Gordon. *Religious Leaders of America.* Detroit: Gale Research, 1991.

Mendelsohn, John, ed. *The Holocaust: Selected Documents in Eighteen Volumes.* 18 vols. New York: Garland, 1982.

Meriwether, Lee. *Jim Reed: "Senatorial Immortal."* Webster Groves, Mo.: International Mark Twain Society, 1948.

Merrill, Milton R. "Reed Smoot: Apostle-Senator," *Utah Historical Quarterly* 28 (1961): 343–50.

Merritt, Richard L. "Woodrow Wilson and the 'Great and Solemn Referendum,' 1920," *Review of Politics* 27, no. 1 (1965): 78–104.

Mervin, David. "Henry Cabot Lodge and the League of Nations," *Journal of American Studies* 4, no. 2 (1971): 201–16.

Messick, Hank, and Burt Goldblatt. *The Mobs and the Mafia: The Illustrated History of Organized Crime.* New York: Crowell, 1972.

Meyer, Alfred G. "The War Scare of 1927," *Soviet Union* 5, no. 1 (1978): 1–25.

Milkman, Ruth, ed. *Women, Work and Protest: A Century of U.S. Women's Labor History.* London: Routledge & Kegan Paul, 1985.

Miller, Edward S. *War Plan Orange: The U.S. Strategy to Defeat Japan, 1897–1945.* Annapolis, Md.: Naval Institute Press, 1991.

Mitscherlich, Alexander. *Doctors of Infamy: The Story of Nazi Medical Crimes.* Translated by Heinz Norden. New York: Schuman, 1949.

Moley, Raymond. *The American Legion Story.* New York: Duell, Sloan & Pearce, 1966.

Mommsen, Hans. *From Weimar to Auschwitz.* Princeton, N.J.: Princeton University Press, 1991.

Moody, Thomas Watson, F. X. Martin, and F. J. Byrne, eds. *A New History of Ireland.* 8 vols. Oxford, England: Clarendon, 1982.

Moquin, Wayne, ed. *The American Way of Crime: A Documentary History.* New York: Praeger, 1976.

Morison, Samuel Eliot. *History of United States Naval Operations in World War II: The Rising Sun on the Pacific, 1931–April 1942.* Boston: Little, Brown, 1948.

Moritz, Charles, ed. *Current Biography 1941.* New York: H. W. Wilson, 1941.

Morley, James William, ed. *Japan Erupts: The London Naval Conference and the Manchurian Incident, 1928–1932: Selected Translations from Taiheiyo Senso e no michi, kaisen gaiko shi.* New York: Columbia University Press, 1984.

Morrison, Elting. *Turmoil and Tradition: A Study of the Life and Times of Henry L. Stimson.* Cambridge: Harvard University Press, 1960.

Moses, Montrose Jonas. *Famous Actor-Families in America.* New York: T. Y. Crowell & Co., 1906.

Moss, Kenneth. "George S. Messersmith: An American Diplomat and Nazi Germany," *Delaware History* 17, no. 4 (1977): 236–49.

Mueller, Gordon H. "Rapallo Reexamined: A New Look at Germany's Secret Military Collaboration with Russia in 1922," *Military Affairs* 40, no. 3 (1976): 109–17.

Murphy, Paul L. *World War I and the Origin of Civil Liberties in the United States.* New York: W. W. Norton & Co., 1979.

Murray, Robert K. *The Politics of Normalcy: Governmental Theory and Practice in the Harding-Coolidge Era.* New York: Horton, 1973.

———. *The 103rd Ballot: Democrats and the Disaster in Madison Square Garden.* New York: Harper & Row, 1976.

Myers, Denys P. *Origin and Conclusion of the Paris Pact: The Renunciation of War as an Instrument of National Policy.* Boston: World Peace Foundation, 1929.

Nahm, Andrew C. *Historical Dictionary of the Republic of Korea.* Metuchen, N.J.: Scarecrow, 1993.

———. *A Panorama of 5000 Years: Korean History.* Elizabeth, N.J.: Hollym International Corp., 1983.

Nairn, Bede, and Geoffrey Serle, gen. eds. *Australian Dictionary of Biography.* 12 vols. Carlton, Victoria: Melbourne University Press, 1976–88.

Nansen, Fridtjof. *Farthest North: Being the Record of a Voyage of Exploration of the Ship Fram, 1893–96.* 2 vols. New York: Harper, 1897.

Nash, Gerald D. "Albert B. Fall and United States Oil Policy in 1921: A Document," *New Mexico Historical Review* 67, no. 2 (1992): 157–66.

Nash, Jay Robert. *Murder among the Mighty: Celebrity Slayings That Shocked America.* New York: Delacorte, 1983.

National Party Conventions. Washington, D.C.: Congressional Quarterly, 1987.

Natkiel, Richard. *Atlas of Battles: Strategy and Tactics, Civil War to Present.* New York: Military Press, 1984.

New Catholic Encyclopedia. 15 vols. 3 supps. New York: McGraw-Hill, 1967–89.

Nixon, Edgar B., and Donald B. Schewe, eds. *Franklin D. Roosevelt and Foreign Affairs.* 17 vols. Cambridge: Belknap Press of Harvard University Press, 1969–83.

Nollen, Scott Allen. *Boris Karloff: A Critical Account of His Screen, Stage, Radio, Television and Recording Work.* Jefferson, N.C.: McFarland & Co., 1991.

Nordstrom, Byron J., ed. *Dictionary of Scandinavian History.* Westport, Conn.: Greenwood, 1986.

Nore, Ellen. *Charles A. Beard: An Intellectual Biography.* Carbondale: Southern Illinois University Press, 1983.

O'Connor, Alfred E. *The First Hurrah: A Biography of Alfred E. Smith.* New York: G. P. Putnam's Sons, 1970.

O'Connor, Francis, ed. *The New Deal Art Projects: An Anthology of Memoirs.* Washington, D.C.: Smithsonian Institution Press, 1972.

O'Connor, Raymond G. *Perilous Equilibrium: The United States and the London Naval Conference of 1930.* Lawrence: University Press of Kansas, 1962.

Offner, Arnold A. "William E. Dodd: Romantic Historian and Diplomatic Cassandra," *Historian* 24, no. 4 (1962), 451–69.

———. *American Appeasement: United States Foreign Policy and Germany, 1933–1938.* Cambridge: Belknap Press of Harvard University Press, 1969.

Ohles, John F., ed. *Biographical Dictionary of American Educators.* 3 vols. Westport, Conn.: Greenwood, 1978.

Olin, Spencer C., Jr. *California's Prodigal Sons: Hiram Johnson and the Progressives, 1911–1917.* Berkeley: University of California Press, 1968.

Ollivier, Maurice, comp. and ed. *The Colonial and Imperial Conferences from 1887 to 1937.* 2 vols. Ottawa: E. Cloutier, Queen's Printer, 1954.

Olson, James Stuart. *Historical Dictionary of the 1920s: From World War I to the New Deal, 1919–1933.* Westport, Conn.: Greenwood, 1988.

Ossietzky, Carl von. *The Stolen Republic: Selected Writings of Carl von Ossietzky.* Translated by John Peet. London: Lawrence & Wishart, 1971.

Ostrower, Gary B. "The American Decision to Join the International Labor Organization," *Labor History* 16, no. 4 (1975), 495–504.

———. "Secretary of State Stimson and the League," *Historian* 41, no. 4 (1979), 467–82.

———. *Collective Insecurity: The United States and the League of Nations during the Early Thirties.* Cranbury, N.J.: Bucknell University Press, 1979.

O'Toole, George J. A. *The Encyclopedia of American Intelligence and Espionage from the Revolutionary War to the Present.* New York: Facts On File, 1988.

Ott, Frederick W. *The Films of Fritz Lang.* Secaucus, N.J.: Citadel, 1979.

———. *The Great German Films.* Secaucus, N.J.: Citadel, 1986.

Owen, Norman G., ed. *Compadre Colonialism: Studies on the Philippines under American Rule.* Ann Arbor, Mich.: Center for South and Southeast Asian Studies, 1971.

Palmer, Friedrich. *This Man Landon.* New York: Dodd, Mead, 1936.

Paneth, Donald. *The Encyclopedia of American Journalism.* New York: Facts On File, 1983.

Partridge, Bellamy. *Amundsen.* London: R. Hale, 1953.

Paschal, Joel Francis. *Mr. Justice Sutherland: A Man against the State.* Princeton, N.J.: Princeton University Press, 1951.

Paul, Rodman W. *The Abrogation of the Gentleman's Agreement.* Cambridge: Harvard University Press, 1936.

Payne, Darwin. *The Man of Only Yesterday: Frederick Lewis Allen, former Editor of Harper's Magazine, Author, and Interpreter of His Times.* New York: Harper & Row, 1975.

Payne, Stanley. *A History of Fascism.* Madison: University of Wisconsin Press, 1995.

Pearlstien, Edward W., comp. *Revolution in Russia! As Reported by the New York Tribune and the New York Herald, 1894–1921.* New York: Viking, 1967.

Pease, Neal. *Poland, the United States, and the Stabilization of Europe, 1919–1933.* New York: Oxford University Press, 1986.

Pelling, Henry. *History of British Trade Unionism.* London: Macmillan, 1992.

Pennell, C. R. *A Country with a Government and a Flag: The Rif War in Morocco, 1921–1926.* Wisbech, England: Middle East and North African Studies, 1986.

Perkes, Dan. *Eyewitness to Disaster.* New York: Gallery Books, 1985.

Perkins, Dexter. *Charles Evans Hughes and American Democratic Statesmanship.* Boston: Little, Brown, 1956.

Perkins, Dorothy. *Encyclopedia of Japan: Japanese History and Culture, from Abacus to Zori.* New York: Facts On File, 1991.

Perkins, Van L. *Crisis in Agriculture: The Agricultural Adjustment Administration and the New Deal, 1933.* Berkeley: University of California Press, 1969.

Petro, Patrice. *Joyless Streets: Women and Melodramatic Representation in Weimar Germany.* Princeton, N.J.: Princeton University Press, 1989.

Phillips, Gordon Ashton. *The Rise of the Labour Party, 1893–1931.* London: Routledge, 1992.

Phipps, Steven P. "The Commercial Development of Short Wave Radio in the United States, 1920–1926," *Historical Journal of Film, Radio and Television* (Great Britain) 11, no. 3 (1991): 215–27.

Polonsky, Antony. *Politics in Independent Poland, 1921–1939.* Oxford: Clarendon Press, 1972.

Porter, David L., ed. *Biographical Dictionary of American Sports: Football.* Westport, Conn.: Greenwood, 1987.

———, ed. *Biographical Dictionary of American Sports: Outdoor Sports.* Westport, Conn.: Greenwood, 1988.

———, ed. *Biographical Dictionary of American Sports: Basketball and Other Indoor Sports.* Westport, Conn.: Greenwood, 1989.

President Wilson's State Papers and Addresses. New York: George H. Doran Co., 1918.

Prouty, Chris, and Eugene Rosenfield, eds. *Historical Dictionary of Ethiopia.* Metuchen, N.J.: Scarecrow, 1982.

Pugach, Noel. "Making the Open Door Work: Paul S. Reinsch in China, 1913–1919," *Pacific Historical Review* 38, no. 2 (1969): 157–75.

Pusey, Merlo J. *Charles Evans Hughes* 2 vols. New York: Macmillan, 1952.

Quint, Howard H., and Robert H. Ferrell, eds. *The Talkative President: The Off-the-Record Press Conferences of Calvin Coolidge.* Amherst: University of Massachusetts Press, 1964.

Ragan, Fred D. "Justice Oliver Wendell Holmes, Jr., Zechariah Chafee, Jr., and the Clear and Present Danger Test for Free Speech: The First Year, 1919," *Journal of American History* 58 (June 1971): 39–43.

Rahnema, Ali. *Pioneers of Islamic Revival.* London: Zed Books, 1994.

Rainbolt, Rosemary. "Women and War in the United States: The Case of Dorothy Detzer, National Secretary, Women's International League for Peace and Freedom," *Peace and Change* 4, no. 3 (1977): 18–22.

Ratliff, William G. *Faithful to the Fatherland: Julius Curtius and Weimar Foreign Policy.* New York: P. Lang, 1990.

Rath, R. John. "The Molding of Engelbert Dollfuss as an Agrarian Reformer," *Austrian History Yearbook* 28 (1997): 173–215.

Rauh, Joseph L., Jr. "A Personalized View of the Court-Packing Episode," *Journal of Supreme Court History* 1990 (1990): 93–98.

Reader's Digest Great Events of the 20th Century: How They Changed Our Lives. Pleasantville, New York: Reader's Digest Association, 1977.

Reich, Bernard. *Historical Dictionary of Israel.* Metuchen, N.J.: Scarecrow, 1992.

Reid, Donald Malcolm. *Cairo University and the Making of Modern Egypt.* Cambridge: Cambridge University Press, 1990.

Reinsch, Paul. *An American Diplomat in China.* Garden City, N.Y.: Doubleday, 1922.

Renschler, Eric, ed. *The Films of G. W. Pabst: An Extraterritorial Cinema.* New Brunswick, N.J.: Rutgers University Press, 1990.

Renwick, Sir Robin. *Fighting with Allies: America and Britain in Peace and War.* New York: Times Books, 1996.

Richardson, Dick. *The Evolution of British Disarmament in the 1920s.* London: Pinter Publishers, 1989.

Richey, Susan. "Comment on the Political Strategy of Christian Pacifists: A. J. Muste, Norman Thomas, and Reinhold Niebuhr," *Towson State Journal of International Affairs* 11, no. 2 (1977): 111–19.

Rieckoff, Harald von. *German-Polish Relations, 1918–1933.* Baltimore: Johns Hopkins University Press, 1971.

Riley, Sam G., ed. *American Magazine Journalists, 1900–1960.* Detroit: Bruccoli Clark Layman, 1995.

Roberts, Adam, and Richard Guelff, eds. *Documents on the Laws of War.* Oxford: Clarendon Press, 1982.

Roberts, Allen. *The Turning Point: The Assassination of Louis Barthou and King Alexander I of Yugoslavia.* New York: St. Martin's, 1970.

Roberts, Nancy L. *American Peace Writers, Editors and Periodicals*. Westport, Conn.: Greenwood, 1991.

Robertson, James C. "The Hoare-Laval Plan," *Journal of Contemporary History* 10, no. 3 (1975): 433–64.

Robinson, Francis, ed. *The Cambridge Encyclopedia of India, Pakistan, Bangladesh, Sri Lanka, Nepal, Bhutan and the Maldives*. Cambridge: Cambridge University Press, 1989.

Rosenmann, Samuel I., ed. *The Public Papers and Addresses of Franklin D. Roosevelt*. 13 vols. New York: Random House, 1950.

Rosenne, Shabtai. *The World Court: What It Is and How It Works*. Dordrecht, The Netherlands: Martinus Nijhoff Publishers, 1995.

Roskill, Stephen W. *Naval Policy between the Wars*. 2 vols. London: Collins, 1968–76.

Rovine, Arthur W. *The First Fifty Years: The Secretary-General in World Politics, 1920–1970*. Leiden, The Netherlands: A. W. Sijthoff, 1970.

Rubin, Joan Shelley. "'Information Please!': Culture and Expertise in the Interwar Period," *American Quarterly* 35 (1983), no. 499–517.

Rumer, Thomas A. *The American Legion: An Official History, 1919–1989*. New York: M. Evans, 1990.

Rupieper, Hermann-Josef. *The Cuno Government and Reparations, 1922–1923: Politics and Economics*. The Hague: M. Nijoff, 1979.

Sadao, Asada. "Japan's 'Special Interests' and the Washington Conference, 1921–22," *American Historical Review* 67, no. 1 (1961–62): 62–70.

Salmond, John A. *Gastonia 1929: The Story of the Loray Mill Strike*. Chapel Hill: University of North Carolina Press, 1995.

Saloutos, Theodore, and John D. Hicks. *Agricultural Discontent in the Midwest, 1900–1939*. Madison: University of Wisconsin Press, 1951.

Salter, Sir Arthur. "The Technique of Open Diplomacy," *Political Quarterly* 3 (1932): 64–65.

Saul, Norman E. *Sailors in Revolt: The Russian Baltic Fleet in 1917*. Lawrence: Regents Press of Kansas, 1978.

Schapsmeier, Edward L., and Frederick H. Schapsmeier. *Henry A. Wallace of Iowa: the Agrarian Years, 1910–1940*. Ames, Iowa: Iowa State University Press, 1968.

Schlessinger, Bernard S. and June H., eds. *The Who's Who of Nobel Prize Winners*. Phoenix, Ariz.: Oryx, 1986.

Schwabe, Klaus. "Woodrow Wilson and Germany's Membership in the League of Nations, 1918–19," *Central European History* 8 (1975): 3–22.

Schwarz, Jordan A. *The New Dealers: Power Politics in the Age of Roosevelt*. New York: Alfred A. Knopf, 1993.

Scobbie, Irene. *Historical Dictionary of Sweden*. Metuchen, N.J.: Scarecrow, 1995.

Scott, James Brown. "Leon Bourgeois, 1851–1925," *American Journal of International Law* 19 (October 1925): 774–76.

Shafer, Robert J., and Donald J. Mabry. *Neighbors—Mexico and the United States: Wetbacks and Oil*. Chicago: Nelson-Hall Publishers, 1981.

Shafir, Shlomo. "George S. Messersmith: An Anti-Nazi Diplomat's View of the German-Jewish Crisis," *Jewish Social Studies* 35, no. 1 (1973): 32–41.

Sheffer, Martin S. *Presidential Power: Case Studies in the Use of the Opinions of the Attorney General*. Lanham, Md.: University Press of America, 1991.

Shideler, James H. *Farm Crisis, 1919–1923*. Berkeley: University of California Press, 1957.

Shotwell, James T. *At the Paris Peace Conference*. New York: Macmillan, 1937.

———, and Marina Salvin. *Lessons on Security and Disarmament from the History of the League of Nations*. New York: King's Crown, 1949.

Shukman, Harold, ed. *The Blackwell Encyclopedia of the Russian Revolution*. Oxford: Basil Blackwell, 1988.

Sinclair, Andrew. *The Available Man: The Life Behind the Masks of Warren Gamaliel Harding*. New York: Macmillan, 1965.

Skidelsky, Robert Jacob Alexander. *Oswald Mosley*. London: Macmillan; reprint, London: Papermac, 1990.

Slichter, Gertrude Almy. "Franklin D. Roosevelt and the Farm Problem," *Mississippi Valley Historical Review* 43, no. 2 (September 1956), 238–58.

Smallwood, James. "Banquo's Ghost at the Paris Peace Conference: The United States and the Hungarian Question," *East European Quarterly* 12, no. 3 (1978): 289–307.

Snow, Edgar. *Scorched Earth.* London: Victor Gollancz, 1941.

Sobel, Robert, and John Raimo. *Biographical Dictionary of the Governors of the United States.* 4 vols. Westport, Conn.: Meckler Books, 1978.

Sontag, John P. "The Soviet War Scare of 1926–27," *Russian Review* 34, no. 1 (1975): 66–77.

Spear, Sheldon. "The United States and the Persecution of the Jews in Germany: 1933–1939," *Jewish Social Studies* 30, no. 4 (1968): 215–42.

Spencer, Thomas T. "The Air Mail Controversy of 1934," *Mid-America* 62 (1980): 161–72.

Sprout, Harold and Margaret. *Toward a New Order of Sea Power: American Naval Policy and the World Scene, 1918–1922.* Princeton, N.J.: Princeton University Press, 1940.

Staudinger, Hans. *The Inner Nazi: A Critical Analysis of "Mein Kampf."* Baton Rouge: Louisiana State University Press, 1981.

Steele, Michael R. *The Fighting Irish Encyclopedia.* Champaign, Ill.: Sagamore Publishing, 1992.

Stenn, David. *Clara Bow: Runnin' Wild.* New York: Doubleday, 1988.

———. *Bombshell: The Life and Death of Jean Harlow.* New York: Doubleday, 1993.

Stern, Sheldon M. "American Nationalism vs. The League of Nations: The Correspondence of Albert J. Beveridge and Louis A. Coolidge, 1918–1920," *Indiana Magazine of History* 72, no. 2 (1976): 138–58.

Stieg, Margaret E. *Public Libraries in Nazi Germany.* Tuscaloosa: University of Alabama Press, 1992.

Stone, Ralph A. *The Irreconcilables: The Fight against the League of Nations.* Lexington: University of Kentucky Press, 1970.

Stroud, Richard H. *National Leaders of American Conservation.* Washington, D.C.: Smithsonian Institution Press, 1985.

Sturdevant, David. *Popular Uprisings in the Philippines, 1840–1940.* Ithaca, N.Y.: Cornell University Press, 1976.

Surface, Frank M., and Raymond L. Bland. *American Food in the World War and Reconstruction Period.* Stanford, Calif.: Stanford University Press, 1931.

Swanson, Jeffrey L. "That Smoke-Filled Room: A Utahn's Role in the 1920 GOP Convention," *Utah Historical Quarterly* 45 (1977): 369–79.

Swanson, Marvin C., ed. *Charles A. Beard: An Observance of the Centennial of his Birth, DePauw University, Greencastle, Indiana, October 11–12, 1974.* Greencastle, Ind.: The University, 1976.

Symons, Julian. *A Pictorial History of Crime.* New York: Crown, 1966.

Taggar, Yehuda. *The Mufti of Jerusalem and Palestine: Arab Politics, 1930–1937.* New York: Garland, 1986.

Tarbell, Ida M. "How about Hughes?" *The American Magazine* 65, no. 5 (March 1908): 451–64.

Taylor, Alan John Percivale, and John Morris Roberts, eds. *Purnell's History of the 20th Century.* 10 vols. New York: Purnell, 1979.

Tenenbaum, Barbara A., ed. in chief. *Encyclopedia of Latin American History and Culture.* 5 vols. New York: Charles Scribner's Sons, 1996.

Thompson, Robert Smith. *A Time for War: Franklin Delano Roosevelt and the Path to Pearl Harbor.* New York: Prentice Hall, 1991.

Timmons, Bascom N. *Portrait of an American: Charles G. Dawes.* New York: Henry Holt & Co., 1953.

Thompson, J. A. "Lord Cecil and the Historians," *Historical Journal* 23, no. 3 (1981): 709–15.

Tokes, Rudolf L. *Bela Kun and the Hungarian Soviet Republic.* New York: Praeger, 1967.

Trani, Eugene P., and David L. Wilson. *The Presidency of Warren G. Harding.* Lawrence: University Press of Kansas, 1977.

Trattner, Walter I., ed. *Biographical Dictionary of Social Welfare in America.* Westport, Conn.: Greenwood, 1986.

Traynor, Dean Elizabeth. *International Monetary and Financial Conferences in the Interwar Period.* Washington, D.C.: Catholic University of America Press, 1949.

The Treaties of Peace 1919–1923. New York: Carnegie Endowment for International Peace, 1924.

Turkus, Burton B. *Murder Inc.: The Story of "The Syndicate."* New York: Da Capo, 1992.

Turley, Charles. *Roald Amundsen, Explorer.* London: Methuen & Co., 1935.

Uldricks, Teddy J. "The Impact of the Great Purges on the People's Commissariat of Foreign Affairs," *Slavic Review* 36, no. 2 (1977): 187–204.

Ullman, Richard H. *Anglo-Soviet Relations, 1917–1921.* 2 vols. Princeton, N.J.: Princeton University Press, 1961–68.

Underwood, Peter. *Karloff: The Life of Boris Karloff, with an Appendix of the Films in Which he Appeared."* New York: Drake Publishers, 1972.

The United States Children's Bureau, 1912–1972. New York: Arno, 1974.

Urofsky, Melvin I., ed. *Documents of American Constitutional and Legal History.* 2 vols. Philadelphia: Temple University Press, 1989.

Van Meter, Robert H., Jr. "The Washington Conference of 1921–1922: A New Look," *Pacific Historical Review* 46, no. 4 (1977): 603–24.

Viets, Henry. "Charles Scott Sherrington, 1857–1952," *New England Journal of Medicine* 246 (1952): 981.

Villard, Oswald G. *Fighting Years: Memoirs of a Liberal Editor.* New York: Harcourt, Brace, 1939.

Vinson, John Chalmers. *William E. Borah and the Outlawry of War.* Athens: University of Georgia Press, 1957.

———. "The Problem of Australian Representation at the Washington Conference for the Limitation of Naval Armament," *Australian Journal of Politics and History* 4, no. 2 (1958): 155–64.

———. *Referendum for Isolation: The Defeat of Article Ten of the League of Nations Covenant.* Athens: University of Georgia Press, 1961.

———. "War Debts and Peace Legislation: The Johnson Act of 1934," *Mid-America* 50, no. 3 (1968): 206–22.

Walker, Samuel. *In Defense of American Liberties: A History of the ACLU.* New York: Oxford University Press, 1990.

Ward, Robert D. "Against the Tide: The Preparedness Movement of 1923–1924," *Military Affairs* 38 (April 1974): 59–61.

Warner, Hoyt L. *The Life of Mr. Justice Clarke: A Testament to the Power of Liberal Dissent in America.* Cleveland: Western Reserve University Press, 1959.

Wasson, Tyler, ed. *Nobel Prize Winners: An H. W. Wilson Biographical Dictionary.* New York: H. W. Wilson Co., 1987.

Weiss, Stuart L. "American Foreign Policy and Presidential Power: The Neutrality Act of 1935," *Journal of Politics* 30, no. 3 (1968): 672–95.

Weissman, Benjamin M. "Herbert Hoover's 'Treaty' with Soviet Russia: August 20, 1921," *Slavic Review* 28, no. 2 (1969): 276–88.

Welker, Robert Henry. *Natural Man: The Life of William Beebe.* Bloomington: Indiana University Press, 1975.

Wheeler, Gerald E. *Prelude to Pearl Harbor: The United States Navy and the Far East, 1921–1931.* Columbia: University of Missouri Press, 1963.

White, William Allen. *The Autobiography of William Allen White.* New York: Macmillan, 1946.

Whitford, Frank. *Bauhaus.* London: Thames & Hudson, 1995.

Whyte, William Farmer. *William Morris Hughes, His Life and Times.* Sydney: Angus & Robertson, 1957.

Williams, Joyce C. "The Resignation of Secretary of State Robert Lansing," *Diplomatic History* 3, no. 3 (1979): 337–44.

Williams, William A., ed. *From Colony to Empire: Essays in the History of American Foreign Relations.* New York: Wiley, 1972.

Williamson, David G. *The British in Germany, 1918–1930: The Reluctant Occupiers.* Oxford, England: Berg, 1991.

Willson, Beckles. *The Paris Embassy: A Narrative of Franco-British Diplomatic Relations, 1814–1920.* London: T. F. Unwin, 1927.

Wilson, Hugh R. *Diplomat between the Wars*. New York: Longmans, Green, 1941.

Wiltz, John E. "The Nye Committee Revisited," *Historian* 23, no. 2 (1961): 211–33.

Wimer, Kurt. "Woodrow Wilson and a Third Nomination," *Pennsylvania History* 29, no. 2 (1963): 193–211.

———. "Woodrow Wilson's Plan for a Vote of Confidence," *Pennsylvania History* 28, no. 3 (1961): 279–93.

———. "Woodrow Wilson's Plans to Enter the League of Nations through an Executive Agreement," *Western Political Quarterly* 11, no. 4 (1958): 800–812.

Winterrle, John. "John Dewey and the League of Nations," *North Dakota Quarterly* 34, no. 3 (1966): 75–88.

Winters, Stanley B., and Robert B. Pynsent, eds. *T. G. Masaryk (1850–1937)*. London: School of Slavonic and East European Studies, University of London. 1989.

Wistrich, Robert S. *Who's Who in Nazi Germany*. London: Routledge, 1995.

World Encyclopedia of Peace. 4 vols. Oxford, England: Pergamon, 1986.

Young, C. Walter. *Japan's Special Position in Manchuria*. Baltimore: Johns Hopkins University Press, 1931.

Zentner, Christian, and Friedemann Bedüftig, eds. *Encyclopedia of the Third Reich*. 2 vols. New York: Macmillan, 1991.

Zinoviev, Grigorii (R. Chappell, trans.). *History of the Bolshevik Party: A Popular Outline by Grigorii Zinoviev*. London: New Park Publications, 1973.

Zivojinoviæ, Dragan R. "The Emergence of American Policy in the Adriatic: December 1917–April 1919," *East European Quarterly* 1, no. 3 (1967): 173–215.

GOVERNMENT DOCUMENTS

AUSTRALIA

Neale, Robert George, ed. *Documents on Australian Foreign Policy, 1937–49*. 13 vols. Canberra: Australian Government Publishing Service, 1975.

CANADA

Canada, The Founders and the Guardians: Fathers of Confederation, Governors General, Prime Ministers—A Collection of Biographical Sketches and Portraits. Ottawa: The Queen's Printer, 1968.

GERMANY

Documents on German Foreign Policy, 1918–1945: From the Archives of the German Foreign Ministry. Washington, D.C.: U.S. Government Printing Office, 1949–1957.

Sontag, Raymond James, and James Stuart Beddie, eds. *Nazi-Soviet Relations, 1939–1941: Documents from the Archives of the German Foreign Office*. Washington, D.C.: U.S. Government Printing Office, 1948.

POLAND

Ministry for Foreign Affairs. *Official Documents Concerning Polish-German and Polish-Soviet Relations, 1933–1939* (London: Hutchinson, 1941). A rare publication of documents by the Polish government-in-exile during the Second World War.

UNION OF SOVIET SOCIALIST REPUBLICS

Report of Court Proceedings: The Case of the Trotskyite-Zinovievite Centre, Heard Before the Military Collegium of the Supreme Court of the U.S.S.R., Moscow, August 19–24, 1936, in re G.E. Zinoviev [and Others] charged under Articles 58(8), 19 and 58(8), 58(11) of the Criminal Code of the R.S.F.S.R. Moscow: People's Commissariat of Justice of the U.S.S.R., 1936.

UNITED KINGDOM

Emergency Powers Act, 16 & 17 Geo. 5, 1926.

Foreign Office. Woodward, Sir Ernest Llewellyn, and Rohan Butler, eds., *Documents on British Foreign Policy, 1919–1939*. 5 vols. London: His Majesty's Stationery Office, 1946–.

Parliament. *Further Documents Respecting Czechoslovakia. Including the Agreement Concluded at Munich on September 29, 1938. Presented by the Secretary of State for Foreign Affairs to Parliament by Command of His Majesty*. Miscellaneous Report No. 8. London: His Majesty's Stationery Office, 1938.

———. Parliamentary Papers. Vol. 30. London: His Majesty's Stationery Office, 1926.

Reparation Commission. *Statement of Germany's Obligations Under the Heading of Reparations, Etc., at April 30th, 1922*. London: His Majesty's Stationery Office, 1922.

————. *Agreements, Concerning Deliveries in Kind to be Made by Germany Under the Heading of Reparations.* London: His Majesty's Stationery Office, 1922.

Statute of Westminster, 22 Geo. 5, c. 4, 1931.

UNITED STATES

Armament Conference Treaties: Treaties and Resolutions, Approved and Adopted by the Conference on the Limitation of Armament, Submitted by the President of the United States for Advice and Consent to their Ratification. Senate Document No. 124. 67th Congress, 2d sess., 1922.

Conditions in Manchuria. Senate Document 55. 72nd Congress, 1st sess., 1932.

Conference on the Limitation of Armament: Address of the President of the United States, Submitting the Treaties and Resolutions Approved and Adopted by the Conference on the Limitation of Armament, Together with the Report of the American Delegation of the Proceedings of the Conference on the Limitation of Armament, Submitted to the President, February 9, 1922. Senate Document No. 125. 67th Congress, 2d sess., 1922.

Court of Inquiry on the Loss of the U.S.S. Shenandoah. Navy Department Report, December 1925, in file "Aviation—Loss of the U.S.S. Shenandoah." Hilary Pollard Jones Papers, Library of Congress.

Department of State. *Papers Relating to the Foreign Relations of the United States: 1921.* 2 vols. Washington, D.C.: U.S. Government Printing Office, 1936.

————. *Papers Relating to the Foreign Relations of the United States: 1923.* 2 vols. Washington, D.C.: U.S. Government Printing Office, 1938.

————. *Papers Relating to the Foreign Relations of the United States: 1930.* 3 vols. Washington, D.C.: U.S. Government Printing Office, 1945.

Enforcement of the Prohibition Laws: Official Records of the National Commission on Law Observance and Enforcement, Pertaining to Its Investigation of the Facts as to the Enforcement, the Benefits, and the Abuses Under the Prohibition Laws, Both Before and Since the Adoption of the Eighteenth Amendment to the Constitution. 5 vols. Washington, D.C.: U.S. Government Printing Office, 1931.

Inaugural Addresses of the Presidents of the United States, From George Washington, 1789, to Richard Milhous Nixon, 1973. House Document 93–208. 93rd Congress, 1st sess., 1974.

London Naval Treaty of 1930. Publications of the United States Department of State, Conference Series No. 2. Washington, D.C.: U.S. Government Printing Office, 1930.

London Naval Conference: Speeches and Press Statements by Members of the American Delegation, January 20–April 29, 1930. Publications of the United States Department of State, Conference Series No. 3. Washington, D.C.: U.S. Government Printing Office, 1930.

United States Congress. House of Representatives. Committee on Foreign Affairs. *Hearings on H.R. 17 and H.R. 6357 (H.R. 6357 Reported Favorably) for the Reorganization and Improvement of the Foreign Service of the United States, and for Other Purposes, January 14–18, 1924.* 68th Congress, 1st sess., 1924.

United States Congress. Senate. *Addresses of President Wilson: Addresses Delivered by President Wilson on his Western Tour, September 4 to September 25, 1919, on the League of Nations, Treaty of Peace with Germany, Industrial Conditions, High Cost of Living, Race Riots, Etc.* Senate Document No. 120. 60th Congress, 1st sess., 1919.

U.S. Statutes at Large, vols. 41, 42, 48.

DISSERTATIONS AND THESES

Andrade, Ernest, "United States Naval Policy in the Disarmament Era, 1921–1927," Ph.D. dissertation, Michigan State University, 1966.

Baldwin, Frank Prentis, Jr., "The Jurisdiction and Authority of the Japanese Kempei in the 1930's," master's thesis, Columbia University, 1967.

————, "The March First Movement: Korean Challenge and Japanese Response," Ph.D. dissertation, Columbia University, 1969.

Barbash, Jack, "Employer Attitudes and Methods in Industrial Disputes," master's thesis, New York University, 1937.

Bowers, Robert E., "The American Peace Movement, 1933–41," Ph.D. dissertation, University of Wisconsin, 1947.

Boyd, Carl Leroy, "The Diplomacy of Hirosji Oshima and German-Japanese Relations, 1934–1939," Ph.D. dissertation, University of California at Davis, 1972.

Boyens, Charles William, "The WPA Mural Projects: The Effects of Constraints on Artistic Freedom," Ph.D. dissertation, Columbia University Teachers' College, 1984.

Brown, Vincent Murray, "Contemporary Appraisal: The National Industrial Recovery Program," Ph.D. dissertation, Georgetown University, 1954.

Butler, Harold Tiffany, "Partisan Positions on Isolationism vs. Internationalism, 1918–1933," Ph.D. dissertation, Syracuse University, 1963.

Buttry, Dolores, "Knut Hamsun: A Scandinavian Rousseau," Ph.D. dissertation, University of Illinois at Urbana-Champaign, 1978.

Caple, Horace B., "Black Playwrights of the Federal Theatre Project during the Great Depression: A Critical Analysis of Select Works, 1935–1939," Ph.D. dissertation, Union Institute, 1911.

Carr, Eleanor, "The New Deal and the Sculptor: A Study of Federal Relief to the Sculptor on the New York City Federal Art Project of the Works Project Administration, 1935 to 1943," Ph.D. dissertation, Institute of Fine Arts, New York University, 1969.

Cebula, James E., "James M. Cox, Journalist and Politician," Ph.D. dissertation, University of Cincinnati, 1972.

Cleaver, Charles G., "Frank B. Kellogg: Attitudes and Assumptions Influencing His Foreign Policy Decisions," Ph.D. dissertation, University of Minnesota, 1956.

Colegrove, John Wesley, "J. H. Scullin: Prime Minister in Adversity," bachelor's honors thesis, University of Queensland (Australia), 1968.

Colgan, Christine Anne, "Warner Brothers' Crusade against the Third Reich: A Study of Anti-Nazi Activism and Film Production, 1933 to 1941," Ph.D. dissertation, University of Southern California, 1985.

Conrad, David Eugene, "The Forgotten Farmers: The AAA and the Southern Tenants, 1933–36," Ph.D. dissertation, University of Oklahoma, 1962.

Contreras, Belisario R., "Treasury Art Programs: The New Deal and the American Artist, 1933 to 1943," Ph.D. dissertation, American University, 1967.

Craig, Douglas Bryden Stuart, "Rehearsal for Revolt: The Ideological Turmoil of the Democratic Party, 1920–1932," Ph.D. dissertation, University of Virginia, 1989.

Criss, Nur Bilge, "Istanbul during the Allied Occupation: 1918–1923," Ph.D. dissertation, The George Washington University, 1990.

Custer, Ben Scott, "The Geneva Conference for the Limitation of Naval Armament, 1927," Ph.D. dissertation, Georgetown University, 1948.

DeBoe, David Cornelius, "The United States and the Geneva Disarmament Conference, 1932–1934," Ph.D. dissertation, Tulane University, 1969.

Dick, Eric Lyle, "Deportation under the Criminal Code and the Immigration Act, 1919–1936," master's thesis, University of Manitoba (Canada), 1978.

Di Piazza, Daniel Dominic, "The Bucareli Conference and United States-Mexican Relations," Ph.D. dissertation, University of Missouri, 1966.

Dowell, Eldridge F., "A History of the Enactment of Criminal Syndicalism Legislation in the United States," Ph.D. dissertation, Johns Hopkins University, two volumes, 1936.

Downing, Marvin L., "Hugh R. Wilson and American Relations with the League of Nations, 1927–1937," Ph.D. dissertation, University of Oklahoma, 1970.

Doyle, Judith Kaaz, "Out of Step: Maury Maverick and the Politics of the Depression and the New Deal," Ph.D. dissertation, University of Texas at Austin, 1989.

Felak, James Ramon, "'At the Price of the Republic': Hlika's Slovak People's Party, 1929–1938," Ph.D. dissertation, Indiana University, 1989.

Ferrell, Robert H., "The United States and the Origins of Kellogg-Briand Pact," Ph.D. dissertation, Yale University, 1951.

Foltz, David A., "The War Crimes Issue at the Paris Peace Conference, 1919–1920," Ph.D. dissertation, American University, 1978.

Goedeken, Edward A., "Charles G. Dawes in War and Peace, 1917–1922," Ph.D. dissertation, University of Kansas, 1984.

Goldman, Michael Abbot, "The War Finance Corporation in the Politics of War and Reconstruction, 1917–1923," Ph.D. dissertation, Rutgers University, 1971.

Goldstein, Brigitte M., "Ludwig Quidde and the Struggle for Democratic Pacifism in Germany, 1914–1930," Ph.D. dissertation, New York University, 1984.

Green, Joseph G., "Joseph Wood Krutch, Critic of the Drama," Ph.D. dissertation, Indiana University, 1964.

Green, Simon Rosengard, "Thomas Garrigue Masaryk: Educator of a Nation," Ph.D. dissertation, University of California at Berkeley, 1976.

Grubbs, Donald H., "The Southern Tenant Farmers Union and the New Deal," Ph.D. dissertation, University of Florida, 1963.

Grumelli, Michael L., "Trial of Faith: The Dissent and Court-Martial of Billy Mitchell," Ph.D. dissertation, Rutgers University, 1991.

Guinsberg, Thomas Nathan, "Senatorial Isolation in America, 1919–1941," Ph.D. dissertation, Columbia University, 1969.

Harbison, Frederick H., "Labor Relations in the Iron and Steel Industry, 1936 to 1939," Ph.D. dissertation, Princeton University, 1940.

Harris, George S., "Political History of Turkey, 1945–1950," Ph.D. dissertation, Harvard University, 1956.

Hight, Eleanor Margaret, "Moholy-Nagy: Photography and the 'New Vision' in Weimar Germany," Ph.D. dissertation, Harvard University, 1986.

Hoover, John Gene, "The Warner Brothers Film Musical, 1927–1980," Ph.D. dissertation, University of Southern California, 1985.

Hurd, Walter C., "The Labor and Industrial Program of the Federal Council of Churches, 1932–1940," master's thesis, Columbia University, 1954.

Johnson, Donald, "American Civil Liberties Union: Origins, 1914–1924," Ph.D. dissertation, Columbia University, 1960.

Jones, John R., "The Foreign Policy of Louis Barthou, 1933–1934," Ph.D. dissertation, University of North Carolina, 1958.

Keating, George, "Three Progressives (Jane Addams, George Perkins, and Hiram Johnson) and the Progressive Profile," master's thesis, Georgetown University, 1971.

Kerwyn, Dr. Jerome G., "Federal Water Power Legislation," Ph.D. dissertation, Columbia University, 1906.

Kleinman, Mark Louis, "Approaching Opposition: Henry A. Wallace, Reinhold Niebuhr and the Emergence of American Liberal Internationalism, 1920–1942," Ph.D. dissertation, University of California at Los Angeles, 1991.

Kneeshaw, Stephen John, "The Kellogg-Briand Pact: The American Reaction," Ph.D. dissertation, University of Colorado, 1971.

Korey, William, "Zinoviev on the Problem of World Revolution, 1919–27," doctoral dissertation, Columbia University, 1960.

Kubek, Anthony, "Japanese-American Relations, 1937–1945," Ph.D. dissertation, Georgetown University, 1956.

Kyvig, David E., "In Revolt against Prohibition: The Association against the Prohibition Amendment and the Movement for Repeal, 1919–1933," Ph.D. dissertation, Northwestern University, 1971.

Lambert, Walter Kraft, "The New Deal Revenue Acts: The Politics of Taxation," Ph.D. dissertation, University of Texas at Austin, 1970.

Lawler, Patricia C., "The Townsend Movement and the Enactment of the Social Security Act of 1935," master's thesis, Columbia University, 1954.

Lingvall, John, "The Lusk Report, 1919," master's thesis, Georgetown University, 1972.

Logoglu, Osman F., "Ismet Inonu and the Political Modernization of Turkey, 1945–1965," Ph.D. dissertation, Princeton University, 1970.

MacRenato, Ternot, "Somoza: Seizure of Power, 1926–1939," Ph.D. dissertation, University of California at San Diego, 1991.

Matthews, Elisabeth Ann, "Meighen and the West, 1921–1926; the National Policy Revisited," master's thesis, Carleton University (Ottawa), 1966.

McKinzie, Richard D., "The New Deal for Artists: Federal Subsidies, 1933 to 1943," Ph.D. dissertation, Indiana University at Bloomington, 1968.

McNally, James Wallace, "The Foreign Policy of Senator William E. Borah," master's thesis, Rutgers University, 1934.

McNeil, Genna Rae, "Charles Hamilton Houston (1895–1950) and the Struggle for Civil Rights," Ph.D. dissertation, University of Chicago, 1976.

Mehler, Barry, "A History of the American Eugenics Society, 1921–1940," Ph.D. dissertation, University of Illinois at Urbana-Champaign, 1988.

Miller, Daniel Edward, "Antonin Svehla and the Czechoslovak Republican Party (1918–1933)," Ph.D. dissertation, University of Pittsburgh, 1989.

Montgomery, Edrene Stephens, "Bruce Barton and the Twentieth Century Menace of Unreality," Ph.D. dissertation, University of Arkansas, 1984.

Neal, Nevin, "A Biography of Joseph T. Robinson," Ph.D. dissertation, University of Oklahoma, 1958.

Olson, James S., "The Reconstruction Finance Corporation, 1932–1940," Ph.D. dissertation, SUNY at Stony Brook, 1972.

Pavich, Paul, "Joseph Wood Krutch: Western Nature Essayist," Seminar Paper, Colorado State University, 1968.

Peretti, Burton William, "Music, Race, and Culture in Urban America: The Creators of Jazz," Ph.D. dissertation, University of California at Berkeley, 1989.

Pettus, Beryl, "The Senatorial Career of Joseph Taylor Robinson," master's thesis, University of Illinois, 1952.

Quinn, Joseph R., "American Recognition of the Soviet Union," Ph.D. dissertation, Georgetown University, 1954.

Romero, Patricia Watkins, "Carter G. Woodson: A Biography," Ph.D. dissertation, Ohio State University, 1971.

Roorda, Eric Paul, "The Era of the Good Neighbor in the Dominican Republic, 1930–1940," Ph.D. dissertation, Johns Hopkins University, 1989.

Rudken, Richard T., "Burton K. Wheeler of Montana: Progressive between the Wars," University of Oregon at Portland, 1961.

Rust, Sharon, "Ayn Rand and the Objectivists: The New Intellectuals," master's thesis, Georgetown University, 1980.

Saunders, Thomas Jeffry, "Weimar, Hollywood, and the Americanization of German Culture, 1921–1933," Ph.D. dissertation, University of Toronto, 1985.

Savage, Hugh James, "Political Independents of the Hoover Era: The Progressive Insurgents of the Hoover Era," Ph.D. dissertation, University of Illinois, 1961.

Schalow, Thomas Richard, "The Role of the Financial Panic of 1927 and Failure of the 15th Bank in the Economic Decline of the Japanese Aristocracy," Ph.D. dissertation, Princeton University, 1989.

Shindo, Charles Jogi, "Voices of the Migrant: Democracy and Culture in the Dust Bowl Works of John Steinbeck, John Ford, and Woody Guthrie," Ph.D. dissertation, University of Rochester (New York), 1992.

Stratton, David H., "Albert B. Fall and the Teapot Dome Affair," master's thesis, University of Colorado, 1955.

Taylor, Paul, "The Entrance of Women in Party Politics: The 1920s," Ph.D. dissertation, Harvard University, 1966.

Totten, Priscilla, "The Reaction of American Women to Margaret Sanger and Birth Control, 1914–1930," master's thesis, Georgetown University, 1978.

Traphagen, Jeanne C., "The Inter-American Diplomacy of Frank B. Kellogg," Ph.D. dissertation, University of Minnesota, 1956.

Trigg, Mary Kathleen, "Four American Feminists, 1910–1940: Inez Haynes Irwin, Mary Ritter Beard, Doris Stevens, and Lorine Pruette" Ph.D. dissertation, Brown University, 1989.

Turner, Elizabeth Hutton, "The American Artistic Migration to Paris between the Great War and the Great Depression," Ph.D. dissertation, University of Virginia, 1985.

Whiteman, Harold B., Jr., "Norman H. Davis and the Search for International Peace and Security, 1917–1944," Ph.D. dissertation, Yale University, 1958.

Winkler, Fred Herbert, "The United States and the World Disarmament Conference, 1926–1935," Ph.D. dissertation, Northwestern University, 1957.

NEWSPAPERS

Arizona Republic

Atlanta Constitution

Brooklyn (New York) *Daily Eagle*

Chicago Daily Tribune

Chicago Sunday Tribune

Chicago Herald-Examiner

Daily News (New York)

Daily Telegraph (London)

Dallas (Texas) *Morning News*

International Herald-Tribune

Los Angeles Times

Melbourne (Australia) *Herald*

Melbourne (Australia) *Sun*

The Nashville Tennessean

New York American

The New York Herald

The New York Herald (European Edition)

New York Herald-Tribune

New York Herald-Tribune (European Edition)

New York Post

The New York Sun

The New York Times

New York Tribune

New York World-Telegram

San Francisco Chronicle

San Francisco Examiner

Seattle Post-Intelligencer

St. Louis Globe-Democrat

St. Louis Post-Dispatch

St. Paul Pioneer-Press (Minnesota)

The Sunday Times (London)

The Times (London)

Tucson (Arizona) *Daily Citizen*

Tucson (Arizona) *Daily Star*

Washington Evening Star

The Washington Post

The World (New York)

UNPUBLISHED MEMOIRS AND ORAL HISTORY COLLECTIONS

"The Reminiscences of Norman Angell," Oral History Memoir, Oral History Research Office, Columbia University

"The Reminiscences of Roger Nash Baldwin," Oral History Research Office, Columbia University

"The Reminiscences of Norman Thomas," Oral History Research Office, Columbia University

"The Reminiscences of Henry A. Wallace," Oral History Research Office, Columbia University

MANUSCRIPT COLLECTIONS
*on microfilm

Agricultural Adjustment Administration Papers, RG 145; National Archives

Joseph Alsop Papers, Library of Congress

American Civil Liberties Papers, G. Seeley Mudd Library, Princeton University

Records of the American Commission to Negotiate Peace, RG 256, National Archives

Hugo L. Black Papers, Library of Congress

William Edgar Borah Papers, Library of Congress

Mark Bristol Papers, Library of Congress

Records of the Brotherhood of Sleeping Car Porters, Chicago Historical Society*

Records of the Brotherhood of Sleeping Car Porters, Newberry Library, Chicago*

Records of the Brotherhood of Sleeping Car Porters, Library of Congress

Heywood Campbell Broun Papers, Library of Congress

Charles Wayland Bryan Papers, Nebraska State Historical Society Archives, Lincoln, Nebraska

Raymond Clapper Papers, Library of Congress

Congress of Industrial Organization Papers, Catholic University of America, Washington, D.C.

Calvin Coolidge Papers, Library of Congress

Eugene V. Debs Control File 77175, Department of Justice Control Files, RG 60, National Archives

William Orville Douglas Papers, Library of Congress

The Federal Theatre Project Collection, Library of Congress

Federal Writers' Project Papers (Records of the Work Projects Administration), RG 69, National Archives

James William Ford File, HQ100-14632, Federal Bureau of Investigation Headquarters, Washington, D.C.

General Records of the U.S. Department of State, RG 59 and RG 84, National Archives

Benjamin Gitlow Papers, J. Murray Atkins Library, University of North Carolina at Charlotte

Warren Gamaliel Harding Papers, Ohio Historical Society*

Gilbert Monell Hitchcock Papers, Library of Congress

Charles Evans Hughes Papers, New York Public Library

Cordell Hull Papers, Library of Congress

Records of the Joint Committees of Congress, Records of the Joint Committee to Investigate Dirigible Disasters, RG 128, National Archives

Hilary Pollard Jones Papers, Library of Congress

Frank Billings Kellogg Papers, Minnesota Historical Society, St. Paul*

Frank Knox Papers, Library of Congress

Philander Chase Knox Papers, Library of Congress

Joseph Wood Krutch Papers, Library of Congress

LaFollette Civil Liberties Committee Papers, National Archives

Fiorello LaGuardia Papers, New York Public Library*

Gertrude Battles Lane Papers, Library of Congress

Clare Boothe Luce Papers, Library of Congress

Ramsay MacDonald Papers, University of Birmingham, England

William Gibbs McAdoo Papers, Library of Congress

Charles Linza McNary Papers, Library of Congress

Henry Louis Mencken Papers, New York Public Library

Papers of the National Association for the Advancement of Colored People*

Records of the National Board of Review of Motion Pictures, New York Public Library

National Recovery Administration Papers, RG 9, National Archives

New Deal Agencies and Black America*

Records of the New York World's Fair, 1939, Inc., New York Public Library

George William Norris Papers, Library of Congress

Frances Perkins Papers, Columbia University, New York

Key Pittman Papers, Library of Congress

Public Works Administration Papers, RG 135, National Archives

Papers of A. Philip Randolph*

Franklin Delano Roosevelt Papers, F.D.R. Presidential Library, Hyde Park, New York

Rose Schneiderman Papers, Robert F. Wagner Labor Archives, New York University

Reed Smoot Papers, Library of Congress

Southern Farm Tenant's Union Papers, Southern Historical Collection, University of North Carolina at Chapel Hill*

William Howard Taft Papers, Library of Congress*

Norman Thomas Papers, New York Public Library*

Records of the United States Senate, RG 46, various Committees, National Archives

Robert F. Wagner Papers, Georgetown University

Records of the Wickersham Commission on Law Observance and Enforcement, RG 10, National Archives

William Allen White Papers, Library of Congress

Alexander Woollcott Miscellaneous Papers, New York Public Library

Records of the Work Projects Administration, RG 69, National Archives: Papers of the Federal Writer's Project, Records of the Central Office, Miscellaneous Publicity Materials, 1935–41. Newspaper clippings, Boxes 4–5.

INDEX

Boldface page numbers denote main entries. *Italic* page numbers indicate illustrations.